Frommer's®
London 2013

by Joe Fullman & Donald Strachan

UNDERGROUND

WILEY

John Wiley & Sons, Inc.

Published by:

JOHN WILEY & SONS, INC.

Copyright © 2013 John Wiley & Sons Ltd, The Atrium, Southern Gate, Chichester,
West Sussex PO19 8SQ, England
Telephone (+44) 1243 779777
Email (for orders and customer service enquiries): cs-books@wiley.co.uk. Visit our Home Page on
www.wiley.com

Editorial Director: Kelly Regan
Production Manager: Daniel Mersey
Editor: Fiona Quinn
Project Editor: Hannah Clement
Photo Research: Cherie Cincilla, Richard H. Fox, Jill Emeny
Cartography: Andrew Murphy

British Library Cataloguing in Publication Data
A catalogue record for this book is available from the British Library
ISBN 978-1-118-28862-7 (pbk); ISBN 978-1-118-33388-4 (ebk); ISBN 978-1-118-33499-7 (ebk);
ISBN 978-1-118-33167-5 (ebk)

Typeset by Wiley Indianapolis Composition Services

Printed and bound in China by RR Donnelley

5 4 3 2 1

CONTENTS

LIST OF MAPS

ABOUT THE AUTHORS

Joe Fullman has lived in London for just over 39 years—or, to put it another way, all his life. It is, as far as he's concerned, the best city in the world, and having worked as a travel writer for more than a decade, he's had the opportunity to compare it to some very distinguished rivals. Joe has written for most of the major guidebook publishers, including *Rough Guides*, *Lonely Planet*, *AA*, *Cadogan*, and, of course, *Frommer's*, and is the author of guides to London (five at the last count including *Frommer's London Free & Dirt Cheap*), England, Berlin, Venice, Las Vegas, Costa Rica, and Belize. Joe wrote the Suggested London Itineraries and Exploring London chapters and worked with Donald on editing the book.

    Donald Strachan is a journalist, writer, and editor who has lived in London for just 19 years—a fact which, as any real local will tell you, disqualifies him from calling himself a "proper" Londoner. However, he has written about the city, and wider European travel, for newspapers worldwide, including the *Sydney Morning Herald* and the *Independent on Sunday,* and is the U.K. *Sunday Telegraph*'s regular contributor on travel-related new technology. He's also authored or co-authored several recent guidebooks to European destinations, including *Frommer's Complete England 2012* and *Florence & Tuscany Day by Day.* Donald wrote The Best of London, London in Depth, and Planning Your Trip to London chapters, and worked on the editing of the whole guide.

    Mary Anne Evans began writing about London's extraordinary wide range of restaurants in the days when posh French had the upper hand and Indian and Chinese restaurants were stuck in the red flock wallpaper era. Many, many meals later, she still champions London as the best city in the world for dining, despite writing about places as far apart as New York, Helsinki, and Albania. She has written guide books on London for *Gayot/Gault Millau* and on Brussels and Stockholm for *Frommer's*. She was editor of *Where London* for 10 years and currently writes on France for *about.com*. Mary Anne wrote the Eating Out in London and Staying in London chapters.

Sian Meades has lived in southeast London for a decade and has spent most of that time window shopping and hunting for the perfect boutiques (new ones keep popping up; it's a fabulous and endless task). She's the editor of the lifestyle website of *Domestic Sluttery* and she won't rest until she's found every single shopping gem in the city. Sian compiled the Shopping chapter.

John Power is a London-based DJ, club promoter, and writer with nearly two decades' experience traversing the bars, clubs, and nightlife of the capital. A confirmed south Londoner, he has written for publications such as *Time Out*, *The Guardian*, *Dummy*, *Kultureflash,* and *le cool* on everything from naked bike riding and the Crystal Palace dinosaurs to acid house raves and pop-up restaurants. John is our resident Nightlife and Entertainment expert.

HOW TO CONTACT US

In researching this book, we discovered many wonderful places—hotels, restaurants, shops, and more. We're sure you'll find others. Please tell us about them, so we can share the information with your fellow travelers in upcoming editions. If you were disappointed with a recommendation, we'd love to know that, too. Please write to:

Frommer's London 2013
John Wiley & Sons, Inc. • 111 River St. • Hoboken, NJ 07030-5774
frommersfeedback@wiley.com

ADVISORY & DISCLAIMER

Travel information can change quickly and unexpectedly, and we strongly advise you to confirm important details locally before traveling, including information on visas, health and safety, traffic and transport, accommodation, shopping and eating out. We also encourage you to stay alert while traveling and to remain aware of your surroundings. Avoid civil disturbances, and keep a close eye on cameras, purses, wallets and other valuables.

While we have endeavored to ensure that the information contained within this guide is accurate and up-to-date at the time of publication, we make no representations or warranties with respect to the accuracy or completeness of the contents of this work and specifically disclaim all warranties, including without limitation warranties of fitness for a particular purpose. We accept no responsibility or liability for any inaccuracy or errors or omissions, or for any inconvenience, loss, damage, costs or expenses of any nature whatsoever incurred or suffered by anyone as a result of any advice or information contained in this guide.

The inclusion of a company, organization or Website in this guide as a service provider and/or potential source of further information does not mean that we endorse them or the information they provide. Be aware that information provided through some Websites may be unreliable and can change without notice. Neither the publisher or author shall be liable for any damages arising herefrom.

FROMMER'S STAR RATINGS, ICONS & ABBREVIATIONS

Every hotel, restaurant, and attraction listing in this guide has been ranked for quality, value, service, amenities, and special features using a star-rating system. In country, state, and regional guides, we also rate towns and regions to help you narrow down your choices and budget your time accordingly. Hotels and restaurants are rated on a scale of zero (recommended) to three stars (exceptional). Attractions, shopping, nightlife, towns, and regions are rated according to the following scale: zero stars (recommended), one star (highly recommended), two stars (very highly recommended), and three stars (must-see).

In addition to the star-rating system, we also use seven feature icons that point you to the great deals, in-the-know advice, and unique experiences that separate travelers from tourists. Throughout the book, look for:

special finds—those places only insiders know about

fun facts—details that make travelers more informed and their trips more fun

kids—best bets for kids and advice for the whole family

special moments—those experiences that memories are made of

overrated—places or experiences not worth your time or money

insider tips—great ways to save time and money

great values—where to get the best deals

The following abbreviations are used for credit cards:

AE American Express	**DISC** Discover	**V** Visa
DC Diners Club	**MC** MasterCard	

TRAVEL RESOURCES AT FROMMERS.COM

Frommer's travel resources don't end with this guide. Frommer's website, **www.frommers.com**, has travel information on more than 4,000 destinations. We update features regularly, giving you access to the most current trip-planning information and the best airfare, lodging, and car-rental bargains. You can also listen to podcasts, connect with other Frommers.com members through our active-reader forums, share your travel photos, read blogs from guidebook editors and fellow travelers, and much more.

THE BEST OF LONDON

London never seems to get tired. It's the greatest paradox of a city with a history spanning two millennia that it stays forever young and energetic. Britain's capital is home to the great art collections of the National Gallery, architectural icons such as Westminster Abbey, and a rich Royal heritage, but it also spawns underground design and musical innovation. It is a city of independent "villages"—Chelsea or Greenwich have little in common with Shoreditch or Soho—and a conurbation of green spaces as well as great buildings.

THINGS TO DO   The old sits alongside the new here—nowhere more so than at Wren's great baroque dome of **St. Paul's Cathedral,** framed by 21st-century skyscrapers—and London is rightly famed for its museums and galleries. Prized collections, ancient and contemporary—from Bloomsbury's **British Museum** to the South Bank's **Tate Modern**—share top billing with small spaces such as the **Sir John Soane's Museum** that could only exist in this city. Ride the **London Eye** observation wheel to get to grips with the city's layout.

SHOPPING   The variety of shopping districts can be bewildering, even for a regular visitor. **Knightsbridge** and **Chelsea** have the chi-chi boutiques, **Mayfair** the finest men's tailors, while the latest in street-level style emerges from **Shoreditch** and the East End, spiritual home of the short-run "pop-up" shop. This is a city with something for every taste or budget, and best buys remain collectables, vintage fashions, and handmade accessories. Street markets as diverse as **Columbia Road** (flowers and niche design) and **Portobello** (antiques, secondhand goods, and fashions) are experiencing a mini-renaissance.

EATING & DRINKING   Whatever your favorite flavor, you'll find it somewhere. As London's center of gravity moves east, so does the dining scene: Nuno Mendes' **Viajante** is the most creative eatery to grace an eastside hotel. British classics **Rules** and **J. Sheekey** are as good as ever, and 2011 saw superstar chef Heston Blumenthal reinvent **Dinner** in Knightsbridge. Areas with lower rents continue to attract skillful chefs to gastropubs and cool cafes, and Spain's culinary influence continues to spawn a new crop of creative tapas bars.

Columbia Road's flower market. PREVIOUS PAGE: **Covent Garden.**

NIGHTLIFE & ENTERTAINMENT When darkness falls, the historic monuments and grand museums fade into the inky night, and a whole new London comes to life. The **West End's** bright lights draw the crowds with mega-musicals and big-name dramas. Less well known is London's growing taste for the offbeat, from cabaret and Charleston revival parties to dubstep, burlesque, and even underground bingo. **Soho** is still buzzing—and the hipster-heavy streets of **Shoreditch, Hoxton,** and **Dalston** are jumping well into the small hours.

THE most unforgettable LONDON EXPERIENCES

o **Flying High on the London Eye:** Take your camera on a ride to the top of London's South Bank observation wheel for a far-reaching shot of the vast cityscape. Any time is a good time to book your "flight," but for a breathtaking photo op, jump aboard in late afternoon as the sun starts to sink and the lights come on across the metropolis. See p. 138.

o **Hanging Out on the Hip Streets of the "New" East End:** London's most fashionable folk haunt the streets and alleyways of East London. Shop the niche designer boutiques and vintage stores of **Shoreditch** (p. 272) and **Columbia Road** (p. 273), dine out on French cuisine at **Les Trois Garçons** (p. 239), drink cocktails at **Nightjar** (p. 311), and dance till the small hours at **Plastic People** (p. 325).

o **Spending an Evening at a West End Theatre:** London is the theatrical capital of the world. The live stages of **Theatreland,** around Covent Garden and Soho, offer a unique combination of variety, accessibility, and economy—and have everything from serious drama to daring musicals. See "The Performing Arts" in Chapter 7.

A flight on the London Eye.

Afternoon Tea at The Ritz.

- **Taking Afternoon Tea:** At the **Ritz Palm Court** (p. 257), the traditional tea ritual carries on as it did in Britain's colonial heyday. The pomp and circumstance of the British Empire live on at the Ritz—only the Empire is missing these days. If the Ritz is fully booked, try **Brown's** or the **Goring;** see "Teatime" in Chapter 5.

- **Climbing the Dome of St. Paul's Cathedral:** Wren's baroque masterpiece, **St. Paul's Cathedral** is crammed full of history, memorials, and architectural detail. But it's the climb up to the Golden Gallery for 360° panoramas across the city that will stay with you forever. Look down, if you dare. See p. 146.

- **Watching the Sunset from Waterloo Bridge:** This famous river crossing is perfectly positioned to watch the embers of the day dissipate behind the Houses of Parliament. The view is so memorable that it moved the Kinks to produce a chart-topping song in 1967, *Waterloo Sunset*, with the lines "As long as I gaze on / Waterloo sunset / I am in paradise." Look east to catch the last rays as they bounce off the dome of St. Paul's Cathedral, the ancient spires of Wren's churches, and the towering glass skyscrapers of the 21st-century city.

THE best FOOD & DRINK EXPERIENCES

- **Sinking a Pint in a Traditional Pub:** From Tudor coaching inns to literary lounges, micro-breweries to indie music taverns, London has a pub for every taste and mood. For an authentic flavor of the capital, seek out beers created in London by breweries such as Meantime, Sambrook, and The Kernel. See "Pubs" in Chapter 7.

- **"Nose-to-tail eating" in the Shadow of London's Meat Market:** St. John, a former smokehouse north of Smithfield, is London's best venue for the serious carnivore. Chef Fergus Henderson can claim to have started the contemporary trend in offal cuisine. His earthy, traditional flavors would delight a reincarnated Henry VIII. The 2011 opening of a restaurant at the **St. John Hotel** saw Henderson repeat the trick in the heart of Theatreland. See p. 238 and p. 347.

o **Mining the Stalls at Borough Market:** The number one weekend port of call for London foodies is this Thursday-to-Saturday produce market under the railway close to London Bridge station—not least for the free samples dished out by vendors keen to market their wares. You'll find stalls selling everything from wild mushrooms and white port to pastries and homemade sweets: It's food heaven. See p. 276.

o **Enjoying Fine Food from the Subcontinent:** London's first Indian restaurant opened in 1810, and the capital now has some of the best South Asian restaurants in the world. At upscale **Amaya** (p. 223), you can enjoy Indian

A traditional London pub.

tapas under cascading crystal chandeliers. Over in the East End, at **Tayyabs** (p. 245), gutsy Punjabi-Pakistani flavors are dished up at bargain prices in a converted Victorian pub. See "Restaurants by Cuisine," p. 260.

o **Chowing down on English cheese:** England produces hundreds of artisan cheeses, and you'll find some of the best places to sample them in the capital. Check out the West Country cheddars, red Leicester, and goat's cheeses at cheesemongers like **La Fromagerie** (p. 292) and **Neal's Yard Dairy** (p. 427)—which also runs entertaining evening tasting sessions open to

Fish stall in Borough Market.

all—as well as on the top-class after-dinner cheeseboard at **The Square** (p. 196).

○ **Eating Sunday Lunch at a Gastropub:** Well-to-do couples and families still observe the traditional ritual of a long, late weekend lunch washed down with a pint of ale or glass of wine. Our favorite spots are in the leafier western reaches of the city, the **Cow** in Notting Hill and the **Pig's Ear** in Chelsea. See p. 220 and p. 230.

THE best LONDON MUSEUMS

○ **British Museum:** When Sir Hans Sloane died in 1753, he bequeathed to England his vast collection of art and antiquities. This formed the nucleus of a huge collection that grew with the acquisitions of the Empire, and has come to include such remarkable objects as the Rosetta Stone and the Parthenon Marbles (which Greece still want back). See p. 96.

○ **National Gallery:** Wandering through the "who's who" of Western painting—from da Vinci to Velázquez to Rembrandt to Cézanne—dazzles the eye at this astounding art museum. The Sainsbury Wing has one of the world's great Renaissance collections. See p. 102.

○ **National Maritime Museum:** The story of Britain is the tale of its relationship with the sea, and a £20m 2011 revamp transformed the world's biggest museum dedicated to seafarers and seafaring. You'll encounter plenty of multimedia exhibits, alongside the likes of the coat that Nelson was wearing when he was shot by a sniper at the Battle of Trafalgar. See p. 172.

○ **Museum of London:** Follow the history of London from Roman times past the Great Fire to the Blitz, the Swinging Sixties, and beyond. The 2010 opening of the Galleries of Modern London propelled this already fascinating museum into the very top rank of the city's cultural spaces. See p. 145.

The Great Court at the British Museum.

Victoria & Albert Museum: Mosaic (left) and the Fashion Gallery (right).

- **Tate Britain:** Sir Henry Tate, a sugar producer, started it all with 70 or so paintings, and the original Tate site now concentrates on British art dating back to 1500. The collection grew considerably when artist J. M. W. Turner bequeathed some 300 paintings and 19,000 watercolors upon his death. It's the best place in the country to view Pre-Raphaelite works, too. See p. 126.
- **Victoria & Albert Museum:** Admire the world's greatest decorative arts. The V&A boasts the largest collection of Renaissance sculpture outside Italy. It is also strong on medieval English treasures and has the greatest collection of Indian art outside India. See p. 127.
- **Sir John Soane's Museum:** The former home of the architect that built the Bank of England is stuffed with curios, sculpture, and serious art—just as he left it on his death in 1837. It's London's best small museum. See p. 108.

THE best FAMILY EXPERIENCES

- **Cruising London's Waterways:** In addition to the grand River Thames, London has a working canal system—with towpath walks, bridges, and wharves—that once kept goods flowing to and from the city's docks. The best value trip is aboard the **Thames Clipper** from Westminster to Greenwich, passing under Tower Bridge, but kids will also love riding a traditional narrowboat from Little Venice to Camden Lock. See p. 422 and p. 424.
- **Asking How, Where, and Why at the Launchpad:** Inside South Kensington's **Science Museum,** the specially commissioned children's area has more than 50 interactive exhibits designed to keep inquisitive minds occupied. Regular free family shows never fail to entertain and amaze. Then there's the main museum collection, the most significant and comprehensive in the

Horse-riding along Rotten Row.

world, with everything from King George III's scientific instruments to the *Apollo 10* space module. See p. 126.

o **Losing Your Way in the World's Most Famous Hedge Maze:** The green labyrinth at **Hampton Court** twists and turns for almost half a mile. When you manage to extricate yourselves from its clutches, stroll through centuries of architectural styles at this stunning palace, home of many an English monarch. With little ones in tow, grab an activity trail and don't neglect the gift shops. See p. 176.

o **Parading Rotten Row on Horseback:** You'll feel like a character from a Victorian novel as you pass **Hyde Park's** joggers, rollerbladers, and cyclists. There's no better way to admire and enjoy the "green lung"—central London's largest and most popular open space. See p. 112.

o **Riding the Routemaster on Heritage Bus 15:** London's traditional hop-on, hop-off buses have been retained in service on two "heritage routes" that criss-cross the capital. Forget the expensive open-top tours: For just £1.35 you can see Piccadilly Circus, Trafalgar Square, St. Paul's Cathedral, the Monument, the Tower of London, and much more. Sit on the front seat on the top deck for the prime panoramas. See p. 425.

o **Going Botanic in Royal Kew:** The **Royal Botanic Gardens,** Kew, house more than 50,000 plants from across the planet, including Arctic and tropical varieties. Youngsters will love the 200m

Treetop walkway in the Royal Botanic Gardens, Kew.

(656-ft.) high Treetop Walkway, up in the Garden's deciduous canopy. After all that greenery, head across the Thames for hands-on engineering displays at the **Kew Bridge Steam Museum.** See p. 182.

THE best FREE & DIRT CHEAP LONDON

- **Visiting the Great Museums:** London's state museums and galleries—including most of the big names—are free to enter. World-class treasure troves where you can roam without charge include the **British Museum, National Gallery, National Portrait Gallery, Horniman Museum, Tate Britain, Tate Modern, Natural History Museum, Science Museum, Victoria & Albert Museum, Museum of London,** and **Sir John Soane's Museum.** And don't forget the **British Library** with its literary gems. See Chapter 4 for listings, and "The Best London Museums," above, for our favorites.

- **Watching Changing the Guard:** The **Buckingham Palace** (p. 97) event has more pomp than any other royal ceremony on earth, but the two daily changes at **Horse Guards** (p. 120), the headquarters of the Queen's Household Cavalry Mounted Regiment, are both more accessible and more fun. See p. 97.

- **Taking in Fresh Air and a City View:** North of the River Thames, **Hampstead Heath** offers miles of woodland trails and the best vistas over low-rise suburbia to the architectural icons of the center. To the south, the heights of **Greenwich Park** enjoy a panoramic sweep that takes in the royal borough's 18th-century maritime architecture and the steel-and-glass of Canary Wharf. Recent freezing winters have even seen the hill used by local snowboarders. See p. 164 and p. 172.

Changing the Guard ceremony.

East End Thrift Store.

o **Dining on the Cheap:** Away from the main tourist drag and the Michelin-starred hotspots, London is surprisingly well equipped with affordable, tasty places to enjoy a full meal for under £15. Among the best are the fiery Szechuan flavors of **Gourmet San** and the West End's venerable budget pitstop, the **Stockpot.** See "Best Places for a Cheap & Cheerful Meal," p. 212.

o **Staying in Style for a Fraction of the Price You Expect:** "Boutique" hotels are encroaching deeper into budget territory than ever before. At **Z Hotel Soho** (p. 348), surrender a little space but none of the chic at a berth in the heart of Soho. For cheaper digs, look east to the likes of Spitalfields' no-frills **Tune Hotel** (p. 371), or Dalston's stylish **Avo** (p. 373).

o **Going to the Library:** The best and most easily accessible of London's specialist (and free) libraries is the **Wellcome Collection,** which houses a grisly cornucopia of medical materials, including books, paintings, and drawings. Staff offer free tours and workshops to help guide you through the collection. See p. 111.

o **Shopping for Vintage Threads:** The **East End Thrift Store** has a warehouse full of vintage clothes for men and women, all at good prices if you hunt hard. See p. 287.

o **Catching a Free Event in the Center of the City:** From the Lord Mayor's Show to the Notting Hill Carnival, almost every major public event in the capital costs nothing to attend. See "London Calendar of Events," p. 43, or call in at the **Britain & London Visitor Centre,** 1 Lower Regent St., SW1 (www.visitlondon.com; ✆ **08701/566-366**), and inquire about what's on while you're here.

THE best HISTORIC EXPERIENCES

o **Meeting the Heroes and Villains of the City's History:** The greats and not-so-greats of English history show their faces at the **National Portrait Gallery** often "warts and all." The gang's all here, from Dr. (Samuel) Johnson to Princess Diana, and a Holbein cartoon of Henry VIII. See p. 104.

o **Taking a Tour of Royal London:** From palaces and parks to the royal art collections, much of London's history, geography, and culture has been shaped by centuries of aristocratic rule. You can see the best of it in a day—including the Queen's favorite grocer, **Fortnum & Mason** (p. 290)—if you plot your itinerary carefully. Come during July or August and you can also view inside **Buckingham Palace** (p. 97). See "Royal London" in Chapter 3.

National Portrait Gallery.

o **Walking in the Footsteps of Sir Christopher Wren:** The architect who rebuilt so much of London after the Great Fire of 1666 is best known for his churches. Walk from **St. Bride's,** on Fleet Street, past his icon, **St. Paul's Cathedral,** to **St. Mary-le-Bow** and beyond to appreciate his genius. See "Saints & the City" in Chapter 4. For expert guides to help you tour, see "Walking Tours & Guided Visits," in Chapter 2.

o **Shopping in the Grandest Department Store of Them All:** And, no, it isn't Harrods. **Liberty of London** was founded in 1875 and moved to its current half-timbered, mock-Tudor home in 1924. London's rediscovered hunger for classic fabrics and vintage style has seen Liberty catapulted right back to the forefront of cool. See p. 290.

Fortnum & Mason.

The steeple of St. Bride's.

Liberty of London.

o **Imagining Domestic Life Through the Ages:** At the **Geffrye Museum** period re-creations of interiors from the spartan 1630s to the flashy 1990s allow visitors to understand how home life has changed. Travel 500 years in an hour in an absorbing visual and personal retelling of the history of middle-class London. See p. 154.

o **Staying at a Classic Mayfair Hotel:** From the Art Deco interiors of **Claridge's** (p. 256), to the liveried door attendants of the **Connaught** (p. 349), nothing screams historic London quite like the city's upscale hotel area. Comfort has never gone out of style here, so start saving right away. See "Mayfair" in Chapter 8.

THE best WAYS TO SEE LONDON LIKE A LOCAL

o **Strolling North London on a Lazy Sunday:** Head for **Hampstead Heath** off Well Walk and take the right fork, which leads to an open field with a panoramic view over central London. Backtrack for lunch at **Wells** (p. 249), before a visit to Hampstead's **Freud Museum** (p. 164) or **Keats House** (p. 166), both of which are open on Sunday until 5pm. Cap it all off with a pint in the **Holly Bush** (p. 315). See "North & Northwest London" in Chapter 4.

o **Joining a Tour Led by a Homeless Resident:** To see the city through a different lens, book a guided walk with **Unseen Tours.** This small social enterprise runs walking tours of neighborhoods like Shoreditch, Covent Garden, and Mayfair, and all are led by homeless and formerly homeless residents of the area. Tours can be raw and personal, obviously, but are also packed with history and anecdote. See p. 426.

o **Bargaining at London's Best Street Market:** A jumble of open-air stalls and warrens of indoor arcades combine to make **Portobello Road** the quintessential West London market. Haggle hard and you'll likely get 10% to 15% off the asking price. Saturday's the best day to come, when even the crowds won't ruin your fun. See p. 277.

o **Spending a Night on the Tiles South of the River:** Young revelers pour into buzzing Brixton after dark, despite the area's historical rep for edginess. Try **Dogstar** for everything from house DJs to cabaret, or the **O2 Academy Brixton** for live performances by the latest indie and rock bands. See p. 309 and p. 320.

Sunday strolling in Hampstead Heath.

o **Feasting on Turkish Food and Nightclubbing in Hip Dalston:** An artsy vibe has overtaken this up-and-coming area just north of Shoreditch. Dalston was long known for its Turkish community, and has the best stretch of *ocakbasi* (open-coal BBQ) dining this side of Istanbul. Eat your fill at **Mangal I,** then dance it all off around the corner at the **Nest.** See p. 248 and p. 324.

o **Volunteering to Maintain London's Natural Spaces:** Give something back—and stay in shape as you do it—by joining London's "Green Gym" for a few hours. See p. 429.

THE best NEIGHBORHOODS FOR GETTING LOST

o **The City:** The "Square Mile" is these days best known for high finance, but the original site of London is still the best place to connect with the city's past. Roam at leisure to discover fragments of Roman walls and a buried amphitheater, alleyways that housed London's first ale houses and coffee shops, Wren's baroque churches, and of course the glass-and-steel towers of the 21st-century skyline. See "The City" in Chapter 4.

o **Southwark's Riverfront:** With its own cathedral and a history separate from its neighbor to the north, Southwark feels like—and once was—a city apart.

Walk the riverside streets from Tower Bridge in the east to Waterloo Bridge in the west and you'll see London's best food market, atmospheric streets lined with old warehouses, and the city's leading modern art museum and performing arts complex. See "The South Bank" in Chapter 4.

o **Royal Greenwich:** Profoundly shaped by the architecture of Sir Christopher Wren and centuries of royal (and naval) patronage, the "village" of Greenwich has more than enough historical sights and museums to fill a day—as well as a great **Indoor Market** (p. 277) and vintage shopping at **The Junk Shop** (p. 279). Round things off with an informal dinner at the **Old Brewery** (p. 317), which is also the home of brewer Meantime. See "Southeast London—Greenwich" in Chapter 4.

o **Mayfair:** Named for a raucous "May Fair" that was finally moved out in 1764, this part of the West End was originally developed as a residential area for noble and royal patrons. It's here you'll find London's grandest addresses, finest luxury hotels, and best upscale shopping streets—but also occasional quiet corners that still retain a "local" feel, as well as a museum dedicated to expat composer Handel. See p. 62.

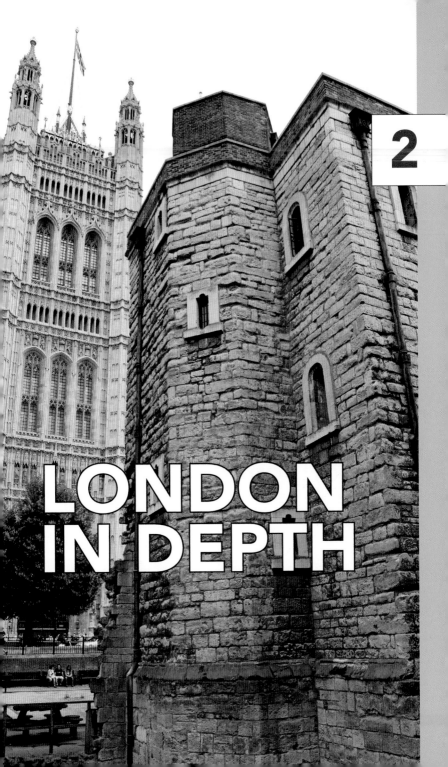

2

LONDON
IN DEPTH

L ondon continues to be the city that sets the trends, rather than merely following them. On the streets of Soho, the trading floors of the Square Mile, the sports stadia of Olympic Park, or the mighty bridges spanning the River Thames, it still feels like London is the fulcrum of the world—just as it was at the height of its power, when half the world was run from Westminster. Expect to discover a city steeped in history and nobility, certainly, but one that's also inventing the future.

Britain's capital is so big—and its residents such a diverse bunch, as Craig Taylor's 2011 book *Londoners* documents—that almost anything we could write about contemporary London life would be true *somewhere* in the city. Londoners dine out more than ever, but at the same time there's unprecedented interest in food preparation at home. High-fashion boutiques sell outfits with staggering price tags, but thrift-store shopping for that unique vintage look has never been more popular. The shiniest new thing always attracts attention, but reverence for the old never disappears. At the same time, temporary **pop-up** retail outlets, often selling trendy clothing, and restaurants are, as the name suggests, popping up all across the city allowing trendsetters to buy and move on, keeping things fresh and vibrant. Rich and poor live closer to each other than ever, as once unheralded neighborhoods like Hackney, Bow, and Bermondsey attract well-heeled, hip, young dwellers.

London practically invented tradition, but in fields as different as food, film, theatre, music, and just about everything else, the city is now, as always, right on the cutting edge.

LONDON TODAY

Cities of eight million residents are rarely "short of news," and in recent years London seems to have generated more than its share of headlines. Riots, strikes, mayoral elections, the 2012 Olympic and Paralympic Games, the Occupy movement—each created news that was amplified by Twitter, Facebook, and other social networks, and shared instantly around the world.

From a PR perspective, the most damaging recent event for London's reputation was the rioting of August 2011. Sparked by a fatal police shooting in Tottenham, in the city's northeast, mass civil disturbance and looting spread to many (mostly outlying) neighborhoods over the course of 3 nights. From Enfield, in the north, to Croydon, south of London, and Hackney to Ealing, a mixture of rage, opportunism, and planned criminality burst onto the streets, spreading like a virus. Scenes of looting, arson, and confrontation were beamed across the globe, then just as suddenly dissipated. The riots left two Londoners dead, and more than 2,000 were subsequently arrested across the city. Politicians and campaigners of every stripe have sought to draw lessons from this unusual event, but it's unlikely that any single interpretation could hold water.

Jewel Tower at the Palace of Westminster.

In the face of continued economic gloom, and upheavals in neighboring European economies, Britain's political system is experiencing turmoil not seen since the 1970s and 1980s. London, naturally, is at the heart of things: Mass student protests against the raising of university fees turned violent in late 2010; tens of thousands of public sector workers took to the streets in November 2011 to protest changes to their pensions. Perhaps the most adept at garnering publicity were the Occupy protesters, who camped for months outside a London icon, St. Paul's Cathedral. Taking their lead from Occupy Wall Street—who themselves were inspired by Spain's *Indignados*—they represented myriad political views, but stood united in opposition to what they perceived as the unfair distribution of wealth and power in Britain.

London's cultural shape has been shifting steadily, the most obvious example being the eastward shift of its center of gravity. Residents—particularly nightlife-loving young Londoners—are rediscovering the areas bordering the original city walls. First came the rebirth of Spitalfields and Shoreditch; then Hoxton and Brick Lane became magnets for the hip; and now the cutting edge is moving northeast—following a path first laid down by the Romans, up the Kingsland Road to Dalston. Come on a weekend and you'll find the streets of these areas as busy at midnight as they are at midday. Startup technology companies gather around Old Street's "Silicon Roundabout," and foster innovation that has attracted government and investment interest in the shape of the Tech City UK initiative (see www.techcityuk.com).

It was therefore appropriate that East London in 2012 was in the global spotlight like never before, as the cameras documented sporting success and failure at the Olympic Park in Stratford. London was the first city to host the Games three times—1908 and 1948 were the previous occasions—and London 2012 represented the only time since World War II that the Olympics returned to a host city. The area will be in the sporting limelight again in 5 years, as 2011 saw London announced as host city of the 2017 World Athletics Championships.

A permanent state of self-transformation continues elsewhere in the city, too, with architects in the Square Mile and its environs looking skyward. A major redrawing of the city's silhouette is in progress: Building is complete on Bishopsgate's 230m (755-ft.) **Heron Tower,** its outer surface coated in energy-generating photovoltaic cells, and is well underway for the nearby 288m (945-ft.) **Pinnacle** building. Across the river, the **Shard of Glass** above London Bridge station is, at 310m (1,017 ft.), the tallest building in the European Union. All dwarf one of the capital's most famous recent skyscrapers, 30 St. Mary Axe, fondly dubbed the "Gherkin" by Londoners for its distinctive, pickle-like shape.

30 St. Mary Axe, also known as the Gherkin.

17

Musically, London is enjoying a mini-renaissance, and the city's urban music is finally holding its own in a market dominated by the U.S. East London's grime scene has spawned headline acts, such as Dizzee Rascal, Tinie Tempah, and Tinchy Stryder. Camden Town's N-Dubz achieved mainstream chart success—band member Tulisa even appeared as a judge on primetime TV talent show *The X Factor*. Dubstep, a fusion of urban music styles, including garage and drum-and-bass, has traveled way beyond its London roots to influence some of the biggest names in U.S. hip-hop and R&B. London's Mobo ("music of black origin") has never been bigger, nationally or internationally. It was also a Londoner, soul singer Adele, who dominated the 2012 Grammy Awards. She won all 6 categories in which she was nominated, thereby confirming her status as the hottest musician on the planet in 2012.

Recent years have seen Londoners grow increasingly interested in the ethics and economics of their food supply—with those at the upper end of the income scale prepared (and able) to pay a premium for a cleaner conscience. However, shopping seasonally and locally isn't straightforward in a metropolis with a taste for food from every corner of the globe. The issues aren't always as clear-cut as they may appear: In spite of the "food miles" gap, an out-of-season tomato reared in Morocco can have a much lower carbon footprint than one grown in a cool English summer. Still, you'll see supermarkets and niche convenience stores such as Planet Organic selling a wide range of seasonal, organic, and Fairtrade goods, as well as produce markets like the one at Borough (p. 276) which is packed to the rafters on weekends. In an upscale restaurant, expect your meat to be reared ethically, your poultry to be free range, and your vegetables and pulses to be organic—and don't be shy about quizzing staff on these points.

It's also increasingly easy to find genuinely local beers. Ales brewed by Meantime, in Greenwich, Brodie's of Leyton, the Camden Town Brewery, Tottenham's Redemption, The Kernel in Southwark, and Battersea's Sambrook are just some of the names available in increasingly more pubs and bars around town. New labels and craft micro-brews seem to appear almost monthly—the

DATELINE

A.D. 47	Romans occupying Britain found Londinium as a garrison and trading settlement.	**1091**	The London Tornado damages London Bridge and St. Mary-le-Bow church.
200	The first city walls are erected by the Romans.	**1189**	Henry Fitz Ailwyn becomes London's first recorded Lord Mayor.
604	St. Paul's Cathedral is established on its current site.	**1212**	The Great Fire of Southwark destroys London Bridge and surrounding streets.
880s	Saxon King Alfred the Great reoccupies the original Roman city.	**1215**	King John signs Magna Carta at Runnymede, granting freedom to the city.
1066	William, Duke of Normandy, invades England, and the Norman Period begins.	**1348–50**	The Black Death kills half of London's population.

Essential London Histories

The definitive and essential historical guide to the city is Peter Ackroyd's *London: The Biography* (2000). The best historically minded travelogue is H. V. Morton's *In Search of London* (1951). Reading-age children will prefer the humorous, but scrupulously accurate take found in Terry Deary's *Loathsome London* (2005), part of the *Horrible Histories* series. For self-guided walking tours based around historical periods, pick up Leo Hollis' *Historic London Walks* (2005). Ed Glinert's *London Compendium* (2004) is a source of lore and trivia organized by district and street.

London Brewers' Alliance website, www.londonbrewers.org, is a good place to keep up with developments. The year 2010 even saw the rebirth of Truman's, once the world's largest brewer. For now it's a niche concern whose beer is brewed in rural Suffolk, northeast of the city, but grand plans are afoot to bring it back to its historic East London home.

THE MAKING OF LONDON
The Ancient City: A.D. 47–1066

Although London almost certainly sprung up in the 1st century A.D., myth and legend hint at Celtic roots much deeper in the clay that lies beneath the city. According to medieval legend, London was founded by a Greek, Brutus, to be the "New Troy" and watched over by Gog and Magog, the last survivors of a race of giants. Wicker effigies of the twin giants have been paraded at the head of the annual **Lord Mayor's Show** for more than 5 centuries (see "London Calendar of Events," p. 43), and carvings are on show at the **Guildhall** (p. 144) year round. Archeological evidence for some prehistoric activity during the Bronze and Iron Ages has been found, dispersed as widely as Uxbridge, Southwark,

1381 Wat Tyler, leader of the Peasants' Revolt, is killed in Smithfield by the Lord Mayor.

1550 London's population reaches 120,000.

1642 The Puritan government orders the closure of playhouses such as the Rose, the Swan, and the Globe.

1649 Charles I is beheaded outside Whitehall Palace, in Westminster.

1675 The Royal Observatory is founded in Greenwich.

1682 A market in "Spital Fields" is granted a Royal Charter.

1694 The Bank of England is founded in the City of London.

1703 The calamitous Great Storm—a hurricane—batters the city with around 120mph winds.

1738 John Wesley is converted to Methodism, on a site now marked by the Aldersgate Flame.

1746 The last ever execution by axe takes place outside the Tower of London.

1753 The Bow Street Runners, London's first detective force, is formed by author and magistrate Henry Fielding.

continues

Beckton, and Carshalton. However, nothing that could be called a "settlement" existed until the Romans arrived around A.D. 47.

According to the 1st-century-A.D. *Histories* of the Roman senator Tacitus, **Londinium** was founded as a garrison and trading settlement—the site on the north bank was probably chosen for twin knolls that served as lookouts, known today as Ludgate Hill and Cornhill. A bloody revolt led by native **Queen Boudicca** (d. A.D. 61) of the Iceni tribe, saw the city sacked a decade later—a deed that earned her a statue in modern-day **Parliament Square.** By A.D. 100, however, the rebuilt town had replaced Camulodunum (modern Colchester) as the capital of the Roman province of Britannia.

The Romans built the first **London Bridge** (p. 137), just yards from the current version, and by A.D. 200 had constructed a London Wall that would remain the city's boundary for more than a millennium; you can still view parts of it in Trinity Place, by Tower Hill, adjacent to a statue of Emperor Trajan (A.D. 53–117), and also at the site of the garrison's fort, now Noble Street, close to the **Museum of London** (p. 145). The Wall and its gates echo in London street names—not least, London Wall—and in the names of long-lived City churches, such as **All Hallows on the Wall** and **St. Giles Cripplegate**.

The City wards of Aldersgate, Aldgate, Bishopsgate, and Cripplegate take their names from Roman gates, while the areas of Houndsditch and Shoreditch on the 21st-century map were Roman defenses dug outside the walls. The Roman Temple of Diana was probably below current St. Paul's Cathedral, the Forum was where Gracechurch Street now meets Lombard Street, and remains of the Basilica lie below **Leadenhall Market.** Until recently, the scanty remnants of a **Temple of Mithras,** discovered in 1952, were on open display on Queen Victoria Street, opposite Sise Lane. (Finds from the Temple also form part of the collection at the **Museum of London,** see p. 145, and plans were announced during 2011 to move the temple back to its original home, soon to be Bloomberg's new European HQ.) The remains of an **Amphitheater** lie below the Guildhall, and you can visit on the same ticket as the **Guildhall Art Gallery**

1810 London's first Indian restaurant opens.	is arrested after a mass gathering on Kennington Common.
1815 The Bethlehem Hospital for the insane—nicknamed "Bedlam"—closes.	**1851** The world is astonished at the exhibits on show at London's Great Exhibition.
1837 Queen Victoria begins her reign, in the same year that London's first rail station—Euston—opens.	**1878** With eerie similarities to the *Marchioness* disaster 111 years later, the *Princess Alice* pleasure boat is struck in the Thames, and 650 souls drown.
1848 The Chartist convention assembles in London and demands political reform. Leading Chartist William Cuffay, mixed-race son of a Kent woman and a freed slave,	**1909** An American, Gordon Selfridge, opens London's iconic department store.

(p. 144). Although little of Roman London remains visible, the modern City of London, the "Square Mile," was essentially mapped out by the Romans.

The Imperial invaders were forced to abandon the city around A.D. 450. New arrivals from the continent, the Saxons, formed their own settlement of **Lundenwic** around the current Covent Garden between A.D. 650 and 850. Little remains of Saxon London save a stone arch at **All-Hallows-by-the-Tower** (p. 153) and in the street known today as **Aldwych**—"old market" in Saxon. Faced with constant Viking attacks, **King Alfred** (849–99) took his people inside the safety of the Roman walls around 886; and when **Edward the Confessor** (1003–66) established an abbey and palace at "West minster" in the 1040s, the double-headed shape of the medieval city was complete.

London in the Middle Ages: 1066–1599

Bustling, medieval London would already have been unrecognizable to a Saxon or Roman. Most of the residents, at least prior to **King Henry VIII**'s (1491–1547) break with the Pope in 1534, were Roman Catholic. The Church was a powerful player in every part of secular life. (The Oscar-winning 1966 film *A Man for All Seasons* dramatizes the politics surrounding Henry's Oath of Supremacy, which was enacted to wrest power from the Church.) The medieval city had more churches than any other in Europe, perhaps 150 packed into the "Square Mile."

In power terms, London was still a double-headed beast: The King or Queen ruled England from palaces in Westminster and Greenwich, but money and mercantilism bought a substantial degree of freedom for the **City of London,** which occupied the land enclosed by the ancient Roman wall. Almost everywhere else that today constitutes "London" was village or open country-side—where **Bloomsbury** (see p. 55) sits was known in the 11th century for its vines and truffle woods. Plague was a regular and devastating visitor; during the **Black Death** of 1348–50, perhaps half of London's population died.

Much of the city was constructed using wood and thatch, and met a fiery end (see below). However, many of London's greatest stone buildings also date

1923 Bolton beat Londoners West Ham in Wembley Stadium's first F.A. Cup Final.	**1981** Race riots blight the inner city borough of Brixton.
1945 Seemingly the entire population takes to the streets to celebrate V.E. Day.	**1986** London's orbital highway, the M25, opens.
1948 London hosts the first postwar Olympic Games.	**1990** Parts of central London are damaged during the Poll Tax Riot.
1952 The Great Smog lasts 5 days and kills 4,000 Londoners.	**1991** John Bird founds the *Big Issue*, a magazine that aims "to help the homeless help themselves."
1953 Queen Elizabeth II is crowned at Westminster Abbey.	**1994** London is linked to Paris by rail via the Channel Tunnel.
1956 The classic red double-decker bus known as the Routemaster hits the streets.	**1996** The IRA breaks a 17-month ceasefire with a Docklands bomb that claims two lives.

continues

from this period. Following the victory of William the Conqueror (r. 1066–87) at the Battle of Hastings, **Romanesque** continental architecture was imported to Britain, where it became known as the **Norman** style. The best example in the city is the 1078 White Tower at the **Tower of London** (p. 150). Londoners associate being "sent to the Tower" with prison and a sticky end, but William and many later royals also used it as a palace and fortress. It's reputedly Britain's most haunted building.

The most significant Norman interior in London is at the **Priory Church of St. Bartholomew the Great** (p. 152), next to Smithfield. This was once part of a much larger monastery. Prior to Henry's **Dissolution of the Monasteries** in 1536–39, London had many powerful religious orders inside and outside its walls. Many survive only in street or neighborhood names: **Blackfriars** was a Dominican priory wedged between Ludgate Hill and the river; and the ruins of the Franciscan monastery of **Greyfriars** occupied the corner of King Edward Street and Newgate Street, opposite St. Paul's Tube station. The site is now a perfumed rose garden on a busy traffic gyratory, and reputedly still haunted by the ghost of **Queen Isabella,** wife and perhaps murderess of King Edward II (r. 1307–27). Whitefriars Street and Carmelite Street, south of Fleet Street, recall a long-vanished **Carmelite** Priory. Nearby, the mysterious **Temple (Round) Church** (p. 152) also dates to the Norman period.

In a separate center farther upstream, **Westminster Abbey** (p. 128) was first used to crown a king in 1066, but is essentially a later **Gothic** building. The French-Gothic style invaded England in the late 12th century, trading round arches for pointed ones—an engineering discovery that, along with flying buttresses, freed church architecture from the need for heavy walls and thick columns. The coming of Gothic allowed ceilings to soar, walls to thin, and windows, vaults, and intricate stone tracery to proliferate. In Britain, it's usually divided into three overlapping periods: **Early English** (1180–1300), **Decorated** (1250–1370), and **Perpendicular** (1350–1550). Westminster Abbey is generally placed among the finest decorated cathedrals in Britain, although later interior additions,

2003 Mass demonstrations take place as up to a million take to London's streets to protest the impending Iraq War.	**2011** Riots and looting spread through many neighborhoods, including Tottenham, Croydon, Enfield, Hackney, and Clapham. Pictures are broadcast across the globe.
2005 July 7 suicide-bomb attacks on three Tube trains and one double-decker bus kill 52.	**2012** London becomes the first city to host a third Olympic Games.
2008 Boris Johnson defeats incumbent Ken Livingstone in the election for Mayor.	

including the fan-vaulted **Henry VII Chapel,** are classic Perpendicular. Many of the great royal names from medieval England are buried inside the Abbey. The hammerbeam ceiling of nearby Westminster Hall inside the **Palace of Westminster** (p. 121) is another prize piece of English Gothic. The **Jewel Tower** (p. 123) is the only other surviving section of the original medieval palace. Parts of the **Guildhall** (p. 144) also date from the Gothic period, as does much of **Southwark Cathedral** (p. 141). The years—and particularly the iconoclasm of the Protestant Reformation—were less kind to London's medieval paintings, although the **Wilton Diptych** (ca. 1399) is one of the stars of the Sainsbury Wing at the **National Gallery** (see p. 102).

Elizabethan music has survived better. The compositions of **William Byrd** (1540–1623) soundtracked both religious ceremonies and courtly intrigues; his *Choral Works* provides an introduction to his devout melodies. The chaotic city streets, however, probably rang more to the tunes of *Songs from the Taverne* (available on CD from Amazon).

It's impossible to understand medieval civic life without grasping the role of the **livery companies,** which emerged during the 13th and 14th centuries. These powerful trade guilds regulated every aspect of the working lives of a skilled laborer; you could only work as a mercer, or a draper, or a fishmonger, or in any other of 70-plus popular trades, with the approval of the appropriate Worshipful Company. Only freemen of a livery company could become Aldermen (council members), and therefore play a role in governing the City from its seat of power, the **Guildhall** (p. 144). The **Lord Mayor of London**—note, not the same person as the recent innovation of a democratically-elected Mayor—could be drawn only from among the Aldermen, a rule that stands to this day; the Lord Mayor's gilded ceremonial coach is one of the prize exhibits at the **Museum of London** (p. 145). Lawyers formed their own kind of company, the **Inns of Court** (see p. 72), and located themselves equidistantly between the twin power centers of Westminster and London. The oldest of the inns, **Lincoln's Inn,** dates to at least 1422—its **Great Hall** was erected in 1490. Among its alumni is

Lincoln's Inn.

poet **John Donne** (1572–1631), whose *Complete English Poems* addresses many contemporary issues.

For the poor, medieval life was, to borrow the words of English philosopher Thomas Hobbes (1588–1679) in *Leviathan* (1651), "nasty, brutish, and short." It was even worse for criminals or anyone who chose the wrong religion: **Smithfield** in the early 16th century was used for burning heretics; convicted counterfeiters ("coiners") were occasionally boiled in oil there; and treasonous rebels were hanged, drawn, and quartered. Traitors' heads were impaled on spikes on city gates or on London Bridge.

Written in 1598, John Stow's *A Survey of London* captured the city as the 17th century beckoned.

Regicide, Plague & Fire: The 1600s

Few centuries in London's history have been as turbulent as the 17th, which saw the people execute a king, die from disease in their tens of thousands, and then lose everything to the most destructive fire in European history. Essentially, the 1600s saw the death of old London and the birth of the modern city—the capital of what had become a fiercely Protestant, anti-Catholic country. It's also the first London century that's well documented, thanks largely to the *Diaries* of Samuel Pepys (written between 1660 and 1669), who lived near the Tower, and the *Diary of John Evelyn,* written by a resident of Deptford, southeast London, between 1641 and 1697.

The 1600s almost started with a bang when, on the night of November 5, 1605, the Gunpowder Plotters planned to blow Parliament and **King James I** (r. 1567–1625) sky high. **Guy Fawkes** (1570–1606) was caught in the act, tortured, and executed—his treachery is remembered each November 5 in **Bonfire Night** celebrations across Britain (see "London Calendar of Events," p. 43). However, the early 17th-century legacy you're most likely to encounter is that of **Inigo Jones** (1573–1652), the architect who first imported the Renaissance ideas of Italian **Andrea Palladio** (1508–80) to England. Jones' "Palladian" **Banqueting House** (p. 93) is all that remains of Whitehall Palace (destroyed in a 17th-century fire, but not *the* Fire). The market building at **Covent Garden** (p. 100) and Greenwich's **Queen's House** (p. 174) were also Jones' designs. South of the river, the **Globe Theatre** (p. 305) was first built by Shakespeare's theatrical company and was a popular stage for performances of the Bard's plays in the early 1600s. The rebuilt Globe Theatre features prominently in he 1998 Oscar-winner *Shakespeare in Love,* a movie that conveys the feel of the city's Elizabethan streets.

Banqueting House.

Shakespeare's equally mysterious, and equally popular, contemporary **Christopher Marlowe** (1564–93), who was murdered in a Deptford tavern in 1593, wrote mainly for the nearby (now vanished) **Rose Theatre.**

The major battles in the **English Civil Wars** (1642–1651)—a convoluted, violent power tussle between king and parliament—happened away from London, but the denouement occurred on January 30, 1649, when **King Charles I** (r.1625–49) was beheaded outside his palace on Whitehall. His son, **King Charles II** (r. 1660–85), was restored as monarch in 1660 after a brief republican interlude, but in 1665 fled the city after the **Great Plague** struck. Around 100,000 died in London's last mass outbreak of bubonic plague, a fifth of the population. Streets that had once provided rich pickings for notorious thieves such as **Moll Cutpurse** (1585–1659) were suddenly empty. Eight thousand Londoners were dying every week at the epidemic's peak in September. Most of the bodies were buried anonymously in mass pits—one giant pit reputedly lies below Greenwich's **National Maritime Museum** (p. 172), another below the **Royal Mint,** opposite **Tower Bridge** (p. 149). As well as diarists Pepys and Evelyn, Daniel Defoe's part-fictional *A Journal of the Plague Year* (1722) summons up the unspeakable horror of those months. There's greater detail in William Bell's classic study, *The Great Plague in London* (1924).

The city in the 1660s was also a perfect storm of fire hazards: Houses were built from wood, streets were narrow, domestic lighting was provided by the candle, and tradesmen like the smith and the baker used open fires from dusk until dawn. It was a disaster waiting to happen . . . and early in the morning of September 2, 1666, at the end of a dry, hot summer, it happened. The **Great Fire of London** started in a bakery on Pudding Lane, and by the following day London Bridge had been consumed. Samuel Pepys watched London burn from the steeple of **All-Hallows-by-the-Tower** (p. 153). It wasn't until Old St. Paul's collapsed in flames, however, that the authorities started pulling down houses to create firebreaks. By the time the fire ended 3 days later on September 5, almost the whole of London had burned.

Officially, just eight souls died, although modern scholars consider a figure in the hundreds more likely. The height of **The Monument** (p. 145) (61.5m/202 ft.) matches the distance from its base to the spot on Pudding Lane where the fire began. The small **Golden Boy of Pye Corner,** mounted on the angle of Giltspur Street and Cock Lane close to **Smithfield Market** (p. 72), marks the spot where the Great Fire ended—although it took many decades before the notion that the Fire was part of either a Dutch or a Catholic plot burned itself out. Liz Gogerly's *Great Fire of London* (2002), aimed at reading-age children, is a succinct description of the disaster.

Much of the reconstruction was overseen by England's most renowned architect, **Sir Christopher Wren** (1632–1723). An astronomer and mathematician by training, Wren rebuilt 51 churches after the Fire, many of which survive. **St. Stephen's Walbrook** and **St. Mary-le-Bow** (p. 153), on Cheapside, are considered his most important ecclesiastical designs. According to tradition, a true "**cockney**" is someone born within earshot of the latter's church bells. Wren's most famous work, the apogee of his **English baroque** style, is **St. Paul's Cathedral** (p. 146), begun in 1675. The designs for the **Royal Observatory** (p. 175), the **Royal Naval College** (p. 174), the **Royal Hospital Chelsea** (p. 125), and the revamp of **Hampton Court Palace** (p. 176), were also entrusted to Wren, as was London's only surviving City gate, **Temple Bar.** Once erected in Fleet Street to mark the City's westernmost reach, it now guards the entrance to Paternoster Square, facing St. Paul's. The 1600s also saw the beginnings of urban life creep into Westminster—**Blooms-bury Square** and **St. James's Square** were among the first to be built—and Rotten Row in **Hyde Park** (see p. 112) became Britain's first artificially illuminated street.

Regular Londoners were perhaps more likely to have enjoyed **Ye Olde Cheshire Cheese** (p. 313), one of the City's oldest inns and another building rebuilt immediately after the Great Fire, or the West End's first theatre,

Fish and chips.

the **Theatre Royal Drury Lane** (p. 306). The theatre originally dates to 1663, but is now on its fourth building. **Nell Gwynne** (1650–87), the King's mistress, was a much-admired actor in the theatre's topical "Restoration comedies," and is interred at nearby **St. Martin-in-the-Fields** (p. 107), designed by Wren acolyte **James Gibbs** (1682–1754). With its courtyard and balconies, Southwark's **George Inn** (p. 317) is another authentic relic of the 17th century.

France's 1685 revocation of the Edict of Nantes caused one of the waves of mass immigration that have punctuated London's history. Thousands of French Protestants, the **Huguenots,** fled for the city to escape persecution. Many set up as silk weavers just outside the walls, in "Spital Fields." Nearby **Fournier Street** was built by and populated with weavers, and survives largely intact; **Dennis Severs' House** (p. 154) imaginatively re-creates an East End Huguenot home. The Huguenots brought with them the custom of serving fried fish with fried potatoes; a couple of centuries later that dish had morphed into that classic "British" staple, "**fish and chips.**"

The Georgian City: 1714–1830

When **Queen Anne** (r. 1702–14) died without an heir, the situation demanded a secure Protestant succession. Parliament turned to Germany's **House of Hanover,** who duly produced four King Georges (I–IV) in a row between 1714 and 1830—a period that's become known, for obvious reasons, as the **Georgian Era.** It wasn't all plain sailing for the Georges, particularly for "insane" **George III** (r. 1760–1820), as the BAFTA-winning movie *The Madness of King George* (1994) dramatizes quite faithfully. He ceded power to the Prince Regent from 1811 (the so-called **Regency Era**).

The Georgians' greatest bequest to London was what is now called the **West End.** The great squares of **Mayfair** and **Marylebone** were laid down in Georgian times: Hanover, Cavendish, Grosvenor, and Berkeley Squares all date from this period. Lambeth-born architect **John Nash** (1752–1835) built the sweeping thoroughfare of **Regent Street,** to connect **Regent's Park** (p. 169) to Carlton House Terrace, overlooking **St. James's Park,** which he also landscaped. The typical white stucco fronts of grand West End terraces owe their look to Nash; he was a prolific and influential builder. He also designed **Marble**

Arch—which occupies the site of a former public gallows at **Tyburn,** last used to hang highwayman John Austin in 1783—and remodeled **Buckingham Palace** (p. 97). **George IV** (r. 1820–30) was the first British monarch to call "Buck House" home. In contrast, British prime ministers were calling **Number 10 (Downing St.)** (p. 123) home from 1735.

Nash wasn't the only great Georgian architect. **Nicholas Hawksmoor** (1661–1736) was heavily influenced by the **baroque** idiom of Wren, and like Wren was a prominent church builder. His six churches are known for their daring towers; the finest examples are **Christ Church, Spitalfields,** and **St. George's, Bloomsbury.** Hawksmoor's churches have reentered popular culture thanks to Peter Ackroyd's 1985 novel, *Hawksmoor,* and Alan Moore's graphic novel, *From Hell.* Both speculate that the churches' designs and locations owe something to Satanism and/or Freemasonry. Later Georgian architects were more restrained and **neoclassical** in their practice. **John Soane** (1753–1837) designed the **Bank of England** (p. 144) and the **Dulwich Picture Gallery** (p. 176), which in 2011 celebrated its 200th anniversary. Soane was also a wonderfully eclectic hoarder—his house and collection are preserved as London's best small museum, the **Sir John Soane's Museum** (p. 108).

That the Georgians succeeded in leaving such a handsome legacy is a wonder in itself. Theirs was a city-society largely without shape or order; streets in Georgian "inner London" were labyrinthine, dark, dangerous, and chaotic. Dissolute rakes would burn their inheritances in no-holds-barred parties at Hellfire Clubs, brothels, gambling dens, or **molly houses** (gay taverns with beds for rent). Coffee houses, which had arrived in London in the 1650s, became hotbeds of sedition. Cockfights were popular urban entertainment, as were raucous fairs, such as the annual **Bartholomew Fair** in Smithfield. Several Acts of Parliament couldn't stop the **Gin Craze** soaking every social stratum in strong alcohol between the 1720s and 1750s. Painter **William Hogarth** (1697–1764) documented and satirized Georgian vice in a remarkable series of paintings and

Illustration of Bartholomew Fair, Smithfield by artist Thomas Rowlandson.

engravings, among them *A Rake's Progress* (1733) and *Gin Lane* (1751). The former is part of the collection at the **Sir John Soane's Museum** (see p. 108); **Tate Britain** (p. 126) and the **Museum of St. Bartholomew's Hospital** (p. 152) also house Hogarth works. Two historical studies in particular cover this subject well: Hallie Rubenhold's *The Covent Garden Ladies* (2005) paints a compelling picture of Georgian London's sexual underworld, while Dan Cruickshank's *Secret History of Georgian London* (2009) also explores the libertine mores of the times.

Polite Georgian society, on the other hand, found refined entertainment at one of the many **pleasure gardens** on London's fringe. For a fee, ladies and gentlemen could eat, drink, stroll, and enjoy orchestral music, masquerades, or fireworks late into the evening. The most celebrated were **Vauxhall Gardens** and **Ranelagh Gardens,** in Chelsea. The **Georgian London blog** (www.georgian london.com) is filled with fascinating tales from the 18th-century streets.

Many of London's upscale areas were once Georgian slums, known as "**rookeries.**" **Seven Dials,** and the area from **Covent Garden** north through the impoverished Parish of St. Giles, was the most notorious—a filthy, lawless den of thieves, prostitutes, gin shops, the diseased, the unfortunate, and the forgotten. The city had no police force: Henry Fielding (1707–54), author of *Tom Jones* and a magistrate, founded the first, tiny, semi-professional force nearby in 1749, the **Bow Street Runners.**

Most law enforcement was carried out by freelance "thieftakers" working for a bounty, many of them as corrupt as the criminals they were chasing. **Jonathan Wild** (1683–1725) was the most notorious thieftaker—and also head of an organized criminal gang—who gained citywide celebrity status for repatriating stolen goods that he himself had arranged to steal. His popularity waned when he became involved in the capture and execution of popular "Robin Hood"–style thief **Jack Sheppard** (1702–24). Wild was eventually rumbled, and followed Sheppard to the Tyburn gallows 6 months later; Wild's corpse was donated to medical science and his skeleton is now part of the **Hunterian Museum** (p. 102) collection, and regularly features in their "talks of the day." The seamy world of Runners and thieftakers is re-created in Andrew Pepper's fictional *The Last Days of Newgate* (2006).

Almost a century later, the lack of a properly trained detective force was a factor in the shambolic investigation of the **Ratcliff Highway Murders** of 1811. Itinerant seaman John Williams was arrested on the flimsiest evidence for the slaughter of two Wapping families. His suicide in prison was deemed proof of guilt by local investigators, but their shoddy handling of the case led indirectly to the **Metropolitan Police Act** of 1829, establishing Britain's first professional police force. As P. D. James' investigation *The Maul and the Pear Tree* (1971) concludes, this development came too late to achieve justice for the victims of 1811. The Ratcliff Highway Murders remained East London's most curious and senseless killings until Jack the Ripper appeared (see p. 30). The name of the road was later shortened to "The Highway" to shake off the stigma.

Perhaps because of their society's general lawlessness, Georgian Londoners showed boundless enthusiasm for public executions. Although burning at the stake ended in 1789, by 1810 there were around 220 separate offenses for which you could be hanged. After the Tyburn gallows were taken down in 1783, hanging usually took place before a huge crowd outside **Newgate Prison.** (London's Central Criminal Court, the **Old Bailey,** stands on the former site of the prison.)

London's gallows were busy in the aftermath of the most violent civil disturbances in London's history, the 1780 **Gordon Riots.** A mob enraged by Parliament's granting of political and civil rights to Catholics, and inflamed by "anti-Popery" speeches from **Lord George Gordon** (1751–93), sacked places of Catholic worship, Catholic homes and businesses, and even Newgate Prison itself. Six days of rioting left 285 Londoners dead.

Wind forward three decades and **Spencer Perceval** (1762–1812) became the only British prime minister to be assassinated—he was shot by a lone gunman inside the Palace of Westminster.

Yet among all this crime and chaos, there was a raw creative energy that later, more restrained and moralistic eras lacked. Literary milestones included the publication of **Dr. (Samuel) Johnson**'s *Dictionary of the English Language* in 1755 and James Boswell's 1791 *Life of Samuel Johnson,* which reinvented biography as a genre. Johnson's residence in Gough Square is preserved as the **Samuel Johnson's House** museum (p. 148); Johnson drank in the nearby **Ye Olde Cheshire Cheese** inn (p. 313) and is interred at **Westminster Abbey** (p. 128). The shocking autobiography of freed slave **Olaudah Equiano** (ca. 1745–97), published in London in 1789, was a contributing factor in the ending of the transatlantic slave trade. **Daniel Defoe** (ca. 1659–1731) wrote *Moll Flanders* (1722), adopted Londoner **Handel** (1685–1759) composed *Messiah* (1741)—his house on Brook Street, Mayfair, is now the **Handel House Museum** (p. 101)—and Spitalfields-born **Mary Wollstonecraft** (1759–97) published *A Vindication of the Rights of Women* (1792), one of the founding tracts of feminism. John Gay's 1728 *The Beggar's Opera* was proletarian London's response to highbrow Italian opera, and a huge popular hit.

Handel House Museum.

The London poetry scene also thrived, from the satires of **Alexander Pope** (1688–1744) to the Romantic odes of **John Keats** (1792–1821). Keats' *The Eve of St. Agnes* (1820) was favored subject matter for the Victorian Pre-Raphaelite painters (see below); he lived in Hampstead for a couple of years, in a residence now preserved as the **Keats House** (p. 166). Less easily pigeonholed was Romantic poet, painter, and illustrator **William Blake** (1757–1827). Blake lived in the city all his life, and wrote the words that later became the hymn *Jerusalem* (1808), usually interpreted as a protest against the country's (and city's) growing industrialization, as well as his defining poetry collection, *Songs of Innocence and Experience* (1789). He was a great observer of the people of his city, such as in his doom-laden poem *London*:

In every cry of every Man,
In every Infants cry of fear,
In every voice: in every ban,
The mind-forg'd manacles I hear.

Peter Ackroyd's *Blake* (1995) is the definitive modern biography. You can see Blake's surreal art at **Tate Britain** (p. 126).

For many, the Georgian years also mark the high point of British painting, with **Joshua Reynolds** (1723–92) and **Thomas Gainsborough** (1727–88) ranking alongside Blake (largely unrecognized in his own lifetime) and Hogarth as the towering figures of the period. Reynolds, who founded the **Royal Academy** (p. 105) in 1768, was a firm believer in the painter's duty to celebrate history, and was influenced by **Classical** art and the paintings of European Old Masters. His sometimes fussy, **baroque** compositions grace the **National Gallery** (see p. 102), **Wallace Collection** (p. 110), **Kenwood House** (p. 166), and **Dulwich Picture Gallery** (p. 176). Reynolds' portrait of Dr. Johnson hangs in the **National Portrait Gallery** (p. 104).

Fashionable, moneyed London society was often the subject matter of Gainsborough's portraiture. He painted celebrated West End *tragedienne* **Sarah Siddons** (1755–1831)—a picture that's now part of the **National Gallery** (p. 102) collection. His **rococo**-tinged work also hangs in the **National Portrait Gallery** (p. 104), the **Dulwich Picture Gallery** (p. 176), and **Kenwood House** (p. 166).

John Constable (1776–1837) is most often associated with idyllic rural landscapes, especially around his home on the Suffolk–Essex border, but he also lived and is buried in Hampstead. His works are on show at **Tate Britain** (p. 126) and the **National Gallery** (p. 102)—where perhaps the most loved image in British art, *The Hay Wain* (1821), hangs. Venetian **Canaletto** (1697–1768) spent almost a decade in London (he lived in Soho), painting and drawing the city. The best place to see his cityscapes is the **British Museum** (p. 96).

The Victorian Age: 1830–1901

No period has left such an indelible mark on the psyche and street-plan of the city as the reign of **Queen Victoria** (r. 1837–1901). The profusion of literature and scholarship, journalism, and satire, even the beginnings of urban photography, mark what's known as the **Victorian Age**—both the best documented and most distorted period before the 20th century.

The 19th century was an era of grand plans and great riches, but also massive disparities of wealth and grinding poverty. Nurse-statistician **Florence Nightingale** (1820–1910) summarized England as "the country where luxury has reached its height and poverty its depth." On returning from the Crimean War (1853–56), she opened London's first nursing school at St. Thomas' Hospital, now the site of the **Florence Nightingale Museum** (p. 134); the hospital will also soon unveil a statue of London's other great Crimean nurse, Jamaican-born **Mary Seacole** (1805–81).

Despair was never far below the surface of Victorian London, and it was among the urban poor of London's East End that it suddenly exploded onto front pages around the globe. **Jack the Ripper** murdered and mutilated at least five prostitutes in Whitechapel between August and November 1888. The fact that he was never caught, as much as the horrific nature of his crimes, secured his place in history. Theories accusing everyone from minor royals and masons to mad doctors and painters have proliferated, but in truth, we'll never know who killed those unfortunate women. **London Walks** (p. 426) runs the best of many walking tours of Ripper locations. Cult graphic novel *From Hell* (1989) remains true to the brutality of the crimes, while steering clear of what has often been sensationalization, if not outright celebration, of a brutal killer; it was made into a passable 2001 film starring Johnny Depp.

Joseph Merrick (1862–90), the "**Elephant Man,**" was another unfortunate resident of the East End. Rescued from a freak show by a surgeon, he spent the rest of his life in Whitechapel's (now Royal) London Hospital, where the **Royal London Hospital Museum** (p. 158) displays items relating to his time there. His remarkable and tragic life was fictionalized in the 1980 David Lynch movie *The Elephant Man,* starring John Hurt.

Ghastly urban legends thrived in the Victorian city—notably that of **Spring-Heeled Jack,** a ghoulish, clawed figure accused in the 1830s of attacking women before leaping away to unnatural heights. Like Jack the Ripper, he was never caught. Unlike the other Jack, he may not even have existed.

Much of this dark side of street life permeates a mountain of great Victorian London writing. **Charles Dickens** (1812–70) is the most celebrated chronicler of the period's fact and fiction, in novels such as *Oliver Twist* (1839) and his satire on London's legal system, *Bleak House* (1853). He was widely known for championing the poor and for incorporating contemporary events into his serialized publications, often with the intention of lampooning pompous or self-righteous public figures. David Lean directed two classic Dickens film adaptations: *Great Expectations* (1946) and *Oliver Twist* (1948). His *Great Expectations* was recently adapted into a new BBC TV miniseries (DVD 2012). The **Dickens Museum** (p. 98) is a must for fans, especially in the wake of celebrations citywide for Dickens' 2012 bicentenary. He's buried in Poet's Corner at **Westminster Abbey** (p. 128). Peter Ackroyd's *Dickens* (1990) was for many years the authoritative modern biography, although Claire Tomalin's *Charles Dickens: A Life* (2011) perhaps supplants it.

The chaotic optimism of the Victorian street was grist to the mill for writers as diverse as **George Eliot** (1819–80)—whose final novel, *Daniel Deronda,* was set largely in the Jewish East End—and **Edgar Allan Poe** (1809–49). In Poe's short story *The Man of the Crowd* (1840), the Victorian street even appears to be the tale's main "character." American **Henry James** (1843–1916) was a shrewd observer of London society in such novellas as *A London Life* (1888) and *In the Cage* (1898). The fears of late Victorian Londoners are captured convincingly by Robert Louis Stevenson's *Strange Case of Dr. Jekyll and Mr. Hyde* (1886), Joseph Conrad's *Secret Agent* (1907), and even Francis Ford Coppola's stylized-Gothic movie, *Bram Stoker's Dracula* (1992): Murder, madness, terrorism, and sex are not new London themes, and were lapped up by a Victorian public reared on "**Penny dreadfuls,**" cheap serial publications filled with lurid fiction.

The poverty described by Henry Mayhew in his *London Labour and the London Poor* (1851) later influenced the Communist writings of **Karl Marx**

Charles Dickens.

GOING underground

Few Victorian innovations have shaped the habits of Londoners as much as the building of their subterranean railway—the London Underground, or **"Tube."** The first line, the Metropolitan Railway, opened between Paddington and Farringdon stations in 1863, closely followed by a rival Metropolitan District Railway that linked South Kensington and Westminster from 1868. The most recent major investments came with the opening of the Victoria Line in the late 1960s, followed by the Jubilee Line in 1979, and its eastward extension in 1999. The network now has almost 250 miles of track linking 260 stations on 11 different lines.

The first true "Tube"—built by boring through the London clay deep under the city (previous lines had been excavated from ground level then covered over)—opened in 1890, along what is now a stretch of the Northern Line. Piecemeal bits and pieces of other lines followed, but it wasn't until 1933 that the sense of a single Underground network began to take shape in the public mind. That was the year the various private railways were amalgamated, and also the year that **Harry Beck's** iconic Tube map first appeared on station walls. The Tube has since become intertwined with the life of the city.

Thousands of Londoners spent night after night underground during World War II, sheltering from the Blitz (see p. 35); **Winston Churchill's Britain at War Experience** (p. 143) attempts to re-create the experience for visitors. Several Londoners were born in the Tube as a result—and in 1943, Bethnal Green station saw the War's worst civilian disaster when 173 people were killed in a crush. The King's Cross Fire of 1987 that killed 31 people struck at the city's nervous system, as well as one of its busiest transport hubs. The July 7, 2005, terrorist bombings—also centered on King's Cross—had a similarly traumatic impact.

The Tube has entered the daily life of the city in many different ways, from the phrase "mind the gap" called by station announcers, and the occasionally poignant "Poems on the Underground" found in some train carriages, to the stoic way Londoners deal with news of the latest Tube strike or a stifling summer journey. As long as you remember essential escalator etiquette—stand on the right, walk on the left—you'll fit right in. If you feel like trumping the locals with some killer Tube trivia, try: Which are the only two station names containing just four letters? (It's Bank and Oval, both on the Northern Line.) Or: How many station names contain all five vowels? (It's two: Mansion House and South Ealing.)

The fascinating **London Transport Museum** (p. 102) is the place to head to learn more about the London Underground. Christian Wolmar's *The Subterranean Railway* (2004) is the definitive book. One of London's best blogs focuses (inevitably) on the Tube: Annie Mole's **Going Underground** (http://london-underground.blogspot.com) is an essential bookmark.

For the practicalities of traveling by Tube, see "Getting Around," p. 417.

and **Friedrich Engels.** Marx lived in the city between 1849 and 1883 and is buried, like George Eliot, in **Highgate Cemetery** (p. 165); his daughter Eleanor committed suicide in the southern suburb of Sydenham in 1898.

Poet **Robert Browning** (1812–89) was born and lived his early years in Camberwell, and married fellow poet, **Elizabeth Barrett Browning** (1806–61), in Marylebone; **Wilkie Collins** (1824–89), author of *The Woman in White* (1860), was a North Londoner whose fiction had a significant influence on the Sherlock Holmes tales of **Arthur Conan Doyle** (1859–1930). Although entirely fictional, 221b Baker Street probably ranks alongside No. 10 Downing Street as London's most famous address. A plaque inside the **Museum of St. Bartholomew's Hospital** (p. 152) commemorates the spot where Holmes and Watson first meet, in 1887's *A Study in Scarlet*.

The Victorian era also spawned Britain's greatest painters, most of whom lived and worked in London. **J. M. W. Turner** (1775–1851) was a native of Covent Garden and a prolific and multitalented artist of the **Romantic Movement**. His mood-laden landscapes and cityscapes were works of ethereal genius. They did not endear him to the strait-laced Royal Academy of Arts, but did have a profound influence on the French Impressionists, especially Monet. **Tate Britain** (p. 126) has the world's best collection of Turner's work, and Turners are also hung at the **National Gallery** (p. 102), **Victoria & Albert Museum** (p. 127), and **National Maritime Museum** (p. 172).

The other great 19th-century painters were members of the so-called **Pre-Raphaelite Brotherhood.** The group endeavored to return art to its "ideal" state before Italian Raphael (1483–1520) picked up a brush, and produced "hyper-real" works rich in symbolism. The major Pre-Raphaelite figures were **Dante Gabriel Rossetti** (1828–82), **William Holman Hunt** (1827–1910), and **J. Everett Millais** (1829–96)—and later figures, such as painter-designer **Edward Burne Jones** (1833–98) and textile designer **William Morris** (1834–96), were also involved in what became a complex web of personal and professional relationships. **Tate Britain** (p. 126) has London's best Pre-Raphaelite works, notably Millais' spectacular *Ophelia* (1852); other examples are displayed at the **Guildhall Art Gallery** (p. 144). Timothy Hilton's *The Pre-Raphaelites* (1985) is the best introduction to the Brotherhood's output. Foreign artists such as **J. A. M. Whistler** (1834–1903) and **Claude Monet** (1840–1926) also documented London's evolving urban landscape in paint, particularly along the River Thames.

Where the Georgians often built for show, the Victorians built with a purpose. In the year that Victoria assumed the throne, **Euston** became London's first mainline railway station: The age of steam had arrived in the capital. As had tourism: Grand hotels such as **Claridge's** (p. 256), the **Savoy** (p. 346), and **Brown's** (p. 349) opened in the 1800s. The major hotel opening of 2011 was of another restored Victorian masterpiece: The **St. Pancras Renaissance Hotel** (p. 343) first graced the rail terminus in 1873.

The **Great Stink of 1858,** when the Thames turned into a stagnant, open sewer, provided confirmation that London's greatest architectural need was for some proper infrastructure. **Joseph Bazalgette** (1819–91) was the driving force behind rebuilding a sewerage system fit for the world's greatest city. He also oversaw the remodeling of London's Embankments into thoroughfares. Stephen Halliday's *Great Stink of London* (1999) is the best account of the life of a Londoner who deserves much wider recognition.

The **Great Exhibition** of 1851 saw the construction of a vast Crystal Palace in Hyde Park as part of a plan to demonstrate the genius of the Victorian mind. The plan worked, and profits from the exhibition funded the construction of the great museums of so-called "Albertopolis," in South Kensington: The **Natural History Museum** (p. 124), the **Science Museum** (p. 126), and the

Victoria & Albert Museum (p. 127). Prince Albert himself, Queen Victoria's husband, died before their completion. The **Royal Albert Hall** (p. 308) was named in his honor in 1871, and the kitsch **Albert Memorial** (p. 114) opposite was unveiled a year later. The other great civic building project of the mid-century was enforced by circumstances. A fire in October 1834 had completely destroyed the old Palace of Westminster. The neo-Gothic palace that stands today was designed by Charles Barry (1795–1860) and executed with considerable embellishments by the master of **Gothic Revival,** Augustus Pugin (1812–52), taking almost 30 years to complete.

Most of London's river bridges, in their current form at least, were also built by the Victorians—including Horace Jones' iconic **Tower Bridge** (1894), whose unfinished hulk looms over one recent *Sherlock Holmes* (2009) movie. *Cross River Traffic* (2005) by Chris Roberts is full of fascinating lore and legend about London's bridges. The **National Gallery** (p. 102) moved into its current Trafalgar Square home, designed by **William Wilkins** (1778–1839), in the first years of Victoria's reign. A more poignant reminder of Victorian values is provided by the *Memorial to Heroic Self-Sacrifice* in **Postman's Park** (p. 153).

Victorian "progress" swept through every sphere of London life. Shopping boomed: **Hamleys** (p. 297) came to Regent Street in 1881; **Harrods** (p. 290) to Knightsbridge in 1849. The electric tram, the omnibus, and the **London Underground** (see below) transformed the population's urban mobility. Theatres were packed out for *The Mikado* (1885) and other "Savoy operas" by **W. S. Gilbert** (1836–1911) and **Arthur Sullivan** (1842–1900). Stage variety entertainment known as **music hall** was the dominant form of entertainment for the masses—**Wilton's** (p. 322) is the oldest standing example of the kinds of venues that Londoners once frequented in their thousands. Philanthropy and collecting became a mark of civilization among the well-to-do. The eclectic **Horniman Museum** (p. 179), which opened in 1901, owes its existence to the interests of tea trader Frederick Horniman (1835–1906). That same year the **Whitechapel**

Harrods.

Art Gallery (p. 160) opened to bring art to the people of that deprived East End borough; the first exhibition included works by the Pre-Raphaelites, Hogarth, and Constable—and was a smash.

As she lay dying on January 22, 1901, Victoria was leaving behind the most powerful and the most complex city on Earth.

From Edwardians to V.E. Day: 1901–45

When **Edward VII** (r. 1901–10) took the throne on Victoria's death, heralding the **Edwardian Age,** he inherited a city and country on the cusp of massive social change. Londoner Virginia Woolf wrote that the "charm of modern London is that it is not built to last; it is built to pass." That was never truer than in the first five decades of London's 20th century.

Trade unions found fertile ground among London's poorly paid and poorly treated workers: A movement that began with the Bow **Matchgirls' Strike** of 1888 reached its peak with Britain's **General Strike** of 1926. Like the newly formed Labour Party, class consciousness was here to stay . . . as was political strife. In the early years of the century, **V. I. Lenin** (1870–1924) lived in the East End, and was a regular on the Bloomsbury scene, as he plotted Russian Revolution. Anarchists fought the police, one encounter ending tragically in the **Siege at Sidney Street** (1911); Donald Rumbelow's *Houndsditch Murders* (1973) explains the event's background and consequences. In 1936, locals of many stripes halted an attempt by Fascists to conduct an inflammatory march through the largely Jewish East End, in a confrontation that's become known as the **Battle of Cable Street.** Ed Glinert's *East End Chronicles* (2005) recounts these and several other upheavals. Written *in situ,* Jack London's 1902 *People of the Abyss* documents the pitiful state of East London at the dawn of the Edwardian Age. Melanie McGrath's *Silvertown* (2002) paints a personal picture of interwar family life. Paul Cohen-Portheim's *The Spirit of London* (1935) is packed with detail and photos of everyday life in the 1930s.

Most revolutionary of all was the struggle for women's suffrage, led somewhat disharmoniously by **Emmeline Pankhurst** (1858–1928) and her daughter **Sylvia** (1882–1960). London was shocked when one suffragette effectively martyred herself, by stepping into the path of a horse owned by **King George V** (r. 1910–36) at the 1913 **Epsom Derby.** The following year, suffragette Mary Richardson slashed Velázquez's *Rokeby Venus* (ca. 1650) in the **National Gallery** (p. 102). By 1928, perseverance had paid off. Women won voting equality with men, and Emmeline was quickly honored with a riverside statue in Victoria Tower Gardens, next to the **Houses of Parliament** (p. 121).

King Edward presided over London's first **Olympics** (1908). However, although he never lived to see it, the King had inherited a country for which the seeds of catastrophic war had already been sown. Both **World War I** (1914–18) and **World War II** (1939–45) saw London bombed from the air, but it was the **Blitz** of 1940–41 that left the most profound scar. The East End bore the brunt, particularly the boroughs of Whitechapel, Bethnal Green, Stepney, and Poplar. This was partly strategic—industry gathered along the East End's River Lea, and Thames docks and warehouses kept the capital in business. It was also ideological: Hitler knew that the East End was London's Jewish heartland. Bombs rained down every night between September 6 and early November, 1940. East Enders largely suffered alone: To keep British morale afloat, the government decreed that their appalling fate should remain concealed from the rest of the country. A particularly devastating raid occurred on the night of December 29, 1940, when 100,000 incendiary bombs set off the city's biggest fire since 1666, destroying almost everything from Cheapside north to Islington. Juliet Gardiner's 2010 book *Blitz* is the definitive study.

You can best get a sense of Britain at war at the **Imperial War Museum** (p. 136) and **Churchill War Rooms** (p. 120), and begin to understand the outpouring of relief when the city took to the streets to celebrate "Victory in Europe" (or "V. E. Day") on May 8, 1945. The sacrifice made by thousands of airmen during the 1940s' aerial Battle of Britain is commemorated by **Westminster Abbey's** RAF Chapel (p. 128). Maureen Waller's *London 1945* (2004) paints a picture of a resilient but ruined city. London gathers in mourning for all British war dead at Edwin Lutyens' 1919 **Cenotaph,** on Whitehall, each **Remembrance Sunday** (the Sunday closest to Armistice Day, November 11), at 11am.

It wasn't just London society that was changing, but also the shape of the city itself. The interwar years saw the mushrooming of suburbia: The rail commuter was born particularly—thanks to the westward expansion of the Metropolitan Railway (see "London's Underground," above)—in Middlesex, northwest of the center. The iconic development of this so-called **"Metro-land"** was E. S. Reid's Harrow Garden Village estate. When it was started in 1929, annual traffic through its new Rayners Lane station was 30,000 passengers. Within 8 years it was 4 million. "Bard of the 'burbs" John Betjeman (1906–84) made a classic BBC documentary, *Metro-land* (1973) that's still available on DVD. The **London Transport Museum** (p. 102) has more information, as does Alan Jackson's *London's Metroland* (2006).

The city center retained its fashionable allure, however. **Selfridges** department store (p. 290) was opened by an ambitious American retailer in 1909; **Liberty of London** (p. 290) moved to its current mock-Tudor HQ in 1924. Oxford Street, Regent Street, and Bond Street were Britain's premier retail lanes, but shopping also became more democratic with the arrival of chain stores such as **Woolworth's.** People from all walks of life would pause their shopping to take tea in a **Lyons Corner House,** although the rich might instead patronize the **Ritz** (p. 351), which opened in 1906.

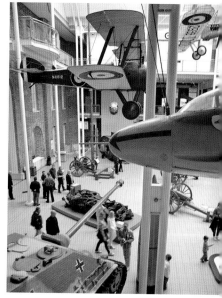

In architecture, the undistinguished grandiose style of the Edwardian Age soon gave way to **Art Deco.** (European-style **Art Nouveau** largely passed the city by.) Outstanding examples of London Art Deco include the 1931 **Daily Express Building,** on Fleet Street, then the center of the newspaper world; the interiors of **Claridge's** (p. 256); and a wing of medieval **Eltham Palace** creatively overhauled for domestic use in the

Imperial War Museum.

1930s; and Michelin House, now **Bibendum** (p. 228), in South Kensington. Look beyond the wear-and-tear, and architect **Charles Holden's** 1920s and 1930s Tube stations, particularly along the outer limits of the Piccadilly Line, are icons of "suburban modernism." Londoners generally agree that one of the best views of their city is to be had from crossing **Waterloo Bridge:** It was constructed in its current form during World War II, and was therefore built almost entirely by women.

The most intriguing London artist of the era was **Walter Sickert** (1860–1942), the leading light of the **Camden Town Group**. His dark portraits documented London's seedier side and owe much to French Post-Impressionism, as well as Sickert's apprenticeship with American J. A. M. Whistler. Sickert was also fascinated with the Jack the Ripper case (see "The Victorian Age," above), and has featured around the edges of many of the wilder conspiracy theories about the killer's identity. Crime writer Patricia Cornwell went as far as to accuse Sickert himself of being the Whitechapel murderer, a claim that's almost unanimously dismissed by experts. You can view Sickert's work in **Tate Britain** (p. 126).

As for the depiction of the city in cinema and literature, you can get a feel for life in Edwardian London from family musical *Mary Poppins* (1964), set in an idealized city of gentlemen bankers and Cockney chimney-sweeps; Dick van Dyke's hilarious attempt at a London accent aside, it's evocative of the first decade of the 20th century. The musical *My Fair Lady* (1956), based on George Bernard Shaw's 1912 play *Pygmalion*, takes a more direct poke at the class system. Multiple Oscar winner *The King's Speech* (2010) tells a slightly fictionalized account of King George VI's ascent to the wartime throne. Thomas Burke's short story collection *Limehouse Nights,* written in 1917, paints a gritty, if sensationalized picture of London's first Chinatown, in what's now Docklands. Interwar London street-life is captured exquisitely by Patrick Hamilton's fictional *Twenty Thousand Streets under the Sky* (1935), and in Virginia Woolf's reportage vignettes written in 1931 and 1932 and collected in *The London Scene.* Rüdiger Görner's literary travelogue, *London Fragments: A Literary Expedition* (2007) is strong on Woolf's London legacy. George Orwell's semi-autobiographical *Down and Out in Paris and London* (1933) examines interwar life lower down the social ladder. Finally, the plays of **Noël Coward** (1889–1973) achieved critical and commercial success between the Wars; the **Noël Coward Theatre** was renamed after him in 2006.

 Five Classic London Movies

The Lavender Hill Mob (1951)
Performance (1970)
The Long Good Friday (1980)
American Werewolf in London (1981)
Bridget Jones's Diary (2001)

From the Aftermath of War to the 21st Century: 1945–2013

Britain's postwar story is largely about the gradual loss of global preeminence and the wild swings of the economic cycle. Years of near-starvation, under food purchasing restrictions known as **rationing,** were followed by a pattern of economic boom followed by economic bust that has endured to the present day. It was a London politician, Prime Minister **Clement Attlee** (1883–1967)—Member of Parliament for Limehouse, in Docklands, and P.M. from 1945–51—whose crusading Labour government established the welfare state and National Health Service, changing British society forever. Attlee and later prime ministers oversaw Britain's loss of Empire—and the subsequent movement of large numbers of its population to London, in the process creating one of the world's most multicultural cities.

Architects have had the most visible impact on the city. War had left large areas of London in ruins and many of the ancient buildings standing today (especially east of St. Paul's Cathedral) owe their survival to piece-by-piece reconstruction. To fill the huge holes created by Hitler's Luftwaffe, and complete the city's sense of self-renewal, grand architectural projects were encouraged. The most controversial were those for buildings in the **Modernist** or **Brutalist** styles: London archetypes include the Barbican Estate (1968)—home to the **Barbican Centre** (p. 307)

> ### Eight Modern London Novels
>
> Patrick Hamilton, *Hangover Square* (1941)
> Colin MacInnes, *Absolute Beginners* (1959)
> Peter Ackroyd, *Hawksmoor* (1985)
> Martin Amis, *London Fields* (1989)
> Zadie Smith, *White Teeth* (2000)
> Monica Ali, *Brick Lane* (2003)
> Zoë Heller, *Notes on a Scandal* (2003)
> Howard Jacobson, *The Finkler Question* (2010)

arts venue—and the **Southbank** complex, built on a site cleared for the 1951 Festival of Britain. Londoners are still divided on the architectural merits of the Southbank Centre's **National Theatre** (p. 305), **Hayward Gallery** (p. 135), and **Royal Festival Hall** (p. 308). When in 1984 Prince Charles criticized a proposed design for the National Gallery's **Sainsbury Wing** as a "monstrous carbuncle," he was echoing these doubts. The Prince got his way at the National, but certainly not everywhere in what is now an architecturally **postmodern** city. The Square Mile, in particular, has seen its skyline renewed by the likes of Richard Rogers' **Lloyds Building** (1986) and Richard Seifert's **Tower 42** (1980)— the tallest building in Britain until 1990, whose top floor now hosts champagne bar **Vertigo 42** (p. 311).

During the years of social, political, and economic turmoil overseen by Prime Minister Margaret Thatcher, who occupied No. 10 Downing Street between 1979 and 1990, even the physical shape of London itself evolved. For the first time in two millennia, the City spread beyond the old Roman wall. The rebirth of **Docklands** in the 1980s as another financial center—anchored by the **Canary Wharf** development and serviced by the **Docklands Light Railway** (p. 418)—saw London look east rather than west for the first time in centuries. "Fleet Street" (shorthand for London's newspaper industry) made a similar pilgrimage east from its historic home on the fringes of the City, just as its heyday was coming to an end. Two contrasting takes on Fleet Street can be found in Michael Frayn's comedic 1967 novel *Towards the End of the Morning* and Charles Wintour's 1989 history, *The Rise and Fall of Fleet Street*. The postscript to the decline of London's newspapers is perhaps yet to be written: The systematic (and illegal) hacking of mobile phones by journalists on at least one tabloid newspaper was one of the big global media stories of 2011. It prompted the parliamentary **Leveson Enquiry** into media ethics, which ran through 2012.

Equally dramatic changes have been seen in the ethnic make-up of the city. The arrival of Caribbean immigrants aboard the **SS *Empire Windrush*** in 1948 was just one small, yet symbolic, part of a wave of immigration from across the British Commonwealth. The old Jewish (and before that, Huguenot) East End ceded to **Banglatown,** now centered around a thriving Brick Lane populated with Bangladeshis and their London-born descendants. Areas such as Notting Hill, Brixton, and Hackney became home to sizable West Indian communities. The expulsion of Asians from East Africa in the early 1970s led many to northwest London.

There was of course discrimination and friction—**race riots** scarred Notting Hill in 1958 and 1976, and Brixton in 1981 and 1985; the high-profile racist murder of a black teenage Londoner in 1993 was the subject of Paul Greengrass' 1999 movie, *The Murder of Stephen Lawrence.* It was only in early 2012 that two of the perpetrators were convicted and sentenced. However, the mostly harmonious integration of people from countries around the globe is one of London's postwar success stories.

In all walks of life, the experience of living in the city has become a multicultural one. The music of the 1960s (see "Swinging Sixties," below), and even the punk and New Wave (although not the ska or reggae) scenes of the 1970s, were largely white in make-up: The **Clash** and the **Sex Pistols** were the most influential London bands of the era. But fast-forward a quarter-century and the "sound of London" is best characterized by the grime-influenced rap of **Dizzee Rascal** (b. 1985), the R&B tones of **Estelle** (b. 1980), and the pop/hip-hop fusion of **N-Dubz**—one of whose members, Tulisa, starred on ratings-topping TV show *The X Factor.* The flavors of London's fashionable areas also betray a distant heritage—Soho's Chinatown, Shoreditch's "Little Hanoi," and Dalston's slew of Turkish restaurants (p. 247) being just three tasty examples. No one has captured suburban London more succinctly than **Hanif Kureishi** (b. 1954), in both his screenplay, *My Beautiful Laundrette* (1985) and debut novel, *The Buddha of Suburbia* (1990).

The postwar art scene in the city was dominated first by the so-called **Independent Group**—forerunners to American Pop Art who were based at London's **Institute of Contemporary Arts (ICA)** in the mid-1950s—then the **School of London** in the orbit of American "adopted Londoner," **R. B. Kitaj** (1932–2007). The best places to enjoy works by leading Independent Group member **Richard Hamilton** (1922–2011) and School of London painter **Francis Bacon** (1909–92) are **Tate Modern** (p. 281) and **Tate Britain** (p. 126). Works by **Frank Auerbach** (b. 1931) and **Lucian Freud** (1922–2011), the other leading lights of the School, grace the latter. Freud's portrait of *Queen Elizabeth II* (2001)—variously labeled "a travesty" and "psychologically penetrating" when it was unveiled—is part of the Royal Collection at the **Queen's**

A London Playlist

Albert Chevalier, *Knocked 'Em in the Old Kent Road* (1892)

Vera Lynn, *A Nightingale Sang in Berkeley Square* (1940)

Lord Kitchener, *London is the Place for Me* (1948)

Ella Fitzgerald, *A Foggy Day in London Town* (1956)

The Kinks, *Waterloo Sunset* (1967)

The Jam, *Down in the Tube Station at Midnight* (1978)

The Clash, *London Calling* (1979)

Flowered Up, *Weekender* (1992)

Pet Shop Boys, *West End Girls* (1985)

Lily Allen, *LDN* (2006)

Gallery (p. 105). Londoners **Antony Gormley** (b. 1950) and **Tracey Emin** (b. 1963) are two of the towering figures of British contemporary art; the **White Cube** gallery in Hoxton is the scene's spiritual home. Chelsea's **Saatchi Gallery** (p. 125) is the place to head to view British contemporary art.

London's film industry reached its peak in the decade after the war. The series of features made between the late 1940s and mid-1950s at Ealing Studios in West London were dubbed **Ealing Comedies.** Movies such as *The Ladykillers* (1955) and *Passport to Pimlico* (1949) won awards worldwide, and launched the acting careers of Londoner **Alec Guinness** (1914–2000) and **Peter Sellers** (1925–80). London continues to provide the backdrop for the likes of Oscar winner *Shakespeare in Love* (1998), twee rom-com *Notting Hill* (1999), bitter assess-ments of modern Britain such as *Naked*

"Platform 9¾" at King's Cross station.

(2003), and even Harry Potter's "Platform 9¾" at King's Cross station—although the movies actually used the more suitably gothic **St. Pancras** for filming. (See also "Five Classic London Movies," above.)

The city is inevitably a favorite subject of feature-length television. Londoners' increased suspicion of politics and politicians is typified by miniseries such as the BBC's *House of Cards* (DVD, 1990) and *State of Play* (DVD, 2003). Alan Moore's dystopian graphic novel—and 2006 feature film—*V for Vendetta* is still more uncompromising on the impact of democracy's disintegration on the streets of London. The stylized "V mask" was adopted by Internet group Anonymous and many of the Occupy protesters who camped outside St. Paul's Cathedral. Nothing portrays the claustrophobia of modern urban life as vividly as Tony Marchant's *Holding On* (DVD, 2005). The successful retelling of *Sherlock* (DVD, 2010–12) and *Whitechapel* (2009–10) in modern garb illustrates how London's history refuses to stay in the past. Smash-hit British primetime spy series *Spooks* (DVD, 2002–11) rarely completes an episode without a panning shot of one iconic London sight or another. *Luther* (DVD, 2010–11)—featuring star of *The Wire,* Hackney-born Idris Elba—takes a walk on the contemporary city's violent side. More realistic, and equally uncompromising, *Top Boy* (DVD, 2011) is set among the criminal gangs of Hackney's impoverished social housing estates.

London's postwar literature spans every genre and style, with an inevitable focus on the experience of urban life. The capital's first prominent postwar "literary movement" was the **Angry Young Men,** who formed a loose grouping in the aftermath of John Osborne's play about disaffection, *Look Back in Anger* (1956). Of all the "Angries," Hackney-born **Harold Pinter** (1930–2008) left the richest written legacy—for which he was awarded the Nobel Prize for Literature in 2005. Sam Selvon's *Lonely Londoners* (1956) was the first high-profile fictional

SWINGING sixties

For a brief spell in the 1960s, it seemed as if London was—once again—at the center of the world. This time it wasn't a vast political empire taking its orders from home-base, however, but a global cultural phenomenon driven by the libertine mores and youthful fashions of Britain's capital.

It all started with the music. The **Beatles** and the **Rolling Stones** both recorded their most memorable work in London during the 1960s, notably the former's 1967 *Sgt. Pepper's Lonely Hearts Club Band* and the latter's *Beggar's Banquet*. (The zebra crossing outside Abbey Road Studios—where the Beatles recorded most of their 1960s' music—remains a popular photo opportunity with fans.) London bands such as the **Kinks,** the **Yardbirds,** and the **Who** straddled the cutting edge and the top of the U.K. charts. Between 1968 and 1969, Jimi Hendrix lived in a flat on Brook Street, next door to the house occupied by composer Handel between 1723 and 1759; it's now the administrative offices of the **Handel House Museum** (p. 101). Venues such as the **Marquee** (now closed) and the **100 Club** hosted gigs and parties that have become legendary. New psychedelic bands including **Pink Floyd** emerged as the decade drew to a close and, like many of the biggest names before them, graced the tiny stage on **Eel Pie Island,** an islet in the Thames close to Twickenham.

Clothing was an essential ingredient in the Sixties' mix. The mod fashions and miniskirts of designer **Mary Quant** (b. 1934) defined the era. Models **Jean Shrimpton** (b. 1942) and **Twiggy** (b. 1949) became the faces of Swinging London. Chelsea's **King's Road** (p. 68) was the boho-chic shopping street par excellence. The Kinks wrote "Dedicated Follower of Fashion" (1966) about **Carnaby Street,** then the epicenter of Soho's style merchants.

Set in Notting Hill, 1970's *Performance*—starring Rolling Stones' lead

Twiggy in 1967.

singer Mick Jagger—is the iconic film of bohemian London. The Beatles' comedy *Hard Day's Night* (1964) and Michelangelo Antonioni's *Blowup* (1966) both capture the spirit of the era. Barry Miles' *London Calling: A Countercultural History of London since 1945* (2010) provides an excellent account of the 1960s' and 1970s' scenes.

When it came to music and fashion, what London did, the world mimicked. But it wasn't all glitz and glamour. Part of the 1960s' mystique is wrapped up in the world of the gangster, among whom the **Kray twins,** Ronald (1933–95) and Reginald (1933–2000), stand out for both their brutality and their mainstream renown. Sharp-suited and dapper, "Ronnie" and "Reggie" were feted in London's East End but finally jailed for the murders of George Cornell (1966) and Jack "the Hat" McVitie (1967), respectively—the former in Whitechapel's **Blind Beggar** pub.

exploration of the West Indian immigrant experience. Books in the genre known as **psychogeography** have been a more recent popular phenomenon. Such contemporary Londoners as **Will Self** (b. 1961), **Peter Ackroyd** (b. 1949), and **Iain Sinclair** (b. 1943) have written about the capital in this vein. Sinclair's *London Orbital* (2002) and Ackroyd's peerless history, *London: The Biography* (2000) are notable examples. The latter's *London Under* (2011) looks below ground for its history. Essential London-focused reads in the modern "street philosophy" genre include Christopher Ross' *Tunnel Visions: Journeys of an Underground Philosopher* (2001) and Alain De Botton's *A Week at the Airport* (2009), which recounts his experiences as Heathrow's writer-in-residence. (See also "Eight Modern London Novels," p. 38.)

WHEN TO GO

CLIMATE You don't come to London for the weather. Yes, it rains, but nowhere near as much as Britain's reputation suggests. Downpours are most likely in the autumn, especially November (2½ in./63mm. on average). It can, however, rain at any time; there's no "dry season" here. Daytime temperatures can range from –1° to 35°C (30° to 95°F), but they rarely stay below 2°C (36°F) or above 26°C (79°F) for too long. Evenings are usually cool, even in summer, but hot July and August days can be muggy—particularly on the Underground, which is not air-conditioned. Note that the British like to keep hotel-room thermostats about 6°C (10°F) below the American comfort level.

London's Average Daytime Temperatures & Rainfall

	JAN	FEB	MAR	APR	MAY	JUNE	JULY	AUG	SEPT	OCT	NOV	DEC
Temp. (°F)	39	39	43	46	52	58	62	62	57	51	44	42
Temp. (°C)	3	3	6	7	11	14	16	16	13	10	6	5
Rainfall (in.)	3.1	2	2.4	2.1	2.2	2.2	1.8	2.2	2.7	2.9	3.1	3.1
Rainfall (mm)	49	39	40	43	47	52	59	57	56	62	59	53

CURRENT WEATHER CONDITIONS The best place to head online for a detailed weather forecast is **www.bbc.co.uk/weather**. Once in the city, you can tune into local radio stations for regular—usually quarter- or half-hourly—weather updates on **LBC** (97.3 FM) or **BBC London** (94.9 FM). Smartphone apps such as **Accuweather** work fine here.

WHEN YOU'LL FIND BARGAINS In short, summer's warmer weather gives rise to many free outdoor music and theatre festivals. But winter offers savings pretty much across the board.

The cheapest time to fly to London is usually during the off season: From late October to mid-December and from January to mid-March. In the last few years, long-haul airlines in particular have offered some irresistible fares during these periods. Remember that weekday flights are often cheaper than weekend fares.

Rates generally increase between March and June, and hit their peak in high travel seasons between late June and September, and in December for the run-up to Christmas and New Year. July and August are also when most Europeans take their holidays, and so as well as higher prices you have to deal with more crowds and limited availability of the best hotel rooms.

You can avoid crowds to some extent, by planning trips for November or January through March. Sure, it may be rainy, gloomy, or cold—or all three—but London doesn't shut down when the tourists thin out a little! In fact, it's a 365-days-a-year tourism city, and the winter season includes some of London's best theatre, opera, ballet, and classical music offerings. Additionally, hotel prices can drop by 20%, unheard of during peak travel times. By arriving after the winter holidays, you can also take advantage of post-Christmas sales, which these days start as early as December 26 or 27. There's usually another major sales period in stores in midsummer.

London Calendar of Events

JANUARY

New Year's Day Parade. London's New Year's Day Parade crowns the capital's festive season with 3 hours of pomp and frivolity. Some 10,000 dancers, acrobats, musicians, and performers assemble in the heart of the city every year for a "celebration of nations." More than 400,000 people regularly gather to admire the floats and entertainers—arrive early to secure a good spot. From Piccadilly to Westminster. www.london parade.co.uk. (C) **020/8566-8586.** January 1.

January Sales. From the exclusive boutiques of Bond Street to the high-street hulks that dominate Oxford Street, London's shops slash prices for the annual January Sales. Shoppers queue for hours to be first into iconic stores such as Harrods and Selfridges, but further discounting in subsequent weeks means browsing for bargains later in the month can be worthwhile. Throughout the month. (Most sales begin December 26 or 27.)

Get into London Theatre. The initiative Get into London Theatre does its best to dispel the gloom of January and lure Londoners from the comfort of their armchairs to the sparkling unpredictability of the capital's **West End.** Some 50 or so productions, from uplifting musicals to searing dramas, offer significant discounts on tickets until February. www.getintolondontheatre.co.uk. (C) **0871/230-1548** to book. Early January to February.

Chinese New Year. London's large Chinese community welcomes the Chinese New Year with a colorful bang. Energetic parades, traditional acrobatics displays, boisterous lion dances, and musical performances are held in Trafalgar Square and Leicester Square. The New Year celebrations are among the biggest in the world outside of China, and as dusk falls the crowds descend on **Chinatown** to feast and drink into the night. Tube: Leicester Sq. One evening in late January/early February.

FEBRUARY

Kinetica Art Fair. Carnivorous lamp-shades and pole-dancing robots might sound like elements of a disturbed person's dream, but Kinetica Art Fair displays exactly these sorts of weird exhibits. Held in central London, it's dedicated to the fantastical flourishes and foibles of kinetic, electronic, and new media art. Ambika P3, 35 Marylebone Rd., NW1. www.kinetica-artfair.com. (C) **020/7392-9674.** Tube: Baker St. Thursday to Sunday in early February.

Imagine Children's Literature Festival. The Imagine Children's Literature Festival, at the **Southbank Centre** (see p. 280) cultural institute, installs a love of literature in demanding tots and discerning teens. The U.K.'s best contemporary children's writers, storytellers, and illustrators enrapture and enthuse young audiences with readings, discussions, and workshops. www.southbankcentre.co.uk/imagine-childrens-festival.

☎ **020/7960-4200.** Tube: Waterloo or Embankment. 2 weeks in mid-February.

London Fashion Week. Design stalwarts and precocious new talents unveil their collections to an audience of press and buyers at London Fashion Week, a biannual fashion festival also held in September. It's a frenetic and fabulous program, but unless you're fashion nobility you're unlikely to be let in. Despite that, the hoi polloi can still enjoy London's flair for unconventional design at a raft of slick complementary events and parties across the city. www.londonfashionweek.co.uk. Mid-February and mid-September.

MARCH

St. Patrick's Day Parade. London's huge Irish community gets out the greenery each March to celebrate at the capital's St. Patrick's Day Parade. Colorful floats, a clatter of marching bands, and community groups jig and jostle their way along a packed route that starts at Hyde Park and ends at **Trafalgar Square.** Official celebrations conclude with Irish musicians performing spirited sets to emotional crowds, as Trafalgar Square's fountains pump out green water. www.london.gov.uk/stpatricksday. ☎ **020/7983-4000.** Tube: Charing Cross. Sunday nearest to March 17.

London Drinker Beer & Cider Festival. Subtle shows of English eccentricity abound at the London Drinker Beer & Cider Festival in **Bloomsbury.** A magnet for ale lovers and cider connoisseurs, it celebrates British booze over 3 alcohol-fueled days. Linger over a menu that includes numerous regional brews that are interesting, if not always enticing: Check out Pressed Rat & Warthog, a beer laced with hints of blackcurrant and plum, or Steaming Billy's Last Bark, a brew dedicated to a deceased dog. Camden Centre, Bidborough St., WC1. www.camranorthlondon.org.uk/ldbf. Tube: King's Cross. Wednesday to Friday in mid-March.

London Handel Festival. The London Handel Festival celebrates the works of George Frederic Handel and his contemporaries, and is based at his one-time place of worship, **St. George's Church** in Hanover Square, as well as other locations throughout London, including the **Royal Academy** (p. 105), **Handel House Museum** (p. 101), and **Wigmore Hall** (p. 309). The festival customarily opens and closes with choral services. www.london-handel-festival.com. ☎ **01460/53500.** Mid-March to late April.

APRIL

London Marathon. More than just a sporting event, the London Marathon is the world's longest street party. Roads along the route come alive with bands, cheering crowds, entertainers, and 30,000 pairs of feet hitting the tarmac along the 26.2-mile course, starting at

Buckingham Palace during the London Marathon.

Greenwich Park (p. 172) and ending on The Mall. www.virginlondonmarathon. com. Sunday in mid-April.

National Gardens Scheme. Londoners open their gardens and homes to the public by partaking in this scheme, which is a nationwide strategy to raise funds for charity. Gardens of quality and character open on set days to botanists, ecologists, and the plain curious. With Londoners' lives so hectic, it's a rare opportunity to meet locals away from the frenetic environs of the city center. www.ngs.org.uk. ✆ **01483/211535.** Set dates through the year but many gardens start to open from April.

MAY

Breakin' Convention. Poppers, lockers, breakers, and krumpers come together for this festival at **Sadler's Wells** (p. 308) theatre every year, for a unique celebration of hip-hop dance. Top talent from London, the rest of the U.K., and abroad lay on nonstop performances, workshops, and demos on stage and in the streets. www.breakinconvention.com. Tube: Angel. Early May.

Regent's Park Open Air Theatre. Forget stuffy auditoriums and enjoy the pleasures of **Regent's Park Open Air Theatre** (p. 169). There's little shelter from sudden downpours, but in good weather the repertoire of high drama, musicals, and Shakespeare sparkles under a canopy of blue skies, towering trees, and natural beauty. www.openairtheatre.org. ✆ **0844/826-4242.** Tube: Regent's Park or Baker St. Mid-May to September.

Chelsea Flower Show. The Chelsea Flower Show is Europe's premier gardening event. Some of horticulture's greatest exponents exhibit imaginative garden designs over a 4.4-hectare (11-acre) site at **Chelsea's Royal Hospital** (p. 125), creating a floral wonderland for the public to explore. Visitors can roam through scores of gardens and exhibitions, with the displays showcasing some of the world's finest examples of botanical

excellence. You'll need to book well ahead to secure tickets. www.rhs.org.uk/ Chelsea. Tube: Sloane Sq. 5 days in late May.

JUNE

Royal Academy of Arts' Summer Exhibition. The Royal Academy of Arts' (p. 105) Summer Exhibition in London is the world's largest open contemporary art exhibition. Paintings, drawings, and models by many distinguished artists jostle with works by the unknown and the emerging. The exhibition spreads over themed rooms, with separate spaces for invited artists and open submissions, so visitors can easily deduce whether a canvas of blotched figures or indistinguishable squiggles is from a supposed master or an overenthusiastic novice. www.royalacademy.org.uk/ summerexhibition. ✆ **020/7300-8000.** Tube: Piccadilly Circus. Early June to mid-August.

Trooping the Colour. Trooping the Colour is a quintessentially English example of pomp and ceremony, which celebrates Queen Elizabeth II's official birthday and sees central London bedecked in flags and regaled by pageantry. Troupes of troops march along **St. James's Park** (p. 106) and The Mall, and the Queen herself can be glimpsed enjoying the spectacle as head of the parade by those lucky enough to secure a good viewing spot (be there by 9am). The write-in lottery for seated tickets in Horse Guards Parade is open January to February. Events begin at 10am and there's a fly-past at 1pm. Also listen out for the 41-gun Royal Salute in **Green Park** (p. 101) at 12:52pm and the 62 Guns at the **Tower of London** (p. 150) at 1pm. www.royal.gov.uk. Saturday in mid-June.

Wimbledon. Whether Londoners are right to claim it as "the world's greatest tennis tournament" is one thing, but the traditional strawberries and cream and infamous rain delays definitely set

Wimbledon (see p. 333) apart from other Grand Slam tournaments. Some of the greatest tennis matches of all time have been fought on Centre Court, a short distance from central London. www.wimbledon.com. ✆ **020/8944-1066.** Tube: Wimbledon Park. Last week June & 1st week July.

Taste of London. London has become increasingly audacious in asserting its status as a culinary capital—decide if the accolade is deserved at this festival. A 4-day celebration held at **Regent's Park** (p. 169), it's attended by dozens of London's top restaurants, all serving delectable sample-sized dishes, and features cooking demonstrations by world-class chefs. www.tastefestivals.com/london. Tube: Regent's Park or Baker St. 4 days in late June.

Greenwich+Docklands International Festival. East London's riverside erupts every summer at this award-winning festival, London's longest-established outdoor extravaganza. Spectacular shows, encompassing theatre and music, fill spaces along the Thames. Performances can vary from the ostentatious and dramatic to the intimate and serene, but all are open to everybody—and free. www.festival.org. ✆ **020/8305-1818.** 10 days in late June to early July.

JULY

Pride Parade. London's Pride Parade has firmly established itself as the biggest event in the U.K.'s gay party calendar. The carnival atmosphere transforms central London with a flamboyant procession of floats, campaigners, community groups, and drag queens representing the full force of Britain's LGBT community. The parade leaves Baker Street at 1pm and heads via Oxford Street to Trafalgar Square, with stage performers from 3pm. Afterwards Soho becomes one big street party. www.pridelondon.org. First Sunday in July.

The Proms. The BBC Henry Wood Promenade Concerts ("the Proms" for short)

at the **Royal Albert Hall** (see p. 308) take over the capital's musical calendar every summer, and can, with some justification, claim to be the world's greatest classical music festival. Over 8 weeks, the majestic venue resounds to dozens of perhaps unexpectedly experimental concerts amid a staple diet of symphony orchestra performances. www.bbc.co.uk/proms. ✆ **0845/401-5040.** Tube: High St. Kensington or South Kensington. Mid-July to mid-September.

AUGUST

V&A Museum of Childhood Summer Festival. This event at the **V&A Museum of Childhood** (p. 159) provides a child-friendly alternative to England's more raucous summer festivals. Youngsters and their keepers gather in the museum's East London venue for a summer fete-style program of live music, outdoor performances, and general jollity. www.vam.ac.uk/moc. ✆ **020/8983-5200.** Tube: Bethnal Green. Sunday in early August.

Notting Hill Carnival. Around a million people throng the pastel-hued streets of West London for the Notting Hill Carnival, Europe's biggest carnival. Fabulous floats make a colorful circuit of the area and sound systems blast out music all day. Sample delicious Caribbean jerk chicken as you savor a soundtrack of calypso, soul, or reggae. www.nottinghill-carnival.co.uk. Tube: Notting Hill Gate. Last Sunday & Monday in August.

SEPTEMBER

London Open House Weekend. Explore the Foreign Office, Mansion House, and other landmark buildings that are normally closed to public view. You can peek inside around 700 of the capital's most famous buildings and best-kept architectural secrets at the London Open House Weekend, part of European Heritage Days. www.londonopenhouse.org (and there is an iPhone app). Weekend in mid-September.

Notting Hill Carnival.

London Design Festival. Londoners aren't shy in claiming their city deserves kudos for its creative flair; judge whether they have justification at the London Design Festival. The capital's premier showcase for the U.K.'s most exciting creative talent, its program of exhibitions, screenings, and workshops across the city reveals the latest developments in British design. www.londondesign festival.com. ℭ **020-7734-6444.** 9 days in mid-September.

Mayor's Thames Festival. With free activities all along the Thames between Westminster Bridge and Tower Bridge, this festival offers everything from a carnival procession to live music, art installations, and street theatre. It culminates in a blaze of color with a fireworks display fired from the river itself. www. thamesfestival.org/festival. ℭ **020/7928-8998.** Weekend in early September.

OCTOBER

Frieze Art Fair. A staggering 68,000 visitors flock to this annual event in a vast marquee in **Regent's Park** (p. 169). Top galleries from more than 20 countries take part, between them representing hundreds of exciting established and emerging artists. Start saving, as all the works on show are for sale. www.frieze artfair.com. ℭ **020/3372-6111.** Tube: Regent's Park or Baker St. 4 days in mid-October.

BFI London Film Festival. With almost 200 films making their U.K. debut at numerous cinemas across the capital, the BFI London Film Festival is the U.K.'s biggest movie event. Exclusive red-carpet premieres gather celebrities and garner press interest, and there's plenty for the public to enjoy, with special screenings, film seasons, talks, and workshops all part of the program. www.bfi. org.uk/lff. 2 weeks in mid-October.

NOVEMBER

Bonfire Night Celebration. Foiled in his attempt to blow up London's Houses of Parliament and murder the protestant King James I on November 5, 1605 (in order to replace him with a Catholic monarch), **Guy Fawkes** was executed and the safety of the King celebrated with the lighting of bonfires throughout the country. The tradition continues to this day, with towns throughout England celebrating Bonfire Night around November 5. As darkness descends families gather around a blazing pyre, often with a smoldering effigy of Fawkes as its centerpiece. Children are distracted from the more macabre connotations of the ceremony by hot dogs, sparklers, and toffee apples, and a huge fireworks display to end the evening. See local press for locations of this year's bonfires (**Victoria Park,** in East London, is a popular destination; see p. 160). On or around November 5.

Lord Mayor's Procession and Show. Be it the Black Death or the Blitz, little has managed to disrupt the Lord Mayor's Procession and Show, which has wound its way round London's streets for almost 800 years. Marking the inauguration of the City of London's new Lord Mayor (not the same office as the Mayor of London), the event's focal point is a parade swaddled in layers of ceremony and pageantry. The parade departs 11am from **Mansion House** to the **Royal Courts of Justice,** returning at 1pm. Fireworks are at 5pm. www.lordmayorsshow.org. Saturday in mid-November.

DECEMBER

Carols by Candlelight. In an impressive 18th-century-style setting at the **Royal** Albert Hall (p. 308), Carols by Candlelight combines traditional Christmas songs with festive music by Handel, Bach, Vivaldi, and Corelli. The **Mozart Festival Orchestra** plays in period costume and special readings accompany the music. www.royalalberthall.com. ℂ **020/7589-8212.** Tube: High St. Kensington or South Kensington. Thursday evening in mid-December.

New Year's Eve Fireworks. As Big Ben strikes midnight, London rings in the New Year with fabulous fireworks over the Thames. A high-spirited crowd turns out to glimpse the iconic London Eye illuminated and to see rockets blaze skywards from barges along the river. www.london.gov.uk/nye. December 31.

Public Holidays

England downs tools for **eight public holidays** (also known as "bank holidays") spread throughout the year: New Year's Day (January 1); Good Friday and Easter Monday (usually April); May Bank Holiday (first Monday in May); Spring Bank Holiday (usually last Monday in May, but occasionally the first in June); August Bank Holiday (last Monday in August); Christmas Day (December 25); Boxing Day (December 26). *Note:* If a marked date such as Christmas Day falls on a Saturday or Sunday, the public holiday rolls over to the following Monday.

RESPONSIBLE TOURISM IN LONDON

Londoners in general are an eco-aware bunch—but don't always practice what they preach. And even the concept of taking a "responsible," "green," or "environmentally friendly" trip here isn't without controversy, particularly if you're traveling by plane. However, there are everyday things you can do to minimize the impact—and especially the carbon footprint—of your travels. Remove chargers from cellphones, laptops, and anything else that draws from the mains, once the gadget is fully charged. If you're shopping, buy seasonal fruit and vegetables or local cheeses from markets (see p. 275) rather than produce sourced by supermarkets from the far side of the world. Ditto with clothes purchases: Vintage threads are a greener alternative to items mass-produced for global chains or brands. London is blessed with some of the best vintage shopping on the planet— you'll find our favorite spots on p. 287. Most importantly, use public transportation to get around town. The city's Tubes and buses are easy to use and efficient; for a comprehensive guide to navigating the city quickly and cost-effectively, see "Getting Around" in Chapter 10.

The **Congestion Charge Zone** (see p. 420) was introduced to discourage car travel within the center, and there's no reason why you should be driving the capital's labyrinthine streets. Another environmental annoyance is the buildup of discarded freesheets throughout the day on buses and trains. Most stations now have paper recycling points near the exit, so if you read a *Metro* or *Evening Standard* on your travels, take it with you and recycle.

Greener even than Tubes and buses are the publically accessible **cycle hire bikes** dotted around town, ideal for short journeys across the center and available to weekend visitors and lifelong residents alike. For details of the **Barclays Cycle Hire** scheme, see p. 423. Provision and marking of dedicated cycle lanes is very hit-and-miss, however, so you'll need to take care and rent (or buy) a helmet if you plan to get around by bike.

Green vacationing also extends to where you eat and stay. Vegetarian food tends to have a much gentler impact on the environment, because it eschews energy- and resource-intensive meat production. The best places around town to sample it are **Mildreds** (p. 211) and **Rasa Samudra** (p. 210). A number of restaurants now specialize in sustainable cuisine; we recommend our favorites on p. 232. Most hotels now offer you the option to use your towels for more than one night before they are relaundered—and of course, you should, because laundry makes up around 40% of an average hotel's energy use. Also, ask for a room that allows you to turn off the air-conditioning whenever you go out. The **Green Tourism for London Scheme** (www.green-business.co.uk) awards grades to hotels that meet various sustainability criteria—businesses that are "actively engaged in reducing the negative environmental and social impacts of their tourism operations." Gold, silver, and bronze award-winners are expected to manage energy effectively, promote public transport and green spaces, and support local cultural activities—and are listed on their website. You'll find yet more green travel inspiration, including ideas for ethical shopping excursions, at **www.visit london.com/green**.

Walking is of course the ultimate green way to see the city. Central London is smaller than you might think, but be sure to pack a good map, because the streetplan conforms to no logical system. There are also several companies offering guided walks of all stripes through the city; our favorites are recommended on p. 426. Of particular note is 2011 responsible tourism award winner **Unseen Tours,** which offers guided city walks led by homeless and former homeless residents of London; see p. 426.

Responsible Travel (www.responsibletravel.com, www.responsiblevacation. com in U.S.) is just one among a growing number of environmentally aware travel agents. They offer a number of "green holidays" across the U.K., including in London. Newspaper green travel sections such as **www.guardian.co.uk/travel/ green** and **www.telegraph.co.uk/travel/hubs/greentravel** are good online places to keep up with the issues and get inspiration. **Vision on Sustainable Tourism** (www.tourism-vision.com) is another excellent news hub. Carbon offsetting (again, not uncontroversial) can be arranged through global schemes such as **ClimateCare** (www.climatecare.org). In the U.K., **Tourism Concern** (www. tourismconcern.org.uk) works to reduce social and environmental problems connected with tourism.

For flexible **volunteering** opportunities that you can build into your city itinerary, see "Voluntourism & Slow Travel," below.

USEFUL LONDON TERMS & LANGUAGE

London has one of the world's most famous argots. **Cockney rhyming slang** emerged from the East End during the 19th century, and consists of words and phrases constructed using a rhyme—a creative process that makes what you're talking about less likely to be understood by the uninitiated. To make the dialect still more obscure, the word that is the original object of the rhyme is often omitted. For example, "bread" meaning money derives from a rhyme with "bread and honey" and "ruby" meaning curry derives from "Ruby Murray," a 1950s' singer. Although some words and phrases have entered common parlance—"barnet," from "Barnet Fair," meaning hair is another—you're unlikely to hear too much pure rhyming slang as you travel the city.

However, London does have a vocabulary of its own, some of it derived from or influenced by Cockney, some disparagingly referred to as "mockney," some related to products, places, and produce that are peculiar to the city, and some just plain slang. You may also notice the liberal use of the F-word on London's streets. Although it certainly isn't considered a polite word, its impact on the local listener is more diluted than in most other English-speaking cities.

Below is a glossary of some London words and phrases you may encounter.

bangers   sausages; usually paired with mashed potato for "bangers and mash"

banging   good; usually applied to music

barking   crazy or mad; coined from a former asylum in the eastern suburb of Barking

barney   an argument or disagreement

bedlam   madness; as in "the roads are bedlam today"; a corruption of "Bethlehem," an asylum formerly at the corner of Moorgate and London Wall, in the City

black cab   an official London black taxi, as opposed to a private hire "minicab"; only black cabs are permitted to tout for fares curbside

Boris bikes   rental cycles that are part of the Barclays Cycle Hire scheme (see p. 423); named after Mayor Boris Johnson, who presided over the scheme's introduction in 2010

brassic   penniless, short of money; derived from rhyming slang, "boracic lint" (a Victorian medical dressing) meaning "skint"

butcher's   a look (from Cockney "butcher's hook"); as in "can I have a butcher's?"

BYO   short for "bring your own"; a restaurant that doesn't sell alcoholic drinks but will happily open any you bring along, sometimes for a small corkage fee

circus   a (usually circular or oval) coming together of streets, as at Piccadilly Circus and Finsbury Circus

clink   a prison; after the former Clink Prison, on the South Bank

damage   the cost or bill; as in "what's the damage?"

dodgy   not to be trusted, suspect; as in "that £20 note looks dodgy"

dosh   money; also "bread" or "dough"

gaff   home; "back to my gaff" means "back to my place"

G 'n' T   gin and tonic; often served with "ice and a slice," i.e. an ice cube and a lemon wedge

gastrocaff a fashionable cafe that nevertheless serves traditional English fried breakfasts

geezer a man; also "bloke" or "fella"

greasy spoon the opposite of "gastrocaff": a basic cafe known for fried food

gutted extremely disappointed; as in "I'm gutted that Arsenal beat Spurs last night"

IPA India Pale Ale; a type of hoppy, light-colored English ale first brewed in the 18th century and lately experiencing a revival

lager straw-colored, fizzy light beer such as Budweiser and Foster's, served colder than traditional ales (although it's a myth that English beers are served "warm"; they should appear at cool cellar temperature)

liquor green parsley sauce served in traditional pie and mash shops

naff cheap looking, or unfashionable

Old Bill the police (also "coppers"); the origin of the nickname isn't totally clear, but see www.met.police.uk/history/oldbill.htm for 13 possible explanations

Porter type of dark, rich, strong ale once popular with London dockers; London brewers Fuller's, The Kernel, and Meantime all brew contemporary versions

pint both a measure of beer and a general term for having a drink; as in "do you fancy going for a pint later?"

quid one pound; "10 quid" or "a tenner" is £10

rabbit talk excessively, as in "what's he rabbiting on about?"; another derivation from rhyming slang, "rabbit and pork" meaning talk

subway a pedestrian underpass; the underground railway is known as "the Tube"

wally a type of pickled gherkin, often paired with fish and chips

3

LONDON NEIGHBORHOODS & SUGGESTED ITINERARIES

n order to get the best out of London, you need to be as informed as possible: To know the hotspots from the not-spots, the bargains from the rip-offs, and the up-and-coming from the down-and-going. Obviously that sort of information can be difficult to pick up during an (all-too-brief) visit, which is where this chapter comes in.

The following pages provide an in-depth introduction to the U.K.'s capital, giving you the low-down on its key areas, and advice on how and where to allocate your time. The chapter is divided into two sections. The first is made up of potted guides to London's main sightseeing neighborhoods, and gives a brief overview of what to expect from each in terms of attractions, eating, nightlife, and accommodation, as well as pointing out recent developments. The second section features three carefully selected itineraries designed to help you get the best out of the city in a limited time.

CITY LAYOUT

Guides to city-planning rarely use London as an example of how things should be done, preferring instead to cite more neatly ordered metropolises with carefully drawn grid plans and formally delineated zones.

London is certainly *not* neat. But then the city wasn't so much planned as made-up, created piecemeal as and when new bits were required. It represents 2,000 years of local projects, individual labors, grand aristocratic ambitions, philanthropic ventures, government schemes, and royal follies—all created with little reference to each other—and then placed on the same patch of ground like the pieces to 500 separate jigsaws.

This history can, unfortunately, make it confusing for visitors to find their way around. Roads don't meet at precise right-angles, but wind and roam, seemingly at random. There appears to be no obvious city center—or conversely, several, each vying for your attention. But this occasionally maddening muddle is also a huge part of London's charm.

One thing the city's great mish-mash layout guarantees is surprises—hidden alleys, unexpected delights, stumbled-upon treasures—as well as the near certainty that you'll get lost at some point (even locals do, all the time). The maps in this book should help keep you on the straight and narrow, but for added peace of mind, it's worth investing in an *A to Z* street atlas, available in all good bookshops, and quite a few central newsagents.

Examined on a map of the U.K., London can look intimidating—a vast urban sprawl. You need to remember, however, that the city comes in two different sizes. There's **Greater London,** which is huge, encompassing some 650 square miles; this part is made up largely of residential suburbs, and most of it can safely be ignored by sightseers. **Central London,** where most of the major attractions are—and where you'll be spending the majority of your time—isn't really so big at all.

FACING PAGE: **Holker Library, Gray's Inn.**

Of course, things aren't entirely straightforward. Central London may be where it's at, but exactly where that is isn't always clear. The areas used in this guide—the West End, West London, Southwest London, and so on—are not for the most part formally recognized zones with marked boundaries, but unofficial identifiers used for the purposes of splitting the city into manageable chunks for readers.

The most important of these areas, from a sightseeing perspective, is the **West End.** Unofficially bounded by the River Thames to the south, Farringdon Road and Farringdon Street to the east, Marylebone Road and Euston Road to the north, and Hyde Park and Victoria station to the west, this is where most of London's major attractions are found, including **Buckingham Palace,** the **British Museum,** or the bars, shops, and theatres of **Soho.** It's also where you'll find the capital's greatest concentration of good hotels and restaurants.

For the purposes of this guide, **Hyde Park** has been nominated as the gateway to **West London.** Its main hotel district lies just to the north, where cheap and mid-range places cluster around **Paddington station,** which serves as the main train link with Heathrow Airport, and thus provides many visitors with their introduction to the city. A limited supply of more expensive, fashionably appointed accommodation is available farther west in the swankier surrounds of **Notting Hill,** site of the famed **Portobello Road Market.**

South of Hyde Park in **Southwest London** are the upscale neighborhoods of **Belgravia, South Kensington, Knightsbridge,** and **Chelsea,** which offer high-class restaurant and hotel options—at high prices.

To the south, across the river, the **South Bank** and **Bankside** present a great line of attractions, including the **London Eye,** the **Southbank Centre, Tate Modern, Shakespeare's Globe,** and **HMS** *Belfast,* which hug the

View of the South Bank and London Eye from Westminster Bridge.

river's edge between Westminster Bridge and **Tower Bridge.** South of this attraction hotspot, however, London's cultural energy fades into sleepy waves of suburbs, with the odd point of interest poking its nose above the surface. There are hotel and B&B options south of the river, which are often a good deal cheaper than those in the center, but you will have to factor in the (often high) transport costs that staying on the outskirts incurs.

There's less choice in the **City,** immediately east of the West End, site of the original Roman settlement of "Londinium," and today one of the world's major financial centers. Although jeweled with historic sites, the City empties out in the evenings and on weekends, and there are better places to base yourself if you're looking for an atmospheric place to stay or a hopping nightlife scene.

Keep heading east or northeast beyond the City and you reach **East London,** the inner part of which is known as the East End. Much of this area is poor and deprived, with postwar tower blocks littering the skyline, but parts—notably the arty enclaves of **Shoreditch** and **Hoxton**—have become increasingly gentrified in recent years. The East End has also been the setting for some of the most ambitious redevelopment schemes of recent times in the capital. In the 1980s and '90s, the **Docklands** area was revitalized and reenergized, while **Canary Wharf** emerged as London's second major center of finance. It's hoped that **Stratford** will enjoy a similar resurgence in years to come following the development of the main London 2012 **Olympic Park** there.

Although primarily residential, **North** and **Northwest London** have more to offer visitors than their southern counterpart, with the great sprawling markets of **Camden** and the wild open spaces and genteel charms of Hampstead among the main draws. **Hampstead** also boasts a fine collection of small hotels and B&Bs, but staying here will mean a deal of traveling back and forth to the center.

Away from the sightseeing center, areas such as **Greenwich, Kew, and Richmond** offer great day-trip opportunities. Although some of these areas are perhaps a bit too far-flung to make convenient bases, Greenwich has good transport links with the center.

NEIGHBORHOODS IN BRIEF

West End

BLOOMSBURY & FITZROVIA Bloomsbury, a world within itself, is bounded roughly by Euston Road to the north, Tottenham Court Road to the west, New Oxford Street to the south, and Clerkenwell to the east. It is, among other things, the academic heart of London. The mighty **British Museum** (p. 96) lies at its center, to the north of which are several colleges, including **University College London,** one of the main branches of the **University of London.** Writers such as Virginia Woolf, who lived in the area, have fanned the neighborhood's reputation as a place devoted to liberal thinking and the arts. The novelist and her husband, Leonard, were unofficial leaders of a group of artists and writers known as the Bloomsbury Group in the early 20th century. However, Bloomsbury is a now fairly staid neighborhood of neat garden squares, with most of the students living outside the area.

The heart of Bloomsbury is **Russell Square,** with its late Georgian terraces surrounding a central park and cafe. Just to the east, the modernist

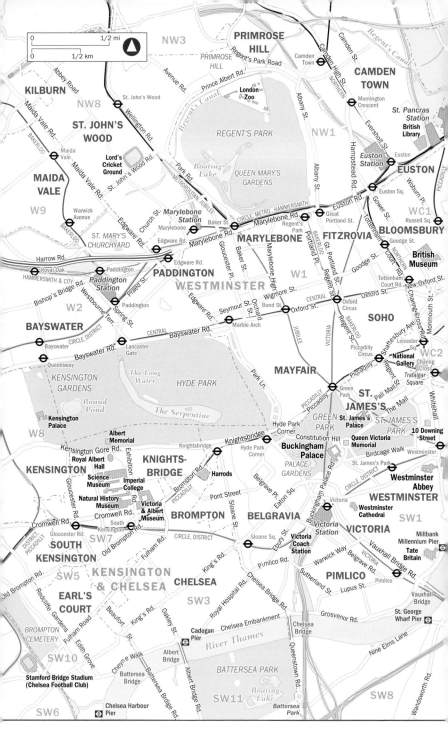

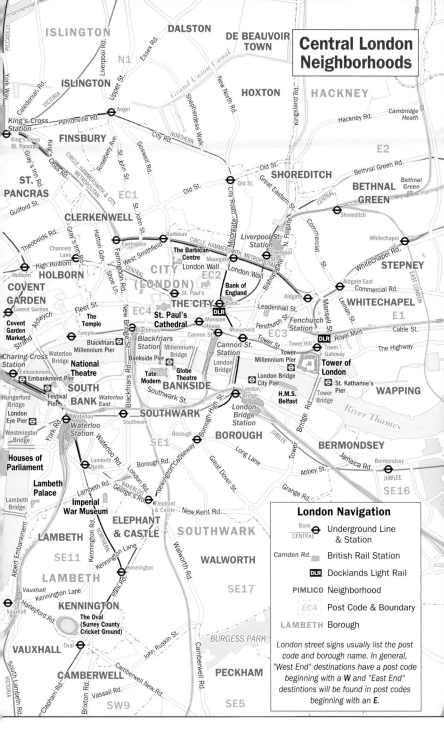

Central London Neighborhoods

ISLINGTON

DALSTON

DE BEAUVOIR TOWN

PICCADILLY

York Way

N1

Essex Rd.

Liverpool Rd.

Caledonian Rd.

ISLINGTON

Pentonville Rd.

Upper St.

Angel

HOXTON

HACKNEY

Kingsland Rd.

Hackney Rd.

Cambridge Heath

King's Cross Station

King's Cross St. Pancras

VICTORIA

City Rd.

NORTHERN

Shepherdess Walk

New North Rd.

Grand Union Canal

FINSBURY

Rosebery Ave.

St. John St.

Goswell Rd.

E2

Gray's Inn Rd.

King's Cross Rd.

CIRCLE, HAMMERSMITH & CITY

METROPOLITAN

Old St.

SHOREDITCH

Great Eastern St.

Bethnal Green Rd.

BETHNAL GREEN

Bethnal Green

ST. PANCRAS

Guilford St.

Theobalds Rd.

EC1

St. John St.

Old St.

Old St.

City Road

Shoreditch

CLERKENWELL

Hatton Gdn.

Farringdon Rd.

Barbican

CIRCLE, HAMMERSMITH, METROPOLITAN

Liverpool St. Station

Liverpool St.

N. Folgate

Commercial St.

CENTRAL

Whitechapel

STEPNEY

Chancery Lane

Gray's Inn Rd.

West Smithfield

The Barbican Centre

Moorgate

London Wall

Bishopsgate

Moorgate

Aldgate East

Commercial Rd.

Leman St.

Whitechapel Rd.

EAST LONDON

HOLBORN

High Holborn

Holborn

Shoe Ln.

CENTRAL

St. Paul's

CITY (LONDON)

EC2

Bank of England

Aldgate

Mansell St.

WHITECHAPEL

E1

Cable St.

COVENT GARDEN

Covent Garden

Fleet St.

EC4

THE CITY

St. Paul's Cathedral

Bank

Leadenhall St.

DLR

Royal Mint

Covent Garden Market

Aldwych

The Temple

New Bridge St.

Mansion House

Fenchurch St. Station

EC3

Tower Hill

DLR

Tower Gateway

The Highway

Charing Cross Station

Strand

Temple

Blackfriars Millennium Pier

Blackfriars Station

Cannon St.

Monument

Tower Millennium Pier

Tower of London

St. Katharine's Pier

WAPPING

Embankment

Embankment Pier

National Theatre

Blackfriars Rd.

Bankside Pier

Millennium Bridge

Cannon St. Station

London Bridge

Tower Bridge

H.M.S. Belfast

River Thames

SOUTH BANK

Festival Pier

Waterloo Bridge

Tate Modern

Globe Theatre

BANKSIDE

Southwark St.

London Bridge City Pier

Tower Bridge

London Eye Pier

Hungerford Bridge

Waterloo East

SOUTHWARK

Southwark

London Bridge Station

BERMONDSEY

Jamaica Rd.

Bermondsey

JUBILEE

Westminster Bridge

Waterloo Station

Waterloo

York Rd.

Lambeth North

Waterloo Rd.

Southwark

BOROUGH

Borough

Long Lane

Tower Bridge Rd.

JUBILEE

SE16

Houses of Parliament

SE1

Borough High St.

Newington Causeway

Great Dover St.

Grange Rd.

Abbey St.

Lambeth Palace

Lambeth Bridge

Lambeth Rd.

Borough Rd.

London Rd.

St. George's Rd.

Elephant & Castle

New Kent Rd.

Imperial War Museum

NORTHERN

ELEPHANT & CASTLE

SOUTHWARK

LAMBETH

Kennington Rd.

Kennington Lane

Walworth Rd.

WALWORTH

SE11

SE17

Albert Embankment

LAMBETH

Park Rd.

Kennington

BURGESS PARK

Vauxhall

Kennington Lane

KENNINGTON

The Oval (Surrey County Cricket Ground)

Harleyford Rd.

Vauxhall

VICTORIA

Oval

John Ruskin St.

Camberwell Rd.

PECKHAM

VAUXHALL

CAMBERWELL

Camberwell New Rd.

SE5

South Lambeth Rd.

Clapham Rd.

Brixton Rd.

Vassall Rd.

SW9

London Navigation

Bank ⊖ CENTRAL	Underground Line & Station
Camden Rd. ⊖	British Rail Station
DLR	Docklands Light Rail
PIMLICO	Neighborhood
EC4	Post Code & Boundary
LAMBETH	Borough

London street signs usually list the post code and borough name. In general, "West End" destinations have a post code beginning with a W and "East End" destinations will be found in post codes beginning with an E.

57

British Museum.

Brunswick Centre, a 1960s'-built residential and shopping center, provides a stark architectural contrast.

Hotel prices have risen in Bloomsbury in the past decade but are still nowhere near the levels of those in Mayfair and St. James's, and there are still bargains to be found, particularly on busy **Gower Street.** In general, Bloomsbury's hotels are comparable in price to what you'll find in Marylebone to the west, but Bloomsbury is arguably more convenient—at its southern doorstep are the restaurants and nightclubs of Soho, the theatre district, and the markets of Covent Garden. If you stay here, it's a 5-minute Tube ride to the heart of the West End.

To the west across Tottenham Court Road is **Fitzrovia,** a rather forgotten stretch of the West End, somewhat overshadowed by its more glamorous neighbors. To those in the know it offers a welcome respite from the crowds and madness of Oxford Street, with many good shops and pubs, particularly on **Charlotte Street.** The area was once the stamping ground for writers and artists such as Ezra Pound, Wyndham Lewis, and George Orwell. The bottom end of Fitzrovia is a virtual extension of Soho, with a cluster of Greek restaurants.

At Fitzrovia's center stands one of the great retro-futurist icons of London, the **BT Tower,** which looks a bit like an enormous spark plug. Opened in the mid '60s, it seemed then to represent the very cutting edge of architectural design, but now looks cheerfully dated. A restaurant once revolved at its summit, now long closed.

COVENT GARDEN & THE STRAND   The flower, fruit, and veg market is long gone (since 1974), but memories of Professor Higgins and his "squashed cabbage leaf," Eliza Doolittle, linger on. **Covent Garden** contains the city's busiest group of restaurants, pubs, and cafes outside of Soho, as well as some of the city's hippest shops, particularly along and around **Neal Street** and **Seven Dials.** The restored market buildings here represent one of London's more successful examples of urban recycling. The main building is now home to a number of shops, as well as a small arts and crafts market, while the former flower market holds the **London Transport Museum** (p. 102).

The area attracts professional street performers, who do their juggling and unicycling by **St. Paul's Church** (p. 108) in front of thronging crowds in summer—and just a few shivering souls in winter. Everywhere you go in the main square, you'll see living statues, buskers, magicians, and on the lower floor sometimes even opera singers moonlighting from the adjacent **Royal Opera House** (p. 308). Appropriately enough, London's **Theatre district** starts around Covent Garden and spills westward over to Leicester Square, Piccadilly Circus, and Soho (see below).

You'll probably come to the Covent Garden area for the theatre or dining rather than for accommodation. There are only a few hotels—although among those few are some of London's smartest.

Running east from **Trafalgar Square,** parallel to the River Thames, the **Strand** forms the southern border of Covent Garden. At one time it bordered the river, but in the 19th century the Victoria Embankment was created to allow for the subterranean construction of Tube lines and sewers to take place, separating the two. Most of the grand mansions and fine houses that once lined its length have—with the honorable exceptions of **Somerset House** (p. 109) and **The Savoy** hotel (p. 346)—been replaced by nondescript offices and chain restaurants.

Covent Garden.

LEICESTER SQUARE & PICCADILLY   Piccadilly Circus and Leicester Square are two of the capital's most famous locations, and yet you can't help feeling that if all London's attractions were of this quality, the city wouldn't receive any visitors at all. A barely-there square, **Piccadilly Circus** is more the confluence of major streets—Regent Street, Shaftesbury Avenue, and Piccadilly—than a venue in its own right. Although its neon billboards have graced a thousand postcards, the reality is underwhelming: a small, partly pedestrianized junction with relentless traffic and crowds; some interesting, if rather overshadowed Regency architecture (which can be seen to better effect on Regent Street); and one small, albeit undeniably pretty statue known to most Londoners as **Eros** (although trivia fans should note that it was meant to be his brother, Anteros, the Greek god of requited love). Visitors who pack its confines throughout the day seem to have a faint "is this it?" look in their eyes as they pose for the obligatory photo.

Leicester Square, just to the east, is larger and fully pedestrianized, and has a bit more going on, but is perhaps even more tawdry, dominated by a cluster of huge cinemas—which are the principal venues for star-laden premiere nights—and mainstream nightlife and eating options.

During the day the square is somewhat of a poor man's Covent Garden, with various low-rent buskers belting out the standards. At night, particularly on weekends, it's a bit too crowded and boozy to be pleasant. An ongoing £18 million redevelopment by Westminster Council has had little effect so far. Some of the newer arrivals—notably the **St. John Hotel** (p. 347)—have hinted at a more upmarket future, while others (M&M's World) have pulled in the other direction, leaving the square more or less where it was. It's convenient for those who want to be at the center of the action. The downside is the expense, the noise, congestion, and pollution.

Much more inviting is **Piccadilly** itself, the grand avenue running west from Piccadilly Circus, which was once the main western road out of London. It was named for the "picadil," a ruffled collar created by Robert Baker, a 17th-century tailor. If you want to do some shopping with a bit of added grandeur, retreat to the elegant, 19th-century **Burlington Arcade** (p. 268). Next door stands the **Royal Academy of Arts** (p. 105), one of the capital's major venues for art exhibitions.

SOHO & CHINATOWN   Just south of the international brands and off-the-peg glamour of Oxford Street—the capital's über-high-street—is somewhere altogether more distinctive: Soho, London's louche dissolute heart. It's a place where high and low living have gone hand in hand since the 19th century, and where today the gleaming offices of international media conglomerates and Michelin-starred restaurants sit next to tawdry clip joints and sex shops. In the 1950s and '60s, its smoky clubs helped give birth to the British jazz and rock 'n' roll scenes—in **Ronnie Scott's** (p. 323), it still boasts one of the capital's foremost jazz venues.

Soho's streets thrum with energy: During the day its pavements are filled with busy people on the make; at night, there's a whiff of sleaze about the place, where illicit entreaties are guaranteed if you wander down the wrong alley—although it's generally a safe area (just keep your wits about you). There are dozens of great places to eat, drink, and hang out, ranging from chic, high-end gastrofests to cheap, late-opening stalwarts such as **Bar**

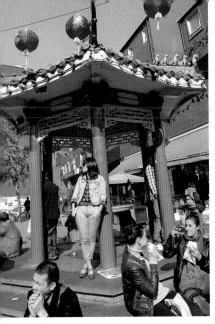
Chinatown.

Italia (p. 329). Many of the best are found on Dean, Frith, and Greek Streets.

Soho is bordered by Regent Street to the west, Oxford Street to the north, Charing Cross Road (lined with second-hand bookshops) to the east, and the **Theatreland** of Shaftesbury Avenue to the south. At its northeastern corner is **Soho Square,** where the central stretch of grass is usually packed with sunbathing workers during sunny lunchtimes, while close to its southern end is Old Compton Street, the longtime home of the capital's gay scene. Keeping it "real" between the two is one of the few remaining street markets in the West End, on **Berwick Street**—even if these days it consists of barely a half-dozen fruit and veg stalls. The British movie industry is centered on Wardour Street, while **Carnaby Street**—a block from Regent Street—was the epicenter of the universe during the Swinging Sixties, but is these days just another shopping street, albeit one with a few quality, independent stores. Running parallel just to the west, **Kingly Street** has some lively bars.

South of Shaftesbury Avenue is London's **Chinatown** . . . although "town" is a slightly grand way of describing what essentially amounts to one-and-a-bit streets lined with restaurants. The main street, **Gerrard Street,** is rather kitsch, with giant oriental-style gates and pagoda-esque phone boxes. However, this is no theme park, but a genuine, thriving community, and one of the most dependable areas for Chinese food.

OXFORD STREET AND MARYLEBONE Pretty much every town in the country has a high street, a collection of shops and businesses aimed at the surrounding community. Where once these would have been locally owned stores, most have now been taken over by national and international chains. **Oxford Street** could be regarded as London's high street, where the biggest chains have their flagship branches and where several of the capital's most prestigious department stores, including Selfridges and John Lewis, are found.

It can be a brutal place, particularly on weekends and the weeks before Christmas, when it is choked with people, traffic, and noise—not to mention numerous pickpockets. Huge volumes of cash are dropped here every day—although not so much of it by Londoners, who try to avoid the crazy, over-commercial maelstrom. Note that often it can be quicker making your way between two destinations on Oxford Street by taking the longer route via the backstreets, rather than fighting your way through human traffic—although the introduction of a Japanese-style diagonal pedestrian crossing system at Oxford Circus has eased problems slightly (very slightly).

North of Oxford Street, the district of **Marylebone** (pronounced Mar-*le*-bone), set between Fitzrovia and Paddington, was once the poor relation of Mayfair to the south, but has become much more fashionable of late—certainly more so than when it was the setting for public executions at the Tyburn gallows (although those did at least attract the crowds). The last executions took place in the late 18th century. Most first-time visitors head here to explore the bafflingly popular **Madame Tussauds** (p. 168) wax-works or walk along **Baker Street** in the imaginary footsteps of Sherlock Holmes. The streets form a near-perfect grid, with the major ones running north–south between Regent's Park and Oxford Street, and are lined with interesting boutiques and restaurants.

Marylebone has emerged as a major "bedroom" district for London, competing with Bloomsbury to its east. The hub of the West End's action is virtually at your doorstep if you lodge here. Once known only for its town houses turned into B&Bs, the district now offers accommodations in all price ranges, catering to everyone from rock stars to frugal family travelers.

MAYFAIR   Once a simple stretch of fields outside the main part of the city where an annual party was held at the start of summer (the "May Fair" that gave the area its name), this is now one of the most exclusive sections of London, filled with luxury hotels, Georgian town houses, and swanky shops—hence its status as the most expensive property on the U.K. version of board game *Monopoly.* Sandwiched between Regent Street and Hyde Park, it's convenient for London's best shopping and reasonably close to the West End theatres, yet removed from the peddlers and commerce of Covent Garden and Soho.

One of the curiosities of Mayfair is **Shepherd Market,** a micro-village of pubs, two-story inns, restaurants, and book and food stalls, nestled within Mayfair's grandness.

This is the place if you're seeking sophisticated, albeit expensive, accommodations close to the high fashion shops of **Bond Street,** the commercial art galleries of **Cork Street,** and the bespoke tailors of **Savile Row.**

At the center of the area, **Grosvenor Square** (pronounced *Grove*-nor) is nicknamed "Little America" because it's home to a statue of Franklin D. Roosevelt and the U.S. Embassy—although a new embassy is due to be constructed in Nine Elms, south of the river in the next few years.

ST. JAMES'S   The neighborhood begins at **Piccadilly Circus** and moves southwest, incorporating the south side of **Piccadilly, Pall Mall, The Mall, St. James's Park,** and **Green Park.** Often called "**Royal London,**" St. James's basks in its associations with everybody from the "merrie monarch" King Charles II to the current Queen Elizabeth II and Prince Charles. This is where you'll find several of the most prestigious royal addresses, including **Clarence House** (p. 99), home of the Prince of Wales, and **St. James's Palace,** the current home of the Princess Royal (Princess Anne) and the official address of the British sovereign—although one they're clearly not very fond of: No reigning monarch has lived here since George III, preferring instead the roomier confines of **Buckingham Palace** (p. 97) down the road.

St James's is where English gentlemen seek haven at that male-only bastion of English tradition, the gentlemen's club, where poker is played, drinks are consumed, and deals are made (the Reform, the Athenaeum, and the St.

Trafalgar Square.

James's Club are some of the most prestigious institutions). Be sure to stop in at **Fortnum & Mason** (p. 290) on Piccadilly itself, the grocer to the Queen. Hotels in this neighborhood tend to be expensive, but if the Queen should summon you to Buckingham Palace, you won't have far to walk.

Trafalgar Square (p. 110) lies at the opposite end of the Mall to Buckingham Palace, marking the district's eastern boundary. It's one of the city's major landmarks and perhaps the closest thing to an official "center" that London possesses. Its north side is taken up by the neoclassical facade of the **National Gallery** (p. 102), while in the middle stands **Nelson's Column,** erected in honor of the country's victory over Napoleon at the Battle of Trafalgar, in 1805.

West London

PADDINGTON & BAYSWATER North of Hyde Park and Kensington Gardens, **Paddington** radiates out from Paddington station, the terminal for the express train service from Heathrow Airport. As such, it's one of the major B&B centers in London, attracting budget travelers who fill the lodgings along **Sussex Gardens** and Norfolk Square. Its eastern boundary, Edgware Road, which runs north of Marble Arch, was first laid out by the Romans, and is now one of the capital's major centers of Middle Eastern culture, lined with Lebanese restaurants and shisha cafes.

Just south of Paddington, north of Hyde Park, and abutting more fashionable Notting Hill to the west, is **Bayswater,** also filled with B&Bs that attract budget travelers. Inspired by Marylebone and elegant Mayfair, a prosperous set of Victorian merchants built terrace houses around spacious squares in this area.

Paddington and Bayswater are "in-between" areas. If you've come to London to see the attractions in the east, including the British Museum, Tower of London, and Theatreland, you'll find yourself commuting a lot, with bus and Tube journeys of 15 to 20 minutes to reach the heart of the action. Stay here for moderately priced lodgings (there are expensive hotels, too) and for convenience to **Hyde Park** (p. 112) and transportation. Accommodation ranges from seedy to swank, so pick your hotel with care; you'll find our favorites starting on p. 337.

KENSINGTON   The Royal Borough lies west of Kensington Gardens and Hyde Park and is traversed by two of London's major shopping streets, **Kensington High Street** and **Kensington Church Street.** Since 1689, when asthmatic William III fled Whitehall Palace for Nottingham House (where the air was fresher), the district has enjoyed royal associations. In time, Nottingham House became **Kensington Palace** (p. 114), and the royals grabbed a chunk of Hyde Park to plant their roses. Kensington Palace was home to the late princesses Margaret and Diana, and in 2013 will be the new home of Prince William and Kate, the Duchess of Cambridge.

During the reign of William III, Kensington Square developed, attracting artists and writers. Thackeray wrote *Vanity Fair* while living here. With all those royal associations, Kensington is a wealthy neighborhood with some very well-to-do hotels and shops. Although it can feel like you've left central London behind on its quiet residential streets, it's just a few Tube stops from High Street Kensington station to the heart of the action.

NOTTING HILL   Fashionable **Notting Hill** is bounded on the east by Bayswater and on the south by Kensington. Hemmed in on the north by the elevated road known as the Westway and on the west by the Shepherd's Bush roundabout, it has many turn-of-the-20th-century mansions and small houses sitting on quiet, leafy, recently gentrified streets, plus a number of hot restaurants and clubs.

Kensington Palace gardens.

In the 1950s the area welcomed a significant influx of Caribbean immigrants, whose cultural heritage is vibrantly celebrated each year at the **Notting Hill Carnival** (p. 46), Europe's largest street party. Hotels are few, but often terrifyingly chic. Although farther out from the center than Paddington and Bayswater, many young professional visitors to London wouldn't stay anywhere else. Notting Hill is also home to **Portobello Road,** the site of London's most famous street **market** (p. 277). Adjacent **Holland Park,** an expensive residential neighborhood spread around the park of the same name, is a little more serene, but also more staid.

SHEPHERD'S BUSH   To the immediate west of Holland Park, this increasingly fashionable area is perhaps best known outside its environs as the home of the giant **Westfield London** (p. 278), one of Europe's largest shopping centers, which sits imperially on the north side of Shepherd's Bush Green, as well as **BBC TV Centre** on Wood Lane. The area has a vibrant cultural scene with a number of well respected music venues—including the Shepherd's Bush Empire and Bush Hall—and a theatre, the Bush Theatre, which specializes in new, often challenging, works.   Most of the hotels around here are in the lower star categories, the notable exception being the awfully glamorous **K West Hotel and Spa** (p. 357).

Southwest London

WESTMINSTER   Westminster has been the seat of first English and then British government since the days of Edward the Confessor (1042–66). Dominated by the **Houses of Parliament** (p. 121) and **Westminster Abbey,** the area runs along the Thames to the east of St. James's Park. Whitehall is the main thoroughfare, linking Trafalgar Square with **Parliament Square.** You can visit the **Churchill War Rooms** (p. 120) and walk by **Downing Street** to see **Number 10,** home to Britain's prime minister (though the street itself is fenced in and guarded these days). No visit is complete without a call at **Westminster Abbey** (p. 128), one of the greatest Gothic churches in the world. It has witnessed a parade of English history, beginning with William the Conqueror's coronation on Christmas Day, 1066, and most recently with the wedding of Prince William and Kate in 2011.

Westminster also encompasses **Victoria,** an area that takes its name from bustling Victoria station. Many B&Bs and hotels have sprouted up here because of the neighborhood's proximity to the rail station, which provides the main fast link with Gatwick Airport.

Westminster Abbey.

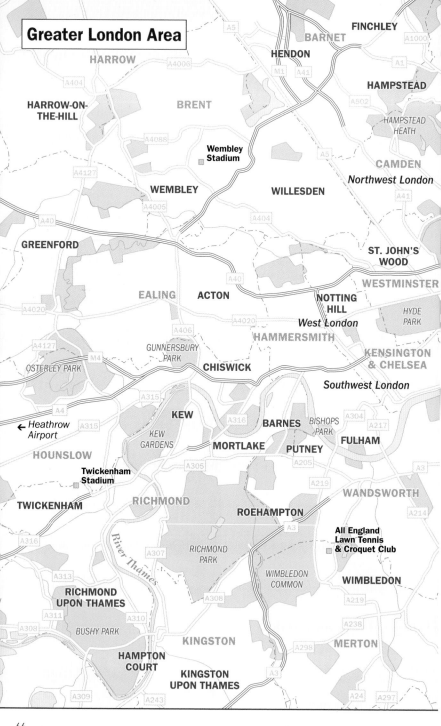

Greater London Area

FINCHLEY

BARNET

HENDON

HARROW

HAMPSTEAD

HARROW-ON-THE-HILL

BRENT

HAMPSTEAD HEATH

Wembley Stadium

CAMDEN

WEMBLEY

WILLESDEN

Northwest London

GREENFORD

ST. JOHN'S WOOD

WESTMINSTER

EALING

ACTON

NOTTING HILL

HYDE PARK

West London

HAMMERSMITH

GUNNERSBURY PARK

KENSINGTON & CHELSEA

OSTERLEY PARK

CHISWICK

Southwest London

← Heathrow Airport

KEW

BARNES

BISHOPS PARK

KEW GARDENS

MORTLAKE

FULHAM

HOUNSLOW

PUTNEY

Twickenham Stadium

RICHMOND

ROEHAMPTON

WANDSWORTH

TWICKENHAM

All England Lawn Tennis & Croquet Club

RICHMOND PARK

WIMBLEDON COMMON

WIMBLEDON

RICHMOND UPON THAMES

River Thames

BUSHY PARK

MERTON

KINGSTON

HAMPTON COURT

KINGSTON UPON THAMES

66

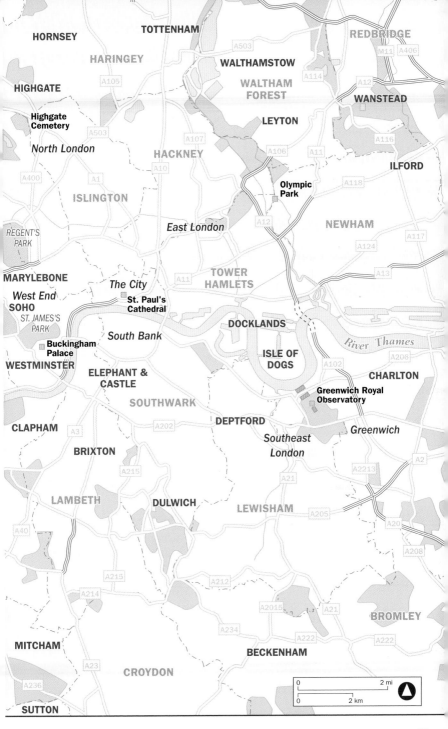

Victoria is cheap (for London) and convenient, if you don't mind the noise and crowds.

The hotels on Belgrave Road fill up quickly. If you've arrived without a hotel reservation, you'll find the pickings better on the streets off Belgrave Road. Your best bet is to walk along **Ebury Street,** east of Victoria station and Buckingham Palace Road. Here you'll find some decent, moderately priced lodgings; we've selected our local favorites starting on p. 337. Since you're near Victoria station, the area is convenient for day trips to **Brighton** (p. 383) and the south coast.

Things are a bit pricier to the southwest in **Pimlico,** the area bordering the river, which is filled with fine Regency squares as well as the 1930's-built Dolphin Square apartment block, where many Members of Parliament (or "MPs") have their London homes.

BELGRAVIA   South of Knightsbridge, this area has long been one of the main aristocratic quarters of London, rivaling Mayfair in grandeur. Its centerpiece is **Belgrave Square,** now home to various foreign embassies.

Packed with grand, formal, and often startlingly expensive hotels, Belgravia is a haven of upmarket tranquility. If you lodge here, no one will ever accuse you of staying on the "wrong side of the tracks." It's also extremely convenient for the western part of central London, just east of the restaurants and pubs of Chelsea, and just west of Victoria station, making it a handy base if you're planning to take day trips.

CHELSEA   Beginning at **Sloane Square,** this stylish Thames-side district lies south and to the west of Belgravia. The area has always been a favorite of writers and artists, including Oscar Wilde, George Eliot, James Whistler, J. M. W. Turner, Henry James, and Thomas Carlyle. Mick Jagger and Margaret Thatcher (not together) have been more recent residents, and the late Princess Diana and the "Sloane Rangers" (a term used to describe posh women, derived from Chelsea's Sloane Square) of the 1980s gave the area more recognition. There are some swanky hotels here, and the merest scattering of modestly priced ones. The main drawback to Chelsea is inaccessibility. Except for Sloane Square, there's a dearth of Tube stops, and unless you like to take a lot of buses or expensive taxis, you may find getting around a chore.

Chelsea's major boulevard is **King's Road,** where Mary Quant launched the miniskirt in the 1960s, Vivienne Westwood devised the punk look in the 1970s, and where today Charles Saatchi's eponymous **Saatchi Gallery** (p. 125) makes the running in the contemporary art world. The road runs the length of Chelsea all the way to **Fulham,** and is at its liveliest on Saturday. King's Road's mainstream shops aren't typical of otherwise upmarket Chelsea, an elegant village filled with town houses and little mews dwellings that only successful types such as stockbrokers and solicitors can afford to occupy.

KNIGHTSBRIDGE & BROMPTON   One of London's swankiest neighborhoods, Knightsbridge is a top residential, hotel, and shopping district just south of Hyde Park. Its defining feature and chief attraction is **Harrods** (p. 290) on the Brompton Road, "the Notre Dame of department stores." Right nearby, **Beauchamp Place** (*Bee*-cham) is a Regency-era, boutique-lined street with a scattering of restaurants. Most hotels around here are in the deluxe category.

Saatchi Gallery.

Knightsbridge, and the equally well-to-do **Brompton** to the south, make up one of the most convenient areas of western London, ideally located if you want to head east to the theatre district or the Mayfair shops, or west to Chelsea or Kensington's restaurants and museums. However, staying here will come at a price.

SOUTH KENSINGTON   If you want to be in the vicinity of the shops, boutiques, and restaurants of Knightsbridge and Chelsea, but don't have the resources for a hotel there, head for South Kensington, where the accommodation is more moderately priced. Southeast of Kensington Gardens, primarily residential **South Kensington** is often called "museumland" because it's dominated by a complex of museums and colleges, including the **Natural History Museum** (p. 124), **Victoria & Albert Museum** (p. 127), and **Science Museum** (p. 126). Just to the north, facing Kensington Gardens, is the **Royal Albert Hall** (p. 308). South Kensington boasts some fashionable restaurants and town house hotels, and is just a couple of stops along the Tube's Piccadilly Line from Green Park.

EARL'S COURT   Earl's Court lies south of Kensington and just west of South Kensington. For decades the favored haunt of visiting Australians (hence its nickname "Kangaroo Valley"), the area is still home to many immigrants—mainly eastern Europeans nowadays—and is also a popular base for budget travelers, thanks to its wealth of B&Bs, inexpensive hotels, and hostels, and its convenient access to central London: A 15-minute Tube ride takes you into the West End. Littered with fast-food joints, pubs, and cafes, it provides a cheap, cheerful base, but little in the way of refinement and no major sights on your doorstep, unless you're visiting the **Earl's Court Exhibition Centre.**

BATTERSEA   Battersea was once an island in the river before being reclaimed by inhabitants of the Thames' southern bank in the Middle Ages. For most of the 19th and 20th centuries, it was an honest working-class district where most of the population were employed in local industries. However, over the past couple of decades, as the number of available properties in Chelsea began to shrink, the tentacles of development reached across the water into Battersea's Victorian terraces. The process of gentrification is now in full swing, particularly along the riverfront.

There are some decent restaurants and hotels here, but you shouldn't go expecting any great bargains—although the presence of the fantastic **Battersea Park** makes it a peaceful alternative to the center.

Not all local redevelopment has been a success, however. The 1930s-built **Battersea Power Station,** one of the great icons of industrial London, its four giant brick towers dominating the local skyline, has stubbornly resisted all attempts to find a new use for it, in a "redevelopment" process that has been ongoing since the 1980s. It's a listed building, which means it can't be torn down, but without anyone willing to pay for its upkeep, the interior has become a gutted shell. Just to its south stands another great icon, the **Battersea Dogs and Cats Home,** the country's most famous center for abandoned pets.

South Bank

Lying south across the Thames from Covent Garden and the Victoria Embankment, this is where you'll find the **London Eye** (p. 138), **National Theatre** (p. 305), and **Southbank Centre** (p. 308; the largest arts center in Western Europe, and still growing).

Although the area's time as a top hotel district may yet come, that day certainly hasn't arrived yet. A few interesting lodgings aside (p. 367), the South Bank is a popular evening destination for culture and dining with plenty of options at **Gabriel's Wharf**, the **Oxo Tower** (p. 272), or the Southbank Centre.

To the east the South Bank bleeds into Bankside, site of **Tate Modern** (p. 281), **Shakespeare's Globe** (p. 305), and **HMS** *Belfast* (p. 136), and today the two areas are generally regarded as forming a single riverside zone linked by a cheery riverside path taking you all the way—via a couple of inland detours at London Bridge—from Westminster Bridge to Tower Bridge.

The area is accessible as never before, reached from its western end via **Waterloo station,** from its eastern end by **London Bridge Station,** and from its central stretch by the new south side entrance to **Blackfriars station.** Also now boasting a revamped north side entrance, Blackfriars has

An entertainer on the South Bank.

become the first London station to span the Thames.

If you're renting an apartment in the city, the South Bank is a great place to pick up some fresh produce from **Borough Market** (p. 276), one of the capital's top foodie markets. The market lies just around the corner from **Southwark Cathedral** (p. 141). The station and its surrounding area have undergone a mass renovation program in recent years, the chief element of which was the creation of **The Shard,** the European Union's tallest building. The 310m (1,017 ft) structure is set to open the capital's highest publicly accessible vantage point, a viewing deck on its topmost 72nd floor—although rumors suggest the entrance fee will be an equally high £20. In 2013, several of the upper floors will be occupied by a new luxury **Shangri-La hotel,** which will add to the area's accommodation choices.

Southwark Cathedral.

Farther south the area quickly becomes much more businesslike, as tourist attractions give way to the residential streets of **Bermondsey, Borough,** and **Lambeth,** where gentrifiers are fighting hard to reclaim the streets from their working-class roots.

The City

THE SQUARE MILE   When Londoners speak of "the City," they mean the original Square Mile that's now Britain's main financial district. The City was the site of "Londinium," the first settlement of the Roman conquerors. Despite its age, the City doesn't easily reveal its past. Although it retains some of its medieval character, much of the City was swept away by the Great Fire of 1666, the Blitz of 1940, and the zeal of modern developers. You can delve deeper into 2,000 years of history at the City's **Museum of London** (p. 145).

Landmarks litter the skyline including **The Monument,** which commemorates the capital's revival after the Great Fire of London (p. 25); the curvy glass skyscraper 30 St. Mary Axe, more commonly known as the "**Gherkin,**" which, less than a decade since it was built, has become one of London's most recognizable icons; and Sir Christopher Wren's masterpiece **St. Paul's Cathedral** (p. 146), the most recognizable icon of all. These will be joined in the coming years by a new set of skyscrapers, each with their own distinctive shape and ready-made nickname (the "Walkie Talkie," the "Cheese Grater," the "Pinnacle" et al), as the City—ever short of space—continues to grow upward. Other attractions include that grand symbol of

British financial might, the **Bank of England** (you can visit its museum; see p. 144) and the Central Criminal Court, better known as the **Old Bailey,** where the country's most serious, high profile crimes are tried. Members of the public can attend trials on a first-come, first-served basis. Line up at the entrances on Newgate Street. Detailed information on the area can be provided by the dedicated **City of London Information Centre** (p. 441).

For all these distractions, the City is largely a functional place, home to many businesses, but few residents, aside from those in the **Barbican** (p. 307) complex. Workers pack out the streets by day, arriving from all corners of the capital and beyond, but depart abruptly come 6pm. On weekends, it can seem ghostly, with few people on the streets, and many restaurants, pubs, and shops shut—although the opening a little while back of **One New Change** (p. 278), a shopping center just opposite St. Paul's, has brought retail life to the area. As such, it can be a bit of a lonely place to base yourself. Most of the hotels are set up for business travelers, not sightseers. However, that can sometimes mean weekend bargains at upscale establishments; see p. 368 for our favorite City hotels.

CLERKENWELL This neighborhood, north and a little west of the City, was the site of London's first hospital, and is the home of several early churches. In the 18th century, Clerkenwell declined into a muck-filled cattle yard, home to cheap gin distilleries and little else. During a 19th-century revival, John Stuart Mill's London Patriotic Club moved here in 1872, and William Morris' socialist press called Clerkenwell home in the 1890s—Lenin worked here editing *Iskra.*

The neighborhood again fell into disrepair, but has recently been reinvented by the moneyed and the groovy. A handful of hot restaurants and clubs have sprung up in **Exmouth Market,** and art galleries line St. John's Square and the fringe of Clerkenwell Green. Lest you think the whole area has become trendy, know that trucks still rumble into **Smithfield Market** throughout the night, unloading thousands of animal carcasses ready for sale at the morning meat market. The area is a good base for young and fashionable visitors, close to the bars and clubs of Hoxton and Shoreditch, and a short walk from the Square Mile itself. At its Western end, **Hatton Gardens** is the jewelry and diamond center of the capital, filled with glittering showcases.

HOLBORN & THE INNS OF COURT The old borough of Holborn (*Ho*-burn), which abuts the Square Mile southeast of Bloomsbury, and **Temple,** south of Holborn across the Strand, represent the heart of legal London—this is where you'll find the city's barristers, solicitors, and law clerks, operating out of four **Inns of Court** (p. 148; legal associations that are part college, part club, and part hotel): **Gray's Inn, Lincoln's Inn, Middle Temple,** and **Inner Temple.** Still Dickensian in spirit, the Inns are otherworldly places to explore, away from London's traffic, with ancient courtyards, mazy passageways, and some of the capital's last remaining gas lamps.

Following the Strand eastward from Aldwych, you'll soon come to **Fleet Street.** In the 19th century, this was the most concentrated newspaper district in the world. In recent times, however, most London newspapers have abandoned Fleet Street for new developments in Docklands.

Temple Bar, Fleet Street.

Where the Strand becomes Fleet Street stands **Temple Bar,** marking the point where the City of London officially begins (the actual Bar has been transported to Paternoster Square, adjacent to St. Paul's).

East London

THE EAST END, HOXTON & DALSTON The East End extends east from the old City walls, encompassing Hoxton, Shoreditch, Spitalfields, Bethnal Green, Whitechapel, Hackney, Bow, Stratford, and other districts. Long one of London's poorest areas, famed for its sprawling 19th-century slums, brutal high rises, and criminal underbelly, the East End is currently regenerating faster than anywhere else in the capital—as exemplified by the creation of the Olympic Park in Stratford (p. 74). True, significant stretches are still impoverished, but there's a real vibrancy about the place. You'll find a growing number of trendy bars, clubs, restaurants, art galleries, and vintage clothing outlets, particularly just north of the Square Mile, in **Shoreditch** and **Hoxton Square**—home to the contemporary art scene's mecca, **White Cube.** The area is also leading the way in new technology; the glut of web-based and tech companies based around the interchange of Old Street and City Road has led to it being dubbed the "Silicon Roundabout."

It's a good spot to base yourself if you want to take advantage of the intense, fluid nightlife, but perhaps a little hectic if you prefer your 8 hours and an early start. Accommodation options have grown (p. 371) and there are plenty of affordable places to eat, particularly in Shoreditch and Dalston. Once rather poorly served by public transport, the area is now easier to reach, following the revamp of an old Tube route that's now part of the Overground rail system, with new stations at Shoreditch High Street, Hoxton, Haggerston, and Dalston Junction.

Immediately east of the City, the redeveloped Spitalfields area boasts a number of great (and historic) markets, including a craft market still trading

When the London Olympic Games and Paralympic Games of 2012 came to an end, the word on everyone's lips was "legacy." Will the games, and in particular the vast Olympic site with its gleaming, cutting-edge stadia and sporting facilities, be of lasting, transformative benefit to a stretch of the East End famed for its urban deprivation and industrial decline? Or will it prove a temporary distraction, leaving behind an array of expensively assembled, but ultimately underutilized and unwanted infrastructure? Is Stratford about to become London's latest up-and-coming area or another failed regeneration project?

Obviously the hope is that the games will ultimately be remembered as just the opening chapter in what turns out to be a much longer and more successful story—the rebirth of this part of the East End. That new narrative began as soon as the Paralympic Games wrapped up on September 9, 2012. How things will pan out, however, and how long the process will ultimately take are far from clear. What is certain is that, having already undergone an enormous transformation to get it ready for the games, the Olympic site will require something of at least a similar scale to get it ready for the future.

Unfortunately, previous Olympic Games don't inspire much confidence. Many former host cities have struggled to find purposes for their shiny new stadia following the games, and there is a genuine fear that, without careful post-Games management, the Olympic Park venues could become a herd of very expensive white elephants.

Thankfully, at the time of writing, the future looks fairly promising even if some of the details still need to be inked in. Transport links to the area have been greatly improved, particularly since the linking of the new Stratford International Station to the DLR system.

in the old **Spitalfields Market** (p. 277) building, despite recent encroaching development; the clothes and jewelry pandemonium of **Petticoat Lane** (officially called Wentworth Street); and the sprawling **flea market** that takes place every Sunday on Brick Lane, selling everything from furniture, clothes, and electrical equipment to CDs, DVDs, and bric-a-brac. See p. 272 for more on the area's thriving street markets.

If you're self-catering, it's also worth checking out **Whitechapel Market** opposite the Royal London Hospital, which caters to the local Asian population, and is a good source of bargain fruit and vegetables.

Brick Lane, incidentally, is a great place for a curry, if you can deal with all the waiters on the street trying to hustle you into their restaurants. You stay round here for the vibe more than for the sights, but attractions you may want to visit include the **Whitechapel Art Gallery** (p. 160) and the **Royal London Hospital Museum** (p. 158).

DOCKLANDS In 1981, in the most ambitious scheme of its kind in Europe, the London Docklands Development Corporation (LDDC) was formed to redevelop the then-moribund dockyards of **Wapping,** the Isle of Dogs, the Royal Docks, and Surrey Docks. The area is bordered roughly by Tower

And the opening of the **Westfield Stratford City** (p. 279), one of Europe's largest urban shopping centers, next to the Olympic Park, has given the area the retail seal of approval.

As for the Olympic infrastructure itself, plans are in place (at least at the time of writing) for six of the eight permanent venues: the **Aquatics Centre** is being transformed into a public swimming venue; the Handball Arena is being repurposed for concerts and exhibitions, to be known as the **Multi-Use Arena;** the Velodrome is becoming a public cycling center named the **Lee Valley VeloPark;** the **ArcelorMittal Orbit Observation Tower** (www.arcelormittalorbit.com) will become a state-operated tourist attraction; while other venues are being turned into venues for hockey and tennis.

Slightly problematically, the future of the biggest venue, the main 80,000-seat athletics stadium, is still in the balance. As things stand, the intention is to try and lease the stadium to one of the local soccer teams.

In the Olympic Park surrounding the venues, the landscaped grounds are to be made publicly accessible and renamed the **Queen Elizabeth II Olympic Park.** A network of cycle paths will be added and several areas will be set aside as wildlife habitats. Meanwhile, the Olympic and Paralympic Village are being transformed into 2,800 new homes and an education campus.

For all the problems—and costs—that hosting London 2012 Games entailed, it would surely be worth it if it left a lasting (there's no other word for it) legacy, transforming Stratford into a standout London neighborhood, its name synonymous with successful urban regeneration and modern, green-aware living.

To keep abreast of the latest developments at the site, check the **Olympic Park Legacy Company's** website, www.legacycompany.co.uk.

Bridge to the west and London City Airport to the east. Despite early setbacks and a couple of ill-timed recessions, the plan was ultimately successful. Many businesses have moved here; Thames-side warehouses have been converted to Manhattan-style lofts, and museums, shops, and an ever-growing list of restaurants have popped up at this 21st-century river city in the making.

Canary Wharf, on the Isle of Dogs, is the heart of Docklands. This 28-hectare (69-acre) site is dominated by a 240m (787-ft.) tower, **One Canada Square,** for many years, the tallest building in the United Kingdom (the title since taken by the "Shard" at London Bridge; see p. 71). The piazza below the tower is lined with **shops** and restaurants. Direct access to the area is provided by the DLR and Jubilee Tube line.

On the south side of the river—although owing to the Thames' meandering nature, actually west of Canary Wharf—Surrey Docks once covered most of the Rotherhithe Peninsula. It too was redeveloped in the 1980s and '90s, and renamed **Surrey Quays,** with a new marina, shopping centers, and several thousand homes. Dockside development also took place farther west at **Butler's Wharf,** where Victorian warehouses have been converted

Shops around Spitalfields Market and Brick Lane.

into offices, workshops, houses, shops, and restaurants. Butler's Wharf is home to the **Design Museum** (until it relocates in 2014; see p. 134).

East of Canary Wharf, but again across the river, the Millennium Dome—the setting for the Millennium Experience, the much derided, under-visited celebration of the year 2000—has since been transformed into the **O2 Arena,** one of the capital's leading entertainment venues. In 2012, the O2 was linked with the ExCel Centre to the east across the river via the capital's first cable car, the **Emirates Air Line,** which takes its passengers on a ride some 60m (200 ft.) above the Thames. More elevated viewing opportunities should be available by the time this guide hits the shelves with the proposed opening of the **Skywalk,** a walkway and viewing platform on top of the O2 Arena.

The Docklands area is fun during the day and is home to some great restaurants, offering good food and a change of pace from the more traditional West End. Chances are you'll venture here for sights and restaurants, not for lodging, unless you have business in the area.

North & Northwest London

ISLINGTON These days Islington, east of King's Cross, has become synonymous with a type of left-leaning, gastropubbing, guacamole-eating gentrification. Once upon a time, however, it was a solidly working-class area, filled with market traders and factory workers who had their entertainment at the area's various Victorian music halls.

Since the 1970s, much of it has undergone wholesale renovation as middle-class professionals began moving in, attracted by the (then) low property prices. However, the renovated Regency squares and Victorian terraces don't tell the whole story. Away from the smart pubs and restaurants of the main thoroughfare, Upper Street, parts of Islington remain severely impoverished.

A primarily residential area, its main formal attraction is **Camden Passage** antiques market (p. 279), as well as its vibrant nightlife, which attracts visitors from all over town; people pack out its pubs, restaurants, and comedy clubs at the weekend.

KING'S CROSS & ST. PANCRAS   Long a seedy area on the fringe of central London, King's Cross is in the midst of a major regeneration program. Millions of pounds are being ploughed into its decaying infrastructure. The process began with the revamp of St. Pancras Station following the transfer of **Eurostar** services—the Channel Tunnel Rail Link—to here from Waterloo.

Train stations are, of course, primarily places you go to be transported somewhere else, not to linger. St. Pancras, however, is an exception, being one of the finest architectural icons of the Age of Steam. If you have some time to spare, do spend a few moments looking around—it's almost worth missing your train for. British Poet Laureate John Betjeman called the 1868 structure, with its huge single span roof—the largest in the world when it was built—gargoyles, and Gothic revival towers, "too beautiful and too romantic to survive."

He almost became a prophet in the 1960s when this landmark was slated for demolition, only to be saved by preservationists. Today the glamorous and restored station is a dazzling entry point into Britain, its grand architecture further enhanced by the reopening in 2011 of the 19th-century Midland Railway Hotel as the St. Pancras Renaissance London Hotel (p. 343).

To the east, King's Cross Station—St. Pancras' more dowdy neighbor—is also being primped and polished. It's been given a new roof and platform, which will soon be followed by the addition of a new concourse and the creation of a large tree-lined square (larger than Leicester Square) in front of the entrance.

St. Pancras station.

These developments will, however, be dwarfed by what's taking place just north of King's Cross. Here a 27-hectare (67-acre) former industrial site is undergoing a massive (to put it mildly) regeneration, which will see the creation of 50 new buildings (a mixture of offices, shops, restaurants, entertainment venues, and galleries), as well as a new campus for the students of Central St. Martin's college—the former building will become the main branch of Foyles (p. 282)—2,000 new homes, 20 new streets (including the largest new London street for a century), 3 parks, and 10 new public squares (including the largest new public square since Trafalgar in 1845). Indeed, the development is so vast that the post office has had to award it its own postcode—N1C—and the whole thing is not due for completion until 2020. In the meanwhile, visitors can enjoy the more sedate, stately pleasures of the **British Library** (p. 161), just to the west on Euston Road.

Once pretty much the last place you'd want to base yourself, King's Cross is now no more (or less) dangerous than anywhere else in central London. The main concerns are more likely to be the crowds spilling out of the various pubs and clubs and milling around the stations.

CAMDEN & PRIMROSE HILL   London's alternative heart lies just northeast of Regent's Park. Since the 1960s, its thicket of clubs and pubs has been at the forefront of a succession of—usually short-lived—musical scenes: Punk, Brit-pop, alt-folk, the embers of which often continue smoldering here some time after the wider blaze has died down. Indeed, Camden can at times resemble a museum of youth movements from across the ages, where tribes of punks, Goths, psycho-billies, and more, proudly congregate to keep the flames of their countercultural obsessions burning.

Camden's various sprawling **markets** (p. 276), which occupy a number of venues north of the Tube station and sell a vast abundance of arts, crafts, and fashions, have turned the area into one of London's major tourist destinations, with tens of thousands pitching up here each weekend. For all its modern mainstream appeal, however, Camden retains a gritty, faintly "dodgy" edge, which is part of its attraction.

It's a noisy, vibrant, crowded, and intense place, and for all those reasons, perhaps not the best to base yourself unless you're here to party. There's still a vibrant music scene played out nightly in the pubs and in more established venues, such as the legendary **Roundhouse** (p. 321), near Chalk Farm Tube station, and **Koko** (p. 320). In any case, Camden doesn't really have much of a hotel scene, although there are some good restaurants. **Camden Lock** provides a gateway to gentler pleasures, offering **narrowboat trips** along the canal to **Little Venice.**

Neighboring **Primrose Hill,** a pretty village of Victorian terrace houses rolling up the hill on the north side of Regent's Park, is much more well-to-do, and has become one of the favorite London addresses for paparazzi-dodging celebrities. Visitors come to explore the high street's fashionable

Little Venice.

The Painted Hall, Old Royal Naval College.

boutiques, and maybe spot a famous face or two. It's not a place to stay, however, as lodgings are few and far between.

HAMPSTEAD   This residential suburb of north London, beloved by Keats and Hogarth, is a favorite excursion for Londoners. Everyone from Sigmund Freud and D. H. Lawrence to Anna Pavlova and John Le Carré have lived here, and it's still one of the most desirable districts in the city. It has a few hotels and B&Bs, although it is quite far from central London. Hampstead's calling card is **Hampstead Heath** (p. 164), nearly 320 hectares (791 acres) of meadows, ponds, and woodland; it maintains its rural atmosphere despite being surrounded by cityscapes on all sides. The "village center" of Hampstead is filled with cafes and restaurants, and there are pubs galore, a few with historic pedigrees.

HIGHGATE   Along with Hampstead, Highgate is another choice north London residential area, particularly on or near **Pond Square** and along Highgate High Street. Once celebrated for its "sweet salutaire airs," Highgate has long been a desirable place for Londoners to live; locals still flock to its pubs for "exercise and harmless merriment" as they did in the old days. Today most visitors come to see **Highgate Cemetery** (p. 165), London's most famous burial ground and the final resting place of Karl Marx and George Eliot.

Southeast London

GREENWICH   In the southeast of London, this suburb, which contains the **prime meridian**—"zero" for the reckoning of terrestrial longitudes—enjoyed its first heyday under the Tudors. King Henry VIII and both of his daughters, Queens Mary I and Elizabeth I, were born here. Greenwich Palace, Henry's favorite, is long gone, though, replaced by a hospital for sailors during Greenwich's second great age, which saw it emerge in the 18th and 19th centuries as one of the country's main naval centers. The hospital became the **Old Royal Naval College** (p. 174), which still stands, although it's now home to the University of Greenwich, the last of the sailors having departed in the 1990s. Greenwich continues to enjoy royal patronage today, however. It was made a "Royal Borough"—one of just four such boroughs in the country—by the Queen in 2012 to mark her Diamond Jubilee. In truth, the only difference visitors will notice will be the new "royal" coat of arms adorning some of the street signs.

Visitors principally come to this lovely port village for nautical sights, including the **National Maritime Museum** (p. 172), which sports a new £20 million wing, and some niche shopping opportunities, especially at **Greenwich Market** (p. 277).

Greenwich is a great place for a daytrip—well worth taking the extra time to **arrive by boat,** which provides the best views of the historic riverside architecture of London's Docklands en route.

ICONIC LONDON

If you're only in town for a short while and want to sample the best the city has to offer, this is the itinerary for you. It takes you on a whistlestop tour past 20 of the city's main attractions. If you don't linger too long in any one place, you could just about get through it all in 1 day—but the itinerary is best spread over 2 or even 3. *Start:* Tube to Westminster.

1 Westminster Abbey ★★★

Begin your tour with one of the country's most potent icons, where most of England's kings and queens have been crowned. Aim to get here when it opens at 9:30am, before the crowds descend. See p. 128.

As you emerge from Westminster Abbey, you confront the symbol of the nation's political power:

2 The Houses of Parliament & "Big Ben" ★

Gaining admission to the debating chambers requires a long wait, which 1-day visitors will have to forgo, but you can admire the massive Gothic Revival pile from the outside. See p. 121.

Walk north along Whitehall until you reach:

3 No. 10 Downing Street

Bear left and look down Downing Street to No. 10. Security concerns mean that it's no longer possible to walk to the prime minister's front door. See p. 123.

Continue north on Whitehall to its end at:

4 Trafalgar Square ★

The hub of London, this is Britain's most famous square and the scene of many a public demonstration. See p. 110.

Pass through Admiralty Arch in the square's western corner, and down the Mall to:

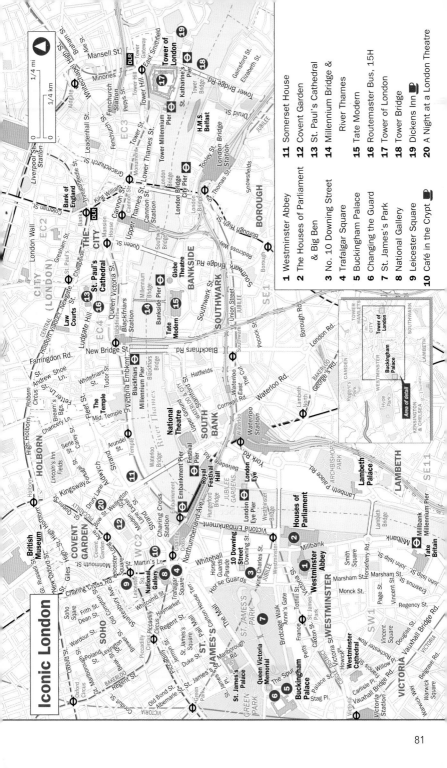

Iconic London

1 Westminster Abbey
2 The Houses of Parliament & Big Ben
3 No. 10 Downing Street
4 Trafalgar Square
5 Buckingham Palace
6 Changing the Guard
7 St. James's Park
8 National Gallery
9 Leicester Square
10 Café in the Crypt 🍴
11 Somerset House
12 Covent Garden
13 St. Paul's Cathedral
14 Millennium Bridge & River Thames
15 Tate Modern
16 Routemaster Bus, 15H
17 Tower of London
18 Tower Bridge
19 Dickens Inn 🍴
20 A Night at a London Theatre 🍴

5 Buckingham Palace ★

If you're not on a 1-day schedule, you can take a look around during the brief summer opening. See p. 97.

6 Changing the Guard

Time it right to catch the Changing the Guard ceremony—it's at 11:30am. However, you'll have to leave after a few minutes if you're sticking to the 1-day schedule. See p. 97.

Retrace your steps to Trafalgar Square, with a detour into adjacent:

7 St. James's Park ★★

Make your way back to Trafalgar Square via a stroll through one of London's most elegant green spaces. See p. 106.

On the north side of the square, you can enter the:

8 National Gallery ★★★

The galleries cover some 8 centuries of the finest art ever created. Even on the most rushed of schedules, try to set aside at least 1 hour. See p. 102.

Head north along Charing Cross Road, and then take a left into:

9 Leicester Square

Make for the "tkts" booth in the center, where you can book reduced-priced tickets for one of this evening's West End shows. See p. 60.

Retrace your steps to Trafalgar Square:

Big Ben.

Changing the Guard.

St. Paul's from Millennium Bridge.

10 Café in the Crypt 🍵 ★★

Stop off for lunch at the atmospheric subterranean self-service dining room in St. Martin-in-the-Fields Church, 6 St. Martin's Place, WC2 (📞 **020/7839-4342**) on the eastern edge of the square.

Suitably fortified, head east along the Strand, past the Savoy Hotel and Theatre as far as Waterloo Bridge and:

11 Somerset House ★★

Those spreading things over several days can visit the **Courtauld Gallery** (p. 99) and **Embankment Galleries.** If you're watching the clock, content yourself with a quick glimpse of the magnificent courtyard. See p. 109.

Head back west along the Strand, and then up Southampton Street to:

12 Covent Garden

If you have the time, enjoy the **street performers** on the **Piazza,** a rummage at the **market,** a mooch about **St. Paul's Church** (p. 108), and a tour of the **London Transport Museum** (p. 102). Or, if you're on a tighter schedule, choose just one of the above.

Head north, up James Street, and take the Piccadilly Line northbound one stop to Holborn. Change to the Central Line and head east two stops to:

13 St. Paul's Cathedral ★★★

Get climbing, up 500 or so steps to enjoy the **panoramic sweep** from the top of the dome. See p. 146.

14 Millennium Bridge & River Thames

This is a bit of a detour, and so is only realistic for those spreading the tour over more than 1 day. Head south from the cathedral courtyard to the pedestrian bridge crossing the River Thames.

Cross the bridge and you'll find yourself at:

15 Tate Modern ★★★

A tour of London's premier museum of modern art should be undertaken only by those with time to spare. See p. 141.

Retrace your steps to St. Paul's Churchyard:

16 Routemaster Bus, 15H

Just outside St. Paul's cathedral, you can board one of the great moving icons of London, the 15H, a shiny red, open-backed Routemaster bus, which runs every 15 minutes as part of a heritage service. See p. 425.

It's a 10- to 15-minute journey to the:

17 Tower of London ★★★

Try to arrive at this 900-year-old symbol of royalty, blood, and gore late in the afternoon, when some of the hordes have departed. But allow yourself a few hours to get your money's worth—it is pretty expensive. See p. 150.

18 Tower Bridge

Once the Tower shuts, head east for a stroll south across London's iconic bridge. See p. 149.

19 Dickens Inn ☕

At the bridge's northern end, on the eastern side, end your sightseeing day with a pint at the Dickens Inn, Marble Quay, St. Katharine's Way, E1 (*℡* **020/7488-2208**), housed in a restored warehouse in **St. Katharine's Dock.** There's a pizza restaurant on the second floor for a quick bite.

Take the Tube from Tower Hill to Bank. Change to the Central Line, alight at Tottenham Court Road and you'll be back in the heart of the West End for:

20 A Night at a London Theatre

Bring things to a close with a night out in the West End, making use of those tickets you picked up earlier.

ROYAL LONDON

The Royal Family may not enjoy quite the same standing as in days gone by—these days the monarch is a ceremonial figure with almost no real power—but they still perform a vital service to the tourist industry. Visitors from all over the world come to marvel at the capital's chocolate-box assortment of royal palaces and homes. Here's a route taking in the highlights. ***Start:*** *Tube to High Street Kensington.*

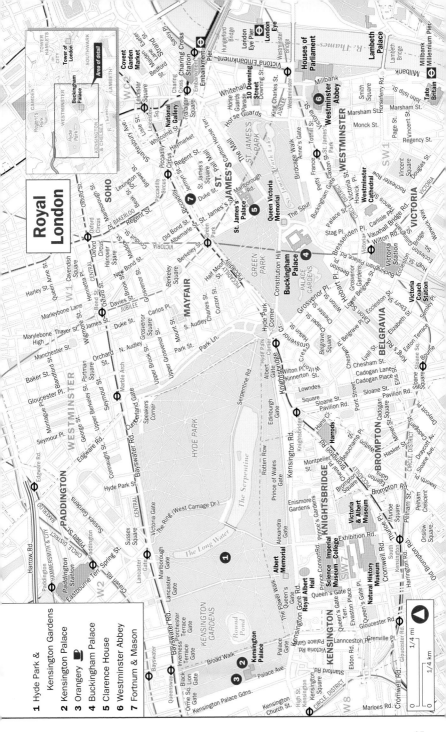

Royal London

1 Hyde Park &
  Kensington Gardens
2 Kensington Palace
3 Orangery
4 Buckingham Palace
5 Clarence House
6 Westminster Abbey
7 Fortnum & Mason

1 Hyde Park ★★★ & Kensington Gardens ★★

From the Tube, turn right and head along Kensington High Street until you reach Kensington Gardens. Seek out some of the royal-related sights, including the **Princess Diana Memorial Fountain** and the fabulously kitsch **Albert Memorial** (p. 114). The **Royal Albert Hall** (p. 308), the main venue for the BBC Proms (p. 46), stands opposite.

2 Kensington Palace ★

Tour the the new "Victoria: Love, Duty and Loss" exhibition and the revamped gardens. See p. 114.

3 Orangery ☕

Enjoy an elegant lunch in Kensington Palace's 18th-century Orangery (an arcade-shaped outhouse originally used for growing citrus fruit). If the weather is fine, sit on the terrace. See p. 259.

Stroll east through the park to Hyde Park Corner, and then past Wellington Arch and through Green Park (p. 101) to:

4 Buckingham Palace ★

If visiting during the summer opening period, you can tour the state rooms. See p. 97.

Head a short way east up the Mall to Stableyard Road, site of:

5 Clarence House

The official home of the Prince of Wales, and the former home of the Queen Mother, is filled with royal knick-knacks. Again, it's only open for a short period in summer. See p. 99.

Head back to the Mall, stroll south across St. James's Park (p. 106), and then south down Storey's Gate to:

6 Westminster Abbey ★★★

Site of numerous royal tombs and the coronation chair. See p. 128.

In the evening catch the Tube to Green Park. Head east along Piccadilly until you reach:

7 Fortnum & Mason

Finish the day with a high-class meal in the Fountain restaurant, set inside the grocer's to the Queen. See p. 290.

Fortnum & Mason

LITERARY LONDON

From Chaucer to Dickens, Shakespeare to Virginia Woolf, London has provided inspiration (and a home) to some of the English language's greatest writers. Follow in their illustrious footsteps on this short walking tour. ***Start:*** *Tube to Euston or King's Cross.*

1 British Library ★★

The country's greatest book repository, where in the permanent collection you can view the original manuscripts of some of the country's finest writers, including Jane Austen, Charlotte Brontë, and Keats. See p. 161.

Head west along Euston Road, and then south down Gordon Street for:

2 50 Gordon Square

A blue plaque marks the headquarters of the Bloomsbury Group, a loose collection of writers, artists, and economists, including Virginia Woolf, E. M. Forster, and John Maynard Keynes, who met here in the early 20th century.

Stroll southeastward through Bloomsbury's lovely garden squares to Doughty Street, and the:

3 Charles Dickens Museum ★

A display of Dickensiana in the great author's only surviving London house. See p. 98.

Head west into Fitzrovia for:

4 Fitzroy Tavern 🍺 ★★

Make some time for a reasonably priced pint in this quaint old pub, part of the Sam Smith's chain, where Dylan Thomas and George Orwell once hung out. It's at 16 Charlotte St., W1 (**☎ 020/7580-3714**).

Saunter south to:

5 Charing Cross Road

Long London's bookselling center, this is lined with secondhand stores and antiquarian dealers, as well as the mighty emporium of Foyles (p. 282). Marks & Co., as immortalized in *84 Charing Cross Road,* is gone, but its former location is marked by a brass plaque.

Continue south to the end of Charing Cross Road, through Trafalgar Square, down Whitehall to:

6 Westminster Abbey ★★★

Poets' Corner contains the grave of Geoffrey Chaucer as well as memorials to many of the country's most celebrated writers, including Shakespeare, Jane Austen, and John Milton. See p. 128.

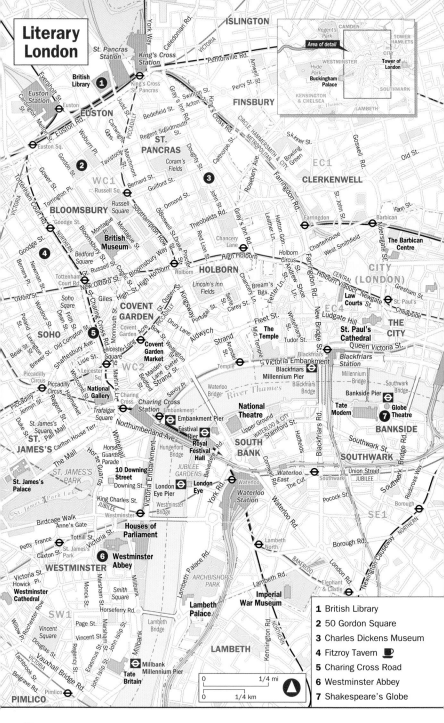

Literary London

1 British Library
2 50 Gordon Square
3 Charles Dickens Museum
4 Fitzroy Tavern ☕
5 Charing Cross Road
6 Westminster Abbey
7 Shakespeare's Globe

In the evening, take the Tube to London Bridge for:

7 Shakespeare's Globe ★

Finish your day of literary delights with dinner and a show at the re-created theatre of England's most famous playwright. See p. 140.

4

EXPLORING LONDON

V isitors to London could be forgiven for thinking that 2013 might be a bit of an anticlimax after all the hype and hoopla of 2012. But while there won't be any celebrations of the scale of the Olympic and Paralympic Games or the Queen's Diamond Jubilee, London in 2013 will still have plenty going on and—thanks in part to the previous year's events—will be looking better than ever.

Major new attractions have opened, such as the Warner Bros. Studio Tour taking visitors on a journey through the sets of the Harry Potter films, while several sightseeing stalwarts—including Kensington Place, the Charles Dickens Museum, and the Victoria & Albert Museum—will have emerged from major revamps. As with any other year, 2012 saw its share of architectural debuts: The National Maritime Museum has a shiny new wing, Tate Modern turned its former oil tanks into subterranean exhibition areas, while the O2 Arena is now linked to the ExCel Centre across the Thames by a 60m (200-ft.) high cable car. In the years to come, these will be joined by a rash of new skyscrapers currently taking shape in the City. Towering over them all, however, is the "Shard" at London Bridge, Europe's tallest building, where the capital's most elevated views are promised from the top-floor observation deck.

Of course, the Olympic and Paralympic Games will be over, but 2013 will see the host of amenities and facilities created for the games being repurposed for the future. The Olympic Park will be prettified, the athletes' village turned into housing, and many of the sporting venues, including the iconic Aquatics Centre, will be opened to the public. These new additions will join the myriad attractions already here, making what was already one of the world's great sightseeing cities just that little bit better.

LONDON'S TOP 10 ATTRACTIONS

Here's our pick of London's top attractions.

British Museum (p. 96): The history and wonders of human civilization packed into one glorious neoclassical building.

Hampstead Heath (p. 64): London's finest open space offering views, ponds, woodland, grassland, kite-flying, birdwatching, and wilderness galore.

National Gallery (p. 102): More than 2,000 masterpieces make this one of the world's great art museums.

Natural History Museum (p. 124): For kids it's all about the dinosaurs, but this "cathedral of nature" provides a great overview of life in all its myriad forms.

FACING PAGE: **St. Paul's from Millennium Bridge.**

Prices & Opening Hours

In the listings below, **children's prices** generally apply to those 15 and under. To qualify for a **senior discount,** you must be 60 or older. Students must present a student ID to get discounts. In addition to closing on public holidays, many attractions close between Christmas and New Year, so always check ahead if visiting at that time. All museums are closed Good Friday, December 25 and 26, and New Year's Day.

Royal Botanic Gardens, Kew (p. 182): The ultimate garden for a nation of gardeners.

St. Paul's Cathedral (p. 146): Sir Christopher Wren's masterpiece is packed with views, inside and out.

Tate Modern (p. 141): Bankside's hymn to the "shock of the new" just got itself a new subterranean extension.

Tower of London (p. 150): This formerly fearsome fortress is now a family-fun favorite.

Victoria and Albert Museum (p. 127): Always evolving and growing, this is perhaps the world's finest collection of decorative arts.

Westminster Abbey (p. 128): Britain's great monument to itself where nearly every monarch of the past 1,000 years has been crowned.

THE WEST END

This is the heart of sightseeing London, as well as the site of the capital's main shopping and entertainment scenes. If you're in town to see the sights, indulge in a little retail therapy, or take in a show, you'll be spending a good deal of time here. Its name suggests a clearly defined area, neatly separated from the rest of London. In fact, the "West End" is more of a concept than a specific location, and its definition varies according to which source you read. If you're not quite sure where you are, look around you. If the crowds are thronging and you can see "Sale!" signs and ads for musicals, you're probably here.

Running through its heart is signature thoroughfare **Oxford Street** (see Chapter 6, Shopping), a grand statement of commercial intent, lined from one end to the other with large, international chain stores. Either side lie some of London's most iconic neighborhoods, each with its own distinct characteristics, including literary Bloomsbury, seedy Soho, and upscale (some would say, snooty) Mayfair. Attractions range from the scholarly (the world-beating collections of the British Museum and the National Gallery, as well as the other museums of the Museum Mile, www.museum-mile.org.uk, stretching from King's Cross to the Thames) to the relaxing (the open spaces of Green Park and St. James's Park) and, of course, the royal—for many visitors, Buckingham Palace is still top of their to-do list.

Apsley House HISTORIC HOME   Standing grandly at Hyde Park Corner, this bulky, 18th-century mansion once marked the western limit of London, which gave rise to its nickname—**No. 1 London.** Today it's best known as the former home of one of Britain's greatest war heroes, the Duke of Wellington, conqueror of Napoleon at Waterloo in 1815, not to mention popularizer of the eponymous boot.

The house is crammed with mementoes of the general's life and boasts numerous art treasures, many of them given to Wellington by European monarchs as thanks for saving their thrones. These include two giant porphyry candelabra from Tsar Nicholas I of Russia, a thousand-piece silver service from the Portuguese court, and a Sèvres Egyptian dinner service from Louis XVIII of France. There is also a collection of paintings bequeathed by King Ferdinand VII of Spain, the highlight being a Goya portrait of the "Iron Duke"—ironically, this was originally intended as a portrait of Joseph Bonaparte, Napoleon's brother and briefly king of Spain, but was hastily repainted when Wellington came marching into Madrid in 1812.

149 Piccadilly, Hyde Park Corner, W1. www.english-heritage.org.uk/daysout/properties/apsley-house/. ✆ **020/7499-5676.** Admission £6.30 adults, £5.70 seniors, £3.80 children 15 and under. Apr–Oct Tues–Sun 11am–5pm; Nov–Mar Sat–Sun 11am–4pm. Tube: Hyde Park Corner.

Banqueting House ★ HISTORIC HOME   This sumptuous dining chamber is the only remaining part of the once-mighty Whitehall Palace. Its commission in the early 17th century by James I marked both the arrival of Renaissance architecture in England and a particular high point for the Stuart Dynasty, which had recently become the first royal family to rule both England and Scotland. However, just a few decades later, in 1649, Banqueting House would provide the setting for the dynasty's lowest ebb when James' successor, Charles I, fresh from his defeat in the English Civil Wars, was executed in front of the building. A restoration ceremony for Charles II was pointedly held here in 1660 to mark the return of the monarchy after Cromwell's brief Puritan Commonwealth.

Today the main attraction of this great feasting hall is not the food—which you won't be able to sample unless you're a visiting head of state—but the ceiling paintings by Rubens which imagine James I crowned amid a swirling mass of cherubic flesh. The house often closes on short notice for official events, so it's best to call in advance.

Insider's tip: Classical concerts are held here on the first Monday evening of each month (August excepted). The website lists the upcoming program; book by calling ✆ **020/3166-6153.**

Whitehall Palace, Horse Guards Ave., SW1. www.hrp.org.uk/banquetinghouse. ✆ **0844/ 482-7777.** Admission £5 adults, £4 seniors and students, free for children 15 and under. Mon–Sat 10am–5pm (last admission 4:30pm). Tube: Westminster or Embankment.

Rubens ceiling in Banqueting House.

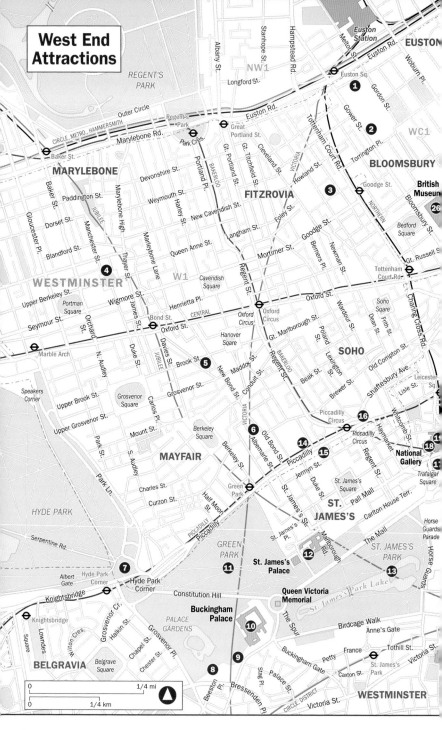

West End Attractions

REGENT'S PARK

NW1

EUSTON

Euston Station

Euston Sq.

①

②

WC1

BLOOMSBURY

③

British Museum

㉖

FITZROVIA

MARYLEBONE

④

WESTMINSTER

W1

Oxford Circus

SOHO

⑤

⑯

Piccadilly Circus

⑥

⑭

⑮

⑱

National Gallery

⑪

Trafalgar Square

MAYFAIR

HYDE PARK

ST. JAMES'S

⑫

St. James's Palace

⑬

ST. JAMES'S PARK

Horse Guards Parade

⑦

Hyde Park Corner

⑪

GREEN PARK

St. James's Park Lake

Queen Victoria Memorial

Buckingham Palace

⑩

Birdcage Walk

BELGRAVIA

⑧

⑨

WESTMINSTER

0   1/4 mi
0   1/4 km

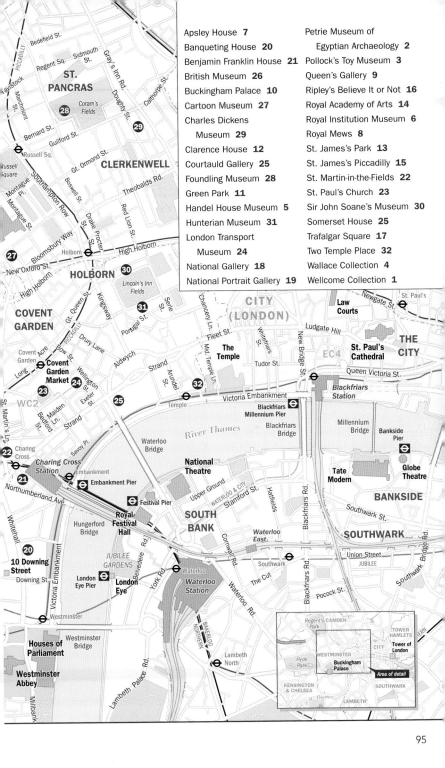

Benjamin Franklin House HISTORIC HOME From 1757 to 1775, this was the home of Benjamin Franklin, one of the "Founding Fathers" of the U.S. and an all-round turn-his-hand-to-anything polymath. Franklin was in his time a politician, an author, a printer, a scientist, and an inventor, but he lived here under yet another guise, that of diplomat sent to argue the colonists' case to the British government, making this modest four-story abode the first, albeit unofficial, U.S. Embassy. Access is only possible as part of a guided tour, or "Historical Experience," given every 45 minutes by a costumed actress playing Polly Hewson, the daughter of Franklin's landlady, which livens things up and helps to gloss over the fact that there aren't many Franklin-related artifacts here. Still, you can see where the great man invented bifocals and, perhaps of slightly less benefit to humankind, the parlor where Franklin—a great fan of fresh air—sat "air bathing" naked by the open windows.

36 Craven St., WC2. www.benjaminfranklinhouse.org. ⓒ **020/7839-2006.** Admission £7 adults, free for children 15 and under. Wed–Sun noon–5pm. Tube: Charing Cross.

British Museum ★★★ ☺ MUSEUM The "BM" has been number one for a long time. It was the country's most popular museum way back in the 1750s (the fact that it was then the country's first and only public museum may have helped) and it's still the most popular, welcoming more than six million visitors every year to its grand neoclassical confines.

If the museum has one central, unifying theme, it's to provide an overview of the development of human culture, illustrated with items from all of the world's major civilizations. If that sounds like a big theme, well this is a big museum, covering some 2 miles of galleries, and impossible to cover in 1 or even 2 days. How you tackle it is up to you.

The collection is arranged along roughly geographical lines, so you could order your tour accordingly, taking in the **Rosetta Stone** from Egypt (the object that finally enabled scholars to decipher hieroglyphics), the **Elgin (or Parthenon) Marbles** from Ancient Greece, or the treasures of a 7th-century Saxon ship burial from **Sutton Hoo,** in nearby Suffolk. But there's so much more—Babylonian astronomical instruments, giants heads from Easter Island, totem poles from Canada, mummies from Egyptian tombs, Chinese sculptures, Indian texts, Roman statues, African art . . . the list goes on. In fact, the museum has more objects in storage than it ever does on display.

And if that wasn't enough, the BM hosts a succession of blockbuster temporary exhibitions, which are often staged in the **Reading Room,** the

British Museum mummy cases.

former home of the British Library. It lies at the center of the **Great Court,** the building's central courtyard, which is topped by a giant glass roof and boasts various cafes and picnic areas.

Of course you could always take the easy option, and let someone else decide what you should see. Free half-hour tours (known as "Eye Opener Tours") to different sections of the museum are given every 15 to 30 minutes from 11am to 3:45pm. The front desk can provide details and floor plans.

Great Russell St., WC1. www.britishmuseum.org. © **020/7323-8299.** Free admission. Sat–Thurs10am–5:30pm; Fri 10am–8:30pm. Tube: Holborn, Tottenham Court Rd., Goodge St., or Russell Sq.

Buckingham Palace ★ ☺ ♨ PALACE   The first house to stand on the site of what is now the principal London home of the monarch was built by the Duke of Buckingham in 1702. It was acquired by George II in 1761 and expanded and renovated throughout the 19th century, first by the flamboyant John Nash for George IV, and later by the more dour Edward Blore (dubbed "Blore the Bore") for Victoria. A new facade—including the famous balcony from where the Royal Family waves to the masses on major royal occasions—was added in 1913.

Although the exterior is rather boxy and uninspiring, the interior has a lot more going on. For 8 weeks in August and September, while the royals are holidaying elsewhere, you can look for yourself. Tours visit a small selection of the palace's 600-plus rooms, including the Grand Staircase, the Throne Room, the Picture Gallery (which displays masterpieces by Van Dyck, Rembrandt, Rubens, and others), and the lavish State Rooms, where the

>
> ## The Guard Doesn't Change Every Day
>
> The ceremony begins at 11:30am sharp every day between May and July, and on alternate days for the rest of the year—in theory, anyway. However, it's often canceled in bad weather, which shows just what an unnecessary ceremony it is. If it looks like it's going to rain, it's probably best to head somewhere else instead.

Queen entertains heads of government with grand formal banquets. You can also take a walk along a 3-mile path through 16 hectares (40 acres) of landscaped gardens.

Outside of the summer months, the only parts of the palace open to the public are the **Queen's Gallery** (p. 105) and the **Royal Mews** (p. 106).

Insider's tip: Remember, if the royal standard isn't flying atop the palace, the Queen isn't at home.

Buckingham Palace is also the setting for a daily dose of public pageantry, **Changing the Guard.** Pretty much every guidebook says the same thing about the ceremony—it's terribly British and a bit dull, and who are we to buck the trend? The needlessly elaborate ceremony for changing the 40 men guarding Buckingham Palace with another contingent from Wellington Barracks only exists for the benefit of visitors these days. It's actually interesting for about 5 minutes—with bearskin-wearing, red-coated soldiers, music from the marching band, shouted orders, and complicated marching patterns. The trouble is the whole thing lasts for around 40 minutes—and if you want a decent vantage point, you need to turn up at least 1 hour early.

Changing the Guard at Buckingham Palace.

A much more accessible piece of pageantry can be seen at the nearby Horse Guards Parade (p. 121) in Whitehall.

At end of the Mall. www.royalcollection.org.uk. *020/7766-7300.* Palace tours £18 adults, £16.50 seniors and students, £10.25 children 5–16, family ticket £47, free for ages 4 and under; Changing the Guard free. Aug 1–Sept 25 (dates can vary), and additional dates may be added. Daily 9:45am–6pm. Changing the Guard daily May–July at 11:30am and alternating days for the rest of the year. Tube: St. James's Park, Green Park, or Victoria.

Cartoon Museum ★★ MUSEUM   This is the capital's first and only museum dedicated to the great British traditions of cartooning, caricaturing, and comics. Displays are arranged chronologically, beginning in the early 18th century with the first British attempts at the new art form of *caricatura*, recently imported from Italy. From here it traces the development of the great cartoonists of the age, such as William Hogarth and George Cruikshank, whose work helped shine a light on the political and social hypocrisies of the day. The displays then take in the great magazine boom of the 19th and 20th centuries, which saw publications such as *Punch* setting the standard for political cartooning, and onto the works of great modern satirists, including Steve Bell and Gerald Scarfe.

The upstairs section is a temple to childhood nostalgia, filled with vintage British comics—*Beano, Dandy, Eagle,* and so on. It's bright, jaunty, and fun—a bit like a cartoon, in fact. The small shop by the entrance (which is free to enter) is a good source of graphic novels and collections of historic cartoons.

35 Little Russell St., WC1. www.cartoonmuseum.org. *020/7580-8155.* Admission £5.50 adults, £4 seniors, £3 students, free for children 17 and under. Tues–Sat 10:30am–5:30pm; Sun noon–5:30pm. Tube: Tottenham Court Rd. or Holborn.

Charles Dickens Museum ★ HISTORIC HOME/MUSEUM   This is the great novelist's only surviving London address, with period-style rooms filled with Dickensiana. Although he lived here for just a few years, from 1837 until 1840, this most prolific of authors still found the time to churn out several classics, including *Nicholas Nickleby, Oliver Twist, Pickwick Papers, Old Curiosity Shop,* and *Barnaby Rudge*. By 2013, the museum should have reopened following its £3 million "Great Expectations" renovation timed to coincide with the bicentenary of Dickens' birth in 2012.

48 Doughty St., WC1. www.dickensmuseum.com. ℰ **020/7405-2127.** Admission £7 adults, £5 students and seniors, £3 children. Daily 10am–5pm. Tube: Russell Sq., Chancery Lane, or Holborn.

Clarence House HISTORIC HOME   This rather staid mansion, built in the 1820s for the Duke of Clarence (later William IV), is the current official residence of Prince Charles and Camilla, the Duchess of Cornwall, although it's perhaps better known for having been home to the late Queen Mother. After her death in 2003, it was redecorated with antiques and art from the Royal collection. Having been closed throughout 2012 as its entrance lay next to one of the venues for the Olympic and Paralympic Games, the house is once again open for a short period in summer. Visitors are taken on a brief guided tour of five of the staterooms, where much of the Queen's collection of art and furniture is on display, along with pieces added by Prince Charles.

Stable Yard Gate, SW1. www.royalcollection.org.uk. ℰ **020/7766-7303.** Admission £8.50 adults, £4.50 children 5–16, free for children 4 and under. Aug 1–Aug 31 (dates subject to change—call first) daily 10am–5:30pm. Tube: Green Park or St. James's Park.

Keeping guard outside Clarence House.

Courtauld Gallery ★ ART MUSEUM   Like a mini National Gallery sequestered in the north wing of **Somerset House** (p. 109), the Courtauld is one of the capital's finest small art museums. It holds an intense collection of works dating from the Renaissance to the 20th century, although the focus is very much on **Impressionism** and **Post-Impressionism** with works by Monet, Renoir, Gauguin, Van Gogh (including his *Self-Portrait with Bandaged Ear*), and Manet (it holds his final painting, *A Bar at the Folies-Bergère*). The Kandinskys on the top floor are also well worth seeking out.

Insider's tip: If money is a bit tight, try to visit on Monday morning when entry is free (until 2pm; excluding public holidays); if you stick around there's also a free 15-minute lecture about the collection at 1:15pm.

Strand, WC2. www.courtauld.ac.uk. ℰ **020/7872-0220.** Admission £6 adults, £4.50 seniors and international students, free for children 17 and under, UK students, and for all Mon till 2pm. Daily 10am–6pm. Tube: Covent Garden, Temple, or Waterloo.

COVENT GARDEN: LONDON'S *best* SQUARE

London doesn't always get its public squares right. For all its charms, there's something rather austere about Trafalgar Square (p. 110), while its neighbor Leicester Square is a tawdry jumble of a place, a syrupy concoction of cinemas and fast food. Covent Garden gets the blend just about right. Its historic architecture, cultural attractions, and superior opportunities for eating, shopping, and live entertainment—as well as its constant thrum of activity—make it a genuinely pleasant place to hang out. But then, it has had a long time to practice. This is London's oldest planned square, laid out by Inigo Jones in the mid-17th century in imitation of an Italian piazza (the square is still often referred to as Covent Garden Piazza). In the 18th century, the addition of the **Royal Opera House** (p. 308) and the **Theatre Royal Drury Lane** (p. 306) saw it firmly established as one of London's prime entertainment areas.

Its character changed over the course of the 19th century as its produce market, which had begun as a small local affair, took over the entire square to become the capital's premier wholesale fruit and vegetable market. Splendid market buildings were erected in the centre of the piazza (for fruit and veg) and on its southern side (for flowers), and thousands of workers were employed. The market thrived throughout the first half of the 20th century. However, by the late 1960s, its enormous size and the consequent ever-growing congestion made its continued presence in central London untenable. In 1974, it was relocated to the suburbs south of the river, leaving behind one of the capital's most enticing pieces of real estate.

For a while, the area looked set to be developed out of existence, buried beneath a mass of office blocks and shopping centers. But sustained public, political, and media pressure resulted in a near miracle—a successful, sensitive redevelopment (a phrase you don't get to write all that often).

Today, the restored central market building sits amid a prettified, pedestrianized square and is home to a merry assortment of cafes, pubs, and shops, as well as a small craft and antiques market, the **Apple Market;** p. 277. The former flower market, meanwhile, has been transformed into the **London Transport Museum** (p. 102), and the surrounding shopping streets—particularly Neal Street and Monmouth Street—boast a selection of quirky independent stores that provide a nice contrast to the chain store bombast of nearby Oxford Street. The open space to the rear of **St. Paul's Church** (p. 108) has become the capital's most celebrated busking stage—the street performer's equivalent of the National Theatre—hosting (in fine weather, at least) a constant parade of buskers, unicyclists, jugglers, magicians, comedians, and other physical performers.

Foundling Museum ☺ MUSEUM   This misery memoir of a museum tells the story of London's first hospital for abandoned children, which was founded in 1741 by the sailor and philanthropist **Thomas Coram.** He was helped in his endeavors by two of the great cultural figures of the day: The satirical artist **William Hogarth** and the composer **George Frederic Handel.** Both used their respective talents to raise money for the enterprise: Hogarth by establishing the country's first public art museum here (you can still see some of his pictures on display); and Handel by conducting musical performances. Over the next 2 centuries, the hospital cared for some 27,000 children, until it relocated outside of the capital in the mid-1950s.

The museum organizes monthly music concerts and plenty of extras for families, including drop-in sessions and activity backpacks. Part of the original site has also been turned into a well-equipped children's park, **Coram's Fields,** which adults can visit only in the company of a child.

Insider's tip: On the first Sunday of each month there's a free talk and classical concert.

40 Brunswick Sq., WC1. www.foundlingmuseum.org.uk. ✆ **020/7841-3600.** Admission £7.50 adults, £5 students and seniors, free children 15 and under. Tues–Sat 10am–5pm; Sun 11am–5pm. Tube: Russell Sq.

Green Park ★ ☺ PARK/GARDEN This most basic of London's great Royal Parks has an almost zen-like simplicity to it. There are no statues, water features, or adventure playgrounds here, just hectares of rolling green lawns and tall trees—plus, in summer, scores of local workers sunning their lunch hour away either on the grass or on the stripy **deckchairs** (£1.50) that are the park's only formal facility. In spring the park's color scheme broadens slightly, when hosts of bright yellow daffodils pop into bloom.

Piccadilly, SW1. www.royalparks.org.uk/Green-Park.aspx. ✆ **030/0061-2350.** Free admission. Open 24 hours. Tube: Green Park.

Handel House Museum ★ HISTORIC HOME/MUSEUM Two musicians, separated by a couple of hundred years, and with profoundly different approaches to their art—albeit both hugely influential in their own way—made their homes on Brook Street, in the heart of Mayfair. The first was George Frederic Handel (1685–1759), the German composer who moved to Britain aged 25 and settled at this address in 1723. He remained here for the rest of his life, creating the scores for many of his most famous works, including *Messiah* and *Music for the Royal Fireworks*.

He was followed in 1968 by the American guitarist, **Jimi Hendrix,** who lived (some of the time) next door at no. 23 with his English girlfriend until his death in 1970. Both properties are now owned by the Handel House Museum, although only Handel's former home is currently open to the public. It's been meticulously restored to its Georgian prime with period fixtures, fittings, and fabrics. Exhibits include two antique harpsichords, various scores, and a canopied bedroom from 1720.

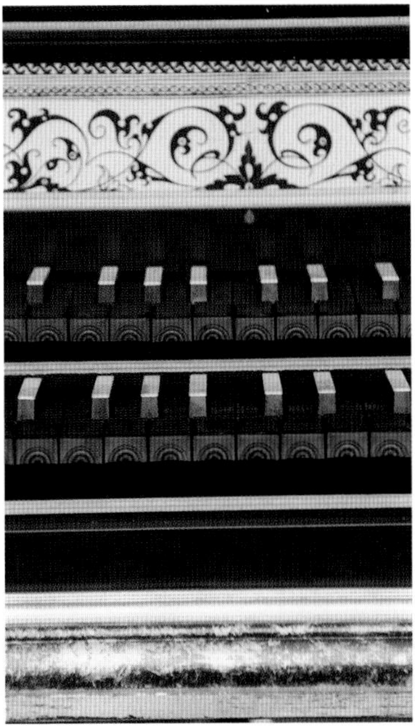

Harpsichord keys, Handel House Museum.

Hendrix's top-floor apartment is currently occupied by the museum's administrative offices, although there is talk of creating a permanent display on his life.

Classical recitals are given every Thursday (plus the occasional Tuesday and Sunday), between 6:30 and 7:30pm and cost £9 (£5 for students). The program is mainly Handel favorites played by harpsichordists, baroque quartets and the like, although Hendrix tunes (done in a classical style, of course) crop up occasionally.

25 Brook St., W1. www.handelhouse.org. ☎ **020/7495-1685.** Admission £6 adults, £5 students and seniors, £2 children 5–15. Free for children 4 and under, and all children on Saturday and Sunday. Tues–Sat 10am–6pm (until 8pm Thurs); Sun noon–6pm. Tube: Bond St.

Hunterian Museum ★ MUSEUM The shiny cases and cabinets of the Hunterian may give it a superficially modern, antiseptic feel, but this is a collection with its roots firmly in the grim and gory past. It's made up of medical oddities and curiosities, most of them assembled in the late 18th century by John Hunter, the physician to "mad" King George III, for the purposes of instructing medical students. Bizarre highlights include body parts pickled in jars (both human and animal), gruesome-looking teaching models (such as the lacquered systems of arteries and veins stuck onto wooden boards), skeletons of "dwarfs" and "giants," and some horror-inducing items of surgical equipment. It's macabrely fascinating stuff. Free guided tours of the collection take place every Wednesday at 1pm, and the museum hosts regular temporary exhibitions, usually with vaguely disquieting titles, such as "The Diary of a Resurrectionist" or "Victorian Dental Practices."

Royal College of Surgeons, 35–43 Lincoln's Inn Fields, WC2. www.rcseng.ac.uk/museums. ☎ **020/7869-6560.** Free admission. Tues–Sat 10am–5pm. Tube: Holborn.

London Transport Museum ★★ ☺ MUSEUM Arranged more or less chronologically, this museum, housed in the swish glass-and-iron confines of Covent Garden's former flower market, traces the history of the capital's transport network from the days of steam and horse power to the green technologies of today. There are some wonderful old contraptions on display, including a reconstruction of an 1829 horse-drawn omnibus, a steam locomotive that ran along the world's first underground railway, and London's first trolleybus.

In addition to all the impressive hardware, the museum has displays on the often-overlooked aesthetics of public transport, particularly the signs, posters, and logos that together provided London Transport with such a clear graphic sensibility in the early 20th century.

There's lots of stuff for youngsters here, too, including a hands-on section where they can climb aboard miniature buses, trams, trains, and tubes, and trails to pick up at the front desk.

Insider's tip: The £13.50 entrance fee entitles you to unlimited visits over a 12-month period—provided you hang on to your ticket.

Covent Garden Piazza, WC2. www.ltmuseum.co.uk. ☎ **020/7379-6344.** Admission £13.50 adults, £10 seniors and students, free for children 15 and under. Sat–Thurs 10am–6pm; Fri 11am–6pm (last admission 5:15pm). Tube: Covent Garden.

National Gallery ★★★ ☺ ART MUSEUM The National's collection of more than 2,300 paintings provides a comprehensive overview of the development of Western art from the mid-1200s to 1900, rivalling any of Europe's other

National Gallery and Trafalgar Square.

great art galleries, such as the Louvre, the Prado, or the Uffizi. It's certainly a good deal more impressive than the original collection, founded by the British Government in 1824, which consisted of just 38 works.

The layout is straightforwardly chronological. Passing through the sturdy neoclassical facade on Trafalgar Square, you turn left to find the oldest works, housed, by way of contrast, in its newest section, the 1990s-built **Sainsbury Wing.** It covers the period from 1250 to 1500, including paintings by such Renaissance and pre-Renaissance greats as Giotto (Room 51), Piero della Francesca (Room 66), Botticelli (Rooms 57 & 58), and Van Eyck (including his famed *Arnolfini Portrait,* Room 65). The basement here is the usual setting for temporary exhibitions, for which tickets typically cost in excess of £12.

The chronology then moves on to the West Wing, covering 1500 to 1600 and filled with European Old Masters, including Titian (Room 12), Raphael (Room 8), and El Greco (Room 10). Next in line is the North Wing (1600–1700), where highlights include three rooms dedicated to Rembrandt (16, 23, and 24) and works by Caravaggio (Room 32) and Velázquez (Room 30). Things culminate in the East Wing (1700–1900), with a celebrated selection of Impressionist and Post-Impressionist paintings, including various water lilies by Monet (Room 43), Van Gogh's *Sunflowers* (Room 45), and Renoir's *The Umbrellas* (Room 44)—some of the most popular (not to say most valuable) paintings in the collection.

If you can't decide where to begin, try joining a free 1-hour "taster tour" of the collection given every day at 11:30am and 2:30pm. If you'd rather move at your own pace, you can pick up an audio tour from the front desk for £3.50. Children's trails are available for £1 from the front desk (or can be downloaded for free in advance from the website).

If you want to see more modern art, head to Tate Modern (p. 141). For a more in-depth look at British art, go to Tate Britain (p. 126).

Insider's tip: The National also lays on plenty of additional free entertainment, including lectures and family events (particularly during the school holidays), and stays open till 9pm on Fridays, when talks and classical music concerts are often staged.

Trafalgar Sq., WC2. www.nationalgallery.org.uk. ☎ **020/7747-2885.** Free admission; fee charged for temporary exhibitions. Sat–Thurs 10am–6pm; Fri 10am–9pm. Tube: Charing Cross or Leicester Sq.

National Portrait Gallery ★★ ☺ ART MUSEUM   Most galleries acquire their collections according to some notion of quality, with the aim of displaying the finest works of a particular artist, movement, or period. Not so the "NPG," where the collection is based not so much on ability as identity. Pictures have been chosen on the basis of who the subject is, not how well they've been captured by the artist. As a result, the works vary hugely in quality, and have been rendered in a great mish-mash of styles and mediums, including oil paintings, sculptures, photographs, and LCD screens. The result is rather jolly and exuberant, like a giant scrapbook of the nation.

The collection is arranged chronologically from top to bottom; so hop on the escalator to start with the earliest pieces, and then wend your way down past the great and the (sometimes not so) good from the mists of history to the present day. You'll pass Tudor kings and queens (including a study of Henry VIII by Holbein), great writers and thinkers (look out for Shakespeare sporting a natty gold earring, a portly looking Samuel Johnson by Sir Joshua Reynolds, and the Brontë sisters as captured by their brother, Bramwell), as well as the musicians, film stars, politicians, and sporting royalty of today. The farther you progress, the more familiar the names will become. However, if you need a little help working out who's who, free "Portrait of the Day" talks are given most Saturdays at noon (and some Wednesdays). This is a great place to hang out on Thursdays and Fridays, when the building (as well as its cafe, bar, and restaurant) stays open till 9pm, laying on art workshops, talks, and concerts—typically classical, jazz, or blues.

Insider's tip: The NPG's **Portrait Restaurant** (p. 257) has one of London's great "secret" views, out over Trafalgar Square.

St. Martin's Place, WC2. www.npg.org.uk. ☎ **020/7306-0055.** Free admission; fee charged for temporary exhibitions. Sat–Wed 10am–6pm; Thurs–Fri 10am–9pm. Tube: Charing Cross or Leicester Sq.

Petrie Museum of Egyptian Archaeology ★ 🏛 MUSEUM   Part of University College London (UCL) campus, this delightful collection of miniature treasures from ancient Egypt makes the perfect companion exhibition to the rather larger and grander items on display in the Egyptian galleries of the nearby British Museum (p. 96). Built up by the famed 19th-century Egyptologist Flinders Petrie, the museum boasts a wonderfully evocative array of finds from the land of the pharaohs, including jewelry, pots, papyrus documents, frescoes, carvings, and some of the world's oldest surviving cloth. Pick up a torch from the front desk and get exploring—the lighting is kept to a minimum to help conserve the delicate items.

University College London, Malet Place., WC1. www.ucl.ac.uk/museums/petrie. ☎ **020/7679-2884.** Free admission. Tues–Sat 1–5pm. Tube: Goodge St. or Euston Sq.

Pollock's Toy Museum ★ ☺ MUSEUM   This museum of vintage playthings occupies two slightly rickety town houses in Fitzrovia, a short walk north of Oxford Street. Although children would seem, on the face of it, to be the museum's ideal clientele, it's probably a little better suited to adults. The overriding emotion induced here is not so much excitement ("ooh, let me play") as nostalgia ("aah, I used to have one of those").

The houses' creaky rooms and narrow stairways are packed with the toys and crazes of yesteryear—puppets, china dolls, dolls' houses, teddy bears, tin soldiers, puppets, and perhaps most importantly, toy theatres. The collection was built up around the stock of Mr. Benjamin Pollock himself—the "last of the Victorian toy theatre makers."

1 Scala St., W1. www.pollockstoymuseum.com. *Ⓒ* **020/7636-3452.** Admission £5 adults, £4 seniors and students, £3 children 3–15, free for children 2 and under. Mon–Sat 10am–5pm (last admission 4:30pm). Tube: Goodge St.

Queen's Gallery ★ ART MUSEUM   This 19th-century chapel is the only part of Buckingham Palace (aside from the Royal Mews; p. 106) that welcomes visitors year round. Today it's dedicated to rotating exhibitions of the wide-ranging treasure trove that is the **Royal Collection.** You'll find special showings of paintings, prints, drawings, watercolors, furniture, porcelain, miniatures, enamels, jewelry, and more. At any given time, you may see such artistic peaks as Van Dyck's equestrian portrait of Charles I; a dazzling array of gold snuffboxes; paintings by Monet; studies by Leonardo da Vinci; or perhaps even the recent and less-than-flattering portrait of the current Queen, by Lucian Freud.

Buckingham Palace, Buckingham Palace Rd., SW1. www.royalcollection.org.uk. *Ⓒ* **020/7766-7301.** Admission £7.50 adults, £6.75 students and seniors, £3.75 children 5–16, free for children 4 and under, £18.75 family ticket. Daily 10am–5:30pm (last admission 4:30pm). Tube: Victoria.

Ripley's Believe It or Not ☺ MUSEUM   The garish, touristy confines of Piccadilly Circus seem like the perfect setting for this latest version of the Ripley's franchise. Dedicated to all that is weird, odd, and—in the case of some of the "craft" exhibits—eminently pointless, its prize displays include a statue of the Beatles carved from a piece of chewing gum, a 16th-century iron maiden (a grisly torture device), "genuine" shrunken human heads, Marilyn Monroe's make-up set, dinosaur eggs, and a 4m (13-ft.) long replica of Tower bridge built from exactly 264,345 matchsticks.

The London Pavilion, 1 Piccadilly Circus W1. www.ripleyslondon.com. *Ⓒ* **020/3238-0022.** Admission £26.95 adults, £24.95 students and seniors, £21.95 children 4–15, free for children 3 and under, £87.95 family ticket. Daily 10am–midnight (last admission 10:30pm). Tube: Piccadilly Circus.

Royal Academy of Arts ★ ART MUSEUM   Established in 1768, the country's first professional art school counted the painters Sir Joshua Reynolds and Thomas Gainsborough among its founding members. Each member has had to donate a work of art, and so over the years the Academy has built up a sizeable collection. Ever-changing highlights are displayed in the **John Madejski Fine Rooms,** which can be visited as part of a free guided tour at 1pm on Tuesday, 1pm and 3pm Wednesday to Friday, and 11:30am on Saturday. The Academy's annual **Summer Exhibition** (p. 45) has been held for more than 200 years, making it the country's oldest (and largest) open art exhibition. Today, however, the main focus of the Academy, and the principal draw for visitors, are its temporary exhibitions (costing upwards of £12), which are usually blockbuster affairs— "Turks," "Degas and the Ballet," and "David Hockney RA: A Bigger Picture" have been some of the recent hits.

Burlington House, Piccadilly, W1. www.royalacademy.org.uk. ✆ **020/7300-8000.** Admission for temporary shows varies from £3–£15.50. Free admission to guided tours of John Madejski Fine Rooms depending on the exhibition. Sat–Thurs 10am–6pm (last admission 5:30pm); Fri 10am–10pm (last admission 9:30pm). Tube: Piccadilly Circus or Green Park.

Royal Institution Museum 👤 MUSEUM   The members of the "RI" have spent the past 200 years pushing at the boundaries of science. Their combined achievements, breakthroughs, and inventions are celebrated at this museum, which emerged from a major revamp in 2008. You can find out about the 14 members who went on to win Nobel prizes, learn about the 10 elements discovered at the institution, explore the preserved 1850s' laboratory of **Michael Faraday** (discoverer of electromagnetism), and look into the scientific future at the exhibition on nanotechnology. You can also poke your head around the door of the hall where the famous annual Christmas lectures—begun by Faraday himself—are given.

21 Albemarle St., W1. www.rigb.org. ✆ **020/7409-2992.** Free admission. Mon–Fri 9am–9pm. Tube: Green Park.

Royal Mews ★ HISTORIC SITE/MUSEUM   This is where the British Royal Family's grandest forms of road transport are stored, including their fleet of Rolls Royces, their carriages, and the horses that pull them, who enjoy luxurious stables adorned with tile walls and gleaming horse brasses. Pride of place goes to the **Gold State Coach,** built in 1761. Decorated with a riotous assortment of gold leaf, painted panels, and sculptures of cherubs, lions' heads, and dolphins, it's the sort of thing that only a monarch could get away with. It's also absolutely huge—3.6m (12 ft.) high, 7m (23 ft.) long, weighing 4 tons (9,960lbs), and requiring eight horses to pull it. As such, it's used only for major occasions. It has transported the monarch to every coronation since George IV's in 1821. The Queen usually uses the smaller Irish State Coach to get to the annual State Opening of Parliament, while her crown travels separately in Queen Alexandra's Coach; both coaches are also on display here, as is the 1902 **State Landau,** the coach in which both princess Diana and Kate rode following their marriages to their respective princes.

Buckingham Palace, Buckingham Palace Rd., SW1. www.royalcollection.org.uk. ✆ **020/7766-7302.** Admission £8 adults, £7.25 seniors and students, £5 children 5–17, free for children 4 and under, £21.25 family ticket. Daily Apr–Oct 10am–5pm, Nov–Dec 10am–4pm. Closed during state visits, royal events and from Christmas–New Year. Tube: Victoria.

St. James's Park ★★ ☺ PARK/GARDEN   With its scenic central pond, tended flowerbeds, and picnic-friendly lawns, it's difficult to believe that this Royal Park was once a swamp near a leper colony. Today it's as elegant a green space as London can muster, and one of the best places in the center of town to watch waterfowl. Its pond is home to more than 20 species, including ducks, geese, and even four pelicans—the descendants of a pair presented to Charles II by a Russian ambassador in 1662—which are all fed daily between 2:30–3.30pm.

The Mall, SW1. www.royalparks.org.uk/parks/st_james_park. ✆ **030/0061-2350.** Free admission. Open 24 hours. Tube: St. James's Park.

St. James's Piccadilly CHURCH   This late 17th-century Anglican church doesn't so much provide a respite from the bustle and commerce of Piccadilly, as form a vibrant part of it. Markets are held in the churchyard (it's antiques on

Central pond in St. James's Park.

Tuesday and general arts and crafts from Wednesday to Saturday) and classical concerts are put on at lunchtime on Mondays, Wednesdays, and Fridays. They're nominally free, although a donation of £3.50 is requested.

The church formed part of the post-Great Fire of London skyline created by Sir Christopher Wren. But unlike almost all his other commissions, this was a new church, not a rebuild, first consecrated in 1684. Wren's master carver Grinling Gibbons created the reredos (a screen decorated with religious icons and placed behind the altar), organ case, and font.

197 Piccadilly, W1. www.st-james-piccadilly.org. (✆) **020/7734-4511.** Free admission. Lunchtime concerts are held on Mon, Wed, and Fri at 1:10pm. Suggested donation £3.50. Evening concerts are on an irregular schedule; check the website of church posters. Tickets cost £10–£22. Tube: Piccadilly Circus.

St. Martin-in-the-Fields ★ CHURCH   Although its setting at the edge of one of London's busiest squares makes the church's name seem almost willfully ironic, St. Martin's was indeed surrounded by fields when first founded in the 13th century. But these had already long gone by the time the current grand 18th-century building was constructed, the work of James Gibbs, a disciple of Christopher Wren. Today, following a £36 million makeover, it looks as good as ever, with an interior adorned with fine Italian plasterwork. A full program of classical concerts (plus the odd bit of jazz) is laid on. Those performed at lunchtime are free (although a £3.50 donation is "suggested"), while evening tickets cost £7 to £26.

Inside, the excellent **Café in the Crypt** (p. 83) enjoys one of the most atmospheric locations in London, its floor made up of numerous gravestones (including those of the highwayman Jack Sheppard, and Nell Gwynne, Charles II's mistress). The crypt is also home to the **London Brass Rubbing Centre** ★ ☺, where children can rub a wide selection of replica brasses (from £4.50), and is open Monday

St. Martin-in-the-Fields.

to Wednesday 10am to 7pm, Thursday to Saturday 10am to 10pm, and Sunday noon to 7pm.

Trafalgar Sq., WC2. www.smitf.org. *(C)* **020/7766-1100.** Mon–Fri 9am–6pm; Sat–Sun 8:45am–7:30pm as long as no service is taking place. Concerts Mon, Tues, and Fri 1pm; Tues and Thurs–Sat 7:30pm. Tube: Charing Cross.

St. Paul's Church CHURCH   A much more modest affair than the great cathedral that shares its name, this 17th-century Inigo-Jones-designed building occupies the western edge of Covent Garden. It's often referred to as the "actors' church," because of its long association with the local theatrical community—the Drury Lane Theatre, the Royal Opera House, and many other theatres lie within its parish. Inside, the walls are adorned with memorial plaques dedicated to such dramatic luminaries as Vivien Leigh, Boris Karloff (better known as Frankenstein's monster), and Noël Coward. Fittingly, the portico at the church's rear provides an impromptu stage for the street performers of Covent Garden's piazza (p. 100). The church also boasts a lovely, peaceful garden.

Bedford St., WC2. www.actorschurch.org. *(C)* **020/7836-5221.** Free admission. Mon–Fri 8:30am–5:30pm; Sun service 11am. Tube: Covent Garden.

Sir John Soane's Museum ★★ HISTORIC HOME/MUSEUM   Perhaps the finest small museum in London, the building is both a repository for a fascinating collection of curios—Egyptian sarcophagi, Greek marbles and bronzes, Roman jewelry, medieval sculptures, Renaissance paintings, and more—and an enchanting demonstration of architectural ingenuity. Both are the work of the eponymous Sir Soane (1753–1837), one of the age's foremost architects and collectors. Soane clearly saw no point in acquiring something if it couldn't be displayed, and so adorned every wall, every surface and even the ceilings of his home with artefacts and artworks. He even designed special fold-out cupboards and panels so as to show off as much as possible. The result is a wonderfully stylish clutter.

The museum plans to restore and open up Soane's (and Mrs Soane's) private apartments on the second floor over the next couple of years, with the project due for completion in 2014.

Insider's tip: On the first Tuesday evening of every month, this most evocative of collections ups the ante by giving visitors the chance to explore its labyrinthine confines by candlelight. Expect to wait in line for at least 1 hour.

13 Lincoln's Inn Fields, WC2. www.soane.org. © **020/7405-2107.** Free admission (donations invited). Tues–Sat 10am–5pm; 1st Tues of each month also 6–9pm. Tours given Sat at 11am; £5 tickets distributed at 10:30am, first-come, first-served (group tours by appointment only). Tube: Holborn.

Somerset House ★★ ☺ HISTORIC SITE/MUSEUM   Until just over a decade ago, most of this grand riverside building was closed to the public. Since its construction in the late 18th century as a replacement for an earlier Tudor palace, it had served primarily as offices, providing working space for a variety of government departments, including the Inland Revenue, the Navy Board, and the Register of Births, Marriages, and Deaths. Following the departure of many of these institutions, and a multi-million pound millennial refit, Somerset House has been turned into one of the capital's leading cultural centers. It's home to the **Courtauld Gallery** (p. 99), a number of temporary exhibition spaces—including the **Embankment Galleries,** the **East Wing Galleries,** and the **Terrace Rooms**—as well as several cafes and restaurants. The highlight of the complex, however, is its central courtyard where in summer children play among 55 water jets that have been programmed to "dance," and in winter skaters slide and topple on a temporary **ice rink** (p. 184). Free 45-minute guided tours of the

Somerset House.

complex are available every Tuesday at 1.15pm and 2.45pm, and every Saturday at 12.15pm, 1.15pm, 2.15pm, and 3.15pm.

Strand, WC2. www.somersethouse.org.uk. © **020/7845-4600.** Free admission to courtyard; charge of around £6 adults for some temporary exhibitions. Daily 10am–6pm. Tube: Temple.

Trafalgar Square ★ SQUARE While undoubtedly London's best known square, boasting numerous, illustrious landmarks—including the **National Gallery** (p. 102), on its north side, **St. Martin-in-the-Fields** (p. 107) on the east, and at its center, **Nelson's Column,** a granite column topped with a statue of Horatio Viscount Nelson (1758–1805), one of the country's most celebrated naval heroes—Trafalgar was until recently a rather congested, unpleasant place. However, significant remodelling over the past decade, which has seen its northern stretches pedestrianized and the former swarms of pigeons sent on their way, has significantly improved its ambience. Which is just as well, as this is where many of the capital's major parades and marches end up. It provides the focus for the festivites for St. Patrick's Day, the New Year's Day Parade, Pride London, Canada Day, and numerous other events (mostly for free; see "London Calendar of Events," in Chapter 10). The square is also the venue for some of the rowdiest New Year's Eve celebrations, held within earshot of the famous bongs of Big Ben.

A few unusual attractions can be found on the square, including an equestrian statue of Charles I, from where all distances from London are measured; the **world's smallest police station**—it has room for just one, rather lonely, officer—and an empty plinth, the "**Fourth Plinth**" (the other three hold statues), on which a succession of temporary artworks is displayed.

Trafalgar Sq., WC2. www.london.gov.uk. No phone. Free admission. Open 24 hours. Tube: Charing Cross.

Two Temple Place ★ ART MUSEUM Opened in 2011 to host temporary exhibitions of publicly owned art from the U.K.'s regional collections, the latest addition to the capital's art scene enjoys a rather grand setting in a Gothic-style mansion built in the late 19th century by William Waldorf Astor (founder of the famous New York Hotel that bears his name). Behind the sturdy Portland stone facade, the interior has a slight strange Victoriana-meets-Disney vibe with the otherwise straightforwardly opulent rooms (lots of marble and mahogany) adorned with bizarre details, such as the statues of characters from *The Three Musketeers* (Astor's favorite book) on the banisters of the main staircase, and the gilded frieze in the Great Hall showing 54 seemingly random characters from history and fiction, including Pocohontas, Machiavelli, Bismarck, Anne Boleyn, and Marie Antoinette.

Temple Place, WC2. www.twotempleplace.org. © **020/7836-3715.** Free admission. Mon & Wed–Sat 10am–4.30pm; Sun noon–5pm. Tube: Temple.

Wallace Collection ★★ 🎁 MUSEUM Located in the palatial town house of one of London's leading aristocratic families, this grand collection comprises a contrasting array of art and armaments. The artworks include such classics as Frans Hals' *Laughing Cavalier* and Rembrandt's portrait of his son Titus. The paintings of the Dutch, English, Spanish, and Italian schools are outstanding. The collection also contains important 18th-century French decorative art, including furniture from royal palaces, Sèvres porcelain, and gold boxes. The European and Asian armaments, on the ground floor, are works of art in their own right.

It's best visited on one of the free "Highlights" tours given at 1pm Monday and Friday; 2.30pm Tuesday and Thursday; and 11.30am and 2.30pm Wednesday, Saturday, and Sunday.

Manchester Sq., W1. www.wallacecollection.org. ☎ **020/7563-9500.** Free admission (some exhibits charge). Daily 10am–5pm. Tube: Bond St. or Baker St.

Wellcome Collection ★★ ☺ MUSEUM The capital's finest museum of medicine was born out of the personal compulsion of Sir Henry Wellcome, a renowned 19th-century pharmacist and collector of historical medical artifacts from around the world. It's divided into two sections. The first, "Medicine Man," comprises Henry's original collection, and is wonderfully strange, consisting of an extraordinary assortment of medical oddities, including ancient Egyptian canopic jars, Roman phallic amulets, South American mummies, a medieval leper clapper, and "secondhand" guillotine blades, as well as a number of "celebrity" items, such as Napoleon's toothbrush, Nelson's razor blade, and Darwin's walking stick. The second section, "Medicine Now," is slightly less bonkers, focusing on modern medical trends and developments, with plenty of hi-tech stuff on genomes, vaccines, nanotechnology, and the like. These are complemented by temporary exhibitions and medically themed artworks, specially commissioned by the museum to highlight and explore aspects of the collection. Free tours of the museum are given on Saturdays and Sundays at 2:30pm.

183 Euston Rd., NW1. www.wellcomecollection.org. ☎ **020/7611-2222.** Free admission. Tues–Wed and Fri–Sat 10am–6pm; Thurs 10am–10pm; Sun 11am–6pm. Tube: Euston Sq., Euston, or Warren St.

WEST LONDON

The major draws of this area are the great stretches of greenery—chief among them Hyde Park and Kensington Gardens—which together make up central London's largest open space. They offer pretty much everything you could want from a park: lots of grassy lawns for sunbathing; shady trees for sitting under reading a book; a lake for boating and swimming; as well as plenty of unusual odds and ends. Perhaps most importantly, the park offers you the chance to get a little bit lost, and to feel (however briefly) that you've left the big city behind.

To the west is the less-visited Holland Park, which has a more quirky vibe, with its free roaming peacocks and Youth Hostel Association (YHA) hostel, while to the northwest are the more well-to-do surrounds of Notting Hill and its famous market snaking along Portobello Road. The Museum of Brands, Packaging, and Advertising here is a real find.

18 Stafford Terrace ⛻ HISTORIC HOME You'll step back into the days of Queen Victoria when you visit this terrace house, which has remained unchanged for well over a century. Built in the late 1860s, the five-story brick structure was the home of Linley Sambourne, a legendary cartoonist for *Punch* magazine, and can be visited only as part of a 1½-hour guided tour. Two types of tour are available: conventional tours and ones led by an actor in period costume.

Insider's tip: It's best to prebook your tour by phone.

18 Stafford Terrace, W8. www.rbkc.gov.uk/subsites/museums/18staffordterrace.aspx. ☎ **020/7602-3316.** Admission £6 adults, £4 seniors and students, £1 children 15 and under. Conventional tours: Wed 11:15am, 2:15pm; Sat–Sun 11:15am; costumed tours Sat–Sun 1pm, 2:15pm, 3pm. Tube: High St. Kensington.

Holland Park ★ ☺ PARK/GARDEN The former estate of Holland House, a 17th-century Jacobean mansion that's now home to the capital's best-situated YHA hostel, the park has an authentic aristocratic air, with manicured lawns, flower beds, and a Japanese water garden, complete with huge, colorful carp and a small waterfall. Haughty peacocks patrol the lawns during the day before retiring to the trees to squawk at each other come nightfall. Somewhat surprisingly, for such a well-tended space, the park also has an area of dense woodland at its northern end. The park's ecology center (✆ **020/7938-8186**) gives regular free nature-themed talks in summer. There are also facilities for children, including an adventure playground.

Holland Park, W8. www.rbkc.gov.uk. (✆ **020/7602-2226.** Free admission. Daily 7:30am–dusk. Tube: Holland Park or High St. Kensington.

Hyde Park ★★★ & Kensington Gardens ★★ ☺ PARK/GARDEN Once a favorite deer-hunting ground of Henry VIII, Hyde Park is today central London's largest park. With the adjoining Kensington Gardens it forms a giant open space, made up of 246 hectares (608 acres) of velvety lawns interspersed with ponds, flowerbeds, trees, meadows, statues, playgrounds, and more. The two parks are divided by a 17-hectare (42-acre) lake known as the **Serpentine.** Paddleboats and rowboats can be rented from the **boathouse** (open Easter–Oct) on the north side (✆ **020/7262-1330**) costing £10 per hour for adults, £5 per hour for children. Part of the Serpentine has also been set aside for use as the **Serpentine Lido** (✆ **020/7706-3422**; open 10am–6pm daily Jun–mid-Sep, weekends May–Oct), where you can swim, provided you don't mind the often rather challenging water temperature. It costs £4 for adults, £3 for children.

Near the Serpentine bridge is the **Princess Diana Memorial Fountain,** the somewhat (perhaps appropriately) troubled monument to the late princess. When first opened in 2004, the giant stone ring's slippery granite surfaces proved singularly unsuited for something intended for paddling, leading to its almost instant closure. It has since reopened with additional safety features.

Princess Diana Memorial Fountain in Hyde Park.

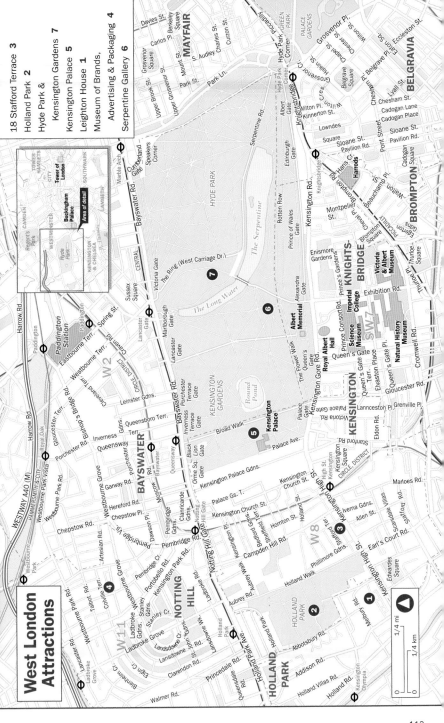

West London Attractions

18 Stafford Terrace **3**

Holland Park **2**

Hyde Park &
  Kensington Gardens **7**

Kensington Palace **5**

Leighton House **1**

Museum of Brands,
  Advertising & Packaging **4**

Serpentine Gallery **6**

At the northeastern tip of Hyde Park, near Marble Arch, is **Speakers Corner,** where people have the right to speak (and more often shout) about any subject that takes their fancy. In the past you might have heard Karl Marx, Lenin, or George Orwell trying to convert the masses; today's speakers tend to be less well known, if no less fervent, and heckling is all part of the fun.

West of the Serpentine, and bordering the grounds of Kensington Palace (see below), are the well-manicured **Kensington Gardens.** Here you can find numerous attractions including the **Serpentine Gallery** (p. 116), a famous statue of **Peter Pan** erected by J. M. Barrie himself, and the **Diana, Princess of Wales Memorial Play-**

Speakers Corner.

ground, a pirate-themed fun area that has proved a more successful tribute to the late Princess of Wales than Hyde Park's fountain. At the park's southern edge is the **Albert Memorial,** a gloriously over-the-top, gilded monument erected by Queen Victoria in honor of her late husband.

Hyde Park, W2. www.royalparks.org.uk/Hyde-Park.aspx and www.royalparks.gov.uk/Kensington-Gardens.aspx. ☎ **030/0061-2100.** Free admission. Hyde Park open daily 5am–midnight, Kensington Gardens open daily 6am–dusk. Tube: Hyde Park Corner, Marble Arch, or Lancaster Gate.

Kensington Palace ★ PALACE   The palace started life as a much simpler (relatively speaking) Jacobean mansion, but was turned into something much grander by Sir Christopher Wren on the orders of William III who acquired it in

Kensington Palace.

the late 17th century. Since then it's been the home of various royals, including Victoria, Princess Margaret (the late sister of the current queen), and perhaps most famously, Diana, Princess of Wales—it was at the palace's gates that the great carpet of flowers was laid in the weeks following her death in 1997.

In 2012, the palace emerged from the initial stages of its most significant revamp in a generation, with new cafes, courtyards, and educational facilities added, and the palace gardens connected to Kensington Gardens (see above) for the first time since the 19th century. In time the interior will be organized into exhibition areas focusing on the lives of four sets of royals: William III, Mary II, and Anne; George II; Victoria; and the princesses Margaret and Diana. The first of these, "Victoria: Love, Duty and Loss," is already open and provides an overview of Victoria's life from the day the 17-year-old princess was awakened in her room in Kensington Palace to be told her uncle, William IV, had died and she was now queen, to her later life as Empress of India and figurehead of an age. Renovation of the palace's private quarters will also take place ready for 2013 when Prince William and the Duchess of Cambridge move into the rooms formerly occupied by Princess Margaret. The palace's magnificent 18th-century **Orangery** (p. 259) is a fine venue for afternoon tea.

The Broad Walk, Kensington Gardens, W8. www.hrp.org.uk/KensingtonPalace. ☏ **0844/482-7777.** Admission £12.50 adults, £11 seniors and students, £6.25 children 5–15, £34 family ticket. Mar–Oct daily 10am–6pm; Nov–Feb daily 10am–5pm. Tube: Queensway or Notting Hill Gate; High St. Kensington on south side.

Leighton House ★ 🎒 HISTORIC HOME   When planning his new house in the mid-19th century, Lord Leighton, the renowned artist and President of the Royal Academy, declared that it should be a "private palace of art" in which he could display his own work, that of his contemporaries (notably the Pre-Raphaelite Brotherhood) and his enormous collection of curios gathered—like a particularly manic magpie—on his travels around Europe and the Middle East. The result, Leighton House, has an interior festooned with artworks and treasures, and is looking as good as it has done in more than a century thanks to a £1.6 million renovation. The glittering (slightly kitschy) glory is the domed **Arab Hall**, housing Leighton's enormous collection of 16th- and 17th-century glazed Middle Eastern decorative tiles, which have been arranged very much according to the artist's aesthetic sense rather than any notions of provenance—or, as his "friend," the artist Burne-Jones put it "all those splendid things from the East built up in such a silly way." But if it is silly, it is also rather grand. Free guided tours of the collection are given every Wednesday at 3pm.

12 Holland Park Rd., W14. www.rbkc.gov.uk/subsites/museums/leightonhousemuseum.aspx. ☏ **020/7602-3316.** Admission £5 adults, £3 seniors, students, and children 15 and under. Wed–Mon 10am–5.30pm. Tube: High Street Kensington.

Museum of Brands, Advertising & Packaging ★ 🎒 MUSEUM   A museum dedicated not so much to things, as to the packets the things come in. These days people are pretty savvy as to the value and appeal of packaging. However, back when the museum's founder, Robert Opie, began his collection—according to legend, in 1963 at the age of 16 with a chocolate wrapper—the idea of appreciating packaging for its own sake was still in its infancy (that great art hymn to packaging, Andy Warhol's *Campbell's Soup Cans* had been produced just the year before). The collection has since grown to vast proportions, comprising some 12,000 items from the past 120 years, including everything from magazine advertisements and washing powder boxes to cereal packets and milk bottles, as well as assorted toys and household appliances. They're all displayed chronologically, from the Victorian era to the present day, like a giant supermarket time tunnel. As you wander through you'll see how logos of some of the country's best known brands have evolved.

2 Colville Mews, Lonsdale Rd., W11. www.museumofbrands.com. ℓ **020/7908-0880.** Admission £6.50 adults, £4 seniors and students, £2.25 children 5–15, £15 family ticket. Tues–Sat 10am–6pm; Sun 11am–5pm. Closed during Notting Hill Carnival. Tube: Notting Hill Gate.

Serpentine Gallery ★ ART MUSEUM   Just southwest of the Serpentine (see above), from which it takes its name, Kensington Gardens' Serpentine Gallery is one of London's leading contemporary art spaces—not to mention a good place to retire to should the British weather curtail your plans for a day of sunbathing or boating. It plays host to a rolling succession of shows, each displayed for a couple of months. Notable exhibitions have featured Henry Moore, Andy Warhol, and Damien Hirst. Over the past decade the Serp has perhaps become best known for commissioning a temporary **pavilion** each summer from one of the world's leading architects (in the Jean Nouvel, Frank Gehry, Daniel Libeskind league), the more avant-garde and "out there," the better. As well as being an artwork in its own right, the pavilion provides a temporary venue for the "Park Nights," a series of concerts, talks, and film screenings that take place on Friday nights. Free art themed talks, known as "Saturday Seminars" are laid on year round at 3pm Saturday.

A new offshoot of the museum, the **Serpentine Sackler Gallery** opened in 2012, just to the north across the lake in Hyde Park. It's housed in the Magazine Building, a surprisingly elegant 19th-century ammunition depot, which has been remodeled by the architect Zaha Hadid, who was also responsible for the aquatic park at the London 2012 Olympic and Paralympic Games. With the addition of a transparent extension for a cafe/restaurant and an outdoor playspace, the new venue is dedicated to putting on ever-changing displays of new art.

Kensington Gardens, W2. www.serpentinegallery.org. ℓ **020/7402-6075.** Free admission. Daily 10am–6pm. Tube: Knightsbridge or Lancaster Gate.

SOUTHWEST LONDON

This stretch of London enjoys a dual nature. It's the moneyed heart of the capital, home to a number of neighborhoods—including Chelsea, Belgravia, and Knightsbridge—that have become bywords for a certain type of designer-shopping, Michelin-starred-eating, multi-million-pound-property-buying wealth. But it's also London's main museum district. Alongside the great department stores and unashamed consumerism of Knightsbridge, sit South Kensington's three great repositories of knowledge: The Natural History Museum, the Science Museum, and the Victoria and Albert Museum, each world leaders in their fields. The road linking them, Exhibition Road, has recently benefitted from a £30 million revamp, which has sought to discourage car use by creating a "shared space" with no sidewalks (traffic and pedestrians use the same surface) and introducing a 20mph speed limit.

Southwest London is also where the country's most important political institution, the Houses of Parliament, can be found, perched regally on the riverbank, as well as two of its finest—albeit contrasting—art museums: Tate Britain, with its unrivaled collection of traditional British art; and the Saatchi Gallery, which specializes in a controversy-seeking array of "is it art?" contemporary offerings.

Battersea Park & Zoo ★ ☺ PARK/ZOO   Often overlooked in lists of London's best parks, this vast patch of woodland, lakes, and lawns on the southern bank of the Thames is the equal of any of its more central siblings. Formerly known as Battersea Fields, the park was laid out between 1852 and 1858 on an old dueling ground. There's a **lake** for boating—and for watching the abundant waterfowl—formal gardens, one of London's largest adventure playgrounds, sports pitches, a new "winter garden," and slightly incongruously, a Buddhist peace **pagoda.** Trails are available from the park office pointing you toward some of the park's 4,000-plus trees.

There's also the **Battersea Park Children's Zoo** (www.batterseaparkzoo.co.uk; ☎ 020/7924-5826), home to various furry (and not-so-furry) critters, including chipmunks, coatis, capuchin monkeys, box turtles, and meerkats. Admission costs £7.95 for adults, £6.95 seniors and disabled visitors, £6.50 children 15 and under, and £26 for a family ticket. It's open daily in summer from 10:30am to 5:30pm and in winter from 10am to 4:30pm.

Queenstown Rd., SW11. www.batterseapark.org. ☎ **020/8871-7530.** Free admission. Dawn till dusk. Tube: Sloane Sq. then no. 137 bus. Rail: Queenstown Rd. or Battersea Park.

Carlyle's House HISTORIC HOME   Thomas Carlyle was one of the foremost historians of the 19th century who made his name with his seminal 1837 study of the French Revolution and his legendary bickering with his wife. As the author Samuel Butler noted at the time: "It was very good of God to let Carlyle and Mrs. Carlyle marry one another, and so make only two people miserable and not four." When Thomas passed away in 1881, his four-story house and its contents were preserved and turned into a museum. It's a veritable Victorian time capsule—the decor and furnishings are more or less exactly as Carlyle left them, and the rooms are filled with relics and mementoes from his life.

24 Cheyne Row, SW3. www.nationaltrust.org.uk/main/w-carlyleshouse. ☎ **020/7352-7087.** Admission £5.10 adults, £2.60 children 6–15, free for children 5 and under. Mar–Oct Wed–Sun and bank holiday Mon 11–5. Closed Nov–Feb. Tube: Sloane Sq. or South Kensington.

Chelsea Physic Garden ★ PARK/GARDEN   This is the second-oldest surviving botanical garden in England after Oxford's, founded by the Worshipful Society of Apothecaries in 1673 for the purpose of growing plants for medicinal study. To this end plant specimens, including trees, began arriving from all over the world, many to grow in English soil for the first time. Some 7,000 plants still grow here, including everything from pomegranate to exotic cork oak. After such a build up, you might be expecting something rather grand and sweeping in the Kew mold. But the Chelsea Physic is a rather small, crowded little place, albeit packed with botanical interest. In the middle is a statue of Sir Hans Sloane, doctor to George II, who provided the freehold—and whose collection of curios provided the basis for the British Museum (p. 96).

66 Royal Hospital Rd., SW3. www.chelseaphysicgarden.co.uk. ☎ **020/7352-5646.** Admission £8 adults, £5 children 5–15 and students. Apr–Oct Wed–Fri noon–5pm; Sun and bank holiday Mon noon–6pm; till 10pm Wed July–Aug. Tube: Sloane Sq.

4

EXPLORING LONDON | Southwest London

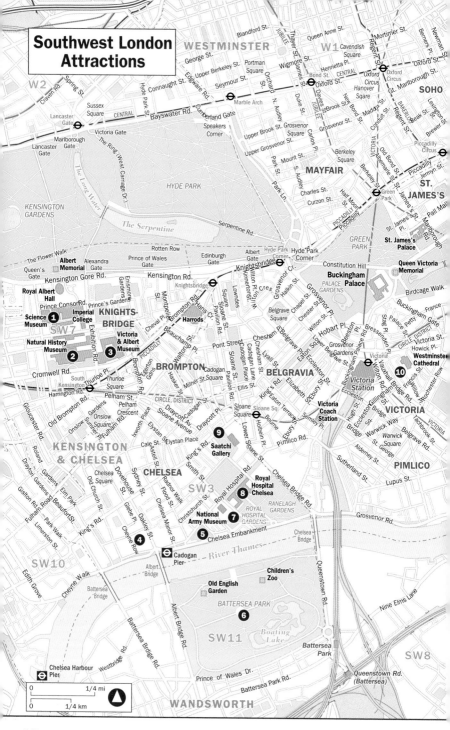

Southwest London Attractions

WESTMINSTER

W1

SOHO

W2

MAYFAIR

ST. JAMES'S

HYDE PARK

KENSINGTON GARDENS

The Serpentine

The Long Water

GREEN PARK

St. James's Palace

Queen Victoria Memorial

Buckingham Palace

KNIGHTS-BRIDGE

SW7

1 Science Museum

2 Natural History Museum

3 Victoria & Albert Museum

Royal Albert Hall

Albert Memorial

Imperial College

Harrods

BROMPTON

BELGRAVIA

VICTORIA

10 Westminster Cathedral

Victoria Station

Victoria Coach Station

PIMLICO

KENSINGTON & CHELSEA

9 Saatchi Gallery

CHELSEA

SW3

8 Royal Hospital Chelsea

7 National Army Museum

5 Chelsea Embankment

SW10

Cadogan Pier

Albert Bridge

River Thames

Chelsea Bridge

4

6 BATTERSEA PARK

Old English Garden

Children's Zoo

Boating Lake

Battersea Park

SW11

SW8

Chelsea Harbour Pier

Battersea Bridge

Prince of Wales Dr.

Queenstown Rd. (Battersea)

| 0 | 1/4 mi |
| 0 | 1/4 km |

WANDSWORTH

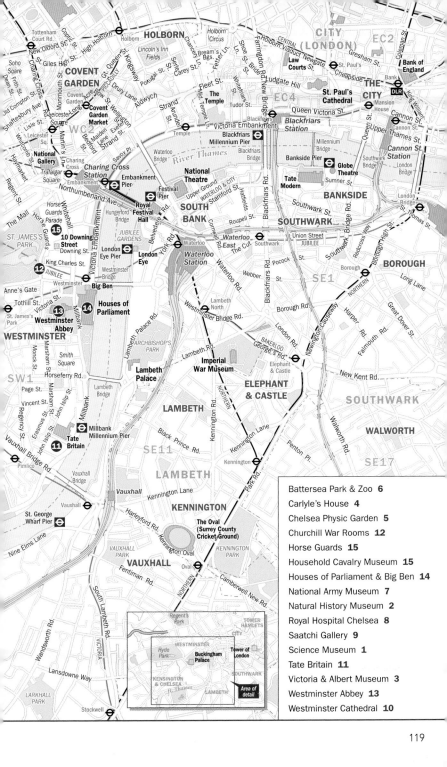

Chelsea Physic Garden.

Churchill War Rooms ★★ HISTORIC SITE/MUSEUM   These cramped subterranean rooms were the nerve center of the British war effort during the final years of World War II, where Winston Churchill and his advisors planned what they hoped would be an Allied victory. In August 1945, with the conflict finally won, the rooms were abandoned exactly as they were, creating a time capsule of the moment of victory.

You can see the **Map Room** with its huge wall maps; the Atlantic map is a mass of pinholes (each hole represents at least one convoy). Next door is Churchill's bedroom-cum-office, with the two BBC microphones via which he tried to rally the nation. Other rooms include Churchill's kitchen and dining room, and the Transatlantic Telephone Room, which is little more than a broom closet housing the special scrambler phone with which Churchill conferred with U.S. President Roosevelt. Visitors are provided with a free audio guide, giving a detailed account of each room's function with accompanying sound effects, including air raid sirens and samples of Churchill's legendary radio broadcasts.

Also in the war rooms is the **Churchill Museum,** the world's first major museum dedicated to the life of Sir Winston Churchill, which opened in 2005 to mark the 40th anniversary of the former prime minister's death. Its centerpiece is a 15m (50-ft.) interactive table on which visitors can explore the events of every year in Churchill's life.

Clive Steps, at end of King Charles St., SW1. www.iwm.org.uk/visits/churchill-war-rooms. ℰ **020/7930-6961.** Admission £15.95 adults, £12.80 seniors and students, free for children 15 and under. Daily 9:30am–6pm (last admission 5pm). Tube: Westminster or St. James's Park.

Horse Guards HISTORIC SITE   North of Downing Street, on the site of the guard house of Whitehall Palace (which burned down in 1698) stands the 18th-century Horse Guards building, the headquarters of the **Household Cavalry Mounted Regiment,** whose soldiers have two principal duties: to protect the sovereign and to provide photo opportunities for tourists—their dandy uniforms of brightly colored tunics and plumed helmets take a great shot.

The ceremony for **changing the guard** here is a good deal more accessible than the more famous one just down the road at Buckingham Palace. It takes place at 11am from Monday to Saturday, and at 10am on Sunday, and lasts around 30 minutes. The mounted sentries are relieved every hour.

If you pass through the arch at Horse Guards, you'll find yourself at **Horse Guards Parade,** formerly the tiltyard (jousting area) of Whitehall Palace, which leads on to St. James's Park. It is here that the Household Cavalry help celebrate the Queen's birthday in June with a military pageant known as "Trooping the Colour" (p. 45).

Most of the building is usually closed to visitors, although a small section has been turned into the **Household Cavalry Museum** (see below).

Whitehall, SW1. ℭ **020/7414-2479.** Free admission. Tube: Charing Cross, Westminster, or Embankment.

Household Cavalry Museum MUSEUM   The Household Cavalry are the Queen's official guard, dispatched to her side on ceremonial occasions. So it is only fitting that it was the monarch herself who turned up to open this small museum in 2008. It's housed in the Horse Guards building on Whitehall (see above), and tells the 350-year history of the cavalry through an assortment of

exhibits, including uniforms, weapons, and standards, as well as some more singular items—such as the Marquess of Anglesey's cork leg; he lost the real one at the Battle of Waterloo. You'll learn that, contrary to public perception, the Household Cavalry are not just ceremonial soldiers, but continue to serve in wars, such as Iraq and Afghanistan, albeit in slightly less gaudy uniforms.

Next to the museum, separated by a glass screen, are the 18th-century stables where you can watch the soldiers feeding, grooming, and shoeing their charges ready for guard duty and parades outside.

Horse Guards, Whitehall, SW1. www.householdcavalrymuseum.co.uk. ℭ **020/7930-3070.** Admission £6 adults, £4 ages 5–16, £15 family ticket. Mar–Sept daily 10am–6pm; Oct–Feb daily 10am–5pm. Tube: Charing Cross, Westminster, or Embankment.

Houses of Parliament & Big Ben ★ GOVERNMENT BUILDING   The image of the **Palace of Westminster** (the official name for the building containing the Houses of Parliament) and

Official guard at the Household Cavalry Museum.

its clocktower known as **Big Ben** (to everyone except pedants, who will tell you that Big Ben is in fact the name of the bell, not the tower) has become an icon of icons. It is the scene most evocative of the capital's timeless nature, and yet all is not as it seems. Although the site has been in use for almost 1,000 years—first as a royal palace, and then from the 16th century onward as the seat of Parliament—most of what you see dates only from the mid-19th century. It was designed in a deliberately medieval-looking, "Gothic Revival" style to replace an earlier structure that burned down in 1834. There are, however, much older sections hidden within, including the 11th-century **Westminster Hall,** which still boasts its 14th-century hammerbeam roof, and the 14th-century Jewel Tower (see p. 123).

On Saturdays throughout the year and during the summer recess (when the politicians are on vacation), all visitors can take a guided tour of the buildings, which takes in various places of interest in the vast 1,000-room complex, including Westminster Hall, the Royal Gallery, and the Queen's Robing Room, where the monarch gets ready for her annual speech to parliament. You are also allowed to pop into the **House of Commons** chamber itself, where the country's 650 elected MPs (Members of Parliament) come to argue over the latest legislation, as well as the secondary chamber, the **House of Lords.** When parliament is sitting, U.K. visitors can arrange guided tours (of both parliament and Big Ben) by contacting their MP.

To see British democracy in (for want of a better word) action, will probably involve a fair bit of waiting around. When the House is sitting—Monday to Thursday and some Fridays during the parliamentary seasons—line up outside the Cromwell Green visitor entrance, usually for a couple of hours (generally less for the Lords). Tickets are allocated on a first-come, first-served basis. Don't expect any great rhetorical fireworks, however. Most debates are sparsely

Big Ben.

Jewel Tower.

NO. 10 (DOWNING STREET): JUST AN ordinary HOME

A snatched glimpse through the railings at the end of the street is as much as you're likely to see these days of the country's most powerful address—No. 10 Downing Street, home of whoever happens to be the current prime minister. The second-most powerful person in the land, the Chancellor of the Exchequer (the finance minister), lives next door at No. 11. There's a connecting door between the two to spare the great officeholders the indignity of having to walk outside whenever they want to talk.

It is not a grand place, certainly not when compared to some of the extravagant residences enjoyed by other state leaders, such as the U.S. White House or France's Elysée Palace. But then, unlike those buildings, it was never designed to be a center of political power, just a simple house on a regular residential street named after the man who built it, George Downing. Its elevation to greatness came about entirely by accident when the country's first prime minister, Robert Walpole, moved here in the early 18th century, once the previous tenant, the improbably named Mr. Chicken, had moved out. A precedent had been set and Britain, being a country that likes to make up traditions and norms as it goes along—this is a country, remember, with no written constitution—decided to stick with it. Every prime minister since has followed in Walpole's footsteps, for no other reason than that it seemed the thing to do.

attended, jargon-heavy, and quite boring—that initial "I'm in the House of Commons" buzz aside.

Frustratingly, tickets for the one proper debate of the week, **Prime Minister's Question Time,** when the leader of the country and the Leader of the Opposition hurl often childish political insults at each other to a pantomime chorus of cheers and boos, have to be arranged in advance, by contacting your embassy or MP.

Across the street is the **Jewel Tower** ★, Abingdon St. (www.english-heritage. org.uk/daysout/properties/jewel-tower/; ⓒ **020/7222-2219**) one of only two surviving buildings from the medieval Palace of Westminster. Despite its name, don't expect to see any jewels. Although originally built in 1365 to house Edward III's treasuretrove, the tower today holds only an exhibition on the history of Parliament. It is open daily from 10am to 5pm April to October and Saturday and Sunday 10am to 4pm November to March. Admission is £3.20 for adults, £2.90 for students and seniors, and £1.90 for children.

Old Palace Yard, SW1. House of Commons ⓒ **020/7219-4272;** House of Lords ⓒ **020/7219-3107.** www.parliament.uk. Free admission to debates. Guided tours: £ 15 adults, £6 children aged 5–15, £37 family ticket. Tours take place Sat 9:15am–4:30pm; Aug–Sept Mon–Tues and Fri–Sat 9:15am–4:30pm, Wed–Thurs 1:15–4:30pm. Tours last 75 min. To attend debates, the House of Commons sits at the following times Mon–Tues 2:30–10:30pm, Wed 11:30am–7:30pm, Thurs 10:30am–6:30pm, Fri 9:30am–3pm. Join line at Cromwell Green entrance. Tube: Westminster.

National Army Museum ★ ☺ MUSEUM   Next to the Royal Hospital Chelsea (p. 125), this tells the colorful story of Britain's armies through four permanent sections—Changing the World 1784–1904; World Wars 1905–1947;

Conflicts of Interest 1969 to present; and the Art Gallery—as well as a similar number of temporary exhibitions. You'll find uniforms worn in every corner of the world by British soldiers, plus weapons, flags, medals, and paintings of military scenes as well as some surprising exhibits, including the skeleton of Napoleon's favorite horse, a bomb-disarming robot from the early 1970s, and a 40 sq. m (430 sq. ft.) miniature recreation of the Battle of Waterloo, featuring 70,000 model soldiers.

Royal Hospital Rd., SW3. www.national-army-museum.ac.uk. (✆ **020/7730-0717.** Free admission. Daily 10am–5:30pm. Closed Good Friday, 1st Mon in May, and Dec 24–26. Tube: Sloane Sq.

Natural History Museum ★★★ ☺ MUSEUM It seems fitting that one of London's great museums should be housed in such a grand building, a soaring Romanesque structure that provides a suitably reverent setting for what is often described as a "cathedral of nature." The museum's remit is to cover the great diversity of life on Earth, although that coverage is by no means uniform. One group of life forms gets a lot more attention lavished on it than any others, much to the delight of visiting youngsters—**dinosaurs.** As you arrive, your first vision will be the giant cast of a diplodocus looming down above you. If you want to see more of these great prehistoric beasts—but with added rubbery skin and jerky movements—then turn left where you'll find a hall filled with fossils and finds, as well as displays of animatronic dinosaurs permanently surrounded by gaggles of wide-eyed children.

The dinosaurs form part of the Blue Zone, one of the four color-coded sections that make up the museum. This zone is primarily concerned with animals, both past and present, and has plenty of other showstoppers, including a 28.5m (94-ft.) model of a blue whale hanging from the ceiling, a saber-tooth tiger skeleton, and an adult-size model of a fetus.

Animatronic raptors at the Natural History Museum.

The Green Zone's galleries focus on the environment, evolution and ecology. Highlights include giant models of insects in the Creepy Crawlies gallery, and a collection of precious stones in the museum's new section, The Vault. The Earth's interior processes are explored in the Red Zone, where you can try and stay upright on an earthquake simulator, and see plastercasts of victims preserved in ash by the volcanic eruption at Pompeii.

The final zone, the Orange Zone, is the museum's latest pride and joy, comprising the eight-story glass-and-steel **Darwin Centre,** the most significant addition to the museum since it opened in 1881. Constructed in 2008 in time for the 150th anniversary of Darwin's *Origin of the Species,* the center is primarily a research institute, but also boasts a number of hi-tech attractions for the public, including the Attenborough Studio (named after Britain's foremost TV naturalist), where talks and audio-visual shows are staged. Free tours are given of the "Spirit Collection"—made up of 22 million preserved specimens arranged on 17 miles of shelving—throughout the day, but to be sure of a place, you should book at the information desk when you arrive. It's for over-8-year-olds only. The museum offers a wealth of resources for younger visitors, including free discovery guides, explorer backpacks, and family workshops.

Cromwell Rd., SW7. www.nhm.ac.uk. ℂ **020/7942-5000.** Free admission. Daily 10am–5:50pm. Tube: South Kensington.

Royal Hospital Chelsea HISTORIC SITE/MUSEUM   Next to the National Army Museum (p. 123), this grand old institution was founded as a home for veterans by King Charles II in 1682, and completed by Sir Christopher Wren 10 years later. There's been little change to Wren's design, except for minor work done by Robert Adam in the 18th century and the addition of stables by Sir John Soane in 1814. Today, the hospital is still home to around 350 veterans, known as Chelsea Pensioners, who make use of various facilities, including extensive gardens (the setting for the annual **Chelsea Flower Show;** p. 45), and wear their distinctive red uniforms and tricorne hats on ceremonial occasions. The small on-site museum tells the story of the building and its pensioners.

Royal Hospital Rd., SW3. www.chelsea-pensioners.co.uk. ℂ **020/7881-5200.** Free admission. Mon–Fri 10am–noon and 2–4pm. Museum and shop closed bank holidays. Tube: Sloane Sq.

Saatchi Gallery ★ ART MUSEUM   If British contemporary art is a balloon, then the Saatchi Gallery is the hot air that's been keeping it aloft for the past 20 years. Having occupied various previous premises, the collection of the British advertising mogul and mega-collector Charles Saatchi, has now taken

Saatchi Gallery.

over a grand three-story former military school. The constantly changing displays of new "challenging" art are free, a welcome rarity for a non-publicly funded museum. Expect plenty of controversy—at least one big story a year or it's not really doing its job.

Duke of York's Headquarters, King's Rd., SW3. www.saatchi-gallery.co.uk. ☏ **020/7811-3070.** Free admission. Daily 10am–6pm. Tube: Sloane Sq.

Science Museum ★★★ ☺ MUSEUM   Founded in the 1850s in the wake of—and largely with leftover contraptions from—the Great Exhibition, the "Museum of Patents," as it was originally known, has grown to become the country's pre-eminent museum of science. It's also one of the capital's great interactive experiences, filled with buttons to press, levers to pull, and experiments to absorb you. There's plenty of impressive hardware on display, beginning, just after the entrance, in the **Energy Hall,** where you can meet the great clunking behemoths of the Industrial Revolution, including steam locomotives and giant beam engines. Beyond, the **Making the Modern World** exhibition celebrates 150 of the most significant icons of industrial progress from the past 250 years, including Charles Babbage's "Difference Engine," the first automatic calculator, Watson and Crick's model of the structure of DNA, and the Apollo 10 command module. On the same floor is the **Legend of Apollo 4D Cinema,** offering viewers a computer-simulated round-trip to the moon, complete with stirring music and a portentous voiceover.

And that's just the start of the museum. On the other floors, you'll find galleries dedicated to medicine and biology (floors 4 & 5), flight (floor 3; the highlight is the **Red Arrows 3D Flight Simulator**), computing (floor 2), and astronomy (floor 1). There's also the ever popular **Launchpad,** where there are more than 50 hands-on experiments to try, as well as an IMAX cinema showing spectacular nature- and space-related epics on a giant screen.

Insider's tip: The museum stages numerous free events, many of them aimed at children. There are daily tours of the galleries led by costumed characters, and workshops and themed days during the school holidays. Adults, meanwhile, can attend child-free science-themed shows at the museum's adjoining **Dana Centre,** 165 Queen's Gate, SW7 (☏ **020/7942-4040;** www.danacentre. org.uk).

Exhibition Rd., SW7. www.sciencemuseum.org.uk. ☏ **0870/870-4868.** Free admission. Daily 10am–6pm (last admission 5.15pm). Closed Dec 24–26. Tube: South Kensington.

Tate Britain ★★★ ART MUSEUM   Fronting the Thames near Vauxhall Bridge, Tate Britain looks like a smaller and more graceful relation of the British Museum. Founded in 1897 by the sugar merchant, Sir Henry Tate (when it was known as the National Gallery of British Art), it now houses the country's finest collection of domestic art with works dating from the 16th century to the present, and most of the country's leading artists represented, including such notable figures as Constable, Gainsborough, Hogarth, Reynolds, Stubbs, and the incomparable William Blake, as well as modern greats including Stanley Spencer, Francis Bacon, and David Hockney. The collection of works by J. M. W. Turner is Tate Britain's largest by a single artist, spread over seven rooms. Turner himself willed most of his paintings and watercolors to the nation.

Free tours of parts of the collection are offered Monday to Friday (at 11am, noon, 2pm, and 3pm) and on Saturdays and Sundays at noon and 3pm, and the

Tate Britain.

first Friday of each month sees the "Late at Tate" event, which involves extended opening hours (till 10pm) and free events, such as talks, film screenings, and live music.

If you want to make an art-filled day of it, the **Tate to Tate boat** service departs from just outside to Tate Modern all day (p. 143).

Millbank, SW1. www.tate.org.uk/britain. 🕿 **020/ 7887-8888.** Free admission; special exhibitions incur a charge of £5–£15. Daily 10am–6pm (last admission 5:15pm). Tube: Pimlico.

Victoria & Albert Museum ★★★ ☺

MUSEUM The V&A (as it's usually known) could justly claim to be the world's greatest collection of applied arts, comprising 7 floors and 150 galleries in which are displayed, at a rough estimate, around four million items of decorative art from across the world and throughout the ages—sculptures, jewelry, textiles, clothes, paintings, ceramics, furniture, architecture, and more. Many of the collections are among the finest of their type. The V&A has the largest collection of Renaissance sculptures outside Italy, the most significant collection of Indian art outside India (in the Nehru Gallery), and the country's most comprehensive collection of antique dresses (in the recently reopened Fashion Gallery). The Photography Gallery can draw on some 500,000 individual images, the William & Judith Bolling Gallery holds one of the world's largest (and most glittering) collections of European jewelry, while the Medieval & Renaissance Galleries take up three floors and offer a cornucopia of crafted objects—stained glass, statuary, metalwork, and tapestries—dating from A.D. 300 to 1600.

That's a huge and potentially overwhelming amount of choice, and it's set to get even worse in the future with new galleries due to open in the next few years, including one dedicated to Europe 1600–1800. Indeed, the museum can be rather confusing at first, particularly as its seems the powers-that-be never quite decided whether to arrange the collection according to geography, chronology, or artistic medium, and so have gone for a sort of hotch-potch of all three, which means you'll find sections entitled "Asia," "Materials & Techniques," or, simply, "Modern." But once you're there it does make sense, kind of. To help you plot your path, your first stop should be the front desk where you can pick up leaflets, floor plans, and themed family trails. If you'd rather somebody else made the decisions for you, free guided tours leave from the grand entrance daily, hourly between 10:30am and 3:30pm. Also look out for the special evening tours, which take place on the first Friday of the month, when the V&A stays open late and lays on special events, including talks and free concerts. Art-based drop-in events are laid on for families on weekends.

Statue gallery in the Victoria & Albert Museum.

Cromwell Rd., SW7. www.vam.ac.uk. (℗) **020/7942-2000.** Free admission. Temporary exhibitions often £12.50. Sun–Thurs 10am–5:45pm; Fri 10am–10pm. Tube: South Kensington.

Westminster Abbey ★★★ CHURCH   The Abbey is not just one of the finest examples of ecclesiastical architecture in Europe, it's also the shrine of the nation where monarchs are anointed before their God and memorials to the nation's greatest figures fill every corner. From the outside, it's a magnificently earnest looking structure, its two great square towers and pointed arches the very epitome of medieval Gothic, while the inside is a cluttered mass of symbols and statuary. The building was begun in 1245 under the reign of Henry II and finally completed in the early 16th century. This replaced an earlier structure commissioned in 1045 by Edward the Confessor (which itself had replaced a 7th-century original) and consecrated in 1065, just in time to play host to Edward's funeral and (following a brief tussle in Hastings) the coronation of William the Conqueror. It has been, with a couple of exceptions, the setting for every coronation since, and it was here in 2011, that Prince William married Kate Middleton.

More or less at the center of the Abbey stands the shrine of Edward the Confessor, while scattered around are the tombs of various other royals, including Henry V, Elizabeth I, Richard III, and the rather splendid Renaissance one made for Henry VII. Nearby is the surprisingly shabby **Coronation Chair,** on which almost every monarch since Edward II, including the current one, has sat.

In **Poet's Corner** you'll find a great assortment of memorials to the country's greatest men (and a few women) of letters, clustered around the grave of Geoffrey Chaucer, who was buried here in 1400. These include a statue of Shakespeare, his arm resting on a pile of books, Jacob Epstein's bust of William Blake, as well as tributes to Jane Austen, Samuel Taylor Coleridge, John Milton, Dylan Thomas, and D. H. Lawrence.

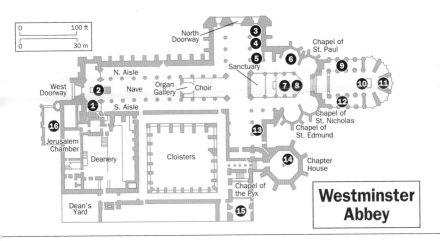

Westminster Abbey

Statesmen and men of science—Disraeli, Newton, Charles Darwin—are also interred in the Abbey or honored by monuments. Near to the west door is the 1965 memorial to Sir Winston Churchill and the tomb of the **Unknown Warrior,** commemorating the British dead of World War I.

More royal relics are on display in the **Abbey Museum,** which is housed in the undercroft. Among its various oddities are the effigies of a number of past royals, including Edward II and Henry VII, which were used instead of the real corpses for lying-in-state ceremonies—they smelled better. It's open Monday through Saturday from 10:30am to 4pm.

If visiting midweek, don't forget to view the garden. First laid out some 900 years ago, it is one of the oldest cultivated gardens in the country, and offers a welcome breath of calming fresh air. It is open only from Tuesday to Thursday from April to September from 10am to 6pm, and from October to March from 10am to 4pm.

Broad Sanctuary, SW1. www.westminster-abbey.org. ✆ **020/7222-5152.** Admission £16 adults, £13 students and seniors, £6 children 11–18, £32 family ticket, free for children 10 and under. Mon–Tues and Thurs–Fri 9:30am–4:30pm (last admission 3.30pm); Wed 9:30am–7pm (last admission 6pm); Sat 9:30am–2:30pm (last admission 1.30pm). Tube: Westminster or St. James's Park.

Westminster Cathedral ★ CATHE-
DRAL This spectacular brick-and-stone
church (1903) is the headquarters of the
Roman Catholic Church in Britain. Adorned
in retro-Byzantine style, it's massive: 108m
(354 ft.) long and 47m (154 ft.) wide. The
interior is very much a tale of two halves with
the black brickwork of the upper part of the
church providing a sombre counterpart to
the gaudy multicolored marble and gold con-
fection of the lower. It's free to look around
most of the cathedral, although you do have
to pay to see the glittering chalices, vest-
ments, and relics (as well as a wooden
scale model of the cathedral) at the Treasures of Westminster Cathedral exhibition
(£5 adults, £2.50 seniors, students, and children), or to ascend the 82m (269-ft.) campa-
nile belltower (£5 adults, £2.50 seniors,
students, and children). Take the elevator to
the top and you'll be rewarded with sweeping
views that take in the Houses of Parliament
and the Gherkin. The cathedral's renowned
choir usually performs daily: You can download the current timetable from the website.

TOP: **Westminster Abbey**;
RIGHT: **Westminster Cathedral.**

Ashley Place, SW1. www.westminstercathedral.org.uk. ℂ **020/7798-9055.** Cathedral free.
Tower £5. Cathedral services Mon–Sat 7am–7pm; Sun 8am–8pm. Tower Mon–Fri 9:30am–5pm;
Sat–Sun 9:30am–6pm. Tube: Victoria.

MUSEUMS: LATE night FEVER

For harassed 9 to 5 workers who feel their cultural lives are suffering, help is at hand. These days, going to a museum is no longer a daytime-only activity. Many of London's attractions—including even zoos and palaces—now offer extended opening times. This can be anything from a few times a year to—in the case of some of London's larger museums—once or twice a week. To sweeten the deal, extra inducements are often offered in the form of food and drink, live music, talks, workshops, tours, and so on. The following attractions all have established "Lates" events:

Attraction	Late Opening Day
British Museum (p. 96)	Friday till 8.30pm
Chelsea Physic Garden (p. 117)	Wednesday till 10pm (July–Aug only)
Courthauld Gallery (p. 101)	Thursday till 9pm (usually one a month)
Handel House Museum (p. 135)	Thursday till 8pm
Hayward Gallery (p. 167)	Thursday & Friday till 8pm
London Canal Museum (p. 167)	Thursday till 7.30pm (first of each month)
London Zoo (p. 102)	Friday till 10pm (selected summer nights only)
National Gallery (p. 104)	Friday till 9pm
National Portrait Gallery (p. 124)	Thursday & Friday till 9pm
Natural History Museum (p. 105)	Friday till 10.30pm (last of each month)
Royal Academy (p. 126)	Friday till 10pm
Science Museum (p. 108)	Wednesday till 10pm (last of each month)
Sir John Soane's Museum (p. 126)	Tuesday till 9pm (first of each month)
Tate Britain (p. 141)	Friday till 10pm (first of each month)
Tate Modern (p. 150)	Thursday & Friday till 10pm
Tower of London (p. 127)	Wednesday tour till 8.30pm (Nov–Feb)
Victoria & Albert Museum (p. 111)	Friday till 10pm (last of each month)
Wellcome Collection (p. 160)	Thursday till 10pm
Whitechapel Gallery (p. 160)	Thursday till 9pm

THE SOUTH BANK

Today the riverside path between Westminster Bridge and Tower Bridge is perhaps the capital's favorite strolling route, taking walkers past a line of attractions, including the London Eye, the Southbank Centre, Tate Modern, Shakespeare's Globe, and HMS *Belfast*, as well as providing great views out across to the undulating facades of the northern bank of the Thames.

City Hall on the South Bank.

The area wasn't always so popular, however. Or rather, it used to be popular for *very* different reasons: In Elizabethan times, this was the bad side of town, where people from the respectable north came to indulge in such disreputable practices as gambling, prostitution, bear baiting, and going to the theatre. Shakespeare's original Globe lay not, as you might have suspected, in the heart of some rarefied center of learning, but in the midst of the city's red-light district.

The region was cleared up in later centuries, and didn't begin to become a center of tourism until the 1950s, when the Royal Festival Hall was built as one of the main venues for the Festival of Britain, the first national cultural event after the war. Various other attractions followed in the ensuing decades, and together they now form one of the city's prime arts hotspots. And things haven't finished yet. Tate Modern has opened a new set of subterranean art spaces in what were the power station's oil tanks, and the next few years should see a bold, assymetrical "ziggurat" extension rising up above the old building. It will, however, be rather overshadowed (as, indeed, is everything else) by the 310-m (1,017 ft) tall "Shard" at London Bridge, the E.U.'s tallest skyscraper, which was due to open at the time of writing.

City Hall GOVERNMENT BUILDING   Adjacent to Tower Bridge, across the water from the Tower of London, the Norman Foster-designed City Hall is the eco-friendly home of the Mayor of London and the London Assembly. Its strange, leaning-back design—as if it's scared of the water—has made the steel-and-glass egg one of the riverside's most recognizable structures. There's a visitor center with a giant walk-on floor photo of the capital where temporary exhibitions are held. The rooftop exhibition space has great views but is usually closed for private events—call in advance.

Queen's Walk, SE1. www.london.gov.uk/city-hall. 📞 **020/7983-4000.** Free admission. Visitor information desk Mon–Fri 9am–5pm; cafe Mon–Fri 8am–8pm. Tube: London Bridge.

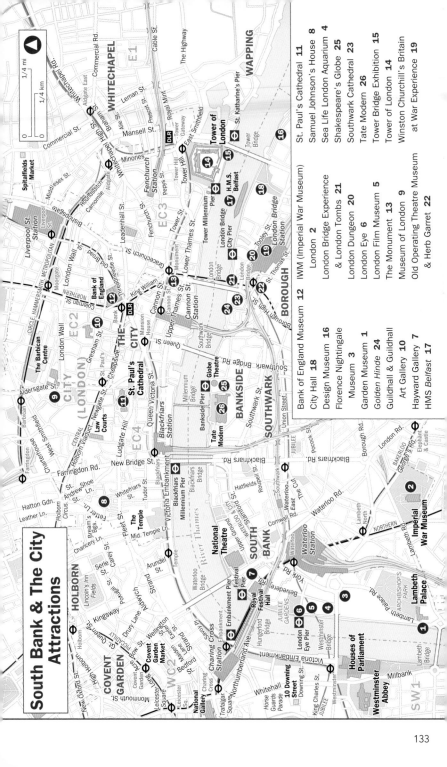

South Bank & The City Attractions

St. Paul's Cathedral **11**
Samuel Johnson's House **8**
Sea Life London Aquarium **4**
Shakespeare's Globe **25**
Southwark Cathedral **23**
Tate Modern **26**
Tower Bridge Exhibition **15**
Tower of London **14**
Winston Churchill's Britain
at War Experience **19**

IWM (Imperial War Museum)
London **2**
London Bridge Experience
& London Tombs **21**
London Dungeon **20**
London Eye **6**
London Film Museum **5**
The Monument **13**
Museum of London **9**
Old Operating Theatre Museum
& Herb Garret **22**

Bank of England Museum **12**
City Hall **18**
Design Museum **16**
Florence Nightingale
Museum **3**
Garden Museum **1**
Golden Hinde **24**
Guildhall & Guildhall
Art Gallery **10**
Hayward Gallery **7**
HMS *Belfast* **17**

Design Museum cafe and shop.

Design Museum MUSEUM   Until its big move to the former Commonwealth Institute Building in Kensington in 2014, the Design Museum will continue to occupy a bright white former banana warehouse by the river. There it will stage a succession of temporary exhibitions based around the work of contemporary designers and movements—consult the website for details of the latest shows. Once ensconced in its new home, however, the plan is to unveil the permanent collection—currently in storage—made up of more than 2,000 everyday objects that also happen to be design classics, including a 1920s' candlestick telephone, a 1950s' red telephone box, and a 1980s' Sony Walkman.

28 Shad Thames, SE1. www.designmuseum.org. 🕾 **020/7940-8790.** Admission £11 adults, £7 students, £10 seniors, free for children 11 and under. Daily 10am–5:45pm (last admission 5:15pm). Tube: Bermondsey or London Bridge.

Florence Nightingale Museum ★ ☺ MUSEUM   This museum celebrates the life and work of one of the great Victorian British women, best known for nursing soldiers during the Crimean War (1853–56). However, you'll learn that the "lady with the lamp's" greatest achievement was probably as a statistician. She used then revolutionary techniques for presenting data, such as pie charts, to prove the importance of sanitation and good hygiene in lowering the death rate of wounded soldiers.

The museum holds many objects owned or used by Nightingale, including clothes, furniture, letters, and even her stuffed pet owl. There are also audiovisual displays on her life and a reconstruction of a Crimean ward scene.

The museum is very much slanted toward families and schoolchildren—parties of whom arrive regularly during term time—and free family events, such as storytellings, art workshops, and trails are put on most weekends. The admission price includes the cost of an audio tour—there are two versions, one for adults and one for children.

St. Thomas' Hospital, 2 Lambeth Palace Rd., SE1. www.florence-nightingale.co.uk. 🕾 **020/7620-0374.** Admission £5.80 adults; £4.80 seniors, students, children aged 5–15, and persons with disabilities; free for children 4 and under; £16 family ticket. Daily 10am–5pm. Tube: Westminster, Waterloo, or Lambeth North.

Garden Museum ★ MUSEUM   Housed in a small medieval church, St. Mary-Lambeth, this offers a celebration of that most British of pastimes—gardening. Its focus is unashamedly domestic, concentrating less on the Capability Browns of the world, with their grand landscaped parks, than on the various unsung heroes of suburbia carefully tending backyard plots. Inside is an assortment of antique gardening implements, a collection of gardening-related art, and a treasure trove of memorabilia.

Outside, the museum's own garden is filled with historic plants that thrive in the microclimate within the church's walls. The churchyard contains two notable memorials from the history of horticulture: The tomb of **Captain Bligh,** whose journey aboard the *Bounty* to Tahiti in the late 18th century to obtain breadfruit trees prompted the famous mutiny against him; and the tomb of John Tradescant, a gardener and plant hunter for King Charles II. A traditional 17th-century knot garden has been laid out in Tradescant's honor.

Insider's tip: Free guided tours are given on the last Tuesday of each month at 2pm. First come, first served.

Lambeth Palace Rd., SE1. www.gardenmuseum.org.uk. ✆ **020/7401-8865.** Admission £6 adults, £5 seniors, £3 students, free children 15 and under. Sun–Fri 10:30am–5:30pm; Sat 10:30am–4pm; closed 1st Mon of month (except bank holidays). Tube: Lambeth North.

Golden Hinde ☺ HISTORIC SITE/MUSEUM   By the river, just around the corner from Southwark Cathedral, is this full-size replica of the ship on which Sir Francis Drake became the first Englishman to circumnavigate the globe in the 16th century. It may seem a touch cozy, but the proportions are accurate—it has even been sailed around the world to prove it. On board it's all very yo-ho-ho, with actors in period costume entertaining you with Tudor maritime tales as you explore the five levels. Understandably, it's very popular with children, and at weekends is usually given over to private birthday parties where everyone dresses up as pirates and buccaneers.

If your kids really want to get a feel for life at sea (or rather, in dry dock), you can sign them up for a "Family Overnight Living History Tour," which run once a month from April to October. Between your arrival (all children must be accompanied by an adult) at 5pm and 10am the next day, you join a crew of Tudor sailors, tending to the ship's needs, eating Tudor food and drink, and sleeping in the (somewhat cramped) cabins in the lower deck.

Pickford's Wharf, Clink St., SE1. www.goldenhinde.com. ✆ **020/7403-0123.** Admission £6 adults, £4.50 seniors, students, and children 15 and under; £18 family. Mon–Sat 10am–5:30pm. Sleepovers cost £42.95 per person—bring sleeping bag. Tube: London Bridge.

Hayward Gallery ART MUSEUM   Opened in 1968, and forming the arts wing of the **Southbank Centre** (p. 308)—which also includes the Royal Festival Hall, the Queen Elizabeth Hall, and the Purcell Room (p. 308)—the Hayward is perhaps the epitome of the concrete brutalist style of architecture for which the Southbank is so derided (or occasionally, admired). Although the outside might not grace many postcards, the interior is a superior art space that presents a changing program of major contemporary exhibits. Every exhibition is accompanied by a variety of educational activities, including tours, workshops, lectures, and publications.

Belvedere Rd., South Bank, SE1. http://ticketing.southbankcentre.co.uk/find/hayward-gallery-visual-arts. ℭ **020/7960-4200.** Admission varies but usually £10 adults, £9 seniors, £8 students, £7.50 children 12–17, free for children 11 and under. Sun–Wed 10am–6pm; Thurs–Fri 10am–8pm. Tube: Waterloo or Embankment.

HMS Belfast ★ ☺ HISTORIC SITE   Moored opposite the Tower of London, between Tower Bridge and London Bridge, HMS *Belfast* is an 11,874-tonne (11,684-ton) World War II cruiser, now preserved as a floating museum run by the Imperial War Museum (see below). Always popular with youngsters, who love climbing between its seven levels of clunking metal decks, the *Belfast* has recently been given an interactive makeover. So in addition to admiring all the hardware on display—including naval guns and anti-aircraft weaponry—it's possible to tackle simulated missions on touch-screen computers in the Interactive Operations Room and place yourself in the midst of a naval battle in the Gun Turret Experience, which uses light, sound, smoke, and even smell effects to tell its story. You can also find out about the more mundane aspects of life at sea—which, in truth, always made up the majority of a sailor's time—by touring the messdeck (where food was served), the cabins where sailors slept sardine-style in hammocks set just 52cm (1ft. 8 in) apart, and the sick bay. Incidentally, the ship's guns have a range of 14 miles, which means they could take out Hampton Court Palace (p. 176) if staff felt so inclined. Children aged 15 and under must be accompanied by an adult.

Morgan's Lane, Tooley St., SE1. www.iwm.org.uk/visits/hms-belfast. ℭ **020/7940-6300.** Admission £14 adults, £11.20 seniors and students, free for children 15 and under. Mar–Oct daily 10am–6pm (last admission 4pm); Nov–Feb 10am–5pm (last admission 4pm). Tube: London Bridge.

IWM (Imperial War Museum) London ★★★ ☺ MUSEUM   From 1814 to 1930, this deceptively elegant, domed building was the Bethlehem Royal Hospital, an old-style "madhouse," where the "patients" formed part of a Victorian freak show—visitors could pay a penny to go and stare at the lunatics. (The hospital's name has since entered the language as "Bedlam," a slang expression for chaos and confusion.) Thankfully, civilization has moved on in its treatment of the mentally ill, although as this museum of warfare shows, nations are still as capable of cruelty and organized madness as they ever were.

The great, gung-ho 38cm (15-in.) naval guns parked outside the entrance give an indication of what you can expect in the main hall (or Large Exhibits Gallery). This is the boys' toys section with a whole fleet of tanks, planes, and missiles on display (including a Battle of Britain Spitfire, a V2 rocket, and a German one-man submarine), and plenty of interactivity for the youngsters, with cockpits to climb into and touch-screen terminals to explore.

After the initial bombast, however, comes a selection of thoughtful, sobering exhibits, focusing on the human cost of war. These include sections exploring life during World Wars I and II on the battlefield and at home, and the "Secret War" exhibition which looks at the use of duplicity, subterfuge, and spying in wartime. On the upper floors, things become more thoughtful still. Floor 3 provides an intense account of the Holocaust, using original artifacts, documents, film, and photographs to examine the first attempt to apply modern industrial techniques to the destruction of people. And, just to remind you that this is not an evil that has been permanently consigned to history, the "Crimes against Humanity" exhibition explores modern genocides. Its central exhibit is a

Main Hall of the Imperial War Museum.

harrowing 30-minute film. These two sections are not recommended for children under 14.

In addition to the permanent collection, the museum usually has one or more temporary exhibitions running (which do incur a charge), and puts on a range of events throughout the year, many suitable for families.

Lambeth Rd., SE1. www.iwm.org.uk. ℭ **020/7416-5320** (info line). Free admission. Daily 10am–6pm. Tube: Lambeth North or Elephant and Castle.

London Bridge Experience and London Tombs ☺ MUSEUM   Head
down beneath the foundations of what has been the capital's prime river crossing for nigh on 2 millennia to find out about the bridge's history and experience a bit of London Dungeon-style gore—heads on spikes, animatronic prisoners, costumed actors playing the roles of Boudicca and William Wallace, and so forth. It bills itself as a "scare attraction" and is big on family fun, if not quite so heavy on intellectual rigor. The admission price rises and falls over the course of the day, and is most expensive between noon and 3pm.

2–4 Tooley St., SE1. www.thelondonbridgeexperience.com. ℭ **0800/043-4666.** Admission £24.50 adults, £22.58 seniors and students aged 15–17, £19 children 5–14. Mon–Fri 10am–5pm; Sat–Sun 10am–6pm. Tube: London Bridge.

London Dungeon ★ ☺ MUSEUM   Set beneath the arches of London
Bridge station, this is a sort of hi-tech haunted house aimed squarely at children and teenagers to whom it delivers a series of "safe" shocks, themed (very loosely) on events and legends from London's history. When it first opened back in the 1970s, it was made up mainly of waxwork tableaux, a bit like the Chamber of Horrors at Madame Tussauds. These days it's a very 21st-century attraction, with plenty of lighting and sound effects adding to the atmosphere, while most of the jolts are provided by costumed actors and fairground-style rides. A list of some of

the dungeon's current "scenes" should give you an idea of what to expect: "Bloody Mary," "Jack the Ripper," "Extremis: Drop Ride to Doom," and "Vengeance 5D Laser Ride."

Depending on your age, you'll find it a terrible piece of kitsch, overpriced nonsense, or a glorious exercise in grand guignol-lite. It's certainly all very tongue-in-cheek, although you should use discretion with very young children.

Insider's tip: The dungeon is pretty pricey, but deals are available on the website where you can also make savings if you book combination tickets to other London attractions, including the London Eye, the Sea Life London Aquarium, and Madame Tussauds.

28–34 Tooley St., SE1. www.thedungeons.com. (℃) **020/7403-7221.** Admission £23.52 adults, £17.52 children 4–15, free for children 3 and under. Times vary; the dungeon is open daily, typically 10am–5pm, but stays open later (till 6:30 or 7pm) during the school holidays. Tube: London Bridge.

London Eye ★★ ☺ OBSERVATION WHEEL The largest observation wheel in Europe, the London Eye has become, just over a decade since it opened, a potent icon of the capital, as clearly identified with London as the Eiffel Tower is with Paris. And indeed, it performs much the same function—giving people the chance to observe the city from above. Passengers are carried in 32 glass-sided "pods," each representing one of the 32 boroughs of London (which lucky travelers get Croydon?), which make a complete revolution every half-hour. Along the way you'll see bird's-eye views of some of London's most famous landmarks, including the Houses of Parliament, Buckingham Palace, the BT Tower, St. Paul's, and, of course, the River Thames itself. "Night flights," when you can gaze at the twinkling lights of the city, are available in winter.

London Eye.

London's best "Bird's-Eye" Views

The **London Eye** (p. 138) is the most obvious of the attractions offering a "bird's-eye" view of the capital, but it's by no means the only vantage point. For centuries before the Eye was built, **St. Paul's Cathedral** (p. 146) has been letting Londoners willing to climb its 500-plus steps gaze out over their city, spread out before them like a 3-D map. Worthy, albeit slightly less elevated, panoramas are also offered from the top of **Westminster Cathedral** (p. 130), the **Monument** (p. 145), the **National Portrait Gallery** restaurant (p. 104), and the **Oxo Tower**—this last one is particularly recommended, because it's free.

At the time of writing, these were set to be joined by some new (rather lanky) kids on the block, including the 60m (200-ft.) high **Emirates Air Line** cable car traversing the Thames between the ExCel Centre and the O2 Arena (p. 76), the 115m (377-ft.) tall **ArcelorMittal Orbit Tower** (www.arcelormittalorbit. com) at the Olympic Park, and—towering above them all—the 310m (1,017 ft.) **Shard,** Western Europe's tallest building. Its 72nd floor observation deck will be London's highest public space.

The Eye is extremely popular, ridden by some 3½ million people every year. Its iconic status was further cemented a few years ago when it became the principal venue for the capital's New Year celebrations, with a 10-minute firework display taking place around the wheel as midnight strikes. Ticket prices are 10% cheaper if booked online.

Millennium Jubilee Gardens, SE1. www.londoneye.com. © **0871/781-3000.** Admission £18.60 adults, £15 seniors, £9.54 children 4–15. Times vary, but Eye is open daily from 10am, usually till 9pm in summer (9:30pm in July–Aug) and till 8.30pm in winter. Tube: Waterloo or Westminster.

London Film Museum ☺ MUSEUM   Housed in the former debating chamber of **County Hall,** the museum's focus is British films, although its rather woolly remit does allow it to feature U.S. blockbusters filmed in this country as well as genuinely domestic product. It's filled with artifacts, memorabilia, and sets from such big screen favorites as *Star Wars, Gladiator, Superman* (including the cape from *Superman Returns*), and *Batman Begins* (including Christian Bale's Batsuit). It also hosts temporary exhibitions, such as the recent retrospective on Ray Harryhausen, the father of stop-motion animation.

County Hall, Westminster Bridge Rd., SE1. www.londonfilmmuseum.com. © **020/7202-7040.** Admission £13.50 adults, £11.50 seniors and students, £9.50 for children 5 to 15, free for children 4 and under. Mon–Fri 10am–5pm; Sat–Sun 10am–6pm. Tube: Waterloo or Westminster.

Old Operating Theatre Museum & Herb Garret ★★ ☺ MUSEUM   Next time you find yourself moaning about a trip to the family doctor, remember it could be *much* worse, as this antique operating theatre shows. Although less than 200 years old, it might as well be from the Stone Age, such have been the advances in medical science. It was once part of St. Thomas' Hospital, but was sealed over and forgotten about for more than a century when the hospital relocated in 1861. Now restored, it provides a grim window in to the past.

Its centerpiece is Europe's oldest operating theatre where operations—mainly amputations—were performed on a simple wooden table without anesthetic or antiseptic. Patients were bound to prevent them struggling free, a box of sawdust was placed beneath them to collect the blood, and then the surgeon got to work, the aim being to sever the limb as quickly as possible to prevent the patient from bleeding to death. The grisly spectacle was watched by medical students in the surrounding seating—this really was a "theatre"—as you can do every Saturday at 2pm, when a demonstration of 19th-century "Speed Surgery" is staged.

The **herb garret,** located above the theatre, was used for drying medicinal plants. It was rediscovered at the same time, and provides a more peaceful, aromatic second act.

9a St. Thomas St., SE1. www.thegarret.org.uk. © **020/7188-2679.** Admission £5.90 adults, £4.90 seniors and students, £3.40 children 15 and under, £13.80 family. Daily 10:30am–5pm. Tube: London Bridge.

Sea Life London Aquarium ★ ☺ AQUARIUM

One of the largest aquariums in Europe, this South Bank attraction boasts 350 species of fish, including everything from British freshwater species to brightly colored tropical clownfish. The tanks are ordered geographically, so you can observe the bountiful riches of the coral reefs of the Indian Ocean, or what lurks in the murky depths of the Atlantic and Pacific oceans, including an array of eels, turtles, squid, jellyfish, and seahorses. As ever, the stars are the sharks. At Shark Walk you can watch these killers of the deep swimming just beneath your feet. Other highlights include a replica tropical rainforest home to a set of crocodiles, and the new Ice Adventure section where you can observe a small colony of Antarctic gentoo penguins alternately hopping clumsily on their replica iceflow or darting through the water with considerably more grace. "Talks & Feeds" take place throughout the day—the rays at 11:30am, the sharks at 2:30pm, and the terrapins at 4:30pm. Tickets are 10% cheaper if booked online.

Sea Life London Aquarium.

County Hall, Westminster Bridge Rd., SE1. www.visitsealife.com/London. © **0871/663-1678.** Admission £19 adults, £14 children 3–15, £60 family. Mon–Thurs 10am–6pm (last admission 5pm); Fri–Sun 10am–7pm (last admission 6pm). Tube: Waterloo or Westminster.

Shakespeare's Globe ★★ HISTORIC SITE/MUSEUM

This is a recent re-creation of one of the most significant public theatres ever built, Shakespeare's Globe, where the Bard premiered many of his most famous plays. The late American filmmaker, Sam Wanamaker, worked for some 20 years to raise funds to re-create the theatre as it existed in Elizabethan times, thatched roof and all. The on-site exhibition, set beneath the building, delves into the world of the Elizabethan theatre with displays on period special effects and clothes. It also tells the story of the Globe's reconstruction, using the material (including goat hair in the plaster), techniques, and craftsmanship of 400 years ago. The new Globe isn't an exact replica: It seats 1,500 patrons, not the 3,000 who regularly squeezed in during the early 1600s, and this thatched roof has been specially treated with a fire retardant—just as well, as a shot from a stage cannon fired during a performance of *Henry VIII* provided the ultimate finale, setting the roof alight and burning the original theatre to the ground.

Insider's tip: Guided tours of the facility are offered throughout the day in the theatre's winter off-season. From May to September, however, Globe tours are available only in the morning. In the afternoon, when matinee performances are taking place, alternative (and cheaper) tours to the rather scanty remains of the **Rose Theatre,** the Globe's precursor (which was torn down in the early 17th century), are offered instead.

See p. 305 for details on attending a play here.

21 New Globe Walk, SE1. www.shakespearesglobe.com. ℂ **020/7902-1400.** Admission and Globe Tour/Rose Tour £13.50/10 adults, £12/9 seniors, £8/7 children 5–15, free for children 4 and under, £35/29 family ticket. Oct–Apr daily 10am–5pm; May–Sept daily 9am–5pm. Tube: Mansion House or London Bridge.

Southwark Cathedral CATHEDRAL   The courtyard at Southwark Cathedral, set back from the Thames, is a particularly welcoming patch of green in the built-up environs of London Bridge. There's been a church on this site since the 7th century. The current version is medieval (with a few 19th-century additions), and was the first church in London to be built in a Gothic style. It took shape slowly over a 200-year period between the early 13th and the early 14th centuries, and by the 17th century lay at the heart of the theatre district, just downriver from the Globe and Rose theatres. It wasn't redesignated as a cathedral, however, until the early 20th century.

Southwark Cathedral.

Inside are memorials to Shakespeare (who is believed to have worshipped here) and Sam Wanamaker—the American actor-director largely responsible for rebuilding the Globe Theatre. Organ recitals are given here on Mondays at 1pm, and classical music recitals on Tuesdays from 3:15 to 4pm. Both are free.

Montague Close, SE1. http://cathedral.southwark.anglican.org. ℂ **020/7367-6700.** Free admission; suggested donation £4. Daily 10am–5pm. Tube: London Bridge.

Tate Modern ★★★ ART MUSEUM
Welcoming more than four million visitors a year, Tate Modern is the world's most popular modern art museum (the free admission helps), and one of the capital's very best attractions. From the day it

opened in 2000, the Tate Modern has received almost as many plaudits for its setting as for its contents. It's housed in a converted 1940s' brick power station, the brooding industrial functionalism of the architecture providing a fitting setting for the often challenging art within. Through the main entrance you enter a vast space, the **Turbine Hall,** where a succession of giant temporary exhibitions are staged—the bigger and more ambitious, the better.

The permanent collection forms a great body of modern art dating from 1900 to the present. Spread over levels 3 and 5, it covers all the big-hitters, including Matisse, Rothko, Pollock, Picasso, Dali, Duchamp, and Warhol. The major movements of the past 100 years—surrealism, minimalism, cubism, abstract expressionism, pop art, and so on—are explored in themed areas called things like "Poetry and Dream" and "States of Flux" which have been designed to highlight the links and relationships between movements and artists. The other floors are given over to temporary exhibitions, for which charges usually apply. Further explanation—always useful where modern art is concerned—is provided by the free 45-minute guided tours of the collection given daily at 11am, noon, 2pm, and 3pm. Audio guides are also available for £3.50 or, if you want to be super-modern, it's even possible to download an explanatory app to your smart phone while at the museum. Tate Modern stays open late on Friday and Saturday, when events, such as concerts and talks, are often put on.

Such has been the Tate Modern's success that a new extension has been built, which should be complete by the time this guide hits the shelves. Taking the form of an asymmetrical pyramid, it's been built using the same type of bricks

LEFT: **Turbine Hall, Tate Modern;** RIGHT: **Tate to Tate boat on the Thames.**

as the original building, making it look as if the power station has simply sprouted a new, angular growth. It will contain a host of new art spaces, some occupying the massive underground oil tanks that once powered the station's turbines.

If this is your day for getting your fill of art, note that you can also visit the Tate Modern's sister, Tate Britain (p. 126), just upriver, by taking the dedicated **Tate to Tate boat** (✆ **020/7887-8888**) from the pier outside. Appropriately enough, the boat's spotted livery was designed by Damien Hirst, aging *enfant terrible* of the London modern art scene. The service takes 20 minutes, and runs every 20 minutes during opening times, stopping en route at the London Eye. Tickets cost £5 adults, £2.50 for children under 16.

Bankside, SE1. www.tate.org.uk/modern. ✆ **020/7887-8888.** Free admission. Sun–Thurs 10am–6pm; Fri–Sat 10am–10pm. Tube: Southwark or London Bridge.

Winston Churchill's Britain at War Experience ☺ MUSEUM   The "Churchill" branding is a bit of a misnomer designed to give the museum name recognition among tourists. The focus of the museum is not great statesmen, or even soldiers, but the ordinary people of London and how they coped during the World War II Blitz, when German bombs rained down on their city night after night. You enter at street level, before descending in a lift down to a replica Underground station, where thousands would gather as darkness fell and the aerial onslaught began.

There's plenty of original World War II material on display, including ration books, documents, sound recordings, and even bombs. Children are particularly well catered for (it's a popular school outing) with worksheets and activity packs, and they have the opportunity to dress up in period costume, complete with gas masks, tin helmets, and ARP (Air Raid Patrol) uniforms. The display finishes with a walk through a replica bombed-out street, as sirens wail and flashlights criss-cross overhead.

64–66 Tooley St., SE1. www.britainatwar.co.uk. ✆ **020/7403-3171.** Admission £12.95 adults, £6.50 seniors and students, £5.50 children 5–15, free for children 4 and under. Apr–Oct daily 10am–5pm; Nov–Mar daily 10am–4:30pm. Tube: London Bridge.

THE CITY

The City is the ancient core of London, where the original Roman settlement was founded nearly 2,000 years ago, and where many great historic structures—including the Tower of London and St. Paul's Cathedral—still stand. However, its status as the U.K.'s financial capital means that it also has London's fastest changing skyline. After all, money has no sentiment or yearning for tradition, and if profit dictates that something old should be torn down and replaced with something new, then all too often that's what happens. Current building trends are very much in an upward direction. The skyscrapers 30 St. Mary Axe (better known as "the Gherkin") and the Heron Tower (currently the City's tallest building) were erected in the past decade, and are to be joined by some even taller companions in the next few years, each with its own ready-made nickname—the "Cheesegrater," the "Helter Skelter," the "Walkie Talkie," and others. You can explore 2,000 years of the City's history at the excellent Museum of London, and find out about the influence of money on the region at the Bank of England Museum.

Bank of England Museum ☺ MUSEUM   This surprisingly arresting look at the history of the Bank of England, banking, and the rise (and several falls) of high finance is located next to the "Old Lady of Threadneedle Street" herself. The displays run broadly chronologically, taking you from the days of handwritten receipts to the computerized mysteries of modern banking. En route, you'll pass a reconstruction of an old stock office as it would have looked in the days of Sir John Soane, the bank's original architect (all that survives of his design is the curtain wall surrounding the site), a colorful assortment of historic banknotes, and the highlight, a solid gold bar worth an estimated £250,000, which you can pick up through a hole in the display case. Alas, no matter how you wiggle it, you won't be able to get it out.

Threadneedle St., EC2. www.bankofengland.co.uk/education/museum. ✆ **020/7601-5545.** Free admission. Mon–Fri 10am–5pm. Tube: Bank.

Guildhall & Guildhall Art Gallery ★ HISTORIC SITE/MUSEUM/ART MUSEUM   The headquarters of the City of London Corporation, the administrative body that has overseen the City's affairs for the past 800 years, the Guildhall's original medieval framework has endured significant repairs following the 1666 Great Fire and World War II (as well as the addition of a rather incongruous concrete wing in the 1970s). Today its Great Hall has a touch of the medieval theme park about it, filled with colorful livery banners and with a (reconstructed) minstrel's gallery from where 3m (9-ft.) statues of mythical giants Gog and Magog gaze down.

East across Guildhall Yard, the **Guildhall Art Gallery** displays a constantly updated selection from the Corporation's 4,000-plus works relating to the capital. The main attraction (there's certainly no missing it) is John Singleton Copley's *The Defeat of the Floating Batteries at Gibraltar, September 1782*, which at 42.5 sq. m (458 sq. ft.) is Britain's largest single oil painting, and takes up two whole stories. Fridays are the best time to visit, when you can join a free tour of the collection at 12:15, 1:15, 2:15, and 3:15pm.

The complex also contains the one-room **Clockmakers' Museum** (www.clockmakers.org), filled with tick-tocking timepieces from throughout history, including John Harrison's 18th-century H5 marine chronometer (the "longitude" clock), the world's first electric clock, and the watch worn by Edmund Hillary on his 1953 ascent of Everest.

Stained-glass window in the Guildhall.

Head down beneath the art museum to visit the scant remains of **London's Roman amphitheater,** which dates from the 2nd century a.d. but remained undiscovered until 1988 (and didn't go on display until 2003). Images of spectators and missing bits have been added to give visitors a better idea of what it once looked like.

Guildhall Yard, Gresham St., EC2. www.guildhallartgallery.cityoflondon.gov.uk/GAG/. ℂ **020/ 7332-3700.** Free admission. Mon–Sat 10am–5pm; Sun noon–4pm. Tube: Bank, St. Paul's, or Moorgate.

The Monument ★ ☺ MONUMENT/MEMORIAL It's hardly a giant by modern standards, and indeed is these days rather obscured by the mid-sized buildings surrounding it, but at 61.5m (9,202 ft.) this is still the world's tallest free-standing column—a boast that probably has more to do with changing building materials than anything else. Designed by Sir Christopher Wren, it was erected in the 1670s to commemorate London's revival following the Great Fire of 1666 (p. 25); hence the golden fiery orb at its top.

You can climb 311 steps to the summit, from where the views are among the finest in the City. Apparently, if the Monument fell over, it would, providing it fell in the right direction, land on the exact spot in Pudding Lane where the Great Fire started.

Fish Street Hill, EC3. www.themonument.info. ℂ **020/7626-2717.** Admission £3 adults, £2 seniors and students, £1 children. Daily 9:30am–5:30pm. Tube: Monument or London Bridge.

Museum of London ★★ ☺ MUSEUM Although the location is rather grim, in the center of a rather unappealing roundabout in London's Barbican district, this museum is an absolute joy, particularly since its recent revamp. Its previous incarnation, though fascinating, was a little stodgy and sedate. A thorough overhaul, however, has added plenty of bells and whistles in the form of videos, touch-screen technology, and audio and lighting effects making it a much more interactive experience. You now get a real sense of the drama of London's story unfolding.

 A Money-Saving Pass

The **London Pass** provides admission to more than 55 attractions in and around London, "timed" admission at some attractions (bypassing the line ups), plus free travel on public transport (buses, Tubes, and trains) and a pocket guidebook. It costs £44 for 1 day, £59 for 2 days, £72 for 3 days, and £95 for 6 days (children aged 5 to 15 pay £29, £44, £49, or £68, respectively), and includes admission to St. Paul's Cathedral, HMS *Belfast*, the Jewish Museum, and the Thames Barrier Visitor Centre—and many other attractions.

This rather pricey pass is useful if you're trying to cram 2 days' worth of sightseeing into a single day. But if you're a slow-moving visitor, who likes to stop and smell the roses, you may not get your money's worth. You can use this guide to calculate whether the London Pass is a good deal for you. It's valid for 12 months, and is also available without the transportation package. Visit the website at www.londonpass.com.

Exhibits in the Museum of London.

Exhibits are arranged so that you can take a chronological stroll through 250,000 years of the capital's history. Upstairs you'll find sections devoted to "London before London" (with flint arrow heads, prehistoric animal skulls, and Bronze- and Iron-Age weapons); Roman London (mosaics, statues, and scale models of the contemporary city); Medieval London (Viking battleaxes and knights' armor); and War, Plague, and Fire (models of Shakespeare's Rose Theatre and the Great Fire, and Cromwell's death mask). The even more whizzy downstairs exhibition spaces bring the story up to date with displays on the "Expanding City: 1666–1850" (including a re-created 18th-century prison cell and a 240-year-old printing press); "People's City: 1850s–1940s" (walk a replica Victorian shopping street); "World City: 1950s–Today" (explore an interactive model of the Thames); and the "City Gallery" where resides the **Lord Mayor's Coach,** a gilt-and-scarlet fairytale carriage built in 1757, weighing in at 3 tons (6,720lbs), which is pulled through the streets each November as part of the Lord Mayor's Show (p. 48).

London Wall, EC2. www.museumoflondon.org.uk. ☏ **020/7001-9844.** Free admission. Daily 10am–6pm. Tube: St. Paul's or Barbican.

St. Paul's Cathedral ★★★ ☺ CATHEDRAL London's skyline has changed dramatically during the past 3 centuries. Buildings have come and gone, architectural styles have waxed and waned, but throughout there has been one constant—the great plump dome of St. Paul's Cathedral gazing beatifically down upon the city. Despite the best intentions of the Luftwaffe and modern skyscraper designers (and honorable mention must go to "the Gherkin"), Sir Christopher Wren's masterpiece is still the defining landmark of the City skyline.

The interior is a neck-craningly large space where the eye is instantly drawn upward to the colorful ceiling, decorated with intricate mosaics of biblical scenes. They were installed in the late 19th century on the orders of Queen Victoria, who

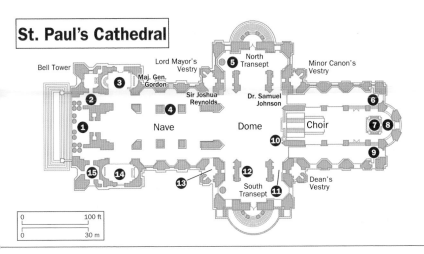

St. Paul's Cathedral

Bell Tower

Lord Mayor's Vestry

Maj. Gen. Gordon

Sir Joshua Reynolds

North Transept

Minor Canon's Vestry

Dr. Samuel Johnson

Nave

Dome

Choir

Pulpit

South Transept

Dean's Vestry

Nelson Monument

0   100 ft
0   30 m

All Souls' Chapel **2**	High Altar **7**
American Memorial Chapter **8**	Lady Chapel **9**
Anglican Martyr's Chapel **6**	Nelson Monument **12**
Chapel of St. Michael & St. George **14**	Pulpit **10**
Dean's Staircase **15**	St. Dunstan's Chapel **3**
Entrance to Crypt (Wren's grave) **11**	Staircase to Library, Whispering Gallery & Dome **13**
Font **5**	Wellington Monument **4**
	West Doorway **1**

thought the cathedral's previously rather dowdy interior needed brightening up. Dotted around at ground level are tombs and memorials to various British heroes, including the Duke of Wellington, Lawrence of Arabia, and in the South Quire Aisle, an effigy of John Donne, one of the country's most celebrated poets and a former dean of St. Paul's. It's one of the few items to have survived from the previous, medieval cathedral, which was destroyed by the Great Fire in 1666; you can still see scorch marks on its base.

The cathedral offers some of the capital's best views, although you'll have to earn them by undertaking a more than 500-step climb up to the Golden Gallery. Here you can enjoy giddying panoramas of the capital, as well as perhaps equally stomach-tightening views down to the floor 111m (364 ft.) below.

Down in the crypt is a bumper crop of memorials, including those of Alexander Fleming, Admiral Lord Nelson, William Blake, and Wren himself—the epitaph on his simple tombstone reads: "Reader, if you seek a monument, look around you."

St. Paul's Churchyard, EC4. www.stpauls.co.uk. ☏ **020/7246-8350.** Cathedral and galleries £14.50 adults, £13.50 seniors and students, £5.50 children 6–18, £34.50 family ticket, free for children 5 and under. Cathedral (excluding galleries) Mon–Sat 8:30am–4pm; galleries Mon–Sat 9:30am–4pm. No sightseeing Sun (services only). Tube: St. Paul's.

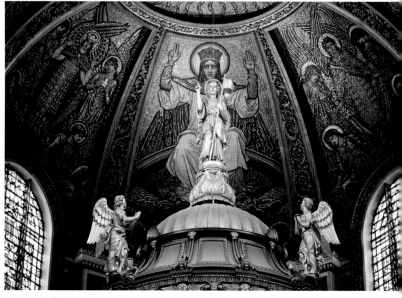

St. Paul's Cathedral.

Samuel Johnson's House ★ HISTORIC HOME   Poet, lexicographer, critic, biographer, and above all, quotation machine, Dr. Samuel Johnson lived in this Queen Anne house between 1748 and 1759. It was here that he compiled his famous dictionary—not as is commonly supposed the first of the English language, but certainly the most influential to that date. His house has been painstakingly restored to its mid-18th-century prime and is well worth a visit. Guided walks taking in many of the local sites associated with Johnson's life, including

Legal London

The bustling former London borough of **Holborn** (*Ho*-burn) is often referred to as "Legal London." It's home to the majority of the city's barristers, solicitors, and law clerks, as well as the ancient **Inns of Court** (Tube: Holborn or Chancery Lane), the beautiful complexes where barristers have their chambers and law students perform their apprenticeships. All barristers (litigators) must belong to one of these institutions: **Gray's Inn,** High Holborn, WC1 (☎ **020/7458-7800**), **Lincoln's Inn** (the best preserved), Serle St., WC2 (☎ **020/7405-1393**), or just over the line inside the City, the **Middle Temple,**

Middle Temple Lane, EC4 (☎ **020/7427-4800**) and **Inner Temple,** Crown Office Row, EC4 (☎ **020/7797-8250**). The Inns' grand interiors can only be visited by prior appointment, but their peaceful gardens and "magnificent ample squares," as Charles Lamb put it in the 19th century, are open to the public, and free. It's well worth wandering the cobbled archaic precincts admiring the various Gothic and Tudor buildings. In the grounds of Inner Temple, look out for the atmospheric, 12th-century **Temple Church,** with its unusual circular nave (see "Saints and the City: A Walk," below).

Temple Bar and Fleet Street, take place on the first Wednesday of the month, leaving from the entrance of the house at 3pm. They cost £5 and no booking is required.

17 Gough Sq., EC4. ☏ **020/7353-3745.** www.drjohnsonshouse.org. Admission £4.50 adults, £3.50 students and seniors, £1.50 children, £10 family ticket, free for children 10 and under. Oct–Apr Mon–Sat 11am–5pm; May–Sept Mon–Sat 11am–5:30pm. Tube: Chancery Lane.

Tower Bridge Exhibition ★ ☺ HISTORIC SITE   Despite its aged appearance, with its great fairytale turrets, London's iconic bridge isn't all that old. It was built in 1894 in a carefully contrived medieval style, so as to be in keeping with the nearby Tower of London. And you won't be surprised to hear that what is today a beloved and iconic monument was—as is so often the case—pretty unpopular when first unveiled.

It's a low bridge equipped with two mighty 1,000-tonne (1,100 U.S.-ton) decks, technically known as bascules, which raise to let ships pass below. This happens around 900 times year. A board next to the bridge announces the time of the next opening and you can also find out on the website.

Now electric, the bridge's lifting mechanism was once powered by hulking great steam hydraulic machinery, which you can view at the bridge's on-site museum, the Tower Bridge Exhibition. This also has a display on the history of the bridge and best of all, provides access to the west walkway along the top of the bridge, providing views up and down the Thames.

Tower Bridge, SE1. www.towerbridge.org.uk. ☏ **020/7403-3761.** Admission £8 adults, £5.60 students and seniors, £3.40 children 5–15, £12.50 family ticket, free for children 4 and under. Apr–Sept daily 10am–6:30pm (last admission 5:30pm); Mar–Apr 9:30am–6pm (last admission 5pm). Tube: London Bridge or Tower Hill/DLR: Tower Gateway.

Tower Bridge.

Tower of London ★★★ ☺ CASTLE   On a sunny summer afternoon, the Tower, one of the best-preserved medieval castles in the world, can be a cheerful buzzing place, filled with happy swarms of tourists being entertained by costumed actors and historically themed events. At such times it can be easy to forget that beneath all the kitschy tourist trappings lies a very real castle with a very brutal and bloody history.

The Tower is actually a compound of structures built at various times for varying purposes. The oldest part is the **White Tower,** begun by William the Conqueror in 1078 to keep London's native Saxon population in check. Later rulers added towers, walls, and fortified gates, until the buildings became like a small town within a city. Although it began life as a stronghold against rebellion, the tower's main role eventually became less about keeping people out, than making sure whoever was inside couldn't escape. It became the favored prison and execution site for anyone who displeased the monarch. Notable prisoners served their last meals here include the "princes in the tower," Lady Jane Grey, and Anne Boleyn, one of several unfortunates who thought that marrying that most unforgiving of monarchs, Henry VIII, was a good idea. A plaque on Tower Green marks the spot where they met their grisly ends.

Displays on some of the Tower's captives can be seen in the **Bloody Tower,** including a reconstruction of the study of Sir Walter Raleigh, the great Elizabethan adventurer who is generally credited with having introduced tobacco-smoking to England. A favorite of Elizabeth I, he was executed by James I, a fervent anti-smoker, having spent 13 years as a prisoner here.

Tower of London.

Royal Armory.

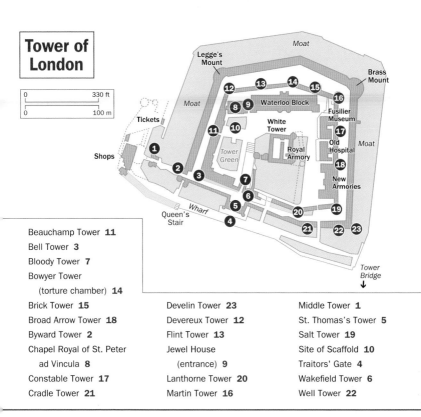

Tower of London

Beauchamp Tower **11**	Develin Tower **23**	Middle Tower **1**
Bell Tower **3**	Devereux Tower **12**	St. Thomas's Tower **5**
Bloody Tower **7**	Flint Tower **13**	Salt Tower **19**
Bowyer Tower (torture chamber) **14**	Jewel House (entrance) **9**	Site of Scaffold **10**
Brick Tower **15**	Lanthorne Tower **20**	Traitors' Gate **4**
Broad Arrow Tower **18**	Martin Tower **16**	Wakefield Tower **6**
Byward Tower **2**		Well Tower **22**
Chapel Royal of St. Peter ad Vincula **8**		
Constable Tower **17**		
Cradle Tower **21**		

In addition to being a prison, the Tower has also been used as a royal palace, a mint, and an armory. Today, however, it's perhaps best known as the keeper of the **Crown Jewels,** the main ceremonial regalia of the British Monarch, which—when not being used—are displayed in the tower's **Jewel House.** It's probably best to tackle this soon after your arrival, as the line ups seem to build exponentially over the course of the day. You hop aboard a travelator for a slow glide past some of the Queen's top trinkets, including the Imperial State Crown (as modeled each year at the State Opening of Parliament), which looks like a child's fantasy of a piece of royal headwear, set with no fewer than 3,000 jewels, including the fourth-largest diamond in the world.

After the jewels, the tower's next most popular draw is probably the **Royal Armory** in the White Tower at the center of the complex where you can see various fearsome-looking weapons, including swords, halberds, and morning stars, as well as bespoke suits of armor made for kings.

 Tower Tips

Tickets are cheaper if booked online: £17 for adults, £9 for children. If buying your ticket at the venue, pick them up at the kiosk at Tower Hill Tube station before emerging above ground—the lines should be shorter. Even so, choose a day other than Sunday—crowds are at their worst then—and arrive as early as you can in the morning, or late in the afternoon.

SAINTS & THE city: A WALK

For somewhere so unashamedly dedicated to Mammon, the financial center of London also offers plenty of spiritual comfort (which no doubt comes in handy when stocks start tumbling). Our favorite historic churches and nearby attractions can be comfortably toured in a day—or an afternoon, if you're quick.

Temple Church ★ CHURCH This "round church" can be reached from the Strand by heading through the arched doorway just to the right of **Prince Henry's Room** at no. 17, one of London's only surviving houses to pre-date the Great Fire of London. The church was built in the late 12th century by the **Knights Templar,** a powerful religious military order during the time of the Crusades. Much restored and rebuilt in subsequent centuries, it has enjoyed a resurgence of interest since being featured in *The Da Vinci Code*. King's Bench Walk, EC4. www.temple church.com. Ⓒ **020/7353-3470.** Admission £3 adults, free to seniors and anyone under 21. Mon, Tues, Thurs & Fri 11am–1pm & 2–4pm, Wed 2–4pm.

St. Bride's CHURCH Founded back in the 6th century, this may be the the city's oldest church (though there are other contenders, see below). The original wooden Saxon church was succeeded by a series of ever grander medieval versions, the last of which was razed to the ground by the Great Fire of London. Rebuilt by Sir Christopher Wren, its distinctive multi-step spire was said to have inspired the design of modern wedding cakes. It's known as the

"Journalists' Church," owing to its proximity to Fleet Street, the old home of the British Press. It lies just off Fleet Street and is rather hemmed in by the surrounding buildings, like a ship trapped in Arctic ice. Fleet St., EC4. www.stbrides.com. Ⓒ **020/7427-0133.** Free admission. Mon–Fri 8am–6pm, Sat 11am–3pm, Sun 10am–1pm & 5–7.30pm.

St. Bartholomew's Museum ★ MUSEUM "Barts" hospital, as it's commonly known, has a small museum of medical curiosities mostly dating from the grim, grit-your-teeth-and-bear-it days before anesthetic and antiseptic. Guided tours of the collection are given at 2pm on Fridays (£5). Outside the entrance, on West Smithfield, note the plaque commemorating **William Wallace** and, across the square, the arches of **Smithfield Market,** the city's great cathedral of meat. North Wing, West Smithfield, EC1. www.bartsandthelondon.nhs.uk. Ⓒ **020/3465-5798.** Free admission. Tues–Fri 10am–4pm.

St. Bartholomew-the-Great ★ CHURCH You enter the 12th-century church of St. Bartholomew-the-Great by

The tower also boasts the only surviving **medieval palace** in Britain, dating back to the 1200s. Comprising St. Thomas's Tower, Wakefield Tower, and Lanthorne Tower, it stands in the riverside wall above **Traitors' Gate,** through which prisoners were brought to the Tower. Within are reconstructed bedrooms, a throne room, and chapel. The tower's latest attraction, the **Fusilier Museum,** tells the story of the Royal Fusiliers, a British army regiment founded at the tower back in 1685.

Be sure to take advantage of the free hour-long tours offered by the iconic guards, the Yeoman Warders—more commonly known as **Beefeaters.** They'll regale you with tales of royal intrigue, and introduce you to the Tower's most passing through a 13th-century gate topped by a 15th-century half-timbered building. Begun in 1123, the church is one of the few examples of large scale Norman architecture left in the city, although the interior is largely Elizabethan.

6–9 Kinghorn St., EC1. www.greatst barts.com. ☎ **020/7606-5171**. Admission £4 adults, children 17 and under £3.50. Mon–Fri 8:30am–5pm, Sat 10.30am–4pm, Sun 8.30am–8pm.

Postman's Park ★ PARK/GARDEN

A tiny refuge of greenery amid all the glass and concrete of the City, this small park boasts one of capital's most curious, and most curiously affecting, memorials—a wall lined with Art Nouveau-style tiles commemorating doomed acts of public bravery.

King Edward St., EC1. Free admission. Daily 8am–dusk.

St. Mary-le-Bow ★ CHURCH

It's said that a true Cockney must be born within range of the sound of this church's famous bells, which is why it's also known as the "Cockney Church." First erected around 1,000 years ago, it was rebuilt by Sir Christopher Wren following the Great Fire and again, in the style of Wren, after World War II. Cheapside, EC2. www.stmarylebow. co.uk. ☎ **020/7248-5139**. Free admission. Mon–Fri 6.30am–6pm.

All-Hallows-by-the-Tower ★

CHURCH Just down the road from, and providing elevated views over, the Tower of London this is another contender for the title of the oldest church in London. When the first church was built here in the 7th century, the site had already been in use for several centuries. You can see Roman, Saxon, and medieval remains at its small crypt museum.

Byward St., EC3. www.allhallowsbythe tower.org.uk. ☎ **020/7481-2928**. Free admission. Mon–Fri 10am–5.30pm, Sat 10am–5pm, Sun 1pm–5pm.

famous residents, the six ravens who live on Tower Gardens. According to legend, if the ravens ever leave the Tower, the monarchy will fall—the birds' wings are kept clipped, just to make sure. The tours take place every half-hour from 9:30am until 3:30pm in summer (2:30pm in winter) and leave from the Middle Tower near the entrance.

Tower Hill, EC3. www.hrp.org.uk/TowerOfLondon. ☎ **0844/482-7777**. Admission £19.80 adults, £17.05 students and seniors, £10.45 children aged 5–15, £55 family ticket, free for children 4 and under. Mar–Oct Tues–Sat 9am–5:30pm, Sun–Mon 10am–5:30pm; Nov–Feb Tues–Sat 9am–4:30pm, Sun–Mon 10am–4:30pm. Tube: Tower Hill/DLR: Tower Gateway.

EAST LONDON

East London has been reinventing itself for as long as anyone can remember: The 1950s saw the erection of the area's defining tower blocks to replace the housing lost to Hitler's bombs; the 1980s and '90s witnessed the wholesale revamp of Docklands following the closure of the Central London Docks; the 2000s have seen pockets of gentrification emerge amid the deprived estates, particularly in Hoxton and Shoreditch, where thriving arts and music scenes have taken off. The latest chapter of renewal was kickstarted by the awarding of the Olympic and Paralympic Games to London in 2012, which has resulted in a great swathe of industrial Stratford being cleared away to make room for a multitude of sporting venues (for more on the future of the Olympic Site, see p. 74).

Perhaps as a result of all this change, many of the museums here have a nostalgic tone, celebrating a variety of lost worlds, including toys at the V&A Museum of Childhood, medicine at the Royal Hospital Museum, domestic life at the Geffrye Museum and Dennis Severs' House, and the docks themselves at the Museum of London Docklands. Only the Whitechapel Art Gallery seems completely of the moment, promoting all that is most "now" in the world of art.

Dennis Severs' House ★ MUSEUM   The Californian Dennis Severs spent 2 decades, between 1979 and his death in 1999, turning his rather dilapidated home next to Spitalfields Market into a replica of a grand, early 18th-century town house. He kitted out each of its ten rooms—cellar, eating parlor, smoking room, and so on—with furniture and decorations appropriate to the period, and even created a back story for the house as the refuge for the fictional Jervises, a family of Huguenots who had fled persecution in France. The rooms have been arranged as if they have just been vacated by their previous occupants, with items carelessly strewn about and food left uncleared, creating what Severs called "snapshots of life." The result is fascinatingly odd, and even a bit pretentious in places. But you do get a real sense of the intensity of Severs' vision in these rooms, which provide an artificial glimpse of an imagined past every bit as compelling as the real thing.

18 Folgate St., E1. www.dennissevershouse.co.uk. © **020/7247-4013.** Admission £10 per person Sunday, £7 per person Monday. Sun noon–4pm; 1st and 3rd Mon of month noon–2pm; closed bank holiday Mon. Tube: Liverpool St./Overground: Shoreditch High St.

Geffrye Museum ★ MUSEUM   For an insight into how Britain's domestic interiors have developed over the past 4 centuries, head to this museum housed in a set of restored 18th-century almshouses. It consists of 11 chronologically arranged period rooms where you can follow the changing tastes in furnishings in English middle-class homes over the generations. There are Jacobean, Georgian, and Victorian interiors, as well as 20th-century rooms, where you'll see luxuriant Art Deco styles giving way to the bleak, utilitarian designs that followed World War II, while newer galleries showcase the decor of the later 20th century. Outside, the chronological theme is continued with a series of four period gardens dating from the 17th to the 20th centuries. The Geffrye is especially charming around Christmas, when each room is dressed in authentic festive style, while from April to October you can visit the herb garden.

136 Kingsland Rd., E2. www.geffrye-museum.org.uk. © **020/7739-9893.** Free admission to period rooms; £2.50 to Almshouses (free for children 15 and under). Tues–Sat 10am–5pm; Sun and bank holidays noon–5pm. Gardens Apr–Oct only. Overground: Hoxton.

A living room in 1935 at the Geffrye Museum.

Museum of London Docklands ★ ☺ MUSEUM   This East London out-post of the Museum of London looks at the history of the capital's river, and in particular the growth and demise of the trading industry that once flourished upon it. Housed in a relic of that industry, a Georgian sugar warehouse, the museum tells the story of the docks from the beginnings of river commerce under the Romans through the glory days of Empire, when London was the world's busiest port, to the closure of the central London docks in the 1970s. It also takes a look at the subsequent regeneration of the area, of which this museum forms a part. The displays focus on both local social aspects—you can walk through "Sailortown," a reconstructed Victorian community—and the global implications of London's rise as a major trading city. The more unsavory aspects of the subject are examined in "London: Sugar and Slavery," and there's also a dedicated hands-on children's section by the entrance, "Mudlarks." Various London-themed family events, many of them free, are staged during the school holidays.

West India Quay, E14. www.museumindocklands.org.uk. ✆ **020/7001-9844.** Free admission. Daily 10am–6pm. Tube: Canary Wharf/DLR: West India Quay.

Ragged School Museum ☺ MUSEUM   "Ragged schools" was the collo-quial name for the free schools that sprang up in London during the 19th century aimed at providing the capital's growing band of destitute children with a basic education—not to mention food and clothes. The name derives from the often unkempt appearance of the children. This was the largest of these schools, opened in 1877 by Dr. Barnardo, the Irish philanthropist who would go on to found more than 100 institutions for homeless children throughout the U.K. Saved from demolition in the 1980s, the building now holds displays on the cul-tural history of the East End and tells the story of these ragged schools. The

**East London
Attractions**

Dennis Severs' House **2**
Geffrye Museum **1**
Museum of London Docklands **8**
Ragged School Museum **7**
Royal London Hospital Museum **4**
Thames Barrier Visitor Centre **9**
V&A Museum of Childhood **5**
Victoria Park **6**
Whitechapel Art Gallery **3**

0   1/2 mi
0   1/2 km

Hackney
Downs

Downs Park Rd.

Pembury Rd.

Hackney
Downs

Dalston Lane

Hackney
Central

Dalston
Kingsland

Dalston Ln.

Graham Rd.

Balls Pond Rd.

KINGSLAND

HACKNEY

Rd.

Richmond Rd.

London
Fields

London
Fields

Englefield Rd.

DALSTON

Mapledene Rd.

Lansdowne Dr.

Mare St.

Well St.

Northchurch
Rd.

Stoke Newington Rd.

Middleton Rd.

Albion Rd.

Essex Rd.

**DE BEAUVOIR
TOWN**

Downham Rd.

Queensbridge Rd.

Brownlow Rd.

Mare St.

New North Rd.

Shepperton
Rd.

St. Paul St.

Lee St.

Pownall Rd.

St. Paul St.

Grand Union Canal

Whiston Rd.

HAGGERSTON

Cambridge Heath Rd.

New North Rd.

Crowley St.

Ply
Park

Pitfield St.

Hoxton St.

Kingsland Rd.

Haggerston
Park

Hackney Rd.

Cambridge
Heath

5

Wharf Rd.

Shepherdess Walk

HOXTON

Geffyre Museum
1

Hackney Rd.

Old Bethnal Green Rd.

**V&A Museum of
Childhood**

City Rd.

NORTHERN

East Rd.

Columbia Rd.

Bethnal Green Rd.

Bethnal
Green

Lever St.

City Rd.

SHOREDITCH

Old St.

Shoreditch

Weaver's
Fields

**BETHNAL
GREEN**

Cambridge Heath Rd.

CENTRAL

Bethnal
Green

Old St.

Great Eastern St.

Bethnal Green Rd.

Old St.

Leonard St.

St. Paul St.

Sclater St.

**ST.
LUKE'S**

Whitecross St.

Bunhill Row

City Road

Worship St.

Appold St.

Sun St.

Quaker St.

Shoreditch

**TOWER
HAMLETS**

Mile End Rd.

Farm St.

Chiswell St.

**Dennis Severs'
House**
2

Hanbury St.

Whitechapel

Sidney St.

**The Barbican
Centre**

CIRCLE, HAMMERSMITH, METROPOLITAN

Moorgate

NORTHERN

**Liverpool St.
Station**

Lamb St.

Brushfield St.

Brick Lane

Old Montague St.

Whitechapel Rd.

**Royal London
Hospital Museum**
4

Barbican

London Wall

Moorgate

Liverpool
Street

Middlesex St.

Commercial St.

Bishopsgate

3

**Whitechapel
Art Gallery**

New Rd.

CENTRAL

Coleman St.

Houndsditch

Camomile

Aldgate East

Commercial Rd.

Cannon St. Rd.

EAST LONDON

St. Paul's

Cheapside

**Bank of
England**

Old Broad St.

Whitechapel High St.

Braham St.

Aldgate

Alie St.

WHITECHAPEL

**THE
CITY**

Bank

Threadneedle St.

Leadenhall St.

Whitechapel High St.

Leman St.

Prescot St.

Shadwell

DLR

Shadwell

**St. Paul's
Cathedral**

Mansion
House

King William St.

Gracechurch St.

Fenchurch
Station

Mansell St.

Cable St.

DLR

Queen Victoria St.

Cannon St.

Fenchurch St.

Pepys St.

Royal Mint St.

SHADWELL

Upper Thames St.

Cannon St.
Station

Monument

Tower St.

Lower Thames St.

Tower Hill

DLR

Tower Hill

Tower
Gateway

The Highway

Wapping
Woods

Millennium
Bridge

**Bankside
Pier**

Queen St.

Monument

Tower Hill

East Smithfield

**Tate
Modern**

Southwark
Bridge

**Globe
Theatre**

**Tower Millennium
Pier**

London
Bridge

**Tower of
London**

WAPPING

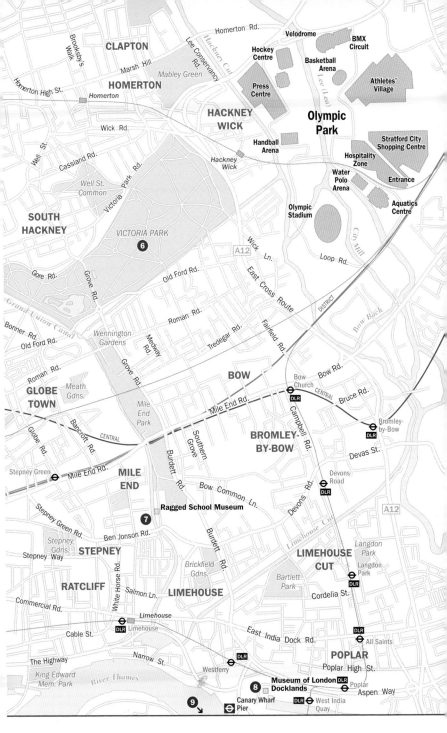

prime exhibit is a replica 1870s classroom where, on the first Sunday of the month, children (and adults) can experience a 45-minute Victorian-style lesson, complete with slate boards, dunces' hats, and plenty of discipline (£2 suggested donation at 2:15pm and 3:30pm). Free themed activities, such as Victorian parlor games, are laid on every Wednesday and Thursday during the school holidays.

46–50 Copperfield Rd., E1. www.raggedschoolmuseum.org.uk. ✆ **020/8980-6405.** Free admission. Wed–Thurs 10am–5pm, first Sun of month 2–5pm. Tube: Mile End.

Royal London Hospital Museum 🎁 MUSEUM

The "London," as it's known locally, has been regarded as one of the city's finest hospitals since its foundation in the 18th century. Its most famous resident was probably Joseph Merrick, better known as the **"Elephant Man,"** who spent his last few years here, having finally left the Victorian freak shows that he called home for much of his life. He died in 1890, aged just 27. Merrick's story—as told in a 20-minute video and illustrated with some of his personal items, including his hat and veil—forms the centerpiece of the hospital's museum, located in its former crypt. Other displays trace the history of the hospital and the development of medicine in general, from the gore-spattered surgery of centuries past to today's world of forensic care.

Royal London Hospital, St. Augustine with St. Philip's Church, Newark St., E1. www.bartsandthelondon.nhs.uk/about-us/museums-and-archives/the-royal-london-museum/. ✆ **020/7377-7608.** Free admission. Tues–Fri 10am–4:30pm. Tube: Whitechapel/Overground: Whitechapel.

Thames Barrier Visitor Centre ☺ ARCHITECTURE

One of the capital's great pieces of modern engineering, the Thames Barrier is the city's primary defense against tidal flooding and comprises ten 20m (66-ft.) steel-and-concrete gates. These can be raised to block the 520m (1706-ft.) span of the river in just 10 minutes. Most of the time you can't see the gates themselves, which rest on

Thames Barrier Park.

V&A Museum of Childhood.

the riverbed, but the piers that raise and lower them are always visible, strung across the river like a row of giant space helmets. At the visitor center you can discover the history of the Barrier's construction and, if you're lucky, perhaps watch a test raise being performed.

Insider's tip: On the north bank of the Thames, opposite the visitor center, next to the barrier, is the 8.8-hectare (22-acre) **Thames Barrier Park.** Established in 2000, it's a very modern open space, scattered with angular hedges and dancing fountains. There's also a riverside promenade and a children's playground. It's open from sunrise to sunset, and is a 5-minute walk from Pontoon Dock DLR station.

Unity Way, Woolwich, SE18. www.environment-agency.gov.uk. © **020/8305-4188.** Admission £3.50 adults, £3 seniors and students, £2 children 5–15, free for children 4 and under. Thurs–Sun and bank holiday Mon 10.30am–5pm. Rail: Woolwich Dockyard.

V&A Museum of Childhood ★★ ☺ MUSEUM A branch of the Victoria and Albert Museum, the U.K.'s national collection of objects relating to childhood is made up of thousands of items dating from the 1600s to the present day.

All shiny and modern-looking following a recent revamp, the museum is split into three main areas, starting to your right just past the entrance with "Moving Toys." The exhibits here are divided into things that can be moved manually (rocking horses, spinning tops, pedal cars, and so on); those powered with springs and cogs (clockwork toys, jack-in-the-boxes); those with circuits and motors (remote control cars and train sets); and those that create the illusion of movement through special effects (such as magic lanterns, zoetropes, and modern video games). On the same floor is the "Creativity" area, which aims to show how toys help children to use their imaginations with displays of puppets, toy theatres, dolls from all of over the world (Barbie, Russian nesting dolls, North American rag dolls), and construction sets such as Lego and Meccano.

Up on floor 1, "Childhood" looks at aspects of growing up through toys that have been designed to give children a taste of adult life: Toy hospitals, toy tea sets, even toy guns, as well as perhaps the museum's most celebrated exhibit, a display of elaborate dolls houses from throughout the centuries—the oldest dating back to 1673.

Understandably, the museum is extremely child-friendly with various interactive areas punctuating the static displays, and free arts and crafts activities laid on every day from 2 to 4pm. It's perhaps best for children aged up to 12, as there's not a great deal aimed at teens.

Cambridge Heath Rd., E2. www.vam.ac.uk/moc. ℂ **020/8983-5200.** Free admission. Daily 10am–5:45pm. Tube: Bethnal Green.

Victoria Park ☺ PARK/GARDEN   The largest and finest open space in East London, this was, when it opened in 1845, the capital's first public park. Bordered by a couple of canals and divided in two by Grove Road, it covers an area of just under 87 hectares (220 acres) and contains two lakes, a number of formal gardens, sports facilities, and a bandstand. Other notable features include a Grade II-listed 1862 drinking fountain and two arches from the pre-1831 London Bridge—now turned into benches. It plays host to large musical events in summers.

A recent £12 million revamp has prettified the park and seen the addition of a new community centre, a lake island (with linking bridges), and a Chinese pagoda. The park also now forms the central section of the **Jubilee Greenway Walkway,** a route marked out with glass paving slabs in honor of the Queen's Diamond Jubilee, and stretching for exactly 60km (37 miles)—one kilometer for each year of her reign—from Buckingham Palace to the Olympic Park.

Grove Rd., E3. www.towerhamlets.gov.uk/victoriapark. ℂ **020/7364-2494.** Free admission. Daily 6am–dusk. Tube: Mile End/Overground: Hackney Wick or Homerton.

Whitechapel Art Gallery ★★ ART MUSEUM   East London's premier art museum reopened a few years back following the most significant revamp since its foundation in 1901. The incorporation of the former library next door has doubled the museum's space, allowing it to stage twice its usual number of mold-breaking temporary exhibitions. For the Whitechapel is no passive regurgitator of accepted trends. Indeed, throughout its history the museum has often played a leading role in the development of artistic movements. In the 1930s, it hosted Britain's first showing of Picasso's *Guernica,* as part of an exhibition protesting the Spanish Civil War. It then shocked postwar audiences by introducing them to Jackson Pollock's abstracts, and pioneered Pop Art in the 1960s. Expect further revelations in the future. It also offers regular free talks, as well as cheap film screenings and concerts. Check the website for the latest details.

77–82 Whitechapel Rd., E1. www.whitechapelgallery.org. ℂ **020/7522-7888.** Free admission. Tues–Sun 11am–6pm. Tube: Aldgate East.

NORTH & NORTHWEST LONDON

This area begins just north of the West End where, across Marylebone Road, lies one of the capital's finest open spaces, Regent's Park. The park has a timeless appeal with its tidy lawns, elegant flower borders, and wildfowl ponds. Its northern corner is occupied by London Zoo, a sightseeing stalwart for 150 years, which

British Library.

has been significantly remodeled in recent years. To the north of the park the tourist scene revolves around two main hubs. The first is Camden, with its sprawling markets, vibrant music scene, and carefully maintained "alternative" image. However, the Jewish Museum aside, it doesn't have much in the way of specific attractions, being more of a shopping and hanging-out, feeling-the-vibe sort of a place. There's a lot more going on in Hampstead, to the northwest, including a great expanse of heathland that rivals Hyde Park for the title of the capital's greatest open space, as well as a decent gathering of museums and galleries, many dedicated to the assortment of writers and artists who have settled in this enclave of middle-class bohemia over the years.

British Library ★★ ☺ MUSEUM

One of the world's great repositories of books, the British Library receives a copy of every single title published in the U.K., which are stored on 400 miles of shelves. In 1996, the whole lot (14 million books, manuscripts, sound recordings, and other items) was moved from the British Museum to the library's new home in St. Pancras. The current building may be less elegant than its predecessor, but the bright, roomy interior is far more inviting than the rather dull, redbrick exterior suggests. Within are a number of permanent galleries, the highlight being the "Treasures of the British Library," where 200 the library's most precious possessions are displayed, including a copy of *Magna Carta* (1215), a Gutenberg Bible, and the journals of Captain Cook.

96 Euston Rd., NW1. www.bl.uk. ✆ **0843/208-1144.** Free admission. Mon and Wed–Fri 9:30am–6pm; Tues 9:30am–8pm; Sat 9:30am–5pm; Sun and bank holiday Mon 11am–5pm. Tube: King's Cross or Euston.

Burgh House HISTORIC HOME/MUSEUM

This Queen Anne home (1703) in the center of Hampstead village was the residence of the daughter and son-in-law of Rudyard Kipling (who often visited). It now plays host to a busy cultural program with various events organized here throughout the year, including local art exhibitions, talks, and walks, as well as classical concerts and recitals.

When no events are taking place (something of a rarity), the main draw for visitors is the **Hampstead Museum,** which illustrates the local history of the area, focusing in particular on the many artists and writers who have made the area their home over the past 2 centuries. Children's trails are available from the front desk.

161

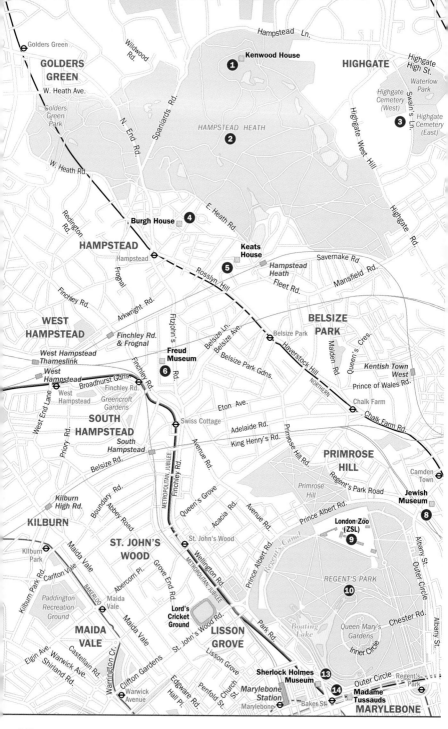

GOLDERS
GREEN

Golders Green

W. Heath Ave.

Golders
Green
Park

Wildwood Rd.

Spaniards Rd.

N. End Rd.

Hampstead Ln.

Kenwood House ①

HAMPSTEAD HEATH

②

HIGHGATE

Highgate High St.

Waterlow Park

Highgate Cemetery (West)

Swain's Ln.

③ Highgate Cemetery (East)

Highgate West Hill

W. Heath Rd.

Redington Rd.

Burgh House ④

HAMPSTEAD

Hampstead

Frognal

Finchley Rd.

Arkwright Rd.

E. Heath Rd.

Rosslyn Hill

Keats House ⑤

Hampstead Heath

Fleet Rd.

Savernake Rd.

Mansfield Rd.

Highgate Rd.

WEST HAMPSTEAD

Finchley Rd. & Frognal

Fitzjohn's Ave.

Belsize Ln.

Belsize Ave.

Belsize Park

BELSIZE PARK

West Hampstead Thameslink

Freud Museum ⑥

Finchley Rd.

Belsize Park Gdns.

Haverstock Hill

Malden Rd.

Queen's Cres.

Kentish Town West

West Hampstead

Broadhurst Gdns.

Greencroft Gardens

Swiss Cottage

Eton Ave.

NORTHERN

Prince of Wales Rd.

Chalk Farm

West End Lane

SOUTH HAMPSTEAD

South Hampstead

Priory Rd.

Belsize Rd.

Adelaide Rd.

King Henry's Rd.

Avenue Rd.

METROPOLITAN JUBILEE

Chalk Farm Rd.

PRIMROSE HILL

Primrose Hill Rd.

Primrose Hill

Regent's Park Road

Camden Town

Jewish Museum ⑧

KILBURN

Kilburn High Rd.

Boundary Rd.

Abbey Road

Finchley Rd.

Queen's Grove

Acacia Rd.

Avenue Rd.

St. John's Wood

Prince Albert Rd.

London Zoo (ZSL) ⑨

Regent's Canal

Albany St.

Outer Circle

Kilburn Park

ST. JOHN'S WOOD

BAKERLOO

Carlton Vale

Maida Vale

Abercorn Pl.

Grove End Rd.

Wellington Rd.

METROPOLITAN JUBILEE

Prince Albert Rd.

REGENT'S PARK

⑩

Paddington Recreation Ground

MAIDA VALE

Maida Vale

Castellain Rd.

Clifton Gardens

Lord's Cricket Ground

St. John's Wood Rd.

LISSON GROVE

Lisson Grove

Park Rd.

Boating Lake

Queen Mary's Gardens

Chester Rd.

Inner Circle

Albany St.

Elgin Ave.

Warwick Ave.

Shirland Rd.

Warwick Avenue

Edgware Rd.

Penfold St.

Church St.

Sherlock Holmes Museum

⑬

Marylebone Station

Baker St.

Marylebone

⑭ Madame Tussauds

MARYLEBONE

Outer Circle

Regent's Park

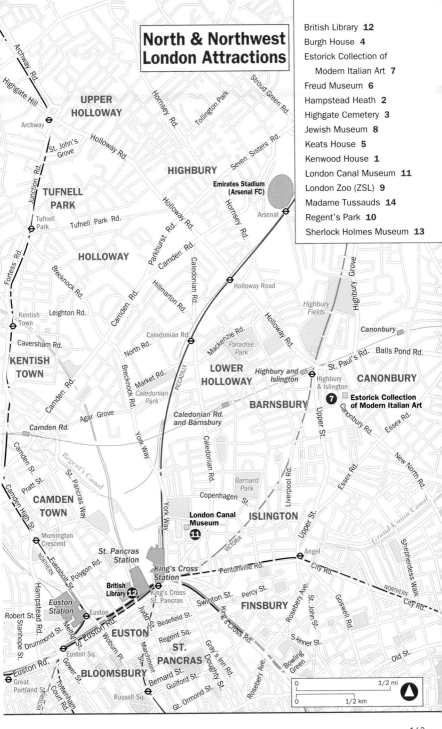

North & Northwest London Attractions

British Library **12**
Burgh House **4**
Estorick Collection of
　Modern Italian Art **7**
Freud Museum **6**
Hampstead Heath **2**
Highgate Cemetery **3**
Jewish Museum **8**
Keats House **5**
Kenwood House **1**
London Canal Museum **11**
London Zoo (ZSL) **9**
Madame Tussauds **14**
Regent's Park **10**
Sherlock Holmes Museum **13**

New End Sq., NW3. www.burghhouse.org.uk. ℰ **020/7431-0144.** Free admission. House and museum Wed–Sun noon–5pm; Sat by appt. Tube: Hampstead.

Estorick Collection of Modern Italian Art 📷 ART MUSEUM   Early 20th-century Italian art is given a rare showcase in this North London Georgian building. The man behind it, Eric Estorick (1913–93), was an American political scientist, writer, and above all, a passionate collector. The year he died, he established a foundation to display his collection. His is one of the finest 20th-century Italian art collections in the world. Powerful images by the main protagonists of the early 20th-century, Italian, avant-garde Futurist movement, including Balla, Boccioni, Carrá, Serverini, and Russolo, are on permanent view, alongside works by figurative artists, such as Modigliani, Sironi, and Campigli.

39a Canonbury Sq., N1. www.estorickcollection.com. ℰ **020/7704-9522.** Admission £5 adults, £3.50 seniors, free for children and students. Wed–Sat 11am–6pm; Sun noon–5pm. Tube: Highbury and Islington.

Freud Museum HISTORIC HOME/ MUSEUM   After he escaped Nazi-occupied Vienna with his family, Sigmund Freud lived, worked, and died (in 1939) in this spacious three-story house. It's now a museum dedicated to his life, with original furniture, letters, photographs, paintings, and the personal effects of Freud and his daughter, Anna (an acclaimed pyschoanalyst in her own right). In the study—kept as it was during his lifetime—and library, you can see the famous couch where all his patients reclined and Freud's large collection of Egyptian, Roman, and Asian antiquities.

20 Maresfield Gardens, NW3. www.freud.org. uk. ℰ **020/7435-2002.** Admission £6 adults, £4.50 seniors, £3 students and children aged 12–16, free for children 11 and under. Wed–Sun noon–5pm. Tube: Finchley Rd.

Freud Museum.

Hampstead Heath ★★★ ☺ PARK/GARDEN   This 320-hectare (791-acre) expanse of high heath is made up of a mixture of formal parkland, woodland, heath, meadowland, and ponds. One of the few places in the big city that feels properly wild, it's a fantastic place to lose yourself on a rambling wander. On a clear day, you can see St. Paul's, the Houses of Parliament, and even the hills of Kent from the prime viewing spot atop Parliament Hill, 98m (322 ft.) up. For years Londoners have come here to sun-worship, fly kites, fish the ponds, swim, picnic, jog, or just laze around.

   Much of the northern end is taken up by the manicured grounds of **Kenwood House** (see below), a great spot for a picnic, where concerts are staged on summer evenings. Along its eastern end are a group of ponds set aside for bathing (there's a ladies pool, a men's pool, and a mixed pool), sailing model boats, and as

TOP: **Swimmers in the mixed pond at Hampstead;** RIGHT: **Flask Walk, Hampstead.**

a bird sanctuary—the heath is one of London's best **birdwatching** locations, where occasional free birdwatching walks are offered.

South of the heath is the leafy, well-to-do **Hampstead Village,** a longtime favorite haunt of writers, artists, architects, musicians, and scientists. Keats, D. H. Lawrence, Shelley, Robert Louis Stevenson, and Kingsley Amis all lived here. The village's Regency and Georgian houses offer a quirky mix of historic pubs, toy shops, and chic boutiques, as exemplified by **Flask Walk.**

Hampstead, NW3. www.cityoflondon.gov.uk. ✆ **020/7482-7073.** Free admission. Open 24 hours. Tube: Hampstead/Overground: Hampstead Heath or Gospel Oak.

Highgate Cemetery HISTORIC SITE A stone's throw east of Hampstead Heath, this beautiful cemetery is laid out around a huge 300-year-old cedar tree and is laced with serpentine pathways. The cemetery was so popular and fashionable in the Victorian era that it was extended on the other side of Swain's Lane in 1857. The most famous grave is that of **Karl Marx,** who died in Hampstead in 1883; his grave, marked by a gargantuan bust, is in the eastern cemetery. In the old western cemetery—accessible only by guided tours, given hourly in summer—are scientist Michael Faraday and poet Christina Rossetti.

Swain's Lane, N6. www.highgate-cemetery.org. ℰ **020/8340-1834.** Western Cemetery guided tour £7 adults, £5 students, £3 children 8–15 (cash only). Eastern Cemetery admission £3 adults, £2 students, free for children 15 and under (cash only). Western Cemetery: Mar–Oct tours Mon–Fri 2pm, Sat–Sun hourly 11am–4pm; Nov–Feb tours Sat–Sun hourly 11am–3pm. Eastern Cemetery: Apr–Oct Mon–Fri 10am–4:30pm, Sat–Sun 11am–4:30pm; Nov–Mar Mon–Fri 10am–3:30pm, Sat–Sun 11am–3:30pm. Both cemeteries closed at Christmas and during funerals. Tube: Archway, and then bus 143, 210, 271, or C11.

Jewish Museum ★ MUSEUM   Reopened to the public in 2010, following a £10 million improvement, this Camden museum retells the often difficult history of Britain's Jewish communities from the time of the first settlers in 1066 to the present, as well as illuminating aspects of Jewish ritual and belief. Most of the items date from after the English Civil Wars, when Oliver Cromwell changed the law to allow Jews to settle in Britain. You can see a variety of historical artifacts, including a 13th-century mikvah (ritual bath), a 17th-century Venetian synagogue ark (discovered in the 20th century being used as a wardrobe in an English castle), and, in the most affecting section, learn about the Holocaust as experienced by a single Auschwitz survivor, Leon Greenman, whose story is cleverly (and movingly) used to represent the plight of an entire people. The downstairs cafe and shop are free to enter.

129–131 Albert St., NW1. www.jewishmuseum.org.uk. ℰ **020/7284-7384.** Admission £7.50 adults, £6.50 seniors and students, £3.50 children 5–15, free for children aged 4 and under. Sun–Thurs 10am–5pm; Fri 10am–2pm. Tube: Camden Town.

Keats House HISTORIC HOME   The poet lived here for only 2 years, but that was approximately two-fifths of his creative life; he died of tuberculosis in Rome at the age of 25 (in 1821). Keats wrote some of his most celebrated works in Hampstead, including *Ode on a Grecian Urn* and *Ode to a Nightingale.* His Regency house, which was thoroughly revamped a few years ago, possesses the manuscripts of his last sonnet (*Bright star, would I were steadfast as thou art*) and a portrait of him on his deathbed in Rome. Regular events, including, inevitably, poetry readings, are organized.

Keats Grove, NW3. www.keatshouse.cityoflondon.gov.uk. ℰ **020/7332-3868.** Admission £5 adults, £3 students and seniors, free for children 15 and under. Easter–Oct Tues–Fri 10am–noon; Nov–Easter Tues–Thurs 10am–5pm. Tube: Hampstead or Belsize Park/Overground: Hampstead Heath.

Kenwood House ★ HISTORIC HOME   Kenwood House was built as a gentleman's country home and was later enlarged and decorated by Scottish architect Robert Adam, starting in 1764. The house contains period furniture and paintings by Turner, Frans Hals, Gainsborough, Reynolds, and more. In summer its lakeside garden stages an acclaimed series of concerts, "Music on a Summer Evening," featuring big-name performers from the worlds of classical, rock, jazz, and musical theatre, and often ending with a big fireworks blowout.

Hampstead Lane, NW3. www.english-heritage.org.uk/daysout/properties/kenwood-house/. ℰ **020/8348-1286.** Free admission. May–Oct daily 11am–5pm; Nov–Apr daily 11.30am–4pm. Tube: Golders Green, and then bus 210; or Hampstead and then bus 603 (Mon–Fri only).

London Canal Museum 😊 🎁 MUSEUM   Set beside Regent's Canal, this tells the story of London's commercial waterways, with displays on canal life, narrow boats, canal horses, locks, and more. The most interesting section deals with the 19th-century ice trade. The museum is located in a former ice warehouse once used by Carlo Gatti, a Swiss immigrant who is credited with having introduced ice cream to the U.K. in the 1850s. He stored his products in subterranean wells kept cool by ice imported from Norway. A variety of activities, including towpath walks are organized, and free trails are provided for children. An mp3 audio tour can be downloaded from the website to play during your visit.

12–13 New Wharf Rd., N1. www.canalmuseum.org.uk. ✆ **020/7713-0836.** Admission £4 adults, £3 students and seniors, £2 children 5–15, free for children 4 and under. Daily 10am–4:30pm (till 7:30pm on the 1st Thurs of month). Tube: King's Cross.

London Zoo (ZSL) ★★ 😊 ZOO   When London Zoo—one of the finest big city zoos in the world—was founded back in 1820, it was purely for the purposes of scientific research. The public were only admitted, almost as an afterthought, a couple of decades later. They clearly liked what they saw, and soon a trip to marvel at the exotic species had become a popular Victorian day out, turning the zoo's most famous inhabitants, notably the enormous elephant, Jumbo, into national celebrities.

In the 20th century, however, attitudes toward zoos changed; people no longer liked seeing large animals living in cramped conditions, and in the early 1990s the zoo, facing dwindling interest, was threatened with closure. An outpouring of public support and a significant redevelopment of the zoo's infrastructure have ensured its survival. The largest animals, including the rhinos and elephants, have been moved to the zoo's more spacious wildlife park in Bedfordshire, while the London premises have been remolded according to the latest theories on captive animal welfare. There are, of course, still plenty of animals here. Big hitters include giraffes, pygmy hippos, lions, tigers and penguins. But the cages of old have, for the most part, been replaced with large, natural-looking enclosures. The importance of conservation, and the zoo's role as a breeding center for rare species, is stressed throughout.

Highlights of the modern London Zoo include the "Clore Rainforest Lookout," a steamy indoor replica jungle inhabited by sloths, tamarin monkeys,

London Zoo.

and armadillos; "B.U.G.S," which apparently stands for Biodiversity Underpinning Global Survival, but does also contain plenty of bugs, including leaf-cutter ants, brightly colored beetles, and giant, scary, bird-eating spiders; and, the current flagship, "Gorilla Kingdom," a moated island resembling an African forest clearing, which provides a naturalistic habitat for gorillas and colobus monkeys. There are always plenty of activities going on here, including keeper talks, feeding times, and "meet the animals" displays. A day-planner is handed out at the front gate, or you can download one from the website.

Insider's tip: Savings of around 10% can be made if you book a family ticket online; these are not available at the front gate.

Outer Circle, Regent's Park, NW1. www.zsl.org/zsl-london-zoo. © **0844/225-1826.** Admission winter season/mid-season/peak-season including donation: £18.50/19.50/20.50 adults, £17/18/19 students and seniors, £15.10/15.50/16.50 children 3–15. Mar–Oct daily 10am–5:30pm; Nov–Feb daily 10am–4pm. Tube: Regent's Park or Camden Town/Bus: C2 or 274.

Madame Tussauds ☺ ♨ MUSEUM   These days, Madame Tussauds is not so much a wax museum as an enclosed amusement park; a weird collage of exhibitions, panoramas, and animatronic trickery. It's the successor to the original Madame Tussauds exhibition founded by the lady herself in the early 19th century, following her escape from revolutionary France. There she had studied the art of wax-modeling, and brought with her death masks made from the guillotined heads of Louis XVI and Marie Antoinette, which formed the basis of the collection. It grew over the decades as models of the noted figures of the day were added, and became hugely popular. The concept behind the exhibition remains largely the same today, with waxworks of the current crop of famous people displayed in a series of tableaux—with names like "A-List Party," "Sports Zone," and "Music Megastars"—albeit now "enhanced" with modern lighting, sound, and motion effects. Highlights include the long-established "Chamber of Horrors," a kind of underground dungeon filled with waxwork torture victims, where costumed actors will try to scare you in the live action section, "Scream."

Madame Tussauds is not for everybody. Its appeal will depend largely on how excited you are at the prospect of having your photo taken next to likenesses of President Obama, David Beckham, and Lady Gaga. And you'll need to be quite excited, as you'll be paying in excess of £25 for a ticket, and may have to wait in line for some considerable time.

Waxwork of Queen at Madame Tussauds.

The Boathouse cafe in Regent's Park.

Insider's tip: It pays to be prepared. Tickets booked online are 10% cheaper than those on the door, and up to 50% if you go for the late saver option which means arriving after 5pm at off-peak times, and after 6pm at peak times. Marylebone Rd., NW1. www.madametussauds.com/London. ℂ **0870/400-3000.** Admission on the door/online £30/27 adults, £25.60/23.10 children 15 and under, £108/97.20 family ticket. Opening times vary throughout the year, but at least daily 9:30am–5:30pm. Tube: Baker St.

Regent's Park ★★ ☺ PARK/GARDEN Designed by 18th-century genius John Nash to surround a palace for the Prince Regent (the palace never materialized), this is the most classically beautiful of all London's parks. Its core is a rose garden planted around a small lake alive with waterfowl and spanned by Japanese bridges; in early summer, the rose perfume is heady in the air. The park is home to the **Open-Air Theatre** (p. 45) and **London Zoo** (p. 167). As at all the Royal Parks, hundreds of deckchairs are scattered around the lawns, ready for sunbathers (£1.50 per hour rental). Rowboats and sailing dinghies are available from **The Boathouse** (ℂ **020/7724-4069**) for £6.50 per adult and £4.40 per child for 1 hour.

Regent's Park, NW1. www.royalparks.gov.uk/The-Regents-Park.aspx. ℂ **030/0061-2300.** Free admission. Daily 5am–dusk. Tube: Baker St., Great Portland St., or Regent's Park.

Sherlock Holmes Museum ♨ MUSEUM In mocked-up Victorian-style rooms in London's most famous fictional address, **221b Baker Street,** you can examine a range of Holmes-related exhibits, including some of the letters written to Conan Doyle's great detective by fans who haven't quite grasped the "fictional" concept, while costumed characters, including a Victorian bobby and maid, guide you around. It's pretty kitschy and touristy, with a well-stocked gift shop—where you can pick up that all important deer-stalker—but worth a visit if you're a Holmes fanatic. It's probably of limited interest to anyone else.

221b Baker St., NW1. www.sherlock-holmes.co.uk. ☏ **020/7224-3688.** Admission £6 adults, £4 children 15 and under. Daily 9:30am–6pm. Tube: Baker St.

SOUTHEAST LONDON

Greenwich

With the great skyscrapers of Canary Wharf to the north, and waves of faceless suburbia to the south, Greenwich seems almost out of place—a royal theme park smuggled into London's backwaters. It makes a great escape from the center of town, with a look and ambience all its own. For the full effect, try arriving by a Thames Clipper boat (p. 424), which shows off the riverside architecture to its best effect.

For centuries Greenwich was a major hub of British seafaring and many of its attractions have a nautical theme, including the Old Royal Naval College, the National Maritime Museum, which traces the history of Britain's mastery of the sea, and the *Cutty Sark,* one of the fastest sailing ships of the 19th century.

Greenwich Park is the real heart of the village, and a wonderful place to unwind, particularly after a hard morning's sightseeing and market shopping. Then head uphill to enjoy a space show at the Royal Observatory—and to get a photo of yourself straddling the Prime Meridian (0° longitude), of course.

British Music Experience ☺ MUSEUM   The O2 Arena at the tip of the Greenwich Peninsula has firmly established itself as the capital's top music venue for arena-level acts over the past half decade. To further cement its status, its top floor is now given over to the British Music Experience, a loose trawl through 7 decades of the U.K.'s popular music history illustrated with various items of memorabilia, including David Bowie's Ziggy Stardust costume, Noel Gallagher's Union Flag guitar, and outfits worn by Jimi Hendrix and Amy Winehouse. It's a straightforwardly populist affair with lots of interactivity—you can take dance lessons at the "Dance the Decades" booth and enjoy drum, guitar, and keyboard tutorials at the "Gibson Interactive Studio," and even record your efforts for posterity on your smart ticket. Good for families, the attraction is perhaps less appealing for serious music fans wanting to delve a little deeper. Think more Madame Tussauds than Rough Trade. But then, the clue is in the name—it's an "experience."

O2 Arena, Millennium Way, SE10. www.britishmusicexperience.com. ☏ **020/8463-2000.** Admission £12 adults, £8 seniors and students, £6 children aged 5–16, free for children 4 and under. Daily 11am–7.30pm (last admission 6.30pm). Tube: North Greenwich.

Cutty Sark ★ ☺ HISTORIC SITE   It's back. The *Cutty Sark,* one of the 19th century's speediest ships, which endured a significant (but thankfully not ruinous) fire in 2007, has finally been restored to its former grandeur and is once again on display in dry dock in the center of Greenwich. The shop was one of a new breed of super-swift craft—known as clippers—built in the mid-19th century with the aim of reducing journey times between Britain and the Far East to aid the ever burgeoning tea trade. For a couple of decades, clippers ruled the waves, consistently lowering the record for the round-Africa route until the opening of the Suez Canal in 1869 rendered them almost instantly obsolete. The

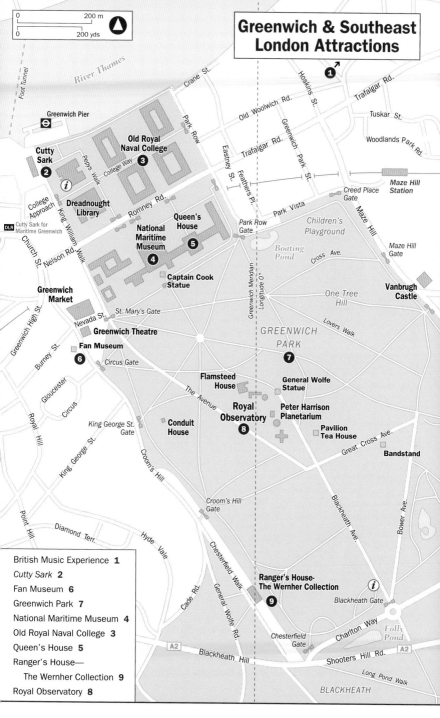

Greenwich & Southeast London Attractions

0 — 200 m
0 — 200 yds

River Thames

Foot Tunnel
Crane St.
Old Woolwich Rd.
Hoskins St.
Trafalgar Rd.
Tuskar St.
Woodlands Park Rd.

Greenwich Pier
Park Row
Trafalgar Rd.
Greenwich Park St.

Cutty Sark ❷
Pepys Walk
College Way
Old Royal Naval College ❸
Eastney St.
Feathers Pl.
Maze Hill

Maze Hill Station

College Approach
Dreadnought Library
Romney Rd.
Park Vista
Creed Place Gate
DLR Cutty Sark for Maritime Greenwich
King William Walk
Nelson Rd.
Church St.

National Maritime Museum ❹
Queen's House ❺
Park Row Gate
Boating Pond
Children's Playground
Maze Hill Gate

Captain Cook Statue
Greenwich Meridian Longitude 0°
Cross Ave.
One Tree Hill
Vanbrugh Castle

Greenwich Market
Greenwich High St.
St. Mary's Gate
Nevada St.
Greenwich Theatre
Lovers Walk

GREENWICH PARK ❼

Burney St.
Fan Museum ❻
Circus Gate
Gloucester Circus

Flamsteed House
General Wolfe Statue

Royal Hill
The Avenue
Royal Observatory ❽
Peter Harrison Planetarium
Pavilion Tea House

King George St. Gate
Conduit House
King George St.
Croom's Hill
Great Cross Ave.
Bandstand

Point Hill
Diamond Terr.
Hyde Vale
Croom's Hill Gate

Blackheath Ave.
Bower Ave.

Chesterfield Walk
Cade Rd.
General Wolfe Rd.
Ranger's House—The Wernher Collection ❾
Blackheath Gate
Blackheath Hill
Chesterfield Gate
Charlton Way
Folly Pond
A2
Shooters Hill Rd.
A2
Long Pond Walk
BLACKHEATH

Cutty Sark was built that same year, arriving just as the party was coming to an end. Today, she is one of only three surviving ships of her type and has been on public display in Greenwich since the 1950s (with the odd restorative gap). The most recent renovation has improved access (lifts have been added) and a new display on the boat's history and construction has been created below the ship's hull. The real joy of visiting, however, is still just exploring the ship's decks and cabins.

King William Walk, SE10. www.cuttysark.org.uk. *C* **020/8312-6608.** Admission £12 adults; £9.50 seniors and students; £5.50 children aged 5–15, free 4 and under. Tues–Sun & public hols 10am–5pm (last admission 4:30pm). DLR: Cutty Sark.

Fan Museum MUSEUM   Two 18th-century Grade II listed houses provide a suitably elegant setting for a museum dedicated to that most genteel of accessories—the hand-held fan. The museum holds one of the world's largest and most important collections, comprising some 3,500 items—more than it can ever display at one time. Alongside a permanent exhibition, detailing the history of fans and fan-making, is a temporary display of fans, which changes three times a year so as to keep the collection in rotation. The very oldest fan dates from the 11th century, although the bulk of the collection is made up of ornate 18th- and 19th-century European creations.

12 Crooms Hill, SE10. www.fan-museum.org. *C* **020/8305-1441.** Admission £4 adults, £3 seniors and students, £3 children 7–15, free for children 6 and under. Tues–Sat 11am–5pm; Sun noon–5pm. DLR/Rail: Greenwich/DLR: Cutty Sark.

Greenwich Park ★ ☺ PARK/GARDEN   The park represents the green heart of Greenwich, around which all its major attractions are grouped. It's been a Royal Park since the 15th century, although the boundary wasn't formally defined until King James I erected a brick wall around it in the early 1600s, much of which still survives. At one time the park adjoined Greenwich Palace, once the capital's leading royal home, and the birthplace of Henry VIII. The palace was abandoned in the Civil War and was subsequently turned into a hospital for maritime veterans, which in time became the **Old Royal Naval College** (see below). No longer the private garden of the Royal Family, the park was opened to the public in the 18th century.

With a hill taking up most of the park's central area, there are great views out over the East London landscape, taking in the Queen's House (see below), the Old Royal Naval College, and beyond to the O2 Centre and Canary Wharf across the river. At the top of the hill, gazing heavenward, sits the **Royal Observatory** (see below), while scattered about the park's handsome lower reaches, you'll find a **deer park,** a children's playground, a pavilion teahouse, and a bandstand. Free guided walks of the park's flower gardens leave from the Park Office in summer.

Greenwich Park, SE10. www.royalparks.gov.uk/Greenwich-Park.aspx. *C* **030/0061-2380.** Free admission. Daily 6am–dusk. DLR/Rail: Greenwich or Maze Hill/DLR: Cutty Sark.

National Maritime Museum ★★★ ☺ MUSEUM   The world's largest maritime museum just got a little bigger. Entry is now via the recently opened, glass-and-stone **Sammy Ofer Wing,** built with a £20 million donation from the eponymous late Israeli shipping magnate. It contains a new cafe and several

View of the city from Greenwich Park.

exhibition spaces, including "Voyagers," perhaps best described as a combination between a traditional museum display and an art piece. Items illustrating stories of Britons at sea surround a 20m (66-ft.) long installation, "The Wave," where maritime-themed images and words are projected in an undulating, wave-like way on to a series of triangular, interlinked screens. Equally up-to-the-minute is the new "Compass Lounge" where visitors can download information about the displays using the "compass card" given to them upon entry.

The rest of the museum is a bit more traditional, dedicated to exploring this island nation's intense relationship with its watery surrounds from the days of the early seafarers to 20th-century naval power. The first two floors are divided into themed sections, including "Maritime London: 1700 to now," "Traders: the East India Company and Asia," and "The Atlantic: Slavery, Trade, Empire." The display cases are filled with nautical oddities—everything from the dreaded cat-o'-nine-tails used to flog sailors until 1879, to Nelson's Trafalgar coat, with the fatal bullet hole in the left shoulder clearly visible—and together the assorted curios, weapons, uniforms, relics, ship models, and paintings tell a convoluted story of naval battles, mercantile expansion, piracy, trade, human trafficking, and the growth (and fall) of an empire.

After all the serious stuff, the top floor provides some light relief with interactive games and experiments, including a ship simulator. Free family events, usually involving storytelling and workshops, are organized at weekends.

Romney Rd., SE10. www.rmg.co.uk/national-maritime-museum/. ⓒ **020/8858-4422.** Free admission. Daily 10am–5pm. DLR: Cutty Sark.

National Maritime Museum.

Painted Hall, Old Royal Naval College.

Old Royal Naval College ★ HISTORIC SITE   The great baroque waterfront facade of this wonderfully grand structure offers perhaps the clearest distillation of Greenwich's charms. UNESCO certainly thought so, describing it as the "finest and most dramatically sited architectural . . . ensemble in the British Isles." It's the work of England's holy trinity of 17th-century architects—Wren, Hawksmoor, and Vanbrugh (mostly Wren, in truth)—and was designed in 1694 as a hospital for veteran sailors, the naval equivalent of the Royal Hospital Chelsea (p. 125). The pensioners moved out in 1873, when the complex became the Royal Naval College. The Royal Navy finally ended its association with the building in 1998, since when it has been home to part of the University of Greenwich. Just three sections are open to the public: the Georgian chapel of **St. Peter and St. Paul,** where organ recitals are often given; the magnificent **Painted Hall** ★ by Sir James Thornhill, where the body of Nelson lay in state in 1805; and the **Discover Greenwich Centre,** which contains an intriguing, interactive exhibition on the history of Greenwich as well as the suburb's tourist information service.

Old Royal Naval College, SE10. www.oldroyalnavalcollege.org. ✆ **020/8269-4747.** Free admission. Daily 10am–5pm. DLR: Cutty Sark.

Queen's House HISTORIC HOME   Viewed from the river, the Queen's House enjoys as elegant a setting as a building could wish for, framed by the great wings of the (later-built) Old Royal Naval College. It was designed in a then-revolutionary, Renaissance-inspired "Palladian" style by Inigo Jones as a summer retreat for King Charles I's wife, Henrietta Maria. It was completed in 1638, just before the Civil Wars put a permanent end to Charles' building programs and forced Henrietta to flee to France. Restored and refurbished under Charles II, the house today boasts a number of galleries and displays, including an exhibition on "Historic Greenwich" and "Art for the Nation," a collection of 200 paintings reflecting Britain's maritime heritage (lots of ships and battles) by such illustrious names as Gainsborough and Hogarth. Between the two are the elegant Tulip Stairs, the first spiral staircase of its kind to be built in Britain.

Greenwich, SE10. www.rmg.co.uk/queens-house. (C) **020/8858-4422.** Free admission. Daily 10am–5pm. DLR: Cutty Sark.

Ranger's House—The Wernher Collection ★ 🏛 MUSEUM   In Greenwich Park, this is one of the country's most unusual 19th-century mixed-art collections. Acquired by a German diamond dealer, Sir Julius Wernher, the collection contains more than 650 exhibits, some dating as far back as 3 b.c. It's an eclectic mix of everything, including jewelry, bronzes, ivory, antiques, tapestries, porcelain pieces, and classic paintings. One salon is devoted to the biggest collection of Renaissance jewelry in Britain, and there are also Limoges enamels and Sèvres porcelain, as well as a few more unusual items, such as enameled skulls and a miniature coffin complete with 3-D skeleton. Don't expect everything to be beautiful—Wernher's taste was often bizarre.

Chesterfield Walk, SE10. www.english-heritage.org.uk/daysout/properties/rangers-house-the-wernher-collection/. (C) **020/8294-2548.** Admission £6.30 adults, £5.70 seniors and students, £3.80 children, free for children 4 and under. Mar–Sept Sun–Wed 10am–5pm. DLR/Rail: Greenwich/DLR: Cutty Sark.

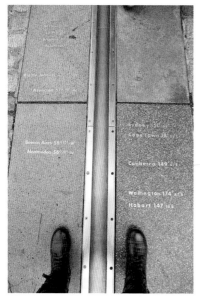

The Prime Meridian outside the Royal Observatory.

Royal Observatory ★★ ☺
HISTORIC SITE/PLANETARIUM The home of **Greenwich Mean Time,** the Observatory was designed by Sir Christopher Wren in the early 18th century and boasts the country's largest refracting telescope (you can look through it, should the British weather oblige, on one of the regular "An Evening with the Stars" events), as well as displays on time-keeping, a camera obsura, and (the only part of the site it's free to visit) an interactive astronomy exhibition. The highlight, however, is the **Planetarium,** the only one in the country where effects-laden star shows are projected onto its ceiling.

Outside you can enjoy one of London's most popular photo opportunities, standing across the **Prime Meridian,** the line of 0° longitude marked in the courtyard, with one foot in the Earth's eastern hemisphere and one foot in the western. At lunch you can set your watch precisely by watching the red **"time ball"** atop the roof, which has dropped at exactly 1pm since 1833, to enable passing shipmasters to set their chronometers accurately.

Blackheath Ave., SE10. www.nmm.ac.uk/places/royal-observatory. ✆ **020/8858-4422.** Admission to observatory £7 adults, £5 seniors and students, free for children aged 15 and under; planetarium £6.50 adults, £4.50 children, £17.50 family. Daily 10am–5pm. DLR/Rail: Greenwich/ DLR: Cutty Sark.

OUTLYING AREAS

Tempting as it is to restrict yourself solely to attractions in the heart of the city, you'd be missing out on some of London's finest treasures. Beyond the heartland are fabulous parks and gardens, vast royal palaces, and quirky little museums and galleries well worth taking the time to visit. The great botanical gardens of Kew and Hampton Court, in particular, are absolute must-sees. Although some of the attractions listed here can be reached only by overground rail, all are within easy reach of central London. Your destination may look far away on the map, but trust us, you'll probably be there in half an hour. And, if you're in no particular hurry, there's no finer way to reach Kew or Hampton Court than on a riverboat from Westminster (p. 424).

Dulwich Picture Gallery ★★ ART MUSEUM   Just 12 minutes by train from Victoria station, this houses one of the country's most significant collections of European Old Masters from the 17th and 18th centuries. The core of the collection was assembled by a pair of London art dealers in the 1790s on behalf of King Stanislaus Augustus of Poland, who thought a royal art collection would be just the thing to enhance his prestige. Unfortunately, he'd rather overestimated his standing, his kingdom was partitioned out of existence before the shipment could be made, and the paintings remained in London. The dealers bequeathed the collection to the independent school, Dulwich College, which commissioned the great Sir John Soane (p. 108) to create the world's first public art museum to display them; it opened in 1817. Soane's cunningly positioned skylights beautifully illuminate the pieces from such figures as Rembrandt, Rubens, Canaletto, Gainsborough, Watteau, and Poussin. Indeed, the *Sunday Telegraph* hailed Dulwich as "the most beautiful small art gallery in the world." Free guided tours of the collection are given at 3pm on Saturdays and Sundays.

Gallery Rd., SE21. www.dulwichpicturegallery.org.uk. ✆ **020/8693-5254.** Admission £5 adults, £4 seniors, free for students, the unemployed, and children 17 and under. Tues–Fri 10am–5pm; Sat–Sun 11am–5pm. Rail: W. Dulwich.

Hampton Court Palace ★★★ ☺ PALACE   The 16th-century palace of Cardinal Wolsey can teach us a lesson: Don't try to outdo your boss, particularly if he happens to be Henry VIII. The rich cardinal did just that, and he eventually lost his fortune, power, and prestige, and ended up giving his lavish palace to the Tudor monarch. Henry's additions include an Astronomical Clock above the Clock Court (still showing the phases of the moon, the position of the sun, and signs of the Zodiac to this day), the aptly named Great Hall with its hammerbeam roof (in Henry VIII's Private Apartments), a Tiltyard (where jousting competitions were held), and a "real tennis" court.

Hampton Court Palace

East Front
& Gardens

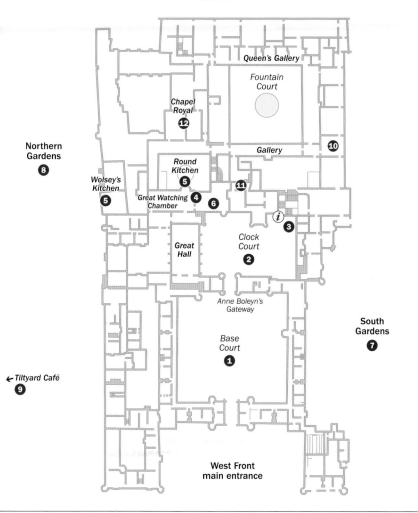

Base Court **1**　　　　　　　　　　Information Centre **3**

Chapel Royal **12**　　　　　　　　　Mary II's Apartments **6**

Clock Court **2**　　　　　　　　　　The Northern Gardens **8**

Georgian Private Apartments **11**　　The South Gardens **7**

Henry VIII's Kitchens **5**　　　　　Tiltyard Café **9**

Henry VIII's Private Apartments **4**　William III's Apartments **10**

Hampton Court Palace.

Although the palace enjoyed prestige in Elizabethan days, it owes much of its present look to William and Mary—or rather, to Sir Christopher Wren. You can parade through their apartments today, filled with porcelain, furniture, paintings, and tapestries. Also, be sure to inspect the **Chapel Royal** (Wolsey wouldn't recognize it), **Henry VIII's Kitchens** where great Tudor feasts are regularly prepared, and the **Base Court** where the latest addition to this composite palace can be found in the form of a replica Wine Fountain built on the foundations of an original discovered in 2008.

The 24-hectare (59-acre) **gardens**—including Tudor and Elizabethan Knot Gardens—are open daily year-round. The most popular section is the serpentine shrubbery **Maze,** also the work of Wren, and accounting for countless lost children every year. A garden **cafe** and restaurant are located in the Tiltyard.

Plenty of family entertainments are laid on throughout the year, and free children's activity trails and audio guides, for both adults and children, are available from the information center.

Insider's tip: Tickets are considerably cheaper if bought online. Below are the walk-up prices.

East Molesey, Surrey. www.hrp.org.uk/HamptonCourtPalace. ℭ **0844/482-7777.** Palace admission £15.95 adults, £13.20 students and seniors, £8 children 5–15, £43.45 family ticket, free for children 4 and under; gardens admission £5.30 adults, £4.60 students and seniors, free for children without palace ticket during summer. Maze: £3.85 adults, £2.75 children 5–15, free for children 4 and under. Cloisters, courtyards, state apartments, great kitchen, cellars, and Hampton Court exhibition Mar–Oct daily 10am–6pm; Nov–Feb daily 10am–4:30pm. Gardens year-round daily 7am–dusk (no later than 9pm). Rail: Hampton Court (30 min. from Waterloo).

Horniman Museum ★★ ☺ MUSEUM   South London's only serious rival to the grand museums north of the river, this charmingly esoteric place is based on the personal collection of Frederick Horniman, a Victorian tea trader. Seemingly with the intent of taking on its competitors all at once, the Horniman has no clear focus, its 350,000 objects made up of all sorts and everything, from African tribal masks to a gigantic, overstuffed walrus, and from musical instruments (it holds one of the country's most important collections) to giant model insects, as well as a small aquarium constructed in waterfall-like tiers. It's divided into three broad categories: natural history, music, and world cultures. Outside, its 6.5 hectares (16 acres) of wonderful grounds now boast a medicinal garden, a food garden, an animal walk (with sheep, goats, and guinea pigs) and a music garden. There's a full range of events and activities, including storytelling and craft sessions for youngsters, along with workshops for adults. Free activity sheets are at the front desk (or online).

100 London Rd., Forest Hill, SE23. www.horniman.ac.uk. *℘* **020/8699-1872.** Free admission except for temporary exhibitions. Museum daily 10:30am–5:30pm. Gardens Mon–Sat 7:30am–dusk; Sun 8am–dusk. Overground: Forest Hill (13 min. from London Bridge station; 24 min. from Shoreditch High St.).

Warner Bros. Studio Tour ★ ☺ ENTERTAINMENT COMPLEX   In 2012, it was the turn of the capital's peripheries to take center stage. East London felt the eyes of the world upon it as never before when it hosted the Olympic and Paralympic Games, while in the far reaches of northwest London a little stardust was sprinkled on the almost archetypically unglamorous town of Watford with the opening of the Warner Bros. Studio Tour. The studio has brought out the big guns (or rather wands) for its "Making of Harry Potter" attraction offering a (mostly) self-guided tour taking in two of the sound stages and many of the sets used in the "most popular film series in history." You'll see the Great Hall, Hagrid's Hut, the Gryffindor Common Room, Dumbledore's Office, and Dragon Alley, as well as props, costumes, and animatronic creatures (Buckbeak the Hippogriff and Fawkes the phoenix among them). The tour takes an estimated 3 hours and has proved hugely popular. Advance booking is essential to guarantee a place.

Aerodrom Way, Leavesden, Hertfordshire, WD25. www.wbstudiotour.co.uk. *℘* **0845/084-0900.** Admission £28 adults, £21 children aged 5–15, free for children 4 and under. Daily 10am–6pm. Rail/Overground: Watford Junction, then shuttle bus running every 15 mins.

Kew ★★ & Richmond ★

About 9½ miles southwest of central London, the pretty suburban "village" of Kew is the site of several attractions, including one of the world's great botanical gardens. Adjacent Richmond is just one stop farther along on the Tube.

Kew Bridge Steam Museum ★ ☺ MUSEUM   This museum is a grimy, industrial counterpoint to all the neatly tended greenery of Kew Gardens (p. 182). Housed in a Victorian pumping station, it provides an overview of the development of London's water supply, from Roman times to the present. The main exhibits are around a dozen giant beam engines that once pumped the nation's water, and which have been recovered and restored to working condition. Most weekends, several of these iron behemoths are "fired up," and set in very noisy motion.

In the Water for Life exhibition you can find out how things have come on, with a display on London's smoother, quieter—but perhaps less exciting—modern distribution techniques, as well as the growth of the capital's sewerage system since the 19th century. It's a surprisingly child-friendly place, with lots of hands-on exhibits—children can sieve sewage for treasure like 19th-century "toshers," control a radio-controlled sewer robot, and take rides on a miniature steam railway, which runs Sundays and bank holidays from April to October.

Green Dragon Lane, Brentford, Middlesex. www.kbsm.org. (€) **020/8568-4757.** Admission £10 adults, £9 students and seniors, £4 children aged 5–15, free for children 4 and under. Tues–Sun and bank holiday Mon 11am–4pm. Rail: Kew Bridge.

Richmond Park ★★ ☺ PARK/GARDEN   The largest of London's Royal Parks, Richmond was, like so many of the others, once a royal hunting ground. Unlike most of the others, however, it still retains a population of around 650 **deer**—the chief royal quarry—who roam at will within the walls in around 1,000 hectares (2,500 acres) of open space, finally free from the attentions of bow-wielding nobles. There's plenty of other wildlife besides, including badgers, rabbits, voles, bats, owls, and butterflies—so much, in fact, that the park been designated a **National Nature Reserve.** Free walks on the lookout for the park's numerous creatures are organized by the **Friends of Richmond Park** (€) **020/8549-8975;** www.frp.org.uk).

Richmond may feel far from the city, but head to **King Henry's Mound**—supposedly a lookout spot erected by Henry VII—and you can enjoy an uninterrupted view (known as the **Long View** ★) all the way to St. Paul's Cathedral. The park is criss-crossed by roads and is open to cars—driving makes a pleasant way to tour its confines when the weather is cold, although be prepared for the

Richmond Park.

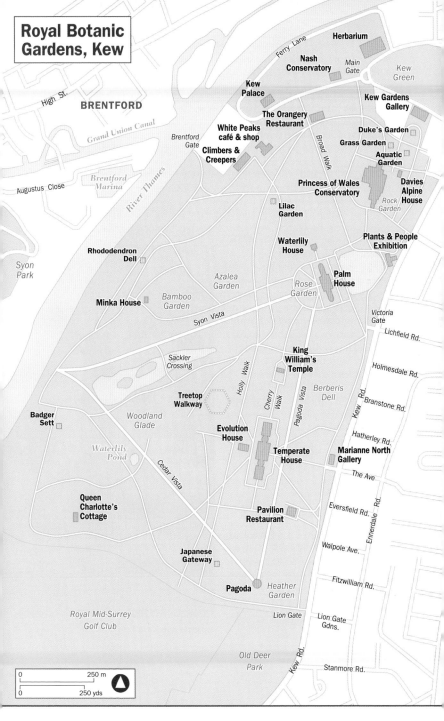

Royal Botanic Gardens, Kew

Herbarium

Ferry Lane

Nash Conservatory

Main Gate

Kew Green

Kew Palace

Kew Gardens Gallery

BRENTFORD

High St.

Grand Union Canal

The Orangery Restaurant

Duke's Garden

Brentford Gate

White Peaks café & shop

Grass Garden

Broad Walk

Climbers & Creepers

Aquatic Garden

Augustus Close

Brentford Marina

Princess of Wales Conservatory

Davies Alpine House

River Thames

Lilac Garden

Rock Garden

Rhododendron Dell

Waterlily House

Plants & People Exhibition

Syon Park

Azalea Garden

Rose Garden

Palm House

Minka House

Bamboo Garden

Syon Vista

Victoria Gate

Lichfield Rd.

Sackler Crossing

King William's Temple

Holmesdale Rd.

Treetop Walkway

Holly Walk

Berberis Dell

Kew Rd.

Branstone Rd.

Badger Sett

Woodland Glade

Cherry Walk

Pagoda Vista

Hatherley Rd.

Waterlily Pond

Cedar Vista

Evolution House

Marianne North Gallery

Temperate House

The Ave

Queen Charlotte's Cottage

Eversfield Rd.

Ennerdale Rd.

Pavilion Restaurant

Walpole Ave.

Japanese Gateway

Fitzwilliam Rd.

Pagoda

Heather Garden

Royal Mid-Surrey Golf Club

Lion Gate

Lion Gate Gdns.

Kew Rd.

Old Deer Park

Stanmore Rd.

0   250 m
0   250 yds

inevitable "deer jams." There's also a **bike hire** shop, **Parkcycle** (www.parkcycle.co.uk), near the Roehampton Gate entrance.

Richmond Park, Surrey. www.royalparks.gov.uk/Richmond-Park.aspx. ℂ **030/0061-2200.** Free admission. Summer 7am–dusk, winter 7:30am–dusk. Tube: Richmond.

Royal Botanic Gardens, Kew ★★★ ☺ PARK/GARDEN These world-famous gardens are home to thousands of elegantly arranged plants, but Kew Gardens, as it's more commonly known, is no mere pleasure garden—it's essentially a vast scientific research center that also happens to be extraordinarily beautiful. The gardens' 121-hectare (299-acre) site encompasses lakes, greenhouses, walks, pavilions, museums, and even a royal palace. Among the 50,000 plants are notable collections of ferns, orchids, aquatic plants, cacti, mountain plants, palms, and water lilies.

No matter what season you visit, Kew always has something to see, with species of shrubs, flowers, and trees from every part of the globe, from the Arctic Circle to tropical rainforests. If the weather's chilly, you can keep warm in the three great hothouses: the **Palm House** (the warmest, with a thick, sweaty mass of jungle plants); the slightly cooler **Temperate House;** and the **Princess of Wales Conservatory,** which encompasses 10 climatic zones, from arid to tropical. But when the sun is out, head to the garden's newest attraction, a 200m (656 ft.) **Treetop Walkway** taking you up into the canopy, some 18m (59 ft.) in the air, for a stroll through chestnut, lime, and oak trees. Other attractions include a bamboo garden, a water lily pond, Treehouse Towers (a tree-themed play area for children aged 3–11), and, providing a chilly contrast to the hot houses, an Alpine glasshouse.

Kew, Surrey. www.kew.org. ℂ **020/8332-5655.** Admission £13.90 adults, £11.90 students and seniors, free for children 15 and under. Apr–Aug Mon–Fri 9:30am–6pm, Sat–Sun 9:30am–7pm; Sept–Oct daily 9:30am–5:30pm; Nov–Jan daily 9:30am–3:45pm; Feb–Mar daily 9:30am–5pm. Tube: Kew Gardens.

Japanese pagoda in Kew Gardens.

ESPECIALLY FOR KIDS

London is a great city for youngsters, filled with parks, museums, and other attractions that will keep them amused for hours. Many also offer child-friendly activities and events. Our top picks are reviewed in detail in the previous sections.

Bank of England Museum (p. 144)
Battersea Park & Zoo ★ (p. 117)
British Library ★★ (p. 161)
British Museum ★★★ (p. 96)
British Music Experience (p. 170)
Buckingham Palace ★ (p. 97)
Coram's Fields (p. 101)
Cutty Sark ★ (p. 170)
Florence Nightingale Museum ★ (p. 134)
Foundling Museum (p. 100)
Golden Hinde (p. 135)
Green Park (p. 101)
Greenwich Park ★ (p. 172)
Hampstead Heath ★★★ (p. 164)
Hampton Court Palace ★★★ (p. 176)
HMS *Belfast* ★ (p. 136)
Holland Park ★ (p. 112)
Horniman Museum ★★ (p. 179)
Hyde Park ★★★ & Kensington Gardens ★★ (p. 112)
Imperial War Museum ★★★ (p. 136)
Kew Bridge Steam Museum ★ (p. 179)
London Brass Rubbing Centre ★ (p. 107)
London Bridge Experience and London Tombs (p. 137)
London Canal Museum (p. 167)
London Dungeon ★ (p. 137)
London Eye ★★ (p. 138)
London Film Museum (p. 139)
London Transport Museum ★★ (p. 102)
London Zoo ★★ (p. 167)
Madame Tussauds (p. 168)
The Monument ★ (p. 145)
Museum of London ★★ (p. 145)
Museum of London Docklands ★ (p. 155)

Princess Diana Memorial Fountain in Hyde Park.

National Army Museum ★ (p. 123)
National Gallery ★★★ (p. 102)
National Maritime Museum ★★★ (p. 172)
National Portrait Gallery ★★ (p. 104)
Natural History Museum ★★★ (p. 124)
Old Operating Theatre Museum & Herb Garret ★★ (p. 139)
Pollock's Toy Museum ★ (p. 104)
Ragged School Museum (p. 155)
Regent's Park ★★ (p. 169)
Richmond Park ★★ (p. 180)

V&A Museum of Childhood.

OUTDOOR ACTIVITIES
Alfresco Ice Skating

Outdoor ice rinks are a relatively recent addition to the winter city, and it's fair to say that Londoners have taken to them like ducks to frozen water—which is to say enthusiastically, if not always gracefully.

Every year more rinks appear, and today visitors to London can skate, spin, step, and stumble in a number of beautiful locations, including the **Natural History Museum** (www.nhm.ac.uk/visit-us/whats-on/ice-rink/; also p. 124) and the grounds of the **Tower of London** (www.toweroflondoniceink.com; also p. 150). Tickets for both are usually around £10 to £15 and are best booked in advance, although there are a few spaces on the day.

Skate at Somerset House ★　The king of the rinks remains the original, in the grandiose courtyard of Somerset House (p. 109). The rink is open annually between late November and late January, with tickets generally costing £15.55 adults £8.45 children for an hour-long skate. DJs spin sounds for the weekend evening sessions. Strand. www.somersethouse.org.uk/ice-rink. ✆ **020/7845-4600.** Tube: Temple.

Cycling

London has never been the most bike-friendly city, but thanks to a pedal-powered mayor things are starting to change. In 2010 London's public bike hire scheme launched. These blue **"Boris bikes"** (as they are colloquially known after the mayor; the official name for the scheme is Barclays Cycle Hire) are now a common sight on the city streets. Anyone can rent one for anything from 30 minutes upwards. See p. 423 for details. To try and encourage use of the bikes, four cycle routes running from outer London to the center have been established. Known as **Barclays Super Highways,** the routes can be downloaded from Transport for London at http://www.tfl.gov.uk/roadusers/cycling/11901.aspx. Keep checking the website as eight more routes are due to open before 2015.

London's many parks offer stress-free cycling routes. Best of the lot for cyclists is probably **Richmond Park** (p. 180).

Alternatively, cycling west along the River Thames from Westminster offers scenic views. Be warned that the cycle path along the river is patchy, and you will often need to detour onto main streets to finish your journey.

For information on **guided cycle tours** of London, see p. 425.

Horse Riding

Hyde Park Stables   Riders of all ages and abilities are welcome at these stables, where horses and ponies are selected for their temperament. With more than 5 miles of bridleways, the Royal Park is a great place to spend an hour or two on horseback. Prices start from £64 per hour for group rides and £69 per hour for semi-private lessons. For more on what to do in Hyde Park, see p. 112. 63 Bathurst Mews, W2. www.hydeparkstables.com. ✆ **020/7723-2813.** Tube: Lancaster Gate.

SIGHTS & ATTRACTIONS BY THEME

AQUARIUM
Sea Life London Aquarium ★ (p. 140)

ARCHITECTURE
Thames Barrier (p. 158)

ART MUSEUM
Courtauld Gallery ★ (p. 90)
Dulwich Picture Gallery ★★ (p. 176)
Estorick Collection of Modern Italian Art (p. 164)
Guildhall Art Gallery ★ (p. 144)
Hayward Gallery (p. 135)
National Gallery ★★★ (p. 102)
National Portrait Gallery ★★ (p. 104)
Queen's Gallery ★ (p. 105)
Royal Academy of Arts ★ (p. 105)
Saatchi Gallery ★ (p. 125)

Serpentine Gallery ★ (p. 116)
Tate Britain ★★ (p. 126)
Tate Modern ★★★ (p. 141)
Whitechapel Art Gallery ★★ (p. 160)

CASTLE
Tower of London ★★★ (p. 150)

CHURCH/CATHEDRAL
All Hallows-by-the-Tower (p. 153)
St. Bartholomew-the-Great (p. 152)
St. Bride's (p. 152)
St. James's Piccadilly (p. 106)
St. Martin-in-the-Fields ★ (p. 107)
St. Mary-le-Bow (p. 153)
St. Paul's Cathedral ★★★ (p. 146)
St. Paul's Church (p. 108)
Southwark Cathedral (p. 141)

Chelsea Physic Garden.

MONUMENT/MEMORIAL

The Monument ★ (p. 145)

MUSEUM

Bank of England Museum (p. 144)
British Library ★★ (p. 161)
British Museum ★★★ (p. 96)
British Music Experience (p. 170)
Cartoon Museum ★★ (p. 98)
Charles Dickens Museum ★ (p. 98)
Churchill War Rooms (p. 120)
Clockmakers' Museum (p. 144)
Dennis Severs' House ★ (p. 154)
Design Museum (p. 134)
Embankment Galleries (p. 109)
Fan Museum (p. 172)
Florence Nightingale Museum ★
(p. 134)
Foundling Museum (p. 100)
Freud Museum (p. 164)
Garden Museum ★ (p. 135)
Geffrye Museum ★ (p. 154)
Golden Hinde (p. 135)
Handel Museum ★ (p. 101)

Horniman Museum ★★ (p. 179)
Household Cavalry Museum (p. 121)
Imperial War Museum ★★★ (p. 136)
Kew Bridge Steam Museum ★ (p. 179)
London Bridge Experience and
London Tombs (p. 137)
London Canal Museum (p. 167)
London Dungeon ★ (p. 137)
London Film Museum (p. 139)
London Transport Museum ★★
(p. 102)
Madame Tussauds (p. 168)
Museum of Brands, Advertising &
Packaging ★ (p. 115)
Museum of London ★★ (p. 145)
Museum of London Docklands ★
(p. 155)
National Army Museum ★ (p. 123)
National Maritime Museum ★★★
(p. 172)
Natural History Museum ★★★
(p. 124)
Old Operating Theatre Museum &
Herb Garret ★★ (p. 139)

4

EXPLORING LONDON

Sights & Attractions by Theme

Somerset House.

British Library.

Detail of mummy case, British Museum.

Stained glass window in Samuel Johnson's House.

OBSERVATION WHEEL

PALACE

PARK/GARDEN

St. James's Park ★★ (p. 106)
Thames Barrier Park (p. 159)
Victoria Park (p. 160)

PLANETARIUM
Royal Observatory ★★ (p. 175)

SQUARE
Covent Garden ★★ (p. 100)
Trafalgar Square ★(p. 110)

ZOO
Battersea Park & Zoo ★ (p. 117)
London Zoo ★★ (p. 167)

Paddle boats on the Serpentine, Hyde Park.

4

EXPLORING LONDON

Sights & Attractions by Theme

EATING OUT IN LONDON

5

L ondon is one of the world's great dining capitals. Here you can experience a global range of cuisines, anything from a traditional English feast to the regional cooking of countries spread around the globe, from Italy to India.

The last few years have been momentous for the London restaurant scene. Top-end places can no longer rest on their laurels; they are dealing with educated, well-traveled, and opinionated customers who know the value of a meal. Prices have stabilized and even lowered in some cases, and every major restaurant now offers good value, set meals.

On top of that, the "gastropub" has become a force to be reckoned with. Young chefs have taken over moribund pubs, filled them with odd pieces of furniture, and now offer top cooking at less-than-top prices. Some are in the city center, but you'll also find many gastropubs in residential neighborhoods outside the usual tourist areas.

A big change in the last few years is the geographic shift from the West End to East London, where new cafes and small restaurants have emerged in what is now a dynamic part of the capital.

But perhaps the greatest coming-of-age for London's restaurants is the acknowledgement from the rest of the world that London is now a gastronomic world-class city. The internationally famous chef Joël Robuchon has described London as "possibly the gastronomic capital of the world," because all that is new and innovative in cooking and the restaurant world now originates in Britain's capital city.

It's all good news for restaurant-goers: Eating out in London offers more choice, more value, and more fun than ever.

BEST BETS

- o **Best Breakfast:** Tradition and British classics are alive and kicking in the splendid Grand Divan at **Simpson's-in-the-Strand.** Nestle in a booth while all around you captains of industry tuck into *Ten Deadly Sins.* See p. 204. Or try a good old-fashioned British deviled kidney at Terence Conran's **Albion.** See p. 242.

- o **Best for Families:** As well as being full of pools and a lush tropical garden, the **Blue Elephant** supplies crayons and paper and face painting at Sunday lunchtime. See p. 230. Highchairs and a family atmosphere at **Locanda Locatelli** might get your children started down the gourmet path. See p. 216.

- o **Best for a New Experience:** If you harbor any doubts about London's inexorable, successful move east, book dinner (way in advance) at **Viajante.** The cool dining room inside the Town Hall Hotel is the setting for unexpected culinary fireworks from Portuguese chef Nuno Mendes. Eating is believing here. See p. 245. At the other side of town, Peter Gordon's **Kopapa** offers his extraordinarily successful style of fusion cooking in a casual Covent Garden setting. See p. 205.

- **Best Budget Eating:** Join the queues for the thick, satisfying udon noodles that come in an array of tastes at **Koya.** See p. 211. Cramped, noisy **Mandalay** happily offers the best (and only) foray into Burmese cooking in London, a mixture of Chinese, Thai, and Indian influences. See p. 219.

- **Best Splurge:** If you want some of the best, most exciting, and up-to-the-minute cooking in London, you can't choose better than **The Square,** where Philip Howard's cooking is as smooth and sophisticated as the setting. See p. 196. Or go for the £125 tasting menu at **L'Atelier de Joël Robuchon,** for a meal where tastes explode on the tongue. See p. 202.

- **Best for Romance:** Eat in the greenhouse surrounded by plants and odd statues and feel a million miles away from it all at **Petersham Nurseries Café,** south of the Thames in serene Richmond. See p. 253. The West End **Greenhouse** is delightful: a fabulous restaurant reached through a quiet garden, where a fountain gently tumbles. See p. 197.

- **Best Service:** Under the suave, experienced guidance of London's most famous restaurant manager, Silvano Giraldin, service at **Le Gavroche,** is the best in London. See p. 193.

- **Best for Sharing:** Tapas bars and restaurants have taken London by storm, as sharing becomes the new trend. **Tapas Brindisa** is owned by Spanish food importer, Brindisa, giving it an ingredients' edge over its competitors. See p. 235. Go for the tempting tasting dishes at the excellent wine bar, **Terroirs.** See p. 206.

- **Best British Cooking: Hix** is the place for great British classics like duck salad with carrots, turnips, and pea shoots, and steak with baked bone marrow. See p. 210. **St. John** has been championing offal and all those bits that are normally discarded. And it's still a huge influence with dishes like potted pork and rabbit, then Arbroath smokie with mash followed by that British dish you don't often encounter: Eccles cake and Lancashire cheese. See p. 238.

- **Best Indian:** Light, flavorful biryanis are just part of the draw of glamorous **Amaya.** The setting is gorgeous, with the cooks in the open kitchen putting on a great performance as they cook the kebabs over coals and throw rotis into the ovens. See p. 223. **Dishoom** may not be as genuine as the old 1990s' Bombay cafes set up by Persian immigrants that it's modeled on, but it's enormous fun. See p. 206.

- **Best Brasserie:** London is teaching the French a thing or

---

Restaurant Prices

Price categories are based on a three-course dinner for one person, without wine.

Very Expensive (££££) = £75+;

Expensive (£££) = £50 to £75;

Moderate (££) = £25 to £50;

Inexpensive (£) = under £25.

But remember these are average prices; you'll find that it's possible to eat almost everywhere (except for high-end, fixed-price restaurants) at the lower end of the price scale.

two about big, bustling, glamorous brasseries. **Les Deux Salons** evokes the Belle Epoque perfectly. See p. 203. One of the most talked about openings of 2012 is **The Delaunay** where ace restaurateurs Jeremy King and Chris Corbin have brought their particular genius to all-day eating. See p. 205.

o **Best Cheeseboard:** For classic French cheeses you can't do better than the top French restaurants, particularly **Le Gavroche** (p. 193), the **Greenhouse** (p. 197), and **The Square** (p. 196). But you'll find unusual cheeses in the new tapas restaurants in London. **The Salt Yard** (p. 216) offers Spanish ewes milk cheeses from La Mancha, as well as a range that runs from Sardinian Pecorino to Gorgonzola from Piedmont.

THE WEST END
Mayfair
VERY EXPENSIVE
Alain Ducasse at the Dorchester ★★★ FRENCH   Alain Ducasse is the name here, but it's talented Jocelyn Herland who earned three Michelin stars in 2010. The plush room centers around a circular table for six, hidden behind a translucent curtain and lit with fiber-optic cables, but it's better to sit in the pretty front room overlooking Hyde Park. This is French haute cuisine, but with a nod toward London's more relaxed style. For the genuine gourmet experience, order what you want and ignore the unfortunate number of high-end dishes with a £10 supplement. The cooking is superb; the quality of the seasonal ingredients shines through in starters such as sautéed lobster, truffled chicken quenelles, and pasta; and a main dish of rich veal from the Limousin region. Desserts are great set pieces, although the cheeseboard is lacking the range a restaurant of this standard should offer. And the wine list? Splendid, but splendidly priced as well.

Inside the Dorchester Hotel, Park Lane, W1. www.alainducasse-dorchester.com. © **020/7629-8866.** Reservations required 2 weeks in advance. Set-price 3 course lunch menu £55, inc 2 glasses of wine, coffee, and water. Set menu 2 courses £60, 3 courses £85, 4 courses £100; tasting menu 7 courses £125. AE, DC, MC, V. Tues–Fri noon–2pm; Tues–Sat 6:30–10pm. Tube: Green Park, Hyde Park Corner, or Marble Arch.

Le Gavroche ★★★ FRENCH   There may be new kids on the block, new cuisines, and new young chefs, but Le Gavroche remains the number one choice in London for classical French cuisine with some masterly updating from Michel Roux, Jr., son of the chef who founded the restaurant in 1966. The famous cheese soufflé is still there, alongside lobster mousse with caviar and a champagne butter sauce. From the main courses: grilled scallops with carrots, salad, and tarragon mustard sauce, or roast veal with creamed morel mushroom sauce and mashed potatoes, and desserts including apricot and Cointreau soufflé. The cheeseboard is exemplary. It's all beautifully presented and served with style. The wine list is a masterclass in top French wines, and is kind to the purse as well on lesser-known varieties. It all takes place in a comfortable, conventional basement dining room that may be too old-fashioned for some, but with its Picassos on the walls, it perfectly sets the scene for a classic meal.

West End
Restaurants

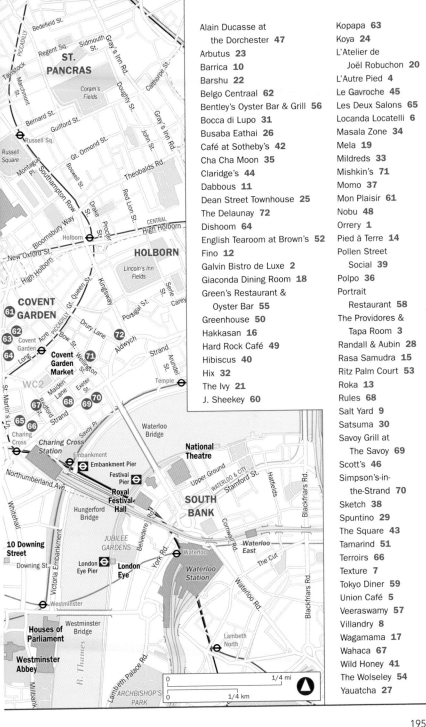

43 Upper Brook St., W1. www.le-gavroche.co.uk. ☏ **020/7408-0881.** Reservations required as far in advance as possible. Main courses £26.90–£54.80; set lunch £52; *Le Menu Exceptionnel* (whole table) £100. AE, MC, V. Mon–Fri noon–2pm; Mon–Sat 6:30–11pm. Tube: Marble Arch.

Hibiscus ★★★ CONTEMPORARY EUROPEAN   The cooking is spectacular here—with enough culinary fireworks to satisfy the most adventurous—while the setting is elegant and understated. Claude Bosi made his name and reputation at his Hibiscus restaurant in Ludlow in Shropshire, and then came to London in 2007 with his wife Claire, who runs front of house. Bosi is now a household name among those who appreciate top cooking. In a real tribute to his skill, he is also something of a chef's chef. His style of cooking includes ingredients that you wouldn't expect in classic French dishes: crab salad comes with turnip, Kentish sea leaves, ginger, and smoked olive oil; Welsh mutton with a walnut crust is served with white bean and prune parfait. This is one to save up for—put yourself into the hands of the master and appreciate an exceptional eating experience.

29 Maddox St., W1. www.hibiscusrestaurant.co.uk. ☏ **020/7629-2999.** Reservations required. Lunch 3 courses £34.95–£43.45, 6-course tasting menu (whole table only) £90, 8-course tasting menu (whole table only) Sat only £100. A la carte 2 courses £60, 3 courses £80. AE, DC, MC, V. Mon–Sat noon–2:30pm and Mon–Thurs 6:30–10pm; Fri–Sat 6–10pm. Tube: Green Park.

Sketch ★★ CONTEMPORARY EUROPEAN   Sketch offers an extraordinary variety of dining experiences. Housed in a converted 18th-century building in Mayfair, it's masterminded by Mourad Mazouz of Momo (p. 199), and Michelin-starred French chef, Pierre Gagnaire. The **Lecture Room and Library** is a riot of color and style with an equally flamboyant menu—this is the place for Gagnaire's most inventive cooking. His style is unique, taking an impressive range of ingredients for each dish so that one course becomes an assemblage of three or four small dishes. For more modest prices and less complex dishes, try the **Gallery,** with videos playing on the walls, loud music, and buzzing atmosphere. Wild sea bass carpaccio with redcurrant jelly and celeriac, and roast lamb with peanut and tandoori sauce, mango and papaya salad, tamarind jus, and dried Paris mushrooms are on the menu. The quirkily decorated **Parlour** offers all-day dining, and becomes a bar at night.

9 Conduit St., W1. www.sketch.uk.com. ☏ **020/7659-4500.** Reservations essential. Lecture Room and Library: Main courses £37–£55; set lunch 2 courses £30, 3 courses £35–£48; 3-course dinner £35; 6-course veg £75, 6-course non veg £75. The Gallery: Main courses £8.50–£35. Parlour: Main courses £10–£17.50; afternoon tea £10.50–£27; with champagne £38–£65. AE, MC, V. Lecture Room and Library Tues–Sat noon–2:30pm and 7–11pm. Parlour Mon–Fri 8am–2am; Sat 10am–2am. Tube: Oxford Circus.

The Square ★★★ FRENCH   One of London's favorite restaurants, The Square has remained consistently true to its aim of serving quality food in a sophisticated, quietly casual setting. The popular chef and co-owner, Philip Howard, has been here since it opened in 1991 and has never failed to deliver the best. Signature dishes such as lasagna of Dorset crab with a cappuccino of shellfish and champagne foam remain on the menu; mains of Pyrenean lamb with curd ravioli, pine nuts, and raisins appear during the winter, along with an unusual red mullet with pumpkin gnocchi, chanterelles, salsify, and Parmesan. The cheeseboard is superb and worth the supplement; desserts such as cheesecake with passion fruit and lime sound simple, but are wonderful exercises in complementary tastes.

THE best WINE BAR FOOD IN TOWN

Wine bars have always been popular in London, with chains such as **Davy's** (www.davy.co.uk), and **Corney & Barrow** (www.corney-barrow.co.uk) leading the way. The independents, however, usually have a quirkier choice of wines.

Bedford & Strand ★ Tucked away in a basement with a packed bar and dining area, the Bedford & Strand, with its odd layout, small corners, and wooden chairs and tables, is a favorite for the after-work crowd. The small wine list is excellent and the food offers straightforward charcuterie and cheese platters, and bistro dishes including classic fish pie or lamb chops. 1a Bedford St., WC2 www.bedford-strand.com. ℂ **020/7836-3033.** Main courses £11–£19.75. AE, MC, V. Mon–Fri noon–midnight; Sat 5.30pm–1am. Tube: Charing Cross.

Cork & Bottle For more than 40 years, Kiwi Don Hewitson has been stocking his popular wine bar with a startlingly wide range of wines from the cheap-and-cheerful to the top end. Order the famous raised ham-and-cheese pie any time of the day, and enjoy the bonhomie of this Sixties basement setting. 44–46 Cranbourn St., WC2. www.thecorkandbottle.co.uk. ℂ **020/7734-7807.** Main courses £8.95 to £21.95. Mon–Sat 11am–11.30pm, Sun noon–10.30pm. Tube: Leicester Sq.

Shampers Since 1977, Londoners have been fed and watered in this wine bar and formal basement restaurant where the wide mix of loyal followers includes City types and those in the entertainment industry. Gravadlax to start and then daily specials along with succulent grills accompany a huge, knowledgeable wine list (with around 50 sold by the glass). 4 Kingly St., W1. www.shampers.net. ℂ **020/7437-1692.** Main courses £11.95–£16.95. Mon–Sat noon–11pm. Tube: Oxford Circus.

Suze ★ Perfectly located, just off Oxford Street on the edge of Mayfair, Suze is run by well-established New Zealanders Tom and Susan Glynn. The selection of antipodean wines is startlingly good and generously priced. The platters of seafood, cheese, and charcuterie, between £6.95 and £17.95, are perfect for sharing. In the summer, grab an outside table and watch the world go by. 41 North Audley St., W1. www.suzeinmayfair.com. ℂ **020/7491-3237.** Main courses £12.95–£17.95. AE, MC, V. Mon–Sat 11am–11pm. Tube: Bond St. or Marble Arch.

6–10 Bruton St., W1. www.squarerestaurant.com. ℂ **020/7495-7100.** Reservations required. Set lunch 2 courses £30, 3 courses £35, 3-course dinner £80; tasting menu £105, £175 with wine. AE, DC, MC, V. Mon–Sat noon–2:45pm. Mon–Thurs 6:30–10pm. Fri–Sat 6:30–10:30pm; Sun 6:30–9:30pm. Tube: Bond St. or Green Park.

EXPENSIVE

Greenhouse ★★ CONTEMPORARY EUROPEAN The secret garden and fountain come as a surprise to first-time visitors. Tucked away in Mayfair, the Greenhouse's pretty dining room looks out onto the greenery. Lyon-born head chef Antonin Bonnet is an inspired master, producing first-class dishes without destroying the natural flavors of his ingredients. His skill in mixing unusual combinations shines through in dishes such as a gutsy, apple-cider-marinated mackerel with horseradish foam and pickled black radish, followed by Scottish venison with spiced pear and smoked celeriac. Vegetarians are well treated with a separate menu that's so tempting it might convert carnivores. The cheeseboard offers one of the largest selections in London; otherwise go for a rich dark chocolate and praline tart with hazelnut ice cream and a milk mousse. The wine list equals the best in the capital, with rare wines a specialty, but it's also kind to less ambitious pockets.

27a Hays Mews, W1. www.greenhouserestaurant.co.uk. ℭ **020/7499-3331.** Reservations required. Set lunch 2 courses £25, 3 courses £29; vegetarian menu £85; tasting menu £90. AE, DC, MC, V. Mon–Fri noon–2:30pm; Mon–Sat 6:30–11pm. Tube: Green Park.

Nobu ★★ JAPANESE   Upstairs in the Metropolitan Hotel, London's original Nobu is still a celebrity haunt—despite the departure of some of the fickle fashion crowd to the louder, flashier **Nobu Berkeley,** where the bar is packed nightly with high spenders. Founded by actor Robert De Niro, restaurateur Drew Nieporent, and chef Nobu Matsuhisa, the original Nobu remains a destination restaurant, its enduring popularity a testament to the skillful cooking of chef Mark Edwards. And it has had a much-needed facelift. All the fireworks are here: stunning appetizers of unusual combinations such as lobster ceviche, shrimp with caviar; new-style sweet shrimp sashimi; plus classic Japanese dishes that Nobu Matsuhisa has famously combined with Peruvian influences. Favorites including black cod with miso are as popular as when Nobu opened in 1997. There's also a small 10-seater sushi bar. For a cheaper option, order the £33 lunch of six dishes with salad, rice, and miso soup.

Inside Metropolitan Hotel, 19 Old Park Lane, W1. www.noburestaurants.com. ℭ **020/7447-4747.** Reservations required 1 month in advance. Main courses £5–£33.50; sushi and sashimi £3–£10 per piece; fixed-price lunch £33. AE, DC, MC, V. Mon–Fri noon–2:15pm; Mon–Thurs 6–10:15pm; Sat–Sun 12:30–2:30pm; Fri-Sat 6–11pm; Sun 6–9:30pm. Tube: Hyde Park Corner. Also at 15 Berkeley St., ℭ **020/7290-9222.**

Scott's ★★ SEAFOOD   Scott's is glamorous and glitzy, a seafood restaurant that's on every celebrity's speed dial. Opened as an oyster warehouse in 1851 by a young fishmonger, John Scott, the restaurant moved to Mayfair in 1968. The dining room is drop-dead gorgeous, oak-paneled with art on the walls and a show-stopping crustacean display in the central bar. Meat eaters are taken care of, as are vegetarians and vegans, but fish is the *raison d'être* here. So it seems perverse to ignore the freshest of oysters, caviar that starts at £80, octopus carpaccio, smoked haddock with colcannon, or a simple, perfectly cooked sea bass. The restaurant has opened the **Mount Street Deli,** 100 Mount St., W1 (www.themountstreetdeli.co.uk; ℭ **020/7499-6843**) opposite, a perfect place for breakfast, a light lunch, or afternoon tea.

20 Mount St., W1. www.scotts-restaurant.com. ℭ **020/7495-7309.** Reservations required. Main courses £17.50–£42. AE, DC, MC, V. Mon–Sat noon–10:30pm; Sun noon–10pm. Tube: Green Park or Bond St.

Tamarind ★ INDIAN   When it opened in 1995, Tamarind was one of the first truly glamorous Indian restaurants in London, and it's still a sophisticated venue for the well heeled and the well traveled. The menu takes traditional Mogul cuisine as its inspiration; selecting the best, freshest market ingredients daily, the team under chef Alfred Prasad produces high-class Indian cooking. Go for the specialist north Indian tandoor dishes—lamb kebab marinated in raw papaya, garlic, green chili, coriander and mint, then perfectly cooked in the charcoal-fired oven—or opt for a curry that modernizes the classics, such as *tali macchi,* pan-fried sea bass with asparagus and mango on a sauce of tomato, mustard, curry leaves, and coconut. Vegetarians are well catered for, especially if they order the *dal makhni,* a black-lentil specialty of northwest India.

20–22 Queen St., W1. www.tamarindrestaurant.com. ✆ **020/7629-3561.** Reservations required. Main courses £17.95–£28; fixed-price lunch 2 courses £18.50, 3 courses £21.50; fixed-price dinner £68; pre- and posttheatre menu £28.50. Sunday lunch 3 courses £32. AE, DC, DISC, MC, V. Sun–Fri noon–2:45pm; Mon–Sat 6–11pm; Sun 6:30–10:30pm. Tube: Green Park.

MODERATE

Hard Rock Café ☺ AMERICAN   This is the original Hard Rock, and it has served more than 12 million people since it opened in 1971. Just like at every other Hard Rock Café, there's usually a line of people waiting to get in. They come partly to take in the now-legendary collection of rock memorabilia, including Eric Clapton's Lead II Fender, to buy the T-shirt at the shop opposite, and to eat starters such as Santa Fe spring rolls and hickory smoked chicken wings, better-than-average burgers, and a wide range of main dishes. There's also a good selection of beers.

150 Old Park Lane, W1. www.hardrock.com. ✆ **020/7514-1700.** Reservations not accepted. Main courses £10.75–£19.45. AE, DC, MC, V. Sun–Thurs 11:30am–12:30am; Fri–Sat 11:30am–1am. Tube: Green Park or Hyde Park Corner.

Momo ★ MOROCCAN/NORTH AFRICAN   Entering, you step into a colorful fantasy of Moroccan life: Stucco walls, wooden screens, rugs, brass lanterns, and low tables take you straight to Marrakech. The menu is authentic as well, built around couscous and tagines bursting with chicken or lamb, preserved lemons, and olives. You might start with a *briouat* of cheese, mint, and potatoes served with quince marmalade, or the chef's specialty of *pastille*—filo pastry parcels filled with sweet-tasting wood pigeon, almonds, and cinnamon, then lamb or fish-of-the-day tagine followed by an orange confit. Informal, onsite **Café Mô** serves a fast lunch (£8.50), all day meze (from £4.50 per dish or meze selections £15.50 to £24.50), and there's a bazaar based on a Moroccan souk, plus an outdoor terrace in summer. The trendy basement **Kemia Bar** serves cocktails to a star-studded clientele.

25 Heddon St., W1. www.momoresto.com. ✆ **020/7434-4040.** Reservations required. Main courses £17–£36; fixed-price lunch £15.50–£19.50; set menu £49. AE, DC, MC, V. Mon–Sat noon–2:30pm and 6:30-11:30pm; Sun 6:30–11pm. Tube: Piccadilly Circus or Oxford Circus.

Pollen Street Social ★★ CONTEMPORARY EUROPEAN/TAPAS   Jason Atherton made his name working for Gordon Ramsay, then left to open his amazingly successful restaurant. It's a large space with an open kitchen, banquette seating, wood floors, and smart brown-and-cream decor. Casual diners make for the lounge bar and a menu of tapas dishes and desserts. Small dishes are also on the restaurant menu, so you can share starters then order a regular main course. Start with scallop ceviche, cucumber, and radish with a soy dressing and apple; Cornish crab with pear and a sweet-and-sour cauliflower and frozen peanut powder; or cauliflower and squid with herbs. Then move on to pork belly with apple, curly kale, mulled blackberries, and cobnut paste or halibut with paella and sprouting broccoli. It's sophisticated cooking in a relaxed, casual venue.

8 Pollen St., W1. www.pollenstreetsocial.com. ℰ **020/7290-7600.** Main courses £22.50–£25. AE, MC, V. Mon–Sat noon–12:45pm and 6–10:45pm. Tube: Oxford Circus.

Wild Honey ★ CONTEMPORARY EUROPEAN   In this posh, and more expensive, Mayfair sibling of Arbutus (p. 208), chef Anthony Demetre and business partner Will Smith have shown once again their uncanny knack of producing just what the punters want. The cooking is market led using impeccably fresh, native, and seasonal ingredients with huge skill. Cornish mackerel with spiced cauliflower, beetroot, pine nuts, and black radish; or foie gras terrine with Yorkshire rhubarb and toasted sourdough, followed by saddle of Norfolk hare with spätzle, curly kale, and Williams pear; or sea bass with grilled artichokes, cavalo nero cabbage, and bergamot testify to the sure touch that produces dishes that both satisfy and intrigue. Cheeses come from the top cheese shop La Fromagerie (p. 292); otherwise finish with the namesake "Wild Honey" ice cream with crushed honeycomb.

12 St. George St., WC1. www.wildhoneyrestaurant.co.uk. ℰ **020/7758-9160.** Reservations required. Main courses £19.50–£23.50; 3-course lunch Mon–Sat £19.95; pretheatre Mon–Fri £22.95. AE, MC, V. Mon–Thurs noon–2:30pm and 5–11pm; Fri–Sat noon–2:30pm and 5–11:30pm; Sun noon–3pm and 6–10:30pm. Tube: Oxford Circus, Bond St., Green Park, or Piccadilly Circus.

St. James's

MODERATE

Green's Restaurant & Oyster Bar ★ SEAFOOD/TRADITIONAL BRITISH   Clubby, comfortable, and definitely part of the Establishment, Green's has been serving its brand of traditional British cooking for more than 30 years. Wood-paneled walls hung with cartoons, a central bar, and seemingly soundproof booths with leather banquettes make Green's a safe bet for its political and power-broking customers. This is the place for potted shrimp with toast, smoked salmon and scrambled eggs; their famous salmon fishcakes; oysters in season; very upscale fish and chips with mushy peas; lamb shank with fennel mashed potatoes; or the occasional discreet foray into contemporary cooking such as monkfish wrapped in bacon with spicy carrot puree. Game is a strength, and the wine list is superb. It could all be rather stuffy but it's not. Staff are attentive, and the experience is all helped along by the urbane presence of the owner, former wine merchant Simon Parker-Bowles.

36 Duke St., St. James's, SW1. www.greens.org.uk. ℰ **020/7930-4566.** Reservations required. Main courses £17–£32.50. Sat brunch menu £20. AE, DC, MC, V. Mon–Sat 11:30am–3pm and 5:30–10:45pm. Tube: Green Park. Also at 14 Cornhill, EC2. ℰ **020/7220-6300.**

The Wolseley ★ CONTEMPORARY EUROPEAN   With its vaulted ceilings and pillars, polished marble, huge chandeliers, and Art Deco interior, the Wolseley looks like a grand Viennese cafe. It's an all-day brasserie that caters for the rich, the famous, media regulars, and ordinary mortals, presided over by Jeremy King and Chris Corbin, two of London's top restaurateurs. Breakfast is a leisurely affair, but it gets pretty busy during lunch, and you can find yourself at a small table away from the main action. The all-day menu takes in light sandwiches, salads, and a *plat du jour*. The lunch and dinner menu runs the gamut from eggs Benedict to salt beef and mustard sandwich, from mussels and chips to a defiantly old-fashioned Wiener Schnitzel. The cooking is above average but not mega, but in this buzzy, bustling atmosphere who cares?

160 Piccadilly, W1. www.thewolseley.com. ℂ **020/7499-6996.** Reservations recommended. Main courses £11.75–£39.75. AE, DC, MC, V. Mon–Fri 7am–midnight; Sat 8am–midnight; Sun 8am–10:45pm. Tube: Green Park.

Piccadilly Circus & Leicester Square

All the selections below (along with those under "Covent Garden & the Strand" and "Soho," elsewhere in this section) are candidates for dining before or after a show in London's Theatreland.

EXPENSIVE

Bentley's Oyster Bar & Grill ★★ SEAFOOD/TRADITIONAL BRITISH Bentley's is a London institution that opened in 1916 and went through various ups and downs, before being rescued by the highly talented and charming Irish chef, Richard Corrigan. Under his expert guidance, Bentley's (according to its many fans) now serves the best fish in London. The **Oyster Bar,** vaguely Arts and Crafts in feel, is a great place for watching the guys shucking oysters behind the bar and dining off the likes of dressed crab, smoked salmon, or smoked eel. In the more formal upstairs **Grill,** divided into the Grill Room and the Rib Room, the menu includes stalwarts such as the rich Bentley's fish soup, but it's worth being more adventurous and trying something like the pan-seared scallops with sardines, horseradish, and lemon pickled grapes. It's all conducted in a genuinely friendly atmosphere, though high-ish prices put off some people.

11–15 Swallow St., W1. www.bentleysoysterbarandgrill.co.uk. ℂ **020/7734-4756.** Oyster Bar: Main courses £11–£24. Grill: Main courses £21.50–£32. AE, MC, V. Oyster Bar: Mon–Sat 7:30–10:30am, noon–midnight; Sun noon–9:30pm. Restaurant: Mon–Fri noon–3pm and 5:30–10:30pm; Sat, Sun 7–10am, noon–2:30pm and 5:30–11pm. Tube: Piccadilly Circus.

Veeraswamy ★ INDIAN In the same ownership as Amaya (p. 223) and Masala Zone (p. 255), this grand old lady of 1926 vintage is one of London's most glamorous Indian restaurants. The Maharajah-like decor is beautiful—with turbans as decoration, chandeliers, and silks of the brightest colors—while the view over Regent Street is unexpectedly glamorous. The cooking is also right up to the minute, with diners led on an exquisite tour through the rich culinary regions of India, from the tandoors of the Northwest Frontier to the coastal specialties of India's seaside states. Fresh mussels in ginger sauce; flash-fried oysters; chicken korma with saffron from Lucknow; spice-covered leg of lamb from north India; Malabar lobster curry—all are dishes that have been carefully sourced and beautifully cooked.

Victory House, 99 Regent St., W1. www.veeraswamy.com. ℂ **020/7734-1401.** Reservations recommended. Main courses £18–£24; lunch and pre-/posttheatre menu Mon–Sat £38–£55; Sun set 3-course menu £24. AE, DC, MC, V. Mon– Fri 12–2:15pm and 5:30–10:30pm; Sat 12:30–2:30pm and 5:30–10:45pm. Sun 12:30–2:30pm and 6–10:15pm. Tube: Piccadilly Circus.

INEXPENSIVE

Cha Cha Moon CHINESE   Restaurateur Alan Yau's uncanny feel for what the public wants to eat has worked yet again with Cha Cha Moon. The man who started Wagamama (p. 255) may soon roll out his latest concept but for the moment, his Ganton Street restaurant is London's trendiest noodle bar. Noodle dishes are cooked in broth, using authentic ingredients, to produce Szechuan chicken with jasmine, coriander, onion, chili, and oil noodles; or Taiwan braised beef with preserved cabbage, mustard greens, and thick noodles from north China. The wok noodle menu produces surprises such as the Singapore dish of Chinese salami, fishcake, and chili sauce. The service can be erratic to say the least, but the restaurant is always popular.

15–21 Ganton St., W1. www.chachamoon.com. ℃ **020/7297-9800.** Main courses £6.30–£9.60. £10 set menu. AE, MC, V. Mon–Thurs 11:30am–11pm; Fri–Sat 11:30am–11:30pm; Sun noon–10:30pm. Tube: Oxford Circus or Piccadilly Circus.

Tokyo Diner 🍴 JAPANESE   This three-storied Japanese interloper into prime Chinatown territory is cheap and friendly, refuses tips, has lasted 20 years, and is open every day of the year from noon to midnight; no wonder it's so popular. Don-buri rice dishes pull in students and the impecunious to fill up on beef and onion braised in sweet Japanese sauce with ginger. Others go for their popular bento box set meals: £14.80 gets you a chicken teriyaki box, in which chicken flambéed in teriyaki sauce is served with rice, vegetables, and pickles. Sushi and soup noodles complete the picture.

2 Newport Place, WC2. www.tokyodiner.com. ℃ **020/7287-8777.** Main courses £6.60–£19.50. Bento box set meals £14.80–£19.90. MC, V. Daily noon–midnight. Tube: Leicester Sq.

Covent Garden & Strand

The restaurants in and around Covent Garden and the Strand are convenient options for West End theatregoers.

VERY EXPENSIVE

L'Atelier de Joël Robuchon ★★★ FRENCH   The London Atelier of Robuchon (the chef with 26 Michelin stars and restaurants around the world), is based on his concept of an informal restaurant. There are three areas: La Cuisine, which is the most conventional; the Le Salon bar; and the moody red-and-black "Atelier." For the most dramatic effect, eat at Atelier's counter. Here you can watch the theatre of the chefs producing tapas-style dishes—small bombshells of taste as in beef and foie gras mini-burger; pig's trotter on parmesan toast; and the signature egg cocotte with wild mushroom cream, all wildly inventive and beautifully presented. The a la carte menu follows the conventional three-course approach, using superb ingredients. Given the skill and the prices, the set lunches are a wonderful, relatively inexpensive way to sample some of London's best cooking.

13–15 West St., WC2. www.joel-robuchon.com. ℃ **020/7010-8600.** Reservations essential. Main courses £19–£38; small tasting dishes £11–£19; Menu Découverte 8 courses £125; Vegetarian Découverte 8 courses £80; lunch and prethreatre 2-course menu £28, 3 courses £32, 4 courses £40. AE, MC, V. Daily noon–2:30pm and 5:30–10:30pm. Tube: Leicester Sq.

EXPENSIVE

The Ivy ★ CONTEMPORARY EUROPEAN   New restaurants with a more exciting vibe, a more adventurous menu, and chicer decor constantly open, but The Ivy manages to remain extremely popular as a favorite London haunt. However since opening the private members' club upstairs, celebrities are thin on the ground in the downstairs restaurant. But mostly there's a genuine welcome, a great buzz, and a menu that stays comfortingly familiar. There's nothing too challenging in starters of smoked salmon; potted ham; or shellfish bisque, and mains of salmon fishcakes; the famous Ivy hamburger; or roast poulet for two. You don't go here for exciting cooking but for the buzz.

1–5 West St., WC2. www.the-ivy.co.uk. © **020/7836-4751.** Reservations required. Main courses £11–£44. Set menu 2 courses £21.75, 3 courses £26.25. AE, DC, MC, V. Mon–Sat noon–11:30pm; Sun noon–10:30pm. Tube: Leicester Sq.

J. Sheekey ★★ SEAFOOD   Tucked into a small alleyway off St. Martin's Lane, J. Sheekey has long been a Theatreland favorite for both the famous (Laurence Olivier and Vivien Leigh) and the not-so-famous. It's a charming dining room with pictures of theatrical greats lining the walls. You can opt for the favorites—Atlantic prawns; the famous Sheekey's fish pie; and if you really want to impress, the *plateau de fruits de mer* (seafood platter) for two—but it's worth trying more unusual dishes like lemon-spiced tiger prawns with mango and coriander salsa or shrimp and scallop burger with spiced mayonnaise. Weekly specials veer away from the familiar menu, with dishes such as fillet of red mullet with spiced crab toast. For dessert, the Yorkshire rhubarb and apple crumble on the winter menu is a must, or go for an excellent British cheeseboard. The more casual **J. Sheekey Oyster Bar,** 33–34 St. Martin's Court (© **020/7240-2565**), is next door, has the same look, and offers Sheekey classics and smaller dishes.

28–32 St. Martin's Court, WC2. www.j-sheekey.co.uk. © **020/7240-2565.** Reservations recommended. Main courses £15.25–£42. Weekend set lunch menu 3 courses £26.50. AE, DC, MC, V. Mon–Sat noon–3pm and 5:30pm–midnight; Sun noon–3:30pm and 6–11pm. Tube: Leicester Sq.

Les Deux Salons ★★ FRENCH/BRASSERIE   The third venture from Michelin-starred Anthony Demetre and Will Smith (see Arbutus, p. 208 and Wild Honey, p. 200) is the kind of smart brasserie that will have the French reaching for their smelling salts. It's large, bustling, decorated with the requisite amount of polished brass, mirrors, and dark wood, evokes the Belle Epoque, and offers a standard of cooking that is now rare in Parisian brasseries. The upper floor is more intimate; downstairs swings along in style. A well-drilled kitchen produces impeccable dishes including Herefordshire snail and bacon pie; thinly sliced veal with tuna mayonnaise and lemon; top French-rated andouillette with mustard sauce; grilled sea bass with Lyonnaise potatoes and wild rosemary; daily specials such as rabbit in mustard; plus desserts of glazed lemon tart with crème Chantilly or warm apple tart with vanilla ice cream. Service is spot on and prices are reasonable. Les Deux Salons is a palpable hit.

40–42 William IV St., WC2. www.lesdeuxsalons.co.uk. © **020/7420-2050.** Reservations recommended. Main courses £11–£22.50. 3 course lunch £15.50, pretheatre menu 3 courses £15.95. AE, MC, V. Daily noon–11pm. Sunday brunch 10am–5pm. Tube: Charing Cross.

Rules ★ TRADITIONAL BRITISH   Here you'll get a genuine taste of traditional London. Opened in 1798 as an oyster bar, the gorgeous, red plush Edwardian interior with drawings and cartoons covering the walls is much as it was when feeding the great and good of the theatrical and literary world—like Charles Dickens and H. G. Wells, Laurence Olivier, and Clark Gable. What keeps Rules alive today is its devotion to top, traditional British cooking. This is the place for a meal of British classics: native Irish or Scottish oysters; the best game only served in season—wild Highland red deer, grouse, snipe, pheasant, and woodcock; and beef from the owner's estate, skillfully prepared and cooked. Puddings (not desserts in this most British of restaurants) might be a rib-stickingly good Golden Syrup sponge pudding, a winter blackberry and apple crumble, or even rice pudding, bringing back childhood memories.

35 Maiden Lane, WC2. www.rules.co.uk. ✆ **020/7836-5314.** Reservations recommended. Main courses £18.95–£32. AE, DC, MC, V. Mon–Sat noon–11:45pm; Sun noon–10:45pm. Tube: Covent Garden.

Savoy Grill at The Savoy ★★★ TRADITIONAL BRITISH   The Savoy Grill is an integral part of the discreet luxury of the Savoy Hotel. Run by Gordon Ramsay, it is everything it should be. The Art Deco-inspired interior is a real gem, with sparkling chandeliers, walls that gleam a deep amber, and black-and-white photographs of past stars including Bogart and Bacall. The menu balances the classics with a lighter modern touch: Cornish crab mayonnaise with apple salad, wild celery, and wafer-thin Melba toast; lobster bisque with brandy butter. Mains of steamed steak and onion pudding; or roast duck breast with foie gras make choosing difficult. At lunch traditionalists opt for the daily trolley that glides around the room. There are desserts such as Eton mess, or rice pudding with poached cherries. This is a return to past glories.

In the Savoy Hotel, Strand, WC2. www.gordonramsay.com. ✆ **020/7592-1600.** Reservations required. Main courses £17–£38. Set price lunch menu £26; pretheatre menu 2 courses £20, 3 courses £26. AE, DC, MC, V. Mon–Sat noon–3pm and 5:30–11pm; Sun noon–4pm and 6–10:30pm. Tube: Charing Cross.

Simpson's-in-the-Strand ★ TRADITIONAL BRITISH   Apart from the odd facelift, Simpson's remains essentially the same as when it first opened in 1828 as a chess club and coffee house called the Grand Cigar Divan, attracting diners such as George Bernard Shaw, Prime Minister Disraeli, and Charlie Chaplin. It's a splendid wood-paneled room with chandeliers, comfortable booths, and an army of formally dressed waiters who serve traditional British food with a pride that recalls the Empire at its height. It's our favorite place for breakfast (although beware the well-named *Ten Deadly Sins*). The lunch and dinner "Bill of Fare" showcases the classics: Brown Windsor soup; fishcakes; and smoked haddock omelet as well as a splendid Beef Wellington. Simpson's Signatures are a history lesson in British tastes: lobster soup; potted shrimps; saddle of lamb. It's generally agreed that the restaurant serves the best roasts in London, carved from a stately silver trolley that trundles around the room.

100 Strand, WC2. www.simpsonsinthestrand.co.uk. ✆ **020/7836-9112.** Reservations required. Main courses £17–£33.50; 3-course fixed-price pretheatre dinner £31; 2-course meal £25.75; breakfast £5.50–£21.50. AE, DC, MC, V. Mon–Fri 7:15–10:30am; Mon–Sat 12:15–2:45pm and 5:45–10:45pm; Sun 12:15–2:45pm and 6–9pm. Tube: Charing Cross or Embankment.

MODERATE

The Delaunay ★★★ 🍴 CONTEMPORARY EUROPEAN Ace restaurateurs, Jeremy King and Chris Corbin, have done it again. In The Delaunay, which opened in early 2012, they've reproduced their fantastically popular and successful The Wolseley (p. 200). A sophisticated David Collins design has brought dark wood, lots of brass fittings, and dark green banquettes, perfectly evoking the grand European cafes of the past. It's open all day, starting with a breakfast of muesli or the full English. The a la carte menu takes in trad Brit dishes like sardines on toast; sandwiches; kedgeree; moules frites; steaks, and Schnitzels, all very reasonably priced. There's afternoon tea, brunch, in fact pretty much everything you could wish for. The addition of the chic Counter with its own entrance, operating as both cafe and takeaway, is just another plus to this great addition to London's dining scene.

55 Aldwych, WC2. www.thedelaunay.com. ⓒ **020/7499-8558.** Main courses £9–£21.75. AE, DC, MC, V. Mon–Fri 7am–midnight, Sat 8am–midnight, Sun 11am–11pm. Tube: Temple or Covent Garden.

Giaconda Dining Room ★ 🎏 CONTEMPORARY EUROPEAN Tucked among the guitar shops of Denmark Street, just off Tottenham Court Road, the Giaconda comes as a surprise. Run by husband and wife Australians, Paul and Tracey Merrony, its bistro-like atmosphere, good cooking, and down-to-earth pricing set it apart. Dishes such as salad of baked beetroot and leek vinaigrette with goat curd to start followed by duck confit with Lyonnaise potatoes and chicory salad, or roast rack of lamb, have Giaconda regulars purring with pleasure (though vegetarians will have a hard time here). A reasonably priced wine list, relaxed atmosphere, and pleasant staff complete the attractive package.

9 Denmark St., WC2. www.giacondadining.com. ⓒ **020/7240-3334.** Main courses £6.50–£20.50. AE, MC, V. Tues–Fri noon–2:15pm Tues–Sat 6–9:15pm. Tube: Tottenham Court Rd.

Mishkin's ★ 🎏 JEWISH/AMERICAN Russell Norman, the genius behind Polpo (p. 212) and Spuntino (p. 211), has done it again. We didn't know it, but a "Jewish deli with cocktails" that would be at home on New York's Lower East Side was just what London needed. The idea might be new to the capital, but the brick-walled, bustling restaurant with its red leather banquettes is instantly recognizable on the London dining scene. Reuben on rye with pastrami, sauerkraut, and Swiss cheese; chopped chicken liver sandwich; great meatballs; an all-day brunch of dishes like latkes; smoked eel, apple sauce and sour cream; or an all-day supper of meat loaf—how could it be anything but a roaring success?

25 Catherine St., London WC2. www.mishkins.co.uk. ⓒ **020/7240-2078.** Main courses £6–£12. AE, MC, V. Mon–Fri 11am-midnight, Sun noon–11pm. Tube: Tottenham Court Rd.

Kopapa ★ PACIFIC RIM/FUSION Peter Gordon, whose style of fusion cooking set London taste buds alight when the New Zealander opened The Providores and Tapa Room (p. 217), is now to be found in a more casual setting. His all-day dining menu starts conventionally enough with eggs on toast and fresh fruit. Then it gets into fusion mode with small plates of plantain, sweet potato and feta tortilla with yogurt; deep-fried spicy chili squid with smoked aioli; or pan-fried scallops with sweet chili sauce and crème fraiche. The eclectic mix of Asian, European, and Middle Eastern ingredients works well, and is more muted than in his Marylebone restaurant. It's comfortable, laid-back, and welcoming with a great drinks list from around the world.

32–34 Monmouth St., WC2. www.kokapapa.co.uk. ✆ **020/7240-6076.** Main courses £6–£12. AE, MC, V. Mon–Fri 11am–midnight; Sun noon–11pm. Tube: Tottenham Court Rd.

Mon Plaisir FRENCH Mon Plaisir is a London institution—a French restaurant still in the same family, which has been dishing up classic food for more than 55 years. The tone is set by the rotund Bibendum model you see on entering, a pewter-topped bar that once graced a Lyonnais bordello, old French posters, and the very French staff. Combining brasserie classics including snails or thick French onion soup with more modern renditions such as scallops with lemon balm, ginger sauce, and onion marmalade, Mon Plaisir walks the fine line between classic and clichéd. And the wine list? Full of French treasures. Its pretheatre fixed-price menu is rightly popular for nearby Shaftesbury Avenue and the shows.

21 Monmouth St., WC2. www.monplaisir.co.uk. ✆ **020/7836-7243.** Reservations recommended. Main courses £16.95–£23.50; lunch menu 2 courses £12.95, 3 courses £15.95; pretheatre menu 2 courses £12.95, 3 courses £14.95. AE, DC, MC, V. Mon–Sat noon–11:15pm. Tube: Covent Garden.

Terroirs ★ FRENCH Hearty rustic French food, good wines (including "natural" wine from small artisan growers, unfiltered and unrefined), and a vibrant atmosphere is what gives Terroirs the edge over other Covent Garden restaurants. The zinc bar in the bistro is a great meeting place for pretheatre drinks. Both dining rooms serve charcuterie that takes in pork and pistachio terrine; rillettes; and Bigorre saucisson; properly kept French cheeses; and tapas-style snacks. It's equally popular for a longer meal, starting with those small plates; or oysters; potted shrimps on toast; herring and warm potato salad; and Dorset crab with mayonnaise, then moving onto *plats du jour* such as bavette steak with shallots, sautéed potatoes, and chanterelle mushrooms.

5 William IV St., WC2. www.terroirswinebar.com. ✆ **020/7036-0660.** Reservations recommended. Small plates £4–£12. Mains £6–£17. AE, MC, V. Mon–Sat noon–11pm. Tube: Charing Cross. Also at Brawn, 49 Columbia Rd., E2 (✆ **020/7729-5629**).

INEXPENSIVE

Dishoom ★ 👪 INDIAN India has provided so much inspiration for London dining that it's difficult to imagine a new experience. Then up pops this wonderful place, modeled on the Bombay cafes of the 1960s. It looks great, with a geometrically tiled floor, marble-topped tables, odd lights and pictures, and its blackboard of rules at the door: "No water to outsiders" and "All castes served." It's clearly hit the spot with the kind of vibe that has attracted London's trendsetters in droves. It swings along from breakfasts of sausage or bacon naan rolls through all-day dining on lightly spiced soups; salads; small plates of vegetable or lamb samosas; fish fingers; or calamari to dinner grills of chicken tikka; sheesh kebab; spicy lamb chops; or one-pot biryani dishes. Finish off with *kulfi* (Indian ice cream) on a stick, or a lassi.

12 Upper St. Martin's Lane, WC2. www.dishoom.com. ✆ **020/7420-9320.** No reservations. Main courses £5.50–£11.50. AE, MC, V. Mon–Thurs 8am–11pm; Fri 8am–midnight; Sat 10am–midnight; Sun 10am–10pm. Tube: Leicester Sq.

LONDON'S top ART GALLERY RESTAURANTS

Cash-strapped museums saw the light long ago, and the best of them opened restaurants that were designed to become destinations in their own right. Now it's the norm to expect top dining along with your priceless artifacts.

National Dining Rooms ★ Overlooking Trafalgar Square, the National Dining Rooms is run by British cooking champion, Oliver Peyton. Dine off a thoroughly British menu of English lamb, Cornish crab, or Scottish beef. It's also a great option for afternoon tea after a round of the Old Masters. Or take the daytime bakery option of excellent sandwiches, cakes and coffee. National Gallery (p. 102), Trafalgar Sq., WC2, www.thenationaldiningrooms.co.uk. ✆ 020/7747-2525. Mains £14.50–£17.50. Sunday menu 2 courses £23.50, 3 courses £26.50. AE, MC, V. Daily 10am–5:30pm (Fri to 8:30pm). Tube: Charing Cross.

Fernandez & Wells ★ Following its other three successful, smaller ventures in Soho, Fernandez & Wells opened its large and smart restaurant/cafe in Somerset House (p. 109). Like the others, it serves breakfasts to early birds, then all-day options like organic farm eggs with sourdough toast; unusual sandwiches such as smoked pork loin, cooked tomato and Manchego cheese at £6; top Spanish hams, and platters of meats and cheese. Somerset House, Strand, WC2. www.fernandezandwells.com. ✆ 020/7420-9408. Dishes £4.50–£9.50. MC, V. Mon–Sat 8am–11pm, Sun 9am–11pm. Tube: Charing Cross.

Wapping Food ★ Housed in a former power station, with a distinctly industrial feel (lofty roof, red-brick walls, and rusting industrial machines). Adventurous dishes such as smoked eel with glazed beetroot, or braised rabbit and fennel stew are very well done and complement the avant-garde exhibitions. Weekends are particularly popular. Wapping Hydraulic Power Station, Wapping Wall, E1. www.thewappingproject.com. ✆ 020/7680-2080. Main dishes £15–£22. AE, MC, V. Mon–Fri noon–3:30pm and 7–11pm, Sat 10:30am–noon and 1–4pm, Sun 10:30am–noon. Overground: Wapping/DLR: Shadwell.

Whitechapel Gallery Dining Room Dine in a light, spacious, former library at this superb art gallery. There's a short, good value menu of small and large dishes to mix and match the sharing plates, or order main dishes such as beef with balsamic shallots, and quails with braised lentils, bacon and aioli. 77–82 Whitechapel High St., E1. www.whitechapelgallery.org. ✆ 020/7522-7888. Main courses £10–£15; set lunches 2 courses £18, 3 courses £23. AE, MC, V. Sun and Tues noon–3:30pm, Wed–Sat noon–2:30pm and 5:30–11pm. Tube: Aldgate East.

Mela ★ ✦ INDIAN This bright, colorful restaurant in Theatreland is a firm favorite with locals, tourists, theatregoers, and vegetarians for its regional Indian cooking and good value. The two-course lunch menu offers three starters, perhaps chicken tikka, or kebab of spiced lamb and vegetables, and four main dishes served with dhal, rice, and naan, all for £9.95. From the main menu, tiger prawns come marinated in saffron, caraway seeds, and coriander; Keralan mixed seafood with a coconut curry evokes the tender flavors of southern India. Add to that friendly service, special deals throughout the year, and a good takeout menu and you have a winner.

152–156 Shaftesbury Ave., WC2. www.melarestaurant.co.uk. (✆ **020/7836-8635.** Reservations required. Main courses £9.95–£29.95; 2-course lunch £9.95, 3 course taster £15.95; 3 course set menu (for 2) £49.95, Veg £ 38.95. AE, MC, V. Mon–Fri noon–11:30pm; Sat 1–11:30pm; Sun noon–10:30pm. Tube: Tottenham Court Rd. or Leicester Sq.

Wahaca MEXICAN   Thomasina Miers won British TV's *Masterchef* competition in 2005, wrote two cookbooks, then opened her first Mexican market food restaurant in 2007 in Covent Garden. There's a long menu of classic tacos; tostadas; and quesadillas; larger plates of burritos and enchiladas deliver flavors that have been carefully researched by the chef in Mexico. Some purists may claim that the food is less "authentic" and generous than the Mexican street venue on which Wahaca is modeled. But the lines still form; and tequilas go down well. Other Wahacas are in Soho, Westfield Shopping Centre (p. 278), and Canary Wharf.

66 Chandos Place, WC2. www.wahaca.co.uk. (✆ **020/7734-0195.** Reservations not accepted. Dishes £3.50–£9.95. AE, MC, V. Mon–Sat noon–11pm; Sun noon–10:30pm. Tube: Covent Garden or Leicester Sq. Other locations throughout London.

Soho

Soho's restaurants offer more options for dining before a show at a West End theatre.

EXPENSIVE

Hakkasan ★ CHINESE/CANTONESE   Opened by the restaurateur Alan Yau (who has done so much to transform London's dining scene), this sexy, moody, subtly lit basement venue serves top-notch modern Cantonese cuisine. During the day, the dim sum is among the best in London—delicate, exquisitely fresh, and beautifully cooked. In the evening top-end ingredients are cooked with subtle skill. Sweet-and-sour Duke of Berkshire pork with pomegranate takes the concept to new heights; stir-fry ostrich comes in yellow bean sauce. From the seafood section, the Chilean sea bass with Szechuan pepper, sweet basil, and spring onion is perfectly treated, the sauce complementing, not overpowering the fish. Even desserts, often the poor relation in Chinese restaurants, are superb. The wine list is a lesson in matching food and wine; ask the knowledgeable waiting staff for advice.

8 Hanway Place, W1. www.hakkasan.com. (✆ **020/7927-7000.** Reservations recommended. Main courses £9.80–£28.80. AE, MC, V. Mon–Fri noon–3pm; Sat–Sun noon–4pm; Sun–Wed 6–11pm, Thurs–Sat 6–11.45pm. Tube: Tottenham Court Rd. Also at 17 Bruton St., W1 (✆ **020/7907-1888**).

MODERATE

Arbutus ★ 🍴 CONTEMPORARY EUROPEAN   Chef Anthony Demetre and front-of-house supremo Will Smith opened Arbutus in 2006 to instant acclaim. The rather awkward two rooms are simply decorated; it's the food that people come for—a successful mix of British tradition and French bistro-style cooking. Ingredients are mainly inexpensive and seasonal, producing dishes such as squid and mackerel burger with razor clams and sea purslane (an edible seashore plant); rabbit with cottage pie, artichokes, carrots, and pancetta; and for the real foodie, lamb tripe parcels or trotters. Desserts are very good: Tarte tatin of English apples with crème fraiche or classic Sicilian lemon tart. It doesn't suit everybody but if you want good food that is out of the ordinary, book here or at sister restaurant Wild Honey (p. 200).

63–64 Frith St., W1. www.arbutusrestaurant.co.uk. © **020/7734-4545.** Reservations required. Main courses £17.95–£19.95; daily 3-course lunch £16.95; Mon–Sat pre- and posttheatre set menu £18.95. AE, DC, MC, V. Mon–Sat noon–2:30pm. Mon–Thurs 5–11pm, Fri–Sat 5–11:30pm; Sun noon–3pm and 5:30–10:30pm. Tube: Tottenham Court Rd.

Barshu ★ CHINESE/SZECHUAN   Barshu glories in fiery hot cooking from Szechuan in southwest China. Equally uncompromising are the ingredients: pigs' kidneys (flash-fried for crispiness), and dry braised ox tendons are not for the faint-hearted. But if you're feeling adventurous, there's plenty to please: beef braised with wild bamboo shoots from Szechuan; stir-fried chicken with dried shiitake mushrooms in a stone pot; Gong Bau chicken with peanuts; and a wonderful crab with enough chilis and garlic to keep your taste buds buzzing for a week. The decor is reminiscent of an old Beijing teahouse, all wooden lattice work and lanterns with tassels. It's very busy and quite cramped—so definitely not the place for a romantic evening or a first date.

28 Frith St., W1. www.bar-shu.co.uk. © **020/7287-6688.** Reservations recommended. Mains £8.90–£28.90. AE, MC, V. Mon–Thurs, Sun noon–11pm; Fri–Sat noon–11:30pm. Tube: Leicester Sq. or Tottenham Court Rd.

Bocca di Lupo ★★ ITALIAN   This hugely popular smart restaurant has an open kitchen, tiled floors, wooden tables, and large paintings of food on the walls. The only downside of its popularity is that it's busy, cramped, and noisy—and you must book in advance. Chef Jacob Kenedy has toured Italy in his search for genuine regional dishes, and the result is a glorious trot around the country. If you want the full tour, go for the small plates and share as many as possible, perhaps tortellini of prosciutto and mortadella with cream and nutmeg from Emilia; and the Venetian fried squid, prawns, and blood orange. More substantial dishes include roast suckling pig and chestnuts, and Ligurian sea bream baked in salt. The all-Italian wine list offers a good selection by the carafe or the glass.

12 Archer St., W1. www.boccadilupo.com. © **020/7734-2223.** Main courses £7–£26.50. AE, MC, V. Mon–Sat 12:30–3pm and 5:30–11pm; Sun 12:45–3:45pm and 5–9pm. Tube: Piccadilly Circus.

Dean Street Townhouse ★ TRADITIONAL BRITISH   Part of the achingly fashionable hotel Dean Street Townhouse (p. 209) dining room fits perfectly into Soho, with a clubby ambience, fashionable Brit-art on the walls, crystal chandeliers, and a long bar: the whole package housed in a four-story Georgian town house. At breakfast media types tuck into boiled eggs and soldiers with a pot of tea. The food is thoroughly British, a wonderful exercise in nostalgia for those brought up on pressed ham and piccalilli or fish and chips. There are more sophisticated dishes like fillet of sea bream with Jerusalem artichokes and almonds. This is traditional cooking at its best: unfussy, unpretentious, and thoroughly worthwhile. A return to the cooking of the past, inside one of the hippest venues in London, is another nice touch of (typically British) irony.

69–71 Dean St., W1. www.deanstreettownhouse.com. ℭ **020/7434-1775.** Reservations required. Main courses £13.50–£32.50; pretheatre (5–7:30pm) 2 courses £16.50, 3 courses £19.50. AE, MC, V. Mon–Thurs 7am–midnight; Fri 7am–1am; Sat 8am–1am; Sun 8am–midnight. Tube: Tottenham Court Rd.

Hix ★ MODERN BRITISH   Mark Hix came to public notice at London institutions Le Caprice and The Ivy (p. 203). He's a clever restaurateur who knows exactly the mood of the moment as well as an excellent chef and a good food writer. The basement bar, Mark's, reminds you of New York, and offers top cocktails and bar snacks. The dining room has mobiles by Damien Hirst, a clubby atmosphere, and stripped down decor. The food is a lesson in all that is good in modern British cookery: winter pies, game, and hotpots prepared with seasonal ingredients and served with vegetables such as Brussels sprouts, swede, and watercress; summer menus of sole with shrimps or lamb with new potatoes.

66–70 Brewer St., W1. www.hixsoho.co.uk ℭ **020/7292-3518.** Reservations recommended. Main courses £15.75–£36.50; pre- and posttheatre 2 courses £17.50, 3 courses £22.50, Sun noon–10:30pm 2/3 courses £17.50/£22.50. AE, MC, V. Mon–Sat noon–11:30pm; Sun noon–10:30pm. Tube: Piccadilly Circus. Also at 36–37 Greenhill Rents, EC1 (ℭ **020/7017-1930**); inside Selfridges (p. 290), and Hix Belgravia inside Belgraves Hotel, Pont St., SW1 (ℭ **020/3189-4850**).

Randall & Aubin ★ SEAFOOD   Randall & Aubin began as a butcher's shop in 1911 selling top quality meat from Paris, and was turned into a restaurant in 1996 by restaurateurs Ed Baines and James Poulton. It's a genuinely lovely setting; the marble surfaces, white tiles, and old wooden furniture fit perfectly into its new incarnation as a restaurant—albeit one that specializes in fish and seafood. It's dishes such as roast halibut with white beans, chorizo, and herb sauce; and grilled sea bass with spring onions, chives, and rosemary salsa and potatoes that please the crowds of loyal fans. Order the *fruits de mer* (seafood) platter to impress, or charm the carnivores in the party with a robust pork belly from the rotisserie. Or do as we like to do: sit at the bar, order champagne, and toy with an oyster.

16 Brewer St., W1. www.randallandaubin.com. ℭ **020/7287-4447.** No reservations. Main courses £10.85–£29.50. AE, DC, MC, V. Mon–Wed noon–11pm; Thurs–Sat noon–midnight; Sun noon–10pm. Tube: Piccadilly Circus or Leicester Sq.

Rasa Samudra ★ 🌶 INDIAN/VEGETARIAN   The famous pink facade has become as widely known as Rasa's Keralan seafood and vegetarian dishes. This is now the flagship of a mini-empire of nine restaurants (six in London), and Rasa founder Das Sreedharan's philosophy of home-cooked food cooked by well-trained chefs is a huge success. In two cramped rooms decorated with artifacts from Kerala, you can start with Rasa's famous snacks and homemade chutneys before trying the *dosas* (savory pancakes) and main dishes such as *moru kachiathu* (sweet mangoes and green bananas cooked with green chilis, ginger, and fresh curry leaves). Highly recommended fish dishes include our favorite, the dish served in toddy shops in Kerala, kingfish cooked in onions, fried chilis, turmeric, and ginger, which comes with cassava steamed in turmeric water. Service is charming; the atmosphere delightful.

5 Charlotte St., W1. www.rasarestaurants.com. ℭ **020/7637-0222.** Reservations required. Main courses £6.50–£12.95; fixed-price dinner £22.50–£30. AE, DC, MC, V. Mon–Sat noon–3pm and 6–11pm; Sun 6–11pm. Tube: Tottenham Court Rd. Other locations throughout London.

Spuntino ★ 🔥 AMERICAN/BURGER   Spuntino looks the part of a New York speakeasy, with an industrial, artfully scruffy interior of rusted ceiling tiles, long U-shaped bar with heavy stools, wooden floor, and light bulbs in wire cages. London restaurateur Russell Norman has embraced New York dining ideas as he did before with Venetian wine bars like Polpo (p. 212). You come here for small plates, which run from imaginative sliders (mini burgers) like beef and marrow meatballs; and lamb and pickled cucumber. It's all well done, even the peanut butter and jelly sandwich for those after a blast from their past. No booking policy means lines at peak times, so arrive unfashionably early or even mid-afternoon for a slightly less rushed experience.

61 Rupert St, W1. www.spuntino.co.uk. No phone. No booking. Main courses £5.50–£10. AE, MC, V. Mon–Sat 11am–midnight; Sun noon–11pm. Tube: Piccadilly Circus.

INEXPENSIVE

Busaba Eathai 🔥 THAI   Restaurateur Alan Yau struck gold once again with his Busaba Eathai concept, where a mix of fans—Londoners, tourists, the young and fashionable—sit at communal tables to eat classy Thai dishes at moderate prices. The private equity firm that bought the chain from Yau currently has seven outlets in London, but is bound to expand further. Favorites on the cleverly composed menu include interesting dishes such as green papaya salad with dried shrimp and tomato; ginger beef with Thai pepper, chili, and spring onion; and chargrilled duck in tamarind sauce with Chinese broccoli. All the branches manage to maintain the same high standards and cheerful, busy service; drinks include wine, Thai beers, as well as lush tropical smoothies.

106–110 Wardour St., W1. www.busaba.com. ✆ **020/7255-8686.** No reservations. Main courses £6.20–£12.40. AE, MC, V. Mon–Thurs noon–11pm; Fri–Sat noon–11:30pm; Sun noon–10pm. Tube: Tottenham Court Rd.

Koya 🔥 JAPANESE   This is the place for fans of those satisfying thick wheat udon noodles. It's a bright, functional room, perfect for a quick meal of noodles served cold with cold sauce to dip; hot noodles in a hot broth; or cold udon noodles with a hot broth. Combinations of taste are excellent; try noodles with smoked mackerel and green leaves. There are also small plates including marinated mushroom; pork belly braised in cider; and rice in a bowl with duck or curry and prawn tempura. Wash it all down with beer, sake, plum wine, or tea.

49 Frith St., W1. www.koya.co.uk. ✆ **020/7434-4463.** No reservations. Main courses £6.70–£14.10. MC, V. Mon–Sat noon–3pm and 5:30–10:30pm; Sun noon–3pm and 5:30–10pm. Tube: Tottenham Court Rd.

Mildreds ★ 🎁 VEGETARIAN   Mildreds may sound like a 1940s' Joan Crawford movie, but it's one of London's most enduring vegetarian and vegan dining spots. The large, airy room with a bar at the front can get very crowded, and you'll probably find yourself sharing a table. The food always hits the spot, using organically grown, seasonal produce. The menu changes daily, but always includes homemade soups, pastas, and salads. There are dishes such as sundried tomato and buffalo mozzarella risotto cake; Sri Lankan sweet potato and cashew nut curry; and unusual side orders. Organic wines are served, and portions are very large. There's no reservations system, so expect to wait.

45 Lexington St., W1. www.mildreds.co.uk. ✆ **020/7494-1634.** No reservations. Main courses £7.95–£10.25. MC, V. Mon–Fri 9am–11pm; Sat noon–11pm. Tube: Tottenham Court Rd.

BEST places FOR A CHEAP & CHEERFUL MEAL

London has its fair share of good, cheap places to eat; you just need to know where to look.

Gourmet San ★ Considered by some as London's best no-frills Szechuan cooking, it's certainly among the fieriest. It's also the place to try out all those unusual ingredients, Szechuan-style. Start with jellyfish with black vinegar, go on to spicy mix of lamb sinew and mix of ox tripe. Or chicken out and order sweet and sour pork; beef fried with cumin; and braised shredded turnips with lamb. 261 Bethnal Green Rd., E2. www.old-place.co.uk. ℂ **020/7729-8388.** Main dishes £6–£12. No credit cards. Daily 4:30–11pm. Tube: Bethnal Green.

Leon ★ This rapidly expanding chain serves "natural fast food" using, where possible, sustainably sourced ingredients. Start with organic porridge topped with melted chocolate and honey at £2.40, then lunch off Moroccan meatballs with rice, or splash out on chili chicken. Stay upstairs for a spot of exotic Carnaby Street people watching. 35 Gt. Marlborough St., W1. www.leonrestaurants.co.uk. ℂ **020/7437-5280.** Main dishes £3.95–£6.75. No credit cards. Mon–Thurs 11am–11pm, Fri–Sat 11am–1am. Tube: Oxford Circus.

Open Kitchen This is the training restaurant for the London City Hospitality Centre (LCHC), so you'll get ambitious cooking with great ingredients at unbelievable prices. Starters (all at £3.50) might include soup of the day, or roast duck with Caesar salad. Then go for slow braised shoulder of lamb stuffed with

apricot and rosemary and accompanied by marquise potatoes, green beans, and red cabbage. Good choices for vegetarians as well. 40 Hoxton St., N1. www.openkitchen.biz. ℂ **020/7613-9590.** Main dishes £6–£7.50. No credit cards. Mon–Fri 10am–2pm and Wed–Fri 5–9pm. Overground: Hoxton.

Stockpot Feeding impoverished Londoners for 50 years, Stockpot is still London's best budget pitstop. Start the day with a hearty British fry-up from £4.95. Then for lunch or dinner—pork escalope in tomato sauce at £5.65, or a good honest shepherd's pie anyone? Everything comes with chips; portions are generous and the atmosphere one of casual bonhomie. 38 Panton St., SW1. www.stockpotlondon.co.uk. ℂ **020/7839-5142.** Main dishes £4.90–£9.90. No credit cards. Daily 7am–11pm. Tube: Piccadilly Circus.

Wong Kei Inevitably known as wonkys, everybody who goes complains about the service and sometimes the food. But somehow it's part of a visit to London. It's huge, cheap, packed, serves a vast and comprehensive Chinese menu that makes you wonder at the size of the kitchen, and the service is reassuringly consistent—always bad. 41–43 Wardour St., W1. ℂ **020/7437-8408.** Main dishes £4.40–£8; set meals £8.50–£13.50. No credit cards. Mon–Sat noon–11:30pm, Sun noon–10:30pm. Tube: Piccadilly Circus.

Polpo ★ ITALIAN Much to many visitors' surprise, London is full of excellent, good-value wine bars, but Polpo is a little different. Modeled on a *bacaro* (Venetian wine bar), the decor is perfect, with stripped brick walls, Victorian tiles, wooden floors, and leather banquettes. A menu of small dishes of regional specialties includes *cicchetti* (Venetian bar snacks) of asparagus, taleggio cheese, and prosciutto ham, salt cod on grilled polenta, or potato and Parmesan crochetta, all between £1 and £2.50. Great breads include the broad bean, ricotta, and mint bruschetta for something different. More substantial tapas-style dishes run from *bresaola* (air-dried beef), and Parmesan to a plate of cold meats, and for fish, perhaps *fritto misto* (mixed fry), or *linguine vongole* (pasta with clams). Order the classic spritz of white wine with Campari or a Bellini. Alas, a no-bookings policy can mean long waits.

41 Beak St., W1. www.polpo.co.uk. ℭ **020/7734-4479.** No reservations. Dishes £1–£14. AE, MC, V. Mon–Sat noon–3pm and 5:30–11pm; Sun noon–4pm. Tube: Piccadilly Circus. Also da Polpo at 6 Maiden Lane, WC2, ℭ **020-7836 8448;** and Polpetto, 2nd floor, French House, 49 Dean St, W1 ℭ **020/7734 1969.**

Satsuma JAPANESE   This canteen with communal wooden benches is the only Japanese restaurant in the Royal China group (p. 219). It's a handy place for a quick but satisfying lunch or a pretheatre meal. It serves a long menu of sashimi, sushi, and dumplings, but is best known for its bento boxes and noodles. You can't go wrong with the Satsuma bento (sashimi of salmon and tuna with a seafood salad, vegetable rolls, yakitori, and more), or a satisfying bowl of ramen, the noodles in a well-seasoned broth with chicken or salmon. Finish with green tea ice cream.

56 Wardour St., W1. www.osatsuma.com. ℭ **020/7437-8338.** No reservations. Dishes £5.80–£16.80. AE, DC, MC, V. Mon–Tues noon–10:30pm; Wed–Thurs noon–11pm; Fri–Sat noon–11:30pm; Sun noon–10pm. Tube: Piccadilly Circus or Leicester Sq.

Yauatcha ★ ASIAN   This Asian eatery, describing itself as a modern reinterpretation of the old Chinese teahouse, is the brainchild of Alan Yau, who won Britain's first Michelin star for Chinese cooking at his top-of-the-range restaurant, Hakkasan (p. 208). At this informal dim sum outlet, service is casual, although it's so popular you may be rushed through your meal to make way for new arrivals. Dim sum, among London's finest, is served for both lunch and dinner, and often takes unusual ingredients such as scallops, Wagyu beef, venison, or king crab. Other notable specialties include a great selection of fish and seafood (Dover sole with shiitake and soya), and a delectable stir-fry rib eye beef in black bean sauce.

15 Broadwick St., W1. www.yauatcha.com. ℭ **020/7494-8888.** Dim Sum £4–£15. Set meal £14.44. AE, MC, V. Mon–Sat noon–11:45pm; Sun noon–10:30pm. Tube: Oxford Circus.

Bloomsbury & Fitzrovia
VERY EXPENSIVE

Pied à Terre ★★★ FRENCH   You could easily walk past the entrance to one of London's best restaurants without a second glance. And once inside, the dark decor is as unassuming as the exterior. But persevere, for Australian chef Shane Osborn has two well-deserved Michelin stars. The set lunch is one of London's greatest bargains. Where else could you get canapés, mackerel with marinated kohlrabi, apple, and vanilla puree, and then roast pork with glazed carrots, white carrot cream, Swiss chard, and mustard sauce for £27.50? Cheese or dessert (including pre-dessert) might be a hazelnut and caramel mousse with sherry jelly and salted peanut ice cream for an extra £6. The a la carte dinner menu is more ambitious producing superb dishes that look as beautiful as they taste. Save up for Pied à Terre; you won't regret it.

34 Charlotte St., W1. www.pied-a-terre.co.uk. ℭ **020/7636-1178.** Set-price 2-course lunch £27.50; set-price 2-course dinner £60 (desserts £14, cheeses £16.50 per person); 10-course dinner £95; vegetarian £85. AE, MC. V. Mon–Fri 12:15–2:30pm; Mon–Sat 6–11pm. Tube: Goodge St. or Tottenham Court Rd.

EXPENSIVE

Roka ★★ JAPANESE   When Rainer Becker opened Roka, the concept of the *izakaya*—where you watch the chefs working on the *robata* (open charcoal grill)—had already been established at his first restaurant, Zuma, in South Kensington. Roka, the little sister, is smaller and less glamorous, but just as stylish. There's plenty of exposed wood, an industrial look, and a counter made from a huge tree trunk that surrounds the theatre of the robata. The menu divides into sushi and sashimi; more complex dishes such as tuna tartar with Sevruga caviar and quail's egg yolk; snacks, salads, and soups (don't miss the stunning beef, ginger, and sesame dumplings); and robata grills of fish, meat, and vegetables. Everything is ultra-fresh and cooked to order. The staff are comfortingly helpful to those unfamiliar with the cooking style, and the wine list is particularly well matched. The trendy **Shochu Lounge Bar** below is the place to be seen.

37 Charlotte St., W1. www.rokarestaurant.com. ℭ **020/7580-6464.** Main courses £4.50–£68; set meals £50–£75. AE, DC, MC, V. Mon–Fri noon–3:30pm and 5:30–11:30pm; Sat 12:30–4pm and 5:30–11:30pm; Sun 5:30–10:30pm. Tube: Goodge St. or Tottenham Court Rd. Also at 40 Canada Sq., E14 (ℭ **020/7636-5229**).

MODERATE

Dabbous ★★ ✒CONTEMPORARY EUROPEAN   Olli Dabbous (pronounced Daboo) began at Le Manoir aux Quat' Saisons outside Oxford, then worked at Michelin-starred Texture (p. 217) before setting up on his own in a big two-storied industrial space. The bar, sensibly in the basement, majors in great cocktails with fashionable infusions and a good menu. The upstairs restaurant buzzes as waitstaff bring small plates of imaginative combinations. Try beef tartar with cigar oil, whisky, and rye; or an unexpected mashed potato with black truffle; roast crab with warm buttermilk and cabbage; or braised veal cheek with spelt, mixed onions, and a light broth. Desserts continue to mix the unusual; when did you last try cucumber and mint in a chilled lemon verbena infusion, or fig leaf ice cream? It's all very well done at good value prices.

39 Whitfield St., London W1. www.dabbous.co.uk. ℭ **020/7323-1544.** Dishes £5–£14. Set tasting menu 7 courses £49 (whole table); set vegetarian menu £45. AE, MC, V. Tues–Sat noon–11:30pm. Tube: Goodge St.

Fino ★ SPANISH/TAPAS   Started by Sam and Eddie Hart, whose parents own the smart country house hotel Hambleton Hall in Rutland Water, Fino introduced London to traditional tapas with a modern twist. The smart basement venue with comfortable banquettes and substantial wooden tables buzzes with well-dressed Brits and knowledgeable Spaniards ordering dishes that emphasize first-rate ingredients cooked with skill. Try clams with sherry and ham, or squid wrapped with pancetta in ink sauce from "la plancha"; or some of the best Spanish cold meats like lomo or chorizo you'll get outside the Iberian peninsula. The brothers have expanded from their first success to open the smaller, but equally

CENTRAL LONDON'S BEST
authentic CHIPPIES

Traditionally cooked in beef dripping and served with mushy peas and a pickled gherkin, Britain's national dish of fish and chips was once a staple for the working classes. But the revival of "retro"-style cooking has brought it racing back into fashion, and you'll find it on the menu of many top restaurants. For a genuine experience, we recommend the following:

The Golden Hind ★ They've been serving breaded or battered fish to a contented mix of regulars and visitors since 1914. The original Art Deco fryer no longer works, but apart from that, this cafe takes you straight back to prewar days. Leave room for a classic steamed sponge pudding and custard. Great frying and you bring your own wine (no corkage). 73 Marylebone Lane, W1. ℂ **0871/332-7803.** Main courses £6.30–£10.70. AE, MC, V. Mon–Fri noon–3pm, Mon–Sat 6–10pm. Tube: Bond St.

Golden Union Fish Bar Just off Oxford Street, it's cheerful and unpretentious, with a take-away counter at the front and a bright jolly cafe with yellow chairs at the back. The menu runs through the fish varieties from pollock to scampi and back accompanied by exemplary chips and mushy peas. Portions are large; extras include the likes of baked beans and there's a limited list of wine and beer. 38 Poland St., W1. www.goldenunion.co.uk. ℂ **020/7434-1933.** Main courses £4.50–£7.50. AE, MC, V. Mon–Sat noon–6pm. Tube: Oxford Circus.

Rock & Sole Plaice ★ One of London's oldest chippies, it opened, according to the owners, in 1871. Crisply battered fish—skate, cod, plaice, halibut, haddock, and lemon sole—are fried in groundnut oil and come with satisfying large chips and mushy peas. Go outside the official lunch hour to ensure a table outside. 47 Endell St., WC2. ℂ **0871/426-3380.** Main courses £9–£12. MC, V. Mon–Sat noon–10:30pm, Sun noon–5:30pm. Tube: Covent Garden.

Sea Shell ★ One of London's most enduring fish and chip shops. With an impressive backlit aquarium, this vast restaurant is as popular as ever (and, according to their website, a favorite of Alain Ducasse). The menu goes beyond the usual chippie, offering deviled whitebait, prawn cocktail, or chargrilled halloumi cheese for starters, and sea bass and wild halibut for mains. Where possible the fish comes from sustainable sources. 49–51 Lisson Grove, NW1. www.seashellrestaurant.co.uk. ℂ **020/7224-9000.** Main courses £12.50–£32.50. AE, DC, MC, V. Tube: Marylebone.

popular, **Barrafina,** 54 Frith St., W1 (www.barrafina.co.uk; ℂ **020/7440-1463.** Tube: Tottenham Court Rd.).

33 Charlotte St., W1. www.finorestaurant.com. ℂ **020/7813-8010.** Tapas £1.50–£21.50 AE, MC, V. Mon–Fri noon–2:30pm and 6–10:30pm; Sat 6–10:30pm. Tube: Goodge St. or Tottenham Court Rd.

INEXPENSIVE

Barrica ★ SPANISH/TAPAS   Barrica looks the part—blackboards chalked up with daily specials, tiled floor, jars of colored pickled vegetables, Spanish posters, hanging hams, and a wall of wine bottles. This excellent tapas bar has an authentic feeling of Spain. The menu offers a tempting selection of dishes from around the country, served in proper small proportions at proper small prices. Those famous hams are here, of course, but also on offer are pork and oxtail meatballs, ham croquettes, and more, plus a substantial dish of the day. They take their wine list seriously, so try an unusual variety or go for their sherry suggestions.

62 Goodge St., W1. www.barrica.co.uk. ⏦ **020/7436-9448.** Tapas £2.75–£15. AE, MC, V. Mon–Fri noon–11:30pm, Sat 1–11:30pm. Tube: Goodge St. or Tottenham Court Rd.

Salt Yard ★ SPANISH/ITALIAN   Joining the slew of new bars and restaurants specializing in tapas and top-quality charcuterie, Salt Yard goes further and champions Italian, as well as the more usual Spanish, sharing dishes. The charcuterie and cheeseboards are reason enough to eat here. Also worth trying is the universally popular confit of pork belly with rosemary-scented cannellini beans, or fresh fish such as tuna carpaccio with broad beans and salsa verde. Gratin of celeriac, cavolo nero (green cabbage), pecorino cheese, and truffle or just a perfectly cooked classic tortilla are good enough to turn anyone into a vegetarian. The Serrano ham, 18 months in curing, is among the best in London. The basement restaurant is usually packed, and in summer seating spills onto the street.

54 Goodge St., W1. www.saltyard.co.uk. ⏦ **020/7637-0657.** Reservations recommended. Tapas £3.75–£9.75; charcuterie or cheese platters £2.55–£14.95. AE, MC, V. Mon–Fri noon–11pm (3–6pm bar snacks only); Sat 5–11pm. Tube: Goodge St. or Tottenham Court Rd.

Marylebone

VERY EXPENSIVE

Locanda Locatelli ★★ ☺ ITALIAN   Giorgio Locatelli earned his first Michelin star at Zafferano (p. 227) and then opened his own restaurant in the Hyatt Regency Churchill Hotel in 2002. Entering from Seymour Street, the setting is sexy with beige leather seating and etched-glass dividers. It's a great place for spotting the A-list of celebrities who love the restaurant. But Giorgio is a family man and children are just as welcome, particularly at Sunday brunch. He's also one of the best Italian chefs in London. The cooking is superb and portions are generous with pastas scoring particularly highly. From a long menu, pan-fried scallops come with celeriac puree and saffron vinaigrette; while the veal cutlet with potato and braised artichoke is meltingly gutsy. Italian cheeses are served with honey; or go for the irresistible tiramisu. The all-Italian wine list is award winning.

8 Seymour St., W1. www.locandalocatelli.com. ⏦ **020/7935-9088.** Reservations required. Main courses £16.50–£31.50. AE, MC, V. Mon–Fri noon–3pm; Sat–Sun noon–3:30pm; Mon–Thurs 6:45–11pm; Fri–Sat 6:45–11:30pm; Sun 6:45–10:15pm. Tube: Marble Arch.

EXPENSIVE

L'Autre Pied ★★ CONTEMPORARY EUROPEAN   The younger sister of the successful Pied à Terre (p. 213), this is now the domain of Andy McFadden from Pied à Terre. The dark red seating, hand-painted walls, and wooden tables make a cozy ambience, ideal for the well-heeled shoppers of Bond Street. The cooking is skillful, with intense flavors brought to the fore in dishes that range from a starter of roast foie gras, with crispy oats and semi dried apple, grapes, and pomegranate, to a deeply satisfying main dish of roasted guinea fowl breast with caramelized apple purée, Brussels sprouts, and the kick of black olives and thyme jus. Vegetarians are well served with imaginative dishes. For dessert the choice might run from vanilla cheesecake with caramelized banana and passion fruit sorbet, to a sharp lime and vodka parfait with mandarin sorbet, coconut foam, and chocolate. It's expensive, but the set lunch and pretheatre dinner is a steal.

5–7 Blandford St., W1. www.lautrepied.co.uk. ✆ **020/7486-9696.** Reservations required. Main courses £15.95–£28.50; fixed-price lunch or pretheatre (6–7pm) set menu 2 courses £18.95, 3 courses £22.50; tasting menu £67.50. AE, MC, V. Mon–Fri noon–2:45pm; Sat noon–2:30pm; Sun noon–3:30pm; Mon–Sat 6–10:45pm. Tube: Bond St.

Orrery ★★ FRENCH   Orrery is a London favorite. Above the smart Conran Shop in Marylebone, the long room was carved out of a former stable block. The menu is classic French, with ingredients imported from regional France—game in season; wild sea bass; chicken from Bresse are all cooked with great skill. Foie gras parfait comes with famous Poîlane bread and apple chutney; an autumn black truffle risotto is flavored with soft herbs and Parmesan. It has an exceptionally good wine list, and the sommelier happily recommends for every pocket. On summer evenings the open-air terrace is a lovely place for drinks and light dishes such as gazpacho or *pâté de campagne.*

55 Marylebone High St., W1. www.orreryrestaurant.co.uk. ✆ **020/7616-8000.** Reservations required. Fixed-price 2-course lunch £22.50, 3-course lunch £25.50; fixed-price dinner £48; tasting menus £55–£59;. AE, DC, MC, V. Mon–Thurs noon–2:30pm; Fri–Sat noon–2:30pm and 6:30–10:30pm; Sun noon–3pm and 6:30–10pm. Tube: Baker St.

Texture ★★ NORDIC   Scandinavian and Nordic restaurants may be relatively rare in London, but they're making an impact. And so with Texture, where Agnar Sverrisson is cooking up a cool storm. The decor is pared down, smart wood, and high ceilings with bright artwork on the walls. Fireworks come in the cooking where classic dishes are given an Icelandic touch, using light flavors rather than traditional French cream sauces. Asian influences appear as well. Try Cornish brill with lemon grass quinoa, barley, and cauliflower touches, or three cuts of lamb with swede. The wine list is one of London's best, with some of the world's top and unusual wines.

34 Portman St., W1. www.texture-restaurant.co.uk. ✆ **020/7224-0028.** Reservations required. Main courses £27.50–£34.50. Set lunch menus 2 courses £19, 3 courses £24, 7-course tasting menu £76. AE, MC, V. Tues–Sat noon–2:30pm and 6:30–11pm. Tube: Marble Arch.

The Providores & Tapa Room ★★ PACIFIC RIM/FUSION   If you've wondered what fusion cooking is all about, book at Peter Gordon's Providores for a sublime example. The New Zealander has been showing how combinations of often relatively unknown ingredients can be fused together to produce a truly memorable gourmet experience. It's the masterly combinations that make each dish such a wonderful discovery. Smoked coconut tamarind noodles with fish dumpling, soba noodles, quail's egg, crispy shallots, and coriander is a glorious meeting of pungent tastes and textures. Pan-fried scallops come with a crisp turnip cake, *kim-chi* (fermented Korean vegetables), orange blossom yogurt with an infusion of orange, and a tongue-tingling pickled prune and shiso salad. Lunch is a la carte, but dinner is a set menu with the savory dishes starter-sized to encourage you to taste as many as possible. The main **Providores** restaurant is upstairs.

The downstairs, low-key **Tapa Room** offers all-day dining, and is a perfect place for breakfast.

109 Marylebone High St., W1. www.theprovidores.co.uk. ✆ **020/7935-6175.** Tapa Room: Tapas £2.40–£14.80. The Providores: Main courses lunch £17–£25; set dinner 2/3/4/5 courses £33/£47/£57/£63. AE, MC, V. Tapa Room Mon–Fri 9–11:30am and noon–10:30pm; Sat 10am–3pm and 4–10:30pm; Sun 10am–3pm and 4–10pm. The Providores Mon–Fri noon–2:45pm and 6–10pm; Sun noon–2:45pm and 6–9:45pm. Tube: Baker St./Bond St.

MODERATE

Galvin Bistro de Luxe ★★ 🍴 FRENCH   The Galvin brothers, Chris and Jeff, opened Galvin Bistro de Luxe in 2005, considered at the time a brave venture after the site had seen off several hopefuls. But their formula of producing some of the best rustic French food to be found in London *and* Paris at reasonable prices in an elegant, buzzing brasserie has proved a winner. Tastes shine through in well-loved dishes such as fish soup with rouille and cheese; sautéed veal kidneys with chanterelle mushrooms and a mustard sauce; and those staples of bistro cooking, *tarte au citron* and apple *tarte tatin*. The fixed-price menu is a steal: Using cheaper cuts and slow cooking, you're treated to the likes of ballotine of pigs head with braised lentils.

66 Baker St., W1. www.galvinrestaurants.com. ✆ **020/7935-4007.** Reservations required. Main courses £18–£25.50; fixed-price menu lunch £19.50, dinner £21.50. AE, MC, V. Mon–Sat noon–2:30pm; Sun noon–3pm; Mon–Wed 6–10:30pm; Thurs–Sat 6–11pm; Sun 6–9:30pm. Tube: Baker St. Also at 35 Spital Sq., E1 (✆ **020/7299-0400**).

Union Café CONTEMPORARY EUROPEAN   We find this place a real haven after shopping in Oxford Street or Marylebone. The buzzing restaurant, part of the upmarket Brinkley's group, is chic with wooden floors, industrial air vents, and an open kitchen. The menu goes the global path: Caesar salad; steamed chicken dim sum with sweet soy sauce; tempting meze plates; linguine with tiger prawns, mussels, and chili. But it's the juicy, tender Union burger with foie gras, chips, and tomato salad that seems to go down best with the punters.

96 Marylebone Lane, W1. www.brinkleys.com/unioncafe.asp. ✆ **020/7486-4860.** Reservations recommended. Main courses £14–£24. AE, MC, V. Mon–Fri noon–3:30pm and 6–10:30pm; Sat 11am–4pm and 6:30–11pm; Sun 11am–4pm. Tube: Bond St.

Villandry CONTEMPORARY EUROPEAN   Delicatessen, food hall, bakery, and restaurant, Villandry offers a lot. It's an industrial minimalist space with a tempting food market area full of meats, cheeses, jams, chutneys, and more. The restaurant at the back can get noisy and overcrowded and Villandry is popular during the day, drawing famous faces, producers from the nearby BBC, and locals. The menu walks a nicely balanced line between traditional and contemporary. Around 16 starters or small dishes, mains including wild mushroom and cep risotto; *moules frites* (mussels and fries); or steak with red pepper relish, plus a daily changing special (lamb cutlets on Tuesday; salmon fish pie on Friday) all please. We prefer the relaxed bar that opens onto outdoor tables at the front for summer dining, and Sunday brunch is good fun.

170 Great Portland St., W1. www.villandry.com. ✆ **020/7631-3131.** Reservations recommended. Main courses £13.80–£21.40; fixed-price dinner 2 courses £30, 3 courses £40. AE, MC, V. Restaurant: Mon–Fri noon–3pm and 6–10:30pm; Sat 6–10:30pm. Food store: Mon–Sat 8am–10pm; Sun 9am–4pm. Tube: Great Portland St.

WEST LONDON
Paddington & Bayswater
EXPENSIVE

Assaggi ★ 🍴 ITALIAN   It's easy to miss the entrance to Assaggi, above a pub in a Georgian terrace. Once upstairs, you're seduced by the airy, simply decorated room with just a dozen tables. What the fiercely loyal clientele appreciates is the joy of simplicity. But simple doesn't mean unskilled: Food is prepared with real love, using whatever is seasonal and fresh. Summer sees the likes of unadorned fish and wonderful vegetables; in winter it's hearty meat and game. Grilled Mediterranean vegetables in virgin olive oil and fresh herbs are always a winning appetizer, followed by such mains as grilled sea bass, or filet of pork with black truffles. Leave room for the favorite dessert, tiramisu.

39 Chepstow Place, W2. (©) **020/7792-9033.** Reservations required. Main courses £18–£25. AE, MC, V. Mon–Sat 12:30–2:30pm and 7:30–11pm. Tube: Bayswater.

MODERATE

Hereford Road ★★ MODERN BRITISH   Once a butcher's shop, this is now a restaurant in the St. John mode of British no-fuss, no-fancy cooking. Chef Tom Pemberton's time at St. John Bread & Wine (p. 238) shows in a menu that takes in potted crab as well as grilled ox heart and roast quail with that most British (but underused) meddler jelly for starters, and moves on to mains of pot-roast duck leg and fennel, or deviled lamb's kidneys and mash. The regulars of Notting Hill have taken this offal-heavy restaurant to their heart.

13 Hereford Rd., W2. www.herefordroad.org. (©) **020/7727-1144.** Reservations recommended. Main courses £10–£14; set lunch, 2 courses Mon–Fri £13, 3 courses £15.50. AE, MC, V. Mon–Sat noon–3pm and 6–10:30pm; Sun noon–4pm and 6–10pm. Tube: Bayswater.

Royal China ★ ☺ CANTONESE/SZECHUAN   The first of the Royal China group to open in London, the Bayswater branch burst on the scene and woke up Londoners (and their children) to the joys of portion-sized dim sum. Competition is now fierce, but Chinese and Londoners still flock here for their dumplings. From a long list, steamed dim sum includes delicious crabmeat in soup, and seafood with minced pork and beef; squid paste or mixed meat fried dumplings live up to expectations, and don't overlook the beef-filled *cheung fun* (rice noodle roll). The dessert varieties include the now famous black sesame dumpling in peanut crumbs. Refurbishment has spruced up the overwhelmingly gold and black lacquer room, which is always heaving. The long evening menu runs the gamut, but it's the daytime dim sum that is the star attraction here.

13 Queensway, W2. www.royalchinagroup.co.uk. (©) **020/7221-2535.** Reservations recommended. Main courses £6.50–£42; fixed-price dinner £30–£38. AE, DC, MC, V. Mon–Thurs noon–11pm; Fri–Sat noon–11:30pm; Sun 11am–10pm. Tube: Bayswater or Queensway.

INEXPENSIVE

Mandalay 🍴 BURMESE   This cramped, family-run cafe is still the only Burmese restaurant in London, drawing a mix of students, locals, and those in the know. The menu takes in influences from China, India, and Thailand too, so you can combine shrimp and vegetable spring rolls; samosas and fritters; as well as spicy lamb curry, sweet-and-sour chicken, and shrimps with bamboo shoots. The small kitchen turns out the dishes with remarkable skill, particularly given the size of the menu. There's a short drinks list, but you go here for the honest food, not a gourmet meal.

444 Edgware Rd., W2. www.mandalayway.com. ℂ **020/7258-3696.** Reservations required at dinner. Main courses £2.90–£7.90. AE, MC, V. Daily noon–2:30pm and 6–10:30pm. Tube: Edgware Rd.

Notting Hill

EXPENSIVE

The Ledbury ★★ EUROPEAN   Australian-born Brett Graham has now earned two Michelin stars at this sophisticated neighborhood restaurant. With an inventive approach to ingredients and taste combinations that show true Aussie innovation, he produces dishes such as flame-grilled mackerel with smoked eel, mustard, and *shiso* (Japanese mint) as a starter, and shoulder of Pyrenean lamb with crushed Jerusalem artichoke and rosemary; and lobster with broccoli and natural yogurt and Indian spices. This is adventurous stuff—and in lesser hands could be a disaster. Here it is some of the best cooking around, and he's just as good at the dessert stage: Try the pavé of chocolate with silky milk purée and an ice cream flavored with that old-fashioned British herb, lovage.

127 Ledbury Rd., W11. www.theledbury.com. ℂ **020/7792-9090.** Reservations recommended. Main courses (lunch) £28.50–£30; set lunch Mon–Fri 2 courses £30, 3 courses £35; set dinner £80; tasting menu £105. AE, MC, V. Tues–Sat noon–2pm; Sun noon–2:30pm; Mon–Sat 6:30–10:15pm; Sun 7–10pm. Tube: Westbourne Park.

MODERATE

The Cow ★ 🎁 MODERN BRITISH/GASTROPUB   Tom Conran's pub is a great mix. It looks like an Irish pub from the outside, and the downstairs bar is just like a regular local boozer. But at the back you'll find the young and hip tucking into the Cow Special (pint of Guinness and six oysters), or the rich Cow fish stew. The upstairs dining room is quieter, a better place to enjoy a compact, attractive menu of British classics including yellow pea soup, mixed with French dishes such as spicy tuna tartare. Pasta makes an appearance, or the pescatorially challenged can order steak or perhaps leg of lamb, but the strength here is the fish and seafood such as smoked eel with a creamy mash or the beautifully presented seafood platter for two.

89 Westbourne Park Rd., W2. www.thecowlondon.co.uk. ℂ **020/7221-0021.** Reservations required. Main courses £17–£23. MC, V. Restaurant daily noon–3pm and 6:30–10:30pm. Bar daily noon–midnight. Tube: Westbourne Grove.

Le Café Anglais ★★ ☺ MODERN BRITISH   This is a grand brasserie in feel with huge windows, high ceilings, and banquette seating, located in Whiteleys shopping center (p. 279). There's also a glamorous all-day cafe and oyster bar, ideal for those seeking an elegant light snack between buying posh frocks. Chef/restaurateur Rowley Leigh started Notting Hill's landmark restaurant, Kensington Place, becoming one of the founding fathers of contemporary British cookery in the process. He's since become a national figure via his food column for the *Financial Times*. There are plenty of his classics on the menu, such as Parmesan custard and anchovy toast for a starter and any of the excellent game dishes. With its wide choice of dishes, set menus, children's meals and parties,

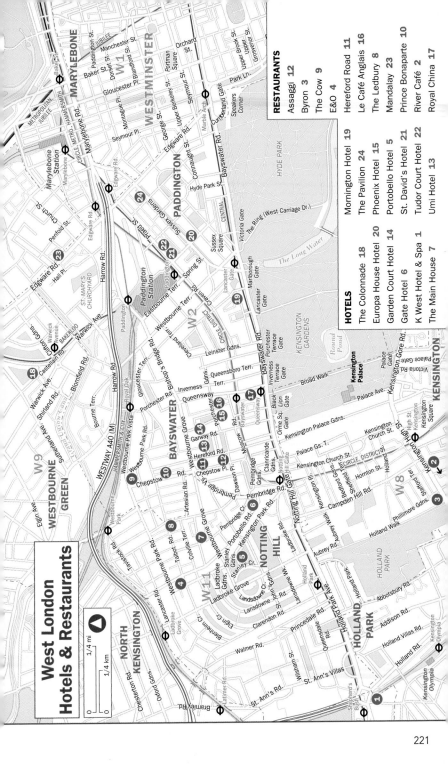

West London
Hotels & Restaurants

1/4 mi

1/4 km

RESTAURANTS

Assaggi **12**
Byron **3**
The Cow **9**
E&O **4**
Hereford Road **11**
Le Café Anglais **16**
The Ledbury **8**
Mandalay **23**
Prince Bonaparte **10**
River Café **2**
Royal China **17**

Mornington Hotel **19**
The Pavilion **24**
Phoenix Hotel **15**
Portobello Hotel **21**
St. David's Hotel **6**
Tudor Court Hotel **22**
Umi Hotel **13**

HOTELS

The Colonnade **18**
Europa House Hotel **20**
Garden Court Hotel **14**
Gate Hotel **6**
K West Hotel & Spa **1**
The Main House **7**

and friendly welcome, Le Café Anglais works hard to create a neighbourhood atmosphere and succeeds; this is a restaurant that pleases everyone.

8 Porchester Gardens, W2. www.lecafeanglais.co.uk. ℂ **020/7221-1415.** Reservations required. Main courses £12.50–£30; set lunch Mon–Fri 2 courses £18.50, 3 courses £22.50; Sun lunch 2 courses £25, 3 courses £30. AE, MC, V. Daily noon–3:30pm; Mon–Thurs 6:30–10:30pm; Fri–Sat 6:30–11pm; Sun 6:30–10pm. Tube: Bayswater or Queensway.

INEXPENSIVE

Prince Bonaparte TRADITIONAL BRITISH/CONTEMPORARY EUROPEAN   Once a local boozer, now a large gastropub with bare brick walls and mismatched furniture, it's a great hit with the bright young things of Notting Hill. There's a large horseshoe-shaped bar at the front, and a dining area and open kitchen at the back. Jazz and blues fill the air, competing with the contented babble. Dishes on a chalkboard offer a mix of all that is modish in gastropub food: smoked haddock and pine nut risotto; pan-fried sea bass with new potatoes and spinach; roast haunch of venison with cream potatoes and braised red cabbage. And there's a good real ale list. The service can be erratic, but the food is good, and the atmosphere relaxed and fun.

80 Chepstow Rd., W2. www.theprincebonapartew2.co.uk. ℂ **020/7313-9491.** Main courses £13–£19.50. AE, MC, V. Mon–Fri noon–3:30pm and 6–10:30pm; Sat noon–4:30pm and 6–10:30pm; Sun noon–9:30pm. Tube: Notting Hill Gate or Westbourne Park.

Ladbroke Grove

MODERATE

E&O ★ ASIAN   Still attracting the likes of Kate Moss and Sir Richard Branson, E&O continues its star-studded path—and it's easy to see why. The dining room with its black chairs, white linen, and dim lights is chic; staff are laid back; the inventive cocktails are a mix of tropical fruit and top spirits (try the ho-chi-minh or bourbon bramble); and the broad pan-Asian menu appeals to everyone. Start with chili salt squid and pork belly in black vinegar, toy with tempura of rock shrimp and jalapeño and sea bass sashimi, and then go for the delectably spiced honey roast duck. Chocolate pudding takes 20 minutes to prepare, but is worth it. Australian restaurateur Will Rickers' empire now stretches all over London, but this is still our favorite for its vibe, and yes, the feeling of dining with . . . well, any star who happens to be in town.

14 Blenheim Crescent, W11. www.rickerrestaurants.com. ℂ **020/7229-5454.** Reservations required. Main courses £6.50–£24. AE, DC, MC, V. Mon–Fri 12–3pm and 6–11pm; Sat noon–11pm; Sun 12:30–10:30pm. Tube: Ladbroke Grove or Notting Hill Gate.

Hammersmith

EXPENSIVE

River Café ★★ ITALIAN   This is one of London's iconic restaurants, an attractive space with an open-plan kitchen and private dining room in a sleek, blue-and-white, canteen-style space. The restaurant continues to attract those after the best rustic Italian cooking in London, despite the tragic death in 2010 of co-founder Rose Gray. Ruth Rogers, whose world famous architect husband Richard co-designed the restaurant, produces authentic home-style cooking. Ingredients are flown in from Italy and France; the seafood and fish arrive daily from Britain's shores. All this comes at a price, but it's one the clientele is happy to pay. This is self-assured, knowledgeable cooking where Parma prosciutto is perfectly paired with bruschetta of broad beans, mint, and Pecorino cheese; and a Tuscan bread soup comes full of robust flavors. For the habitués, the wood-fired oven has produced new classics such as herb-stuffed pigeon roasted on bruschetta in Chianti with peas and prosciutto.

Thames Wharf, Rainville Rd., W6. www.rivercafe.co.uk. ℂ **020/7386-4200.** Reservations required. Main courses £13–£38. Set lunch 2 courses £25, 3 courses £31, 4 courses £39. AE, DC, MC, V. Mon–Thurs 12:30–2:15pm and 7–9pm; Fri 12:30–2:15pm and 7–9:15pm; Sat 12:30–2:30pm and 7–9:15pm; Sun noon–3pm. Tube: Hammersmith.

SOUTHWEST LONDON
Belgravia
EXPENSIVE

Amaya ★★ INDIAN   Theatrical, with its chefs working at the open kitchen and charcoal grill; beautiful, with pink sandstone and black granite worktops, chandeliers of cascading crystals, and colorful modern art; and seductive, with its rosewood and red bar—it's not surprising that Amaya is such a hit. And that's before you taste the food. Chef Karunesh Khanna not only has a Michelin star, he also specializes in tapas-style Indian food, so go in a group to share as many of the array of dishes as possible. Try prawns with tomato and ginger; marinated leg of lamb; lamb seasoned with cardamom, mace, and ginger cooked over charcoal; and a range of vegetarian dishes such as tandoor-cooked broccoli in yogurt sauce. Biryanis are a specialty: light, delicately seasoned, and baked in a pastry-sealed pot.

Halkin Arcade, Motcomb St., SW1. www.amaya.biz. ℂ **020/7823-1166.** Reservations required. Main courses £19–£24; set-price lunch £19.50–£32, set-price dinner £42–£70. AE, DC, MC, V. Mon–Sat 12:30–2:15pm and 6:30–11:30pm; Sun 12:45–2:45pm and 6–10:30pm. Tube: Knightsbridge.

Palm ★ ☺ AMERICAN/STEAK   Walk into the long buzzing bar and you'll find a TV at one end showing North American sports. Two adjacent dining rooms follow the decor of the other Palms in this American group: casual yet smart, with wooden floors and walls covered in caricatures of famous or faithful customers. The menu goes beyond the normal steakhouse, with classic Italian dishes (Palm's founders were Italian immigrants) such as veal marsala, and fresh seafood and burgers, but steak is what Palm is all about. It's expensive, but go for the Prime New York Strip, arguably the best steak you've ever tasted. Start with sesame-seared yellowfin tuna and finish with key lime pie. The welcome is as big as the portions; there's a good children's menu and a reasonably priced wine list.

1 Pont St., SW1. www.thepalm.com/london. ℂ **020/7201-0710.** Reservations recommended. Main courses £14–£50. AE, DC, MC, V. Mon–Sat noon–11pm; Sun noon–9pm. Tube: Knightsbridge or Sloane Sq.

Knightsbridge
VERY EXPENSIVE
Dinner by Heston Blumenthal ★★ TRADITIONAL BRITISH   Heston Blumenthal of the Fat Duck in Bray, hit the ground running with his London

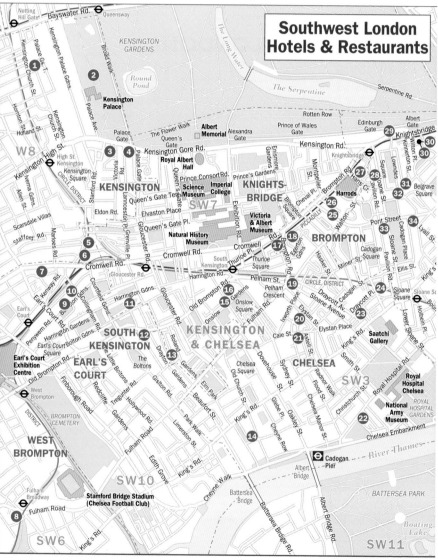

RESTAURANTS

Amaya **31**

Bar Boulud **29**

Bibendum &
   the Oyster Bar **19**

Blue Elephant **8**

Cambio de Tercio **12**

Cassis Bistro **17**

Cinnamon Club **46**

Clarke's **1**

Dinner by Heston
   Blumenthal **29**

Gordon Ramsay **22**

The Goring **41**

Jenny Lo's
   Teahouse **39**

Koffmann's **30**

Marcus Wareing at
   the Berkeley **30**

The Orange **35**

The Orangery **2**

Palm **34**

Pig's Ear **14**

Racine **18**

Rex Whistler
   Restaurant **47**

Tom Aikens **20**

Tom's Kitchen **21**

Zafferano **32**

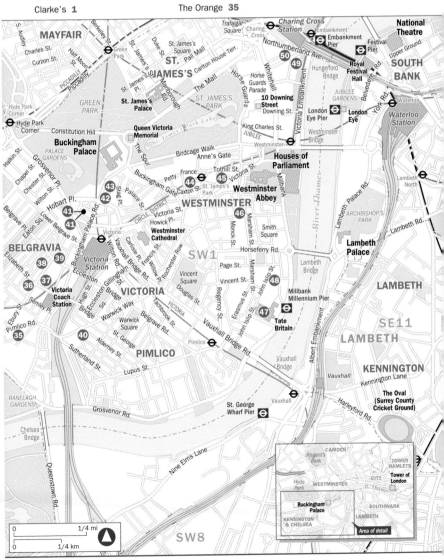

restaurant. The dining room looks over Hyde Park on one side and into an open kitchen on the other. The decor is fine; but it's the food that is the star here. The dishes are based on Britain's culinary past, from savory porridge (ca. 1660) and broth of lamb (ca. 1730) to powdered duck breast (ca. 1670) and cod in cider (ca. 1940). Finish with a sublime dessert—tipsy cake from 1810 perhaps? Don't worry; this is an extremely serious, profoundly satisfying rerendering of historic recipes with modern cooking and techniques. Take the starter of meat fruit (ca. 1500), which looks exactly like a tangerine until you cut through the mandarin jelly to discover a perfect chicken liver parfait. Dinner comes at a price and wine is expensive. But this is a unique experience in a crowded marketplace.

Inside Mandarin Oriental Hyde Park, 66 Knightsbridge, SW1. www.dinnerbyheston.com. ☎ **020/7201-3833.** Reservations required. Main courses £23–£33; 3-course set lunch Mon–Fri £32. AE, DC, MC, V. Daily noon–2:30pm and 6:30–10:30pm. Tube: Knightsbridge.

Marcus Wareing at the Berkeley ★★★ FRENCH   Diners at this claret-colored, cosseting restaurant are treated to all the goodies expected from one of London's top venues. Marcus Wareing began as a protégé of Gordon Ramsay but then took over the restaurant independently and blossomed. The three-course, fixed-price lunch menu at £38 is relatively inexpensive, but the dishes—wood pigeon with tomato, black pudding, and lettuce followed by perhaps chicken with root vegetables—don't stretch the kitchen. So if you can, blow the budget and go a la carte. Start with foie gras with sorbet, walnuts, dates, and a milk tuile, and then follow with flavorful mutton, caper, raisins, cabbage, and spices. The kitchen delivers dishes that are beautifully constructed in looks and full of rich flavors that never overpower. Don't expect a quick meal; delicious extras—smooth velouté as a pre-starter, lip-tingling granitas between courses, and pre-desserts—keep you guessing as to what might come your way next.

Inside Berkeley Hotel, Wilton Place, SW1. www.marcus-wareing.com. ☎ **020/7235-1200.** Reservations required. Lunch menu 2 courses £30, 3 courses £38; a la carte menu £80; prestige menu or vegetarian menu £98; weekend menus £85 and £120. AE, MC, V. Mon–Fri noon–2:30pm; Mon–Sat 6–11pm. Tube: Hyde Park Corner or Knightsbridge.

EXPENSIVE

Koffmann's ★★ FRENCH   Pierre Koffmann, one of London's most feted chefs, returned in 2010 in a move that encapsulates the merry-go-round of London's restaurants. Koffmann opened La Tante Claire in Royal Hospital Road in 1977, now occupied by Gordon Ramsay (p. 229), moved to what is now Marcus Wareing at the Berkeley (p. 226), and then disappeared for a few years before returning—to what was once Gordon Ramsay's Boxwood Café. Here he's left behind haute cuisine to return to his Gascon roots. Earthy, honest, bourgeois French cooking, top ingredients, and one of the most skilled chefs combine to deliver a near-perfect dining experience for contemporary tastes. A rich Provencal fish soup, or snails and mushrooms in creamy sauce and mashed potatoes, followed by his signature dish of pig's trotter stuffed with sweetbreads and morels bring sighs of contentment. Staff under Eric Garnier (from Racine; p. 228) are delightfully welcoming, and the set 3-course lunch for £25.50 is a bargain.

Inside Berkeley Hotel, Wilton Place, SW1. www.the-berkeley.co.uk/pierre-koffmanns-french-restaurant.aspx. ☎ **020/7235-1010.** Reservations required. Main courses £22–£60; set lunch 2 courses Mon–Sat £21.50, 3 courses £25.50; Pre/posttheatre 3-course menu £38. AE, MC, V.

Mon–Fri noon–2:30pm; Sat–Sun noon–3pm; daily 6–10:30pm. Tube: Hyde Park Corner or Knightsbridge.

Zafferano ★★ ITALIAN   There's something honest and satisfying about this restaurant, where decor consists of little more than ocher-colored walls, immaculate linens, and a bevy of diligent staff. The light modernized interpretation of classic Italian cuisine features such dishes as Tuscan ham with celeriac and mustard fruits; roast chicken with lemon and capers; and herb-crusted roast sea bass with grapes and green olives. The seemingly simple dishes rely on the freshest of ingredients and skillful, accurate cooking. The owners pride themselves on one of the most esoteric and well-rounded collections of Italian wine in London: You'll find as many as 20 different vintages each of Brunello and Barolo, and about a dozen vintages of Sassicaia.

15 Lowndes St., SW1. www.zafferanorestaurant.com. ☎ **020/7235-5800.** Reservations required. Main courses £9–£25; Set-price lunch 2 courses £21, 3 courses £26; set-price dinner menu 2/3/4 courses £36.50/£46.50/£51.50. AE, MC, V. Mon–Fri noon–2:30pm; Sat–Sun 12:30–3pm; daily 7–11pm (until 10:30pm Sun). Tube: Knightsbridge.

MODERATE

Bar Boulud ★★ FRENCH   French-born, U.S.-raised, superstar chef Daniel Boulud opened the doors of his first London venture to universal approval in 2009. It's in the Mandarin Oriental, but with its own entrance, and has an attractive decor of red banquette seating, an open kitchen, and a real buzz. You won't encounter the Michelin three-star cuisine of his New York restaurant, but hearty, rustic cooking. A charcuterie counter rightly takes pride of place—Daniel Boulud was born in Lyon. Feast on classic French bistro fare such as a *petit aioli* of seafood and vegetables with a perfect garlic mayonnaise; a coq au vin that had us rushing home to dig out the French recipe books; homemade sausages; and for dessert, a rich dark chocolate and raspberry gateau. The wine list is built around the chef's favorite Burgundy and Rhône wines. Prices are very reasonable for this part of London and level of glamour.

In the Mandarin Oriental Hyde Park, 66 Knightsbridge, SW1. www.barboulud.com. ☎ **020/7201-3899.** Reservations recommended. Main courses £9–£27.50; 3-course fixed price £23. AE, MC, V. Daily noon–3pm and 5–11pm (10:30pm on Sun). Tube: Knightsbridge.

Cassis Bistro ★★ FRENCH/PROVENCALE   Marlon Abela is something of a star—a restaurateur who owns top restaurants in London (including the Greenhouse, p. 197), New York, Greenwich, Connecticut, and Boston. His latest London venture is this bistro in fashionable Brompton Cross. It's very refined, as you'd expect, with an open fireplace, oak floors, and banquettes. There's a zinc-topped bar area, the bistro itself, and summer terrace seating. Chef David Escobar comes with the best credentials—he was last at Michelin three-star Maison Lameloise in Chagny-en-Bourgogne. The menu is a Provencal dream with a playful touch. Start with seared tuna carpaccio with a red grape and tomato marinade, and then recall sun-drenched holidays with a lobster linguine or roast duck breast with chick pea galette and Niçoise olive sauce. Good cocktails and Provencal wines are an added bonus.

232 Brompton Rd., SW3. www.cassisbistro.co.uk. ☎ **020/7581-1101.** Reservations recommended. Main courses £11–£31; set lunch 2 courses £17, 3 courses £20. AE, DC, MC, V. Mon–Fri noon–11pm; Sat 11:30am–11pm; Sun 11:30am–10pm. Tube: Knightsbridge.

Racine ★ FRENCH The chef, Henry Harris, is as English as they come, but the cuisine at this bustling French restaurant puts you right in the heart of Paris. Francophiles flock to this brasserie with its wooden floors, dark-leather banquettes, mirrors, and black-and-white-clad waiters. Seasonal dishes are featured on the ever-changing menu from Harris, who serves what he loves to cook and eat. When he opened in 2002, this was a new departure—bistro food with a highly professional edge. Today, and despite competition, Racine is one of London's enduring favorites. Come here for classics such as Bayonne ham with celeriac remoulade; foie gras with caramelized apple and Calvados; grilled rabbit with mustard sauce; and classic duck confit with Puy lentils. Expect true, robust flavors and a minimum of pretentiousness.

239 Brompton Rd., SW3. www.racine-restaurant.com. Ⓒ **020/7584-4477.** Main courses £16.50–£28.50; set-price lunch 2/3 courses £15.50/£17.75; Sun 2 courses £18–£20. MC, V. Mon–Fri noon–3pm and 6–10:30pm; Sat noon–3:30pm and 6–10:30pm; Sun noon–3:30pm and 6–10pm. Tube: Knightsbridge.

Kensington & South Kensington
VERY EXPENSIVE

Tom Aikens ★★★ FRENCH The refurbishment of Tom Aikens' eponymous restaurant has produced a more informal space with bare wooden tables, mismatched china, and concrete walls etched with food related quotes. And the punters seem to like it. What hasn't changed is his remarkable style: a modern interpretation of haute French cuisine, produced with confidence and skill, though with less gourmet flourishes than before. Lobster comes with pickled cucumber and yogurt granita; Kentish lamb with ewes' cheese, anchovy, and confit garlic. The cooking shows harmony and cohesion, as exemplified by turbot with crisp chicken skin, cress, and sorrel. The end result is supremely satisfying, and it is beautifully presented.

43 Elystan St., SW3. www.tomaikens.co.uk. Ⓒ **020/7584-2003.** Reservations required. Set lunch 2 courses £24, 3 courses £29; a la carte menus 2 courses £40, 3 courses £55; tasting menu 6 courses £55, 8 courses £75 (whole table). AE, DC, MC, V. Mon–Fri noon–2:30pm; Mon–Sat 6:45–11pm. Tube: South Kensington.

EXPENSIVE

Bibendum & the Oyster Bar ★ FRENCH Glamorous, elegant, and still fashionable after so many years, **Bibendum** stands out as a reliable London icon. You can't miss the Art Deco exterior with its huge windows, dramatic tiling, and stained glass starring the rotund Bibendum. In the light and airy upstairs dining, well-drilled staff serve a loyal lunchtime clientele with a good value menu of French favorites from the kitchen of chef Matthew Harris. Beetroot and horse-radish-cured herrings with warm potato salad; mussels with cream and chives; roast rump of lamb with Savoyard potatoes, and daube of beef are dishes designed to satisfy. Dinner is a more expensive affair: perhaps foie gras terrine with Armagnac jelly followed by roast pheasant with morels, foie gras, and spätzle. At street level, the pretty **Oyster Bar** is the place for shellfish presented in traditional French style on ice-covered platters; oysters in season; and light dishes, accompanied by a short wine list.

81 Fulham Rd., SW3. www.bibendum.co.uk. © **020/7581-5817.** Reservations required in Bibendum, not accepted in Oyster Bar. Main courses £18.50–£29.75; fixed-price lunch 2 courses £26.50, 3 courses £30, Sundays 2/3 courses £30/£32; cold seafood platter in Oyster Bar £29.95 (minimum 2 people). AE, DC, MC, V. Bibendum Mon–Fri noon–2:30pm and 7–11pm; Sat 12:30–3pm and 7–11pm; Sun 12:30–3pm and 7–10:30pm. Oyster Bar daily noon–11pm (Sun 10:30pm). Tube: South Kensington.

MODERATE

Cambio de Tercio ★★ CONTEMPORARY SPANISH   Vibrantly colored in blood reds, deep pinks, and bright yellows, and adorned with equally vibrant stylized paintings of bull fighting, this is not the best place for the shy and retiring. But it is the place for exciting, modern Spanish cooking from a menu with wide appeal. It offers conventional dishes such as fried squid; prawns with garlic-parsley oil; and five sorts of top Iberian ham. But it also takes you on a different journey. With many of the dishes available in tapas size, you'll be tempted to forgo the straight three-course route for a series of small dishes, perhaps what is described as the famous deconstructed Spanish chorizo omelet from El Bulli; or ox tail caramelized in red wine with green apple. Order equally exciting main dishes like grilled cod with braised pig's head and onions. Or take the plunge and go for the exceptional value £37 seven-course tasting menu (whole table).

163 Old Brompton Rd., SW5. www.cambiodetercio.co.uk. © **020/7244-8970.** Main courses £17.50–£23; 7-course tasting menu £37. AE, DC, MC, V. Mon–Fri noon–2:30pm; Sat–Sun noon–3pm; Mon–Sat 7–11:30pm; Sun 7–11pm. Tube: Gloucester Rd. or South Kensington. Also at 174 Old Brompton Rd., SW7 (© **0207370-3685**) and 108–110 New King's Rd., SW6 (© **020/7371-5147**).

Clarke's ★ CONTEMPORARY EUROPEAN   Now awarded a well-deserved MBE, Sally Clarke remains one of London's favorite chefs. The pretty restaurant overlooking Kensington Church Street is bright and modern, with additional space in the basement—where tables are more spacious and private. Seasonality has always been the driving force of her cooking. She sources the best ingredients from Britain and as far afield as Italy. The menu, which changes weekly, emphasizes chargrilled foods with seasonal vegetables. So a winter meal might begin with salad of steamed mussels that incorporates shaved fennel and blood oranges in a citrus vinaigrette; slow-baked duck with orange and sage glaze, roast celeriac and red watercress salad.

124 Kensington Church St., W8. www.sallyclarke.com. © **020/7221-9225.** Reservations recommended. Main courses £22–£24; fixed-price 3-course meal £42.50. AE, DC, MC, V. Mon–Fri 12:30–2pm; Sat noon–2:30pm; Mon–Sat 6:30–10pm. Tube: High St. Kensington or Notting Hill Gate.

Chelsea

VERY EXPENSIVE

Gordon Ramsay ★★★ FRENCH   Whatever may be happening in the fiery chef's empire elsewhere, a meal here remains one of London's great pleasures. From the moment you walk in the door, you are cosseted, and made to feel special. The menu has changed under head chef Clare Smyth—someone to take note of—while retaining the subtlety and delicacy of the master. Try, for example, ravioli of lobster, langoustine, and salmon with a lemongrass and chervil velouté; or sautéed foie gras with roasted veal sweetbreads. The emphasis is on retaining the essential flavors of top ingredients while delivering exquisite tastes. This is a top restaurant with complex dishes that reflect its reputation: sea bass with oyster beignet and caviar velouté; wild venison with celery braised with truffle, pear, and smoked pork belly. The wine list is masterly; the sommelier quietly knowledgeable; the service charming. A rare experience.

68 Royal Hospital Rd., SW3. www.gordonramsay.com. (C) **020/7352-4441.** Reservations essential (1 month in advance). A la carte menu 3 courses £95; fixed-price 3-course lunch £45, 7-course dinner £125. AE, DC, MC, V. Mon–Fri noon–2:30pm and 6:30–11pm. Tube: Sloane Sq.

MODERATE

Blue Elephant ★ ☺ THAI   After 25 years, the Blue Elephant has moved from the greenery-filled, semi tropical restaurant in Fulham to the more sophisticated setting of Imperial Wharf in Chelsea. It's just as luxurious and elegant with the interior modeled on the royal Sarn Rom residence in Bangkok. The bar has a replica of the royal barge of Thailand. The new restaurant has a cookery school and a heated summer terrace overlooking the river. The menus have been altered as well, and are now based on the splendid past, present, and future. Try *Ma Auan*, steamed minced chicken with crab and foie gras from the Cooking of the Past menu, or perhaps order *Isaac Carpaccio*, which is spicy raw slices of beef with fiery papaya salad, olive oil, rock salt, and Parmesan cheese from the Thai Kitchen of Tomorrow menu.

The Boulevard, Imperial Wharf, Townmead Rd., SW6. www.blueelephant.com. (C) **020/7385-6595.** Reservations required. Main courses £18–£28; set lunch 2 courses £14, 3 courses £18; Memories of Siam tasting menu £45; Sun brunch £30. AE, DC, MC, V. Mon–Sat noon–2:30pm, 7–11pm; Sun noon–3:30pm and 6:30–10:30pm. Tube: Fulham Broadway.

Pig's Ear ★ 👜 MODERN BRITISH/GASTROPUB   The packed bar serves excellent traditional beers, and dishes such as risotto or roast guinea fowl in the back dining room. The Blue Room serves meals that are more sophisticated: smoked salmon mousse; a good charcuterie plate for starters; slow-cooked pork belly with horseradish mash, carrots, and parsnip crisps as a typical main. It's a posh gastropub, befitting its posh location in Chelsea, but it's friendly and casual and you're always made to feel welcome.

35 Old Church St., SW3. www.thepigsear.info. (C) **020/7352-2908.** Reservations required in restaurant. Main courses £13.75–£25. AE, DC, MC, V. Mon–Fri 12:30–3pm and 6–10pm; Sat 12:30–10:30pm; Sun 12:30–9pm. Tube: Sloane Sq.

Tom's Kitchen ★ TRADITIONAL BRITISH   High octane, hugely busy, and wildly popular, this former pub has been turned into a brasserie from top chef Tom Aikens (p. 228), and is a great all-day venue. The menu is a rundown of all that is good in London's more casual venues: full English breakfast, butternut squash soup; spicy crab cake; excellent pastas and salads; mains such as roast lamb rump or fish and chips; and the dramatic baked Alaska flamed at the table.

27 Cale St., SW3. www.tomskitchen.co.uk. (C) **020/7349-0202.** Reservations required. Main courses £7.50–£30. AE, MC, V. Mon–Fri 8–11:45am and noon–3pm; Sat–Sun 10am–4pm; daily 6–11pm (10:30pm on weekends). Tube: South Kensington. Also at Somerset House, Strand, WC2, ((C) **020/7845-4646**).

Westminster & Victoria

EXPENSIVE

Cinnamon Club ★★ INDIAN   This former Victorian library is a gorgeous, stately building with wooden paneling, high ceilings, and a book-lined gallery. It's a suitably grand setting for the many MPs (Members of Parliament) who seem to regard it as their club. And it's a suitably theatrical setting for the exciting modern Indian cooking from executive chef Vivek Singh. European ingredients, Indian spicing, classical cooking techniques, and Western-style presentation make for a heady mix. Such a balancing act could be disastrous in less skilled hands, but here it produces some of the most innovative Indian cooking. Try carpaccio of cured salmon; tandoor salmon with green pea relish; baked prawns with special spices and tomato lemon sauce; tandoori partridge breast with pickling spices. Go conventional at breakfast with a perfect, light kedgeree—the dish of fish, rice, eggs, parsley, and cream brought back from the Raj by British colonials.

Old Westminster Library, 30–32 Great Smith St., SW1. www.cinnamonclub.com. ℂ **020/7222-2555.** Main courses £14–£25; set meal pre- and posttheatre 2 courses £22, 3 courses £24; tasting menu £75. AE, DC, MC, V. Mon–Fri 7:30–9:30am, noon–2:45pm, and 6–10:30pm; Sat noon–2:45pm and 6–10:30pm. Tube: St. James's Park or Westminster. Also at Cinnamon Kitchen, 9 Devonshire Sq., EC2, (ℂ **020/7626-5000**).

MODERATE

The Orange ★ ☺ GASTROPUB/CONTEMPORARY EUROPEAN   The Orange is a smart gastropub with four delightful rooms for overnight stays. There's a heaving bar downstairs, with a dining room adjoining and a second dining room upstairs. It serves a clever menu that has the wealthy nearby residents of Pimlico coming back again and again. Oysters or spiced butternut soup with chive cream might start the meal. Wood-fired pizzas, conveniently served in two sizes, are popular with the families who regularly eat here, while mains such as grilled rib eye with chips, or rainbow trout with dill potatoes satisfy the parents. It's fun, cheerful, and the staff go about their business with great charm.

37–39 Pimlico Rd., SW1. www.theorange.co.uk. ℂ **020/7881-9844.** Main courses £9–£26; set 3-course menu £35. AE, MC, V. Mon–Thurs 8–11:30pm; Fri–Sat 8am–midnight; Sun 8am–10:30pm. Tube: Sloane Sq.

Rex Whistler Restaurant ★★ CONTEMPORARY EUROPEAN   This famous landmark restaurant was the pioneer of museum dining, becoming famous for its superb comprehensive wines and its extraordinary 1926 Whistler mural, *The Expedition in Pursuit of Rare Meats.* Today's menu is an exciting one, championing British cooking and using fresh seasonal ingredients for dishes such as marrow mousse with chutney and marrow fritters; or duck breast with a Swiss chard gratin and bitter orange sauce. The first Friday of the month sees a special menu with wine at £70 per person. Afternoon tea is a good bet here.

Tate Britain, Millbank, SW1. www.tate.org.uk; ℂ **020/7887-8825.** Main dishes £12.95–£18.50. AE, MC, V. Daily 11:30am–3pm and 3:15–5pm; Sat–Sun 10–11:15am. Tube: Pimlico.

INEXPENSIVE

Jenny Lo's Teahouse 🍴 CANTONESE/SZECHUAN   This teahouse is really a small, fun cafe, ideal for inexpensive lunches. It was opened by Jenny Lo, daughter of late Ken Lo, the tennis-playing restaurateur whose Memories of

DINING green ON ECO-FRIENDLY FARE

Eco-friendly dining has become a serious pastime in London. At such cafes, gastro-pubs, and small restaurants, much of the fresh produce served comes from near London. All ingredients are carefully sourced for sustainability and green farming practices. Diners in these places expect the waiters to know the provenance of the food—don't be shy to ask. Leading green restaurants include:

Duke of Cambridge ★ The only gastropub in the UK certified by the Soil Association. The modern Brit menu is an all-organic extravaganza, showcasing ingredients from independent producers with 80% coming from near London. If it's not seasonal, it's not on the menu. So sit back, order the likes of beetroot and cumin soup with crème fraiche in winter, and rack of lamb with Jersey royals, runner beans, and salsa verde in summer. 30 St. Peter's St., N1. www.dukeorganic.co.uk. ℓ **020/7359-3066.** Main courses £12.75–£19.50. MC, V. Mon–Sat 12:30–3pm and 6:30–10:30pm, Sun 12:30–3:30pm and 6:30–10pm. Tube: Angel.

Daylesford Organic This posh Chelsea cafe specializes in seasonal produce, including vegetables from their own kitchen garden. Tuck into soup of the day, fish, or roast beef with horseradish and mustard dressing, along with organic cakes, pastries, and breads. It's smart, very Chelsea, and has a farm shop for those without their own acres in central London. 44B Pimlico Rd., SW1. www.daylesfordorganic.com. ℓ **020/7881-8060.** Main courses £9.95–£13.95. AE, MC, V. Mon–Sat 8am–7pm, Sun 10am–4pm. Tube: Sloane Sq.

Water House Stylish and tucked away behind apartment houses beside the Regent's Canal, Water House prides itself on its carbon-neutral credentials. It serves Italian influenced dishes like smoked mackerel Niçoise; excellent risottos; salads and pastas, as well as slow-braised lamb shank. Ethically sound, it boasts filtered tap water instead of bottled, and a wormery for all those kitchen leftovers, which is the proper eco alternative to a doggy bag. 10 Orsman Rd., N1. www.waterhouserestaurant.co.uk. ℓ **020/7033-0123.** Main courses £12–£16. Mon–Fri, Sun noon–4pm, Tues–Sat 6–10pm. Train: Haggerston.

China brought upper-class Chinese cooking to London. Ken Lo cookbooks contribute to the dining room decor of black refectory tables set with paper napkins and chopsticks. The menu offers a good range of well-cooked dishes such as vermicelli rice noodle (noodles topped with grilled chicken breast and Chinese mushrooms). Rounding out the menu are stuffed Peking dumplings, chili-garnished spicy prawns, and wonton soup with slithery dumplings.

14 Eccleston St., SW1. www.jennylo.co.uk. ℓ **020/7259-0399.** Reservations not accepted. Main courses £7.50–£9.50. No credit cards. Mon–Fri noon–2:55pm; Mon–Sat 6–9:55pm. Tube: Victoria.

THE SOUTH BANK

Bankside

EXPENSIVE

Le Pont de la Tour ★ FRENCH Once the flagship of Sir Terence Conran's dining empire, now owned by D&D London, Le Pont de la Tour is still a destination restaurant for the great and the good. It's housed in a 19th-century warehouse and

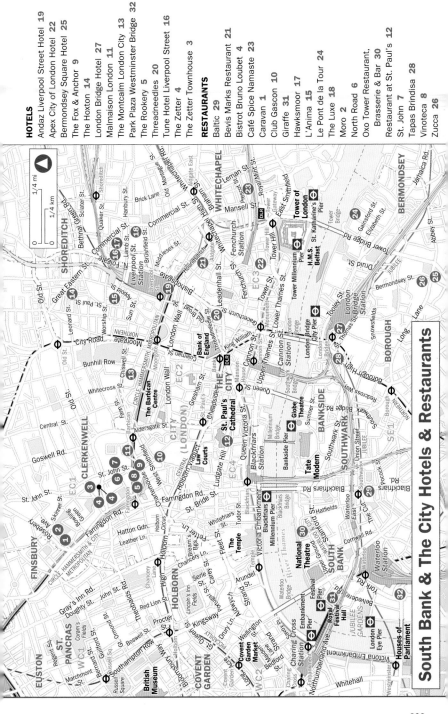

South Bank & The City Hotels & Restaurants

233

the views of the river and Tower Bridge are splendid. This is the place for City types at lunch, but becomes more mellow with couples and groups in the evenings. The **Bar and Grill** offers a brasserie-style menu with choices like smoked duck breast starter followed by rib eye steak, while a jazz pianist plays in the evenings and at Sunday brunch. The **Restaurant** has smart decor of oak furniture surrounded by pictures of early 20th-century Parisian cafe life: It hums like a well-oiled machine. Try lobster bisque for starters and roast pheasant in season for the main. Beware the many supplements on the menu; the wine list is predictably pricey.

36d Shad Thames, Butler's Wharf, SE1. www.dandlondon.com. ✆ **020/7403-8403.** Reservations highly recommended in the Bar and Grill; recommended in the Restaurant. Bar and Grill main courses £5.50–£20.50; Restaurant 2-course lunch £ 27.50, 3-course lunch £31.50; 3-course dinner £44.50; Sun 3-course lunch £28.50. AE, DC, MC, V. Bar and Grill Mon–Fri noon–3pm and 6–11pm; Sat noon–4 and 6–11pm; Sun noon–4 and 6–10pm. Restaurant daily noon–3pm and 6–11pm. Tube: Tower Hill or London Bridge.

Oxo Tower Restaurant, Brasserie & Bar ★★ INTERNATIONAL   The Oxo Tower is one of London's top dining spots—literally, as it's on the eighth floor of Oxo Tower Wharf. Stunning views up and down river make the terrace one of summer's most sought-after venues. Both the Brasserie and the Restaurant share the same chic, 1930s'-liner decor, and the same contemporary ethos in the cooking. The **Brasserie** is more casual, offering all the current modish mixes of tastes, spices, and inspirations such as chargrilled, Moroccan-spiced quail followed by teriyaki salmon with soba noodle salad. Dishes on the **Restaurant** menu use more luxury ingredients: langoustines; foie gras; sea bass with crab, samphire, truffle beurre blanc, and fennel salad; and wild game in season. It's all seasonally led, with carefully sourced British ingredients to the fore. The refurbished **bar** with its excellent food has become one of London's most desirable meeting places.

22 Barge House St., SE1. www.harveynichols.com/restaurants. ✆ **020/7803-3888.** Reservations recommended. Main courses £21.50–£35; 3 courses £35. AE, DC, MC, V. Mon–Fri noon–2:30pm and 6–11pm; Sat noon–2:30pm and 5:30–11pm; Sun noon–3pm and 6:30–10pm. Tube: Blackfriars or Waterloo.

Waterloo, Southwark & Borough
MODERATE

Baltic ★ ▮ EASTERN EUROPEAN   This is one of our favorite places after a visit to the Old Vic theatre, particularly when the actors arrive to eat. It's cool in decor (minimalist with roof lights and upholstered chrome chairs) but hot on atmosphere—with a continuous, contented buzz and good jazz. The menu here mixes Polish, Russian, and Hungarian influences to great effect. Gravadlax salmon marinated in vodka with potato latkes; marinated herring; or Polish black pudding for starters, and then our favorite to follow: a rich goose leg with beetroot, spring onions, and redcurrant is cooked with self-confident skill. There's live jazz on Sundays, and great cocktails from the bar staff, who mix unusual ingredients such as rhubarb jam or beetroot with proper Eastern European vodkas.

74 Blackfriars Rd., SE1. www.balticrestaurant.co.uk. ✆ **020/7928-1111.** Main courses £15–£17; set meal 2 courses £14.50, 3 courses £17.50; AE, MC, V. Mon–Fri noon–3pm and 5:30–11:15pm; Sat–Sun noon–4:30 and 5:30–10:30pm. Tube: Southwark.

Tapas Brindisa ★ SPANISH/TAPAS   Borough Market brings a steady stream of customers to the area—folk who regard good food as one of life's necessities—so Tapas Brindisa, which sources its food directly from Spain, is constantly busy. Add to that a no-bookings policy and a relatively small dining space, and you'll find yourself with a long wait at popular times. But customers agree that it's worth it, for plates such as traditional black rice with squid and aioli; sautéed white beans with Swiss chard and morcilla sausage; chili garlic prawns; and clams with butter beans and bacon. Charcuterie is top class, (but beware, it can push up the bill); there's also a selection of cured fish and specialty cheeses you won't find elsewhere. Partner it with a fino sherry or hearty Rioja.

18–29 Southwark St., SE1. www.brindisa.com. (✆ **020/7357-8889.** Tapas plates £4–£21.50. AE, MC, V. Fri–Sat 9–11am, noon–4pm, and 5:30–11pm; Mon–Thurs11am–3pm and 5:30–11pm, Fri 9–11am, noon–4pm, and 5:30–11pm; Sun 11am–10pm. Tube: London Bridge. Also at 46 Broadwick St., W1, (✆ **020/7534-1690)**; and Casa Brindisa, 7–9 Exhibition Rd., SW7, (✆ **020/ 7590-0008**).

Zucca ★ 🎁 ITALIAN   Zucca is the real thing—an Italian restaurant that opened in 2009 in increasingly trendy Bermondsey and which provides excellent Italian food, an all-Italian wine list, value prices, and a cheerful and professional staff. The setting is minimal with a full open-plan kitchen—a setting where the concentration is, quite rightly, on the food. So what's best to order? Start with "Zucca" *fritti* (pumpkin slices battered and fried) before moving on to pappardelle pasta with pork and fennel ragout, then veal chop with spinach and lemon or black squid with white polenta. These dishes pack a real punch. If you're unfamiliar with Italian wines, ask the waiting staff—they really know their stuff.

184 Bermondsey St., SE1. www.zuccalondon.com. (✆ **020/7378-6809.** Main courses £8–£16. MC, V. Tues–Fri noon–3pm and 6–10pm; Sat noon–3:30pm and 6–10pm; Sun noon–3.30pm. Tube: London Bridge.

THE CITY
Spitalfields
EXPENSIVE

L'Anima ★★ ITALIAN   This chic, high-ceilinged restaurant and bar sporting exposed stonework and white upholstered furniture has been so popular since its opening that it has now doubled in size. The bar is the place for a snack, but you need to book the restaurant to appreciate fully chef Francesco Mazzei's pure, and contemporary, Italian cooking. Many dishes come from his home in southern Italy, from Calabria, Puglia, Sicily, and Sardinia, and he also incorporates Moorish influences. From the starter menu, try *fritto misto* or beef carpaccio with truffle sauce and watercress salad. Move on to a homemade risotto or pasta before a startlingly good fish stew with Sardinian couscous. The clientele is mainly on expense accounts.

1 Snowden St., Broadgate West, EC2. www.lanima.co.uk. (✆ **020/7422-7000.** Main courses £15–£36. AE, DC, MC, V. Restaurant Mon–Fri 11:45am–3pm and 5:30–11pm; Sat 5:30–11:30pm. Bar Mon–Fri 9am–1am; Sat 5:30pm–1am. Tube: Liverpool St.

MODERATE

Hawksmoor ★ AMERICAN/STEAK   With its bare brick walls, wooden tables, and walls covered with photographs, Hawksmoor is every bit the New York steak joint. Its food won't disappoint steakhouse aficionados either. Hawksmoor prides itself on top-quality, perfectly aged, generous portions of beef, sourced from the well-known London butcher, Ginger Pig (p. 291), dry-aged for at least 35 days and cooked exactly to order. All the prime cuts are here: Porterhouse; bone-in prime rib; Chateaubriand; all perfectly seared on the outside, perfectly tender inside. There are other main dishes, such as a fish of the day and whole grilled lobster. Starters are pretty good too: The potted smoked mackerel with toast goes down well, and the prawn cocktail is a lovely retro number. Talking of cocktails, bar staff mix a mean mint julep.

157 Commercial St., E1. www.thehawksmoor.com. ✆ **020/7247-7392.** Main courses £13–£35. AE, MC, V. Mon–Fri noon–3pm and 6–10:30pm; Sat 11am–3pm and 6–10:30pm; Sun 11am–4:30pm. Tube: Liverpool St. Also at 11 Langley St., WC2, (✆ **020/7247-7392**), & 10–12 Basinghall St., EC2 (✆ **020/7397-8120**).

The Luxe ★ CONTEMPORARY EUROPEAN   John Torode has expanded from his original venture, Smiths of Smithfield, into the refurbished Spitalfields Market, where restaurants sit cheek-by-jowl in the modernized Victorian structure. Torode's four-storey Luxe offers a multi-purpose restaurant experience. The cafe buzzes all day, and is a favorite place of ours for breakfast. There's a basement music and cocktail bar, and upstairs is a dining room, complete with open kitchen, exposed brick walls, and silk wallpaper recalling the area's Huguenot silk-weaving heritage. Start with gravadlax with caper berry, shallot, and parsley salad, and then move on to slow roast belly of pork with mash and green sauce. For dessert go the blueberry cheesecake with lemon curd or chocolate pudding route.

109 Commercial St., E1. www.theluxe.co.uk. ✆ **020/7101-1751.** Main courses £13.75–£28.50. AE, MC, V. Restaurant Mon–Fri noon–3pm; Sun noon–4pm; Mon–Sat 6–9:30pm. Cafe-bar Mon–Sat 9am–11:30pm; Sun 9:30am–10pm. Tube: Liverpool St.

Clerkenwell & Farringdon

EXPENSIVE

Club Gascon ★★ FRENCH   Pascal Aussignac set up Club Gascon in Smithfield in 1998, bringing the rich tastes of his native southwest France to a city that took to his Gascony cooking with an enthusiasm that never waned. The menu features modest-sized, beautifully presented dishes that encourage sharing rather than the conventional three-course approach. The seasonal menu is divided into themed sections, so "Land and Sea" might feature scallops with artichokes, violet sauce, and blueberries, or beef with caviar sauce, while "Pasturelands" offers rabbit and octopus with a confit fennel and chorizo. It's adventurous, perfectly balanced cooking. Adjacent **Cellar Gascon** (✆ 020/7600-7561) offers more casual dining, but of an equally high standard where daily specials such as Monday's winter duck confit, and fish pie on a Friday, keeps loyal punters happy.

57 West Smithfield, EC1. www.clubgascon.com. ✆ **020/7796-0600.** Reservations required. Main courses £10.50–£23.50; set lunch £25; set meal 4 courses £55, 5 courses £70. AE, MC, V. Mon–Thurs noon–2pm and 7–10pm; Fri noon–2pm and 7–10:30pm; Sat 7–10:30pm. Tube: Barbican.

MODERATE

Bistrot Bruno Loubet ★★ FRENCH   A collective cheer went up among London's restaurant-goers when Bruno Loubet returned to the capital after 8 years in Australia. And when this star of 1990s' London opened Bistrot Bruno Loubet in the adventurous and funky **Zetter** hotel (p. 369), nobody was disappointed. The all-day bistro hits the spot with a short, gutsy menu. Classic bistro dishes are given a twist in starters such as guinea fowl boudin blanc on cassoulet beans, or snails and meatballs with wild mushrooms, while a main dish of daube of beef Niçoise with herbs and ricotta gnocchi, and a perfect pan-fried sea bream with cauliflower and parsley puree in squid ink demonstrates that London restaurants are the equal of Paris's best. There's a bar at the front, an open kitchen at the back, and large windows looking out onto St. John's Square.

St. John's Sq., 86–88 Clerkenwell Rd., EC1. www.thezetter.com/en/restaurant. ✆ **020/7324-4455.** Main courses £15–£20.50. AE, MC, V. Breakfast Mon–Fri 7–10:30am, Sat–Sun 7:30–11am; daily noon–2:30pm; Mon–Sat 6–10:30pm; Sun 6–10pm. Tube: Farringdon.

Caravan ★ INTERNATIONAL   Exmouth Market has become one of London's fashionable dining streets, particularly favored by media types working locally. Caravan fits in perfectly with its industrial decor and its creative, exciting cooking. The chef is Miles Kirby, a New Zealander who learnt much from Peter Gordon at Providores (p. 217). You can choose individual main dishes (perhaps veal Schnitzel with gypsy potatoes), but we recommend going down the tapas-style, small plate-sharing route for a mix of tastes—such as tomato and chili soup with cucumber yogurt; squid pancake with Japanese brown sauce, mayonnaise and seaweed salt; or oxtail with crème fraiche polenta. Weekend brunch is one of the best in London.

11–13 Exmouth Market, EC1. www.caravanonexmouth.co.uk. ✆ **020/7833-8115.** Small plates £4.50–£8. Main dishes £12.50–£16. AE, MC, V. Mon–Fri 8–11:30am and noon–10:30pm; Sat 10am–4pm and 5–10:30pm; Sun 10am–4pm. Tube: Farringdon.

Moro ★★ NORTH AFRICAN/SPANISH   When it opened in 1997, Moro's Spanish and North African cooking helped put Exmouth Market on London's gastronomic map. Moro remains a local favorite and standards are as high as ever. The large, plain, wooden-floored room buzzes—though be warned, it can get very noisy when it fills in the evenings. The wood-burning oven and charcoal grill produce hearty dishes such as lamb chops with date and parsnip salad and pumpkin pilaf; or a roasted guinea fowl with sage-flavored yogurt. Such blends of sweet and savory characterize Moorish (and Moro's) cooking. Save room (portions are generous) for desserts such as yogurt cake with pistachios and pomegranate, and one of their many recommended sherries by the glass. Tapas served all day at the bar make a great option to a full meal; outside tables fill quickly in summer.

34–36 Exmouth Market, EC1. www.moro.co.uk. ✆ **020/7833-8336.** Reservations recommended. Main courses £15.50–£19.50; tapas £3.50–£14.50. AE, DC, MC, V. Mon–Sat 12:30–2:30pm and 7–10:30pm. Tapas served all day. Tube: Farringdon.

North Road ★★ CONTEMPORARY EUROPEAN/SCANDINAVIAN   Nordic cooking is notoriously under-represented in London, but this venture from Danish chef Christoffer Hruskovase should convince Londoners to look north. Suitably Scandinavian and minimal, the restaurant is both welcoming and smart. The Nordic influence comes not so much from the ingredients (which are British), as with the cooking approach, which uses less butter and cream and the *sous-vide* vacuum method (cooking in airtight plastic bags in a water bath) to keep the essentials of ingredients intact. Start with veal sweetbread with cabbage, followed by wild sea bass with celeriac and celery. Norfolk deer with beetroot comes rolled in hay (a Viking preservation technique), giving a smoky taste that's enhanced by smoked bone marrow. Desserts also surprise: Try the rhubarb with rye bread and milk ice cream. Vegetables and foraged herbs are used extensively. You'll find the clean, light tastes here refreshingly different.

60–73 St. John St., EC1. www.northroadrestaurant.co.uk. (②) **020/3217-0033.** Reservations recommended. Main courses £19.50–£24. Set lunch and pretheatre 2 courses £22, 3 courses £25; 5-course chef tasting menu £60, 7-course £67. AE, MC, V. Mon–Thurs noon–2:30pm and 6–10:30pm; Fri noon–2:30pm and 6–11pm; Sat 6–11pm. Tube: Barbican or Farringdon.

St. John ★★ MODERN BRITISH   "Nose to tail eating" characterizes Fergus Henderson's no-nonsense approach. All parts of the animal are used—neck, tongue, trotters, tail, liver, and heart—to produce dishes for which devotees travel miles: deep-fried sprats with tartare sauce; snails and oakleaf; or, for the truly dedicated, rolled pig's spleen and bacon. It's a genuine seasonally led menu—in winter chitterlings and radishes or braised rabbit, turnips, and aioli will keep out the cold. The ingredients are the best, the cooking is superb, and the dish is what it says on the menu. The restaurant is a plain, whitewashed room in a former smokery. Other pluses are a bar for a thoroughly British "elevenses" or a quick lunch, an excellent wine list, and baked goods to take home. There's a sister restaurant in Spitalfields, **St. John Bread & Wine ★**, 94–96 Commercial St., E1 (www.stjohnbreadandwine.com; (②) **020/7251-0848;** Tube: Liverpool St.).

26 St. John St., EC1. www.stjohnrestaurant.co.uk. (②) **020/7251-0848.** Reservations required. Main courses £12.40–£18.20. AE, DC, MC, V. Mon–Fri noon–3pm; Sun 1–3:30pm; Mon–Sat 6–11pm. Tube: Farringdon.

INEXPENSIVE

Vinoteca WINE BAR/INTERNATIONAL   Primarily a wine bar, Vinoteca showcases 300 bottles from around the world chosen for both quality and value for money. The kitchen offers similarly good value, with a menu that ranges from a selection of Spanish cured meats with almonds and olives to a tempting list of dishes such as deep fried squid and chili mayonnaise; crab salad with fennel, samphire, and aioli; or oven roast pork tenderloin with coleslaw, black beans, and corn salsa. Wine suggestions for each dish are spot on. You can only book at lunch; otherwise join the crowds after work and perch on a bar stool while waiting in front of the open kitchen for a table.

7 St. John St., EC1. www.vinoteca.co.uk. (②) **020/7253-8786.** Reservations recommended (lunch only). Main courses £5.50–£15.95. MC, V. Mon–Sat noon–11pm; Sun noon–5pm. Tube: Farringdon. Also at 15 Seymour Place, W1 ((②) **020/7724-7288**) and Beak St, W1 (②) **020/3544-7411.**

Tower Hill

MODERATE

Bevis Marks Restaurant ★ JEWISH   Bevis Marks has moved from its beautiful venue attached to London's 18th-century synagogue to a larger restaurant.

The menu is an interesting mix of traditional Ashkenazi dishes and those with Asian influences. On the starter menu, chicken soup with matzo balls sits happily beside mustard-cured salmon gravadlax with deconstructed tartare sauce. Main dishes continue down the same path: Poached haddock comes with steamed potatoes and vegetables cooked in a court bouillon, or go for the classic salt beef and chips with beet and horseradish relish. Desserts offer seasonal comforts such as rhubarb crumble and cinnamon ice cream. There's an interesting selection of Israeli bottles on a pricey wine list.

Bevis Marks, EC3. www.bevismarkstherestaurant.com. ℰ **020/7283-2220.** Main courses £18.50–£25.95. AE, MC, V. Mon–Thurs noon–3pm and 5:30–10pm; Fri noon–3pm. Tube: Aldgate or Liverpool St.

Café Spice Namaste ★★ INDIAN   Walk into this large restaurant divided into two dining rooms and you're instantly cheered up by its hot Indian colors and fanciful decor. Chef Cyrus Todiwala has always been a chef with a mission—he was the first to bring Parsee dishes to London, and to create his own spice mixes, chutneys, and pickles. Today he champions organic, seasonal, and locally produced ingredients. The original Parsee menu has broadened to encompass the whole of India, with dishes such as chargrilled Keralan Syrian duck tikka marinated in yogurt with tamarind, chili, and spices; a beef tikka of Buccleuch-farmed cattle; and a classic Goan curry of prawns served with rice and a dried shrimp and onion salad.

16 Prescot St., E1. www.cafespice.co.uk. ℰ **020/7488-9242.** Reservations recommended. Main courses £13.95–£19.50. AE, DC, MC, V. Mon–Fri noon–3pm and 6:15–10:30pm; Sat 6:30–10:30pm. Tube: Aldgate East or Tower Hill.

EAST LONDON
Docklands
MODERATE

The Narrow ★ 🍴 MODERN BRITISH/GASTROPUB   With a stunning riverside location, open fire in winter, terrace, and large conservatory, the Narrow couldn't fail to be popular. Add the undoubted talent of Gordon Ramsay's kitchen team and you have a winner. The bar menu is everything you'd expect from a traditional pub: fish and chips; sausages; Scotch egg served with that English staple, HP (brown) sauce. The restaurant menu majors in dishes of modernized classics such as beetroot cured salmon with horseradish for starters, and slow-cooked duck with braised red cabbage for mains. Interesting beers from breweries such as Adnams or Meantime in Greenwich, cheerful service, and good value for money—it's not surprising that the Narrow is packed with contented diners.

44 Narrow St., E14. www.gordonramsay.com. ℰ **020/7592-7950.** Reservations required for the restaurant. Main courses £9.50–£17.50; set lunch and pretheatre 2 courses £18, 3 courses £22; bar snacks £3.50–£13. AE, MC, V. Mon–Sat noon–11pm; Sun noon–10:30pm. DLR: Limehouse.

Shoreditch
EXPENSIVE

Les Trois Garçons ★ 🍴 FRENCH   Walk into Les Trois Garçons and you enter a fantasy, or possibly a nightmare, according to your taste. The interior of

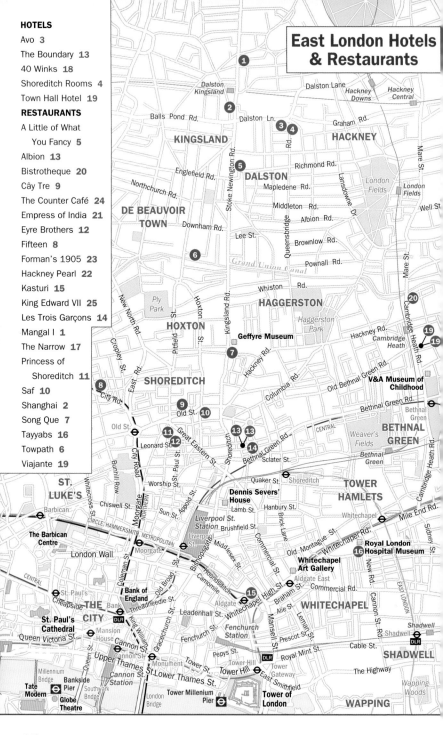

**East London Hotels
& Restaurants**

this former Victorian pub is full of glittering, lurid-colored and crystal chandeliers, old handbags hung from the ceiling, stuffed animals, and general bric-a-brac. The three "garçons," Hassan Abdullah, Michel Lassere, and Stefan Karlson opened the restaurant 10 years ago and have not looked back since. The menu is equally flamboyant, offering dishes that some find sublime and others just too over the top. Try their famous foie gras cured in Sauternes and cooked *au torchon* (in a tea towel), or perhaps fish and shellfish with couscous, chorizo, samphire, carrots and Pernod and lemon sauce. This expensive restaurant is the place to go if the culinary world seems drab and boring.

1 Club Row, E1. www.lestroisgarcons.com. © **020/7613-1924.** Reservations essential.Set menu 2 courses £40.50, 3 courses £47; tasting menu £63.50 (whole table only). AE, MC, V. Mon–Sat 6pm–midnight. Tube: Liverpool St./Train: Shoreditch High St.

MODERATE

Eyre Brothers ★ PORTUGUESE/SPANISH   On the borders between trendy Shoreditch and the more staid City, Eyre Brothers attracts diners from both camps. The restaurant is elegant with wooden walls and partitions, interesting art on the walls, and the comfortable feeling that comes from a staff that knows exactly what it's doing. The cooking is a mix of Iberian influences plus inspiration from the former Portuguese colony of Mozambique. Try superb Iberico hams; truffled globe artichoke with poached egg and three different beans; marinated pork casseroled with clams accompanied by fried potatoes; baked salt cod. The open fire is used for meats including rib steak, and the fish catch of the day. The tapas bar is great for a quick, cheaper meal. There's also a good list of wines, and of course many sherries.

70 Leonard St., EC2. www.eyrebrothers.co.uk. © **020/7613-5346.** Reservations required. Main courses £15–£27. Tapas £5–£7.50 AE, DC, MC, V. Mon–Fri noon–3pm and 6:30–10:45pm; Sat 7–10:45pm. Tube: Old St./Train: Shoreditch High St.

Fifteen ★★ ITALIAN   Jamie Oliver, bestselling cookbook author, TV personality, and international restaurateur of note, opened Fifteen in 2002 with the laudable aim of training disadvantaged young people as chefs. Today the redbrick Victorian building has been smartened up, but the kitchen is still a training ground. The downstairs restaurant serves a daily changing Italian menu, using impeccably sourced ingredients from Britain and Italy. Start with a simple mozzarella with tomatoes and basil, or perhaps a satisfying ravioli of veal ragu. Mains of Sicilian fisherman's stew, or lamb with fennel, olives, pine nuts, and gremolata show how well the kitchen can perform. The street-level **Trattoria** is more casual, with an a la carte menu. Weekend brunch here is a pleasant, relaxed meal to linger over.

15 Westland Place, N1. www.fifteen.net. © **0871/330-1515.** Reservations required. Restaurant: main courses £11.50–£29; breakfast £2–£11; set lunch Mon–Fri 2 courses £26, 3 courses £30, 4 courses £35. Trattoria: main courses £9–£18.50. AE, MC, V. Mon–Sat 7:30–10:45am and noon–3pm; Sun 8am–11am, noon–3pm and 6–10pm. Tube: Old St.

INEXPENSIVE

Albion TRADITIONAL BRITISH/CAFE   Sir Terence Conran's Boundary Project is all-embracing: Within the trendy **Boundary** hotel (p. 371) there's a smart basement restaurant, summer rooftop terrace bar, and the Albion shop, bakery, and cafe. Don't be fooled by the retro decor with its wood and leather banquettes, industrial lights, and white tiles. Despite its description as a "caff," this is a posh joint where the punters wear trendy trainers rather than cloth caps. Being Sir Terence, it's all extremely well done. You can eat all day on good old British classics—omelet, potted shrimps, deviled kidneys, or rump steak. Free Wi-Fi is the icing on the sticky toffee pudding.

2–4 Boundary St., E2. www.albioncaff.co.uk. © **020/7729-1051.** No reservations. Main courses £4.75–£12.50. AE, MC, V. Daily 8am–11:30pm. Tube: Liverpool St./Train: Shoreditch High St.

Cây Tre VIETNAMESE   Vietnamese restaurants are flourishing in East London, and Cây Tre in Shoreditch follows a stylish path so beloved in this trendy area. Its formula is simple and winning: top Vietnamese cooking at value-for-money prices. The long menu takes in spring rolls done various ways; Indochinese beef filet slices prepared like ceviche in lemon juice; spectacular fish such as lobster baked in salt and chili; as well as favorites including duck with Asian greens and plum sauce. Each dish is packed with flavor; not surprisingly, Cây Tre is a favorite spot with many top London chefs. Sister restaurant, **Viet Grill,** 58 Kingsland Rd., E2 (© **020/7739-6686;** Train: Hoxton), is close by.

301 Old St., EC1. www.vietnamesekitchen.co.uk. © **020/7729-8662.** Main courses £5.50–£22; set dinner £22.50 (min. 2 people). MC, V. Daily noon–3pm Mon–Thurs 5:30–11pm; Fri–Sat 5:30–11:30pm. Tube: Old St. Also at 42–43 Dean St., W1. (© **020/7317-9118**).

Princess of Shoreditch ★ MODERN BRITISH/GASTROPUB   This handsome old pub close to Old Street has been beautifully transformed. The downstairs bar fills up with City types at lunchtime downing pints of Wandle ale from Battersea brewery, Sambrooks, and tucking into soup of the day (£5.50); fish and chips (£11.95); and pies (£10.50). Up the spiral staircase, the dining room is a more serious affair with an extended menu, and attracts more serious diners. Propose the deal over prawn and lobster cocktail, discuss it while eating lamb rump with celeriac purée and crispy potatoes, and clinch it over rhubarb crumble. Popular with families and groups of friends at weekends.

76 Paul St., EC2. www.theprincessofshoreditch.com. © **020/7729-9270.** Main courses £11.50–£20. AE, MC, V. Mon–Thurs noon–3pm and 6:30–10pm; Fri noon–3pm and 6–10:30pm; Sat–Sun 10am–4:30pm and 6–10:30pm. Tube: Old St.

Saf VEGAN   Forget staid food and worthy-looking customers, Saf is a smart designer restaurant with a particularly good line in botanical cocktails incorporating herbs and edible flowers, named "Tipping the Velvet," "A Decadent Dram," and the like. The kitchen takes the food seriously, cooking below 48°C (118°F) to keep nutrition and flavors intense and dishes exciting. Dinner could be chili and garlic-marinated butternut squash filled with herb cheese served with fennel salad and balsamic fig compote followed by Thai red curry with tofu in a spiced coconut curry soup served with black rice. Staff are friendly; service is slick; the place jumps. For an all-day Saf, visit Whole Foods Market in Kensington.

152–154 Curtain Rd., EC2. www.safrestaurant.com. © **020/7613-0007.** Main courses £8.10–£15.50. AE, MC, V. Mon–Sat 6–11pm. Tube: Old St. Also at the Barkers Building, Whole Foods Market, W8. (© **020/7368-4555**).

Song Que VIETNAMESE   Kingsland Road remains the headquarters of London's Vietnamese restaurants, so there is plenty of competition in the area. Song

THE best PIE & MASH

A plateful of meat in a pastry pie, mash and gravy, or parsley sauce, was once a traditional working-class staple. It never hit the culinary heights, but remains one of those much-loved, much-vaunted traditions that everybody talks about but few have experienced. There are a few traditional pie and mash shops left and as it's become quite trendy, some new places have opened. Many of the old-fashioned ones serve jellied eels, perhaps an acquired taste. But for a slice of old London customs, try one of the following:

Clarks ★   With its old-fashioned windows and PIE AND MASH sign, Clarks looks a little incongruous in this rapidly gentrifying area, but is the real McCoy and seems to attract as many trendsetters as it does old hands. Its pies and mash have good amounts of meat in them, come with loads of gravy and a friendly smile. 46 Exmouth Market, EC1. ✆ **020/7837-1974.** No credit cards. Mon–Thurs 10:30am–4pm, Fri–Sat 10:30am–5pm. Tube/Rail: Farringdon.

F. Cooke   F.Cooke sticks to tradition in a delightful setting with wooden tables and chairs. Broadway Market is gentrifying fast, like a lot of the formerly working-class East End, so it's good to see this stalwart holding its own among the boutiques, craft shops and restaurants springing up here. 9 Broadway Market, E8. ✆ **020/7254-6458.** Pies from £2.50–£3.75. No credit cards. Mon–Thurs 10am–6pm, Fri–Sat 10am–7pm. Tube/Rail: Liverpool St.

M. Manze ★   This claims to be the oldest continuously running pie shop. It was established in 1902 and serves pies, mash, and eels (the latter both jellied and stewed) from recipes used by the founding grandfather. Those addicted to the wholesome, old-fashioned fare, can order online and get their pies delivered, but it's not the same. 87 Tower Bridge

Rd., SE1. www.manze.co.uk; ✆ **020/7407-2985.** Pie and mash from £2.85–£5.20. MC, V. Mon 11am–2pm, Tues–Thurs 10:30am–2pm, Fri–Sat 10am–1:30pm. Tube: Tower Hill; DLR: Tower Gateway.

Pieminister   A small chain from Bristol supplies market stalls, shops, delis and pubs throughout the U.K.. Its London outpost at Gabriel's Wharf has outside tables for summer riverside dining. Pies come in all guises, including sweet pies and seasonal pies for Christmas or special events. Prices are equally sweet at around £4.25. 56 Upper Ground, SE1. www.pieminister.co.uk. ✆ **020/7928-5755.** Daily 10am–5pm. Tube/Rail: Waterloo.

Square Pie ★   Smart and sassy, Square Pie sells excellent pies in just the right locations, in Spitalfields Market, Canary Wharf, and Westfield Shopping Centre. Prices are a bit higher than most of its competitors (pie, double mash, side dish, and gravy weighs in at £7.49) but as they are so good at feeding hungry city workers, commuters, and shoppers, they're rightly popular. Spitalfields Market, 105c Commercial St., E1. www.squarepie.co.uk. ✆ **020/7375-0327.** Pies £3.79–£7.49. MC, V. Mon–Fri 10:30am–4:30pm. Sat–Sun 10:30am–5:30pm. Tube/Rail: Liverpool St.

Que holds its own—although not for its decor, which is more garish cafe than chic London venue. The vast menu includes reliable *pho* noodle soups with the well-flavored, aromatic broth full of meat and herbs. Barbecued quail is another favorite for its deeply satisfying, well-cooked meat. At night the lineups are long; the best time to go is at lunch.

134 Kingsland Rd., E2. www.songque.co.uk. ℂ **020/7613-3222.** Main courses £6.70–£14.80. MC, V. Mon–Fri noon–3pm and 5:30–11:30pm; Sat 5:30–11:30pm; Sun noon–11pm. Train: Hoxton.

Whitechapel

INEXPENSIVE

Kasturi INDIAN   Kasturi is a favorite with curry fans and those after healthy Indian food. Its Pakhtoon cooking comes from the northwest frontier of India, where rich ghee and butter is replaced with natural meat and vegetable juices. But don't worry; this doesn't mean tastes are watered down. Gutsy flavors permeate dishes such as spicy lamb cakes with coriander, mint, and ginger; crab Masala; and specialties including Jeera chicken—marinated chicken sautéed in ginger, garlic, and cumin. The decor is as bright and fresh as the cooking.

57 Aldgate High St., EC3. www.kasturi-restaurant.co.uk. ℂ **020/7480-7402.** Reservations recommended. Main dishes £9.10–£11.95; set menus £17.95–£19.95. AE, MC, V. Mon–Sat noon–3pm and 6–11pm. Tube: Aldgate.

Tayyabs ★ INDIAN   This Pakistani/Punjabi-inspired restaurant goes from strength to strength. In a former Victorian pub, it's on two levels and near enough to the City for savvy bankers to make it their local lunch spot. Tayyabs's gutsy food at low prices provides a welcome change from the more tourist-orientated Brick Lane Indian restaurants. Punjabi meat curries, flavorful kebabs, and their now well-known marinated lamb chops are the staples; or go for the daily specials. It's unlicensed with no corkage, so take your own bottle.

83 Fieldgate St., E1. www.tayyabs.co.uk. ℂ **020/7247-9543.** Main courses £6.50–£28. AE, MC, V. Daily noon–midnight. Tube: Aldgate East or Whitechapel.

Bethnal Green

VERY EXPENSIVE

Viajante ★★ CONTEMPORARY EUROPEAN   When he was performing culinary miracles at various East London venues, Portuguese-born Nuno Mendes was the darling of diners desperately seeking the next big thing. Now he's resurfaced inside the **Town Hall Hotel** (p. 372). In a restaurant with a kitchen so open it feels like you're in somebody's living room, this El Bulli-trained chef serves dishes that will either knock your socks off or leave you scratching your head. From the first *amuse bouche* that is sublime—through dishes that pair braised octopus with potatoes, chorizo, and eggs; slow-cooked pig neck with savoy cabbage, fried capers, and grated egg—the surprises keep coming. This is supremely skillful, playful, flawlessly executed cooking. Now that El Bulli has closed, this is your best bet for an adventure. The Corner Room is a cheaper options and has a no bookings policy.

Inside Town Hall Hotel, Patriot Sq., E2. www.viajante.co.uk. ℂ **020/7871-0461.** Reservations required. Lunch menus 3 courses £28, 6 courses £65, 9 courses £80; Dinner 6 courses £65, 9 courses £80, 12 courses £90. AE, MC, V. Mon–Thurs noon–2pm and 6–9:30pm; Fri–Sun 6–9:30pm. Tube: Bethnal Green.

MODERATE

Bistrotheque ★ FRENCH   Bistrotheque is now a fixture on the capital's fashionable dining scene, attracting diners from way out west and beyond. And with good reason. The sparse, white industrial upstairs space is striking with bold flower arrangements and generous-sized windows. Staff work hard to keep diners satisfied with dishes that take a straightforward route. Starters might include smoked mackerel with cucumber and dill, or soup of the day; mains run from half a garlic roast chicken to roast bream with fennel and black olives. It's difficult to choose between puddings such as white chocolate cheesecake with griottines in kirsch and the excellent cheese selection. Cocktails are a feature in the bar. Weekend brunch with a live pianist is a real draw.

23–27 Wadeson St., E2. www.bistrotheque.com. ✆ **020/8983-7900.** Main courses £13.50–£19.50; 3-course set menu £21. AE, MC, V. Bar Tues–Sat 6pm–midnight; Sun 6–11pm. Restaurant Mon–Thurs 6:30–10:30pm; Fri 6:30–11pm; Sat 11am–4pm and 6:30–11pm; Sun 11am–4pm and 6:30–10:30pm. Tube: Bethnal Green.

Hackney

MODERATE

Empress of India ★ MODERN BRITISH/GASTROPUB   This brasserie draws foodies like a magnet to the now chic area of Victoria Park "village." The "Empress" as it's known, is smart with wooden paneling, chandeliers of mussel shells, and a mural of 18th-century Mogul India. A long zinc bar caters for drinks and snacks. The kitchen is strong on seasonal ingredients and all the fish is bought daily at Billingsgate Market. Take your pick from the changing specials chalked up on a blackboard and start your meal with root vegetable soup with cardamom oil, oysters, or a satisfying terrine, before moving on to a winter-warming beef cheek and turnip, or steak and chips. The well-priced menu includes desserts at £5 each, perhaps blueberry and almond tart with thick clotted cream. There's a good tea list, a children's menu, and a Sunday roast lunch with all the trimmings.

130 Lauriston Rd., E9. www.theempressofindia.com. ✆ **020/8533-5123.** Reservations recommended. Main courses £11–£29. AE, MC, V. Mon–Sat, noon–3:30pm, 6–10:15pm; Sat–Sun 10am–10:15pm (9:30pm on Sunday). Overground: Homerton.

Hackney Wick/Stratford

MODERATE

Forman's 1905 🍴 TRADITIONAL BRITISH/FISH   You may not have heard of Forman's, but you've probably tasted their smoked salmon somewhere in London—perhaps at Gordon Ramsay or the Dorchester. Forman's is an established East End smokery (opened in 1905) run by generations of the same family. The present owner, Lance Forman, is a formidable character who, when forced to move from his smokery due to the Olympic Park construction, struck a very good deal and built a new smokery right opposite the Stadium. Also in the large building is a gallery and event space. Start with their London cured smoked salmon, and follow with sea bass with truffle mash and vanilla froth.

Stour Rd., E3. www.formans.co.uk/restaurant. ✆ **020/8525-2365.** Main courses £11.50–£19.50. MC, V. Restaurant Thurs–Fri 7–11pm; Sat 10am–2pm and 7–11pm; Sun noon–5pm. Gallery and Bar Thurs–Fri 5–9pm; Sat–Sun noon–5pm. Overground: Hackney Wick.

5

East London

EATING OUT IN LONDON

INEXPENSIVE

The Counter Café ★ 🍴 TRADITIONAL BRITISH/TAPAS   The two-storied Stour Space is home to various artists' studios and the Counter Café. Offering great views over the Regent's Canal to the Olympic Stadium, it has a shabby chic industrial decor, long tables and chairs as well as a sofa, fun atmosphere, and good food. Not surprisingly, it's extremely popular. Start the day with a great breakfast or brunch, or go for a pie at lunch. On Thursday to Sunday evenings, it becomes a bar serving tapas.

4a Roach Rd., E3. www.thecountercafe.co.uk. ✆ **07834/275-920.** Main courses £3.50–£8. AE, MC, V. Mon–Wed 7:30am–5pm; Thurs–Fri 7am–11pm; Sat 9am–11pm; Sun 9am–5pm. Overground: Hackney Wick.

Hackney Pearl ★ 🍴 TRADITIONAL BRITISH   The Hackney Pearl is a well-loved, locally popular cafe-restaurant created out of two former shops. It's friendly and casual, the decor a mix of recovered items—Formica tables, odd wooden dressers, and chalkboard menus—producing just the right creative vibe for a neighborhood inhabited by many artists. The daytime cafe menu takes in soups, salads, Panini, or steak and chips. On Monday and Tuesday evenings, a glass of wine and a main course costs £11; Sundays see the Pearl lay on traditional roasts such as Suffolk lamb or pork belly. The beer comes from the Meantime Brewery in Greenwich; wines have a fixed markup with good varieties around the £20 mark. All in all, the "Pearl" is worth the (substantial) detour from the beaten track.

11 Prince Edward Rd., E9. www.thehackneypearl.com. ✆ **020/8510-3605**. Main courses £5.50–£13.50. MC, V. Daily 10am–11pm. Overground: Hackney Wick.

King Edward VII 🍴 TRADITIONAL BRITISH/PUB   Originally the King of Prussia that renamed itself in 1914 due to politics, this 19th-century listed building is everything an old pub should be. It's large, wood-paneled and has Chesterfield sofas, wooden tables and chairs, and open fires. The food is good: oysters, crab mayonnaise on toast, or grilled Old Spot ham to start; sausage and mash with onion gravy, beer battered fish and chips, venison burger, or the most expensive on the menu, Barnsley lamb chop with braised fennel and fondant potato. Prices are honest; there's a good beer menu for Real Ale fans and you're entertained with music on Thursday's open mic night and a Sunday quiz.

47 Stratford Broadway, E15. www.kingeddie.co.uk. ✆ **020/8534-2313.** Main courses £8–£13. MC, V. Mon–Wed noon–11pm; Thurs–Sat noon–midnight; Sun noon–11:30pm. Tube: Stratford; Overground: Hackney Wick.

Dalston

INEXPENSIVE

A Little of What You Fancy 🍴 MODERN BRITISH   This pretty, quirky cafe with its odd bits of attractive furniture opened in September 2010 on rapidly gentrifying Kingsland Road. The area is known for its Turkish and Vietnamese restaurants, but British cooking was remarkable by its absence until "ALOWYF" landed here. Open all day, its brand of fresh, local food produces Scottish oatmeal porridge with lavender and honey for breakfast, roast chicken or open sandwiches for lunch, and more complex dishes such as slow-braised oxtail with wine, herbs, and garlic for dinner. Don't overlook the fabulous cakes, which you can eat here or take out.

464 Kingsland Rd., E8. www.alittleofwhatyoufancy.info. ℰ **020/7275-0060.** Main courses £6.50–£17.50. MC, V. Tues–Wed 9am–11pm; Thurs–Fri, 9am–midnight; Sat 10am–midnight; Sun noon–6pm. Overground: Dalston Junction or Dalston Kingsland.

Mangal I ★ ✦ TURKISH You can tell you're in prime territory for *ocakbasi* (open-coal barbecue cooking) in Stoke Newington Road from the aroma of cooking meat that wafts through the air. Follow your nose just off the main road and you come to Mangal I. The kelim-hung room might not be the greatest in looks, but it cooks and serves a succulent mound of meat and vegetables. Feast on the mixed meze while you're waiting for the herbed lamb *sis* or spicy minced kebabs to appear. You should book and expect delays in service at busy times.

10 Arcola St., E8. www.mangal1.com. ℰ **020/7275-8981.** Main courses £9–£15. No credit cards. Daily noon–midnight. Overground: Dalston Kingsland. Also at 4 Stoke Newington Rd., N16.

Shanghai 🍴 CHINESE/CANTONESE A Chinese restaurant in a former Art Deco pie and mash shop—Shanghai sums up London's eclectic, even eccentric, restaurant scene. The interior remains as before; it's a long room with wooden booths, tiled walls, and a marble-topped bar. But replacing the standard East End fare of the past is a regional Chinese menu that takes in a long all-day dim sum menu; rice pots with mushrooms; Cantonese chicken and sausage; *congees* (Chinese rice pudding); slow-cooked duck with orange peel, herbs, and oyster sauce; and crispy eel fillet lightly battered. The food is good as is the buzz and the decor. Oh, and if you're a group of exhibitionists, the incongruous, wildly popular karaoke room beckons.

41 Kingsland Rd., E8. www.shanghaidalston.co.uk. ℰ **020/7254-2878.** Dim sum £1.20–£7.20. Main courses £7.20–£35. Set lunch Mon–Fri £7.50; set dinners £16–£19.80. MC, V. Daily noon–11pm. Overground: Dalston Kingsland.

Towpath 🍴 ITALIAN/INTERNATIONAL You won't find this little cafe easily; it's on the towpath of the Regent's Canal, and so was first "discovered" by joggers, cyclists, and people from the narrowboats. Set up by food writer Lori De Mor and her photographer husband Jason Lowe, it serves great dishes from local ingredients (paella, tortillas, roast lamb), coffee from Florence, and delicious desserts. There's one table indoors; otherwise it's a summer venue with mismatched outdoor seating and places on a pontoon. It's deliberately low-key, but has become quite the place to people watch.

Regent's Canal towpath between Whitmore Bridge and Kingsland Road Bridge, N1. No phone. Main courses £3–£8. No credit cards. Tues–Fri 8am–dusk; Sat 9am–dusk; Sun 10am–dusk. Overground: Haggerston.

NORTH & NORTHWEST LONDON

Camden Town

EXPENSIVE

York & Albany ★ CONTEMPORARY EUROPEAN Camden Town is not known as a gastronomic destination, so the locals were very excited when Gordon Ramsay reopened this derelict pub as a fine dining restaurant with rooms. It's a relaxed place that offers the best dining in the area. Top seasonal ingredients drive the menu, as in tagliatelle with crab, or organic salmon ceviche with avocado, chili, and lime. Equally imaginative are mains such as chargrilled poussin with burnt lemon chimichurri sauce. Steamed treacle sponge and custard for two brings out the greedy; the tiramisu is perfect. The only downsides are the sometimes-slapdash service and the noise level when the place is full. The early set supper menu, however, is a bargain. It's a wonderful breakfast place and a small courtyard makes summer dining a treat. Eating wood-fired pizzas at the bar is a favorite Camden Town pastime.

127–129 Parkway, NW1. www.gordonramsay.com/yorkandalbany. (✆ **020/7388-3344.** Reservations recommended. Main courses £9.50–£26. Set menus and early supper 2 courses £18, 3 courses £21. AE, MC, V. Mon–Fri 7–10:30am, noon–3pm, and 6–11pm; Sat 7–11:30am, 12:15–3pm, and 6–11pm; Sun noon–8:30pm. Tube: Camden Town.

Hampstead
MODERATE

Wells ★ CONTEMPORARY EUROPEAN/GASTROPUB   Close enough to Hampstead Heath (p. 164) to attract walkers with their dogs and families, this place is also the local for many of Hampstead's decidedly upmarket residents. The old Georgian building is made up of a bar plus three rooms in the restaurant serving the same menus. The decor is chic enough for any smart gastropub; add to that the feel of a country retreat and it's not surprising that this is a winner. Dishes such as ham hock terrine with gribiche sauce; and smoked haddock with poached quail egg and champ potato sit happily beside rib-eye steak and chips; and sea bass with beans, sautéed potatoes, and chorizo with a chili sauce. Sunday lunch is a family occasion, and beers come on tap for the devoted.

30 Well Walk, NW3. www.thewellshampstead.co.uk. (✆ **020/7794-3785.** Reservations recommended. Main courses £10.95–£24. MC, V. Mon–Fri noon–3pm and 6–10pm; Sat noon–4pm and 7–10pm; Sun noon–4pm and 7–9:30pm. Bar open daily noon–11pm. Tube: Hampstead.

Islington
INEXPENSIVE

Ottolenghi ★★ INTERNATIONAL   The cool, sleek, white interior of this traiteur-cum-cafe has become the meeting place for the chattering classes of Islington. There are currently four Ottolenghi outlets in London, and a new more expensive restaurant, **Nopi** (21–22 Warwick Street, W1; (✆ **020/7494-9584**). But the Islington branch is the flagship, with seating at long tables and a kitchen that produces some of the best Mediterranean-influenced food in town. It's open all day for healthy and hearty lunches of superb salads; snacks from the mounds of meringues, tarts, and cakes; and dinners such as sea bass with baba ganoush, pomegranate, and shallots. Devotees buy the owner Yotam Ottolenghi's cookbooks (he's also a food columnist on the *Guardian* newspaper). If you visit just one cafe in London, make it this one.

287 Upper St., N1. www.ottolenghi.co.uk. (✆ **020/7288-1454.** Reservations recommended at dinner. Main courses £8–£12. AE, MC, V. Mon–Sat 8am–11pm; Sun 9am–7pm. Tube: Angel or Highbury & Islington. Other locations throughout London.

Pasha TURKISH   Once a kebab shop, now a restaurant with chandeliers, leather seats, and tables laid with candles, Pasha is a favorite with locals who know their *borek* from their *dolma*. It's a step up from the usual London Turkish

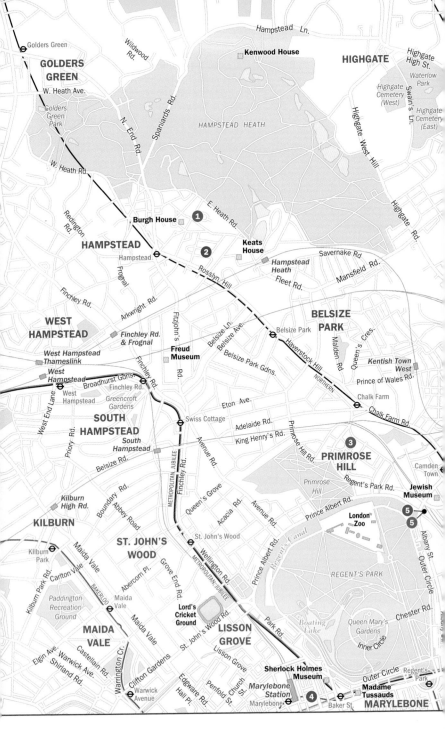

GOLDERS GREEN

HIGHGATE

Golders Green

Wildwood Rd.

Kenwood House

Highgate High St.

W. Heath Ave.

Highgate Cemetery (West)

Waterlow Park

Golders Green Park

N. End Rd.

Spaniards Rd.

HAMPSTEAD HEATH

Highgate Cemetery (East)

Swain's Ln.

W. Heath Rd.

Highgate West Hill

Highgate Rd.

Redington Rd.

Burgh House **1**

E. Heath Rd.

HAMPSTEAD

Keats House **2**

Savernake Rd.

Hampstead

Frognal

Rosslyn Hill

Hampstead Heath

Fleet Rd.

Mansfield Rd.

Finchley Rd.

Arkwright Rd.

Fitzjohn's Ave.

Belsize Ln.

BELSIZE PARK

WEST HAMPSTEAD

Finchley Rd. & Frognal

Freud Museum

Belsize Ave.

Belsize Park

Queen's Cres.

Kentish Town West

West Hampstead Thameslink

Finchley Rd.

Belsize Park Gdns.

Haverstock Hill

Malden Rd.

Prince of Wales Rd.

West Hampstead

Broadhurst Gdns.

NORTHERN

West Hampstead

Finchley Rd.

Greencroft Gardens

Eton Ave.

Chalk Farm

West End Lane

SOUTH HAMPSTEAD

Swiss Cottage

Adelaide Rd.

Chalk Farm Rd.

Priory Rd.

South Hampstead

King Henry's Rd.

Avenue Rd.

Primrose Hill Rd.

PRIMROSE HILL **3**

Camden Town

Belsize Rd.

Boundary Rd.

Abbey Road

METROPOLITAN JUBILEE

Finchley Rd.

Queen's Grove

Primrose Hill

Regent's Park Rd.

Jewish Museum

Kilburn High Rd.

Acacia Rd.

Avenue Rd.

Prince Albert Rd.

5

KILBURN

Kilburn Park

St. John's Wood

London Zoo

5

Maida Vale

Carlton Vale

ST. JOHN'S WOOD

Grove End Rd.

St. John's Wood

Albany St.

Outer Circle

Kilburn Park Rd.

Abercorn Pl.

Wellington Rd.

Prince Albert Rd.

Regent's Canal

REGENT'S PARK

BAKERLOO

Maida Vale

METROPOLITAN JUBILEE

Chester Rd.

Paddington Recreation Ground

Maida Vale

Lord's Cricket Ground

St. John's Wood Rd.

Park Rd.

Boating Lake

Queen Mary's Gardens

MAIDA VALE

Castellain Rd.

LISSON GROVE

Lisson Grove

Inner Circle

Elgin Ave.

Warwick Ave.

Shirland Rd.

Clifton Gardens

Edgware Rd.

Penfold St.

Church St.

Sherlock Holmes Museum

Outer Circle

Regent's Park

Warrington Cr.

Warwick Avenue

Hall Pl.

Marylebone Station

4

Madame Tussauds

MARYLEBONE

Marylebone

Baker St.

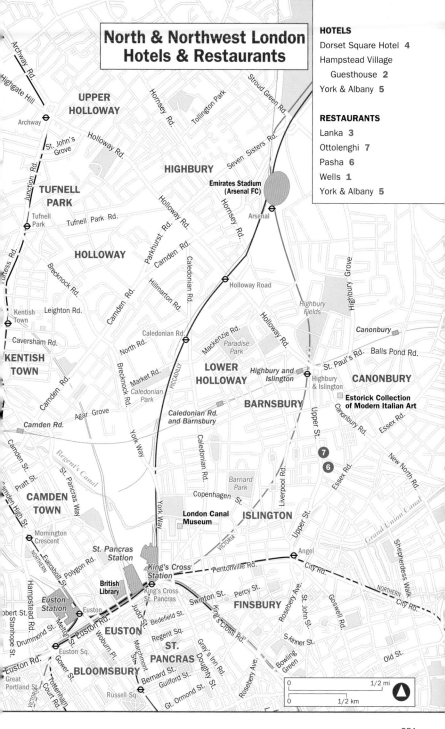

North & Northwest London Hotels & Restaurants

HOTELS
Dorset Square Hotel **4**
Hampstead Village
Guesthouse **2**
York & Albany **5**

RESTAURANTS
Lanka **3**
Ottolenghi **7**
Pasha **6**
Wells **1**
York & Albany **5**

restaurant, open from breakfast to dinner. The slow-cooked shoulder of lamb in a rich mix of tomatoes, onions, and oregano is tender to a fault; while dishes that veer away from Turkey, like baked sea bass with spinach, crushed new potatoes, and lemon olive oil, show that the kitchen can compete with many a French restaurant. Good ingredients, skilled cooking, a relaxed, friendly ambience, and good value prices.

301 Upper St., N1. www.pasharestaurant.co.uk. ℂ **020/7226-1454.** Main courses £9.50–£17.95; set meze lunch £9.95; dinner £12.95. AE, MC, V. Mon–Sat noon–11:30pm; Sun noon–11pm. Tube: Angel or Highbury & Islington.

SOUTHEAST LONDON

Greenwich

MODERATE

Inside CONTEMPORARY EUROPEAN   Tucked away from the main tourist area, this is a proper neighborhood restaurant with a loyal local following. The decor is plain and simple but the atmosphere buzzes with contentment. Culinary inspiration is wide, ranging from Asian tastes as in tagliatelle with tiger prawns, chili, parsley, and garlic, to classic French in foie gras terrine with red onion chutney. It's excellent cooking using top ingredients in favorite dishes like confit pork belly with braised red cabbage, Puy lentils, and cumin roast parsnips in a thyme jus. Apple and quince tart with Cornish clotted cream perfectly demonstrates why Brits are so proud of their traditions. Set menus are a steal and an added bonus is a well-priced wine list.

19 Greenwich South St., SE10. www.insiderestaurant.co.uk. ℂ **020/8265/5060.** Main courses £12.50–£17.95. AE, MC, V. Set-price menus midweek-lunch 2 courses £12.95, 3 courses £17.95; weekend-lunch 2 courses £18.95, 3 courses £23.95; dinner 2 courses £19.95, 3 courses £24.95. Tues–Fri noon-2:30pm and 6:30–11pm; Sat 11am–2:30pm and 6:30pm–11pm; Sun noon–3pm. DLR/Rail: Greenwich.

Old Brewery MODERN BRITISH   The handsome Old Brewery, owned and run by the Meantime Brewery and supplying some of London's restaurants and pubs with its particular amber nectar, is a cafe by day and a restaurant by night. Huge shiny vats full of brewing beer (this is a working brewery) adorn one end; large windows and wooden tables and chairs fill the main space. There's also a small bar and outdoor seats in a walled courtyard. It has a solid, dependable menu with dishes such as deviled whitebait with caper mayonnaise, and fish and chips, or steak, all with recommended beers to try. It's a great place for true beer buffs, who can also book the brewery tour.

Pepys Building, Old Royal Naval College, SE10. www.oldbrewerygreenwich.com. ℂ **020/3327-1280.** courses £11.50–£18.50. MC, V. Cafe: Daily 10am–5pm. Bar: Mon–Sat 11am–11pm; Sun noon–10:30pm. Restaurant: Mon–Sat 6–11pm; Sun 6–10:30pm. DLR: Cutty Sark.

Rivington Grill MODERN BRITISH   The restaurant, next door to Greenwich Picturehouse, is smart with a mirror-lined mezzanine and a fashionably brown decor, though it lacks the glamour you might expect from a venue owned by the proprietor of The Ivy (see p. 203). But the food works. It's a modish mix of classic native dishes: roast pumpkin soup, Cornish crab, oysters, comforting smoked salmon, or eggs Benedict on toast to start; followed perhaps by steak and kidney pudding, fish and chips with mushy peas, or grilled meats. Desserts include that British favorite spotted dick with custard as well as mulled pear with brandy cream. Thoroughly comforting and thoroughly British, it does a mean line in sausages (and has a special Monday night sausage menu), and is a great place for breakfast. Good wine and beer list and an outside terrace make up for any shortcomings in the atmosphere.

178 Greenwich High Rd., SE10. www.rivingtongrill.co.uk. ✆ **020/8293 9270.** Main courses £11.50–£28.50. Set-menu Sun lunch 3 courses £19.75. AE, MC, V. Mon–Wed 5pm–11pm; Thurs–Sat 10am–11pm; Sun 10am–10pm. DLR/Rail: Greenwich. Also at 28–30 Rivington St, EC2. ✆ **020/7729 7053.**

OUTLYING AREAS
Richmond
EXPENSIVE
Petersham Nurseries Café ★★ CONTEMPORARY EUROPEAN   Go southwest to Richmond, and you'll come across Petersham Nurseries—and in a greenhouse full of odd furniture, artifacts, and sweet-smelling plants, you'll find

---

 ## THE best PARK EATERIES

Wandering through London's parks on a warm summer day is one of the capital's great pleasures. Some have the added attraction of a good meal.

Pavilion Tea House   Near the Royal Observatory, the Pavilion offers some of the best views in London along with soups, salads, and sandwiches as well as dishes like shepherd's pie and fish cakes. Greenwich Park, Blackheath Gate, SE10. www.companyofcooks.com. ✆ **020/8858-9695.** Main courses £4.95–£6.60. MC, V. Mon–Fri 9am–5:30pm, Sat–Sun 9am–6pm. Rail/DLR: Greenwich.

Drawing Room Eatery ★★   In the grounds of Fulham Palace is the Bishop of London's former home right by the river, where you can eat your soup, pastas, bagels, and sandwiches on the terrace or in the elegant interior. Bishop's Ave., SW6. www.fulhampalace.org. ✆ **020/7610-7160.** Main courses £3.95–£10.90. MC, V. Summer 8am–6pm, winter 10am–4pm. Tube: Putney Bridge.

Garden Café   You can sit smelling the scent of Regent's Park's roses over breakfast or dishes from smoked salmon to rib-eye steak. Inner Circle, NW1. www.companyofcooks.com. ✆ **020/7935-5729.** Main courses £7.50–£13.50. MC, V. Oct–April 9am–4pm, May–Sep 9am–9pm. Tube: Baker St. or Regent's Park.

Lido Café   Right in central London, Hyde Park's wonderful Serpentine lake has the advantage of the Lido Café. It's best outside on a warm day for breakfast, lunch, and all day dishes such as fish and chips, little pizzas, and slow cooked chicken. South side of the Serpentine, Hyde Park, W2. www.companyofcooks.com. ✆ **020/7706-7098.** Main courses £5.65–£12.80. MC, V. Daily 8am–dusk. Tube: Hyde Park Corner or Knightsbridge.

the new Australian chef, Greg Malouf who's stepped into the very large shoes of Skye Gyngell. Malouf, known for his modern middle eastern cooking, is changing the menu. Currently the cafe's daily lunch might include crab cakes with rocket and spicy Thai *nam jim* dressing; wild sea bass with poached artichokes and spinach in caper and mint dressing; or rich classic fillet of beef with roasted beetroots, sweet potatoes, and salsa verde. For a less expensive treat try the **Teahouse** and its homemade sandwiches, soups, cakes, and flapjacks, washed down with whole leaf Chinese teas and English nectars.

Church Lane, Richmond. www.petershamnurseries.com. ℂ **020/8605-3527.** Reservations required (as far in advance as possible). Main courses £15.50–£33. Set lunch 2/3 courses £24.50/£28.50. AE, DC, MC, V (no credit cards in the Teahouse). Cafe Tues–Sun noon–3pm; Teahouse Mon–Sat 9am–5pm; Sun 11am–5pm. Closed Jan. Tube: Richmond.

FAMILY-FRIENDLY RESTAURANTS

London's restaurants are becoming ever more family friendly, and many these days pull up highchairs as soon as you arrive. However, if you're eating out with children, take with you any entertainment you may need (coloring books or games). Many establishments provide children's menus; otherwise try asking for a simple pasta or chicken dish—and if you have two or more kids, most places will allow them to share adult-size main dishes. If you're going in the evening, go early when restaurants are less rushed and the noise level is reasonable.

Below are some restaurants that cater very well for children. Others we recommend for family eating include **Blue Elephant** (p. 230), **Locanda Locatelli** (p. 216), **The Orange** (p. 231), and **Le Café Anglais** (p. 220). London's art gallery eateries are also well set up for families (p. 207), and children usually enjoy a trip to a London "chippy" for authentic fish and chips (p. 215).

West End

COVENT GARDEN

Belgo Centraal ☺ BELGIAN   Go for the atmosphere in this cavernous basement where mussels *marinières* with fries—plus 100 Belgian beers including 11 Trappist varieties for the grown-ups served by waiters dressed as monks—are the main attractions. Take a freight elevator past the busy open kitchen and into the converted cellar. If you don't fancy any of the nine kinds of mussels (steamed, in a half-shell, or in huge bowls), go for a spiced spit-roast chicken basted in Belgian beer, wild boar sausages with *stoemp*—Belgian mashed spuds and cabbage—or a typical Belgian *waterzooï* stew. On their "Beat the Clock" offer, Monday to Friday 5 to 6:30pm, you pay the price of the time you order (ask for the special Beat the Clock menu, 6pm is £6, and so on). A great atmosphere, those monks, coloring sheets and pencils, and a £4.95 two-course children's menu (mussels or roast chicken with chips or mash, and dessert) bring in families.

50 Earlham St., WC2. www.belgo-restaurants.co.uk. ℂ **020/7813-2233.** Main courses £9.95–£17.95; express lunch noon–5pm £7.95. AE, DC, MC, V. Mon–Thurs noon–11pm; Fri–Sat noon–11:30pm; Sun noon–10:30pm. Tube: Covent Garden. Other locations throughout London.

SOHO

Masala Zone ☺ 🍴 INDIAN   Having cornered the market in luxury Indian food, the owners of Amaya (p. 223) and Veeraswamy (p. 201) took on the cheaper end with a winning formula of home-cooked food and street snacks served amid contemporary decor. There are now Masala Zones all around town, each one decorated differently with enough glitz to keep children amused. Order fresh Indian lemonade or a mango and coconut lassi while you study the menu. You can snack on *puris* (puffed wholewheat biscuits served with different fillings), bhajis, or samosas; or go for a more substantial thali, a whole meal of curry with rice, vegetables, dhal, raita, and chapatis (freshly made Indian bread). There's a special menu and highchairs.

9 Marshall St., W1. www.masalazone.com. ✆ **020/7287-9966.** Main courses £11–£16. MC, V. Mon–Sat noon–11pm; Sun 12:30–10:30pm. Tube: Oxford Circus.

BLOOMSBURY & FITZROVIA

Wagamama ☺ 🍴 JAPANESE   This basement restaurant, handy for the British Museum, was the first of the immensely successful Wagamama chain of pan-Asian noodle restaurants started in 1992 by Alan Yau. He sold the business and moved on to open several other landmark London restaurants, including Hakkasan (p. 208). The Bloomsbury venue is noisy and crowded, and you may have to wait for a seat. The original udon and soba noodles, grilled or in broth, plated or in large bowls, with meat, chicken, vegetables, or salmon and *gyoza* (steamed dumplings) are still there, but now there's more choice and rice dishes have joined the menu. Expect communal tables, coloring sheets and pencils, and special noodle dishes for children. Service is brisk and friendly; the atmosphere is casual.

4 Streatham St., WC1. www.wagamama.com. ✆ **020/7323-9223.** Reservations not accepted. Main courses £7.10–£13.50. AE, MC, V. Sun–Thurs noon–10pm; Fri–Sat noon–11pm. Tube: Tottenham Court Rd. Other locations around London including Tower of London.

South Bank

WATERLOO, SOUTHWARK & BOROUGH

Giraffe ★ ☺ INTERNATIONAL   You feel better as soon as you walk into any of Giraffe's user-friendly restaurants. Upbeat, and playing music that older children will know even if you don't, it's a hit with families. The noise drowns out any wails, and the menu has something for everyone: burgers; spiced chicken fettuccine; jambalaya risotto; Thai duck stir fry; noodles; sausage, beans, and mash; and BBQ chicken wraps. There are often meal deals, plus information on dishes suitable for vegetarians, those that contain nuts, and so on. Decor is colorful; the welcome genuine. The Southbank Centre location is the chain's biggest restaurant, with great river views and an ideal location for the London Eye.

Behind Royal Festival Hall, Riverside Level 1, Belvedere Rd., SE1. www.giraffe.net. ✆ **020/7928-2004.** Main courses £8.45–£15.95; from 5pm 2 courses £9.95. AE, MC, V. Mon–Fri 8am–11pm; Sat 9am–11pm; Sun 9am–10:30pm. Tube: Waterloo. Other locations throughout London.

West London
KENSINGTON & SOUTH KENSINGTON

Byron ☺ AMERICAN   Just the place for a family meal, this chain of burger joints serves "proper hamburgers." The decor and atmosphere is casual (exposed brick walls, bare light fittings, and a young clientele in scruffy jeans); there's a children's menu of two courses (good hamburgers or chicken filet, and ice cream), and youngsters can color their menu and turn it into a paper plane afterwards. There's a knickerbocker glory for a grown-up (well, nearly grown-up) dessert.

222 Kensington High St., W8. www.byronhamburgers.com. ✆ **020/7361-1717.** Main courses £6.75–£10.75. AE, MC, V. Mon–Thurs noon–11pm; Fri noon–11:30pm; Sat 11am–11:30pm; Sun 11am–1:30pm. Tube: High St. Kensington. Other locations throughout London.

TEATIME

Formal afternoon tea in London is a relaxing, civilized affair. Elegantly served on delicate china, there are dainty finger sandwiches, fresh-baked scones served with jam and clotted cream, and an array of small cakes and pastries. An attentive waiter is ready to refill your pot of tea. At many places, you can gild the lily with a glass of champagne. It makes a great alternative to pretheatre dining.

Afternoon tea, a British institution since the 18th century, was traditionally taken around 4pm, although today it's an all-afternoon affair in the top London spots. High tea, originally a working-class alternative to dinner, is a grander affair and available in some venues.

Interesting West End alternatives to top London hotels include Momo's **Mô Café** (p. 199), where you're transported to Morocco with mint tea and whichever very sweet pastry you might fancy. Or try **Chai Bazaar,** part of Indian restaurant **Chor Bizarre,** 16 Albemarle St., W1 (www.chorbizarre.com; ✆ **020/7629-9802;** Tube: Green Park), for Indian teas matched with Indian desserts. High tea here costs £9.50.

West End
MAYFAIR

Café at Sotheby's 🎁   You don't have to be bidding for an Old Master to eat at this charming small cafe, decorated with black-and-white photographs and located just off the main foyer of the illustrious auction house. It's open all day for great breakfasts and light lunches (the wine list is overseen by the head of Sotheby's International Wine Department, Serena Sutcliffe, M.W.). But set afternoon tea is our favorite meal here. It's a classic cream tea, and you can watch the auction fun on a big screen.

Sotheby's, 34–35 New Bond St., W1. www.sothebys.com. ✆ **020/7293-5077.** Reservations for lunch recommended. Afternoon tea £8.50. High tea £12.50. AE, MC, V. Mon–Fri 9:30–11:30am, noon–2:45pm, and 3–4:45pm. Tube: Bond St.

Claridge's ★   Make for the Foyer or the Reading Room for an afternoon tea in fabulous, glittering Art Deco surroundings. A pianist accompanies the mix of tea lovers and tourists who sit, suitably dressed (no jeans, trainers, or the like) in elegant chairs for one of London's rituals. You can choose from 30 different teas, and partake of (it's the sort of venue that encourages that kind of phrase) finger sandwiches, scones with jam and cream, and pastries that look as delicate as they taste. The reckless or those bent on seduction go for the Champagne Tea.

55 Brook St., W1. www.claridges.co.uk. © **020/7629-8860.** Reservations essential. Jacket and tie required for men after 6pm. Afternoon tea £38, with champagne £49–£62. AE, DC, MC, V. Daily 3–5:30pm. Tube: Bond St.

English Tearoom at Brown's ★★   One of our favorite places for a posh afternoon tea, Brown's has upped the ante with two tea sommeliers who take you through the 17-strong list of teas, and a policy of replenishing any of the delights in front of you at no extra charge. The now requisite, albeit fabulous, range of sandwiches on offer in London's top hotels is augmented by some of the best fruit-cake you'll find and an assortment of gluten- and nut-free items. It's all elegantly conducted in a wood-paneled room with a plaster ceiling and an open fire.

Brown's Hotel, Albemarle St., W1. www.brownshotel.com. © **020/7518-4155.** Reservations recommended. Afternoon tea £39.50, with champagne £49.50–£52.50. AE, DC, MC, V. Mon–Fri 3–6pm; Sat–Sun 1–6pm. Tube: Green Park.

ST. JAMES'S

Ritz Palm Court ★★★   This remains the top place for afternoon tea in London—and the hardest to get into without reserving way in advance. It's a spectacular stage setting, complete with marble steps and columns, a baroque fountain, and little gilded chairs. Nibble on a smoked salmon sandwich and egg mayonnaise roll and then pig out on the chocolate cake. But you're really here to feel like a duchess.

Inside Ritz Hotel, 150 Piccadilly, W1. www.theritzlondon.com. © **020/7493-8181.** Reservations required at least 8 weeks in advance. Jeans and sneakers not accepted. Jacket and tie required for men. Afternoon tea £42–£53, with champagne £64. AE, DC, MC, V. Five seatings daily at 11:30am, 1:30, 3:30, 5:30, and 7:30pm. Tube: Green Park.

TRAFALGAR SQUARE

Portrait Restaurant ★   The views south over London's landmarks from the fifth floor of the **National Portrait Gallery's** (p. 104) Ondaatje Wing are spectacular. It's known for its cooking, but we like it best for afternoon tea when it's quieter and you get the chance to see the London Eye, Big Ben, and Nelson almost eye-to-eye on his Column. Afternoon tea is a feast featuring seasonal treats such as mince pies and chocolate, cherry, and vanilla cream log at Christmas.

In the National Portrait Gallery, Trafalgar Sq., WC2. www.searcys.co.uk/national-portrait-gallery. © **020/7312-2490.** Reservations recommended. Afternoon tea £19.95; with glass of champagne £29.95. MC, V. Daily 3.30-4.45pm. Tube: Leicester Sq. or Charing Cross.

The City

Restaurant at St. Paul's ★   Perfect for afternoon tea after a quick trot around St. Paul's Cathedral, the restaurant in the vaulted crypt is a bastion of good British cooking. And as such, its afternoon tea is impeccable. Cream teas with dollops of strawberry jam and clotted cream, and a traditional afternoon tea complete with cucumber cheese and Battenberg cake.

St. Paul's Cathedral, EC4. www.restaurantatstpauls.co.uk. © **020/7248-2469.** Afternoon tea £9.95–£15.05, with glass of English rosé sparkling wine £21.95. MC, V. Daily noon–4:30pm. Tube: St. Paul's.

COFFEE & cake

There was a time when the only cup of coffee that could pass muster with a caffeine aficionado was at the splendid survivor in Soho, **Bar Italia** (p. 329). Then a wave of young, well-trained baristas jetted in, mostly from Australia and New Zealand, and changed the face of London's coffee houses for ever. They're all very serious, using top coffee roasts and the best techniques; there are often tasting notes to accompany the brew. Try any of the following:

The Espresso Room ★ A tiny room, but always packed. Go especially for their milky lattes; and for sweeteners they offer rich Costa Rican brown sugar. They use Has Bean and Square Mile beans, and herbal teas. Often busy with the staff from the children's hospital opposite, they also sell great daily soups, sandwiches, and cakes for around £3–£6. 31–35 Gt. Ormond St., WC1. www.the espressoroom.com. *© **07760/714883.** No credit cards. Mon–Fri 7:30am–5pm. Tube: Russell Square.

Flat White This small but hip joint, just by Berwick Street Market, is a magnet for Antipodeans who also make up the staff. Like many, they use superior Square Mile coffee roaster beans and offer around ten different coffees, plus juices and shakes. Croissants and porridge are served all day; lunch offers salads and unusual toasted sandwiches such as fried chorizo and roast pepper. 17 Berwick St., W1. www.flatwhitecafe. com. *© **020/7734-0370.** No credit cards. Mon–Fri 8am–7pm, Sat–Sun 9am–6pm. Tube: Leicester Sq. or Tottenham Court Rd.

Department of Coffee and Social Affairs The Dept. used to be an architectural ironmongers; now it's an industrial chic coffee shop that packs in the punters. A few doors away from Prufrock, it serves hand-ground beans that change often, coming from around the globe. There are also tasty sandwiches and home-made cakes. 14–16 Leather Ln., EC1. www.departmentofcoffee.co.uk. No phone. MC, V. Mon–Fri 7:30am–5pm, Sat–Sun 10am–4pm. Tube: Farringdon/ Chancery Lane.

Prufrock Coffee The UK's first World Barista Champion, Gwylim Davies, is the hero here, serving great flat whites and espressos to go with the cakes and sandwiches. They've expanded from their original small space in the menswear shop, Present at 140 Shoreditch High St., to this new spacious cafe, which also runs a barista training course for individuals, professionals and groups. 23–25 Leather Ln., EC1. www.prufrock coffee.com. *© **020/7404-3597.** AE, MC, V. Mon–Fri 8am–6pm, Sat 10am–4:30pm, Sun 11am–4pm. Tube: Chancery Lane/ Farringdon.

Tina, We Salute You 🎒 Once a cupcake stall, now a Dalston favorite, the decor is as quirky as the name. Walls painted with works of art, a large sofa and table inside, and outdoor tables attract trendy locals for traditional breakfasts, sandwiches, and a selection of coffee and cakes. 47 King Henry's Walk, N1. www.tinawesaluteyou. *© **020/3119-0047.** Main courses £3.60–£6. No credit cards. Tues–Fri 8am–7pm, Sat 9am–7pm, Sun 10am–7pm. Rail: Dalston Kingsland.

The Other Café and Gallery 🎒 This is a haven of calm in a street dominated by small shops. The owner is an artist selling his and other people's work in the basement, beside a dining room that feels just like somebody's 1950s' lounge. A comprehensive all-day menu and excellent coffees are offered, along with a large sofa and table for surfing the net in the upstairs part. 48 Balls Pond Rd, N1. *© **07787/269-499.** Dishes £4.55–£6.95. No credit cards. Mon, Wed, Thurs 8:30am–6pm, Fri–Sat 9am–7pm, Sun 9am–6pm. Rail: Dalston Kingsland.

Southwest London

KENSINGTON

The Orangery   Just north of, but part of **Kensington Palace** (p. 114), the Orangery is a long, narrow garden pavilion built in 1704 for Queen Anne. Rows of potted orange trees bask in sunlight from soaring windows, and tea is served amid Corinthian columns, Grinling Gibbons woodcarvings, and urns and statuary. The menu includes soups, salads, and sandwiches. But it's afternoon tea that brings out the great aunts. The array of different teas is served with high style, accompanied by fresh scones with clotted cream and jam, and Belgian chocolate cake.

In the gardens of Kensington Palace, W8. www.hrp.org.uk/KensingtonPalace. ✆ **020/7376-0239.** Reservations not accepted. Afternoon tea £14.85, with champagne £33.75. MC, V. Daily noon–6pm. Tube: High St. Kensington.

VICTORIA

The Goring ★★   Still family-owned after a century in business, this favorite, comfortable hotel offers afternoon tea in the lounge, and in the summer on the sunny terrace overlooking the private garden. It's a clubby sort of place, with regulars propping up the very popular, convivial bar all day long. Straying a little from the format, tea has Jaffa cakes, and mulled wine and pear jelly with cinnamon cream. It's as suitable for your great aunt as it is for your next romantic interest.

Beeston Place, Grosvenor Gardens, SW1. www.goring.com. ✆ **020/7396-9000.** Afternoon tea £35; champagne tea £45. AE, DC, MC, V. Daily 3:30–4:30pm. Tube: Victoria.

Northwest London

PRIMROSE HILL

Lanka 🍴   Primrose Hill is just the place for a brisk afternoon walk, and Lanka just the place for tea afterwards. This cafe serves light lunches, but the reason to come here is the cakes and pastries. They're produced by chef Masayuki Hara, using Japanese flavors such as sesame and ponzu alongside more familiar tastes. Teas come from Sri Lanka and are a revelation. The shop sells portions and whole cakes to take away.

71 Regent's Park Rd., NW1. www.lanka-uk.com. ✆ **020/7483-2544.** Individual cake portions £1.50–£4.20. MC, V. Tues–Sat 9am–5.30pm; Sun 9am–5pm. MC, V. Tube: Chalk Farm.

Outlying Areas

KEW

Original Maids of Honour   The first shop was opened in Kew in 1860 and since then the Newens family has been serving generations of locals and visitors to nearby Kew Gardens with a delightfully old-fashioned menu of meat pies, sandwiches, and salads. Go for the afternoon tea for a nostalgic trip back to the days when nannies took their charges to this cozy teashop with its bottle glass windows, chintz-covered chairs, and cheerful staff.

228 Kew Rd., Kew. www.theoriginalmaidsofhonour.co.uk. ✆ **020/8940-2752.** Set tea £6.45–£14.95; with champagne £48.95. MC, V. Daily 8:30am–6pm. Tube: Kew Gardens.

RESTAURANTS BY CUISINE

AMERICAN

Byron (Kensington & South Kensington, £, p. 256)
Hard Rock Café (Mayfair, ££, p. 199)
Hawksmoor ★ (Spitalfields, ££, p. 236)
Mishkin's ★ (Covent Garden, ££, p. 205)
Palm ★ (Belgravia, £££, p. 223)
Spuntino ★ (Soho, ££, p. 211)

ASIAN

(See also Cantonese, Chinese, Japanese, Szechuan, and Thai)
Bevis Marks ★ (Tower Hill, ££, p. 238)
E&O ★ (Ladbroke Grove, ££, p. 222)
Yauatcha ★ (Soho, £, p. 213)

BELGIAN

Belgo Centraal (Covent Garden & Strand, ££, p. 254)

BRITISH—MODERN

A Little of What You Fancy (Dalston, £, p. 247)
The Cow ★ (Notting Hill Gate, ££, p. 220)
Empress of India (Hackney, ££, p. 246)
Hereford Road ★★ (Paddington & Bayswater, ££, p. 219)
Hix ★ (Soho, ££, p. 210)
Le Café Anglais ★★ (Notting Hill Gate, ££, p. 220)
The Narrow ★ (Docklands, ££, p. 239)
Old Brewery (Greenwich, ££, p. 252)
Pig's Ear ★ (Chelsea, ££, p. 230)
Portrait Restaurant ★ (Trafalgar Square, ££, p. 257)
Princess of Shoreditch ★ (Shoreditch, ££, p. 243)
Rivington Grill (Greenwich, ££, p. 252)

BRITISH—TRADITIONAL

Albion (Shoreditch, £, p. 242)
Bentley's Oyster Bar & Grill ★★ (Piccadilly Circus & Leicester Square, £££, p. 201)
Counter Café (Hackney Wick/Stratford, £, p. 247)
Dean Street Townhouse ★ (Soho, ££, p. 209)
The Delaunay ★★★ (Covent Garden, ££, p. 205)
Dinner by Heston Blumenthal ★★★ (Knightsbridge, £££, p. 223)
Forman's 1905 (Hackney, ££, p. 246)
Green's Restaurant & Oyster Bar ★ (St. James's, ££, p. 200)
Hackney Pearl ★ (Hackney, £, p. 247)
King Edward VII (Stratford, £ p. 247)
Randall & Aubin ★ (Soho, ££, p. 210)
Rules ★ (Covent Garden & Strand, £££, p. 204)
St. John ★★ (Clerkenwell & Farringdon, ££, p. 238)
Savoy Grill ★★★ (Covent Garden & Strand, £££, p. 204)
Simpson's-in-the-Strand ★ (Covent Garden & Strand, £££, p. 204)
Tom's Kitchen ★ (Chelsea, £££, p. 230)

BURMESE

Mandalay (Paddington & Bayswater, £, p. 219)

CANTONESE

Hakkasan ★ (Soho, £££, p. 208)
Jenny Lo's Teahouse (Westminster & Victoria, £, p. 231)
Royal China ★ (Paddington & Bayswater, ££, p. 219)
Shanghai (Dalston, £, p. 248)

KEY TO ABBREVIATIONS:
££££ = Very Expensive   £££ = Expensive   ££ = Moderate   £ = Inexpensive

CHINESE

(See also Cantonese and Szechuan)

Cha Cha Moon (Leicester Square, £, p. 202)

Hakkasan ★ (Soho, £££, p. 208)

CONTEMPORARY EUROPEAN

Arbutus Restaurant ★ (Soho, ££, p. 208)

Clarke's ★★ (Kensington & South Kensington, ££, p. 229)

Dabbous ★★ (Fitzrovia, ££, p. 214)

The Delaunay ★★★ (Covent Garden, ££, p. 205)

Giaconda Dining Room ★ (Covent Garden & Strand, ££, p. 205)

Greenhouse ★★ (Mayfair, £££, p. 197)

Inside (Greenwich, ££, p. 252)

L'Autre Pied ★★ (Marylebone, £££, p. 216)

The Ledbury ★★ (Notting Hill Gate, £££, p. 220)

The Ivy ★ (Covent Garden, ££, p. 203)

The Luxe ★ (Spitalfields, ££, p. 236)

North Road ★★ (Clerkenwell & Farringdon, ££, p. 237)

The Orange (Westminster & Victoria, ££, p. 231)

Petersham Nurseries Café ★★ (Richmond, £££, p. 253)

Pollen Street Social ★★ (Mayfair, ££, p. 199)

The Pig's Ear ★ (Chelsea, ££, p. 230)

Rex Whistler Restaurant at Tate Britain ★★ (Pimlico, ££, p. 231)

Prince Bonaparte (Notting Hill Gate, £, p. 222)

Sketch ★★ (Mayfair, ££££, p. 196)

Union Café (Marylebone, ££, p. 218)

Viajante ★★ (Bethnal Green, ££££, p. 245)

Villandry (Marylebone, ££, p. 218)

Wild Honey ★ (Mayfair, ££, p. 200)

The Wolseley ★ (St. James's, ££, p. 200)

York & Albany ★ (Camden Town, £££, p. 248)

EASTERN EUROPEAN

Baltic ★ (Waterloo, Borough & Southwark, ££, p. 234)

ENGLISH AFTERNOON TEA

Café at Sotheby's (Mayfair, ££, p. 256)

Claridge's ★ (Mayfair, £££, p. 256)

English Tearoom at Browns ★ (Mayfair, ££, p. 257)

The Goring ★ (Victoria, ££, p. 259)

Lanka (Primrose Hill; £, p. 259)

The Orangery (Kensington & South Kensington, £, p. 259)

Original Maids of Honour (Kew, £, p. 259)

Portrait Restaurant ★ (Trafalgar Square, ££, p. 257)

Ritz Palm Court ★★★ (St. James's, £££, p. 257)

FRENCH

Alain Ducasse at the Dorchester ★★★ (Mayfair, ££££, p. 193)

Bar Boulud ★★ (Knightsbridge, £££, p. 227)

Bibendum & the Oyster Bar ★ (Kensington & South Kensington, £££, p. 228)

Bistrot Bruno Loubet ★★ (Clerkenwell & Farringdon, ££, p. 237)

Bistrotheque ★ (Bethnal Green, £, p. 246)

Cassis Bistro ★★ (Knightsbridge, £££, p. 227)

Club Gascon ★★ (Clerkenwell & Farringdon, £££, p. 236)

Galvin Bistrot de Luxe ★★ (Marylebone, ££, p. 218)

Gordon Ramsay ★★★ (Chelsea, ££££, p. 229)

Hibiscus ★★★ (Mayfair, ££££, p. 196)

Koffmann's ★★ (Knightsbridge, £££, p. 226)

L'Atelier de Joël Robuchon ★★★ (Covent Garden, ££££, p. 202)

Le Gavroche ★★★ (Mayfair, ££££, p. 193)

Le Pont de la Tour ★ (Bankside, £££, p. 232)

Les Deux Salons ★★ (Covent Garden and Strand, £££, p. 203)

Les Trois Garçons ★ (Shoreditch, £££, p. 239)

Marcus Wareing at the Berkeley (Knightsbridge, ££££, p. 226)

Mon Plaisir (Covent Garden & Strand, ££, p. 206)

Orrery ★★ (Marylebone, £££, p. 217)

Pied à Terre ★★★ (Bloomsbury & Fitzrovia, £££, p. 213)

Racine ★ (Knightsbridge, ££, p. 228)

The Square ★★★ (Mayfair, ££££, p. 196)

Terroirs ★ (Covent Garden & Strand, ££, p. 206)

Tom Aikens ★★★ (Kensington & South Kensington, ££££, p. 228)

FUSION

Kopapa ★ (Covent Garden, ££, p. 205)

The Providores and Tapa Room ★★ (Marylebone, ££, p. 217)

GASTROPUBS

The Cow ★ (Notting Hill Gate, ££, p. 220)

Empress of India (Hackney, ££, p. 246)

The Narrow ★ (Docklands, ££, p. 239)

The Orange (Westminster & Victoria, ££, p. 231)

Pig's Ear ★ (Chelsea, ££, p. 230)

Princess of Shoreditch ★ (Shoreditch, £, p. 243)

The Wells ★ (Hampstead, ££, p. 249)

INDIAN

Amaya ★★ (Belgravia, £££, p. 223)

Café Spice Namaste ★★ (Tower Hill, ££, p. 239)

Cinnamon Club ★★ (Westminster & Victoria, ££, p. 231)

Dishoom (Covent Garden & Strand, £, p. 206)

Kasturi (Whitechapel, ££, p. 245)

Masala Zone (Soho, £, p. 255)

Mela ★ (Covent Garden & Strand, ££, p. 207)

Rasa Samudra ★ (Soho, ££, p. 210)

Tamarind ★ (Mayfair, £££, p. 198)

Tayyabs ★ (Whitechapel, £, p. 245)

Veeraswamy ★ (Piccadilly Circus, ££, p. 201)

INTERNATIONAL

Caravan ★ (Clerkenwell & Farringdon, £, p. 237)

Giraffe (Waterloo, Borough & Southwark, £, p. 255)

Orrery ★★ (Marylebone, £££, p. 217)

Ottolenghi ★ (Islington, £, p. 249)

Oxo Tower Restaurant ★★ (Bankside, £££, p. 234)

Vinoteca (Clerkenwell & Farringdon, £, p. 238)

ITALIAN

Assaggi ★ (Paddington & Bayswater, £££, p. 219)

Bocca di Lupo ★★ (Soho, ££, p. 209)

Fifteen ★★ (Shoreditch, ££, p. 242)

L'Anima ★★ (Spitalfields, £££, p. 235)

Locanda Locatelli ★★ (Marylebone, £££, p. 216)

Polpo ★ (Soho, £, p. 212)

River Café ★★ (Hammersmith, £££, p. 222)

Salt Yard ★ (Bloomsbury & Fitzrovia, £, p. 216)

Towpath (Dalston, £, p. 248)

Zafferano ★★ (Knightsbridge, £££, p. 227)

Zucca ★ (Waterloo, Borough & Southwark, ££, p. 235)

JAPANESE

Koya (Soho, £, p. 211)

Nobu ★★ (Mayfair, £££, p. 198)

Roka ★★ (Bloomsbury & Fitzrovia, £££, p. 214)

Satsuma (Soho, ££, p. 213)

Tokyo Diner (Leicester Square, £, p. 202)

Wagamama (Bloomsbury & Fitzrovia, £, p. 255)

JEWISH

Bevis Marks ★ (Tower Hill, ££, p. 238)

Mishkin's ★ (Covent Garden, ££, p. 205)

MEXICAN

Wahaca (Covent Garden & Strand, £, p. 208)

MOROCCAN

Momo ★ (Mayfair, ££, p. 199)

NORTH AFRICAN

Momo ★ (Mayfair, ££, p. 199)

Moro ★★ (Clerkenwell & Far-ringdon, ££, p. 237)

PACIFIC RIM

The Providores and Tapa Room ★★ (Marylebone, ££, p. 217)

PORTUGUESE

Eyre Brothers ★ (Shoreditch, ££, p. 242)

SCANDINAVIAN

North Road ★★ (Clerkenwell & Far-ringdon, £££, p. 237)

Texture ★★ (Marylebone, £££, p. 217)

SEAFOOD

Bentley's Oyster Bar & Grill ★★ (Pic-cadilly Circus, £££, p. 201)

Forman's 1905 (Hackney, £, p. 246)

Green's Restaurant & Oyster Bar (St. James's, ££, p. 200)

J. Sheekey ★★ (Covent Garden & Strand, £££, p. 203)

Randall & Aubin ★ (Soho, ££), p. 210)

Scott's ★★ (Mayfair, £££), p. 198)

SPANISH

Barrica ★ (Bloomsbury & Fitzrovia, ££, p. 215)

Cambio de Tercio ★★ (Kensington & South Kensington, ££, p. 229)

Eyre Brothers ★ (Shoreditch, ££, p. 242)

Fino ★ (Soho, ££, p. 214)

Moro ★★ (Clerkenwell & Farringdon, ££, p. 237)

Salt Yard ★ (Soho, £, p. 216)

STEAK

Hawksmoor ★ (Spitalfields, ££, p. 236)

Palm ★ (Belgravia, £££, p. 223)

SZECHUAN

Barshu ★ (Soho, ££, p. 209)

Jenny Lo's Teahouse (Victoria, £, p. 231)

Royal China ★ (Paddington & Bay-swater, £££, p. 219)

TAPAS

Barrica ★ (Bloomsbury & Fitzrovia, ££, p. 215)

Counter Café (Hackney Wick/Stratford, £, p. 247)

Fino ★ (Soho, ££, p. 214)

Pollen Street Social ★★ (Mayfair, ££, p. 199)

Salt Yard ★ (Soho, £, p. 216)

Tapas Brindisa ★ (Waterloo, Borough & Southwark, ££, p. 235)

THAI

Blue Elephant ★ (Fulham, ££, p. 230)

Busaba Eathai (Soho, ££, p. 211)

TURKISH

Mangal I (Dalston, £, p. 248)

Pasha (Islington, ££, p. 249)

VEGETARIAN

Mildreds ★ (Soho, £, p. 211)

Rasa Samudra ★ (Soho, ££, p. 210)

VIETNAMESE

Cây Tre (Shoreditch, £, p. 243)

Song Que (Shoreditch, £, p. 243)

PRACTICAL MATTERS: THE RESTAURANT SCENE

HOURS   Restaurants in London keep varied hours, but in general, lunch is served from noon to 2pm and dinner from 6:30 to 9:30pm, although more restaurants are staying open later these days. Sunday is the usual closing day for restaurants, but there are exceptions. (Many also close for a few days around Christmas, so call ahead during the holidays.)

PRICES   Price categories above are based on a three-course dinner for one person, without wine. Very expensive (££££) = £75+; Expensive (£££) = £50 to £75; Moderate (££) = £25 to £50; Inexpensive (£) = under £25. But remember these are average prices; you'll find that it's possible to eat almost everywhere (except for high-end, fixed-price restaurants) at the lower end of the price scale.

RESERVATIONS   Nearly all establishments, except pubs, cafes, and fast-food joints, prefer or require reservations. Almost invariably, you get a better table if you book in advance. For a few of the best, you must reserve weeks in advance, even before leaving home. (Always confirm your reservation nearer the time; some restaurants may ask for a telephone number and call you to confirm.) However, if you don't have reservations, even at a "reservations required" restaurant, it's worth checking; if they have room, you won't be turned away. If you're staying in one of London's top hotels, you might get lucky by asking the concierge for help with hard-to-get reservations.

   Restaurant booking websites are useful, both for specific restaurants and if you're uncertain of where to eat. **Top Table** (www.toptable.com) has a large selection of London restaurants. You enter details (number of people, location, and so on), check the list and details like a typical menu, reviews, any special offers, and then book online. **Open Table** (www.opentable.com) runs a similar service.

RESTAURANT DEALS   Look to the Internet for occasional impressive discounts on London dining. Websites promoting special deals include **Lastminute.com** and **Squaremeal.co.uk**. It's also worth subscribing to regular newsletters such as those emailed weekly by **Lovefoodlovedrink.co.uk** and **Travelzoo.com**, and signing up to deals websites such as **KGB Deals** (www.kgbdeals.co.uk/london), **LivingSocial** (www.livingsocial.com), or **Groupon** (www.groupon.com). For a top meal at reasonable prices, many destination restaurants offer set-price lunch deals, as well as limited, but top-quality pre- and posttheatre menus; see details in the reviews above. Some London and U.K. newspapers run promotions (usually during January and February) offering lunch or dinner from £5 or £10. Keep an eye on local press.

TAXES & TIPPING   Charges for service, as well as any minimums or cover charges, must be made clear on the menu, and all prices shown must include 20% VAT. Most restaurants add a 10% to 15% service charge to your bill. But beware: Some may add the service charge, but still leave the total blank on your credit card payment, a deplorable practice that's fortunately not widespread. If nothing has been added, leave a 10% to 15% tip as long as you were happy with the service.

6

SHOPPING

Londons shopping scene never stays still for long—from secret pop-up shops and sample sales to huge shopping malls transforming the east end, the city's retailers and its trends are ever-changing.

There's always something new and there's always somewhere different to shop, which makes shopping in London constantly exciting. Nothing is predictable—not even a simple walk down the high street.

But it's the streets just behind the high street that have changed the most. Once home to nothing but offices and the odd sandwich shop, you'll now find unusual brands to browse, more boutique shops, and more interesting labels. Not quite vintage and not quite high street, it's an eclectic mix all offered at high-street prices.

The high street itself has mellowed a little and it's no longer only about big shops and big names (although you'll still find plenty dominating streets and malls). Instead, Londoners are welcoming smaller brands and encouraging more unique stores, while the high street is letting the new kids play on their turf.

Mass-produced foreign products are no longer where it's at. The recent financial crisis has stopped many of us shopping for the sake of it, making us think about our cash and where it's going, which has allowed excellent smaller British brands to take advantage of that.

We want something special, but now we want it with the convenience of having it immediately. For that reason, the main shopping streets in London have become that little bit more special. London has always been full of surprises and that's one thing that will always stay the same.

THE WEST END

Oxford Street is undeniably the West End's main shopping attraction. Start at the westernmost end by Marble Arch for an enormous branch of budget clothes chain **Primark** at no. 499 (www.primark.co.uk; ℂ **020/7495-0420;** Tube: Marble Arch) and further on fashion favorite department store, **Selfridges** (see p. 290). **Topshop** (p. 289), right in the centre of Oxford Street at Oxford Circus, remains a must-visit (as does the impressive crossroads outside), and the giant branches of **New Look** (p. 289) and **H&M** at 1 Oxford Circus, W1 (www. hm.com; ℂ **0844/736-9000;** Tube: Oxford Circus) offer good value clothes if you tire of the department stores. The quality of the shops heads downhill the closer you are to Tottenham Court Road—around here it's mainly bargain basement tat and cheap souvenirs. Only the brave attempt Oxford Street at the weekend; weekday mornings are best for your own sanity.

PREVIOUS PAGE: **Fortnum & Mason.**

Oxford Circus.

If the crowds are too much, you'll find more peaceful high-street shopping in nearby **Marylebone.** This is where London's top plastic surgeons are based if you're looking for some extreme shopping adventures. It's impossible not to fall in love with the quaintness of Marylebone High Street. The foodie shops and interior brands ooze class and a quirky kind of elegance; make sure you pop into **Rococo,** at no. 43 (www.rococochocolates.com; ✆ **020/7935-7780;** Tube: Regent's Park), for some chocolate samples—sometimes they're free.

Regent Street (www.regentstreetonline.com), leading south off Oxford Circus, is more toward the high end of "high street," typified by the affordable luxury of chain stores such as **Mango** at nos. 106–112 (www.mango.com; ✆ **020/7434-3694**) and **French Connection** at nos. 249–251 (www.french connection.com; ✆ **020/7493-3124**). Boutique lifestyle shop **Anthropologie** (p. 293) is expensive in comparison to its U.S. equivalent. Head to the world-famous department store **Liberty** (p. 290), a London landmark of designer treasures inside a mock-Tudor building. You're now at the top of **Carnaby Street** and although it's not quite the Sixties' style mecca it once was you'll enjoy a good few hours of shopping—especially if you veer off into the **Newburgh Quarter.** The area is also home to **Kingly Court,** a cute little piazza of independent shops and vintage boutiques. The area can be overpriced and very busy, but it makes a good place to people-watch.

Parallel to Regent Street, the **Bond Street** area connects Piccadilly with Oxford Street, and is synonymous with the luxury rag trade. It's not just one street, but a whole area, mainly comprising New Bond Street and Old Bond Street. It's the flagship location for the best designers—you'll find **Prada** at 17–18 Old Bond St. (www.prada.com; ✆ **020/7647-5041**), **Chanel** at 26 Old Bond St. (www.chanel.com; ✆ **020/7493-5040**), **Gucci** at 34 Old Bond St. (www.gucci.com; ✆ **020/7629-2716**) and British fashion house **Burberry** at 21–23 New Bond St. (www.burberry.com; ✆ **020/3402-1500**). **Tiffany** at 25 Old Bond St. (www.tiffany.co.uk; ✆ **020/7409-2790**) is quite at home nestled among designer jewelry shops. Make sure you stop off at **Dover Street Mar-**

ket—not a market at all, but actually a designer shop housing all sorts of fashionable folk under the same roof.

Burlington Arcade (www.burlington-arcade.co.uk; Tube: Piccadilly Circus), a glass-roofed Regency passage leading off **Piccadilly,** looks like a period exhibition, and is lined with mahogany-fronted shops and boutiques. Lit by

wrought-iron lamps, its small, upscale stores specialize in fashion, gold jewelry, Irish linen, and cashmere. If you linger until 5:30pm, you can watch the **beadles** (the last London representatives of Britain's oldest police force) ceremoniously place the iron grills that block off the arcade until 9am, at which time they remove them to start a new business day. Over the road at the Queen's grocers **Fortnum & Mason** (p. 290), make sure to catch the clock that moves on the hour in a rather charming display.

Nearby **Jermyn Street** (Tube: Piccadilly Circus), on the south side of Piccadilly, is a tiny two-block street devoted to high-end men's haberdashers and toiletries shops; many have been doing business for centuries.

TOP: **Turnbull & Asser.** BOTTOM: **Neal's Yard, Covent Garden.**

Several hold Royal warrants, including **Turnbull & Asser,** 71–72 Jermyn St. (✆ 020/7808-3000; www.turnbullandasser.com), where HRH Prince Charles has his PJs made. To the northwest, **Savile Row** is where you'll find London's finest tailors and at the bottom of St. James's Street at no. 3 is **Berry Bros & Rudd** (www.bbr.com; ✆ 0800/280-2440; Tube: Green Park), the world's oldest wine store.

The West End theatre district borders two more shopping areas: the not-ready-for-prime-time **Soho** (Tube: Tottenham Court Rd. or Leicester Sq.), where sleazy sex shops are slowly morphing into cutting-edge designer boutiques—check out clothing exchange **Bang Bang,** 9 Berwick St. (✆ 020/7494-2042), for designer bargains (they also have a branch on Goodge Street, see p. 287)—and **Covent Garden** (Tube: Covent Garden), a shopping haven stocked with fashion, food, books, and everything else. The original Covent Garden market-place has overflowed its boundaries and eaten up the surrounding neighborhood; it's fun to shop the narrow streets. Just off trendy **Neal Street** and **Seven Dials, Neal's Yard** is a stunning splash of color on rainy days. It's mainly cafes, but you can pick up organic toiletries from **Neal's Yard Remedies** at no. 15 (www.neals yardremedies.com; ✆ 020/7379-7222). You'll discover **Shu Uemera** on **Neal Street** at no. 24 (www.shuuemura.co.uk; ✆ 0207/240-7635) a glamorous false eyelash emporium specializing in dramatic feather eyelashes. **Monmouth Street** is somewhat of a local secret and stores specialize in everything from lingerie to bespoke perfumes and vintage clothing. Make sure to take in **Charing Cross Road** and get your nose into one of the many secondhand bookshops. You can't avoid **Foyles** (p. 282) (and nor should you), but the smaller shops have good secondhand options and well-priced first editions if you're particular about your Pulitzers.

WEST LONDON

If you're heading west, the first place you should find yourself in is **Notting Hill.** Of course, one of the main draws for shopping in West London is **Portobello Market** (p. 277). Every Saturday the whole of Portobello Road turns into a sea of antiques, cool clothing, and even cooler shoppers. You might even spot a celebrity or three.

Some of the best boutiques in London are also here. The independent shopping scene thrives; this is an area where people want to be unique, but still look expensive and well-groomed. Expect one-off boutiques housing designer labels you've never heard of, quirky housewares, and more than a handful of retro record shops. Stick to Portobello for antiques, but head to **Westbourne Grove** and **Ledbury Road** for the fancy boutiques.

The area is also full of organic food stores, with **Whole Foods** (p. 293) having its flagship home here. West Londoners take their food seriously. It does come at a price, but the quality is good so make sure you pick up a few bits. Pop into **Melt** (p. 292) on Ledbury Road for some of the best chocolate in London.

West London is also home to two American-style shopping malls. **Westfield** (p. 278) takes up residence in Shepherd's Bush and **Whiteleys** (p. 279) sits in Bayswater. They're huge, they have everything, and they're busy. If it's raining (it probably will be at some point during your visit) and you still want your ubiquitous high-street shops, come here.

SOUTHWEST LONDON

The home of **Harrods** (p. 290), **Knightsbridge** (Tube: Knightsbridge) is probably the second-most famous London retail district (Oxford Street just edges it out). **Sloane Street** is traditionally regarded as a designer area, but these days it's more "upscale high-street," and nowhere near as luxurious as **Bond Street** (see above). This is where you can grab some aromatherapy from **Jo Malone,** 150 Sloane St. (www.jomalone.co.uk; ☎ **0870/192-5121;** Tube: Sloane Sq.), a haven for bespoke perfumes.

Walk southwest on **Brompton Road**—toward the V&A Museum (p. 127)—and you'll find **Cheval Place,** lined with designer shops, and **Beauchamp Place.** It's top end, but with a hint of irony. Expect to see little lapdogs poking their heads out of bags.

Walk along Brompton Road and you'll connect to **Brompton Cross,** another hip area for designer shops made popular when Michelin House was refurbished by Sir Terence Conran becoming the **Conran Shop.** Seek out **Walton Street,** a tiny snake of a street running from Brompton Cross back toward the museums, that specializes in things you don't need but suddenly really want. You'll also be near **King's Road** (Tube: Sloane Sq.); once a beacon of Sixties cool, this is now a haven for designer clothes and housewares. About a third of King's Road is devoted to independent fashion shops, another third houses design-trade showrooms and stores for household wares. Scandinavian designs are prominent here and a must at no. 205 is **Design House Stockholm** (www.designhousestockholm.com; ☎ **020/7352-8403**). The remaining third of the street is a mix of dress shops and shoe boutiques. The clothes stores tend to suit a more mature customer (with a more mature budget), but you'll have fun shopping here if you remain oblivious to shop assistants who can be a little on the snooty side.

V&A Museum shop in Kensington V&A museum.

The outskirts of South London are a bit of an odd bag, because the shopping areas are so widely separated. You can easily get to each area by train or bus (usually from London Bridge or Victoria stations), but they're not as easily accessible as parts of Central London. One place to head is **Crystal Palace** (Overground: Crystal Palace) for its cute collection of vintage shops and indie stores. Check out the **Bookseller Crow** (p. 281) for unique children's books and friendly service, and then **Crystal Palace Antiques** (p. 279). Don't forget to visit **Vintage Hart** (p. 288), a vintage shop nestled in the corner of the White Hart Pub.

Herne Hill (Rail: Herne Hill) and **Dulwich** (Rail: North Dulwich) merge slightly, and both attract a "yummy mummy" crowd—posh mums with posh buggies—but the shops also benefit from a local community vibe. It's certainly worth browsing here, in preference to **Clapham**—which apart from a few gems such as **Lisa Stickley** (p. 286) is unlikely to wow you.

Brixton has also had a bit of a facelift recently and trendy Dulwich-dwellers are likely to be found relaxing in Brixton Village. It's a strange market that's a mix of stalls selling fresh meat and veg, bijou bakeries, and coffee shops. It doesn't entirely make sense, but it works and pulls in a crowd. Avoid after 4pm—all of the shops are shutting by then and the restaurants tend to not reopen until the evening.

The best place for shopping in London's far southwest is **Chiswick** (Tube: Turnham Green), which has always had a thriving artsy community. This is where you'll find modern little galleries on the corner of residential streets (be sure to check out the **Treatment Rooms**—a house/gallery covered in mosaics). Unique houseware retailers such as **Eco** as well as temporary pop-up shops make the trip worthwhile despite it still being a mostly residential suburb. Start your browsing along **Devonshire Road** and follow your senses.

Finally, don't forget the museums in nearby **South Kensington.** They have fantastic gift shops. If you're looking for jewelry and gifts the **V&A** (p. 127) is a must-visit and the **Science Museum** shop (p. 126) is perfect for inquisitive youngsters. Make sure to view the collections too—they're free, and have some world-class exhibits.

Kensington High Street (Tube: High St. Kensington) is the hangout of the classier breed of teen, one who has graduated from Carnaby Street (see above). While there are a few staples of basic British fashion here, most of the stores feature items that can be described as modern classics with a twist. From Kensington High Street, you can walk up **Kensington Church Street.** Like Portobello Road, this is one of the city's main shopping avenues for antiques, offering everything from antique furniture to Impressionist paintings.

Insider's Tip: Kensington might scream money, but there are still places to pick up a bargain. The charity shops here (particularly along Kensington Church Street) are full of designer bargains. Where else is London's upper crust going to drop off last season's clobber? It might not be good enough for them, but if you're looking for cut-price Gucci garments and Pucci prints, this is where you'll find them. That's not to say you'll be paying pennies for your wares, but you can pick up a vintage bargain and do your bit for charity at the same time.

THE SOUTH BANK

The South Bank isn't an obvious shopping destination. Empty at first glance, it hides secret artsy and design shops that take their lead from nearby museums and galleries. The **OXO Tower,** Bargehouse St., (℃ **020/7021-1600;** Tube: Waterloo) has a collection of upscale boutiques in its lower floors, which are much more interesting than the selection in the tired Gabriel's Wharf area. **Hay's Galleria,** 2 Battle Bridge Lane (℃ **020/7403-3583;** Tube: London Bridge), is cute, if rather sparse—you'll find a toy shop and a ubiquitous Starbucks, but not much

Hay's Galleria shopping arcade.

else, although **Riverside Bookshop** (Unit 18–19, Hay's Galleria, SE1. ℃ **020/7378-1824;** Tube: London Bridge) is certainly worth a look. Much better is the **Southbank Centre shop** (p. 280) which has had a huge revamp and now spans two floors; it's packed full of art and design goodies. **Borough Market** (p. 276) brings foodie crowds in their droves, as does **Tate Modern** (p. 281) with its fabulous shop for creative visitors and locals.

The South Bank might be more of a summer destination but something delightful happens to the area over Christmas. There's a German **Christmas Market,** which stretches along the whole South Bank, offering festive delights. Everything from seasonal food to Christmas decorations can be bought, all before going to see Santa himself. There's also a **Slow Food Market** (www.slowfood.org.uk) in winter offering roasted meats, chutneys, and festive foods that you'll want to savor with your mulled wine.

THE CITY & EAST LONDON

The financial district itself doesn't really offer much in the way of shopping, especially at the weekend when everything tends to be shut. However, the shopping centre **One New Change** (p. 278) is attracting a rich crowd for its luxury goods—it's opposite the eastern end of St. Paul's Cathedral. You'll also find a handful of tailors in the area, and there are several high-end brands in the nearby **Royal Exchange** (www.theroyalexchange.com; Tube: Bank). Despite the beautiful building, it's really not a shopping destination in itself.

Wander west from St. Paul's and you'll wind up in the jewelry district around **Hatton Garden** (Tube: Chancery Lane/Farringdon). On Saturdays it's a sea of nervous men hunting the perfect engagement ring. If you're not in the market for fancy finger adornments, **Lamb's Conduit Street** isn't far away. It's a beautiful street, full of history (and several appearances in classic literature), and now independent shops and restaurants. Make sure you pop to **Persephone** (p. 282) for unique womens' literature, and next door at no. 47 pick up food goodies from **Kennards** (www.kennardsgoodfoods.com; ✆ 020/7404-4030).

Continue your adventure east on **Commercial Street** (Tube: Liverpool St./Overground: Shoreditch High St.) in Shoreditch, where you'll find the best vintage shops in the city. They're on almost every street, and new ones seem to appear daily alongside pop-up stores just here for the weekend. Make sure you hit **Absolute Vintage** at 15 Hanbury St. (www.absolutevintage.co.uk; ✆ 020/7247-3883; Tube: Liverpool St./Aldgate East) and the smaller **Blondie** (p. 287) around the corner, on the way to the antiques market in **Spitalfields** (p. 277).

A short stroll north, **Columbia Road** is more than just a flower market (p. 276)—in many ways, the main attractions are the artist studios that line the street. Head up every single one of those staircases you see. If the door is open, you're allowed in. You'll find artists at work and shops such as **J&B—The Shop** at no. 158 (www.buddug.com; ✆ 07704/708577; Overground: Shoreditch High St.), selling handmade notebooks and unusual jewelry. Once you're done with the studios and shops—**Ryan Town** (p. 293) sells fabulous paper cut designs. And from 3pm on Sundays, everything at the flower market will be going cheap.

Still in the mood for more shops? Then **Westfield Stratford** (p. 279) isn't far away. The younger sister to the Westfield Shepherd's Bush (p. 278) is a huge pull for the East with its convenient transport links.

Columbia Road flower market.

NORTH LONDON

Shoppers can split north London in two: Camden has its market and heavy metal and Goth shops; Primrose Hill and its surrounds has perfect little streets full of local finds. The two could not be more different, but both are equally enticing.

Primrose Hill (Tube: Chalk Farm) is Camden's northern neighbor, and the Cinderella to North London's ugly sister. Everything is pretty, perfect, and rather posh. The original cupcakery **Primrose Bakery,** 69 Gloucester Ave. (www. primrosebakery.org.uk; ℂ 020/7483-4222), is here, and the area is popular with fashion celebs such as Kate Moss and Sienna Miller. Designer stores, chi-chi art galleries, and overpriced clothes are what you'll find in this part of town. Some might claim that there's not much substance, but if you're willing to search, there are beautiful interiors shops, and great frocks in **Anna,** 126 Regent's Park Rd. (www.shopatanna.co.uk; ℂ 020/7483-0411).

Camden (Tube: Camden Town) is anything but dull. Even if the bustling leather-clad crowds aren't your thing, it's worth a stroll just for the spectacle: street-food stalls and Goths in full make-up at lunchtime against a backdrop of Camden Lock and the canal. **Camden Market** (see below) itself has changed somewhat since a devastating fire in 2008. The refurbishment has tidied things up a little, although some might argue that some of the charm has gone with it. The stalls are more settled now, **the Stables** area is more exciting, and everything is just perhaps a little more refined; it still has some rough and ready Camden charm, but also a wider appeal.

Angel—in Islington, south and east of Camden—bridges the gap between indie cool, and luxury and boutique style. Head to **Camden Passage** for the best of vintage (it's best to avoid the confusingly sometimes trade-only Decorexi). The

Camden Lock.

weekend market stalls are interesting, but the real charm lies in the street's small shops. Upscale vintage and specialized antiques flank both sides, leading up to Essex Road and Upper Street. Both these major thoroughfares have shops lining them: **Essex Road** is good for independent designers; **Upper Street** sticks to high-street and specialist chains such as a branch of **Joy** (p. 288) and **Oliver Bonas,** at nos. 147–148 (www.oliverbonas.com; ℭ **020/7424-5305**).

The area leads up to **Stoke Newington**—a trendy neighborhood, which is something of a shock next to its rougher Dalston neighbor. Here you'll find organic grocery stores and everything a young hipster could want whether it's vinyl records or mid-century clothing and furniture.

SOUTHEAST LONDON
Greenwich & Blackheath

Although many London stores are open on Sundays, the best weekend shopping is still the stalls of Greenwich's flea and craft markets. The ideal way to arrive is to float downstream on a boat from Embankment or Westminster piers (see "River Cruises on the Thames," p. 424). The trip takes about a half-hour. Both the DLR station (Cutty Sark) and the pier are minutes from the indoor craft market, **Greenwich Market** (see below). Greenwich town center isn't very big: Follow the signs—or the crowd—and you'll find the market bursting with art and crafts, both global and local. The shops around the outside are also worth a browse. Be sure to walk through the food section when you're done, if only to try the *churros* filled with *dulce de leche* (milk caramel).

You're now only 5 minutes from Greenwich rail station, on Greenwich High Road, from where there's a train back to the center of London every half-hour until about 11:30pm. Make sure you check out the shops around the rest of Greenwich first. **Joy's** (p. 288) flagship store is here. Buy pies and tarts at **Rhodes Bakery,** 37 King William Walk (www.rhodesbakery.co.uk; ℭ **020/8858-8995**), or vintage accessories and retro music from **Beehive,** 322 Creek Rd. (ℭ **020/8858-1964**). If you have time for a rummage through secondhand books, head to **Halcyon,** 1 Greenwich South Street (www.halcyonbooks.co.uk; ℭ **020/8305-2675**).

MALLS & MARKETS
Markets

London can't quite compete with the flea markets of Paris, but it does increasingly hold its own. London's markets are smaller, more niche, and perhaps slightly too expensive—but they are lots of fun. Take cash with you (and keep it somewhere safe), as most markets are a bit of a walk from any ATMs. Do haggle if you find something you like. Most items can be bought for cheaper than their price tag so ask for something for nothing, and get a bargain.

Bermondsey Antiques Market ★★ This South London market is a treasury of furniture and hidden antique gems. But it comes at a price; the price being your beauty sleep. It's open only on Fridays, starts at 4am, and continues through to 1pm. Unfortunately for night owls, the best time to get here is early in the morning. Bermondsey Sq., SE1. www.bermondseysquare.co.uk/antiques. ℭ **020/7351-5353.** Tube: Bermondsey.

Billingsgate Market ★ One of the most exciting markets in London is, however, not exactly a tourist destination. If you have a love of seafood, and early mornings, this is the perfect market for you, but you'll need to be up with the birds and aiming to arrive before 7am for the best bargains. Bear in mind that this is a real fish market and you're shopping with restaurant owners. It's no frills but you'll get the freshest seafood in the country at the best prices. They're open Tuesday to Saturday 5am to 8:30am, but avoid the day after a public holiday (p. 48), when the market is shut as there's no fish to sell. Trafalgar Way, E14. www.billingsgate-market.org.uk. ✆ **020/7517-3548.** Tube/DLR: Canary Wharf.

Borough Market ★★★ One of the largest outdoor food markets in the world, Borough market sells a mammoth variety of delectables from across the globe. Best buys are the more unusual items and British-reared meats, rather than standard food-market fare, which is aimed at tourists with money to burn. If you're buying foodie gifts to take home, make sure you

Borough Market stall.

check what you're allowed to take back through customs, or just nibble your way around the entire market and have a very tasty (if pricey) lunch. The market is open Thursday 11am to 5pm, Friday noon to 6pm, and Saturday 9am to 5pm. Try to avoid Saturday lunchtimes, when everyone in London seems to descend. Southwark St., SE1. www.boroughmarket.org.uk. ✆ **020/7407-1002.** Tube: London Bridge.

Camden Market and the Stables ★ This market has had a revamp since the 2008 fire, but it hasn't lost any of its grungy charm. There's no doubting that Camden isn't the prettiest area in London, but it is cool in its dinginess. If you're looking for an alternative shopping scene, head here for all the silver jewelry and PVC clubwear you'll ever need. It's best to avoid the food stalls selling questionable lunchtime offerings, though. Most stalls are open every day of the year except Christmas day. Many stay open well past 6pm. Camden High St., NW1. ✆ **020/7974-6767.** Tube: Camden Town.

Columbia Road Flower Market ★★ This East London flower market really is worth the trip (unless you suffer from hayfever). The flowers are beautiful, but it's the shops on either side of the road that deserve the most attention. Make sure you go in every open door—they're studios and usually full of lovely things. **Vintage Heaven,** 82 Columbia Rd. (www.vintageheaven.co.uk; ✆ **01277/215968**), has all sorts of tea sets and a little tea room out back. One or two shops on Columbia Road are open during the week, but most only open on weekends. The market itself is open from 8am until 4pm every Sunday. Columbia Rd., E2. www.columbiaroad.info. ☏ **07708/921550.** Tube: Old St./Overground: Hoxton.

Covent Garden ★★   Right in the middle of town, Covent Garden conveniently offers several markets running Monday through Saturday from 10am to 6pm. The best way to tackle them is to dive straight in and explore the area, stopping to watch the human statues and magicians along the way. **Apple Market** is the bustling market in the courtyard, where traders sell pretty much everything. Some of the merchandise is truly unusual, and you'll even find a palm reader to tell you your fortune. Craftspeople sell their own wares except on Monday, when antiques dealers take over for the day. Out back, on the corner of Southampton Street, is **Jubilee Market** (☏ **020/7836-2139**), also an antiques market on Monday; Tuesday to Sunday, it's a fancy, hippy-style market with cheap clothes and books. At the indoor section of Covent Garden Market (in a superbly restored hall) specialty shops sell fashion and herbs, gifts and toys, books and dollhouses, cigars, and there's also the **Real Food Market,** which includes excellent food stalls, particularly in the run-up to Christmas. The Piazza, WC2. www.coventgarden londonuk.com. ☏ **020/7836-9136.** Tube: Covent Garden.

Greenwich Indoor Market ★★   A haven for craft and vintage lovers, this is a real gem of a market. Open Wednesday through Sunday it's great for gift buying. There are little boutiques and cute shops around the outside (open all week), and a food market at weekends. There are smaller markets nearby as well—a farmers' market in nearby Blackheath station car park (Sunday only, from 10am to 2pm), and **Greenwich Clocktower Market** (www.clocktowermarket.co.uk) on Greenwich High Street whose outdoor area doesn't look like anything special at first but it has some packed antiques' stalls and is constantly growing. Greenwich Market, SE10. www.greenwichmarket.net. ☏ **020/8269-5096.** DLR: Cutty Sark.

Marylebone Farmers' Market ★ 📷   This is a nifty little market on Sundays (10am to 2pm). It's not cheap (we're at the fancy end of town now), but if you want good organic produce, you should come here. Although nowhere near as big as **Borough Market** (see above), it is classy. And with **La Fromagerie** (p. 292) and **Ginger Pig** (p. 291) right next door, you have some great culinary treats to hunt down. Car park, Cramer St., W1. www.lfm.org.uk. No phone. Tube: Baker St.

Portobello Market ★★   This is the market for West Londoners, spanning the whole of Portobello Road, and made world famous by Richard Curtis' movie *Notting Hill.* It's much more diverse than Curtis made it look, and it'll take you all day to walk down. You'll pass through cheap tat, leather goods, antiques, and craft stalls. Take your time, enjoy, and haggle like you've never haggled before. It's open Monday to Wednesday and Friday from 8am to 6:30pm; Thursday 8am to 2pm; and Saturday 6am to 6:30pm. Portobello Rd., W10. www.portobellomarket.org. ☏ **020/8960-5599.** Tube: Notting Hill Gate.

Spitalfields Market & UpMarket ★   Spitalfields is one of the best allrounders in London. The well-chosen boutiques fit in with the fashionable locals, but the old market is among the best for vintage clothing and antiques. The cool **Sunday UpMarket** (www.sundayupmarket.co.uk) is a 5-minute walk away at the Old Truman Brewery on Brick Lane and if you're looking for more personal homemade items and unique clothes, this is the place for you. It's open on Sundays from 10am to 5pm. There's only one ATM nearby, and there's always a long

Sunday secondhand street market near Brick Lane.

line of people, so come with cash. The food at both markets is tasty and more interesting than the curry houses, so make sure you arrive hungry. Commercial St., E1. ✆ **020/7247-8556.** Tube: Liverpool St./Overground: Shoreditch High St.

Malls

Canary Wharf   They're a stylish bunch in Canary Wharf, and highlights of this center include swanky homewares from **The White Company** and dresses from **Whistles.** Make sure you pop into **Space NK** for some of the best toiletries around. Maps are dotted around the confusingly laid out center but you will still get lost. The plus side to this area is that unless you hit the madness of the office lunch break, it's always quiet, leaving you plenty of leisurely browsing time—even at weekends. 1 Reuters Plaza, E14. www.canarywharf.com. ✆ **020/7477-1477.** Tube/DLR: Canary Wharf.

One New Change   The City was one area that was crying out for a decent shopping center, and it finally has one. It's surprisingly eclectic, and unsurprisingly expensive. High-end high street, overpriced suits, and all sorts of poshness are going on here: **Hobbs** and **Jigsaw** take care of the women, while **All Saints** and **Hugo Boss** look after the guys. The shops are populist but the brands are all about making a statement, which is exactly what City folk want. 1 New Change, EC4. www.onenewchange.com. No phone. Tube: St. Paul's.

Westfield ★★★   The biggest central mall, Westfield has revolutionized shopping in West London. If you're looking for high-street and high-end clobber, you'll find it all here. There is also an excellent selection of restaurants (**Wahaca** does decent Mexican street food; see p. 208). It doesn't matter if you take a trip at weekends or on a Monday, Westfield will always be busy, and it'll take you an entire weekend to visit every shop. Ariel Way, W12. http://uk.westfield.com/london. ✆ **020/3371-2300**. Tube: Shepherd's Bush.

Westfield Stratford City   The expansion of the Westfield shopping group has started the makeover of east London. It's more of the same, but it's a huge coup for the area—Stratford isn't exactly known for its shopping. Canary Wharf (see above) might be a little quiet for some so if you're planning on doing some serious spending this is a better choice. Olympic Park, E20. http://uk.westfield.com/stratfordcity. ✆ **0208/221-7300**. Tube/DLR: Stratford.

Whiteleys ★   This Bayswater center is a bit more upscale than its Westfield neighbor. It's also a little more fashion-centered, so expect to spot cute pop-up shops and brands you've not heard of before. It's smaller but all the better for it. The shopping centers in London don't have too much soul, but this one at least tries to have a personality. 144 Queensway, W12. www.whiteleys.com. ✆ **020/7229-8844.** Tube: Bayswater or Queensway.

SHOPPING A TO Z
Antiques & Collectibles

Alfie's Antique Market   This is the biggest and one of the best-stocked conglomerates of antiques' dealers in London, crammed into the premises of a 19th-century store. It has more than 370 stalls, showrooms, and workshops in over 3,252 sq. m (35,004 sq. ft.) of floor space. A whole antiques' district has grown up around Alfie's along Church Street. 13–25 Church St., NW8. www.alfiesantiques.com. ✆ **020/7723-6066.** Tube: Marylebone or Edgware Rd.

Camden Passage ★★   Angel is best known for busy Upper Street and trendy Essex Road, so it's surprising to stumble upon such a cute little passageway packed with antiques' stalls and shops on Wednesdays and Saturdays. There are some surprising finds here, but most popular are the stalls selling on-trend tea sets, and the jewelry stands so full you can't see the table. You'll have to do a bit of digging to find the best stuff, but that's half the fun. Camden Passage, N1. www.camdenpassageislington.co.uk. No phone. Tube: Angel.

Crystal Palace Antiques ★★★   In South London, a few stops on the train from London Bridge, you'll find four floors of antiques. Crystal Palace Antiques is housed in a Victorian warehouse in the heart of a beautiful suburb of London. It's one to make a day of. Furniture and large items are often the best purchases, so check you can get them home before you buy. Be willing to spend if you come here, because you're likely to want everything you clap eyes on. Junction of Westow Hill & Jasper Rd., SE19. www.crystalpalaceantiques.com. ✆ **020/8480-7042.** Overground: Crystal Palace.

The Junk Shop ★★★ 🎁   Greenwich has been hiding a little secret since the outdoor market closed. To non-locals, this shop looks small, but follow the precarious stairs inside and you'll find a cavern of vintage and antiques' stalls, all manned by friendly dealers. Excellent prices, good banter and bartering, and unusual items make this shop a must-visit if you like your wares old and your shops secret. 9 Greenwich South St., SE10. ✆ **020/8305-1666.** DLR/Rail: Greenwich.

Grays Antiques and Grays Mews   These markets have been converted into walk-in stands with independent dealers. There are two floors, two buildings, and more than 200 dealers selling everything you could imagine from all over the world. If it's antique, you'll no doubt find it here. There's a cafe in each building too—shopping for priceless finds is thirsty work. 58 Davies St. and 1–7 Davies Mews, W1. www.graysantiques.com. ✆ **020/7629-7034.** Tube: Bond St.

Art, Crafts & Museum Stores

Blade Rubber Stamps　This unique little shop has gained a bit of a following in the crafty and stationery-loving camps. They sell all things stamp related (the rubber kind, not postage). It's only been open since 1993, but it feels like it's been part of London for centuries. Visit after a trip to the nearby British Museum (p. 96). 12 Bury Place, WC1. www.custom.bladerubberstamps.co.uk. ✆ **0845/873-7005.** Tube: Holborn.

Camden Arts Centre　The Camden Arts Centre is the hub of art in North London and aims to "put you in direct contact with artists." Alongside the art, it has a cafe, bookstore, and studios in addition to its exhibition galleries, where the displays are frequently changed. Arkwright Rd., NW3. www.camdenartscentre.org. ✆ **020/7472-5500.** Tube: Finchley Rd./Overground: Finchley Rd. & Frognal.

Contemporary Applied Arts　This association encourages traditional and progressive contemporary artwork. Many of Britain's best-established craftspeople, as well as promising talents, are represented within their space. The gallery houses a diverse display of glass, ceramics, textiles, wood, furniture, jewelry, and metalwork—all by contemporary artisans. A program of special exhibitions focuses on innovations in craftwork; these exhibitions turn around quickly. 2 Percy St., W1. www.caa.org.uk. ✆ **020/7436-2344.** Tube: Tottenham Court Rd.

Drink, Shop & Do ★★★　The title of this shop sums up its ethos. Get yourself a drink, do some shopping, and then do some . . . doing. This is the latest crafty venue in the city, but the focus is on the cafe and shopping with this one—although they also run regular craft classes. They also have a night club next door for drinking, shopping, and dancing. 9 Caledonian Rd., N1. www.drinkshopdo.com. ✆ **020/3343-9138**. Tube: King's Cross.

Grosvenor Prints　London's largest stock of antique prints, ranging from the 17th to the 20th centuries, is on sale here. Views of London are the biggest-selling items, which is perfect if you're looking for a reminder of your trip. Some prints depict significant moments in the city's history, including the Great Fire of 1666. The British are great animal lovers, so expect plenty of prints of dogs and horses as well. 19 Shelton St., WC2. www.grosvenorprints.com. ✆ **020/7836-1979.** Tube: Covent Garden.

The Make Lounge　London's premier craft venue now has a shop that sells crafts from the lesson teachers, as well as unique jewelry, and crafting books and magazines. You'll also find craft kits to continue your new hobby after your class, including wool, jewelry kits, and embroidery thread. It's a small shop in an ever-expanding business, but perfectly suited to crafters new and old. 49–51 Barnsbury St., N1. www.themakelounge.com. ✆ **020/7609-0275.** Tube: Angel or Highbury & Islington/Overground: Caledonian Rd. & Barnsbury.

The Southbank Centre Shop ★★★　What was once a small and perfectly formed design shop has had a makeover and expansion and now sprawls across two gorgeous floors. You'll find it difficult to leave here without spending money. The emphasis is on housewares, but you won't find anything boring in this shop. It's not cheap, but the designers focus on British and you'll find designs exclusive to the Southbank venue. Festival Terrace, SE1. www.southbankcentre.co.uk. © **020/7921-0773.** Tube: Waterloo.

Tate Modern ★★   If you're an art lover, you should definitely swing by Tate Modern for a browse in their shop. It's a great store, full of prints and more art books than you'll ever be able to carry. Everything is inspired by the exhibitions, and if you see a piece of art you like when you're walking around, be sure to note the number so you can pick up a much more affordable postcard version to send home; it's easier than trying to sneak Monet's *Water Lilies* into your bag. Bankside, SE1. www.tate.org.uk/modern. © **020/7887-8888**. Tube: Southwark.

V&A Shop ★★★   The V&A has the best museum shop in London, perfect for design lovers. It stocks everything from exotic jewelry inspired by the exhibitions to their own line of toiletries and reclaimed prints. They take design seriously, and it's celebrated in every single item in the shop. It's worth the trip to the museum just for the shop, even if you don't have time to look around the (mostly free) exhibits. Cromwell Rd., SW7. www.vam.ac.uk. © **020/7942-2000.** Tube: South Kensington.

Beauty, Cosmetics & Perfume

Angela Flanders ★★   This tiny Columbia Road shop sells bespoke perfumes and home scents. Try the English Rose perfume; it's basically the countryside in a bottle. As with the rest of Columbia Road, you can only rely on finding it open on weekends. 96 Columbia Rd., E2. www.angelaflanders-perfumer.com. © **020/7739-7555.** Tube: Old St./Overground: Hoxton

D.R Harris ★ 👔   This little shop is over 200 years old and holds the warrant to HRH Prince of Wales. Real bristle shaving brushes, soaps wrapped in paper, and high quality colognes: This is a great place to browse and pick up gifts for traditionalists. It's a real slice of a London that once was. 29 St James's St., SW1. www.drharris.co.uk. © **020/7930-3915**. Tube: Green Park.

Miller Harris ★★   Arguably the most famous perfumers in London. Their Nouvelle Edition is incredibly popular although hard to get your hands on. Their scents make their way into candles and boy products as well. The Miller Harris scent obsession even goes as far as tea—there's a perfumed tea room at the back of the store. 21 Bruton St., W1. www.millerharris.com. © **020/7629-7750.** Tube: Green Park.

Lush ✋   You don't need a guidebook to find Lush—you'll be able to smell it a street away. The toiletries are known for their strong scent and you'll either love it, or barely be able to stand in the shop. Come here for cute gifts, bath oils, and presents for girly girls. 1–3 Quadrant Arcade, 80–82 Regent St., W1. www.lush.co.uk. © **020/7434-3953.** Tube: Piccadilly Circus. Other locations throughout London.

Books, Maps & Stationery

Blackwell's   Although smaller than Foyles over the road, it has a particularly good selection of academic books. This is an excellent bookshop if you know what you're looking for. 100 Charing Cross Rd., WC2. http://bookshop.blackwell.co.uk. © **020/7292-5100.** Tube: Tottenham Court Rd.

Bookseller Crow on the Hill ★★★   Right at the heart of the Crystal Palace community, this is much more than just a store that sells books. Their range is fantastic (especially the children's section) and they're very friendly. Browse, buy, and leave happy. 50 Westow St., SE19. www.booksellercrow.co.uk. ☎ **020/8771-8831**. Overground: Crystal Palace.

Books for Cooks 🎁 Passionate about nothing but cookery books? If you hang out in the kitchen (or want to be inspired to start) this shop is a joy to spend time in. They even have a cafe and host regular events. 4 Blenheim Crescent, W11. www.booksforcooks.com. ☎ **020/7221-1992.** Tube: Ladbroke Grove.

Daunt Books ★★ Daunt specializes in travel books and it has an enormous selection of them. It's a beautiful building, one that you'll want to spend hours browsing in. The only problem will be taking the inspiration too far and booking yourself a trip within minutes of leaving. 83 Marylebone High St., W1. www.daunt books.co.uk. ☎ **020/7224-2295.** Tube: Baker St. Other locations throughout London.

Foyles ★★ Foyles has an impressive array of hardbacks and paperbacks, as well as travel maps, new records, CDs, videotapes, and sheet music. The store also has a jazz cafe and music venue that hosts regular live performances alongside the literary events. Foyles is an institution in London, and despite it no longer having piles of books all over the place, its popularity and success is largely down to the passionate people who work here. 113–119 Charing Cross Rd., WC2. www. foyles.co.uk. ☎ **020/7437-5660**. Tube: Tottenham Court Rd. or Leicester Sq. Other locations throughout London.

Hatchards On the south side of Piccadilly, Hatchards offers a wide range of books on all subjects and is particularly renowned in the areas of fiction, biography, travel, cookery, gardening, art, history, and finance. In addition, Hatchards is second-to-none in its range of books on royalty. 187 Piccadilly, W1. www.hatchards. co.uk. ☎ **020/7439-9921**. Tube: Piccadilly Circus or Green Park.

Magma ★ Part bookshop, part gift store and housewares shop, Magma is excellent at selling cool things that you don't need. All sorts of trendy coffee-table books and stationery items are tucked away inside. It's all a little bit too-cool-for-school, but luckily the stock is good. 8 & 16 Earlham St., WC2. www.magmabooks.com. ☎ **020/7240-8498**. Tube: Covent Garden.

Map House of London An ideal place to find an offbeat souvenir, the Map House sells antique maps and engravings, plus a vast selection of old prints of London and England, both original and reproduction. The cost of a century-old original engraving begins at £24. 54 Beauchamp Place, SW3. www.themaphouse.com. ☎ **020/7589-4325.** Tube: Knightsbridge.

Paperchase One of the most popular stationery stores, this shop on Tottenham Court Road is a mecca for paper lovers. It's expensive, but the choice is excellent, especially the greetings cards and notebooks. If you're a fan of scribbling, you'll find it very easy to spend your money here. 213–215 Tottenham Court Rd., W1. www.paperchase.co.uk. ☎ **020/7467-6200**. Tube: Goodge St. Other locations throughout London.

Persephone ★★★ 🎁 Want something unique that no one else will have on their shelves? Even the most discerning bookworm will find something special in Persephone. They source out-of-print texts by women, and then edit and bind them in their own fashionable endpapers. You won't find the latest Margaret Atwood in here, but you'll discover something new and rare. It's a book lover's haven. 59 Lamb's Conduit St., WC1. www.persephonebooks.co.uk. ☎ **020/7242-9292.** Tube: Holborn or Russell Sq.

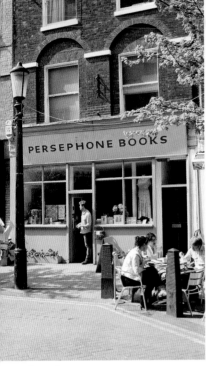

Persephone.

Smythson ★★ The most iconic (and upscale) stationery shop in London, Smythson is stylish, elegant, and has a price tag to make you wince. The leather-bound diaries and notebooks are the perfect gifts for fashionable folk. You'll also discover stationery events and sometimes even graphology going on in the West London branch. 135 Sloane St., SW1. www.smythson.com. ✆ 020/7730-5520. Tube: Sloane Sq. Other locations throughout London.

Stanfords ★ Established in 1852, Stanfords is the world's largest map shop. Many maps, including worldwide touring and survey maps that are unavailable elsewhere, are stocked here. It's also an excellent travel bookstore. 12–14 Long Acre, WC2. www.stanfords.co.uk. ✆ 020/7836-1321. Tube: Covent Garden.

Waterstones ★ The biggest bookstore in Europe and the flagship store of a giant chain seen countrywide is still a fantastic place to shop. Staff tend to know their stuff. It spans five floors meaning that even over Christmas it isn't too crowded. The fifth-floor restaurant and bar, **5th View** (www.5thview.co.uk) offers excellent food and stunning views. 203–206 Piccadilly, SW1. www.waterstones.com. ✆ 020/7851-2400. Tube: Piccadilly Circus. Other locations throughout London.

Clothing & Accessories
CHILDREN

Amaia ☺ With descriptions like "easy-to-wear" and "elegant" you'd be forgiven for thinking that Amaia was a high-end designer boutique. And it is. Not for adults, though—it's for the well-groomed children of London used to the finer things in life. 14 Cale St., SW3. www.amaiakids.co.uk. ✆ 020/7590-0999. Tube: South Kensington.

Elias & Grace ★★★ ☺ Where do you go for the best dresses you can buy your little ones? Elias & Grace is in the fancy "village" of Primrose Hill. You'll find everything from designers Chloe and Marni, all perfectly sized for your mini-you. 158 Regent's Park Rd., NW1. www.eliasandgrace.com. ✆ 020/7449-0574. Tube: Chalk Farm.

Frogs and Fairies ☺ Buying shoes for children is often a nightmare (and they grow out of clothes in minutes) but Frogs and Fairies makes it fun with the latest styles and giant games to keep youngsters busy. 223 Blackstock Rd., N5. www.frogsandfairies.co.uk. ✆ 020/7690-1341. Tube: Arsenal.

Sasti ☺ If you're looking for something original, Sasti is an affordable children's boutique. It has one-off outfits for newborns and toddlers, so you can buy bright prints and cute outfits without spending hundreds. 281 Portobello Rd., W10. www.sasti.co.uk. ✆ **020/8960-1125.** Tube: Ladbroke Grove.

JEWELRY

Comfort Station ★★★  No jewelry brand does quirky elegance quite like Comfort Station. From their necklaces holding tiny pages of poetry, to the earrings with the coordinates for Hope (a town in Devon) and Love (in Barbados), all their pieces are special. Each one has a story to tell, and yet items rarely go over the £100 mark. You'll also find the range in **Anthropologie** (p. 293). 22 Cheshire St., E2. www.comfortstation.co.uk. ✆ **020/7033-9099.** Tube: Liverpool St./Overground: Shoreditch High St.

Lazy Oaf ★ If you want something different (and well-priced), Lazy Oaf is it. Whether it's a brooch that announces that you're a lousy dancer, or a necklace with a slightly offensive slogan, Lazy Oaf will inspire you to buy something out of the ordinary and just a little bit cheeky. 19 Foubert's Place, W1. www.lazyoaf.co.uk. ✆ **020/7287-2060.** Tube: Oxford Circus.

Lazy Oaf.

Kabiri ★★★ This high end jewelry store doesn't take itself too seriously. Everything is colorful and playful, often not cheap, although you'll find a few pieces under £50. It's a fun place to shop and very stylish indeed. 37 Marylebone High St., W1. www.kabiri.co.uk. ✆ **020/7224-1808.** Tube: Baker St.

Tatty Devine ★★ Tatty Devine started the acrylic jewelry trend way before anyone else, and is still very good at it. Everything is handmade, super cool, and covetable. A dinosaur skeleton around your neck might not be subtle . . . but that's a good thing, right? Cute, whimsical, and fun is what Tatty Devine do best. They have a branch near Seven Dials in Covent Garden, but the flagship store is in the East End. 236 Brick Lane, E1. www.tattydevine.com. ✆ **020/7739-9191.** Tube: Liverpool St./Overground: Shoreditch High St.Also at 44 Monmouth St., WC2.

LINGERIE

Bravissimo If you're rather gifted in the chest department, Bravissimo is the ideal place for lingerie shopping. They specialize in larger sizes (from a D to an L cup) and offer an excellent (and free) measuring service. They have a wide range of styles, as well as their own clothing range, Pepperberry. 28 Margaret St., W1. www. bravissimo.com. ✆ **0207/462-5620**. Tube: Oxford Circus.

Bordello ★★   Scratchy lace is not desirable any time of the year, and Bordello have raised the bar when it comes to where the ladies of London buy their smalls. It's expensive here, but everything is sexy and screams luxury. If you're looking for very special lingerie, it should be the first place you visit—and it'll probably be the last place as well. 55 Great Eastern St., EC2. www.bordello-london.com. ✆ **020/7503-3334**. Tube: Old St./Overground: Shoreditch High St.

Myla ★★★   If you like your silk fine, your lace of the very best quality and your wallet a little lighter, Myla is the small shop for you. Their lingerie is simply beautiful. Sexy garments of the highest quality don't come cheap (expect to pay hundreds for a bra in some cases) so try and catch them when there's a sale on. 77 Lonsdale Rd., W11. www.myla.com. ✆ **020/7792-8880**. Tube: Ladbroke Grove.

Rigby & Peller ★   The most famous of lingerie brands, Rigby & Peller are corsetiers to the Queen and an institution amongst London women. Their bra-fitting is regarded as the very best in town and that part is free, which should soften the blow of their hefty garment prices. Still, you're paying for the very best in London. 22A Conduit St., W1S. www.rigbyandpeller.com. ✆ **0845/076-5545**. Tube: Green Park.

MEN

Folk ★★★   Folk is far too stylish for its own good, but that's the appeal. Trendy designers and a preppy look are the trademark style of this shop. They do a small line in women's clothes, but the focus is very much on the guys. 49 Lamb's Conduit St., WC1. www.folkclothing.com. ✆ **020/7404-6458**. Tube: Holborn.

Ozwald Boateng ★★   If you're after swanky threads and a suit cut better than anywhere else, Savile Row should be your first stop—and Ozwald Boateng knows his way around a pattern. Expect a perfect fit, lush fabric, and a price tag to make your eyes water. 30 Savile Row, W1. www.ozwaldboateng.co.uk. ✆ **020/7440-5231**. Tube: Piccadilly Circus.

Peckham Rye   Funky tailoring and accessories—all with a bit of a twist—are what to expect when you shop in Peckham Rye. If you can carry off yellow check, you'll have a blast. Skinny ties, woolen scarves, and a distinct Swinging Sixties' vibe are all here for you to browse. 11 Newburgh St., W1. www.peckhamryelondon.com. ✆ **020/7734-5181**. Tube: Oxford Circus.

Paul Smith ★★   Sharp shirts and stripes are very much the order of the day in Paul Smith. The British designer is known for his smart design often dashed with a little sense of humor. His shirts are very popular (it's helpful if you're a fan of color) and you'll find a quirky range of accessories. It's not cheap, but classic style and good tailoring rarely is. 122 Kensington Park Rd., W11. www.paulsmith.co.uk. ✆ **020/7727-3553**. Tube: Notting Hill. Other locations throughout London.

SHOES & ACCESSORIES

Accessorize ★★   This high-street chain store is perhaps the best on the high street for easy-to-wear, well-priced accessories and jewelry. You'll find one in most main train stations and airports, and on almost every major shopping street. Where there are people, there's an Accessorize—which is a good thing, because they have a fantastic range of items to complete an outfit. Hats, bags, and leather gloves are the best buys, and if you're in town make sure you hit their January sale, where most things are half price. 1 Piccadilly, W1. www.accessorize.com. ✆ **020/7494-0566.** Tube: Piccadilly Circus. Other locations throughout London.

James Smith & Sons ★★★   This is an authentic London institution. Specializing in umbrellas, it's been open since 1830 and is still a family business. They make their own brollies, and the shop is nothing short of spectacular to look at. It's also very handy if you get caught in the rain that England is known for. 53 New Oxford St., WC1. www.james-smith.co.uk. ✆ **020/7836-4731.** Tube: Tottenham Court Rd.

Kate Kanzier ★ 👜   Kate Kanzier might be the best value shoe shop in the whole of London. The shop sells fashionable brogues in every color you could imagine, for around £30 a pair. The quality probably isn't first rank, but when you're paying so little for a favorite among London's most fashionable, you can't complain. 67–69 Leather Lane, EC1. www.katekanzier.com. ✆ **020/7242-7232.** Tube: Farringdon.

Kurt Geiger   One of London's very best shoe shops. The mix of convenience of lots of brands under one roof, and the stylish designs mean you'll come out with more shoes than you can wear on your feet. Their men's section is on a par with everything else. They have excellent sale sections so keep your eyes peeled for half price peep toes. 1 James St., W1. www.kurtgeiger.com. ✆ **020/7240-6269.** Tube: Covent Garden.

Lisa Stickley ★★   This range of accessories has become so popular that there's also a range at the department store **Debenhams** (see below), and pieces in the **Tate Modern** shop (p. 281). A mix of typography and floral patterns are their trademark and the bags are especially popular. 74 Landor St., SW9. www.lisa stickleylondon.com. ✆ **020/7737-8067.** Tube: Clapham North.

Lulu Guinness   This self-taught British bag designer launched her business in 1989. Many of the world's greatest retail outlets, including **Fortnum & Mason** (p. 290), sell her signature bags, which have been immortalized in the fashion collection at the **V&A Museum** (p. 127). She's popular with British celebrities. 3 Ellis St., SW1. www.luluguinness.com. ✆ **020/7823-4828.** Tube: Sloane Sq.

Luna & Curious ★★★ 👜   Have you ever thought to yourself, "I wish I could buy sexy designer tights and false paper eyelashes shaped like horses in the same shop?" Well, strange as it sounds, it works well at Luna & Curious. The only way to describe it is as an accessory shop, but it feels more special than that. The beautiful things make you feel like you're shopping in Wonderland, and you're not (always) charged hundreds for the privilege. 24–26 Calvert Ave., E2. www.shopluna andcurious.com. ✆ **020/7033-4411.** Tube: Liverpool St./Overground: Shoreditch High St.

The Old Curiosity Shop ★★ 👜   Men are rarely well-catered for in the shoe department, but this shop is one of the most special in the city. It is the very "curiosity shop" that Charles Dickens based his novel on. They stick to traditional styles and the men's selection is better than the women's. With such a beautiful building, steeped in so much history, it's worth popping in even if you aren't planning to buy. 13–14 Portsmouth St., WC2. www.curiosityuk.com. ✆ **020/7405-9891.** Tube: Holborn.

The Old Curiosity Shop.

VINTAGE

Bang Bang ★★★ 🎁 The flashy designer-clad mannequins in the window make this Goodge Street store stand out among the secondhand computer shops and lunchtime pitstops. It specializes in designer clothes and high-end high-street, but all at bargain prices. You'll find cut-price Armani and cheap Topshop under the same roof, but the stock changes regularly. Best bargains are the accessories and tailored items. Although prices are fair and everything is excellent quality, staff can be a little surly. 21 Goodge St., W1. ✆ **020/7631-4191.** Tube: Goodge St.

Blondie ★ This is the sister store to the larger **Absolute Vintage** at 15 Hanbury St. (www.absolutevintage.co.uk; ✆ **020/7247-3883**). Don't let the small stature of the shop put you off—it has some real gems inside. Everything is arranged by color, so you can head straight to the red polka dots or little black dresses. There's also an enormous shoe collection (mostly in smaller sizes, which is always the way with vintage) and a wide selection of Dior sunglasses. 114–118 Commercial St., E1. ✆ **020/7247-0050.** Tube: Liverpool St./Overground: Shoreditch High St.

East End Thrift Store Another vintage shop that's worth the trip to East London is inside a large warehouse off the unattractive Stepney Green Road. Inside you'll find a massive array of vintage clothing, all well priced, but of varying quality and styles. Men do well here, thanks to an excellent selection of shirts, but vintage newbies might have to do a bit of hunting to find easier-to-wear items. Assembly Passage, E1. www.theeastendthriftstore.com. ✆ **020/7423-9700.** Tube: Stepney Green or Whitechapel.

Emporium ★★   A trip over the river to Greenwich takes you to this classy vintage shop. Men fare slightly better for browsing (the best stuff for women is secreted in protective covers), but the accessories cabinet is an Aladdin's cave of treasures. 330–332 Creek Rd., SE10. ⓒ 020/8305-1670. DLR: Cutty Sark.

Peekaboo Vintage   This vintage range was made popular by the concession in Oxford Street's Topshop. The store in the Newburgh Quarter fits in well with its neighbors and houses a truly beautiful range of vintage frocks, but you certainly pay the price for its popular name. 2 Ganton St. W1. www.peekaboovintage.com. ⓒ 020/7434-4142. Tube: Oxford Circus.

Rokit   There are three locations for this small chain, but the most central and best stocked is in Covent Garden. The trick here is to browse at leisure, looking for that perfect item—that's when vintage shopping really becomes fun. You'll find the best buys in leather, denim, and 1970s' fashions. 42 Sheldon St., WC2. www.rokit.co.uk. ⓒ 020/7836-6547. Tube: Covent Garden. Other locations throughout London.

East End Thrift Store.

Vintage Hart ★★ 📖   A quality vintage shop inside a quality pub? That's certainly a unique selling point, and one that Vintage Hart is lucky to boast. The small shop makes up for its lack of size with excellent quality and unique garments for women. The owners are friendly and helpful plus, after you've made your purchases, you can have lunch and a drink in the excellent pub. White Hart, 96 Church Rd., SE19. www.vintagehart.co.uk. ⓒ 07949/552926. Overground: Crystal Palace.

WOMEN

Fever ★★★ 📖   Tucked just off Oxford Street, this is a shop for dress lovers. The designs are classic, vintage inspired, and very reasonably priced. What's more unusual about the beautifully designed shop is their vintage section where you can buy the vintage originals so pretty that they inspired the mainstream ranges. 52 Eastcastle St., W1. www.feverdesigns.co.uk. ⓒ 020/636-6326. Tube: Oxford Circus.

Joy ★★   If you have a thing for dresses, this is the shop for you. Day dresses, flirty dresses, little black dresses—Joy excels in them. They're unique, but still well-priced. Apart from the odd exception that creeps into three figures, everything is around the £50 mark. They have their own clothing range called Louche but the thorn in their side is a frankly tacky range of housewares and gifts. The flagship branch in Greenwich is in a stunning old public baths building. 9 Nelson Rd., SE10. www.joythestore.com. © **020/8293-7979.** DLR: Cutty Sark. Other locations throughout London.

New Look   You can still get great London style even if you're on a tight budget. New Look is the place to start: It's one of the best value chains on the British high street, and stocks items that will last more than three wears. Its range is not at the cutting edge, but dresses tend to stay under £30. As with all of Oxford Street, avoid on the weekends if possible. 502–504 Oxford St., W1. www.newlook.com. © **020/7290-7860.** Tube: Marble Arch. Other locations throughout London.

Topshop ★★   This shop is enormous (although surprisingly easy to navigate). The versatile and ever-changing merchandise is aimed at younger shoppers, but that doesn't stop many fashionable women in their thirties and forties from shopping here. The shop also has a men's floor, and an entire floor of accessories; women's shoes, vintage clothing, and other designer concessions are housed in the basement. 216 Oxford St., W1. www.topshop.co.uk. © **0844/848-7487.** Tube: Oxford Circus. Other locations throughout London.

Department Stores

Contrary to a popular belief held by some visitors to the city, **Harrods** is not the only department store in London. The department store is far more mainstream these days; plenty are upscale, but you can usually still find a bargain in most. They're also getting better at catering for a younger shopper, and the concessions and food halls are generally the best instore sections.

Debenhams   If you want all the high-street shops in one place, Debenhams is the place to come. The designer range offers exclusive brands at high-street prices. Avoid the cafes; head for the housewares and clothes (the underwear section is particularly excellent). You won't be wowed by unique finds, but it's dependable. 334–348 Oxford St., W1. www.debenhams.com. © **0844/561-6161.** Tube: Bond St. Also at Westfield (p. 278).

Fenwick ★   Fenwick (with a silent "w") dates back to 1891. It's a stylish store that offers a large collection of designer womenswear. The perfume and toiletries

---

 All Under One Roof

Between the high-street shops, the one-off boutiques, and the department stores, lies a strange retail beast known as the "collective shop." These are the stores that grab a selection of the very best of fashion, and spread it out over several floors—meaning you're spoilt for choice whenever you visit. U.S. chain **Urban Outfitters,** 42–56 Earlham St., WC2 (www.urbanoutfitters.co.uk; © **020/7759-6390;** Tube: Covent Garden), does this just right, and London has

its own take on the format, with some stunning homemade shops doing the same. Over in West London, the **Shop at Bluebird,** 350 King's Rd., SW3 (www. theshopatbluebird.com; © **020/7351-3873;** Tube: South Kensington), is chock-full of designers, and **Dover Street Market** excels at eclectic fashion choices. It stocks apparently every fashionable designer that might take your fancy.

department is excellent although it comes at a price (in very pretty packaging). 63 New Bond St., W1. www.fenwick.co.uk. ℂ **020/7629-9161.** Tube: Bond St. or Oxford Circus.

Fortnum & Mason ★★ Catering to well-heeled clients as a full-service department store since 1707, Fortnum & Mason has chilled out a bit in recent years and is better than ever. Offerings include one of the most exciting delicatessens in London, as well as stationery, gift items, porcelain, and crystal. The perfume section offers unique and rare items, all available for smelling. You'll find the items here traditional, elegant, and pricey. Make sure you stop at one of the restaurants if you can, book in for afternoon tea, or at the very least have a quick tipple in the wine bar hidden on the bottom floor behind the vegetables. 181 Piccadilly, W1. www.fortnumandmason.com. ℂ **020/7734-8040.** Tube: Piccadilly Circus.

Harrods Harrods remains a London institution, but it's not what you'd call cutting edge. However, it's as entrenched in history as Buckingham Palace and racing at Ascot, and is still an elaborate emporium. There's now a pet emporium so you can purchase diamond collars for your pooch and gold food dishes for your kitty (there's even a few pets to cuddle). You'll also find a traditional barber, a jewelry department, and a section dedicated to younger customers. Hungry after all that shopping? You'll also have a staggering 24 eateries and bars to choose from. 87–135 Brompton Rd., SW1. www.harrods.com. ℂ **020/8479-5100.** Tube: Knightsbridge.

Harvey Nichols Known as "Harvey Nicks" to locals, this is a store favored with those happy in the fancy town houses of West London. Once a favorite of the late Princess Diana, the shop has its own gourmet food hall and fancy restaurant, the **Fifth Floor,** and is crammed with the best in designer home furnishings, gifts, and fashions for all, although women's clothing is the largest segment of its business. You're unlikely to find a bargain here, but that's not why you shop in Harvey Nicks. 109–125 Knightsbridge, SW1. www.harveynichols.com. ℂ **020/7235-5000.** Tube: Knightsbridge.

John Lewis This department store remains one of the most tried-and-true outlets in London and throughout the U.K. Their motto is that they are never knowingly undersold, and they mean it. There are always bargains to be had and they excel in housewares. Whatever you're looking for, ranging from Egyptian cotton bedding to clothing and jewelry, you'll find it. The Food Hall has a solid and well-deserved reputation, but it doesn't quite match the one at Selfridges (see below) further up Oxford Street. 278–306 Oxford St., W1. www.johnlewis.com. ℂ **020/7629-7711.** Tube: Oxford Circus. Other locations throughout London.

Liberty ★★★ The glorious building and quirkiness of the stock makes Liberty the most popular destination in town. Not afraid to do something new, and always full of exciting designers it's exclusive without being stuffy. The Tudor-style splendor that includes half-timbering and interior paneling houses six floors of fashion, china, and home furnishings. The famous Liberty Print fabrics cover everything—upholstery, scarves, ties, luggage, gifts, and much more. The shoe section isn't much to shout about, and the cafe is massively overpriced, but excellent stationery and toiletry departments more than make up for that. 210–220 Regent St., W1. www.liberty.co.uk. ℂ **020/7734-1234.** Tube: Oxford Circus.

Selfridges ★ Those iconic yellow bags scream fashion, and Selfridges do it better than anywhere else. You'll get lost in here (you're meant to, but there's a Champagne bar so don't complain). Since it was founded in 1858, Selfridges has

Liberty.

adapted to changing times and always been one to push trends. Stroll through the "Wonder Room" for luxurious jewelry, and enjoy the shoe section—it's one of the best in London. Even if you don't care about fashion, you can't come here without heading to the staggering food hall. And don't leave without checking out their innovative window displays (especially at Christmas). 400 Oxford St., W1. www.selfridges. com. ✆ **0800/123-400.** Tube: Bond St.

Food & Drink

Camellia's Tea House   This little cafe is the perfect pitstop if you're shopping in central London. In the very top corner of Kingly Court, it's calming even on a busy Saturday. It's not just afternoon tea and cake, though; you'll also find a vast array of teas from around the world on sale. There's a tea for every mood and occasion, including teas to make you dream and to cure tummy ailments. Pick up a pretty teapot or two as well; the china here is beautiful. 212 Kingly Court, W1. www.camelliasteahouse.com. ✆ **020/7734-9939.** Tube: Oxford Circus.

Hope and Greenwood ★★   Retro candy is very trendy at the moment, and Hope and Greenwood make the sweet treats of yesteryear a pleasure to buy. The shop in Covent Garden is like a little time warp, full of cola bottles, coconut ice, and traditional British fudge to take home. 1 Russell St., WC2. www.hopeand greenwood.co.uk. ✆ **020/7240-3314.** Tube: Covent Garden.

Gerry's ★★   If you're a fan of interesting booze, you'll be like a kid in a tipsy candy store in Gerry's. It's a Soho landmark and houses every spirit you can think of. Some see it as just another bottle shop, but to locals it's beloved, and especially handy if you're trying to find a special gift for friends who sneer at duty-free bargains. 74 Old Compton St., W1. www.gerrys.uk.com. ✆ **020/7734-2053.** Tube: Piccadilly Circus or Leicester Sq.

Ginger Pig ★★★   If you're looking for the best meat money can buy, head to Ginger Pig. Renowned countrywide, the shops consistently win awards for their produce, and rightly so. Animals are reared on Ginger Pig's own farms on the Yorkshire Moors, and the meat is the capital's freshest outside of Smithfield market. Be sure to try one of the sausage rolls—they're the best in London. 8–10 Moxon St., W1. www.thegingerpig.co.uk. ✆ **020/7935-7788.** Tube: Baker St. Other locations throughout London.

Laduree ★★   Who knew little squidgy discs of meringue would become so popular? This shop on the corner of Burlington Arcade is tiny, but what it lacks

Macarons in Laduree, Burlington Arcade, Piccadilly.

in size it more than makes up for in brash and gaudy interior. Don't be put off, the Aladdin's cave decor is precisely why people love it here. That and the *macarons*, which are famous all across Europe. The vibrant rows of treats are too tempting to ignore. Buy one in each color. 71–72 Burlington Arcade, W1. www.laduree.fr. ✆ **020/7491-9155**. Tube: Green Park/ Piccadilly.

La Fromagerie ★★ It's the cheese room that makes this shop special. Ignore the little grocery displays when you enter and head straight to the good stuff. Remember to close the door behind you, because the temperature is set perfectly for their vast range of British and Continental cheeses. *Insider's tip:* For cheese lovers visiting Greenwich, the **Cheese Board,** 26 Royal Hill (✆ **020/8305-0401;** www.cheese-board.co.uk), can't quite rival La Fromagerie, but is excellent nonetheless. 30 Highbury Park, N5. www.lafromagerie.co.uk. ✆ **020/7359-7440.** Tube: Arsenal. Also at 2–6 Moxon St., W1.

Melt ★ This chocolate shop in Notting Hill is a West London favorite. It will tempt you with caramels and sweet treats, and if you're lucky, you'll even be able to peek into the kitchen where the chocolates are made. The proprietors run workshops (must be pre-booked), and their chili chocolate is something special. It's not cheap, but if you have a sweet tooth and you're exploring West London, make this a priority stop. 59 Ledbury Rd., W11. www.meltchocolates.com. ✆ **020/8962-0492.** Tube: Notting Hill Gate.

Persepolis ★★★ One of the friendliest stores in south London, Persepolis is a Peckham landmark and local treasure. Although primarily a Persian grocery store, this shop is a hub of the Peckham community. Come here for authentic baklava, herbs and spices that you've never heard of, and a cup of Persian tea. The owner, Sally, is as cheery as she is bonkers (enjoy the little notes she leaves around the shop) and has written two fabulous recipe books. 28–30 Peckham High St., SE15. www.foratasteofpersia.co.uk. ✆ **020/7639-8007**. Rail: Peckham Rye.

Whole Foods   The flagship Whole Foods store in Kensington is a bit of a treat if you have the money to enjoy it. Full of tasty (mostly organic) goods, this is a real haven for foodies. It feels like an indoor market (without the haggling) and you'll find every type of food you could wish for. You won't be able to walk past the cakes without sampling something sweet, but avoid it at lunchtimes when it draws a huge office crowd and gets too busy. 63–97 Kensington High St., W8. www. wholefoodsmarket.com. ✆ **020/7368-4500.** Tube: High St. Kensington.

Gifts & Souvenirs

Maiden ★   Maiden is all about exciting and unexpected gifts—unique items from pretty dinner trays to wooden toy soldiers. There's nothing ordinary in here; Maiden excels in the weird and wonderful in a way that only East London can. 186 Shoreditch High St., E1. www.maidenshop.com. ✆ **020/7998-0185.** Overground: Shoreditch High St.

Muji   An emporium for Japanese wares, this chain store is known for its bargain offerings. Among its merchandise, the frugal shopper will find everything from "simple and functional" chic clothing to housewares, most of it in a minimalist style. The bath soaps and candles are a delight, coming in such unusual scents as grapefruit and mandarin orange. Funky umbrellas and a host of other ever-changing wares also tempt shoppers. 157 Kensington High St., W8. www.muji.co.uk. ✆ **020/376-2484.** Tube: High St. Kensington. Other locations throughout London.

Ryan Town ★★★   There are iconic shops in London's east end, and then there's Rob Ryan. In the center of Columbia Road market (and as such, only open on weekends), this shop devoted to the paper cut artist is famous across the design world. The whimsical and sentimental artworks adorn everything from greetings cards to cushions. Prices vary from £3 for a greetings card to £300 for an original print, but you'll find it hard to resist the romantic pieces. 126 Columbia Rd., E2. www.misterrob.co.uk. ✆ **020/7613-1510.** Tube: Old St./ Overground: Hoxton.

Interiors

See also "Art & Crafts," earlier in this section.

Anthropologie ★   This lifestyle shop from across the pond dominates Regent Street. It's huge, beautiful, and has a living wall covered in lichen and exotic flowers. If you're familiar with the American version, you'll baulk at the prices, but it's hard not to be charmed by the designs and the vibe of this West End branch—think chintzy florals with a modern twist alongside overpriced kitchenware. You'll have fun browsing in here, even if you don't spend any money. 58 Regent St., W1. www.anthropologie.eu. ✆ **020/7529-9800.** Tube: Piccadilly Circus. Also at 131–141 King's Rd., SW3.

Divertmenti   There's something so very stylish about simple kitchenware that just works well. Divertmenti focus on that, and they do it brilliantly. Everything is chic, well-priced, and practical. There's also a cookery school attached if you're really into your chopping and roasting. 33/34 Marylebone High St., W1. www. divertimenti.co.uk. ✆ **020/7935-0689.** Tube: Bond St./Baker St.

Heal's   Very much the king of interiors on the high street at the moment, Heal's stands tall above the rest of the interiors shops on Tottenham Court Road. Solid, dependable, and enough quality design to nod to a trend without ever feeling "faddy." If you're a fan of mid-century design as well as dark wood and leather then you'll love shopping in here. Be careful when ordering furniture—a lot of it is bulky so double check your luggage allowance and delivery costs. 196 Tottenham Court Rd., W1. www.heals.co.uk. ℰ **020/7636-1666.** Tube: Goodge St.

Labour and Wait ★★   Established in 2003, this Spitalfields store offers useful items that have gone out of style in many households—enamel bread bins, rope doorstops, galvanized steel watering cans and buckets, and even stylish (yes, stylish) brooms. The shop is a showcase for specialist makers from around the world, many of whom manufacture items based on their traditional and original designs. Items are both new and vintage. The shop lies around the corner from Brick Lane, and is open only Saturday 1 to 5pm, and Sunday 10am to 5pm. 18 Cheshire St., E2. www.labourandwait.co.uk. ℰ **020/ 7729-6253.** Tube: Liverpool St./Overground: Shoreditch High St.

Snowden Flood ★★★   One of the most popular London designers, Snowden Flood's shop is part of the

Labour and Wait.

wonderful collection of shops in the OXO Tower. Her striking ceramic designs, often featuring iconic London landmarks, are becoming as recognizable as the buildings themselves. Pick up a platter for £40, or a more modestly priced mug for little over a tenner. Watch out for sale items, the range is hugely collectable.

 London's Tin Pan Alley

If you're a little bit musical—or can at least play a few guitar chords—head to **Denmark Street** (Tube: Tottenham Court Rd.), just off Charing Cross Road. The little alleyway is littered with guitar and music shops, as well as some serious recording studios. If the shops are quiet and the guys behind the counters are feeling nice, you'll be allowed to play about with the kit. **Rockers** at no. 5 (ℰ **020/7240-2610**) isn't quite as friendly

as **Hanks** at no. 24 (www.hanks guitarshop.com; ℰ **020/7379-1139**). Pop into the **12 Bar** next door for a drink and some live music when you're done (www.12barclub.com; ℰ **020/7240-2120**) or grab dinner at the tiny bistro **Giaconda Dining Room** (p. 205). Denmark Street is always going to be a bit touristy—and a little sure of itself—but it's a whole lotta fun if you know your way around a six-string.

And don't visit on Mondays—that's Snowden's "design day." Unit 1.01, Oxo Tower Wharf, Barge-house St., SE1. www.snowdenflood.com. ✆ **020/7401-8710.** Tube: Southwark.

Twenty-Twentyone ★★★ This shop is all about the contemporary. If you're looking for an unusual cheese grater, this is where you come. If you don't want a standard foot stool, you head here. If you want a surprising interior gift, you'll find it on the shelves of this tiny Islington shop. 274–275 Upper St., N1. www.twentytwentyone.com. ✆ **020/7288-1996.** Tube: Highbury & Islington/Angel.

Music

Collectors should browse **Notting Hill;** the handful of record stores near Notting Hill Gate Tube station are excellent. Also browse **Soho** around Wardour Street and near the Tottenham Court Road Tube stop. Sometimes dealers show up at Covent Garden on the weekends.

Dress Circle ★ This store is unique in London in that it's devoted to musical theatre and standards vocalists such as Frank Sinatra and Judy Garland. After half a century, recordings in the U.K. enter the public domain—hence the lower prices on rereleased CDs of West End and Broadway musicals from the 1950s. New releases, of course, cost at least three times more. Karaoke recordings and even theatrical souvenirs are sold—perhaps a Bette Davis doll as Margo Channing in *All About Eve.* 57–59 Monmouth St., WC2. www.dresscircle.co.uk. ✆ **020/7240-2227.** Tube: Covent Garden.

Duke of Uke ★★★ This fabulously named shop sells all things ukulele. It sells banjos and standard guitars as well, but really it's all about the uke. There are great events (p. 320) here as well, so keep your eyes (and ears) open. 88 Cheshire St., E2. www.dukeofuke.co.uk. ✆ **020/3583-9728.** Tube: Whitechapel or Aldgate East.

Flashback ★★ This small, cramped store deep in Islington is devoted to golden oldies. For the music lover, especially the devotee of the hits of yesterday, it's a gem and a discovery—and one of the best places in London to spend an afternoon browsing secondhand vinyl. 50 Essex Rd., N1. www.flashback.co.uk. ✆ **020/7354-9356.** Tube: Angel.

Sporting/Camping Goods

Bobbins Bicycles ★ Not exactly the most energetic of bike shops, but if you're looking for a bit of gentle

Duke of Uke.

exercise, head to Angel for the very best line in vintage-inspired cycles. 397 St. John St., EC1. www.bobbinbicycles.co.uk. ℭ **020/7837-3370.** Tube: Angel.

Decathlon ★★   If you're a runner on a budget, this is where you go. They have a huge range of stylish sportswear, but it doesn't come with the celebrity endorsed price-tag attached. You'll find good sports gear at impressively low prices. Canada Water Retail Park, Surrey Quays Rd., SE16. www.decathlon.co.uk. ℭ **020/7394-2000.** Tube: Canada Water.

Ellis Brigham   The most popular skiing and snowboarding store in Central London, this is your one-stop shop for all winter activities. Whether you need goggles, sun block, or the whole snow kit, you'll find it here. 3 Southampton St., WC2. www.ellis-brigham.com. ℭ **020/7395-1010.** Tube: Charing Cross or Covent Garden.

Field and Trek ★★   A small outdoors store, absolutely packed with camping goodies. Better value than most in London, too. 42 Maiden Lane, WC2. www.fieldandtrek.com. ℭ **0844/332-5893.** Tube: Covent Garden.

Sweaty Betty   If you're into your yoga, Sweaty Betty has everything you need. It's not cheap, but they do manage to make Lycra and gym wear look good. 125 King's Rd., SW3. www.sweatybetty.com. ℭ **020/7349-7597.** Tube: Sloane Sq. Other locations throughout London.

Technology & Cameras

Apple   Either you're an Apple fan or you're not. Whichever camp you fall into, tech lovers flock to this place. It's minimalist, full of things to play with, and staffed by people who know their stuff. Prepare to get in line when new products are released. 1 The Piazza, Covent Garden, WC2. www.apple.com. ℭ **020/7447-1440.** Tube: Covent Garden. Also at 235 Regent St., W1.

Camera Café ★★   The Camera Café is a cute little place just by the British Museum where they'll sell you a coffee and let you play about with their second-hand cameras. There's free Wi-Fi, too. If you're a photography fanatic, seek this place out. 44 Museum St., WC1. www.cameracafe.co.uk. ℭ **07887/930-826.** Tube: Holborn.

Lomography ★★   Lomo photography is big in the U.K. Highly saturated color images and funky replica vintage cameras make this a cool and fairly simple hobby to pick up: You can buy a camera for £50 and start shooting straight away. The Lomo shop has the biggest selection in London and some excellent

---

 ### Electrical Heaven

The best stretch in London for browsing electrical and electronic goods is **Tottenham Court Road,** the main thoroughfare separating the West End from Bloomsbury. If you've forgotten your phone charger, or need a new battery, or are hunting a replacement mp3 player, this is where to come. Unless you're willing to haggle, however, expect to pay over the odds in the area's smaller independent outlets, particularly if you're not especially tech-savvy. The real bargains are to be had in the larger stores. It's unlikely that you'll find a better deal here than you would online, but at least you can touch and feel before you buy—and the item is right there if you need it right now. Once you've decided what to buy, visit three shops, ask them to write down their quotes, and play them off against each other. It works.

examples of Lomography to inspire you. 3 Newburgh St., W1. www.lomography. com. 📞 **020/74341466.** Tube: Oxford Circus.

Toys, Comics & Games

Compendia ★ ☺ If you like classic games, Compendia will sort you out faster than you can say "Checkmate," with wooden backgammon sets, checkers boards, and even a hand-carved chess set or two. They do sell other games here, but steer clear of mainstream board games, which are very expensive. 10 The Market, SE10. www.compendia.co.uk. 📞 **020/8293-6616.** DLR: Cutty Sark.

Forbidden Planet ★★★ They're not strictly toys. They're collectables. However you phrase it, Forbidden Planet is the world's largest sci-fi and fantasy retailer, specializing in comic books, graphic novels, and erm . . . toys. If you want a model of a Dalek, you come here. 179 Shaftesbury Avenue. www.forbiddenplanet.com. 📞 **0207/420-3666.** Tube: Tottenham Court Rd.

Paddington Bear at Hamleys.

Hamleys ☺ Possibly the finest toy shop in the world—more than 35,000 toys and games on seven floors of fun and magic. The huge selection includes soft, cuddly stuffed animals as well as dolls, radio-controlled cars, train sets, model kits, board games, outdoor toys, computer games, and more. Just don't ever think it's a good idea to visit in the school holidays. 188–196 Regent St., W1. www.hamleys.com. 📞 **0844/855-2424.** Tube: Oxford Circus or Piccadilly Circus. Also at St. Pancras International station, NW1.

Play Lounge ★★ ☺ There's nothing dull about this toy shop aimed at young adults and grown-up "kids." If you like your Japanese figurines and interesting comics, you'll find something to keep you occupied. The shop is tiny, but it's packed from floor to ceiling with goodies. If you want a pop-up book and a scary Tim Burton-inspired collectable, you'll find both. It's pricey sometimes, but they stock small toys and games on the counter that are perfect for pocket money. 19 Beak St., W1. www.playlounge.co.uk. 📞 **020/7287-7073.** Tube: Oxford Circus.

Pollock's Toy Museum ★★ ☺ The key part to this traditional toy shop is that it's attached to its own museum (p. 104), so you can buy cute presents and toys (including magic sets) and then have a wander around the exhibition, which costs around £5. It's a lovely, old-fashioned shop—and you won't find a single video game. 25 Scala St., W1. www.pollockstoymuseum.com. 📞 **020/7636-3452.** Tube: Goodge St. Also at 44 The Market, WC2.

PRACTICAL MATTERS: THE SHOPPING SCENE

HOURS London keeps fairly uniform store hours. The norm is 10am opening and 6pm closing Monday to Saturday, with a late Thursday night until 7 or 8pm. Most of the more central stores stay open until 8pm most days, or 9pm on a Thursday. However, the upscale stores along Bond Street usually shut earlier—around 6pm.

On a Sunday, shops in England are allowed to trade for 6 hours; and many central stores open at 12 noon. A handful of shops open earlier for browsing only, thus extending their opening hours without breaking the law.

TAXES & SHIPPING Value-added tax (VAT) is Britain's sales tax, and is currently at its highest ever rate, a whopping 20% on most goods. It must be included in any quoted consumer price, so the number you see on the price tag is exactly what you'll pay at the register. Non-E.U. residents can claim back much of the tax by applying for a VAT refund (see "How to Get Your VAT Refund," p. 299). In Britain, the minimum expenditure to qualify for a refund is £50. Not every store honors this minimum, but it's far easier to qualify for a tax refund in Britain than some other countries in the European Union.

Vendors at flea markets may not be equipped to provide the paperwork for a refund, so if you're contemplating a major purchase and are counting on one, ask before you buy. Be suspicious of any dealer who tells you there's no VAT on antiques. This was once true, but things have changed—and pricing should reflect this. Negotiate a price you're comfortable with first, and then ask for the VAT refund.

VAT is not charged on goods shipped directly out of the country. Many London shops will help you beat the VAT by shipping for you. But watch out: Shipping may be even more expensive than the VAT, and you might also have to pay import duties if you're shipping your stuff to North America.

You can ship your purchases on your flight home by paying for excess baggage (rates vary by airline), or have your packages shipped independently, which is generally less expensive than shipping it through the airlines. However, you can avoid the VAT upfront *only* if you have the store ship directly for you. If you ship via excess baggage or an independent shipping company, you still have to pay the VAT and apply for your refund.

DUTY-FREE AIRPORT SHOPPING Shopping at airports is big business. Heathrow is virtually a shopping mall these days, and designer shops are especially prevalent at Terminal 5. Prices at the airport for items such as souvenirs and confectionery are, of course, higher than on the streets of London, but duty-free prices on luxury goods are usually fair. Sales at these airport shops are made for those passing through Heathrow en route to other destinations—usually home. Perfumes and aftershaves, as well as designer accessories, are where the best bargains are to be had.

Global Refund (www.globalrefund.com) is your best bet for getting VAT refunds at the airport (see box above). Shop where you see the Global

HOW TO GET YOUR VAT refund

Residents of countries outside the European Union are entitled to claim VAT back on major purchases. However, you *must* get your VAT refund form from the retailer. You can't get this form from the airport, so *don't* leave the store without it. It must be completed by the retailer at the time of purchase. After you've asked whether the store does VAT refunds and determined their minimum, request the paperwork.

Fill out your form and then present it—with the goods, receipts, and passports—at the Customs office in the airport. You should allow an hour to stand in line, and do remember that you're required to show the goods, and so put them in your carry-on luggage.

Once the paperwork has been stamped, you have a couple of options. You can mail the papers (remember to bring a stamp) and receive your money as a credit card refund; or you can go to the Cash VAT Refund desk at the airport and claim your refund in cash. If you accept cash other than sterling, you will lose money on the conversion. Many stores also charge a fee for processing your refund, so that will be deducted from the total you receive. But since the VAT in Britain is 20%, it's worth the trouble to get the money back for a major purchase.

Note: If you're heading to other countries in the European Union, you should file all of your VAT refunds together as you depart your final E.U. destination.

Refund Tax-Free Shopping sign, and ask for a Global Refund Tax-Free check when you purchase your items.

SALES   Traditional sale periods have changed in the face of financial crisis, you can find a bargain during most months. It's rare that you can walk down a street without getting enticed by sale posters in a window. However, the **January sale** is still the big shopping event of the year. Boxing Day in England (December 26), following the Christmas shopping spree, marks the beginning of year-end clearance sales, which often run through January. On Boxing Day itself, many shops open early (some as early as 5am, although people start lining up much earlier). You'll also find that some stores try to cash in on bargain-hunting Christmas shoppers by starting their sales midway through December. The discounts usually increase again after Christmas, but if you want the good stock, get in early. Sharpen your elbows and get shopping.

There are also several **designer sample sales** that are worth looking out for. They're often advertised in the local press, but you can also find the best ones by signing up to email alerts from the London edition of **Daily Candy** (www.dailycandy.com) or **Emerald Street** (www.emeraldstreet. com). Expect long lines of people, and fashionistas fighting over the best pieces—understandable given that most are discounted by 70%. Stock is often replenished daily, but it varies from sale to sale so if you want the best stuff arrive at least an hour before opening. You should also expect to pay to get in, but this is usually around the £2 mark, which tends to cover the costs for the venue and very busy staff. Make sure you keep an eye out for the massive costume and fancy dress sales from **Angels,** 119 Shaftesbury Ave., W1 (www.fancydress.com; ✆ **020/7836-5678;** Tube: Tottenham Court Rd.). They're rare, and you'll have to line up for hours; but if you're a fan of dressing up, it's one sale you do not want to miss. You'll find details of any sales in the London press, but if they have one coming up it'll be plastered all over the website too.

ENTERTAINMENT & NIGHTLIFE

Few cities in the world can match London when it comes to entertainment and nightlife. It overflows with history and tradition, with theatres and venues that measure their lifetimes in decades. From the grand old opera houses and theatres of the West End, to clubs and bars in the City's fashionable eastern quarter, and global sports events to cool pool halls, London oozes possibilities and excitement.

Despite all its visible history, London is very much alive and constantly in flux — away from the classical palaces of entertainment, you'll find a very different London. This is a London that takes place in basements and spaces that have been left behind, out of sight sometimes, but with a pulse that can be felt all over the city. Never standing still, this is a London where clubs, bars, and even whole districts drift in and out of fashion in bewilderingly quick time, sometimes frustrating, but always exciting. The Tube may not run all night, but thanks to relaxed licensing laws, a city that once closed down at 11pm now parties on well into the small hours.

Weekly publications such as *Time Out* carry full entertainment listings, including information on restaurants, nightclubs, and bars. You'll also find listings in all the daily newspapers, and the *Guide* distributed every Saturday inside the *Guardian* newspaper is an invaluable source of up-to-date information.

THE PERFORMING ARTS

The theatrical capital of the world, London is home to some of the most famous companies on the planet, often housed in glorious buildings with rich and long histories. The number and variety of productions, and the standards of acting and directing, are unrivaled, and a London stage has also become the first port of call for many Hollywood stars looking to prove their thespian skills. Accommodating both the traditional and the avant-garde, London theatres are, for the most part, accessible and reasonably affordable.

Getting Tickets

To see specific shows, especially hits, purchase your tickets in advance. Ticket prices vary greatly depending on the seat and venue—from £25 to £85 is typical. Occasionally gallery seats (the cheapest) are sold only on the day of the performance, so you'll have to head to the box office early in the day and return an hour before the performance to line up, because they're not reserved seats.

Founded in 2000, **London Theatre Direct** (www.londontheatredirect.com; ✆ **0845/505-8500**) represents a majority of the major theatres in the city and tickets for all productions can be purchased in advance, either over the phone or via their website. Alternatively try the **Society of London Theatre** (www.officiallondontheatre.co.uk; ✆ **020/7557-6700**), whose ticket booth (**"tkts"**) on the southwest corner of Leicester Square is open Monday to

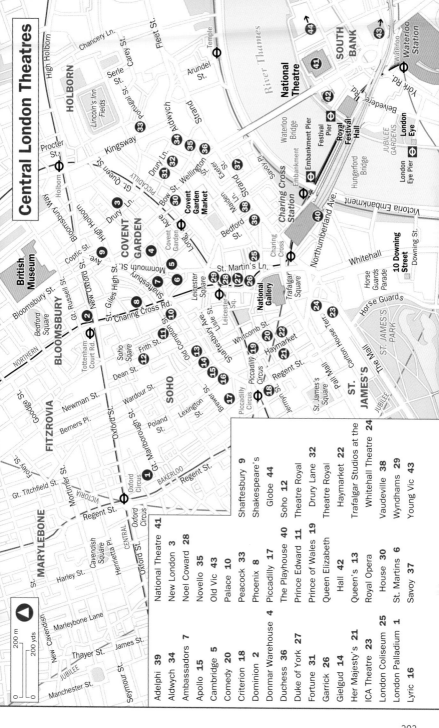

Central London Theatres

Adelphi **39**
Aldwych **34**
Ambassadors **7**
Apollo **15**
Cambridge **5**
Comedy **20**
Criterion **18**
Dominion **2**
Donmar Warehouse **4**
Duchess **36**
Duke of York **27**
Fortune **31**
Garrick **26**
Gielgud **14**
Her Majesty's **21**
ICA Theatre **23**
London Coliseum **25**
London Palladium **1**
Lyric **16**

National Theatre **41**
New London **3**
Noel Coward **28**
Novello **35**
Old Vic **43**
Palace **10**
Peacock **33**
Phoenix **8**
Piccadilly **17**
The Playhouse **40**
Prince Edward **11**
Prince of Wales **19**
Queen Elizabeth
 Hall **42**
Queen's **13**
Royal Opera
 House **30**
St. Martins **6**
Savoy **37**

Shaftesbury **9**
Shakespeare's
 Globe **44**
Soho **12**
Theatre Royal
 Drury Lane **32**
Theatre Royal
 Haymarket **22**
Trafalgar Studios at the
 Whitehall Theatre **24**
Vaudeville **38**
Wyndhams **29**
Young Vic **43**

Saturday 10am to 7pm and Sunday 11am to 4pm. You can purchase all tickets here, although the booth specializes in half-price sales for shows that are undersold. These tickets must be purchased in person—not over the phone. A £2 service fee is charged. For phone orders, you should call **Ticketmaster** (www. ticketmaster.co.uk; ✆ **0870/060-2340**).

Visitors from North America can try **Keith Prowse,** 234 W. 44th St., Ste. 1000, New York, NY 10036 (www.keithprowse.com; ✆ **212/398-4175** in the U.S.) to arrange tickets and seek information before they leave home. Their London office is at 39 Moreland St., EC1 (✆ **0844/209-0382;** Tube: Angel). They'll mail your tickets, fax a confirmation, or leave your tickets at the appropriate production's box office. Instant confirmations are available for most shows. A booking and handling fee of up to 20% is added to the price.

If you're staying at a first-class or deluxe hotel with a concierge, you can also call and arrange tickets before you arrive, putting them on a credit card.

Many of the major theatres, such as the **National** (see below), offer reduced-price tickets to students and those under 18 on a standby basis, but not to the general public. When available, these tickets are sold 30 minutes prior to curtain. Line up early for popular shows, as standby tickets go fast. Of course, you must show a valid student ID.

TheatreFix (www.theatrefix.co.uk) is a website set up to help and encourage those aged 16 to 26 to attend London theatres. Sign up to the service and you can get cheap entry to many productions, as well as valuable advice if you're making your first trip to the city.

Finally, if you decide to check out the theatre on a whim—and you're not too fussy—**Lastminute.com** is a safe bet to pick up late tickets at discounted rates.

Warning: Beware of scalpers (ticket touts) who hang out in front of theatres. Many report that they sell forged tickets, and their prices can be outrageous.

Long-Running Shows

In recent years the **musical** has come to dominate London's theatre heartland, to both the delight of audiences and the chagrin of many traditional producers. Latterly the trend for new musicals has been for two specific genres. First, there are those based around popular rock and pop acts, such as *We Will Rock You* at the **Dominion Theatre,** 268–269 Tottenham Court Rd., W1 (www. dominion theatre.co.uk; ✆ **020/7927-0900**), featuring adaptations of songs by rock band Queen, and *Mamma Mia!* based on the music of Abba. Second are stage adaptations of films: Musical versions of *Dirty Dancing, Shrek, Lion King, Flashdance,* and *Legally Blonde* have been packing in the crowds.

Those on the hunt for more traditional fare needn't despair, and long-running West End mainstays such as *Les Misérables* still play to appreciative crowds. Also, you're almost always guaranteed to find at least one Andrew Lloyd Webber production being performed somewhere in London, and currently both *Phantom of the Opera* and its sequel *Love Never Dies* occupy major London houses. And no guide to London theatre is complete without mentioning Agatha Christie's *The Mousetrap,* now in the 59th year of a record-shattering nonstop run. Since its premiere in 1952, this murder-mystery play has been performed more than 24,000 times, first at the Theatre Royal and now at **St. Martin's Theatre,** West

St., WC2 (www.stmartins-theatre.co.uk). It has become as intrinsic a part of London as the ravens at the Tower of London.

Major Theatres & Companies

Donmar Warehouse ★★★ Although its auditorium only seats 250 people, the Donmar Warehouse is still one of London's most important and acclaimed theatres. For the past two decades—under the artistic directorship of Sam Mendes, Michael Grandage, and now Josie Rourke—the Donmar has staged some of London's most memorable productions with several, such as *Frost/Nixon,* going on to tour internationally. It's renowned for an emphasis on performing new works and contemporary reworkings of the classics, so catching a performance here should be high on the priority list of any visiting theatre lover. 41 Earlham St., WC2. www.donmarwarehouse.com. ℂ **020/7240-4882.** Tube: Covent Garden.

National Theatre ★ Home to one of the world's greatest stage companies, the Royal National Theatre is not one but three theatres—the **Olivier,** reminiscent of a Greek amphitheatre with its open stage; the more traditional **Lyttelton;** and the **Cottesloe,** with its flexible stage and seating. The National presents the finest in world theatre, from classic drama to award-winning new plays, including comedies, musicals, and shows for young people. A choice of at least six plays is on offer at any one time.

It's also a full-time theatre center, with bars, cafes, restaurants, free foyer music and exhibitions, short early-evening performances, bookshops, backstage tours, riverside walks, restaurants, and terraces. South Bank, SE1. www.national theatre.org.uk. ℂ **020/7452-3000.** Tube: Waterloo, Embankment, or Charing Cross.

Old Vic ★★ The Old Vic has stood on its site near Waterloo Station for more than 190 years, and since 2004 has been under the stewardship of actor Kevin Spacey. His tenure and aim to "inject new life" into London theatre has generally been regarded as a success. Spacey's star power has enabled him to attract Hollywood names alongside powerhouse directors of the caliber of Trevor Nunn. Productions range from modern classics through to Shakespearean tragedies and modern farces. 103 The Cut, SE1. www.oldvictheatre.co.uk. ℂ **020/7928-2651.** Tube: Waterloo.

Shakespeare's Globe In May 1997, the new Globe Theatre—a replica of the Elizabethan original, thatched roof and all—staged its first slate of plays (*Henry V* and *A Winter's Tale*) yards away from the site of the 16th-century theatre where the Bard originally staged his works. Productions vary in style and setting; not all are performed in Elizabethan costume. In keeping with the historic setting, no lighting is focused just on the stage, but floodlighting is used during evening performances to replicate daylight in the theatre (Elizabethan performances took place in the afternoon). Theatregoers sit on wooden benches of yore—in thatch-roofed galleries—but these days you can rent a cushion to make yourself more comfortable. About 500 "groundlings" can stand in the uncovered yard around the stage, just as they did when the Bard was here.

Due to the Globe's open-air nature the schedule can be affected by weather and so check the website beforehand. New Globe Walk, Bankside, SE1. www.shakespeares globe.com. ℂ **020/7902-1400**. Tube: Mansion House or Southwark.

Pretheatre Dining

For a full rundown of London's best Theatreland restaurants, see the sections on "Soho" and "Covent Garden" in Chapter 5. Our particular pre-show favorites are **Rules** (p. 204), for old English ambience and traditional yet impeccable cooking; **J. Sheekey** (p. 203), for theatrical interiors and some of the best seafood in the West End; **L' Atelier de Joël Robuchon** (p. 202), for Michelin-starred cooking and a great value, pretheatre set menu; **Les Deux Salons** (p. 203), for a theatrical dinner; and **Mon Plaisir** (p. 206), for the full Gallic experience, including French onion soup and *fruits de mer* platters.

Theatre Royal Drury Lane   Drury Lane is one of London's oldest and most prestigious theatres, crammed with tradition—not all of it respectable. This, the fourth theatre on the site, dates from 1812; the first was built in 1663. Nearly every star of London theatre has taken the stage here at some time. It has a wide-open repertoire but leans toward musicals, especially long-running hits. Guided tours of the backstage area and the front of the house are given Monday, Tuesday, Thursday, Friday at 2:15 and 4:15pm, plus 10:15am and 11:45am Wednesday and Saturday. The box office is open Monday to Saturday from 10am to 8pm. Catherine St., WC2. www.reallyuseful.com. ✆ **0844/871-8810.** Tickets £15–£45. Tube: Covent Garden.

Fringe Theatre

Some of the best theatre in London is performed on the "fringe"—at the dozens of venues devoted to alternative plays, revivals, contemporary drama, and musicals. These shows are usually more adventurous than established West End productions, and they're cheaper. Most offer discounted seats (often as much as 50% off) to students and seniors. Fringe theatres are scattered around London, so check listings in *Time Out* or websites such as **Run-Riot.com** or **LeCool.com**, both of which cover leftfield theatre.

Almeida ★★★   The Almeida is known for its adventurous stagings of new and classic plays. The theatre's legendary status is validated by consistently good productions at lower-than-average prices. The Almeida is also home to the **Festival of Contemporary Music** (also called the Almeida Opera) from mid-June to mid-July, which showcases everything from atonal jazz to 12-tone chamber orchestra pieces. Almeida St., N1. www.almeida.co.uk. ✆ **020/7359-4404.** Tickets £6–£30. Tube: Angel or Highbury and Islington.

Lyric ★   A vibrant, modern theatre, the Lyric, under the artistic directorship of David Farr, has made a name for itself with a lively, eclectic, and often controversial schedule. From world-class children's theatre to experimental performances that have seen audiences spy upon actors in a neighboring tower block . . . a night at the Lyric is never dull. With an open-air terrace and a great pizza restaurant too, there's lots to love about this proudly local theatre. Lyric Sq., King St., W6. www.lyric.co.uk. ✆ **0871/221-172.** Tube: Hammersmith.

Tricycle   Focusing on experimental and left-leaning works of political theatre, the Tricycle can often be as heavy-going as it is rewarding. Productions such as *Nuremburg*, *Guantanamo*, and *Bloody Sunday* certainly lack laughs, but the

The Cut Bar at the Young Vic.

Tricycle has played an important role in bringing difficult or ignored subjects to the stage. To date Tricycle productions have gone on to be staged in both the British Houses of Parliament and on Capitol Hill—this lively, anarchic theatre continues to punch above its weight. Check the website for innovative offers such as "Pay What You Can," designed to encourage attendance by those not usually drawn to the theatre. 269 Kilburn High Rd., NW6. www.tricycle.co.uk. ℂ **020/7328-1000.** Tube: Kilburn.

Young Vic ★★ Long known for presenting both classical and modern plays, the Young Vic tends to nurture younger talent than its sister theatre, the Old Vic (see above), and places a greater emphasis on working with young and emerging directors. Productions here could be almost anything, and are priced depending on the show—discounted tickets are available for students and anyone aged 26 or under. A recent addition to the Young Vic is its much loved in-house bar and restaurant, **The Cut,** the perfect place to meet before a play or to discuss its merits (or otherwise) afterwards. 66 The Cut, SE1. www.youngvic.org. ℂ **020/7922-2922.** Tube: Waterloo or Southwark.

Classical Music, Opera & Dance

Currently, London supports a sometimes unwieldy yet impressive five major orchestras—the **London Symphony,** the **Royal Philharmonic,** the **Philharmonia Orchestra,** the **BBC Symphony,** and the **BBC Philharmonic**—as well as several choirs, and many chamber groups and historic instrument ensembles. Also look for the **London Sinfonietta,** the **English Chamber Orchestra,** and the **Academy of St. Martin in the Fields.**

Barbican Centre ★★★ Standing fortress-like on the fringe of the City of London, the Barbican is the largest art and exhibition complex in Western Europe. Roomy and comfortable, it's the perfect setting for enjoying music and theatre, and is the permanent home address of the **London Symphony Orchestra,** as well as host to visiting orchestras and performers of all styles, from classical to jazz, folk, and world music.

In addition to its hall and two theatres, the Barbican Centre encompasses the **Barbican Art Gallery,** the **Curve Gallery,** and foyer exhibition spaces; Cinemas One and Two; the **Barbican Library,** a general lending library that places a strong emphasis on the arts; the rooftop Conservatory, one of London's largest greenhouses; and restaurants, cafes, and bars. Silk St., EC2. www.barbican.org.uk. ℂ **020/7638-8891.** Tube: Barbican or Moorgate.

Royal Albert Hall   Opened in 1871 and dedicated to the memory of Queen Victoria's consort, Prince Albert, this circular building is one of the world's most famous auditoriums. With a seating capacity of 5,200, it's a popular place to hear music by major world-class performers from both the classical and pop worlds.

Since 1941, the hall has hosted the **BBC Henry Wood Promenade Concerts** (p. 46), known as "the Proms," an annual series that lasts for 8 weeks between mid-July and mid-September. The Proms incorporate a medley of mostly British orchestral music, and have been a national favorite since 1895. Although most of the audience occupies reserved seats, true aficionados usually opt for standing room in the orchestra pit, with close-up views of the musicians on stage. The final evening (the "Last Night of the Proms") is the most famous, when rousing favorites *Jerusalem* and *Land of Hope and Glory* echo through the hall. After its 8-year restoration, the Albert Hall now allows tours of both Front of House £8.50 and Backstage £12. Kensington Gore, SW7. www.royalalberthall.com. ✆ **020/7589-8212.** Tube: South Kensington.

Royal Opera House   The Royal Ballet and the Royal Opera are at home again in this magnificently restored theatre. The entire northeast corner of one of London's most famous public squares has been transformed, finally realizing Inigo Jones' original vision for his colonnaded Covent Garden. Performances at the Royal Opera are usually sung in the original language, but supertitles are projected. **The Royal Ballet,** which ranks with top companies such as the Kirov and the Paris Opera Ballet, performs a repertory with a tilt toward the classics, including works by earlier choreographer-directors Sir Frederick Ashton and Sir Kenneth MacMillan. Tickets start from £9. Bow St., WC2. www.roh.org.uk. ✆ **020/7304-4000.** Tube: Covent Garden.

Sadler's Wells ★   One of London's premier venues for dance and opera, Sadler's Wells occupies the site of a series of theatres, the first built in 1683. The original facade has been retained, but the interior was completely revamped in 1998 with a stylish, cutting-edge design. The new space offers classical ballet, modern dance of all degrees of "avant-garde-ness," and children's theatrical productions, usually including a Christmas ballet. Rosebery Ave., EC1. ✆ **0844/412-4300.** www.sadlerswells.com. Tube: Angel.

Southbank Centre ★★   Its brutalist concrete exterior may not be to everyone's taste, but there's no denying that the Southbank Centre contains three of the most acoustically perfect concert halls in the world: the **Royal Festival Hall,** the **Queen Elizabeth Hall,** and the **Purcell Room.** Together, the halls present more than 1,200 performances a year, including classical music, ballet, jazz, popular music, and contemporary dance. The **Hayward Gallery** is also located here (p. 135).

The Centre itself usually opens daily at 10am, and offers an extensive array of things to see and do, including free exhibitions and musical performances in the foyers. Food and drink are also served at venues including the **Skylon Bar and Grill** (www.skylonrestaurant.co.uk; ✆ **020/7654-7800**), a restaurant on Level 3 serving modern Continental cuisine with panoramic views of the River Thames. Less formal eating is available at the **Riverside Terrace Café** on Level 2. South Bank, SE1. www.southbankcentre.co.uk. ✆ **0871/663-2500.** Tube: Waterloo or Embankment.

Wigmore Hall An intimate auditorium, Wigmore Hall offers an excellent series of voice recitals, piano and chamber music, early and baroque music, and jazz. With at least 400 performances a year, plus workshops and community projects, Wigmore Hall is a vitally important venue, ensuring new generations are introduced to the joys of classical music. 36 Wigmore St., W1. www.wigmore-hall.org.uk. ✆ **020/7935-2141.** Tickets £10–£35. Tube: Bond St. or Oxford Circus.

THE BAR SCENE
Bars & Cocktail Lounges

Academy It may no longer serve the best cocktail in town, but there's still plenty to enjoy at this Seventies kitsch-inspired bar formerly known as LAB. A thick cocktail book lies on every table, its contents perfected over 10 years of mixing and muddling: If you're in London long enough, you may want to work your way through it all, from classics to house specialties such as the Soho Lady. DJs spin house music Wednesday to Saturday, ensuring a lively atmosphere at this Soho institution. 12 Old Compton St., W1. www.labbaruk.com. ✆ **020/7437-7820.** Tube: Leicester Sq.

Alibi As Shoreditch has become ever more popular, many of those originally drawn to this arty enclave of East London have been pushed out. Dalston and Bethnal Green mopped up the overspill, and now hold the title of London's hippest areas. The Alibi is the best among a number of bars to open in Dalston in 2010, and implements a policy of giving interesting record labels and promoters a small space in which to throw big parties. 91 Kingsland High St., E8. www.thealibi london.co.uk. ✆ **020/7249-2733.** Tube: Old St. and then bus 243/Overground: Dalston Kingsland or Dalston Junction.

Book Club A much-needed shot in the arm for an area that has become increasingly commercialized, the Book Club offers up a lively mix of art exhibitions, club nights, poetry slams, thinking, and drinking. It's a different yet winning combination, and judging by the crowds that spill out into the street, one that the locals have taken to with open arms. 100 Leonard St., EC2. www.wearetbc. com. ✆ **020/7684-8618.** Tube: Old St./Overground: Shoreditch High St.

Callooh Callay A fun and remarkably unpretentious cocktail bar hemmed in on all sides by Shoreditch's lively pubs and clubs. The drinks menu features everything you would expect to find, though take the time to chat to any of the bar's knowledgeable staff and you'll soon find yourself going off-menu as they mix up a drink to suit your taste. Whilst the front bar is pleasant enough, for the full experience head through the concealed door disguised as a wardrobe to the more atmospheric back room (officially a members' bar so you will need to call ahead). 65 Rivington St., EC2A. www.calloohcallaybar.com ✆ **020/7739-4781.** Tube: Old Street.

Dogstar The Dogstar earned its special place in London's nightlife history as the first DJ pub in the city. Over the years, the Dog has had its ups and downs, but its recent owners have performed wonders. Nowadays the place not only looks great, but also is once again a thriving venue with everything from bands and DJs through to cabaret, comedy, and theatre attracting a buzzing local crowd. 389 Coldharbour Lane, SW9. www.thedogstar.co.uk. ✆ **020/7733-7515.** Tube: Brixton.

Ice Bar.

Gordon's Wine Bar  Gordon's can lay claim to being one of London's oldest and, in the eyes of those who have fallen for its charms, most inimitable wine bars. Descend the stairs into the bar's grotto-like basement and if you're lucky enough to find a table, settle in for an evening of wine, sherry, and cheese. The service isn't always impeccable, but you can't fault the atmosphere, hence the eclectic mix of office workers, students, and artistic sorts who pack it out most nights. 47 Villiers St., WC2. www.gordonswinebar.com. ✆ **020/7930-1408.** Tube: Charing Cross or Embankment.

Ice Bar A novelty, yes, but London's only bar constructed entirely from imported Swedish ice is still worth checking out. For obvious reasons the temperature is always kept at a chilly −15°C (5°F), so you'll want to wrap up tight in the silver cape and hood they provide. 31–33 Heddon St., W1. www.belowzerolondon.com. ✆ **020/7478-8910.** Admission Mon–Wed and Sun £12; Thurs–Sat £15. Tube: Oxford Circus.

Loungelover Expensive, garish, but also ever popular, Loungelover is adjacent to and run by the same people as the equally colorful restaurant **Les Trois Garçons** (p. 239). It's a warren of rooms, each with its own identity; the effect has been compared to a walk through a film set. The elegant cocktails are among the most original creations in London, often with quirky names. Food is available on tapas-like platters. Even if you're only stopping in for a drink, make a reservation because space is limited. 1 Whitby St., E1. www.loungelover.uk.com. ✆ **020/7012-1234.** Tube: Old St./Overground: Shoreditch High St.

Mark's Bar ★★ Attached to noted restaurant **Hix** (p. 210), this dark and stylish bar offers up a slice of Manhattan deep in the heart of Soho. Its imaginative drinks menu, devised by Nick Strangeway, is packed full of historical curiosities that "hark back to another era before the Temperance Movement had reared its ugly head." Leave your mojitos at the door and instead try something a little different, such as the 19th-century inspired "Punch à la Regent." 66–70 Brewer St., W1. www.hixsoho.co.uk. ℂ **020/7292-3518.** Tube: Piccadilly Circus.

Nightjar ★★   Hidden away just a stone's throw from Old Street roundabout is subterranean cocktail speakeasy, The Nightjar. It might not be much to look at from the outside but once you've found the place, you can settle into a dark corner and treat yourself to one (or several) of the drinks from their impressive menu of elegant and inventively presented cocktails. 129 City Road, EC1V. www.barnightjar. com. ℂ **020/7253-4101.** Tube: Old Street.

Phoenix Artist Club 👥   The favored watering hole of many a London actor, this basement bar has seen plenty of decadent sights over the years. This is where Laurence Olivier made his stage debut in 1930, although he couldn't stop giggling even though the play was a drama. Live music is featured occasionally, but the hearty welcome, good beer, and friendly patrons from ages 20 to 50 are what make this theatre bar a worthwhile detour. It's "members only" after 8pm, but arrive early, find yourself a secluded spot, and you'll be able to drink long into the night. 1 Phoenix St., WC2. www.phoenixartistclub.com. ℂ **020/7836-1077.** Tube: Tottenham Court Rd.

69 Colebrooke Row ★★★   Showing that size certainly isn't everything, 69 Colebrooke Row is one of London's smallest bars and a must-visit for true cocktail aficionados. Serving up exquisite bespoke beverages, Tony Conigliaro is widely regarded as one of the U.K.'s finest drink creators, and applies the same sense of experimentation and scientific play to the bar that chefs such as Heston Blumenthal have brought to the kitchen. 69 Colebrooke Row, N1. www.69colebrookerow. com. ℂ **07540/528-593.** Tube: Angel.

The Social   While most bars in the West End exist solely to speed the separation of your money from your wallet, this curiously thin bar has much nobler aims. Founded by the team behind the Heavenly record label, The Social offers up great new bands, surprise big-name DJs, a decent selection of beers, and the guarantee that come 10pm on a Friday night the place will be jumping. Now entering its second decade, The Social shows no sign of slowing down, which is just how it will hopefully continue. 5 Little Portland St., W1. www.thesocial.com. ℂ **020/7636-4992.** Tube: Oxford Circus.

Vertigo 42 ★ 📷   For a truly unique London experience head to Vertigo 42, the champagne bar at the top of Tower 42 (until 1990 the tallest building in London). At around 180m (some 600 ft.), the bar offers panoramic views across all of London. Although the price of drinks may match the bar's own vertiginous heights, for special occasions few spots can match it. Tower 42, 25 Old Broad St., EC2. www.vertigo42.co.uk. ℂ **020/7877 7842.** Tube: Bank or Liverpool St.

Worship Street Whistling Shop ★★ 📷   Just as the likes of Heston Blumenthal have revolutionized the British dining experience, combining both ultramodern cooking techniques with a rediscovery of past menus, we're increasingly seeing a more experimental and inventive approach to the science of mixology. If you're looking to slake your thirst with something beyond a mojito then definitely add The Worship Street Whistling Shop to your checklist. Re-creating long forgotten drinks and applying new techniques to create libations never possible before, the alchemists behind the bar create liquid gold every time. 63 Worship St., EC2A. www.whistlingshop.com. ℂ **020/7247-0015.** Tube: Old Street.

Late Nights at the NHM

Generations of children have stood in the great hall at the **Natural History Museum** (p. 124) and gawped at the giant Diplodocus that greets them. Thanks to a monthly late-night opening, adults can now have the place to themselves between 6 and 10:30pm, and enjoy a bite to eat, some soft music, and a glass or two of wine beneath the fossilized remains of the great beast itself. After-hours events happen on the last Friday of every month, with everything from photographic exhibitions to lectures alongside an eye-opening opportunity to see one of London's great Victorian edifices in a whole new light. Check **www.nhm.ac.uk** for details of upcoming events.

Pubs

The quintessential British experience of dropping into the "local" for a pint of real ale or bitter is a great way to soak up the character of the different villages that form London. As bars and clubs have mushroomed over the past two decades, the pub may have lost some of its grip on the British psyche and the Great British local is an increasingly rare and endangered beast, but gems still exist. Hunt one down and you'll find yourself in the best place to catch the area's gossip or sports talk—and, of course, enjoy the finest ales, stouts, ciders, and malt whiskies in the world. General opening hours are noon until 11pm, although recent changes to licensing laws mean that many pubs now stay open later—and even in those that don't you're unlikely to be rushed from the premises.

Insider's tip: Websites such as **Beer-intheevening.com** and **Fancyapint.com** host user reviews of nearly every London pub.

THE WEST END

French House A remnant from Soho's louche past, the French House is a curious creature. No pint glasses and no mobile phones are the rules of this house, and woe-betide anyone who tries to flout either. A favorite of writers, poets, and actors over the years, the French House makes few concessions to modernity—and that's just the way its bohemian patrons like it. 49 Dean St., W1. www.frenchhousesoho.com. ⓒ **020/7437-2477.** Tube: Leicester Sq.

Harp ★ Wedged between Covent Garden and Trafalgar Square, the Harp is a much-loved traditional pub offering an authentic experience, the winner of several awards over the years. Break up the shopping trip with a

French House.

leisurely pint or two from their interesting range of ales and lagers. 47 Chandos Place, WC2. www.harpcoventgarden.com. ✆ **020/7836-0291.** Tube: Leicester Sq. or Charing Cross.

Seven Stars   This tranquil little pub facing the back of the Royal Courts of Justice dates back to 1602 and is run by Roxy Beaujolais, author of the pub cookbook, *Home From the Inn Contented.* With its listed rooms and ancient charm this is a pleasant spot to linger over pub food and real ales with litigants, barristers, reporters, and pit musicians from West End shows. In mild weather, the law courts' stone balustrade under the trees provides customers with a long bar and beer garden. 53 Carey St., WC2. www.fullers.co.uk. ✆ **020/7242-8521.** Tube: Chancery Lane or Temple.

Ye Olde Cheshire Cheese   You could be forgiven for thinking Ye Olde Cheshire Cheese was built for a BBC TV costume drama, but there has been a public house on this site for several centuries now. The present building and its maze-like interior dates back to the 17th century, and for a living slice of olde London it's hard to beat, even if just for a quick drink. 145 Fleet St., EC4A. ✆ **020/7353-6170.** Tube: Chancery Lane or Temple.

THE CITY

Counting House   Located bang in the heart of the City, London's financial district, the Counting House is, suitably enough, housed in a former bank. Popular with local financiers, you may need to pay a visit to your own bank beforehand if you're planning on eating because the prices match the location. Still, as watering holes go, this is a rather impressive one and its size, imposing architecture, and great glass-domed ceiling offer a drinking experience unlike most London pubs. 50 Cornhill, EC3V. ✆ **020/7283-7123.** Tube: Bank.

Craft Beer Co.   One of the pioneers of craft beer in the city, the Craft Beer Co. opened its doors back in 2006 and has gone on to become one of the most highly rated bars in the world. With 16 cask ales on tap at any one time, not to mention a range of bottled brews from around the world, this is the place to go in London if you're in search of something a little more interesting than a pint of Carling. 82 Leather Lane, EC1. www.thecraftbeerco.com. Tube: Farringdon.

Wilmington Arms   Located a short hop from bustling Exmouth Market, the Wilmington is a quality pub serving Clerkenwell locals a fine selection of seasonal ales, lagers, and decent, unfussy pub food in comfortable surroundings. Settle into the comfy sofas, and work your way through the day's newspapers, while the pub's well-stocked jukebox provides the soundtrack. If that all sounds a little too sedate, head out back where you can catch up-and-coming indie bands or comedians on most nights. 69 Rosebery Ave., EC1. www.thewilmingtonarms. co.uk. ✆ **020/7837-1384.** Tube: Farringdon.

Ye Olde Mitre Tavern 🏨   Ye Olde Mitre is the name of a working-class inn built here in 1547, when the Bishops of Ely controlled the district. Despite being slap bang in the heart of London, one of those historical anomalies that are so prevalent in Britain meant that until the 1930s it was considered part of Cambridgeshire. Hidden away and hard to find, it's a rough gem of a pub well worth searching out. 1 Ely Court, EC1. www.fullers.co.uk. ✆ **020/7405-4751.** Tube: Chancery Lane.

WEST LONDON

Churchill Arms   Stop here for a nod to the Empire's end. Loaded with Churchill memorabilia, the pub hosts a week of celebration leading up to Churchill's birthday on November 30. Decorations and festivities are also featured for Halloween, Christmas, and St. Paddy's Day, helping to create the homiest village pub atmosphere you're likely to find in London. 119 Kensington Church St., W8. www.fullers.co.uk. ℂ **020/7727-4242.** Tube: Notting Hill Gate or High St. Kensington.

Dove   Where better to relax by the Thames than at the pub where James Thomson composed *Rule Britannia* and part of his lesser-known *The Seasons*. To toast Britannia, you can hoist a pint of Fuller's London Pride or ESB. 19 Upper Mall, W6. www.fullers.co.uk. ℂ **020/8748-9474.** Tube: Ravenscourt Park.

Ladbroke Arms   Previously honored as London's "Dining Pub of the Year," the Ladbroke Arms is still highly regarded for its food. An ever-changing menu includes roast cod filet with lentils and salsa verde; and aged bone-in rib steak with mustard, peppercorn, and herb and garlic butter. With background jazz and rotating art prints, the place strays from the traditional pub environment. The excellent Eldridge Pope Royal is usually on tap. 54 Ladbroke Rd., W11. www.capital pubcompany.com. ℂ **020/7727-6648.** Tube: Notting Hill Gate.

Old Ship   With three different cask beers on rotation at any one time, plus a varied selection of bottled beers and wine and a well-appointed kitchen, the Old Ship ticks a lot of boxes. Check the pub's website for details of the many events they hold from whisky-tasting to carol concerts. It's also easy to see why the Old Ship has topped several polls for alfresco dining. 25 Upper Mall, W6. www.oldshipw6. com. ℂ **020/8748-2593.** Tube: Ravenscourt Park.

Churchill Arms.

Princess Victoria Although "best pub in Shepherd's Bush" probably wouldn't be the most highly regarded award in landlord circles, it's one that the Princess Victoria would win hands down every time. Renovated and recently reopened, this grand old pub with its huge centerpiece horseshoe-shaped bar, is a great addition to an area that tends toward more down-at-heel establishments. Its food is fairly priced, imaginative, and delicious, and the bar carries a great selection of lagers, ales, and wines. 217 Uxbridge Rd., W12. www.princessvictoria.co.uk. (C) **020/8749-5886.** Tube: Shepherd's Bush.

NORTHWEST LONDON

Euston Tap ★ Pubs attached to train stations are often fairly dispiriting affairs, functional spaces for transient drinkers. The Euston Tap throws all that on its head. Occupying a small but curiously grand lodge in front of the station it attracts not just those temporarily marooned by London's woeful transport network but discerning ale drinkers from across the city. An ever changing list of rare lagers and ales ensures that there's always something new on the menu and a reason to visit again and again. West Lodge, 190 Euston Rd., NW1. www.eustontap.com. (C) **020/7387-2890.** Tube: Euston.

Holly Bush ★★ The Holly Bush is the real thing: authentic Edwardian gas lamps, open fires, private booths, and a tap selection of Fuller's London Pride, Adnams, and Harveys. Hidden away in a quiet area of Hampstead, the Holly Bush provides a warm welcome to those who find it. After a hard day's shopping or walking on Hampstead Heath, settle into one of its snugs and revive yourself with a quality pint and traditional pub food from its well-regarded kitchen. 22 Holly Mount, NW3. www.hollybushpub.com. (C) **020/7435-2892.** Tube: Hampstead.

North London Tavern It's fair to say that Kilburn has come a long way in the past decade. This part of northwest London is now only 50% composed of discount pound shops, with the other 50% made up of quality bars, restaurants, and clubs. The North London Tavern is a prime example of the area's regeneration, and this formerly down-at-heel pub is now one of the area's best with a well-stocked bar that keeps the locals watered, whilst the comfortable dining room serves quality food to an appreciative crowd. 375 Kilburn High Rd., NW6. www.north londontavern.co.uk. (C) **020/7625-6634.** Tube: Kilburn.

NORTH LONDON

Auld Shillelagh Church Street in Stoke Newington has more than its fair share of decent establishments, but for sheer effort the Auld Shillelagh wins hands down. As befits an Irish pub, Guinness flows smoothly behind the bar, but the varied off-the-wall club nights are what really pull in the crowds: from country-themed Sons of Lee Marvin through to Bowie Bar, a night dedicated to the music of the Thin White Duke. In the summer, the sizeable garden out back makes this pub an even more attractive proposition. 105 Stoke Newington Church St., N16. www.theauldshillelagh.com. (C) **020/7249-5951.** Bus: 73.

BrewDog Camden Bar The past few years have seen an explosion (not literally, thankfully) of micro-breweries and craft beer bars in the U.K. The BrewDog Brewery has been at the forefront of this, giving real ales a much needed, punky makeover. Their new bar in Camden exemplifies the spirit of the company—it's loud, fun and full of young people. Although it might appear a million miles away from the ale enthusiasts' stereotype, don't make the mistake of thinking ales aren't taken seriously here. There's a huge, ever-changing range of bottled and draft beers to work through. 113 Bayham Street, NW1. www.brewdog.com/bars/camden. *℃* **020/ 7284 0453.** Tube: Chalk Farm or Camden Town.

Lock Tavern   You're lucky if you can find a space inside the Lock Tavern—the garden and roof terrace fill up within seconds when the sun shines, and the place is home to some of the most painfully trendy people ever to have spent hours perfecting a nonchalant, messed-up look. Despite this, if you're young (or just young at heart) the Lock Tavern remains one of the best pubs in the area, and well worth a visit after an expedition to Camden Market (p. 276). The pub's association with some of the best promoters in London—and the annual Field Day Festival, held every August in Victoria Park and featuring some of the biggest leftfield and indie bands around—ensure that you'll often find some of the coolest DJs slumming it behind the decks. 35 Chalk Farm Rd., NW1. www.lock-tavern.co.uk. *℃* **020/7482-7163.** Tube: Chalk Farm.

EAST LONDON

Britannia ☺   At first glance you'd never guess the Britannia was run by the same people as the Griffin in Shoreditch. As light, airy, and comfortable as the Griffin is not, the Britannia boasts one of the best pub gardens in London, a huge, green space that backs onto stately Victoria Park. In the summer they frequently make the most of it by screening classic films. With no Tube station nearby it can be a bit of a pain to get to, but on a sunny summer day, it's worth the effort. 360 Victoria Park Rd., E9. www.thebritanniapub.co.uk. *℃* **020/8533-0040.** Overground: Hackney Wick.

Camel 🍴   The pie's the thing at the Camel, a small but friendly backstreet hostelry that has made a name for itself serving up some of the best pub grub in the East End. On winter weekends few places can match this cozy, intimate space for a warm welcome, and some justly famous home-cooked pies draw in those in the know from across the city. 277 Globe Rd., E2. www.thecamele2.co.uk. *℃* **020/8983-9888.** Tube: Bethnal Green.

Mason & Taylor   For a true taste of the city head to Mason & Taylor, a modern looking bar that is particularly focused on the beers produced by London's growing number of craft beer brewers. Camden Town Brewery and the Kernal Brewery are particularly well stocked but whatever your tipple you'll be sure to find something that hits the spot from the selection of 12 different beers on tap and an ever-changing roster of bottled ales. 51–55 Bethnal Green Road, E1. www.masonandtaylor.co.uk. *℃* **020/7749-9670.** Tube: Bethnal Green.

Palm Tree 🍴   Although Mile End won't be on most tourists' checklists, those engaged in a spot of East End sightseeing could do a lot worse than stop off here. Tucked away by the Regent's Canal, the Palm Tree attracts a friendly mix of old locals, young students, and those who just appreciate a decent pint in a traditional pub. The live jazz sessions on Saturday nights are a particular draw, and make this place well worth a trip off the beaten path. 127 Grove Rd., E3. *℃* **020/8980-2918.** Tube: Mile End.

Prospect of Whitby   One of London's most historic pubs, the Prospect was founded in the days of the Tudors, taking its name from a coal barge that made trips between Yorkshire and London. Come here for a tot, a noggin, or whatever measure you drink, and soak up the atmosphere. The pub has quite a pedigree:

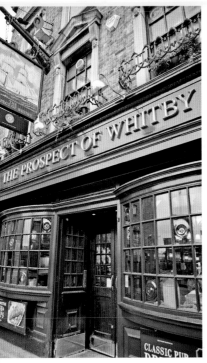
Prospect of Whitby.

Dickens and diarist Samuel Pepys used to drop in, and painter Turner came here for weeks at a time studying views of the Thames. In the 17th century, the notorious Hanging Judge Jeffreys used to get drunk here while overseeing hangings at the adjoining Execution Dock. Tables in the courtyard overlook the river. 57 Wapping Wall, E1. ✆ **020/7481-1095.** DLR: Shadwell/Overground: Wapping.

SOUTHEAST LONDON

Florence ★ A grand old pub with an equally impressive garden, The Florence is an oasis of calm and quality ales in this part of southeast London. With its own micro-brewery on site you know they take their beer seriously here. Just a stone's throw away from Herne Hill station, lazily passing away a sunny afternoon in the garden with a pint of their own-brewed Weasel is one of life's true pleasures. 131–133 Dulwich Road, SE24. www.capitalpubcompany.com/the-florence. ✆ **020/7326-4987.** Rail: Herne Hill.

Gipsy Moth The food is variable and space inside is at a premium, but on a hot summer's day you'll find few nicer spaces to take the weight off your feet than the Gipsy Moth's sizeable garden. Situated right next to the *Cutty Sark* (p. 170)—and within a stone's throw of the Old Royal Naval College—it provides a welcome rest after a day spent taking in Greenwich's sights. 60 Greenwich Church St., SE10. www.thegipsymothgreenwich.co.uk. ✆ **020/8858-0786.** DLR: Cutty Sark.

Old Brewery The Meantime Brewery in Greenwich has long been responsible for providing London's drinkers with quality ales. In 2010, it decided to cut out the middleman and opened its own bar-restaurant-cafe in the grounds of the Old Royal Naval College (p. 174). Whether you want to take a tour of the microbrewery and see award-winning brewers in action, or just relax in the lovely outdoor space, this is just the place. There are more than 50 different beers on offer. Old Royal Naval College, SE10. www.oldbrewerygreenwich.com. ✆ **020/3327-1280.** DLR: Cutty Sark.

THE SOUTH BANK

George Inn With its historic courtyard, wooden beams, and associated trappings, the George is many tourists' idea of an authentic English pub—indeed, it's even run by the National Trust. For that very reason it's often busy, and many locals give it a clear steer. Worth popping in for one pint, but not the best for an evening's drinking. 77 Borough High St., SE1. www.nationaltrust.org.uk/george-inn/. ✆ **020/7407-2056.** Tube: Borough or London Bridge.

King's Arms Just a few minutes' walk from Waterloo Station, tucked away down a road of handsome cottages, the King's Arms is the perfect mid-commute stop-off. A decent selection of beers including Cornwall's Doom Bar on tap and a well-respected kitchen ensure the pub's two cozy bars soon fill up on weeknights. In summer months you'll find the crowd spilling out of the front. 25 Roupell St., SE1. *℃* **08721/077-077.** Tube: Waterloo.

Royal Oak A real ale fan's delight, the Royal Oak often stocks several draught beers you won't find anywhere else in London—and for that reason is always busy. It's not exclusively for beer buffs though, and the pub itself is a remarkably pleasant inn with tasty, simple food and a friendly crowd. 44 Tabard St., SE1. www.harveys.org.uk. *℃* **020/7357-7173.** Tube: Borough.

Royal Oak.

SOUTHWEST LONDON

Bread & Roses Fancy furthering the cause of international socialism while enjoying a decent pint? If so, the Bread & Roses in Clapham is the pub for you. Owned and run by the Battersea and Wandsworth Trades Union council and the Workers Beer Company, this is about as right-on a pub as you can imagine. Even if you don't tend to break into a rendition of the *Internationale* after a few jars, there's lots to recommend here, with live bands and DJs playing rock 'n' roll, reggae, and soul at the weekend and comedy and quiz nights throughout the week. 68 Clapham Manor St., SW4. www.breadandrosespub.com. *℃* **020/7498-1779.** Tube: Clapham North or Clapham Common.

Draft House Northcote ★★★ For anyone serious about their ales, a visit to the Draft House is a must. It's an attempt to recapture all the best qualities of a British pub, and thereby create the perfect example. At any one time you'll find dozens of lagers, ales, and beers from all over the world on offer—and to help you in your quest to try them all, the Draft House is one of the only pubs in London to serve half-pint measures. 94 Northcote Rd., SW11. www.drafthouse.co.uk. *℃* **020/7924-1814.** Rail/Overground: Clapham Junction.

Powder Keg Diplomacy ★ Even if there was nothing else to recommend it Powder Keg Diplomacy in Clapham would still be worth a visit just to gawk at its over-the-top Victorian-era decorations. As it stands there's a lot more to this pub than its colonial trappings and, with a strong emphasis on supporting local small breweries and giving traditional British cocktails a modern twist, don your pith hat and hunt it out. 147 St. John's Hill, SW11. www.powderkegdiplomacy.co.uk. *℃* **020/7450-6457.** Rail/Overground: Clapham Junction.

A home FROM HOME

If you're spending time in London but miss home (or just that all important cup match) then you're in luck. One of the most multicultural cities in the world, London plays host to communities from countless nations and you're never far from a familiar accent. There are parts of west and southwest London where you'll find the majority of the community are Australian, and certainly between Shepherd's Bush and Clapham you'll not have to look far to find a welcoming bar. The **Walkabout** chain of pubs (www.walkabout.eu.com) is probably the most ubiquitous with bars all over London, and you're guaranteed to find all the major Oz sporting events being shown when they're not hosting touring bands.

South Africans in search of some home comforts (or just a pint of Castle) should head to **The Aardvark** (351 Rotherhithe Street, London, SE16; © **020/7394-8644;** Tube: Canada Water) in Rotherhithe, southeast London, where you'll be able to sate your appetite for biltong and boerie rolls whilst watching the latest Currie Cup matches. If you're looking to catch up with the latest goings on in the NFL or NBA, then **Bodean's BBQ** chain (www.bodeansbbq.com) is your best bet, with venues in Soho, Clapham, Fulham and Tower Hill. Not only will you be able to knock back a cold brew whilst watching the latest U.S. sports action, but you'll be able to fill your belly with Bodean's healthy sized portions of BBQ'ed pork and slaw.

Priory Arms   A genuine freehouse (that is not tied to one particular brewery), the Priory is one of South London's best loved pubs. With five real ales on tap at any one time, you know they take their beer seriously and the regulars—who come from all over London—love them for it. Quiz nights on Sunday, a competitive poker league on Thursdays, and quality, affordable seasonal food nightly completes the picture of this tightly run pub. 83 Lansdowne Way, SW8. www.theprioryarms.co.uk. © **020/7622-1884.** Tube: Stockwell.

THE CLUB & MUSIC SCENE
Live Music

Every night in hundreds of venues across London, you'll find live music being played, from international superstars to those making their first hesitant steps from their garages. The *Guide,* a supplement inside Saturday's *Guardian,* offers up-to-date listings covering everything from rock and pop through to jazz, folk, and blues. Online guides such as **Spoonfed** (www.spoonfed.com) are often a good place to find more leftfield events. Most small venues will allow you to purchase tickets on the night, but for larger and more popular events you may have to buy way in advance. Most venues have ticketing information on their own websites; failing that, check **SEEtickets.com**, **WeGotTickets.com**, or **Ticketweb.co.uk**.

ROCK & POP
Bush Music Hall ★★   One of London's more beautiful venues, this former Victorian music hall has a small capacity, but bands and punters alike love its

"Duke of Uke" & the Rise of the Ukulele

A curious phenomenon of recent years has been the rise and rise of the humble ukulele. For years this relation of the banjo was the preserve of flat-capped comic George Formby. It has experienced an unlikely revival, and now the likes of Amanda Palmer and Noah and the Whale incorporate its distinctive plucked sound. The **Ukulele Orchestra** of **Great Britain** is also becoming a fixture at the U.K.'s major summer music festivals. If you want to get the uke habit, head for **Duke of Uke,** 88 Cheshire Street, E2. (www.dukeofuke. co.uk; 🕾 **020/3583-9728**), to satisfy all your banjo and uke cravings, and to get advice and tips on playing.

unique ambience. In recent years it's become a favored venue for larger acts to perform one-off, often secret shows with the likes of Suede performing here in 2010 before their headline dates at the larger O2 Arena. 310 Uxbridge Rd., W12. www.bushhallmusic.co.uk. 🕾 **020/8222-6955.** Admission £5–£20. Tube: Shepherd's Bush.

CAMP   Set up by James Priestly, the man behind the legendary Secret Sundaze parties, the CAMP (City & Arts Music Project) may lack the niceties of other venues, but already in its short life this rough-and-ready basement has hosted some of the most anticipated gigs of recent times. Expect to hear all manner of edgy, underground music here—from visiting American indie bands to homegrown dubstep and techno DJs. 70–74 City Rd., EC1. www.thecamplondon.com. 🕾 **020/7253-2443.** Admission from free to £10. Tube: Old St.

Koko ★   This venue has gone by a variety of names over the years, first as a theatre before becoming a famous live music venue. Koko now hosts the weekly NME club night every Friday that showcases up-and-coming indie bands, with Saturdays dedicated to more dance-music-oriented events, and live bands throughout the week. Despite having a capacity of just 1,500, Koko has made a name for itself hosting special one-off gigs by name acts such as Madonna, Prince, and Red Hot Chili Peppers. 1a Camden High St., NW1. www.koko.uk.com. 🕾 **0870/432-5527.** Admission £8–£20. Tube: Mornington Crescent.

Macbeth   If you fancy catching not the next, but possibly the third or fourth, big thing then The Macbeth is as good a bet as any. On first impressions it could pass for any old London pub that has somehow avoided the avaricious grasp of the property developers, slightly run down, with just the curious frescoes on the wall marking it out. Come sundown it transforms into one of London's best new live venues hosting everything from punk bands and vintage rockers, through to electronic noiseniks and arena selling bands slumming it under an assumed name. 70 Hoxton Street, N1. www.themacbeth.co.uk. 🕾 **020/7749-0600.** Admission free–£5. Tube: Old Street.

O2 Academy Brixton ★   For many indie and rock bands a night at Brixton Academy represents a true measure of success. With a capacity of just under 5,000, it's one of London's most impressive venues, and that's reflected by the high caliber of artists that occupy its stage most nights. Voted best London venue by the readers of indie bible *NME* 12 times, this former Art Deco cinema is now a rock institution. Shows at the Academy tend to sell out well in advance and scalpers outside the venue charge a hefty premium, so look ahead and book through the venue's website. 211 Stockwell Rd., SW9. www.o2academybrixton.co.uk. ✆ **020/7771-3000.** Admission £15–£40. Tube: Brixton.

Roundhouse ★★ Housed in a Victorian steam-engine repair shed, the Roadhouse in Camden is a cultural venue, presenting live music from emerging young talent, and even theatre and dance. Famous for all-night psychedelic raves in the 1960s, it reopened in 2006 attracting a new young London crowd. In days of yore Jimi Hendrix, Paul McCartney, and The Who performed here and now it plays host to today's rising stars, urban festivals, and innovative performances. Chalk Farm Rd., NW1. www.roundhouse.org.uk. ✆ **0844/482-8008.** Admission £5–£50. Tube: Chalk Farm.

Scala This former Art Deco cinema is now one of London's best music venues. With four floors, three bars, and a capacity just short of 1,200, Scala plays host to a wide range of club nights and live music events from indie, rock, and pop through to hip-hop, electronica, and drum and bass. Acts such as Coldplay, the Chemical Brothers, and Robbie Williams have all graced its stage. Advance booking is advisable. 275–277 Pentonville Rd., N1. www.scala-london.co.uk. ✆ **020/7833-2022.** Admission £10–£30. Tube: King's Cross.

Union Chapel ★★★ 📷 You'd be hard pressed to find a more beautiful setting for a concert than this 19th-century Islington church. Settle in on one of the wooden pews and let yourself be awestruck by the surroundings. To suit the venue's natural ambience, music here tends toward the more reflective end of the spectrum with folk, ambient electronica, and acoustic pop and rock. Compton Ave., N1. www.unionchapel.org.uk. ✆ **020/7359-4019.** Admission from free to £30. Tube: Highbury and Islington.

The Roundhouse.

Union Chapel.

Wilton's Music Hall ★★  London's oldest surviving music hall, Wilton's, which opened in the 1850s, was for many years one of east London's most vibrant venues hosting all manner of bawdy entertainment. Years of neglect left the venue close to being demolished but recent efforts to secure the venue's future have seen it once again become a vital part of the capital's entertainment scene, hosting live gigs, theatre productions, and comedy events in what is one of London's most spectacular and atmospheric venues. Graces Alley, E1. www.wiltons.org.uk. 020/ 7702 9555. Admission from free to £30. Tube: Aldgate East.

JAZZ & BLUES

Blues Kitchen One of London's only dedicated blues bars, Camden's Blues Kitchen is the place to listen to stripped-down music from the Mississippi Delta while enjoying a plate loaded with authentic Cajun cooking. Hosting DJ nights, real Blues legends from the States, and the occasional indie star looking to reconnect with their roots, the Blues Kitchen is a lively alternative to the identikit indie nights of most Camden venues. 111–113 Camden High St., NW1. www.theblueskitchen.com. 020/7387-5277. Admission from free to £3. Tube: Camden Town.

Café Oto Experimental is the watchword at Café Oto—on some nights the casual visitor might be forgiven for wondering if the sound is music at all, let alone jazz. For anyone open to some left-field sonic experiences, however, Café Oto is a delight, and one of the few venues in London where acclaimed musicians can be sure to find an

Marshall Allen performing at Café Oto.

appreciative audience for even their most challenging works. 18–22 Ashwin St., E8. www.cafeoto.co.uk. © **020/7923-1231.** Admission £5–£10. Overground: Dalston Kingsland or Dalston Junction.

Ronnie Scott's Jazz Club　Inquire about jazz in London, and people immediately think of Ronnie Scott's, the European vanguard for modern jazz. Only the best English and American combos, often fronted by top-notch vocalists, are booked here. In the Main Room, you can watch the show from the bar or sit at a table and order dinner. The Downstairs Bar is more intimate; among the regulars may be some of the world's most talented musicians. Reservations are recommended. 47 Frith St., W1. www.ronniescotts.co.uk. © **020/7439-0747.** Admission £10–£50. Tube: Leicester Sq. or Tottenham Court Rd.

Vortex ★　If Ronnie Scott's is the sanitized, tourist-friendly face of London's jazz scene, the Vortex in Dalston is the real deal, and the place where you're as likely to find yourself seated next to a jazz musician as watching them. Now firmly settled in its new home, the club offers an exciting mix of internationally acclaimed established players and up-and-coming talent, catering for jazz fans of all persuasions, from the traditional to the more leftfield. Advance booking is recommended. 11 Gillett Sq., N16. www.vortexjazz.co.uk. © **020/7254-4097.** Admission £8–£15. Overground: Dalston Kingsland or Dalston Junction.

Nightclubs

Cable　With its warren-like maze of tunnels and railway arches, the area around London Bridge has long been home to some of London's best underground clubs. The current king of SE1, Cable has quickly become a byword for quality underground dance music, from house, disco, and techno through to dubstep and drum and bass and its success has led to the opening of a sister club next door, the 500-capacity Relay. 33 Bermondsey St., SE1. www.cable-london.com. © **020/7403-7730.** Admission £5–£15. Tube: London Bridge.

Corsica Studios ★★★ 👔　It shares a Tube station with **Ministry** (p. 324), but in every other respect Corsica Studios is a world away from its internationally famous neighbor. Housed under the railway arches behind the Coronet, it harks back to the days before clubbing became corporate and safe. Although the club may seem rather Spartan on first impression, that's because those involved know that a good PA, a dark space, and a few lights are all that the best

---

 London Pleasure Gardens

The concept of the "pleasure garden," a leafy, open retreat for Londoners to escape from the pressures of the city, dates back to the Victorian era. Needed now more than ever the **London Pleasure Gardens** (www.londonpleasure gardens.com; DLR: Pontoon Dock)—opened in 2012 as part of the Olympics-inspired regeneration of east London—has reclaimed a huge swathe of the riverside, transforming it into a new cultural hub in the heart of the city. With concert stages, floating restaurants, cocktail bars, open-air cinema spaces, and lots more beside, the London Pleasure Gardens offers year-round entertainment, from the mainstream to the avant-garde.

DJs need to work their magic. From techno and electronica, through to leftfield disco and experimental rock, Corsica Studios provides a haven for those seeking underground sounds. For this reason, it's regularly voted among the U.K.'s best small clubs. 5 Elephant Rd., SE17. www.corsicastudios.com. © **020/7703-4760.** Admission £5–£15. Tube: Elephant & Castle.

Fabric ★ While other competitors have come and gone, Fabric continues to draw in the big crowds. Consistently ranked as one of the best clubs on the planet, every weekend it plays host to the biggest DJs in town. On some crazed nights, at least 2,500 crowd into this mammoth place. It has a trio of dance floors, bars wherever you look, unisex toilets, and a sound system that you feel as much as hear. Friday nights tend to veer toward live performances, dubstep, drum and bass, and electro music, while Saturday nights feature the best techno and house DJs from around the world. Open Friday 9:30pm to 5am, Saturday 10pm to 7am. 77a Charterhouse St., EC1. www.fabriclondon.com. © **020/7336-8898.** Admission £15–£20. Tube: Farringdon.

Ginglik 👫 Unlikely as it seems, hidden away in a former block of Victorian toilets underneath Shepherd's Bush Green is one of London's best clubs. Favoring more underground styles of music from electronica and techno through to leftfield hip-hop and funk, Ginglik inspires a lot of love and devotion from its regulars who travel from all over London to party at long-running club nights such as I Love Acid and Size Doesn't Matter. During the week comedy and live nights rule, with an ever changing line-up of new talent. 1 Shepherds Bush Green, W12. www.ginglik.co.uk. © **020/8749-2310.** Admission £5–£8. Tube: Shepherd's Bush.

Ministry of Sound It's been a while since London's first superclub was considered cool and these days the venue itself is just one small part of the Ministry's global brand. However, the club still has the international reputation to attract the biggest names in house music to this unloved corner of South London, and glammed-up crowds continue to pack out the venue's three rooms. It can be a pricey night out and you'll need to dress up but as the place where London's underground club culture first came of age it's well worth a visit. Open Friday 10pm to 5am and Saturday 11pm to 7am. 103 Gaunt St., SE1. www.ministryofsound.com. © **0870/060-0010.** Admission £10–£20. Tube: Elephant & Castle.

The Nest ★ Shoreditch has ruled over London's nightlife for much of the past decade, but the area's increased commercialization has driven many of its artier denizens to seek out new haunts in Bethnal Green, Dalston, and London Fields. But whilst the area is a hotbed for pop-up parties in abandoned or appropriated spaces, there are still relatively few proper venues to check out. Luckily the one that is there, The Nest, is one of the best around. Live events during the week usually feature bands at the cutting edge of whatever scene is current, and weekends are given over to respected techno, house, and disco DJs. With the kind of line-ups you'd expect to see at Fabric (see above) and not in the basement of a former furniture shop the club is usually full by midnight, but well worth checking out. 36 Stoke Newington Rd., N16. www.ilovethenest.com. © **020/7354-9993.** Admission £5–£10. Overground: Dalston Kingsland or Dalston Junction.

Notting Hill Arts Club West London has been left behind in the cool stakes, but this remains one of the hippest nighttime venues in London. Located

Notting Hill Arts Club

close to the HQs of many big record labels, you'll often find a music industry crowd here checking out the latest buzz bands, and Thursday night's YoYo party can see the likes of Mark Ronson take to the decks. Most clients are younger than 35, and come from a wide range of backgrounds. The music is eclectic, varying from night to night—from jazz and world music through to electro, hip-hop, and indie. 21 Notting Hill Gate, W11. www.nottinghillartsclub.com. ✆ **020/7460-4459.** Admission £5–£15. Tube: Notting Hill Gate.

Plan B Thirty years on from the Brixton Riots, and a lot has changed in this part of south London. Although the area remains far from gentrified, it now boasts several of London's best clubs, bars, and venues. Leading the pack is Plan B, where an uncluttered dance floor, excellent sound system, and forward-thinking club nights have made it a destination for clubbers from across the city. From hip-hop and house through to disco and dubstep, you'll often find the venue being used as an official after-party location for bands playing nearby O2 Academy Brixton (p. 320). 418 Brixton Rd., SW9. www.plan-brixton.co.uk. ✆ **020/7733-0926.** Admission from free to £10. Tube: Brixton.

Plastic People ★★ 📷 For much of London's clubbing cognoscenti, this 200-capacity basement in Shoreditch is simply the best this city has to offer—and it's easy to see why. With probably the sharpest sound system in town and a crowd who know their music, Plastic People manages to attract DJs more used to playing to parties numbered in the thousands. For dubstep, techno, or house, few other venues can compare to a night at Plastic People. 149 Curtain Rd., EC2. www.plasticpeople.co.uk. ✆ **020/7739-6471.** Admission £5–£15. Tube: Old St./Overground: Shoreditch High St.

Queen of Hoxton The latest in a long line of venues to have occupied this space, the Queen of Hoxton is the first to have made a success of it. With a decent-sized basement bar, a comfortable ground floor, and a rooftop garden, it attracts a young, dressed-up, trendy crowd who dance long into the night to a mixture of electro, disco, and house on weekends, with up-and-coming electronica and indie bands taking over the basement midweek. 1–5 Curtain Rd., EC2. www.thequeenofhoxton. co.uk. ℭ **020/7422-0958.** Admission £3–£10. Tube: Liverpool St./Overground: Shoreditch High St.

XOYO XOYO (pronounced "X-O-Y-O") was launched in 2010 to much fanfare and no little disaster, but despite an opening week that saw power cuts, closures, and general chaos, the venue has established itself as a valuable addition to London clubland. Thanks to the involvement of some top-rank promoters—such as Eat Your Own Ears and Bugged Out!—XOYO has become the place to check out exciting new bands from around the world and dance till the morning in the company of big-name DJs. 32–37 Cowper St., EC2. www.xoyo.co.uk. ℭ **020/7490-1198.** Admission £5–£15. Tube: Old St.

Queen of Hoxton.

Comedy Clubs

Amused Moose Three times winner of London's Best Comedy Club award, the Amused Moose in Soho is one of London's most established and best-loved comedy nights. Every Saturday night expect to be entertained by comedians both old and new. If you fancy having a go yourself, the club runs comedy workshops and classes most weeknights. 17 Greek St., W1. www.amusedmoose.com. ℭ **020/7287-3727.** Admission £10. Tube: Tottenham Court Rd.

Comedy Café Now in its second decade, the Comedy Café in Shoreditch serves up an appetizing menu of decent food, good cocktails, and some of the best comic talent around. Wednesday night is "New Acts Night" where you can expect to see eight first timers try their hand at the comedy business, while Thursday through Saturday sees established talent take to the stage with four different comics on each night. Popular with parties, advance booking is usually recommended and various deals are available for groups. 66–68 Rivington St., EC2. www.comedycafe.co.uk. ℭ **020/7739-5706.** Admission from free to £16. Tube: Old St.

Comedy Store This is London's showcase for established and rising comic talent. Inspired by comedy clubs in the U.S., the venue has given many comics their start, and today a number of them are established British TV personalities. The club opens 1½ hours before each show. Tuesday to Sunday, doors open at 6:30pm and the show starts at 8pm; on Friday and Saturday, an extra show starts at midnight (doors open at 11pm). *Insider's tip:* Go on Tuesday when the humor is more cutting edge. 1a Oxendon St., off Piccadilly Circus, SW1. www.thecomedystore. co.uk. ✆ **0844/847-1728.** Admission £13–£20. Tube: Leicester Sq. or Piccadilly Circus.

99 Club With shows running 7 nights a week, 52 weeks a year, you know the people behind the 99 Club are serious about their comedy. It's regularly voted one of the best places in London for alternative stand-up, and those on stage range from award-winning TV regulars through to emerging talent. 28a Leicester Sq., WC2. www.99clubcomedy.com. ✆ **07760/488-119.** Admission £8–£16. Tube: Leicester Sq.

Up The Creek Opened by the late, great comic Malcolm Hardee, Up The Creek in Greenwich has hosted some of the biggest names in British comedy from Jimmy Carr to Harry Hill and Al Murray. A favored venue for those trying out new material, this is a great spot to catch both up-and-coming and established talents especially in the run up to the Edinburgh Festival. Shows run from Thursday through Sunday, and although you can book in advance, you can normally just turn up and expect to get in. 302 Creek Rd., SE10. www.up-the-creek.com. ✆ **020/8858-4581.** Admission £5–£10. DLR: Cutty Sark.

Dance Clubs & Cabaret

Bathhouse 🎁 Unless you happen to work in the City, the Bathhouse isn't the easiest place to find—but trust us, it's worth the effort. This former Victorian opium den reopened in 2010 after an extensive renovation had brought it back to its decadent best. Now home to some of London's best cabaret nights—including wildly popular burlesque and rock 'n' roll sensation, the **Boom Boom Club**—you'll find a mixed crowd of open-minded office workers and dressed-up burlesque scenesters taking in the live shows, or dancing through the night as DJs play from inside a giant golden birdcage. 8 Bishopsgate Churchyard, EC2. www. thebathhousevenue.com. ✆ **020/7920-9207.** Admission £9–£45. Tube: Liverpool St.

Box Within weeks of opening The Box in Soho had already generated its fair share of tall and scandalous stories with everyone from the Royal Family to popstars and models in attendance. Described as "Britain's seediest club," it is fair to say that the entertainment on offer is not for the priggish or faint hearted. Still with some of the biggest names in cabaret gracing its stage, it's quite an experience—just expect to pay through the nose to enjoy it. 11 Walker's Court, W1. www. theboxsoho.com. ✆ **020/7434-4374.** Tube: Leicester Square.

Proud Cabaret While its larger sister club in Camden flirts with burlesque, as the name suggests Proud Cabaret is a more committed affair. Modeled on early 20th-century speakeasies, the venue offers wining, dining, and risqué entertainment from some of the scene's biggest performers. It's a more upscale affair, and representative of a trend that has seen cabaret become mainstream in recent years, not always with the approval of those at the scene's grassroots. If you want to experience old-fashioned glamour and glitz, advance booking is recommended. 1 Mark Lane, EC3. www.proudcabaret.com. ✆ **020/7283-1940.** Admission £10–£50. Tube: Monument.

A star of Proud Cabaret.

The Gay & Lesbian Nightlife Scene

Admiral Duncan   A popular, fun, and above all lively pub in the center of Soho, the Admiral Duncan has long been one of London's most popular gay bars, and most nights you'll find the pub packed with shot-downing regulars. 54 Old Compton St., W1. ✆ **020/7437-5300.** No cover. Tube: Piccadilly Circus or Leicester Sq.

Dalston Superstore ★★   Cafe by day, disco bar by night, this Superstore is a welcome addition to trendy Dalston, providing a space for gays, lesbians, and their straight friends to party away from the mainstream scene. It's packed most nights with a friendly, arty, and open-minded crowd, and the music is much the same as at any cutting-edge bar in this part of town, with disco, electro, and underground house. 117 Kingsland High St., E8. www.dalstonsuperstore.com. ✆ **020/7254-2273.** No cover. Overground: Dalston Kingsland or Dalston Junction.

Eagle   Another lively pub in the "Vauxhall village," the Eagle boasts several raucous nights including cruise party Bootcamp, gay wrestling night Grapple, and on Sunday, the famous Horse Meat Disco, where gays, bears, and clued-up straight disco lovers party to classic sounds. 349 Kennington Lane, SE11. www.eagle london.com. ✆ **020/7793-0903.** Admission £3–£10. Tube: Vauxhall.

Edge   Few bars in London can rival the tolerance, humor, and sexual sophistication found here. The first two floors are done up with decorations that, like an English garden, change with the seasons. Dance music can be found on the crowded, high-energy lower floors. Three menus are featured: A funky daytime menu, a cafe menu, and a late-night menu. Clientele ranges from flamboyantly gay to hetero pub-crawlers. 11 Soho Sq., W1. www.edgesoho.co.uk. ✆ **020/7439-1313.** Tube: Tottenham Court Rd.

Fire One of the biggest gay clubs in London, Fire goes all night throughout the weekend, from Friday night right through to Monday morning, pumping out house and electro of various flavors to a devoted, full-on crowd. It's hot and sweaty, but not to worry . . . shirts soon come off at this hedonists' playground. The contrast between those staggering out of Fire on a Monday morning and commuters heading to work is one of the more surreal London sights. 34–41 Parry St., SW8. www.fireclub.co.uk. ✆ 020/3242-0040. Admission £6–£12. Tube: Vauxhall.

George & Dragon A great deal of "Queer as Folk" life is shifting from Vauxhall and Soho to increasingly fashionable Shoreditch. Its epicenter is this pub where the late Alexander McQueen used to show up and Boy George still drops in. London's *Evening Standard* raved, "it's possibly the best pub in the world . . . ever." It's also been accused of "attracting flotsam," being "grotty," and looking "green and slimy." Regardless of what the spin is, the place is a subcultural phenomenon. Expect a kitsch decor of pink walls, a talking horse head on the wall, cowboy hats, and a sequined guitar worthy of Elvis. 2–4 Hackney Rd., E2. ✆ 020/7012-1100. No cover. Overground: Shoreditch High St.

Heaven This club, housed in the vaulted cellars of Charing Cross railway station, is a long-running London landmark, and one of the biggest and best-established gay venues in Britain. Painted black and reminiscent of an air-raid shelter, the club is divided into different areas, connected by a labyrinth of catwalk stairs and hallways. With the closing of the iconic Astoria, Heaven now hosts **G-A-Y**, on Thursdays, Fridays, and Saturdays. The biggest gay and lesbian party in the

LATE-night EATS

Tinseltown If you don't trust those dubious-looking sausages that get served up on the streetside but fancy a proper bite then check this American-style diner that serves up flamegrilled burgers and milkshakes to a post-club crowd—it's the perfect stop on the way home from Fabric for late night clubbers in need of a quick fix. 44–46 St. John St., EC1. www.tinseltown.co.uk. ✆ 020/7689-2424. Tube: Farringdon. Open till 4am Fri & Sat, 3am Sun, 5am Mon–Thurs.

Bar Italia Serving revelers 24 hours a day for decades, Bar Italia is a Soho institution. Over the years this has been a popular haunt of pop- and rock-stars relaxing after a show and even if Soho might not quite serve the avant-garde community it once did, Bar Italia remains an icon of continental cool. 22 Frith St.,

W1. www.baritaliasoho.co.uk. ✆ 020/7437-4520. Tube: Tottenham Court Rd.

Beigel Bake ★ If you're on Brick Lane, ignore the overrated curry houses and head here, where at weekends you'll find a long but fast-moving line of people trailing out of Beigel Bake, where generations of clued-up Londoners have been heading to get their late-night fix of salt-beef specials. 159 Brick Lane, E1. ✆ 020/7729-0616. Tube: Liverpool St.

Damascu Bite You're never far from a kebab shop in London, but they're normally a last resort after a boozy night. Damascu Bite may be open 24 hours but its chicken shish are a cut above the competition and really far too good for just drunken revelers. 21 Shoreditch High St., E1. ✆ 020/7247-0207. Tube: Old St./Overground: Shoreditch High St.

U.K. if not Europe, G-A-Y has featured performances from big name pop acts including Madonna and the Spice Girls. The Arches, Villiers St., WC2. www.heaven nightclub-london.com. ✆ **020/7930-2020.** Admission £12–£20. Tube: Charing Cross or Embankment.

Royal Vauxhall Tavern ★   The Royal Vauxhall Tavern was here long before Vauxhall became London's gay village, but even back in the late 1890s it was home to some of London's most colorful cabaret. London's oldest surviving gay venue, the Royal Vauxhall is a much-loved institution and an essential stop-off before hitting one of the local clubs. It's open 7 nights a week and you're likely to find all manner of fun inside from camp burlesque and cabaret to bingo, comedy, and plain old-fashioned discos. 372 Kennington Lane, SE11. www.theroyalvauxhalltavern. co.uk. ✆ **020/7820-1222.** Admission £5–£15. Tube: Vauxhall.

ALTERNATIVE ENTERTAINMENT

Alt-Cinema

Visiting the cinema—in central London at least—can be an expensive experience, especially those on Leicester Square. Plus, given that mainstream Hollywood films are shown at most theatres, you could be in any city. Scratch beneath the surface, however, and you'll find alternative cinematic experiences.

Curzon in Mayfair   The Curzon caters for true cineastes with screenings of foreign and art-house films, Q&As with directors, and one-off screenings of classics. If you fancy enjoying the silver screen away from popcorn-chomping hordes then this is the place to go. 38 Curzon St., W1. www.curzoncinemas.com. ✆ **0871/703-3989**. Admission £8.50–£12.50. Tube: Green Park.

Prince Charles Cinema   If you like audience participation, and have a high tolerance for the camp, head here on the last Friday of every month for "Sing-A-Long with *Grease*" (www.singalonga.net), a long-running and inspired combination of fancy-dress karaoke and a classic film. Film choices may vary from *The Sound of Music, The Commitments,* or *The Rocky Horror Show.* Films are shown at 8:30pm with occasional lunchtime viewings throughout the month. The cinema also shows mainstream movies. 7 Leicester Place, WC2. www.princecharlescinema. com. ✆ **020/7494-3654**. Admission £15. Tube: Leicester Sq.

Secret Cinema ★★   Every few months the Secret Cinema hosts a large-production extravaganza in a different venue, bringing a film to life on an epic scale. You're given a theme to ensure you dress appropriately. On arrival you're catapulted into a complete reproduction of the film's universe—it's spectacular. Buying tickets in advance is a must. Venues vary. www.secretcinema.org. Admission from £30.

Bingo

Long the preserve of octogenarians in drafty village halls, bingo has enjoyed an unexpected renaissance, and a number of alternative bingo nights have sprung up.

Underdog   Those in search of a full house can choose between a number of flavors including Australian Rules Bogan Bingo, which runs weekly on Thursdays from 8pm at The Underdog Bar in Camden. You'll be treated to an irreverent night of Aussie stereotypes, fast-paced bingo action, and even a weekly air guitar competition. 16a Clapham Common, SW4. www.theunderdogbar.co.uk. *©* **020/7978-2691**. Tube: Clapham Common.

Underground Rebel Bingo Club ★   The anarchic mix of music, drinking, dancing, shouting, and of course bingo makes up the now international Underground Rebel Bingo Club. With parties popping up all over the planet keep an eye on the website for news of "secret" parties in London. Venues vary. www.rebel bingo.com. Admission from £5.

Cool Karaoke

London has plenty of places where enthusiastic amateurs can do terrible things to popular songs. Despite the British reputation for reserve, you'll find karaoke nights in pubs and bars all over the city, not to mention dedicated karaoke bars.

Hip-Hop Karaoke   For an evening of memorable karaoke, head to the Social (p. 311), a place to channel your inner Jay-Z. Let loose your best Kanye West impersonation or go old school and bust out your favorite Run DMC rhymes in a raucous, yet friendly atmosphere. The Social, 5 Little Portland St., W1. www.southern hospitality.co.uk. *©* **020/7636-4992.** Tube: Oxford Circus.

Hot Breath ★   Head east to one of the funniest karaoke nights in town, running monthly. Out-of-tune singing is just half the fun, so leave your inhibitions at the door and prepare to get involved in everything from synchronized dancing, through to hot dog eating competitions, while making liberal use of the dressing-up box. Bethnal Green Working Men's Club, 44 Pollard Row, E2. www.thehouseofhotbreath. com. *©* **020/7739-2727.** Tickets usually cost £5 to £10. Tube: Bethnal Green.

Literary Events

A growing number of literary events have brought books out of silent libraries and into London's noisy nightclubs.

Although numbers have decreased in recent years, London still boasts an impressive number of bookshops—ranging from the esoteric to the populist—and many regularly hold literary evenings. **Waterstones** (www.waterstones. com), the largest chain of bookshops in the U.K., has stores dotted all over London, and their website lists all upcoming instore events.

Websites such as **Flavorpill** (www.flavorpill.com/london) and **Londonist** (www.londonist.com) carry information on forthcoming literary events.

Book Slam   The capital's premier regular literary event takes place on the last Thursday of every month at the **Clapham Grand.** Heavyweight authors such as Hanif Kureishi and Nick Hornby have all guested alongside a variety of book-loving pop- and rock-stars. Expect everything from poetry and book readings to live music and DJs. Clapham Grand, 21–25 St. John's Hill, SW11. www.bookslam.com. *©* **020/7223-6523.** Tickets are usually £10. Rail/Overground: Clapham Junction.

Ten-Pin Bowling

Ever since Jeff Bridges played the role of "the Dude" in *The Big Lebowski*, ten-pin bowling has been the coolest sport on Earth. London now has the bowling lanes to match where music, drinking, and dancing are all part of the fun.

All-Star Lanes   Bloomsbury and Brick Lane are two of London's best bowling lanes, where you'll not only be able to skid across the floor in your best bowling shirt but also catch DJ sets from the likes of legendary record shop Rough Trade's staff. www.allstarlanes.co.uk. 95 Brick Lane, E1, ✆ **020/7426-9200.** Tube: Aldgate East; and Victoria House, Bloomsbury Place, WC1, ✆ **020/7025-2676.** Tube: Holborn.

Bloomsbury Lanes With a hot tub in the basement, private lanes and regular nights featuring both big name DJs, and up and coming bands Bloomsbury Lanes provide everything for a fun night out. If you're just interested in bowling though avoid weekend nights when it gets very busy and the music very loud. Tavistock Hotel, Bedford Way, WC1. www.bloomsburybowling.com. ✆ **020/7183-1979.** Tube: Russell Sq.

SPECTATOR SPORTS
Annual Sporting Events
THE BOAT RACE

Taking place on either the last Saturday of March or the first Saturday of April, the Boat Race is an annual rowing competition between teams from Oxford and Cambridge Universities. The two "eights" race up one of the nicer stretches of the Thames, from Putney Bridge to Chiswick Bridge. First held in 1829, the event now attracts thousands of people to the riverside. Although the race itself only lasts around 20 minutes, it does provide a perfect excuse for a free day out in West London, and the chance to ensconce yourself in one of the several fine pubs that line the route. The choice spots are generally considered the **Star & Garter,** 4 Lower Richmond Rd., SW15 (www.thestarandgarter.com; ✆ **020/8788-0345;** Tube: Putney Bridge/Rail: Putney), which overlooks the start and is so popular it actually sells tickets in advance through its website, and the **Ship,** 10 Thames Bank, Ship Lane, SW14 (✆ **020/8876-1439;** Rail: Mortlake), right by the finish line. Wherever you choose to perch, arrive early because the prime spots soon fill up. For more information and to check exact dates and times, see **www.theboatrace.org**.

THE LONDON MARATHON

Held every April, the 26-mile London Marathon (www.virginlondonmarathon.com) winds its way from Greenwich and Blackheath in the southeast of London, across the river at Tower Bridge and west toward The Mall and Buckingham Palace. The annual event shames even the laziest local into struggling out of bed and the route is always lined with huge crowds cheering on anyone mad enough to attempt the race—especially anyone dressed in a ridiculously impractical costume. If you wish to take part, you need to apply up to 8 months in advance, and must usually be sponsored by a charity. Then it's just a question of waiting to see whether you're selected by the massively oversubscribed lottery. A word of warning: Due to the size and duration of the event, many roads in Central, East, and Southeast London are closed for much of the day, and so plan accordingly.

WIMBLEDON

The air of genteel respectability, the punnets of plump strawberries, the frequent bad weather, and the general failure of the local talent to win anything . . . few events are more English than the Championships at the All England Lawn Tennis Club—or "Wimbledon" for short. The world's oldest Grand Slam tennis tournament takes over Southwest London for two weeks each June and early July. Tickets to show courts are incredibly hard to come by: Unless you're lucky enough to bag a corporate ticket, you need to enter the public ballot via the official Wimbledon website. Entry to the ballot is normally opened up the August before the next tournament and closes in December—and as you would expect, it's always massively oversubscribed. During the tournament itself, 500 tickets are released daily for Centre Court and Court 2, another 500 for No. 1 Court. It has become something of a tradition in itself for eager fans to camp outside overnight to be first in line. See **www.wimbledon.org**.

General Spectator Sports

CRICKET

After years in decline, the national summer sport has enjoyed a resurgence of late. The England team is performing well, and a new, shorter form of the game known as **"20/20"** attracts a younger, livelier audience. Now is a great time to catch a game, whether a county or cup match, or one of the annual international "Test Matches" in which England plays against Australia, Bangladesh, India, New Zealand, Pakistan, South Africa, Sri Lanka, or the West Indies.

The cricket season begins in March and ends in September. Lord's and the Oval generally each host at least two international matches in summer, with the full 5-day test matches being followed by a shorter One Day International. Tickets for all matches can be purchased via the grounds' respective websites. For all the latest news and details of forthcoming international matches, check the England & Wales Cricket Board website, **www.ecb.co.uk**.

Lord's Cricket Ground ★ Considered "the home of cricket," the game has been played on this patch of North London since 1814, the base of both the Middlesex Cricket Club and the England and Wales Cricket Board, Lord's plays host to at least two international test matches each summer and is a must visit for any cricket fan passing through the capital. St. John's Wood Rd., NW8. www.lords. org. ✆ **020/7432-1000.** Tube: St. John's Wood.

Oval Cricket Ground South of the river, this cricket ground is somewhat less prestigious than Lord's but still has a long and rich history dating back to the mid 1800s. Home to Surrey Cricket Club, The Oval also traditionally hosts the final international test of each summer. Kennington, SE1. www.thekiaoval.com. ✆ **020/ 7820-5700**. Tube: Oval.

FOOTBALL

From mid-August through mid-May, football (soccer) dominates London like no other sport, often monopolizing both the front and the back pages of local and national newspapers. On any given weekend, thousands of teams—from local pub sides to the international stars of the Premier League—can be found kicking a pigskin around a field. London's biggest clubs pull in tens of thousands of fans each week, and even second- and third-tier clubs regularly play to crowds of 15,000 or more.

Matches traditionally kick off at 3pm on Saturdays, although the demands of TV have transferred several to Sundays or even Monday evenings. Details of forthcoming fixtures can be found in any (literally any) newspaper or online at websites such as **BBC Sport** (http://news.bbc.co.uk/sport) or **Football365** (www.football365.com).

Tickets for the top matches can be very expensive, and are hard to procure. Matches in the lower divisions are not only more affordable, but also frequently attract a noisier and more passionate crowd—and are a real introduction to London weekend life.

Arsenal   One of London's oldest and most successful clubs, Arsenal might not have enjoyed much silverware over the past few years but still rarely finish outside of the top three. Their new home, The Emirates Stadium, may not yet have the history or atmosphere of older grounds but is one of the best to visit. The Emirates Stadium, Drayton Park., N5. www.arsenal.com. 𝒞 **020/7619-5003**. Tube: Arsenal.

Chelsea   Fueled by Russian billionaire Roman Abramovich's fortune Chelsea have gone from being nearly bankrupt to one of the most successful teams in the country and have been winners or runners up of the English premier league seven times over the past decade. Stamford Bridge, Fulham Road, London, SW6. www.chelseafc.co.uk. 𝒞 **0871/984-1905**. Tube: Fulham Broadway.

Queen's Park Rangers (QPR)   A trip to watch newly promoted QPR should cost you between £15 and £25 depending on the match. Often you can pay at the turnstile, although check the club website to make sure. Loftus Road Stadium, South Africa Rd., W12. www.qpr.co.uk. 𝒞 **020/8743-0262**. Tube: Shepherd's Bush.

RUGBY

Although doomed to be forever overshadowed by football, rugby union (the unarmored forbear of "American Football") is an attractive option for anyone determined to take in a sporting event. There are fewer rugby clubs than football clubs active in the city—and certainly none that can match attendances with even second-tier football clubs.

Twickenham   A rugby match at the majestic national stadium is an experience you won't forget. Tickets for the annual **Six Nations Tournament** (during February and March; see www.rbs6nations.com) are like gold dust, but HQ (as Twickenham is known) also hosts numerous exhibition matches and friendlies from the Army vs. Navy and the Sevens Tournament in May, through to the Autumn Internationals series in November against the Southern Hemisphere powers. To check dates and purchase tickets go to the RFU website (www.rfu.com), which has details of forthcoming matches. Expect to pay around £10 to £20 for tickets to exhibition matches, and anywhere from £60 to £120 for major internationals. 200 Whitton Rd, Twickenham, TW2. www.rfu.com/TwickenhamStadium. ☎ **0870/143-2400.** Rail: Twickenham.

Harlequins   A short punt away from Twickenham is The Stoop, home to Harlequins Rugby Club. Their fortunes have fluctuated over the years but they're currently ensconced in the English Premier League and you'll be sure of seeing a good standard of game here. Langhorn Drive, Twickenham, TW2. www.quins.co.uk. ☎ **020 8410 6000.** Rail: Twickenham.

8

STAYING IN LONDON

When it comes to hotel openings and revamps in London, the capital goes from strength to strength. Recession? What recession? The 2012 Olympic factor has certainly helped and barely a month goes by without a new boutique hotel or a multi-million pound refurbishment being announced or completed—London is a boomtown for accommodation.

At the cheapest and most expensive ends of the spectrum, the city's offering is hard to beat. The grand hotels of Mayfair still offer the kind of gracious service and country-house ambience that are copied around the world, and the more recent rise of the no-frills crashpad has been a welcome development in a city where rooms remain among the most expensive on the planet.

BEST BETS

- **Best for Families:** For a high-end break with children, The **Goring** is hard to beat, with a basket of essentials for babies, a bedtime library, furry sheep and activity pack, and the chance to decorate cakes in the kitchens. See p. 359. At the other end of the price scale, the **Hart House Hotel** has such a variety of family rooms that they can accommodate any brood. See p. 353.

- **Best Value:** The new **Z Hotel** is stylish, right in the center of the action in Soho and great value. See p. 348. Out east, the **Hoxton** is regularly booked months in advance, and is as popular with locals as with tourists. See p. 371. You can have a whole floor to yourself in Notting Hill's The **Main House** for the price of a studio elsewhere. See p. 356.

- **Best Splurge: 45 Park Lane** offers the wow factor and the best of modern comforts with large rooms, great views over Hyde Park, and Wolfgang Puck's CUT restaurant. See p. 350. For those with itchy feet, the **St. Pancras Renaissance,** right next to Eurostar in King's Cross, recalls the days of the grand Victorian traveler with its magnificent interiors. See p. 343.

- **Most Romantic:** A converted pumping station might not sound like the thing to set the pulse racing, but the canopy beds and Georgian elegance of **30 Pavilion Road** have made it a much sought-after honeymoon location. See p. 363. The open fireplaces and rich fabrics of the **41 Hotel** are just part of what's making it *the* secret treat for traveling couples. See p. 359.

- **Best Service:** Time and again, you'll hear guests raving over the staff members at the **Covent Garden Hotel**—they're always helpful, and knowledgeable about a district with plenty of hidden treats. See p. 345. Service at the **Mornington Hotel** is very good for such a reasonably priced place. See p. 354.

FACING PAGE: **St. Pancras Renaissance London Hotel.**

London Hotel Price Categories	

Room rates quoted include VAT and service unless otherwise stated. At the smaller family-owned hotels, breakfast is often included, while it comes as extra at the top end of the scale.

Very Expensive	£250 and up
Expensive	£150–£250
Moderate	£120–£150
Inexpensive	Under £120

○ **Best for Food:** The grand lady of Mayfair, **Claridge's** has shaken off the past with a magnificent refurbishment and the inclusion of Gordon Ramsay at Claridge's, where Art Deco opulence and 21st-century culinary genius meet. See p. 349. Making a splash in London's restaurant scene, the modern bistro cookery of Bruno Loubet at the **Zetter** is hard to beat. See p. 369.

○ **Best for Business Travelers: Andaz** combines a City location with business-savvy staff, but its elegant setting and top-notch bar and restaurant make it feel more like a cool West End hangout. See p. 368. Film and media types flock to the **Soho Hotel** in the heart of London's creative hub. See p. 347.

○ **Best Location:** The **Corinthia** is at the heart of royal London, with sweeping views of the Thames and the London Eye from its rooms. See p. 358. If it's the 24-hour city you want, there's no beating the **Dean Street Townhouse,** right in the middle of Soho with a restaurant so packed with media celebrities that the star-struck don't need to walk out of its doors. See p. 348.

○ **Best Design: Rough Luxe** typifies the new London style—a mix of bare walls, ornate wallpaper, quirky antiques, and modern artworks. See p. 344. To get a dose of minimalist Manhattan-style chic, head to the **Sanderson**. See p. 347.

○ **Most Quirky:** No TV, no phones, no room service. It doesn't seem to matter at **40 Winks** where the two tiny rooms are a kind of fashionable time machine. See p. 372. If all London pubs had the kind of cozy yet high-tech rooms boasted by the **Fox & Anchor,** it would completely change the London hotel scene. See p. 370.

○ **Best Discoveries:** In trendy Dalston, the new, tiny boutique **Avo Hotel,** delivers a five-star experience at two-star prices. See p. 373. In chic Spital-fields, the inexpensive **Tune Hotel** may be basic, but it offers clean, comfortable bedrooms and a thoroughly surprising garden. See p. 371.

THE WEST END

If you can afford it, staying in the West End is still the quintessential London experience.

In **Mayfair** you'll be staying in London's top historic hotels. **Bloomsbury** teams quiet, tree-lined streets and Georgian terraces with access to Oxford Street shopping and Theatreland, while near-neighbor **Covent Garden** is nois-ier, smarter, and right at the heart of the action. **Marylebone** is more "villagey" than either. If London's just one port of call on a larger trip then consider **King's**

Cross; it's not the prettiest of central locations, but unparalleled transport links to the north of Britain and continental Europe make it a fine base. Turn-of-the-century London with the gentleman's clubs, royal buildings, and gracious hotels is on show in **St. James's** (at decidedly 21st-century prices). But for the full-on, 24-hour, everything-on-your-doorstep feeling, it has to be **Soho.** Just remember to bring your credit card, and earplugs.

Best for: All the glorious whirl of world-class theatre, historic sights, and shopping that spans the full range from the dirt-cheap to the wallet-batteringly expensive.

Drawbacks: All this comes at a price—don't expect to stay in the West End cheaply or, in hotels at the less expensive end, for your room to be particularly spacious or quiet.

Bloomsbury

VERY EXPENSIVE

Chancery Court Hotel ★★ This opulent landmark 1914 building opened as a hotel in 2003 and has retained some of the best architectural features of its Edwardian heyday while adopting cutting-edge comforts. The glamorous and exceedingly comfortable rooms are all furnished with fine linens and decorated in hues of cream, red, and blue. Some of the best are on the sixth floor, opening onto a cozy interior courtyard hidden from the world outside. The building has been used as a backdrop for such films as *Howard's End* and *The Saint* by filmmakers drawn to its soaring archways and classical central courtyard.

252 High Holborn, London WC1V 7EN. www.chancerycourthotel.com. ☎ **020/7829-9888** or 800/468-3571 in the U.S. and Canada. Fax 020/7829-9889. 358 units. £169–£374 double. Rates include English breakfast. AE, DC, MC, V. Parking £35/day. Tube: Holborn. **Amenities:** 2 restaurants; 2 bars; health club & spa; concierge; room service; babysitting. *In room:* A/C, TV, minibar, hair dryer, Internet (£15/day).

EXPENSIVE

The Academy ★ With a pretty, private garden out back, this row of converted Georgian houses offers a sense of sanctuary just yards from the bustle of Bloomsbury and Oxford Street. The original architectural details —glass panels, colonnades, and intricate plasterwork on the facade—contribute to the classic air (this is the area where Virginia Woolf and the other members of the literary Bloomsbury Set would wander). Rooms mix a smart Georgian ambience with 21st-century touches such as MP3 docking stations—those at the rear are at a premium because of their garden views; they're also quieter, even allowing for the double-glazing of the front rooms. *Note:* There are no elevators in this four-floor hotel.

21 Gower St., London WC1E 6HG. www.theetoncollection.co.uk/academy. ☎ **020/7631-4115.** Fax 020/7636-3442. 49 units. £120–£395 double. AE, DC, MC, V. Tube: Tottenham Court Rd., Goodge St., or Russell Sq. **Amenities:** Bar; room service. *In room:* A/C, TV, minibar, hair dryer, MP3 docking station, Wi-Fi (free).

Grange Blooms Hotel ★ Even though it's in the heart of London, the hotel has a country-home atmosphere, complete with fireplace, period art, and copies of *Country Life* in the magazine rack (and happily a lift). This restored 18th-century town house has a pedigree: It stands in the former grounds of Montague House (now the British Museum, see p. 96). The small- to medium-sized

West End Hotels

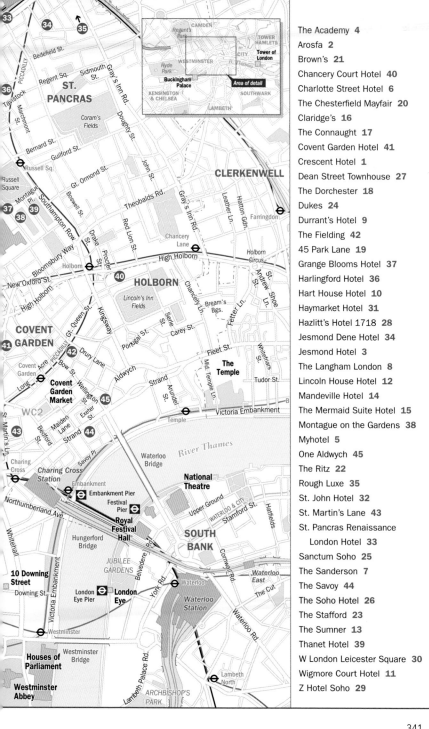

bedrooms (four have four-poster beds, six have king-size beds) are individually designed with traditional elegance, in beautifully muted tones. Some rooms have a literary theme—the Dickens room is full of old Victorian prints and pictures. Rooms 1 & 2 have balconies overlooking the walled garden where guests can take morning coffee or a light meal.

7 Montague St., London WC1B 5BP. www.grangehotels.com. ℂ **020/7323-1717.** Fax 020/7636-6498. 26 units. £78–£270 double. AE, DC, MC, V. Tube: Russell Sq. **Amenities:** Restaurant; bar; room service. *In room:* TV, minibar, hair dryer, Internet (£10/day).

Montague on the Gardens ★★ English country-house style within sight of the British Museum makes the Montague a winning combination for traveling culture buffs. It's a little way back from the busy West End streets but still just a short walk from theatres and Oxford Street. Guest rooms are individually sized and decorated; most aren't huge, but all are cozy and spotless. Some beds are four-posters, and most sport half-canopies. Bi-level deluxe king rooms would be suites in many hotels.

15 Montague St., London WC1B 5BJ. www.montaguehotel.com. ℂ **020/7637-1001** or 877/955-1515 in the U.S. and Canada. Fax 020/7637-2516. 100 units. £165–£275 double. AE, DC, MC, V. Tube: Russell Sq. **Amenities:** 2 restaurants; bar; fitness center; concierge; room service. *In room:* A/C, TV, fax (in some rooms), hair dryer, Wi-Fi (free).

Myhotel ★ Defiantly untypical in an area renowned for staid, chintzy accommodations, Myhotel is a London terrace house on the outside with a modernist Asian-style interior aimed at the young, hip traveler. It's designed according to feng shui principles; so, for example, the mirrors are positioned so you don't see yourself when you first wake up. (That's feng shui rule one, and probably a good rule, feng shui or no feng shui.) Rooms are small, but are havens of comfort, taste, and tranquility, with excellent, sleep-inducing beds. Tipping is discouraged, and each guest is assigned a personal assistant responsible for his or her happiness.

11–13 Bayley St., Bedford Sq., London WC1B 3HD. www.myhotels.co.uk. ℂ **020/7667-6000.** Fax 020/7667-6044. 77 units. £169–£279 + VAT double. AE, DC, MC, V. Tube: Tottenham Court Rd. or Goodge St. **Amenities:** Restaurant; bar; room service. *In room:* A/C, TV, hair dryer, Wi-Fi (free).

MODERATE

Arosfa ★ 🏠 This tiny Georgian town house hotel is a cut above many of the other Gower Street hotels with touches like fresh fruit in the rooms and black-and-white photographs and colorful art on the walls. It was once the home of pre-Raphaelite artist, Sir John Everett Millais. It's within walking distance of the British Museum and Theatreland and has small, neat, simple rooms and decent-sized marble bathrooms. The young staff is welcoming; there's a garden at the back and a lounge. The apartment taking up the whole of the top floor sleeping six is ideal for a family.

83 Gower St., London WC1E 6HJ. www.arosfalondon.com. ℂ **020/7636-2115.** Fax 020/7323-5141. 17 units. £70–£180 double. Rates include Continental or English breakfast. MC, V. Tube: Goodge St. *In room:* TV, hair dryer, Wi-Fi (free).

INEXPENSIVE

Jesmond Hotel The friendly and welcoming Beynon family has been running the hotel since the 1980s when they converted what was their own house into a bed and breakfast. Some of the rooms are large enough to sleep five people. Otherwise, like all the hotels in this listed area, rooms are relatively small, but neat and comfortable. Ask for one with an ensuite bathroom, and request a room at the back if you're a light sleeper. The pretty peaceful garden is a real bonus.

63 Gower St, London WC1E 6HJ. www.jesmondhotel.org.uk. © **020/7636-3199.** Fax 020/7323-4373. 15 units. £80–£100 double. Rates include English breakfast. AE, MC, V. Tube: Holborn or Russell Sq. **Amenities:** Breakfast room. *In room:* TV, hair dryer, Wi-Fi (free).

Thanet Hotel   The family-owned Thanet is an affordable option on a quiet Georgian terrace between Russell and Bloomsbury Squares, although it no longer charges the same rates it did when it appeared in *Frommer's England on $5 a Day*. For the most part, rooms are small and adequately furnished, and some have original fireplaces. Ask for one of the refurbished rooms overlooking the back if you're a light sleeper. The ground-floor breakfast room has street views. Wi-Fi is free but sometimes patchy.

8 Bedford Place, London WC1B 5JA. www.thanethotel.co.uk. © **020/7636-2869.** Fax 020/7323-6676. 16 units. £115 double. Rates include English breakfast. AE, MC, V. Tube: Holborn or Russell Sq. **Amenities:** Breakfast room. *In room:* TV, hair dryer, Wi-Fi (free).

King's Cross

VERY EXPENSIVE

St. Pancras Renaissance London Hotel   This hotel has been lovingly restored into an opulent reinterpretation of the golden age of railway hotels. Gilbert Scott's iconic Gothic hotel above St. Pancras station stood unused for 76 years and narrowly escaped being torn down. The centerpiece is the sweeping double staircase that whisks you from the ornate vault of the lobby (more like a medieval church than a hotel) into luxuriously wide corridors and a maze of grand halls and intimate lounges. The attention to detail is so extraordinary—every surface gleams with Gothic ornamentation and period wallpaper—that the modern rooms, though large and perfectly serviceable, are a bit of a let-down. But this is as much hotel as spectacle; a place to sip martinis in style, to explore at leisure, and to plan that European adventure.

Euston Rd., London, NW1 2AR. www.stpancrasrenaissance.com. © **020/7841-3540.** 245 units. £306–£834 double. AE, MC, V. Valet parking £50/day. Tube: King's Cross St. Pancras. **Amenities:** Restaurant; bar; pool; gym; spa; concierge; room service. *In room:* A/C, TV/DVD, minibar, CD player, Wi-Fi (£15/day).

EXPENSIVE

Rough Luxe ★ 👔   Despite the setting in a row of Georgian town houses, the decor of this small boutique hotel, just minutes from St. Pancras station, is almost industrial, resembling the interior of a warehouse art gallery. No two rooms are alike. Three units come with private bathroom, with glass-enclosed showers and "rainfall" shower heads. Decades of wallpaper and paint were peeled away, leaving distressed walls of hand-painted mosaic wallpaper and plaster. Many of the antiques found throughout were purchased at the auction of the Savoy Hotel's throwaways.

1 Birkenhead St., London WC1H 8BA. www.roughluxe.co.uk. ℂ **020/7837-5338.** Fax 020/7837-1615. 9 units (3 with bathroom). £189–£289 double. Rates include continental breakfast. AE, MC, V. Tube: King's Cross St. Pancras. **Amenities:** Breakfast room. *In room:* TV, hair dryer, Wi-Fi (free).

INEXPENSIVE

Crescent Hotel   Overseas visitors after somewhere with that at-home feeling in central London go for the Crescent. Why? Partly because the owners treat this Georgian house as an extension of their own home—with delightful decorative touches. Partly it's the leafy gardens and the use of the nearby tennis courts. But mainly it's because guests who have been coming here for decades give the Crescent that home-from-home feel. Bedrooms range from small singles with shared bathrooms to more spacious twin and double rooms with private bathrooms. There's a tiny Garden Yard for outdoor tea and coffee in the summer.

49–50 Cartwright Gardens, London WC1H 9EL. www.crescenthoteloflondon.com. ℂ **020/7387-1515.** Fax 020/7383-2054. 27 units, 18 with bathroom (some with shower only, some with tub and shower). £105 double with bathroom; £122 family room. Rates include English breakfast. MC, V. Tube: Russell Sq., King's Cross, or Euston. **Amenities:** Tennis courts (in Cartwright Gardens). *In room:* TV, Wi-Fi (£3/1 day, £6/2–3 days, £10/4 days and over).

Harlingford Hotel 🍴   Made up of three 19th-century town houses, the Harlingford is more spacious than many of its neighbors, decorated with antiques and modern pictures and with a delightful lounge. And the staff seems genuinely concerned about the welfare of the guests. The most comfortable rooms are on the second and third levels, but there are some steep stairs and no elevator and an eccentric array of staircases and meandering hallways. Lower-floor rooms are darker and have less security.

61–63 Cartwright Gardens, London WC1H 9EL. www.harlingfordhotel.com. ℂ **020/7387-1551.** Fax 020/7387-4616. 43 units. £112 double. Rates include English breakfast. AE, MC, V. Tube: Russell Sq., King's Cross, or Euston. **Amenities:** Tennis courts (in Cartwright Gardens). *In room:* TV, hair dryer, Wi-Fi (free).

Jesmond Dene Hotel   The Jesmond Dene is a small but neat B&B. It offers good value, is surprisingly quiet, and is known for helpful, friendly service. Like many of its close neighbors mentioned above, it may not be the place for a 2-week holiday, but for a base to explore London that's handy for day trips, you could do worse. It is in the King's Cross area which offers unparalleled travel links—you can be in Paris or the Lake District within 3 hours—but at the cost of a scruffy, noisy district.

27 Argyle St., London WC1H 8EP. www.jesmonddenehotel.co.uk. ℂ **020/7837-4654.** Fax 020/7833-1633. 20 units, some with private bathroom. From £70 double without bathroom, from

£100 double with bathroom. AE, DC, MC, V. Tube: King's Cross. **Amenities:** Breakfast room. *In room:* TV, Wi-Fi (free).

Covent Garden

VERY EXPENSIVE

Covent Garden Hotel ★★★ The phrase most often used by guests who've stayed here is "expensive, but worth it." The former hospital building lay neglected for years until it was reconfigured in 1996 by hoteliers Tim and Kit Kemp—whose flair for interior design is legendary—into one of London's most charming boutique hotels. Upstairs, accessible via a dramatic stone staircase, soundproof bedrooms are furnished in English style with Asian fabrics, many adorned with hand-embroidered designs. Each room has a clothier's mannequin, the hotel's decorative trademark. The staff is among the most knowledgeable in London—always useful in an area thronged with theatres, galleries, and rare bookshops. The bar makes a very good meeting place.

10 Monmouth St., London WC2H 9HB. www.firmdale.com. ℰ **020/7806-1000** or 888/559-5508 in the US & Canada. Fax 020/7806-1100. 58 units. £260–£365 double. AE, DC, MC, V. Tube: Covent Garden or Leicester Sq. **Amenities:** Restaurant; bar; exercise room; concierge; room service; babysitting. *In room:* A/C, TV/DVD, minibar, hair dryer, movie library, CD player, Wi-Fi (£20/day).

One Aldwych ★★★ One Aldwych is an object lesson in how to combine old-school London elegance with state-of-the-art facilities. Guests bask in an artfully simple layout that includes stylish minimalist furniture, big bay windows, masses of flowers, and lashings of contemporary art. The sumptuous bedrooms are decorated with elegant linens and rich colors, raw-silk curtains and deluxe furnishings, while flowers and fresh fruit appear daily. On Friday and Saturday evenings, movies are shown in the screening room. And, unusually for such a smart hotel, sustainability is taken seriously; the glorious swimming pool has chlorine-free toilets and the in-house Axis restaurant uses local produce.

1 Aldwych, London WC2B 4BZ. www.onealdwych.com. ℰ **020/7300-1000** or 800/745-8883 in the U.S. and Canada. Fax 020/7300-1001. 105 units. £230–£470 double. AE, DC, MC, V. Parking £37/day. Tube: Temple or Covent Garden. **Amenities:** 2 restaurants; 3 bars; pool (indoor); health club; concierge; room service; babysitting. *In room:* A/C, TV/DVD, minibar, hair dryer, MP3 docking station, CD player, CD library, Wi-Fi (free).

St. Martin's Lane ★★★ "Eccentric and irreverent, with a sense of humor," is how Ian Schrager described his cutting-edge Covent Garden hotel, which he transformed from a 1960s' office building into a chic enclave. This was the first hotel that Schrager designed outside the U.S. and the mix of hip design and a sense of cool have been imported across the pond. Whimsical touches abound, for example, a string of daisies replaces "do not disturb" signs. Rooms are all white, but you can use the full-spectrum lighting to make them any color. Floor-to-ceiling windows in every room offer panoramic views of London.

45 St. Martin's Lane, London WC2N 4HX. www.stmartinslane.com. ℰ **020/7300-5500** or 800/697-1791 in the U.S. and Canada. Fax 020/7300-5501. 204 units. £229–£330 double. AE, DC, MC, V. Tube: Covent Garden or Leicester Sq. **Amenities:** Restaurant; 2 bars; exercise room; concierge; room service; babysitting. *In room:* A/C, TV/DVD, minibar, hair dryer, movie library, Wi-Fi (£15/day).

The Savoy ★★ After a 3-year, £200 million restoration, the Savoy has settled into its role of providing glitzy, high-octane business. Updating such an iconic hotel—at various times home to Coco Chanel, Humphrey Bogart, Marlene Dietrich, Oscar Wilde, and Churchill's war cabinet—was tricky but it's lost none of its turn-of-the-century appeal with rich fabrics and acres of gold leaf on display, and a very subtle updating to draw the 21st-century *belle monde* back to their spiritual home. No two rooms are the same, despite their mix of Art Deco and Edwardian palettes. If you can, take one of the Edwardian rooms near the rear—the combination of Thames views and a real fireplace is London at its finest. The Savoy Grill (p. 204) is as grand as ever.

Strand, London WC2R 0EU. www.fairmont.com/savoy. ✆ **020/7836-4343.** Fax 020/7420-6040. 268 units. £350–£775 double. AE, DC, MC, V. Tube: Embankment or Charing Cross. **Amenities:** 3 restaurants, including Savoy Grill (p. 204); 2 bars; exercise room; concierge; room service; babysitting. *In room:* A/C, TV/DVD, minibar, hair dryer, movie library, CD player, Wi-Fi (£10/day).

MODERATE

The Fielding ★ 🛍 If you remember The Fielding from the old days, you'll be delighted that this firm favorite among theatre-goers was sold on and has had a much-needed renovation. The Fielding is a little slice of Dickensian London in the heart of Covent Garden. Named after local novelist Henry Fielding of *Tom Jones* fame, it's on a pedestrian street lined with 19th-century gas lamps. Rooms, which differ in size, are now prettily decorated in natural tones with splashes of bright colors, and bathrooms are well equipped. Some rooms have small steps down to a writing area and the bathroom. The paintings and prints on the walls reflect its proximity to Covent Garden opera and ballet. There's no breakfast room, but no shortage of good cafes and restaurants in the area.

4 Broad Court, Bow St., London WC2B 5QZ. www.thefieldinghotel.co.uk. ✆ **020/7836-8305.** Fax 020/7497-0064. 25 units. £168–£192 double. AE, DC, MC, V. Tube: Covent Garden. *In room:* A/C, TV, hair dryer, Wi-Fi (free).

Soho

VERY EXPENSIVE

Charlotte Street Hotel ★★ 🛍 In Fitzrovia, but just a short walk from Soho Square, this town house has been luxuriously converted into a high-end hotel that is London chic at its finest, with a private screening room and a sophisticated blend of stately English manor house and contemporary decor. The latter, overseen by the independent hoteliers, the Kemps, has made the hotel a hit with the movie, fashion, and media crowd. Midsize to spacious bedrooms have fresh, modern, English interiors with strong colors. Guests can relax in the elegant drawing room and library with a log-burning fireplace.

15–17 Charlotte St., London W1T 1RJ. www.firmdale.com. ✆ **020/7806-2000** or 888/559-5508 in the US, and Canada. Fax 020/7806-2002. 52 units. £250–£340 double. AE, MC, V. Tube: Tottenham Court Rd. or Goodge St. **Amenities:** Restaurant; bar; exercise room; room service. *In room:* A/C, TV/DVD, CD player, minibar, hair dryer, Wi-Fi (£20/day).

Sanctum Soho ★ 🛍 If you're after a thoroughly modern boutique hotel in the heart of Soho, look no further. All the usual boutique touches are on show here—an edgy mix of antiques and hi-tech, bedrooms done up in glass-beaded wallpaper and Art Deco mirrors—but the Sanctum ups the ante with its buzzing roof terrace and underground cinema. The location is a real draw, with Regent

Street and Soho shopping on the doorstep. But be warned, for all its reputation as a sanctuary, this is a far-from-quiet hotel.

20 Warwick St., London W1B 5NF. www.sanctumsoho.com. *C* **020/7292-6100.** Fax 020/7434-3074. 30 units. £230–£550 double. AE, DC, MC, V. Tube: Piccadilly Circus. **Amenities:** Restaurant; bar; spa; concierge; room service; cinema; roof terrace with hot tub. *In room:* A/C, TV, minibar, Wi-Fi (free).

The Sanderson ★   Travelers used to the sleek glitz of Manhattan design hotels will feel at home at the Sanderson. All the signature Ian Schrager touches are here—Philippe Starck furnishings, acres of glass, and an ambience halfway between a high-end design gallery and a 1970s' nightclub. Your bed is likely to be an Italian silver-leaf sleigh attended by spidery polished stainless-steel night tables and draped with a fringed pashmina shawl. The hotel, located in a former corporate building near Oxford Street, north of Soho, comes with a lush bamboo-filled roof garden, a large courtyard, and a spa.

50 Berners St., London W1T 3NG. www.sandersonlondon.com. *C* **020/7300-1400** or 800/697-1791 in the U.S. and Canada. Fax 020/7300-1401. 150 units. £307–£449 + VAT double. AE, DC, MC, V. Tube: Oxford Circus or Tottenham Court Rd. **Amenities:** Restaurant; 2 bars; health club & spa; concierge; babysitting. *In room:* A/C, TV/DVD, minibar, hair dryer, CD player, Wi-Fi (£15/day).

The Soho Hotel ★★★   Entering The Soho Hotel always gets hearts racing: The sleek lobby with its giant cat sculpture and hip staff; the buzz from the bar and the restaurant. *Tatler* called it "the most glamorous hotel in the world," which might be pushing it but there's no denying it's a magnet for the glitterati. And behind the glitz it's a well-run, deceptively spacious hotel. Rooms are big for Soho, and individually designed in granite and oak. There are four penthouses on the fifth floor with tree-lined terraces opening onto panoramic sweeps of London. All the famous Kemp (see Covent Garden Hotel above) touches can be found, from boldly striped furnishings to deep bathtubs for a late-night soak.

4 Richmond Mews, London W1D 3DH. www.firmdale.com. *C* **020/7559-3000** or 888/559-5508 in the US & Canada. Fax 020/7559-3003. 91 units. £295–£380 double. AE, MC, V. Tube: Oxford Circus or Piccadilly Circus. **Amenities:** Restaurant; bar; exercise room; concierge; room service. *In room:* A/C, TV/DVD, hair dryer, CD player, Wi-Fi (£20/day).

St. John Hotel ★★ 🎽   The rise of the restaurant with rooms continues, and this offering from the much-lauded St. John (p. 238), epitomizes all that is best in this category. In the very heart of the city, just off Leicester Square, the former posttheatre eatery, Manzi's, has been converted into a shrine to Modern British cooking, with some cozy—and for the area, reasonably priced—rooms. Bedrooms are simple in white wood with turquoise floors, but this is a hotel for exploring—an elegant cocktail bar and great pre- and posttheatre dining should keep you from your room for a night or two at least.

1 Leicester St., London WC2H 7BL. www.stjohnhotellondon.com. *C* **020/3301 8020.** 15 units. £240–£330 double. AE, DC, MC, V. Tube: Leicester Sq. **Amenities:** Restaurants; bar. *In room:* Wi-Fi (free).

W London Leicester Square ★★   W London is so deliberately chic it sharply divides opinion: You either love it or hate it. You enter the hotel past an enormous W into a large space with nothing but doormen. Take the lift to the first floor to an impressive, lofty reception with low-key check-in desks. There are buzzing public spaces, a serous gym, Screening Room, popular bar, and a pan-Asian two-story restaurant with an additional street entrance. Rooms are minimal and chic, with long windows and a second outer decorated glass wall to give privacy. Color schemes are mainly white and gray, with splashes of red, and gold bed coverings. It is undeniably fashionable in every way (rooms are classified in terms like "Wonderful," "Cool Corner," "Wow Suite" etc.); if you're a traditionalist after cozy comfort, this is not for you.

10 Wardour St, London W1D 6QF. www.wlondon.co.uk. © **020/758-1000;** [fax] 020-7758-1001. 192 units. From £335 double. AE, DC, MC, V. Tube: Oxford Circus or Piccadilly Circus. **Amenities:** Restaurant; 2 bars; exercise room; concierge; room service; Wi-Fi (free in public areas). *In room:* A/C, TV, minibar, hair dryer, MP3 docking station, Wi-Fi (£16/24 hrs).

EXPENSIVE

Dean Street Townhouse ★★★ ▮▮ Deep in the heart of town, this boutique hotel in a restored four-story Georgian town house is a fashionable base for exploring Theatreland and the nightlife of Soho. Formerly the home of the Gargoyle Club, it has been converted to a hotel with its Georgian architecture more or less preserved. Atmosphere and location are the draws here—the price is that rooms are small even for central London. Bedrooms have four-poster beds, hand-painted wallpaper, and other retro-chic touches. Amenities from the trendy Cowshed range in the bathrooms include toothbrushes, toothpaste, and combs. There's an innovative all-day dining room with a weekly, changing menu of seasonal British food (p. 209). But dress accordingly as this is a magnet for celebrities, the media, and the posttheatre crowd. Book in advance—you won't get a last-minute bargain here.

69–71 Dean St., London W1D 3SE. www.deanstreettownhouse.com. © **020/7434-1775.** 39 units. £90–£410 double. AE, MC, V. Tube: Oxford Circus or Tottenham Court Rd. **Amenities:** Restaurant (p. 209); bar. *In room:* TV/DVD, minibar, hair dryer, MP3 docking station, Wi-Fi (free).

Hazlitt's Hotel 1718 ★ ▮▮ Character, character, character; some hotels don't have it, however hard they try, but Hazlitt's has it in spades. You step from the heart of buzzing Soho into what feels like an untouched Georgian literary salon. Public areas are bookish and calm, decorated in a lived-in 18th-century style, while the rooms mix up antiques, ancient portraits, glorious free-standing baths, and fireplaces. Soho's a 24-hour kind of area, so unless you're a heavy sleeper, opt for a room facing the back.

6 Frith St., London W1D 3JA. www.hazlittshotel.com. © **020/7434-1771.** Fax 020/7439-1524. 30 units. £179–£255 + VAT double. AE, DC, MC, V. Tube: Leicester Sq. or Tottenham Court Rd. **Amenities:** Concierge; room service. *In room:* A/C, TV, minibar, hair dryer, Wi-Fi (free).

INEXPENSIVE

Z Hotel Soho ★ ▮▮ The team behind Z Hotels produces five-star quality at three-star prices, challenging the cheap chains. What is sacrificed is space: Rooms are small, your suitcase goes under the bed and clothes hang on hooks on the walls. But you do get stylish decor, triple-glazed windows, good bathrooms with frosted glass walls and top toiletries, goose feather pillows, best quality bed linen, a chic wood and marble decor, and a 42-inch TV with Sky, bang in the middle of Soho. The only criticism concerns the hard mattresses. Created from 12 derelict town houses over five floors, you reach your room via an elevator and an open-air corridor of wooden walls that gives a real Scandinavian feel. State-of-the-art

Wi-Fi, a 24-hour cafe, rapid check-in and check-out, and a Lanson champagne bar complete the package. Plans include 15 new hotels in and around London.

17 Moor St, London W1D 5AP. www.thezhotels.com. ✆ **020/3551-3700.** 85 units. £102. AE, MC, V. Tube: Oxford Circus or Tottenham Court Rd. **Amenities:** 2 bars; cafe. *In room:* A/C, TV/DVD, hair dryer, MP3 charger, Wi-Fi (free).

Mayfair
VERY EXPENSIVE

Brown's ★★   Often imitated but rarely bettered, Brown's takes on the English country-house ambience with Chippendale and chintz, and sees off young pretenders year after year. Founded the year Queen Victoria took the throne by Lord Byron's manservant James Brown, Brown's occupies 14 Georgian town houses just off Berkeley Square. Its guest rooms, completely renovated, vary considerably in decor, but all show restrained taste in decoration and appointments; even the washbasins are antiques. Rooms range in size from small to extra spacious; some suites have four-poster beds. Don't leave without trying their afternoon tea (p. 257), which is a London institution.

30 Albemarle St., London W1S 4BP. www.brownshotel.com. ✆ **020/7493-6020.** Fax 020/7493-9381. 117 units. £585–£735 + VAT double. AE, DC, MC, V. Off-site parking £50/day. Tube: Green Park. **Amenities:** Restaurant; bar; health club & spa; concierge; room service. *In room:* A/C, TV/DVD, minibar, hair dryer, MP3 docking station, Internet (£15/day).

Claridge's ★★★   No hotel epitomizes the rebirth of London's grand old hotels quite like Claridge's. Sure, it still boasts the Art Deco finery and a history stretching back to 1812, but Gordon Ramsay's flagship restaurant and two hip bars have made it a favorite with the fashion and media sets. Much of its 1930s' style remains, with the hotel's strong sense of tradition and old-fashioned "Britishness" intact; in spite of the gloss and the hip clientele, afternoon tea (p. 256) remains a quintessentially English experience. The rooms are the most varied in London, ranging from the costly and stunning Brook Penthouse—complete with a personal butler—to the less expensive superior queen rooms with queen-size beds.

Brook St., London W1A 2JQ. www.claridges.co.uk. ✆ **020/7629-8860.** Fax 020/7499-2210. 203 units. £339–£659 double. AE, DC, MC, V. Parking £50/day. Tube: Bond St. **Amenities:** 2 restaurants; 2 bars; health club & spa; concierge; room service; babysitting. *In room:* A/C, TV/DVD/VCR, minibar, hair dryer, Wi-Fi (free).

The Connaught ★★★   Built as a home-away-from-home for the denizens of Britain's stylish country houses, no hotel has updated the classic British style with quite as much élan as the Connaught. Leaded skylights, liveried doormen who seem to know every guest's name, and shady, masculine bars and restaurants are the picture of restrained 21st-century glamour, while the rooms are spacious Edwardian gems. Traditionalists opt for the Old Wing; the more contemporary minded go for the New Wing—it's where the Connaught's mix of the old and new is most successful.

Carlos Place, London W1K 2AL. www.the-connaught.co.uk. ✆ **020/7499-7070**. Fax 020/7495-3262. 122 units. £339–£369 double. AE, DC, MC, V. Parking £48/day. Tube: Green Park. **Amenities:** 2 restaurants; 2 bars; health club & spa; concierge; room service; babysitting. *In room:* A/C, TV/DVD, minibar, hair dryer, MP3 docking station, Wi-Fi (free).

8

STAYING IN LONDON

The West End

The Dorchester ★★★ Few hotels have the time-honored experience of "the Dorch," which has maintained a tradition of fine comfort and cuisine since it opened in 1931. Breaking from the neoclassical tradition, the most ambitious architects of the era designed a building of reinforced concrete clothed in terrazzo slabs. The Dorchester boasts guest rooms outfitted with Irish linen sheets on comfortable beds, plus all the electronic gadgetry you'd expect, along with plump armchairs, cherry wood furnishings, and, in many cases, four-poster beds piled high with pillows.

53 Park Lane, London W1A 2HJ. www.thedorchester.com. ✆ **020/7629-8888** or 1 800/727-9820 in the U.S. Fax 020/9629-8080. 250 units. £265–£695 double. AE, DC, MC, V. Parking £50/day. Tube: Hyde Park Corner or Marble Arch. **Amenities:** 5 restaurants, including Alain Ducasse (p. 193); 3 bars; health club & spa; concierge; room service; babysitting. *In room:* A/C, TV/DVD, fax, minibar, hair dryer, CD player, Internet (£20/day).

45 Park Lane ★★★ The grand double-height entrance and restaurant stretching beyond provide the first "wow" factor in the Dorchester Collection's latest opening. With a glam Hollywood look, Thierry Despont's elegant, luxurious design provides a contrast to the neighboring Dorchester's glitz. Public rooms are Art Deco-inspired with angular lights, light marble floors, leather seating, and plenty of silk curtains. Bedrooms are equally sumptuous, large, and kitted out with bespoke desks, huge beds, and the crispest linen. High-tech amenities include iPads and large Bang & Olufsen TVs. Bathrooms have mirrors with TV screens, marble baths, rain showers, and enough towels to kit out a football team. Some of the upper floor rooms have balconies; all look over Hyde Park and beyond. Outstanding extras include a media room with 103-inch 3-D screen, 3-D glasses, and surround sound for your latest film or the family photo album. This is high-end London at its finest.

45 Park Lane, London W1K 1PN. www.45parklane.com. ✆ **020/7493 4545** or 1-800/727-9820 in the U.S. Fax 020/7319-7455. 45 units. From £395 + VAT double. AE, DC, MC, V. Parking £50/day. Tube: Hyde Park Corner. **Amenities:** Restaurant; bar; 24-hour fitness studio; free entry to The Dorchester's Spa; concierge; room service; library; private Media Room. *In room:* A/C, TV/DVD, minibar, hair dryer, Wi-Fi (free).

EXPENSIVE

The Chesterfield Mayfair ★★ Only in super-expensive Mayfair could the Chesterfield be considered a bargain, but it serves up that ritzy grand hotel feeling at a better price than the Connaught or the Dorchester. The hotel, once home to the Earl of Chesterfield, still sports venerable features, including richly decorated public rooms featuring woods, antiques, fabrics, and marble. The secluded Library Lounge is a great place to relax, and the glassed-in conservatory is a good spot for tea. The guest rooms are dramatically decorated and make excellent use of space including generous closets.

35 Charles St., London W1J 5EB. www.chesterfieldmayfair.com. ✆ **020/7491-2622** or 877/955-1515 in the U.S. and Canada. Fax 020/7491-4793. 107 units. £160–£375 double. AE, DC, MC, V. Tube: Green Park. **Amenities:** 1 restaurant; bar; use of nearby health club; concierge; room service; babysitting. *In room:* A/C, TV/DVD, minibar (in suites only or on request), hair dryer, Wi-Fi (free).

INEXPENSIVE

The Mermaid Suite Hotel Technically in Mayfair, but in the northernmost end just off Oxford Street, this is a great find for shopaholics. A steep flight of

STAYING IN LONDON   The West End

stairs takes you up to a tiny reception area. Bedrooms however are a decent size, light and airy, and with adequate bathrooms. You take breakfast at the downstairs Italian restaurant, Il Pizzaiolo, under the same ownership; you also get 10% discount on other meals there. The hotel is basic but honest and for Mayfair (technically), a great bargain.

3-4 Blenheim St., London W1S 1LA. www.mermaidsuite.com. © **020/7629-1875.** Fax 020/7499-9475. 30 units. £90–£130 double. MC, V. Tube: Oxford Circus. **Amenities:** Restaurant. *In room:* TV, hair dryer, Wi-Fi (£7.50/24 hrs).

St. James's
VERY EXPENSIVE

Dukes ★★ Sitting in the famous cozy bar at Dukes, with barman Alessandro mixing a martini while the gas lamps splutter into life in the courtyard outside, is one of London's great experiences. Or choose the Champagne Lounge, or in summer, the cigar and cognac garden. Dukes is the least flashy of the St. James's hotels, providing elegance without ostentation in what was presumably someone's *Upstairs, Downstairs* town house. It caters to those looking for charm, style, and tradition in a hotel, and its tranquil location in a leafy alley keeps the 21st century at bay. Each well-furnished guest room is decorated in the style of a particular English period, ranging from Regency to Edwardian.

35 St. James's Place, London SW1A 1NY. www.dukeshotel.com. © **020/7491-4840.** Fax 020/7493-1264. 90 units. £360–£440 double. AE, DC, MC, V. Parking £58/day. Tube: Green Park. **Amenities:** Restaurant; bar; health club & spa; concierge; room service; babysitting. *In room:* A/C, TV/DVD, minibar, hair dryer, Wi-Fi (free).

Haymarket Hotel ★★★ Although completely modernized and perhaps the most sophisticated small hotel in the city, much of the elegant 19th-century John Nash architecture remains. The understated Georgian entrance, right by the Haymarket Theatre, hides a surprisingly bold and colorful hotel. Public areas are a riot of turquoise, fuchsia, mango, and even acid green while rooms are classy in black and white. Bedrooms are sumptuously elegant with fine linens and the latest amenities. There's even an indoor pool lounge.

1 Suffolk Place, London SW1Y 4HX. www.firmdale.com. © **020/7470-4000** or 888/559-5508 in the U.S. and Canada. Fax 020/7470-4004. 50 units. £265–£340 double. AE, DC, MC, V. Tube: Charing Cross or Piccadilly Circus. **Amenities:** Restaurant; bar; pool (indoor); exercise room; concierge; room service. *In room:* A/C, TV/DVD, hair dryer, CD player, Wi-Fi (£20).

The Ritz ★★★ Few hotels can say that they've entered everyday language, but the Ritz has become synonymous with luxury. A major restoration brought the hotel's original turn-of-the-century style some way into the 21st century: It's still a glitzy mix of gold-leafed molding, marble columns, and potted palms, but new carpeting and air-conditioning have been installed in the guest rooms, and an overall polish has put the Ritz back center-stage. The Belle Epoque guest rooms, each with its own character, are spacious and comfortable. Many have marble fireplaces, elaborate gilded plasterwork, and a decor of soft pastel hues. Opt for a corner room: They're grander and more spacious. Its afternoon tea (p. 257) is legendary.

150 Piccadilly, London W1J 9BR. www.theritzlondon.com. © **020/7493-8181** or 877/748-9536 in the U.S. and Canada. Fax 020/7493-2687. 135 units. From £300 + VAT double. Children 15 and

under stay free in parent's room. AE, DC, MC, V. Parking £56/day. Tube: Green Park. **Amenities:** 2 restaurants, including Palm Court (p. 257); bar; health club & spa; concierge; room service; babysitting. *In room:* A/C, TV/DVD, fax, hair dryer, Internet (£25/day).

The Stafford ★★★ Famous for its American Bar, its St. James's address, and its Edwardian decor, the Stafford competes well with Dukes for a tasteful, discerning clientele. All the guest rooms are individually decorated, reflecting the hotel's origins as a private home. Many singles contain queen-size beds. Some of the deluxe units offer four-posters for a Henry VIII touch. Much has been done to preserve the original style of these rooms, including preserving the original A-beams on the upper floors. The converted stables of the Carriage House rooms offer a trip back to historic London but no 18th-century horse ever slept with the electronic safes, stereo systems, and quality furnishings that these rooms feature.

16–18 St. James's Place, London SW1A 1NJ. www.kempinski.com/london. ✆ **020/7493-0111.** Fax 020/7493-7121. 105 units. £290–£740 double. AE, DC, MC, V. No parking. Tube: Green Park. **Amenities:** Restaurant; bar; exercise room; concierge; room service; babysitting. *In room:* A/C, TV/DVD, hair dryer, CD player, Wi-Fi (free).

Marylebone

VERY EXPENSIVE

The Langham London ★★★ Halfway between the high-end shopping of Bond Street and the greenery of Regent's Park, the Langham is an opulent and practical choice in central London. Comfortable guest rooms are attractively furnished, featuring French provincial furniture and red oak trim. The bathrooms, and the English breakfast, are bigger and better than most. The hotel is within easy reach of Mayfair as well as Soho's restaurants and theatres. Sure, it's expensive; but the Langham is popular for its beguiling mix of old and new: Any place that's home to the Art Deco elegance of afternoon tea's birthplace, the **Palm Court**, *and* a spa as sleek as the Chuan Spa water spa, will always win hearts.

1c Portland Place, London W1B 1JA. http://london.langhamhotels.co.uk. ✆ **020/7636-1000** or 800/223-6800 in the U.S. and Canada. Fax 020/7323-2340. 380 units. From £215 double. AE, DC, MC, V. Tube: Oxford Circus. **Amenities:** 2 restaurants; bar; pool (indoor); health club & spa; concierge; room service. *In room:* A/C, TV/DVD, minibar, hair dryer, Wi-Fi (free for simple browsing and emails, then £20/day).

EXPENSIVE

Durrant's Hotel ★ If you like the idea of Brown's' (see above) quintessential English charm, but it's outside your price range, Durrant's is a reasonable alternative. This historic hotel with its Georgian-detailed facade is snug, cozy, and traditional with pine-and-mahogany-paneled public rooms. During the 100 years they've owned the hotel, the Miller family has incorporated several neighboring houses into the original structure. Guest rooms have elaborate cove moldings, comfortable furnishings, and good beds. For a fresh, country chintz look, and more space, ask for a refurbished room.

26–32 George St., London W1H 5BJ. www.durrantshotel.co.uk. ✆ **020/7935-8131.** Fax 020/7487-3510. 92 units. £216–£326 double; £265 family room for 3. AE, MC, V. Tube: Bond St. or Baker St. **Amenities:** Restaurant; bar; concierge; room service; babysitting. *In room:* A/C (in most), TV, hair dryer, Wi-Fi (£10/day).

Mandeville Hotel ★★ The jewel in the crown of Marylebone Village—one of London's best-kept secrets and a charming warren of independent shops, neighborhood restaurants, and busy bars—is the refurbished Mandeville. This once-staid property is now a hot address. One of London's leading decorators, Stephen Ryan, was brought in to restyle the lobby, restaurant, and bar. Bedrooms too have had a makeover and are thankfully free of the chintz of some Marylebone hotels—rich autumnal tones and masculine furnishings are the order of the day here.

Mandeville Place, London W1U 2BE. www.mandeville.co.uk. ℭ **020/7935-5599.** Fax 020/7935-9588. 142 units. £127–£339 double. AE, DC, MC, V. Tube: Bond St. **Amenities:** Restaurant; bar; exercise room; concierge; room service. *In room:* A/C, TV, minibar (in some), hair dryer, Wi-Fi (£13/day).

The Sumner ★ 🛏 It's no wonder this Georgian town house hotel is so popular—boutique hotels on quiet streets just minutes from Hyde Park and Oxford Street are pretty rare. Retaining much of its original architectural allure, standard rooms are midsized and attractively furnished, while deluxe rooms feature artwork and better furnishings. All guest rooms are designer-decorated and luxuriously appointed, and there's also an elegant sitting room with a working fireplace.

54 Upper Berkeley St., London W1H 7QR. www.thesumner.com. ℭ **020/7723-2244.** Fax 087/0705-8767. 20 units. £210–£258 double. Rates include buffet breakfast. AE, MC, V. Tube: Marble Arch. *In room:* A/C, TV, fridge, minibar, hair dryer, Wi-Fi (free).

MODERATE

Hart House Hotel ★ ☺ Hart House, run by the Bowden family for 44 years, is a long-standing favorite of Frommer's' readers. In the heart of the West End, this well-preserved Georgian mansion lies within walking distance of West End shopping and dining. The rooms—done in a combination of furnishings, ranging from antique to modern—are spick-and-span, each one with its own character. Favorites include no. 7, a triple with a big bathroom and shower; no. 3 is large, sleeps four and is at the back. For singles, no. 11 is a brightly lit aerie. Hart House has long been known as a good, safe place for traveling families, with many triple rooms and special interconnecting family units.

51 Gloucester Place, London W1U 8JF. www.harthouse.co.uk. ℭ **020/7935-2288.** Fax 020/7935-8516. 15 units. £145–£185 double; £150–£225 triple. Rates include English breakfast. MC, V. Tube: Marble Arch or Baker St. *In room:* TV, hair dryer, Wi-Fi (£5/stay).

Wigmore Court Hotel 🏃 Conveniently placed, this hotel, part of the Minotel group, is near the famous fictional address of Sherlock Holmes—Baker Street. It's also close to Oxford Street and Madame Tussauds. The somber Georgian house has been converted into a B&B suitable only for serious stair climbers (there's no elevator). Traffic noise is audible, so request a room in the rear. Bedrooms, many quite spacious, are comfortably furnished. Most units contain double or twin beds, plus a small bathroom.

23 Gloucester Place, London W1U 8HS. www.wigmore-hotel.co.uk. ℭ **020/7935-0928.** Fax 020/7487-4254. 19 units. £110–£135 double. MC, V. Tube: Marble Arch. **Amenities:** Guest kitchen. *In room:* TV, Wi-Fi (free).

INEXPENSIVE

Lincoln House Hotel ★   Lincoln House has bags of character that make it feel like a house rather than a hotel. Built in the late 18th century, this refurbished and tastefully decorated hotel with a delightful maritime theme is a converted town house, just a 5-minute walk to Marble Arch Tube and Hyde Park. Midsize bedrooms are completely modernized but decorated in a traditional fashion. All have showers; some also have baths. The downstairs restaurant serves a good-value simple dinner as well as breakfast. Half of the hotel is air conditioned.

33 Gloucester Place, London W1U 8HY. www.lincoln-house-hotel.co.uk. ℂ **020/7486-7630.** Fax 020/7486-0166. 24 units. £109–£129 double. AE, DC, MC, V. Tube: Marble Arch. **Amenities:** Restaurant. *In room:* TV, fridge, hair dryer, Wi-Fi (free).

WEST LONDON

West London offers a range of hotels in different areas. **Paddington** and **Bayswater** are full of terraced family-run hotels that may not offer glamour but are very close to Hyde Park and the West End. **Notting Hill** has upscale boutiques, celeb-rich restaurants, and the famous Portobello Road market. Hotels here are more expensive, but more elegant. Nearby **Maida Vale** is West London's prettiest neighborhood with canals, coffee shops, and calm wide streets for those after peace and quiet.

Best For: Staying in a mainly residential, leafy district.

Drawbacks: Some areas, like Paddington, are impersonal due to the massive railway station.

For a **map** of West London hotels, please see "West London Hotels & Restaurants" (p. 221 in Chapter 5).

Paddington & Bayswater

EXPENSIVE

Phoenix Hotel ★   Well situated near the ethnic mix of Queensway, this member of the Best Western chain occupies a series of 1850s' town houses. The atmosphere is always welcoming and the public rooms, from bar to lounge, give an impression of comfort and space. Well-furnished bedrooms keep to a smart international standard, with a palette of muted tones. Twin rooms are bigger than doubles if size is a consideration.

1–8 Kensington Gardens Sq., London W2 4BH. www.phoenixhotel.co.uk. ℂ **020/7229-2494** or 800/528-1234 in the U.S. and Canada. Fax 020/7727-1419. 125 units. £130–£165 double. Rates include continental breakfast. AE, DC, MC, V. Tube: Bayswater. **Amenities:** Bar; room service. *In room:* TV, hair dryer, Wi-Fi (free).

MODERATE

Mornington Hotel ★   There's nothing flashy about the Mornington, but a 2010 refurbishment and staff who win plaudits from guests make it the best value in the area. Touches like a 24-hour reception and bar, a guest computer with printer (free access), and iron and ironing board in room are thoughtful additions. Just north of Hyde Park and Kensington Gardens, the hotel has a Victorian exterior and Scandinavian-inspired decor. The area isn't London's most fashionable, but it's close to Oxford Street, and to the ethnic restaurants of Queensway. Renovated guest rooms are tasteful and comfortable.

12 Lancaster Gate, London W2 3LG. www.morningtonhotel.co.uk. ℂ **020/7262-7361** or 800/633-6548 in the U.S. and Canada. Fax 020/7706-1028. 70 units. £89–£199 double. Some rates include breakfast. AE, DC, MC, V. Parking nearby £25/day. Tube: Lancaster Gate. **Amenities:** Bar; gym. In room: TV, hairdryer, Wi-Fi (free).

INEXPENSIVE

Europa House Hotel ☺ This family-run hotel attracts visitors who want a room with a private bathroom but at shared-bathroom prices. Like most hotels along Sussex Gardens, some bedrooms are a bit cramped, but they're well maintained with solid furniture. An ongoing refurbishment program means that, though standards vary, there are some nicely up-to-date accommodations here with good bathrooms. There are two good family rooms each with four beds.

151 Sussex Gardens, London W2 2RY. www.europahousehotel.com. ℂ **020/7723-7343.** Fax 020/7224-9331. 20 units. £98 double; from £128 family room. Rates include English breakfast. AE, DC, MC, V. Free parking (if available, ask when booking). Tube: Paddington. In room: TV, hair dryer, Internet (free).

Garden Court Hotel The hotel has been family-run for more than 50 years, is meticulously managed, and set in a tranquil Victorian garden. Most accommodations are spacious, with good lighting, shelf and closet space, and comfortable furnishings. Rooms without ensuite facilities generally share a bathroom with the occupants of only one other room. There are many homelike touches throughout the hotel, including ancestral portraits and silk flowers. Rooms open onto the square in front or the gardens in the rear.

30–31 Kensington Gardens Sq., London W2 4BG. www.gardencourthotel.co.uk. ℂ **020/7229-2553.** Fax 020/7727-2749. 32 units, 24 with bathrooms. £85–135 double. Rates include English breakfast. MC, V. Tube: Bayswater. In room: TV, hair dryer, Wi-Fi (£2.50/day or £5/whole stay).

St. David's Hotel Another very reasonable garden square B&B, St. David's has been completely renovated by the family which has been running it since 1980. Only a 2-minute walk from Paddington station, the hotel was built when Norfolk Square knew a grander age. The bluebloods are long gone, but the area is still safe and recommendable. Refurbished bedrooms are well maintained and furnished comfortably, a few with original features like fireplaces and wooden shutters. Some bathrooms are very small, but you can't beat the price. Make sure you try the cooked breakfast—it always wins plaudits.

14–20 Norfolk Sq., London W2 1RS. www.stdavidshotels.com. ℂ **020/7723-4963.** Fax 020/7402-9061. 70 units. £65 double without bathroom, £80 double with bathroom. Rates include English breakfast. AE, MC, V. Tube: Paddington. In room: TV, Wi-Fi (free).

The Pavilion ★ Could this be London's most colorful hotel? Brother-and-sister team Danny and Noshi Karne have taken a nondescript B&B and transformed it into a kaleidoscope of funky fabrics, eccentric antiques, and themed rooms. When they get it right—the elegant Chapter & Verse room, or the faded glamour of the Silver Salon—it's a glorious change from the cookie-cutter hotels that dominate Bayswater. The less tasteful rooms, such as the explosion of fake fur that makes up the Honky Tonk Afro room, are only for the very brave. The hotel's idiosyncrasies make it a magnet for designers and musicians. Breakfast is served in your room from 8am.

34–36 Sussex Gardens, London W2 1UL. www.pavilionhoteluk.com. ☏ **020/7262-0905.** Fax 020/7262-1324. 30 units. £100 double. Rates include continental breakfast. MC, V. Parking £10/day. Tube: Edgware Rd. *In room:* TV, Wi-Fi (free).

Tudor Court Hotel Originally built in the 1850s and much restored and altered, this Victorian structure is now a small hotel of tranquility and comfort, a 2-minute walk from Paddington station. Bedrooms are compact to midsize, completely restored, and traditionally furnished, with single, double (or twin), triple, and family rooms available. Pod bathrooms with shower are well maintained and spotlessly clean. Family owned since 1989, the hotel really is concerned with guests' comfort, making this one a winner. The breakfast, cooked by the owner to order, is a great start to the day.

10–12 Norfolk Sq., London W2 1RS. www.tudorcourtpaddington.co.uk. ☏ **020/7723-6553/5157.** Fax 020/7723-0727. 38 units. £99-£120 double. Rates include English breakfast. AE, DC, MC, V. Nearby paying car park. Tube: Paddington. *In room:* TV, hair dryer, Wi-Fi (free).

Notting Hill

EXPENSIVE

Portobello Hotel ★ The quintessential Portobello Hotel tale is the night that Kate Moss and Johnny Depp allegedly took a champagne bath here. It sums up the hotel—glamorous, bubbly, and expensive. Made up of two 1850s' town houses, the Portobello is home to a wild variety of rooms. The cheapest are tiny but at the top end expect Chippendales, claw-foot tubs, or round beds tucked under gauze canopies (no. 16 has a full-tester bed facing the garden). Since windows are not double-glazed, request a room in the quiet rear.

22 Stanley Gardens, London W11 2NG. www.portobellohotel.com. ☏ **020/7727-2777.** Fax 020/7792-9641. 24 units. £195–£320 double. Rates include continental breakfast. AE, MC, V. Tube: Notting Hill Gate or Holland Park. **Amenities:** Restaurant; bar; room service. *In room:* A/C (some rooms), TV, minibar, hair dryer, Internet (free).

MODERATE

The Main House ★★ 🍴 The term home-from-home is bandied around all too frequently, but the Main House deserves the tag. Each guest gets a high-ceilinged floor of this Notting Hill town house to themselves, decorated in rare style from on-the-doorstep Portobello Road market—expect gilded mirrors, watercolors of elegantly dressed 1930s' women, and similar antiques. Some extra little touches make this place unique: Early morning tea or coffee in the room; a wonderfully cheap deal on chauffeur service; mobile phones to keep your call costs down; helpful maps, books, films, and umbrellas to borrow; and gleaming wood floors swathed in animal skins (reflecting owner Caroline Main's time as an explorer).

6 Colville Rd., London W11 2BP. www.themainhouse.co.uk. ☏ **020/7221-9691.** 4 suites. £120–£150 suite. MC, V. Parking £2.50/hr. Tube: Notting Hill Gate. **Amenities:** Bikes; access to health club & spa; room service; Internet (free). *In room:* TV, hair dryer.

Umi Hotel ★ 😊 🎒 Location, location, location; given its proximity to Hyde Park, Portobello Road, and hip (and pricey) Notting Hill's browsing and dining, this charming little hotel is a true find. It's located in side-by-side row houses on a quiet square. Don't expect luxury—although the decor is modern and inviting, it's pretty basic. But that's just fine, given that the basics are so good. Rooms are small but spotless and breakfast includes fresh and Fair Trade produce. Added bonus: The hotel offers both single rooms and family rooms that can sleep four. Ask for one of the rooms at the front for the gorgeous view over the square's garden.

16 Leinster Sq., London, W2 4PR. www.umihotellondon.co.uk. © **020/7221-9131.** Fax 020/7221-4073. 117 units. £160–£185 double. AE, DISC, MC, V. Tube: Bayswater or Queensway. **Amenities:** Restaurant; bar; cafe; concierge. *In room:* TV, Wi-Fi (£3/hr).

INEXPENSIVE

Gate Hotel   This antique-hunters' favorite is the only hotel along the length of Portobello Road—and because of rigid zoning restrictions, it will probably remain the only one for many years to come. It has seven cramped but cozy bedrooms over its four floors, and be prepared for some very steep stairs. Especially intriguing are the wall paintings that show the original Portobello Market: Every character looks plucked straight from a Dickens novel.

6 Portobello Rd., London W11 3DG. www.gatehotel.co.uk. © **020/7221-0707.** Fax 020/7221-9128. 7 units. £85–£105 double. Rates include continental breakfast (served in room). AE, MC, V. Tube: Notting Hill Gate or Holland Park. **Amenities:** Room service. *In room:* TV/DVD, hair dryer, Wi-Fi (£10/whole stay).

Maida Vale/Little Venice

EXPENSIVE

The Colonnade ★ ☺   Tree-shaded streets and canalside walks characterize pretty Little Venice, and the Colonnade's Victorian charm fits in perfectly. Each midsize bedroom is individually decorated, and many feature four-poster beds and small terraces. Tasteful fabrics and antiques evoke town-house living. The least desirable units are two small basement bedrooms, impeccably furnished but subject to rumblings from the Underground. Families might want to opt for the spacious two-level JFK suite. It's an easy walk to buzzing Notting Hill or Lord's Cricket Ground.

2 Warrington Crescent, London W9 1ER. www.theetoncollection.co.uk/colonnade. © **020/7286-1052.** Fax 020/7286-1057. 43 units. £110–£240 double. AE, DC, MC, V. Tube: Warwick Ave. **Amenities:** Room service. *In room:* A/C, TV, minibar, hair dryer, CD player, Wi-Fi (free).

Shepherd's Bush

VERY EXPENSIVE

K West Hotel & Spa ★★ 🎁   It's no accident that K West's name evokes the design hotels of Miami Beach—this is a little slice of Stateside glamour in an unlikely setting off the Shepherd's Bush roundabout that attracts a distinctly cool crowd, especially media mavens visiting the nearby BBC and touring musicians. The latter can be seen rocking all night long in the chic K Lounge and recovering the next day with an Asian head massage in the spa. Swanky suites and elegant bedrooms in an avant-garde neutral style attract the cosmopolitan guests. Behind the scenes there's a real commitment to energy saving too.

Richmond Way, London W14 0AX. www.k-west.co.uk. © **020/8008-6600.** Fax 020/8008-6650. 220 units. £129–£319 double. AE, DC, MC, V. Parking £5/3 hr., £1.50/each hour after that. Tube: Shepherd's Bush. **Amenities:** Restaurant; bar; health club & spa. *In room:* A/C, TV/DVD, hair dryer, CD player, MP3, Wi-Fi (£15/day).

SOUTHWEST LONDON

Southwest London is a popular choice. **Knightsbridge** is the smartest with classic town houses and high-end restaurants, Hyde Park for a garden, and Harrods as the local store. **Kensington** and **Chelsea** are also heavy on grand Edwardian accommodation, but with less flash, and less expense. **Victoria** and **Pimlico** are cheaper still with plenty of smaller hotels and B&Bs. **Westminster** puts you at the heart of British politics and royal grandeur. Live like a visiting dignitary here but don't expect to do it on the cheap.

Best For: First-time visitors wanting to see the classic attractions of shopping, royal life, and green spaces.

Drawbacks: Some areas like Victoria can be very busy with commuters at peak times.

For a **map** of Southwest London hotels, please see "Southwest London Hotels & Restaurants" (p. 224 in Chapter 5).

Westminster

VERY EXPENSIVE

Corinthia Hotel London ★★★ 📷 Opened in April 2011 as the Corinthia Hotels' flagship property, the triangular-shaped building has retained the huge spaces, marble columns, and ceilings of its sumptuous past as the Metropole Hotel. Bringing it right up-to-date is the commissioned art work and eye-catching lighting like the Baccarat chandelier that dominates the central Lobby Lounge—a great meeting place, which serves a lovely afternoon tea. Bedrooms are amongst the largest in London, decorated in natural colors; each has a media hub and a Nespresso machine; bathrooms have wall-mounted TV screens. The restaurants are equally grand: Northall serves British traditional dishes while Massimo is the inspiration of Italian chef Massimo Riccioli. Recall the 1930s' Jazz age in the Bassoon bar. The flagship Espa Life on four floors is now London's most glamorous and spacious spa.

Whitehall Place, London SW1A 2BD. www.corinthia.com. ☏ **020/7930 8181**. Toll free USA 1-877-842-6269. Fax 020/7321 3001. 294 units. £339–£680 plus VAT double. AE, DC, MC, V. Tube: Embankment. **Amenities:** 2 restaurants; 2 bars; 24-hr gym; spa; concierge; room service. *In room:* A/C, TV/DVD, minibar, hairdryer, media hub, Wi-Fi (free).

Royal Horseguards Hotel ★★ 📷 The Royal Horseguards Hotel was once the National Liberal Club, built in the 1880s, then turned into the headquarters of the Secret Service during World War I. All political ties may have been severed, but the building still has some remarkable original architectural features like large spaces and high ceilings, sumptuous fabrics, a magnificent staircase, and glazed patterned tiling. Bedrooms are large and comfortable, the whole package still a little gentlemen's club-like in feel. The views are magnificent and the restaurant—a converted library—harks back to the hotel's illustrious past. You can dine on the terrace in good weather.

2 Whitehall Court, London SW1A 2EJ. www.guoman.com/theroyalhorseguards. ☏ **0871/376-9033** or 0845/305-8332. Fax 0871/376-9133 or 0845/305-8371. 282 units. £250–£480 double. AE, DC, MC, V. Tube: Embankment. **Amenities:** Bar; restaurant; gym; concierge; room service. *In room:* A/C, TV/DVD, minibar, hairdryer, Wi-Fi (free).

EXPENSIVE

Sanctuary House Hotel This is a sightseer's dream—a classic neighborhood hotel, complete with its own traditional pub, just yards from Westminster Abbey, the Houses of Parliament, and the London Eye. Accommodations have a rustic feel, but with first-rate beds. Downstairs, the in-house pub/restaurant offers old-style British food that has ignored changing culinary fashions, dishes like roast beef, Welsh lamb, and Dover sole that pleased the palates of Churchill and his contemporaries. Naturally, there's always plenty of beer on tap.

33 Tothill St., London SW1H 9LA. www.fullershotels.com. © **020/7799-4044.** Fax 020/7799-3657. 34 units. £155–£185 double. AE, DC, MC, V. Tube: St. James's Park. **Amenities:** Restaurant; pub; room service. *In room:* A/C, TV, hair dryer, Wi-Fi (free).

MODERATE

DoubleTree by Hilton Hotel London – Westminster ★ Next to Tate Britain and Parliament, this purpose-built inn formerly known as the Mint Hotel Westminster has a vast array of rooms at the heart of tourist London. The best units are the 67 City Club rooms or the 16 suites, but all are comfortable, with a fresh, light, and contemporary design. Business clients predominate during the week, but on weekends rates are often slashed to bargain prices. Ask about this when booking. Try for a guest room opening onto the Thames or Parliament.

30 John Islip St., London SW1P 4DD. http://doubletree1.hilton.com/. © **020/7630-1000,** UK toll free **0800/8900-111.** Fax 020/7233-7575. 460 units. £119–£159 double. AE, DC, MC, V. Tube: Pimlico or Westminster. **Amenities:** Restaurant; 2 bars; exercise room; concierge; room service. *In room:* A/C, TV/DVD/CD player, hair dryer, Wi-Fi (free).

Victoria, Belgravia & Pimlico

VERY EXPENSIVE

41 Hotel ★★★ 📖 This is the very antidote to chain hotels—30 individually designed rooms, with nice touches such as open fireplaces and scented candles. 41 Hotel is best suited to couples or those traveling alone—especially women. Public areas are furnished with antiques and rich fabrics and always have fresh flowers. Guests can read, relax, or watch TV in the library-style lounge, where a complimentary continental breakfast and afternoon snacks are served each day. Guest rooms are individually sized, but all feature elegant black-and-white color schemes and large beds with Egyptian-cotton linens.

41 Buckingham Palace Rd., London SW1W OPS. www.41hotel.com. © **020/7300-0041** or 877/955-1515 in the U.S. and Canada. Fax 020/7300-0141. 28 units. £275–£295 double. Rates include welcome drink, continental breakfast, afternoon snacks, and evening canapés. AE, DC, MC, V. Tube: Victoria. **Amenities:** Bar; access to nearby health club; concierge; room service; babysitting. *In room:* A/C, TV/DVD, hair dryer, CD player, MP3 docking station, Wi-Fi (free).

The Goring ★★★ ☺ There are plenty of family-run hotels in London, but The Goring is the very best. It's close to Buckingham Palace, the royal parks, and Westminster Abbey (one reason why Kate Middleton chose the Goring as her hotel the night before she married Prince William); an excellent staff; and understated splendor. Guest rooms offer luxurious bathrooms with extra-long tubs and red marble walls, and the beds are among the most comfortable in town. Queen Anne and Chippendale are the decor styles, all beautifully maintained. The rooms overlooking the garden are best. Touches such as a basket of essentials for babies, bedtime story library, a gift bag of a furry sheep and special activity pack, and the chance to decorate cakes in the kitchen make this an ideal family hotel. Business travelers may baulk (others will cheer) at a ban on mobile phones and laptops in the lounge or restaurant, where you can take afternoon tea (p. 259).

15 Beeston Place, London SW1W 0JW. www.thegoring.com. © **020/7396-9000.** Fax 020/7834-4393. 69 units. £420–£850 double. AE, DC, MC, V. Parking £45/day. Tube: Victoria. **Amenities:** Restaurant; bar; access to nearby health club; concierge; babysitting. In room: A/C, TV/DVD, hair dryer, movie library, CD player, CD library, Wi-Fi (£5.25/hour; £15.75/day).

Rubens at the Palace ★★ 🍴 The very British Rubens is popular with Americans and Europeans seeking traditional English hospitality and the latest creature comforts. Its location is one of the best in town—directly across the street from Buckingham Palace and only a 2-minute walk from Victoria station. The size and decor of the guest rooms vary, but all feature grand comfort. Housed in a private wing, each of the eight "Royal Rooms" is named for an English monarch and decorated in the style of that ruler's period.

39 Buckingham Palace Rd., London SW1W 0PS. www.rubenshotel.com. © **020/7834-6600** or 877/955-1515 in the U.S. and Canada. Fax 020/7828-5401. 161 units. £192–£310 double. AE, DC, MC, V. Tube: Victoria. **Amenities:** 2 restaurants; bar; access to nearby health club; concierge; room service; babysitting. In room: A/C, TV/DVD, minibar (some suites only), hair dryer, movie library, Wi-Fi (free).

EXPENSIVE

St. Ermin's Hotel ★★ 🎁 The beautifully renovated hotel has a racy past. Converted from a mansion block into a hotel in 1899, it was the place where Churchill founded SOE (Special Operations Executive). More notoriously, it housed MI6 and the bar was the place where, allegedly, Guy Burgess and Kim Philby handed over secrets to their Russian counterparts during the Cold War. If that's not intriguing enough for you, then just see the decor. The hotel is set back from the street with a pretty, tree-lined entrance. Walk inside and you're greeted by acres of white swirling plasterwork, grand high ceilings and quirky artifacts. The glamour continues in good-size bedrooms with silk walls and gorgeous bed linen. The 41 suites have luxury "wet rooms" with a roll top bath and rain shower. Smart Caxton Grill serves modern British cuisine; the bar serves cocktails and history and there's an outside terrace for fine weather drinks.

Caxton St., London SW1H 0QW. www.sterminshotel.co.uk. © **0800/635-0438;** in the USA © **877-218-6004.** Fax 0207/976-0710. 331 units. From £139 double, from £369 suite. AE, MC, V. Tube: Victoria. **Amenities:** Restaurant; bar; concierge; room service. In room: A/C, TV, DVD (suites only), minibar; hair dryer, MP3 docking stations, Wi-Fi (£15/24 hrs).

MODERATE

B&B Belgravia ★ In its first year of operation (2005), this elegant town house won a Gold Award as "the best B&B in London." Design, service, quality, and comfort paid off. The prices are reasonable, the atmosphere in this massively renovated building is stylish, and the location is grand: Just a 5-minute walk from Victoria station. The good-size bedrooms are luxuriously furnished. There is also a DVD library, and tea and coffee are served 24 hours a day. Late risers may want to avoid Room 1—it's above the breakfast room and isn't the quietest. Unusually for London, pets are welcome.

64–66 Ebury St., London SW1W 9QD. www.bb-belgravia.com. ✆ **020/7259-8570.** Fax 020/7259-8591. 17 units. £135-£145 double; £165–£175 family room. Rates include English breakfast. AE, MC, V. Tube: Victoria. **Amenities:** Breakfast room. *In room:* TV, Wi-Fi (free).

Lime Tree Hotel The Davies family, veterans of London's B&B business, have transformed a dowdy guesthouse into a cozy hotel for travelers on a budget. The simply furnished bedrooms are scattered over four floors (with no elevator) of a brick town house; each has been refitted with new curtains and cupboards. The front rooms have small balconies overlooking Ebury Street; units in the back don't have balconies but are quieter with a view of the hotel's small rose garden. Rooms tend to be larger here than other hotel rooms offered at similar prices. Six rooms come with a tub/shower combination, the rest with shower only.

135–137 Ebury St., London SW1W 9QU. www.limetreehotel.co.uk. ✆ **020/7730-8191.** Fax 020/7730-7865. 25 units. £125–£170 double. Rates include English breakfast. AE, DC, MC, V. No children 4 or under. Tube: Victoria or Sloane Sq. **Amenities:** Breakfast room. *In room:* TV, hair dryer, Wi-Fi (free).

The Windermere ✔ This award-winning small hotel is an excellent choice near Victoria station. The Windermere was built in 1857 as a pair of private dwellings on the old Abbot's Lane linking Westminster Abbey to its abbot's residence used by the kings of medieval England. A good example of early Victorian classical design, the hotel has plenty of English character. All rooms have a private bathroom—some with shower, others with tubs—and come in a range of sizes, some accommodating up to four lodgers. Lower-floor rooms facing the street tend to be noisy at night.

142–144 Warwick Way, London SW1V 4JE. www.windermere-hotel.co.uk. ✆ **020/7834-5163.** 19 units. £145–£205 double. Rates include English breakfast. AE, MC, V. Tube: Victoria. **Amenities:** Restaurant; bar; room service. *In room:* TV, hair dryer, Wi-Fi (free).

INEXPENSIVE

Morgan House Hotel This Georgian house has a convenient address, and its rooms are often fully booked all summer. Guest rooms are individually decorated and have orthopedic mattresses. Many are small to midsize, while others are large enough to house up to four people. Hallway bathrooms are well maintained and adequate for guests who don't have their own private facilities. A hearty English breakfast is served in a bright, cheerful room, and there's a small courtyard.

120 Ebury St., London SW1W 9QQ. www.morganhouse.co.uk. ✆ **020/7730-2384.** 11 units, 4 with private bathroom. £84–£108 double. Rates include English breakfast. MC, V. Tube: Victoria. **Amenities:** Breakfast room. *In room:* TV, hair dryer, Wi-Fi (free).

Knightsbridge

VERY EXPENSIVE

The Beaufort ★★ Personal service, a quiet location minutes from Harrods, and genuinely hospitable little touches have made the Beaufort one of the best of the Knightsbridge boutique hotels. The two converted 1870s' town houses sit in a quiet cul-de-sac. Each guest room is tasteful and bright, individually decorated in a modern color scheme, and adorned with well-chosen paintings by London artists. Rooms come with earphone radios, flowers, and a selection of books—the junior suites offer use of a mobile phone and a personal fax/answering machine. Bedrooms are small, but a grand lounge (with free afternoon tea) is a recompense. Ask for a room at the front—they're larger and lighter than those at the back.

33 Beaufort Gardens, London SW3 1PP. www.thebeaufort.co.uk. ℂ **020/7584-5252.** Fax 020/7589-2834. 29 units. £216–£312 double. Rates include afternoon cream tea and drinks 3–11pm daily. AE, DC, MC, V. Tube: Knightsbridge. **Amenities:** Bar; access to nearby health club; room service; babysitting. *In room:* A/C, TV, hair dryer, CD player, Wi-Fi (free).

The Berkeley ★★★

The Berkeley's winning formula remains intact—a modern building decorated in classic Art Deco grand style but with the kind of understated, helpful service that sets it apart from stuffier neighbors. Inside you'll find an environment inspired by French classical design but with a contemporary edge. Each room offers high-end style, but most elegant of all are the suites, many of which have luxurious, marble-and-tile-trimmed baths. Some of the suites also have iPads for guests' use.

Wilton Place, London SW1X 7RL. www.maybournehotelgroup.com or www.the-berkeley.co.uk. ℂ **020/7235-6000** or 800/599-6991 in the U.S. and Canada. Fax 020/7235-4330. 214 units. £299–£329 double. AE, DC, MC, V. Tube: Knightsbridge or Hyde Park Corner. **Amenities:** 3 restaurants, including Koffmann's (p. 226) and Marcus Wareing (p. 226); 2 bars; health club & spa concierge. *In room:* A/C, TV/DVD, hair dryer, CD player, CD library, Wi-Fi (free).

The Capital ★★★

A luxury shopper's and gourmet's delight, the Capital manages, year after year, to combine boutique hotel charm with the amenities you'd expect in a far larger establishment. Only 45m (148 ft.) from Harrods department store, this family-run town-house hotel is also at the doorstep of London's "green lung," Hyde Park. Famed designer Nina Campbell furnished the spacious bedrooms with sumptuous fabrics, art, and antiques. David Linley, nephew of the Queen, also assisted in the design. The liveried doorman standing outside has welcomed royalty, heads of state, and international celebrities.

22 Basil St., London SW3 1AT. www.capitalhotel.co.uk. ℂ **020/7589-5171.** Fax 020/7225-0011. 49 units. £300–£400 double. AE, DC, MC, V. Parking £40/24 hrs. Tube: Knightsbridge. **Amenities:** Restaurant; bar; access to nearby health club; concierge; babysitting. *In room:* A/C, TV, minibar, hair dryer, Wi-Fi (free).

Knightsbridge Hotel ★★ 🍃

Located on a quiet, traffic-free, tree-lined street, this charming small and comfortable hotel in a high-rent district has a loyal regular following. Built in the early 1800s as a private town house, the Knightsbridge has been updated with such luxe touches as granite-and-oak bathrooms, an honor bar, and Frette linens. Most bedrooms are spacious and furnished with traditional English fabrics. The best rooms are nos. 311 and 312 at the rear, each with a pitched ceiling and a small sitting area. The hotel is fabulously located between fashionable Beauchamp Place and Harrods, with many of the city's top museums close at hand.

10 Beaufort Gardens, London SW3 1PT. www.firmdale.com. ℂ **020/7584-6300** or 888/559-5508 in the U.S. and Canada. Fax 020/7584-6355. 44 units. £235–£330 double. AE, DC, MC, V. Tube: Knightsbridge. **Amenities:** Self-service bar; room service; babysitting. *In room:* TV/DVD, minibar, hair dryer, CD player, Wi-Fi (£20).

EXPENSIVE

Aster House ★★★ ✦ Only in Knightsbridge could a B&B fit into the "expensive" category, but this former winner of the London Tourism Award for best B&B is as good as ever. Within an easy walk of Kensington Palace and the museums of South Kensington, it's a friendly, inviting, and well-decorated lodging on a tree-lined street. The area surrounding the hotel, Sumner Place, looks like a Hollywood stage set of Victorian London. Rooms range from spacious to Lilliputian, with some beds draped with fabric tents for extra drama, and each room is individually decorated in the style of an English manor-house bedroom.

3 Sumner Place, London SW7 3EE. www.asterhouse.com. ✆ **020/7581-5888.** Fax 020/7584-4925. 14 units. £195–£295 double + VAT. Rates include buffet breakfast. MC, V. Tube: South Kensington. *In room:* A/C, TV, minibar, hair dryer, Wi-Fi (free).

30 Pavilion Road ★★ 🎒 A leafy rooftop restaurant, understated country-house ambience, and the most British of personal service—it's no surprise that many of the guests of this converted pumping station are repeat visitors. At this Knightsbridge oasis, you press a buzzer and are admitted to a freight elevator that carries you to the third floor. Upstairs, you encounter handsomely furnished rooms with antiques, tasteful fabrics, comfortable beds (some with canopies), and often a sitting alcove. Some of the bathtubs are placed in the room instead of in a separate unit.

30 Pavilion Rd., London SW1X 0HJ. www.searcys.com/30-pavilion-road/bed-breakfast. ✆ **020/ 7584-4921.** Fax 020/7823-8694. 10 units. £229–£258 double; £310 family room. Rates include continental breakfast. AE, DC, MC, V. Tube: Knightsbridge. **Amenities:** Room service. *In room:* A/C, TV, Wi-Fi (free).

Kensington
VERY EXPENSIVE

Baglioni Hotel ★★★ Arguably West London's chicest address, the Baglioni, part of the Italian hotel chain, is the personification of *la dolce vita* in London. This pricey hotel attracts those who were born to shop (Harrods is a 10-min. walk away, Kensington High Street, only 5). Of the 67 stunning and luxuriously furnished bedrooms, 49 are suites. The best and most elegant bedrooms open onto Kensington Gardens. What an enclave: Ebonized wood floors and deluxe furnishings in mocha, taupe, and black are just part of the allure, although it means rooms are dark and cocoon-like in need of some extra lighting. Suites come with their own espresso machine, and the room service is highly skilled.

60 Hyde Park Gate, London SW7 5BB. www.baglionihotels.com. ✆ **020/7368-5700.** Fax 020/7368-5701. 67 units. £279–£500 double. AE, MC, V. Parking £38/day. Tube: High St. Kensington. **Amenities:** Restaurant; bar; babysitting; concierge; room service. *In room:* A/C, TV/DVD, minibar, hair dryer, movie library, CD player, CD library, Internet (free).

The Bentley ★★★ Following an 8-year renovation, this hotel is for those who prefer opulence to minimalism. Located in the heart of Kensington, the Bentley is the Rolls Royce (or at least, the Bentley) of London hotels. Six hundred tonnes of marble were imported from Turkey, Africa, and Italy to adorn the place. Gorgeous silk fabrics fill its spacious rooms and suites, each with a luxe marble-lined bathroom with walk-in shower and Jacuzzi. The fixtures are gold plate, and the bedrooms have deep pile carpets and Louis XIV accessories. The Imperial Suite even boasts a grand piano. Unusually there is a Turkish hammam.

27–31 Harrington Gardens, London SW7 4JX. www.thebentley-hotel.com. ☎ **020/7244-5555.** Fax 020/7244-5566. 64 units. £185–£330 double. AE, MC, V. Tube: South Kensington. **Amenities:** 2 restaurants; bar; fitness room; health club & spa; concierge; babysitting. *In room:* A/C, TV, DVD on request, minibar, hair dryer, Internet (£16.99/day).

The Milestone ★★★   A firm favorite with Frommer's' readers, The Milestone epitomizes everything good about the classic London hotel—understated elegance, service that regularly goes that extra mile, cozy public rooms decorated with fresh flowers, dark woods, antique furnishings, fabric wall coverings, and a location close to some genuine London landmarks. Guest rooms and suites are spread over six floors and vary in size, decor, and shape (some rooms are quite small). For an iconic view, request a room overlooking the palace and Kensington Gardens.

1 Kensington Court, London W8 5DL. www.milestonehotel.com. ☎ **020/7917-1000** or 877/955-1515 in the U.S. and Canada. Fax 020/7917-1010. 62 units. £250–£360 double. AE, DC, MC, V. Tube: High St. Kensington. **Amenities:** Restaurant; bar; health club; concierge; room service; babysitting. *In room:* A/C, TV/DVD/VCR, fax, minibar, hair dryer, CD player, MP3 docking station, Wi-Fi (free).

EXPENSIVE

Parkcity Hotel ★★★   Entering the Parkcity is always a surprise—it's a modern, sleek-lined wolf in historical sheep's clothing. The staid Victorian frontage gives way to a thoroughly up-to-date hotel. Much better equipped than many of the hotels in the area (it has a business center and a gym), and with a friendly staff, the hotel has a good repeat customer base. All rooms are bright and airy with a pleasingly modern sheen, but in the summer avoid those overlooking the patio if you want peace and privacy. The basement dining room only serves breakfast; ask for a table overlooking the garden.

18–30 Lexham Gardens, London W8 5JE. www.theparkcity.com. ☎ **020/7341-7090.** Fax 020/7835-0189. 62 units. £149–£219 double. AE, MC, V. Tube: Gloucester Rd. **Amenities:** Bar; exercise room; concierge; room service; Wi-Fi (free in public areas). *In room:* AC, TV/CD player, minibar, Wi-Fi (free).

INEXPENSIVE

Easyhotel ✦   This is the hotel that brought budget airline thinking to London's accommodation scene. Rooms are tiny (if spotlessly clean) at 6 to 7 sq. m (65–75 sq. ft.), with most of the space taken up by standard double beds. Ask for a room with a window to lessen the claustrophobia. A flatscreen TV is in every unit, but it costs an extra £5 fee to use it. Still, if all you're looking for in a hotel is somewhere to rest your head it's hard to argue with the price. Housekeeping service costs an optional £10 per day, there is no elevator, and checkout time is 10am. You must book by credit card through the hotel website.

14 Lexham Gardens, London W8 5JE. www.easyhotel.com. ☎ **020/7706-9911.** 47 units. £39–£99 double. MC, V. Tube: High St. Kensington or Earl's Court. *In room:* A/C, TV, Wi-Fi (£10/24hrs).

Chelsea

VERY EXPENSIVE

The Cadogan ★★   Historic without being stuffy, the Cadogan combines small-hotel friendliness with big-hotel standards. Best known as the spot where Oscar Wilde was arrested for so-called indecent acts, this late-Victorian terra-cotta brick hotel had grown a bit stale before design doyenne Grace Leo-Andrieu stepped in. Today you get "stardust" wallpaper in the Drawing Room, Chanel-style tweeds on the upholstery, ostrich feathers strewn across pillows, and cheeky silver wallpaper in the very room (no. 118) where Wilde met his fate. The spacious and individually decorated bedrooms come in many styles and arrangements, even studios, and some have two bathrooms. Rooms and suites are either contemporary with smooth lines and bold splashes of color or Edwardian style with period details and country-house furnishings.

75 Sloane St., London SW1X 9SG. www.cadogan.com. ℂ **020/7235-7141.** Fax 020/7245-0994. 64 units. £175–£435 double. AE, DC, MC, V. Tube: Sloane Sq. or Knightsbridge. **Amenities:** Restaurant; bar; use of tennis courts; exercise room; concierge; use of private garden. *In room:* A/C, TV/DVD, minibar, hair dryer, Wi-Fi (free).

Draycott Hotel ★★★   The Draycott offers British gentility, style, and charm. Guests are greeted like old friends by a staff that is both hip and cordial. The hotel took its present-day form when a third brick-fronted town house was added to a pair of interconnected houses that had been functioning as a five-star hotel since the 1980s. That, coupled with tons of money spent on English antiques, rich draperies, and an upgrade of those expensive infrastructures you'll never see, including security, has transformed this place into a gem. Bedrooms are outfitted differently, each with haute English style and plenty of fashion chic. As a special feature, the hotel serves complimentary drinks—tea at 4pm daily, champagne at 6pm, and hot chocolate at 9:30pm.

26 Cadogan Gardens, London SW3 2RP. www.draycotthotel.com. ℂ **020/7730-6466** or 800/747-4942 in the U.S. and Canada. Fax 020/7730-0236. 35 units. £255–£345 + VAT double. AE, DC, MC, V. Tube: Sloane Sq. **Amenities:** Bar; access to nearby health club & spa; room service. *In room:* A/C, TV/DVD, minibar, CD player, MP3 docking station, Wi-Fi (free).

San Domenico House ★★   Reclining in a four-poster bed, antiques scattered around the room, it's hard to believe that you're in a B&B. A redbrick Victorian town house that has been tastefully renovated in recent years, San Domenico House is in the heart of Chelsea near the shops of Sloane Square and the King's Road. Bedrooms come in varying sizes, ranging from small to spacious, but all are opulently furnished with flouncy draperies, tasteful fabrics, and sumptuous beds. The rooftop terrace is ideal for breakfast or an evening drink.

29 Draycott Place, London SW3 2SH. www.sandomenicohouse.com. ℂ **020/7581-5757** or 800/324-9960 in the U.S. and Canada. Fax 020/7584-1348. 16 units. £255–£335 double. AE, DC, MC, V. Tube: Sloane Sq. **Amenities:** Babysitting; room service; Wi-Fi (free in lobby). *In room:* A/C, TV/DVD, minibar, hair dryer, Wi-Fi (free).

South Kensington & Earl's Court

VERY EXPENSIVE

Blake's Hotel ★★★   Actress Anouska Hempel's opulent and highly individual creation remains one of London's best small hotels. No expense was spared in converting this former row of Victorian town houses into one of the city's most original places to stay. It offers an Arabian Nights atmosphere: The richly appointed lobby boasts British Raj-era furniture from India, and individually decorated, elaborately appointed rooms contain such treasures and touches as Venetian glassware, cloth-covered walls, swagged draperies, and even Empress Josephine's daybed. Live out your fantasy: Choose an ancient Egyptian funeral barge or a 16th-century Venetian boudoir. Rooms in the older section have the least space and aren't air-conditioned, but are chic nevertheless.

33 Roland Gardens, London SW7 3PF. www.blakeshotels.com. ℂ **020/7370-6701** or 800/926-3173 in the U.S. and Canada. Fax 020/7373-0442. 48 units. £269–£349 + VAT double. AE, MC, V. Parking £4/hr. Tube: Gloucester Rd. **Amenities:** Restaurant; exercise room; room service; babysitting. *In room:* TV, minibar, hair dryer, Wi-Fi (free).

EXPENSIVE

Number Sixteen ★★ Modern yet cozy is the description guests frequently use. The scrupulously maintained front and rear gardens make this one of the most idyllic spots on the street. Rooms are decorated with an eclectic mix of English antiques and modern paintings, although some of the decor looks a little faded. Accommodations range from small to spacious and have themes such as tartan and maritime. If the weather's good take breakfast in the garden, with its bubbling fountain and fishpond.

16 Sumner Place, London SW7 3EG. www.firmdale.com. ℂ **020/7589-5232** or 888/559-5508 in the U.S. and Canada. Fax 020/7584-8615. 41 units. £225–£300 double. AE, DC, MC, V. Parking £39/day. Tube: South Kensington. **Amenities:** Honor bar; access to nearby health club; room service; babysitting. *In room:* TV, minibar, hair dryer, Wi-Fi (£20/24 hrs).

The Rockwell ★★ 🏙 Proof that London high style doesn't always come with a high price tag. This independently owned bastion of deluxe comfort occupies a converted Georgian manse in South Kensington. Its bedrooms, tricked out with oak furnishings and Neisha Crosland wallpaper, combine traditional English aesthetics with modern design. Large and inviting, they feature the finest Egyptian cotton, feather pillows, and merino wool blankets. All are bright and airy with large windows and simple lines, but the garden units with their own private patios are particularly appealing.

181-183 Cromwell Rd., London SW5 0SF. www.therockwell.com. ℂ **020/7244-2000.** Fax 020/7244-2001. 40 units. £162–£210 double. AE, DC, MC, V. Tube: Earl's Court or Gloucester Rd. **Amenities:** Restaurant; bar; access to nearby gym; room service. *In room:* A/C, TV, minibar, Internet (free).

MODERATE

Base2Stay 🍃 Visitors who value their independence, and bang for their buck, go for Base2Stay—no-frills apartment accommodations with no hidden extras. What you get are stylish, comfortably furnished rooms with small kitchenettes. The cheapest rooms contain bunk beds, and suites can be made from interconnecting rooms. Living may be stripped to the basics, but this is no hostel, as there is a 24-hour reception and a daily maid service. Green credentials are impeccable too: 60% of waste is recycled, and electrical devices are low-energy.

25 Courtfield Gardens, London SW5 0PG. www.base2stay.com. ℂ **020/7244-2255** or 800/511-9821 in the U.S. and Canada. Fax 020/7244-2256. 67 units. £122 bunk beds; £97–£220 double. AE, MC, V. Tube: Earl's Court. *In room:* A/C, TV, kitchenette, Wi-Fi (free).

INEXPENSIVE

Henley House ★★ 🎁 This B&B stands out from the pack around Earl's Court—and it's better value than most. The redbrick Victorian row house is on a communal fenced-in garden entered by borrowing a key from the reception desk. The decor is bright and contemporary; a typical room has warmly patterned wallpaper, chintz fabrics, and solid-brass lighting fixtures. The friendly staff members are happy to take bewildered newcomers under their wing, so this is an ideal place for London first-timers.

30 Barkston Gardens, London SW5 0EN. www.henleyhousehotel.com. ℂ **020/7370-4111.** Fax 020/7370-0026. 21 units. £75–£159 double. Rates include continental breakfast. AE, DC, MC, V. Tube: Earl's Court. *In room:* TV, hair dryer, Wi-Fi (free).

THE SOUTH BANK

The South Bank, stretching from Westminster Bridge to London Bridge takes in museums, theatres, and galleries. Hotels in prime spots such as **Waterloo** and the **South Bank** are closer to the London Eye, Tower Bridge, and world-class arts venues than most of their West End counterparts.

Best For: Walks along the Thames and taking in the world-class theatre and concerts on the South Bank.

Drawbacks: In some areas you may feel out of the action.

For a **map** of South Bank hotels, please see "South Bank & The City Hotels & Restaurants" (p. 233 in Chapter 5).

Expensive

Bermondsey Square Hotel ★★ 🎁 At one time no one would think of staying in Bermondsey, in southeast London, but times are changing and this hotel, the first boutique hotel in the area, is part of the neighborhood's renaissance. Local galleries, boutiques, bars, and restaurants are thriving. Overlooking one of London's largest antiques markets, this cool hotel caters to both foodies drawn to Alfie's Bar & Kitchen and fashionistas attracted to well-equipped and decorated designer-chic bedrooms. Rooms on the penthouse floor are named for hit songs from the 1960s, including "Lucy" and "Jude."

Bermondsey Sq., Tower Bridge Rd., SE1 3UN. www.bermondseysquarehotel.co.uk. ℂ **020/7378-2450.** Fax 020/7378-2460. 79 units. £129–£350 double. AE, MC, V. Tube: London Bridge, and then bus 78. **Amenities:** Restaurant; bar; concierge; room service. *In room:* A/C, TV/DVD, minibar, hair dryer, MP3 docking station, Wi-Fi (free).

London Bridge Hotel ★★ There's no doubt the London Bridge Hotel puts you right in the thick of things—the river, Borough Market, and the South Bank are all just seconds away. A former telephone exchange building, this 1915 structure was successfully recycled into a bastion of comfort and charm. Bedrooms are completely up to date and offer homelike comfort and plenty of amenities. Rooms in the front have double-glazing on windows to cut down on noise. The Quarter Bar and Lounge are handy meeting places for Londoners.

8–18 London Bridge St., London SE1 9SG. www.londonbridgehotel.com. ℂ **020/7855-2200.** Fax 020/7855-2233. 140 units. £143–£384 double. Children 11 and under stay free in parent's room. AE, DC, MC, V. Tube: London Bridge. **Amenities:** 2 restaurants; bar; access to nearby health club; babysitting. *In room:* A/C, TV/DVD, minibar, hair dryer, Wi-Fi (free).

Park Plaza Westminster Bridge ★ ✦   Perfectly located for the South Bank and opposite the Houses of Parliament, this new modern hotel is a real plus. Not the most beautiful from the outside, inside it's designed around a huge central atrium. The best rooms have views over Parliament, the London Eye, or out toward south London. For families, the well-designed studio rooms come with self-catering facilities like a microwave and refrigerator and a living area with a pull-out sofa bed. It's spacious, smart, and well-thought out with all the expected high tech amenities. All the restaurants and bars interconnect on the first floor. You can choose from the main brasserie, sushi and sashimi bars, a patisserie, and a lounge for all-day tapas. Unusually, the hotel has a swimming pool.

200 Westminster Bridge Road, London SE1 7UT. www.parkplaza.com/westminster. ℂ **0844/415 6780.** Europe toll free 800/169 6128. Fax 0844/415 6791. 1019 units. £109–£409 + VAT double. AE, DC, MC, V. Tube: Waterloo. **Amenities:** 2 restaurants; bar; pool; fitness center; spa; concierge. *In room:* A/C, TV, minibar, hair dryer, Wi-Fi (free).

THE CITY

Hotels in and around the **Square Mile** mainly cater for businessmen, but are increasingly geared toward leisure visitors. The City's hip neighbors—**Shoreditch** and **Clerkenwell**—have injected real cool into the area.

Best For: Great weekend rates and quiet nights.

Drawbacks: As some of the City is a business area, you might find it quiet at weekends and in the evening.

For a **map** of City hotels, please see "South Bank & The City Hotels & Restaurants" (p. 233 in Chapter 5).

Very Expensive

Andaz Liverpool Street Hotel ★★   The Andaz has the best of both worlds—tradition and modernity under an elegant Victorian roof. The original hotel, designed in 1884 by Charles Barry (known for his work on the Houses of Parliament), is an opulent gem with grand public areas, and a 2007 refit brought it bang up to date without losing the period charm. The hotel's exterior is a Victorian glory, complete with a stained-glass dome. Bedrooms are contemporary and comfortable, with state-of-the-art bathrooms and color schemes of dark red and white. Touches like a free non-alcoholic minibar and free local landline telephone calls add to the excellent package.

40 Liverpool St., London EC2M 7QN. www.andaz.com. ℂ **020/7961-1234** or 800/228-9000 in the U.S. and Canada. Fax 020/7961-1235. 267 units. £145–£360 + VAT double; AE, DC, MC, V. Tube: Liverpool St. **Amenities:** 5 restaurants; 5 bars; health club; room service. *In room:* A/C, TV/DVD, minibar, hair dryer, MP3 docking station, Wi-Fi (free).

The Montcalm London City ★★   In the mid-18th century, the Brewery that houses the new Montcalm was London's largest beer producer. Today its huge vaulted ceilings and cast-iron columns take you straight back to its industrial past. Corridors take you round odd corners and over an enclosed iron bridge. Rooms have been cleverly converted, some retaining industrial features. Colors are browns and greens, and as well as all the high tech you'd expect, each room has an aroma machine of different scents. The London City Suites opposite the main hotel have kitchenettes for longer stays. It may seem somewhat remote at weekends, but it's very near the Barbican (p. 307) and a short walk to Spitalfields (p. 277).

52 Chiswell St., London EC1Y 4SD. www.themontcalmlondoncity.co.uk. ℂ **020/7614-0100.** Fax 020/7374-2577. 235 units. £99–£350 double. AE, DC, MC, V. Tube: Moorgate. **Amenities:** 2 restaurants; 2 bars; health club & spa; concierge; room service. *In room:* A/C, TV, minibar, hair dryer, MP3 docking station, Wi-Fi (free).

Threadneedles ★★   Threadneedles is the boutique business hotel par excellence. In the heart of the financial district, within walking distance of the Bank of England (the "Old Lady of Threadneedle Street") this converted Victorian bank radiates all the grandeur and solidity of the City. Chunky oak doors, soaring marble columns, and walnut walls speak of its past, but the bedrooms are packed with contemporary comforts including roomy limestone baths and Egyptian-cotton and duck-down duvets on the beds.

5 Threadneedle St., London EC2R 8AY. www.theetoncollection.co.uk. ℂ **020/7657-8080.** Fax 020/7657-8100. 69 units. £220–£415 double; discounts of about 50% offered for stays on Fri and Sat nights. AE, DC, MC, V. Tube: Bank. **Amenities:** Restaurant; bar; concierge; room service; babysitting. *In room:* A/C, TV, minibar, hair dryer, Wi-Fi (free).

The Zetter ★★★   It was only a matter of time before a hotel blended the edgy Shoreditch scene with the creature comforts demanded by City types. This converted Victorian warehouse features seven rooftop studios with patios and panoramic views of the London skyline, including a sky-lit atrium flooding its core with natural light. Many original features were retained, blending tradition with a chic, urban modernity. The eco-friendly refurbishment features recycled timber and bricks, and "smart" rooms that turn off heating and lighting when not in use. Bedrooms, ranging from small to midsize, are spread across five floors, and open onto balconies that circle the atrium. Unplastered brick walls reach up to "floating" ceilings and customized wallpaper panels. Secondhand furnishings are set beside classic modern pieces. Ask for a room at the rear of the hotel—they back onto a quiet square.

St. John's Sq., 86–88 Clerkenwell Rd., London EC1M 5RJ. www.thezetter.com. ℂ **020/7324-4444.** Fax 020/7324-4445. 59 units. Mon–Thurs £222–£342 double; Fri–Sun £185–£342 double. AE, DC, MC, V. Tube: Farringdon. **Amenities:** Restaurant (p. 369); bar; concierge; room service. *In room:* A/C, TV/DVD, CD player, MP3 docking station, Internet (free).

The Zetter Townhouse ★★★   In sharp contrast to the contemporary Zetter, the Zetter Townhouse, in the square behind, occupies two 18th-century town houses in a large square. Behind the elegant facade there's a delightful, very chic, quirky, and slightly tongue-in-cheek hotel. You walk into a bar, crowded with a jumble of objects accumulated by an invented Great Aunt Wilhelmina. It's relaxed, fun, comfortable, and inescapably cool in feel. Bedrooms are delightful with retro Roberts's radios and antique furniture. Book no. 4 if you fancy a four-poster decorated with Union Jacks. Bathrooms have fashionably distressed mirrors and REN toiletries. Food comes courtesy of Bruno Loubet (p. 237) and cocktails include nettle gimlet and twinkle.

49-50 St. John's Sq., London EC1V 4JJ. www.thezettertownhouse.com. ℂ **020/7324-4567.** Fax 020/7324-4456. 13 units. £246–£294 double. AE, DC, MC, V. Tube: Farringdon. **Amenities:** Bar; room service. *In room:* A/C, TV/DVD, MP3 docking station, Internet (free).

Expensive

Apex City of London Hotel The modern hotel stands next to St. Olave's church with views over the peaceful garden on one side. Mainly a business hotel (so emptier at weekends), its relaxed feel, informal restaurant, and colorful public lounges make it friendlier than many of its neighbors. Bedrooms are smart with pretty cushions and curtains softening the blocks of color; tea- and coffee-making facilities and free mineral water plus nibbles are thoughtful touches. Bathrooms have walk-in power showers and Elemis toiletries. Good inexpensive bar snacks and drinks, and the restaurant, with its modern British cooking, is also very sensibly priced, with a fixed price dinner menu from £15.95. A well-equipped gym will help work off the calories.

No. 1 Seething Ln., London EC3N 4AX. www.apexhotels.co.uk. ℂ **020/7977-9500.** Fax 020/7702-2217. 179 units. £99–£340 + VAT double. AE, DC, MC, V. Tube: Tower Hill. **Amenities:** Restaurant; bar; concierge; room service. *In room:* A/C, TV, DVD (in most rooms), minibar, hair dryer, MP3 docking station, Wi-Fi (free).

Malmaison London This Victorian mansion block—once a nursing home—overlooks a leafy cobbled square and is the London showcase for the boutique hotel chain known for clever contemporary designs, state-of-the-art facilities, and, as always, a little brasserie serving French classics. On the southern rim of once-workaday, now trendy, Clerkenwell, Malmaison is decorated in dark teak wood; has tall, glowing floor lamps; tasteful fabrics in neutral shades; and a portrait and bust in the lobby of Napoleon and Josephine, who spent many a "wanton night" at the original Château Malmaison outside Paris. The dark-wood guest rooms are individually designed and larger than average for central London.

18–21 Charterhouse Sq., London EC1M 6AH. www.malmaison.com/hotels/london. ℂ **020/7012-3700.** Fax 020/7012-3702. 97 units. £225–£295 double. AE, MC, V. Tube: Barbican or Farringdon. **Amenities:** Restaurant; bar; concierge; room service. *In room:* A/C, TV/DVD, minibar, CD player, CD library, Wi-Fi (free/30 min., and then £10/day).

The Rookery ★ 🎐 Quirky and eccentric, the Rookery is a great choice for travelers who want a hotel with the atmosphere of Dickens' or Dr. Johnson's London. Opened in the late 1990s, it salvaged three of the few remaining then-derelict antique houses in Clerkenwell. The result is a delightful maze of crooked floors, labyrinthine hallways, and antique furnishings that mix the fun with the functional. According to a spokesperson, "We went out of our way to make the floors creak" as part of its charm. Bedrooms are delightful and quirky, furnished with carved 18th- and 19th-century bed frames, and lace or silk draperies.

Peter's Lane, Cowcross St., London EC1M 6DS. www.rookeryhotel.com. ℂ **020/7336-0931.** Fax 020/7336-0932. 33 units. £179–£255 + VAT double. AE, DC, MC, V. Tube: Farringdon. **Amenities:** Concierge; room service. *In room:* A/C, TV, minibar, Wi-Fi (free).

Moderate

The Fox & Anchor ★ 🎐 The traditional English pub just got hip. Entering from Smithfield meat market, you'd be forgiven for thinking this was just a great little inn—brass fittings, etched glass, and acres of mahogany—but upstairs houses six classy rooms. Wood-floored and modern, with high-end flatscreen TVs, sound systems, and huge free-standing baths, they're more glamorous than your usual room-above-a-pub. The meat market location has its pros and cons. Con: it can be a little noisy. Pro: the breakfast is a carnivore's dream.

115 Charterhouse St., London EC1M 6AA. www.foxandanchor.com. ✆ 020/7550-1000. Fax 020/7250-1300. 6 units. £115–£205 double. Rates include breakfast. AE, DC, MC, V. Tube: Barbican or Farringdon. **Amenities:** Restaurant; bar. *In room:* TV, minibar, Wi-Fi (free).

Inexpensive

The Hoxton ★ ✦   The appeal of the Hoxton is straightforward—reasonable prices and quality service in a district best known for hotels whose prices are out of the range for those without an expense account. It's not just room rates that are competitive: Cheap calls to North America and supermarket prices for the minibar food are proof that budget airline tactics can work in a hotel. Of course there are downsides; the price means bedrooms are utilitarian and none too roomy, and booking in advance is vital. The Hoxton's popularity as a Shoreditch post-club crashpad means it can be noisy at the weekends; but for a reasonably priced stay at the heart of the Shoreditch scene, there's no better option.

81 Great Eastern St., London EC2A 3HU. www.hoxtonhotels.com. ✆ 020/7550-1000. Fax 020/7550-1090. 208 units. £69–£249 double. Rates include light breakfast. AE, DC, MC, V. Tube: Old St. **Amenities:** Grill; bar; access to nearby gym (£7). *In room:* TV, fridge, hair dryer, Wi-Fi (free).

Tune Hotel Liverpool Street ✦   Tune's appeal lies in its location in the middle of trendy Spitalfields, simple but spotlessly clean rooms (some without windows, so check when you book), power shower in the pod bathrooms, and straightforward pricing policy. You pay for the room, then add on items like towels, use of TV, hairdryer, safe etc. It feels a little like a hostel, but a very friendly one. There's a coffee machine and snacks and a large garden. There's also the **Tune Hotel Westminster** at 118–120 Westminster Bridge Road, SE1 7RW (✆ 020/7633 9317; Tube: Waterloo) and more planned to open in 2013.

13-15 Folgate St., London E1 6BX. www.tunehotels.com/uk. ✆ 020/7456-0400. Fax 020/7456-0409. 183 units. £35–£95 double. AE, MC, V. Tube: Old St. **Amenities:** Garden. *In room:* A/C, TV (£3/24 hrs, £10/unlimited), hairdryer (£1), Wi-Fi (£1.50/1 hr, £3/24 hrs, £10/unlimited).

EAST LONDON

21st-century London is moving east. The gentrification of the old East End has brought interesting new design hotels, hip crashpads, and historic conversions of old buildings. Improved transport links make it a hop, skip, and a jump from central London.

Best for: Fashion-conscious travelers after a new scene.

Drawbacks: Not for the cautious who might find it all a little too cutting-edge.

For a **map** of East London hotels, please see "East London Hotels & Restaurants" (p. 240 in Chapter 5).

Expensive

The Boundary ★ 🎁   With Sir Terence Conran at the helm you'd expect something rather special from this converted East End warehouse, and you won't be disappointed. The 17 rooms are a design junkie's dream (and include an iPad for guests' use), many boasting pieces specially created for the hotel, alongside chunky, reclaimed bathroom suites. And unlike many new boutique hotels, rooms are spacious and airy. Plus there's enough going on downstairs (and up) to make this somewhere you won't want to leave. There's a French restaurant in the basement, a roof terrace for barbecues and East London views, and Albion (p. 242), a great bakery/cafe for lazy weekend breakfasts.

2–4 Boundary St., London, E2 7DD. www.theboundary.co.uk. © **020/7729-1051.** Fax 020/7729-3061. 17 units. £170–£260 + VAT double. AE, DC, MC, V. Tube: Liverpool St. or Old St. **Amenities:** 3 restaurants, including Albion (p. 242); bar; room service. *In room:* TV, minibar, Wi-Fi (free).

Shoreditch Rooms ★★ 🏠 Fitting perfectly into the once grungy, now hip surroundings of Shoreditch, this is the latest venture from Soho House, which also owns Dean Street Townhouse (p. 209). The industrial space, shared with Cowshed Pharmacy, feels more like a club than a hotel. And most people use the hotel's accommodation to gain access to adjoining members-only and ultra-fashionable Shoreditch House with its rooftop restaurants and swimming pool, bars, and club scene. But you're not shortchanged on the rooms which are a good size with king-size beds, simply and sparsely furnished with a retro-style telephone and DAB radio, and an open-draw dresser. Colors are fresh, there's sisal matting on the floor, and slatted wooden walls, rather New England in feel. Small balconies in some rooms look over the thoroughly urban scene.

Ebor St., London E1 6AW. www.shoreditchhouse.com. © **020/739-5040.** 26 units. £60–£265 double. AE, MC, V. Tube: Liverpool St. or Old St. **Amenities:** 2 restaurants; bar; gym. *In room:* TV, minibar, hairdryer, Wi-Fi (free).

Town Hall Hotel ★★ There were sharp intakes of breath when this grand hotel opened in 2010 on an ordinary Bethnal Green side street: An imposing design hotel, with one of the hippest young chefs doing the food, this far east? The gamble paid off, and London's East End finally has the luxury accommodation it needed. The former Bethnal Green Town Hall has been converted into a palace of design and taste. Rooms are somber and clean-lined with beautiful mid-century design pieces. The Viajante restaurant (p. 245) is the hottest ticket in town, but you can get a taste of the chef's superb cooking at the more casual, walk-in, no-reservations Corner Room restaurant. The bar has a great creative staff and the smart pool and spa are a rare treat for East London.

8 Patriot Sq., London E2 9NF. www.townhallhotel.com. © **020/7871-0460.** Fax 020/7160-5214. 98 units. £162–£192 double. AE, DC, MC, V. Tube: Bethnal Green. **Amenities:** 2 restaurants; bar; indoor pool; exercise room; spa. *In room:* A/C, TV/DVD, hair dryer, Wi-Fi (free).

Moderate

40 Winks ★ 🏠 If you want your stay to feel like a piece of period drama, this is the hotel for you. Interior decorator David Carter turned his elegant Queen Anne town house into a romantic, eclectic dressing-up box. Originally used for fashion shoots and filming, the house is a centuries-spanning whirl of antiques, wild ornaments, and luxurious touches. The two rooms are much loved by the fashion and Hollywood crowd (don't even think of trying to book during London Fashion Week), and the rest of the house is shared with the owner. No TV, no phone, no credit cards; it's not for the business traveler, but for an adventurous romantic, this is a dream.

109 Mile End Rd., London E1 4UJ. www.40winks.org. © **020/7790-0259.** 2 units. £175 double. Rates include continental breakfast. No credit cards. Free parking. Tube: Stepney Green. *In room:* MP3 docking station, Wi-Fi (free).

Inexpensive

Avo ★ ☺ 🍴 🛍 Nothing sums up the gentrification of Dalston and the East End like charming Avo boutique B&B hotel. It was a general shop and post office until a large supermarket opened next door. So the family turned the property into a stylish small hotel. Contemporary designed rooms have lots of wood, black tiles, and subtle lighting, fine Egyptian cotton sheets, and luxurious fabrics sourced from India. Sparkly bathrooms with Elemis toiletries are a cut above the average. There's a top floor apartment for families. Breakfast in the dining room includes organic and gluten-free options. Three times a week, you can watch organic chocolatier Niko B making chocolates in the kitchen, taste, then buy them. The welcome is charming, the art stylish. Long live gentrification.

82 Dalston Lane, London E8 3AH. www.avohotel.com. ☎ **020/3490 5061.** 6 units. £79–£99 double. Rates include continental breakfast. MC, V. Rail: Dalston Kingsland. *In room:* TV/DVD, MP3 docking station, Wi-Fi (free).

NORTH & NORTHWEST LONDON

Regent's Park is a fine area for green spaces, while **Hampstead** is home to a multitude of tiny, family-run B&Bs.

Best For: Feeling like a local.

Drawbacks: You need to use public transport into the center of London.

For a **map** of North and Northwest London hotels, please see "North & Northwest London Hotels & Restaurants" (p. 250 in Chapter 5).

Regent's Park

EXPENSIVE

Dorset Square Hotel ★★ Just steps from Regent's Park, this is one of London's best and most stylish "house hotels"—it even overlooks Thomas Lord's (the man who set up London's first private cricket club) first pitch. The first property of the Kemps (see the Soho Hotel, p. 347), they sold it, then reacquired it, and have just reopened after a refurbishment. Expect all the usual style, from a drawing room with open fireplace to swathes of glorious fabrics and one-off and bespoke objects gathered from around the world. Bedrooms follow the same individual style and are beautifully equipped.

39–40 Dorset Sq., London NW1 6QN. www.firmdalehotels.com. ☎ **020/7723-7874.** Fax 020/724-3328. 38 units. £190–£380 double. AE, DC, MC, V. Parking £35/day, free on weekends. Tube: Baker St. or Marylebone. **Amenities:** Restaurant; bar; concierge, room service. *In room:* A/C, TV, minibar, hair dryer, MP3 docking station, Wi-Fi (£20/day).

York & Albany ★ Chef-entrepreneur Gordon Ramsay has taken a derelict 19th-century pub and transformed it into a classy modern British restaurant with rooms. Though, as one guest pointed out, "It feels like the hotel is an afterthought, rather than the main course." Rooms are a typically London mish-mash, clean and white but dotted with antiques and objets d'art. They can also be noisy and certainly aren't the largest in this price bracket. Fabulous for a short break—the Sunday lunch and the proximity to Regent's Park and Camden make it great for lazy weekends—but not your best bet for an extended city stay.

127–129 Parkway, London NW1 7PS. www.gordonramsay.com/yorkandalbany. ☎ **020/7387-5700.** Fax 020/7255-9250. 9 units. £155–£225 double; AE, MC, V. Tube: Camden Town.

Amenities: Restaurant (p. 373); bar; room service. *In room:* A/C, TV/DVD, hair dryer, CD player, Wi-Fi (free).

Hampstead

INEXPENSIVE

Hampstead Village Guesthouse 🎁 Set on a quiet, tree-lined street within walking distance of Hampstead Heath and tons of restaurants, the Hampstead Village Guesthouse is ideal for those after a quieter London. It's not as remote as it sounds, though; a 15-minute Tube ride will get you to Leicester Square. Rooms are cozy, cluttered, and certainly not large, and the bathrooms are smaller still, but you get what you pay for, and prices are reliably low. No credit cards, so make sure you pick up cash before you arrive.

2 Kemplay Rd., London NW3 1SY. www.hampsteadguesthouse.com. ✆ **020/7435-8679.** 10 units. £90–£100 double. AE, MC, V. Parking £15/day. Tube: Hampstead. *In room:* TV, fridge, hair dryer, Wi-Fi (free).

NEAR THE AIRPORTS

Heathrow

Among the chain hotels, the **Heathrow Airport Hilton,** Terminal 4, Hounslow TW6 (www1.hilton.com; ✆ **020/8759-7755**), wins out for its unrivaled access—a covered walkway takes you to the terminal. However, the **Holiday Inn,** Sipson Way, Bath Rd., Hayes, Middlesex UB7 (www.ichotelsgroup.com; ✆ **020/8990-0000**), is better value and the **Radisson Edwardian,** 140 Bath Rd., Hayes, Middlesex UB3 (www.radisson.com; ✆ **020/8759-6311**), has the best facilities, with elegant Edwardian furnishings and a fabulous spa and pool.

Gatwick

At Gatwick, the **Hilton London Gatwick Airport,** South Terminal, Gatwick Airport, West Sussex RH6 (www1.hilton.com; ✆ **01293/518080**), is bland and uncomplicated, but is under increasing pressure from **Yotel,** South Terminal, Arrivals Concourse, Gatwick Airport, West Sussex RH6 (www.yotel.com; ✆ **020/7100-1100**), a Japanese-style capsule hotel that's great value if you're just looking for a bed and a shuttle. Or treat yourselves to the sprawling, neo-Tudor, comfortable **Manor House Hotel,** Bonnetts Lane, Ifield, Crawley, Sussex RH11 (www.manorhouse-gatwick.co.uk; ✆ **01293/518046**), which is family-run and quirky.

Luton

For ease of access, the **Express by Holiday Inn,** 2 Percival Way, Luton LU2 (www.hiexpress.com; ✆ **01582-589100**), is hard to beat—it's nearest the terminal, with utilitarian rooms and free airport shuttle. If you want to explore the area, try **Live and Let Live,** Pegsdon, Hitchin, Herts SG5 (www.theliveand letlive.com; ✆ **01582-881739**). The pub offers seven basic rooms on the edge of the pretty Chiltern Hills.

Stansted

The **Radisson Blu,** Waltham Close, Stansted Airport, Essex CM24 (www. radissonblu.co.uk; ✆ **0127/966-1012**), ticks all the boxes. Its ultra-modern design fits well with the sci-fi airport look, rooms are modern and spacious, and a covered walkway runs the 10-minute walk to the terminal.

PRACTICAL INFORMATION

The Big Picture

London is a huge, sprawling city, so decide what you want to see and do before choosing a hotel. Sightseers and theatre-goers find that either the **West End** or the **South Bank** brings everything within walking distance; lovers of wide open spaces and the landmark museums opt for **West London;** and hipper, younger travelers have a range of options on the fringes of the **City** and in trendy **East London.**

However be warned of London's idiosyncratic ways: for example, air-conditioning is far from standard, and in cheaper hotels heating can be patchy. Call ahead to check whether your room is climate controlled.

The venerable age of many of London's best hotels means that rooms are smaller, and more variable, than in other modern cities; and some still have charges for international phone calls and Wi-Fi access, in particular the larger hotels.

The standard of rooms across the city is better now than it has ever been. Unfortunately, it hasn't made prices any easier to swallow. Travelers to the city each year have found some hoteliers unembarrassed about over-charging and poor service.

London boasts some of the most famous hotels in the world. But even at the luxury level you may be surprised at what you don't get. Many of the grand gems lack modern conveniences standard in luxury hotels worldwide. The best have modernized, but others retain distinctly Edwardian amenities. Although London has an increasing number of sleek, high-tech palaces, these hotels can lack the personal service and spaciousness that characterize the grand old favorites.

The biggest change to the London hotel landscape has been the rise of the **boutique hotel.** The best of them offer the charm of a B&B with the facilities of much larger hotels, but sufficient numbers of very ordinary small hotels have rebranded themselves "boutique" as to make travelers wary. We've sorted the wheat from the chaff, concentrating on reasonably priced choices with the best that each category has to offer.

Getting the Best Deal

There are good, cheap options other than hotels. London has many B&Bs, and the best of them offer a much friendlier, family welcome than at a budget hotel. Just don't expect all of the hotelier's bells and whistles. For this option, try the **London Bed and Breakfast Agency** (www.londonbb.com; ✆ 020/7586-2768), an established agency for inexpensive accommodations in private homes for around £30 to £100 per person per night, based on double occupancy (although some rooms will cost a lot more). At **London B&B** (www.london bandb.com; ✆ 800/872-2632 in the U.S. and Canada) homes and unhosted apartments are inspected for quality and comfort, amenities, and convenience.

Online travel booking sites such as **Travelocity, Expedia, Orbitz, Priceline,** and **Hotwire** sometimes have excellent deals, or book hotels through **Hotels.com, Quikbook** (www.quikbook.com), **LateRooms.com** (www.laterooms.com), and **Travelaxe** (www.travelaxe.com). **TripAdvisor.com** or **HotelShark.com** offer independent consumer reviews of hotels, though there are doubts about authenticity. It's always a good idea to **get a confirmation number** and **make a printout** of any online booking transaction.

During certain peak periods, including the high season (approximately April through October), school holidays, sporting events, and royal occasions, rooms in all kinds of hotels are snapped up early. Book ahead.

Alternative Accommodations

If you're staying for more than a couple of weeks, consider self-catering accommodation or apartment rental. The reputable **Coach House London Rentals,** 2 Tunly Rd., London SW17 7QJ (www.rentals.chslondon.com; ℂ **020/8133-8332**) represents over 75 properties, from studio flats for friendly couples to spacious homes sleeping up to 12. The minimum length of a stay is 5 nights, and you can book airport transfers. **Housetrip.com** is a young company with excellent short-term rental properties around Europe. It's safe and reliable and easy to use. **University Rooms** (www.londonuniversityrooms.co.uk), started by a young Cambridge graduate, has rooms in university hostels in major university cities. Its London properties are central, vetted, and very good value. Rooms are mainly available in vacations, which are the peak traveling months of June to September.

At **AirBnB.com,** owners rent out everything from single rooms to whole houses, but with a user-rating and verification system that discourages scammers. **9flats.com** has rooms in houses and apartments to rent in some of the trendiest parts of London like Shoreditch, Stratford, and Islington. Its rates are good and the information on what you get comprehensive. **Viveunique.com** offers more upscale lets, all personally vetted. It also offers a bespoke service on airport transfers, theatre tickets and more and suits corporate clients.

For the freedom of an apartment but with a little more hotel-style glitz, **Uptown Reservations,** 8 Kelso Place, London W8 5QD (www.uptownres.co.uk; ℂ **020/7937-2001**), features upscale furnished rooms and suites in private homes in some of the city's best postcodes. See a slice of London life and share space with the hosts themselves, many of whom are artists, diplomats or, in some rare cases, lords of the realm who need a little extra pocket money. **Onefinestay.com** is another great bet with characterful homes to stay in—they offer space in private homes (or even whole houses) while owners are away, backing it up with add-on hotel-style services such as chefs and maids.

Low-cost airlines and improving London hostels have encouraged "flashpacking": ultra-cheap, no-luggage short breaks in hostels and the cheapest hotels. **Hostelbookers.com** is consistently good for finding these bargain accommodations, but be ready to share facilities.

House-swapping is becoming a more popular and viable means of travel; you stay in their place, they stay in yours, and you both get an authentic view of the area, the opposite of the escapist retreat that many hotels offer. Try **Home-Link International Home Exchange** (www.homelink.org), the largest and oldest home-swapping organization, founded in 1952, with over 11,000 listings worldwide ($119/£115 for annual membership). It has a number of properties available for exchange in London.

For female-only accommodation and travel advice, see "Women Travelers," p. 442.

SIDE TRIPS FROM LONDON

9

ondon offers so much that you might be hard-pressed to find time to leave the capital. However, for those visitors who want to glimpse more of what England has to offer, in this chapter we suggest some delights that you can visit in a day—from the royal castle of Windsor, to the prehistoric standing stones at Stonehenge, the Georgian spa city of Jane Austen's Bath, the university towns of Oxford and Cambridge, and the modern-day pleasures of Brighton with its pebbly beach, only a stone's throw from London.

WINDSOR ★ & ETON

21 miles W of London

Windsor is a charming, largely Victorian town, with lots of brick buildings and a few remnants of Georgian architecture. All this is completely overshadowed of course by its great castle, which dominates the area like a giant crown of stone. Windsor Castle has been the home of the Royal Family for some 900 years, a pedigree that makes it an enticing target for day-trippers from London. Despite the inevitable crowds this is a sight you should not miss; the State Apartments are especially lavish, adorned with some exceptional paintings from the Royal Collection.

Essentials

GETTING THERE Trains make the 35-minute trip from Paddington station in London to **Windsor & Eton Central** (opposite the castle entrance) every 20 minutes or so, with one change at Slough. Trains run at similar intervals for the 1-hour trip from Waterloo direct to **Windsor & Eton Riverside** station (a short walk from the castle). The off-peak round-trip cost is £9.50 from Paddington and £9.50 from Waterloo.

VISITOR INFORMATION The **Royal Windsor Information Centre** is at the Old Booking Hall, Windsor Royal Shopping center on Thames Street in the center of town (www.windsor.gov.uk; ✆ 01753/743900). It is open May through August, Monday to Friday 9:30am to 5:30pm, Saturday 9:30am to 5pm, and Sunday 10am to 4pm; and September through April, Monday to Saturday 10am to 5pm and Sunday 10am to 4pm.

TOURS **City Sightseeing Open Top Bus Tours** (www.city-sightseeing.com; ✆ 01708/866000) make 45-minute loops of Windsor and Eton with 11 hop-on-hop-off stops (Jan–March daily 10am–5pm, March–May daily 10:30am–4pm, Jun–Sep daily 10am–5pm, Oct daily 10:30am–4pm, Nov–Dec daily 10:30am–3:30pm). Tickets are £10.50 for adults, £5 for children and £9 concessions, family tickets available for 2 adults and up to three children for £25, all valid for 24 hours. The most appealing way to see the area is by **boat,** which departs from Windsor Promenade, Barry Avenue, for a 40-minute round-trip. The cost is £5.40 for adults, £2.70 for children.

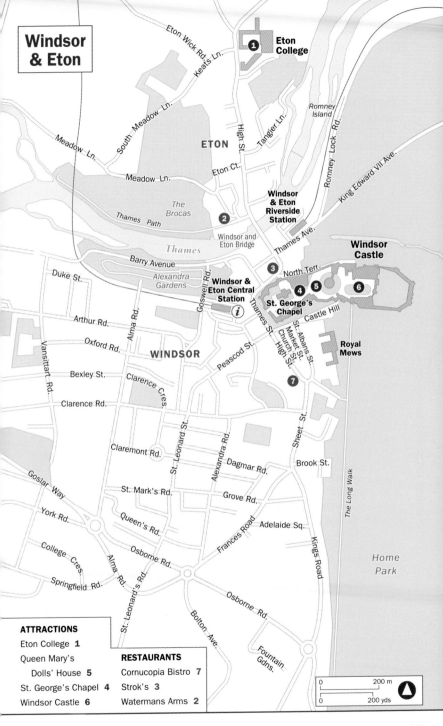

Windsor & Eton

ETON

Eton Wick Rd.

Keats Ln.

South Meadow Ln.

High St.

Tangier Ln.

Romney Island

Romney Lock Rd.

King Edward VII Ave.

Meadow Ln.

Meadow Ln.

Eton Ct.

Eton College ❶

The Brocas

Thames Path

Thames

Windsor & Eton Riverside Station

Thames Ave.

❷

Windsor and Eton Bridge

Barry Avenue

Alexandra Gardens

Goswell Rd.

Windsor & Eton Central Station ⓘ

❸ North Terr.

Windsor Castle

❹ ❺ ❻

St. George's Chapel

Castle Hill

Duke St.

Arthur Rd.

Alma Rd.

Oxford Rd.

WINDSOR

Peascod St.

Thames St.

St. Albans St.

Market St.

Church St.

High St.

Royal Mews

Bexley St.

Clarence Cres.

Clarence Rd.

Vansittart Rd.

Sheet St.

❼

Claremont Rd.

St. Leonard St.

Alexandra Rd.

Dagmar Rd.

Brook St.

The Long Walk

St. Mark's Rd.

Grove Rd.

Goslar Way

Queen's Rd.

Frances Road

Adelaide Sq.

Home Park

York Rd.

Osborne Rd.

Kings Road

College Cres.

Alma Rd.

St. Leonard's Rd.

Springfield Rd.

Osborne Rd.

Bolton Ave.

Fountain Gdns.

ATTRACTIONS

Eton College **1**

Queen Mary's
   Dolls' House **5**

St. George's Chapel **4**

Windsor Castle **6**

RESTAURANTS

Cornucopia Bistro **7**

Strok's **3**

Watermans Arms **2**

0 — 200 m
0 — 200 yds

Tours are operated by **French Brothers,** Clewer Boathouse, Clewer Court Rd., Windsor (www.boat-trips.co.uk; ✆ **01753/851900**). A "combined bus and boat trip" ticket costs £15 for adults and £7 for children.

Exploring Windsor

Windsor Castle ★★★ ☺   Looming high above the town on a chalk ridge, Windsor Castle is an awe-inspiring site, an enormous hulk of stone dating back to the days of William the Conqueror. The history and art here are undeniably impressive, but what really draws the crowds is the association with the Royal Family; this is no ruin or museum, but one of the three homes of Queen Elizabeth II. Indeed, Windsor is the world's largest inhabited castle and the Queen is often in residence, especially at weekends (when the royal standard flies). Getting a glimpse of the Queen is not that hard, as the town's clued-up hoteliers often have advance warning of when Her Majesty comes and goes. Even if you don't see the Queen, the Windsor **Changing the Guard ★** at 11am (see below) offers more pageantry than the London version. The guard marches through the town, stopping traffic as it wheels into the castle to the tunes of a full regimental band; when the Queen is not here, a drum-and-pipe band is mustered. From April to July, the ceremony takes place Monday to Saturday at 11am. In winter, the guard is changed every 48 hours Monday to Saturday. It's best to call ✆ **020/7766-7304** for a schedule.

Originally constructed in wood in the 1080s, Henry II (r. 1154–89) started to rebuild the castle in stone in the 12th century. Today many parts of the castle (but not all) are open to the public, including the precincts and the **State Apartments.** On display in the latter are many works of art, armor, three Verrio ceilings, and several 17th-century Gibbons carvings. Several works by Rubens adorn the King's Drawing Room. In the relatively small King's Dressing Room is a Dürer, along with Rembrandt's portrait of his mother and Van Dyck's triple portrait of Charles I. Of the apartments, the **grand reception room,** with its Gobelin tapestries, is the most spectacular.

The elegant **Semi-State Rooms ★★** are open only from the end of September until the end of March. They were created by George IV in the 1820s as part of a series of royal apartments designed for his personal use. Seriously damaged by fire in 1992, they have been returned to their former glory, with lovely antiques, paintings, and decorative objects. The Crimson Drawing Room is evocative of the king's flamboyant taste, with its crimson silk damask hangings and sumptuous art. The **Drawings Gallery** shows revolving exhibitions from the Royal Library.

Enlightening behind-the-scenes tours of the **Great Kitchen** (30 min.) are offered (selected dates Jan, Feb, Aug, Sep) at an additional cost. In August and September, you can also climb the **Round Tower** for views over the Great Park and all the way to London.

Insider's Tip: Although the ticket price (see below) includes a 2-hour audio guide, we recommend a free guided tour of the castle precincts (30 min.) departing from the admissions office. Guides recapture the rich historical background of the castle. Family activity trails are also available.

Castle Hill. www.royalcollection.org.uk. ✆ **01753/83118.** Admission £17 adults, £15.50 students and seniors, £10.20 children 16 and under, free 4 and under, £44.75 family of 5 (2 adults and 3 children 16 and under). Daily Mar–Oct 9:45am–5:15pm; Nov–Feb 9:45am–4:15pm. Last admission 3pm. Closed for periods in Apr, June, and Dec, when the royal family is in residence.

Queen Mary's Dolls' House 😊 A palace in perfect miniature, the Dolls' House was given to Queen Mary in 1923. The house, designed by Sir Edwin Lutyens, was created on a scale of 1-to-12, with contributions made by some 1,500 tradesmen, artists, and authors. It took 3 years to complete. Every item is a miniature masterpiece; each room is exquisitely furnished, and every item is made exactly to scale. Working elevators stop on every floor, and there is running water in all five bathrooms.

For admission and entry details, please see Castle above.

St. George's Chapel ★★★ A perfect expression of the Medieval Perpendicular style, this chapel contains the tombs of ten sovereigns. The present St. George's was founded in the late 15th century by Edward IV on the site of the original Chapel of the Order of the Garter. You first enter the nave, which contains the tomb of George V (1936) and Queen Mary (1953). Off the nave in the Urswick Chapel, the Princess Charlotte memorial provides a touching moment; if she had survived childbirth in 1817, she, and not her cousin Victoria, would have ruled the British Empire. In the north nave aisle is the tomb of George VI (1952) while the altar contains the remains of Edward IV (1483) and Edward VII (1910). In the center is a flat tomb, containing the vault of the beheaded Charles I (1649), along with Henry VIII (1547) and his third (and son-providing) wife, Jane Seymour (1537). The latest royal burials here (in the King George VI Memorial Chapel) were of Queen Elizabeth The Queen Mother and Princess Margaret in 2002. It's open Monday to Saturday 10am to 4pm. Closed Sundays and for a few days in June and December.

For admission and entry details, please see Castle above.

Eton College ★★ Eton is the home of arguably the most famous public school in the world (non-Brits would call it a private school). The school was founded by 18-year-old Henry VI in 1440, and since then 20 prime ministers have been educated here, as well as such literary figures as George Orwell, Aldous Huxley, Ian Fleming, and Percy Bysshe Shelley. Prince William was a student, as was prime minister David Cameron. The real highlight inside is the Perpendicular **College Chapel,** completed in 1482 with its 15th-century paintings and reconstructed fan vaulting.

The history of Eton College is depicted in the **Museum of Eton Life,** located in vaulted wine cellars under College Hall (originally used as a storehouse by the college's masters). The displays include a turn-of-the-20th-century boy's room, schoolbooks, and canes used by senior boys to apply punishment—the brutal fagging and flogging that characterized much of the school's history. Note that admission to the school and museum is by **guided tour only.**

Keats Lane, Eton, Windsor. www.etoncollege.com. ✆ **01753/671000.** Admission £7 adults, £6 children 8–13. Mar 25–Apr 15 and early Jul–early Sep daily 10:30am–4:30pm; late Apr–Jun and early Sept–early Oct Wed & Fri–Sun 1:30pm–4:30pm. Dates vary every year and Eton may close for special occasions; call ahead. **Insider's tip:** Parking is likely to be a problem, so turn off the M4 at exit 6 to Windsor; you can park here and take an easy stroll past Windsor Castle and across the Thames Bridge. Follow Eton High St. to the college.

Where to Eat

For traditional pub grub, such as fish and chips or a Ploughman's lunch, with real ales from the local Windsor & Eton Brewery, head to the Tudor pub **Watermans**

Cornucopia Bistro, Windsor.

Arms, Brocas St., Eton, (www.watermans-eton.com; ✆ **01753/861001**), just over the bridge to Eton. Best of all is the beef and Guinness pie. A Sunday roast costs £8.95.

Strok's at Sir Christopher Wren's House Hotel, Thames St., (www.sir christopherwren.co.uk; ✆ **01753/442422**), with its garden terraces and a conservatory, is the perfect place for an elegant, albeit pricey, lunch. Try the tongue-tingling foie gras parfait followed by goat's cheese tortellini, and wild seabass risotto, with roasted peppers, tiger prawn, and confit cherry tomato.

Cornucopia Bistro ★★, 6 High St., (www.cornucopia-bistro.co.uk; ✆ **01753/833009**), is justly regarded as the best deal in town; this simple French restaurant is usually full—book ahead if you can. The exquisite food includes perfectly steamed mussels, venison and red wine pâté, or buttery lamb shank. Set menus cost £12.90 to £14.90 for three courses.

Shopping

Windsor Royal Shopping, the shopping center at the main railway station (www.windsorroyalshopping.co.uk; ✆ **01753/797070**), has a concentration of shops, mostly the usual chains but also locally owned **Simply Windsor Gifts** (www.simplywindsorgifts.co.uk; ✆ **07799/622649**).

A colorful traditional English perfumery, **Woods of Windsor,** 50 High St. (www.woodsofwindsor.co.uk; ✆ **01753/868125**), dates from 1770. It offers soaps, shampoos, scented drawer liners, and hand and body lotions, all prettily packaged in pastel-floral and bright old-fashioned wraps.

Stock up on the Queen's vittles, produced from her estates, at the **Windsor Farm Shop,** Datchet Rd., Old Windsor (www.windsorfarmshop. co.uk; ✆ **01753/623800**), and head for a picnic in the park. The steak-and-ale pies are tasty or try the 15-year-old whisky from Balmoral Castle in Scotland.

BRIGHTON

52 miles S of London

Brighton is a party place and it's where Londoners flee for a day out, or for a fun weekend. One of England's first great seaside resorts, Brighton went through a bad time when its clientele started holidaying abroad. Now it's back—bigger and brighter than ever. It has taken on the ambience of London, with boutique lodgings, hip nightspots, and trendy shops. It's not for everyone though: Once you're here there's little respite from the crowds, and the beaches are shingle. Yet you can't help but love it.

When he arrived in 1783, fun-loving Prince Regent, the Prince of Wales (later George IV) helped to raise Brighton to its lofty position. The town blossomed with attractive town houses and smart squares and crescents. The Prince Regent's Royal Pavilion summer home is still here, and despite being surrounded by old-time fun—the beach-front lined with bars, fish and chip shops, and cheap souvenir stalls, and the pier with its amusements—Brighton is fashionable once again.

Essentials

GETTING THERE   Fast trains leave Victoria and London Bridge stations roughly every 15 minutes; the journey is less than an hour. Buses from London's Victoria Coach Station take about 2 hours.

If you're driving, the M23 (signposted from central London) leads to the A23, which takes you straight into Brighton.

VISITOR INFORMATION   The **Tourist Information Centre,** 4–5 Pavilion Buildings (www.visitbrighton.com; © **01273/290337**), is next to the Royal Pavilion shop. It's open from March to October Monday to Saturday 10am to 5pm. Sunday hours are from 10am to 4pm.

Exploring Brighton

Brighton's **promenade** ★★ exists on two levels: There's the wide path and cycleway that runs along King's Road, above the level of the beach; and there's the beachfront path, which is awash with cotton candy sellers and mini carousels, bars, and shellfish stalls. It runs from **Brighton Pier** (a Victorian structure now featuring a rollercoaster and other hair-raising, over-water rides, bars, and restaurants) to the entrance of the old West Pier (where the I360 (p. 384) is going up). Star attractions are the **Brighton Smokehouse,** where fish are smoked in a beach hut and you can buy a hot kipper sandwich for £2.80, and the free **Brighton Fishing Museum** (www.brightonfishingmuseum.org.uk; © **01273/723064**) with a fishing boat and lots of memorabilia and old photos. You'll find music pouring out of bars, bands playing on the beach, rollerbladers whizzing by, and people out for a stroll.

A mile or so east of the city, tucked beneath the chalky cliffs, is the modern **marina.** It's Britain's biggest, with 1,600 moorings. But this is also a massive entertainment complex with more than 20 restaurants, mostly chains, including Marco Pierre White's, bars, a modest outlet mall, a 26-lane bowling alley, movie theatre, children's playgrounds, and bicycle hire. It's an easy walk from town, there's a 24-hour bus (No. 7), plenty of free parking, or you can take the miniature **Volks Electric Railway** for £3 or less (www.volkselectricrailway.co.uk; © **01273/292718**), Britain's first electric train, which started running in 1873.

Brighton Museum & Art Gallery ★★   Once the Royal Pavilion's magnificent stable block in the park adjoining the Pavilion, this is now a treasure trove of beautiful and curious things. A recent £10 million redevelopment has created a bright, white environment to showcase one of the most important collections of decorative arts in England outside London. And it's free. The first thing you come to is the 20th-century Decorative Art and Design gallery where Salvador Dali's Marilyn Monroe Lips sofa rubs shoulders, as it were, with some exquisite pieces by Charles Rennie Mackintosh. Farther on you find the history of Brighton, from its beginnings to the dark days of World War II bombings, while upstairs are modernist paintings, including works by Walter Sickert, and a cafe.

Royal Pavilion Gardens. www.brighton-hove-rpml.org.uk. ✆ **03000/290900.** Free admission. Tues–Sun 10am–5pm.

1360 Tower ★★   The South Coast's highest viewing tower, this new Brighton landmark (due to open 2013) is on the site of the entrance to the now-derelict West Pier. The slim tower's circular, spaceship-like viewing deck is also its elevator, carrying crowds up to the 150m (492-ft.) summit.

King's Rd. www.brightoni360.co.uk. ✆ **01273/321499.** No further details available.

The Royal Pavilion at Brighton ★★★   From the outside, the Pavilion appears a bit garish, a melee of vaguely eastern-looking domes, painted an unattractive beige, that you suspect might house an entertainment complex. Yet the place is a pleasure palace of another kind.

This was the Royals' idea of a seaside hideaway. It's a phantasmagorical collection of Oriental architecture, furniture, and fittings; a playful place that fitted in with the resort's somewhat wild reputation even when it was built. It was created for the Prince Regent, later King George IV, between 1787 and 1823. Queen Victoria later stayed here, but both it and Brighton were a little too much for her prim and proper tastes. The dining room is simply superb, the 24-seat table

The Royal Pavilion at Brighton.

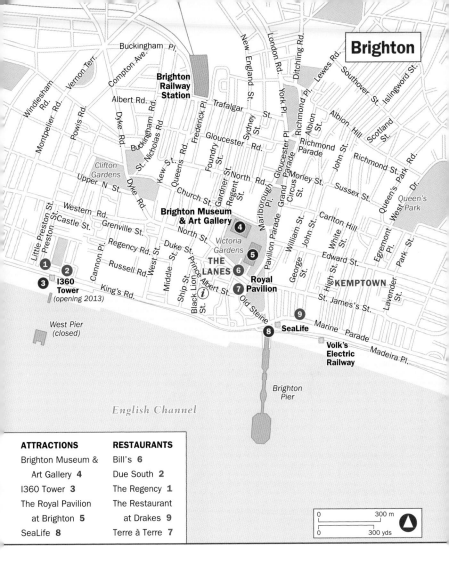

Brighton

ATTRACTIONS	RESTAURANTS
Brighton Museum & Art Gallery **4**	Bill's **6**
	Due South **2**
I360 Tower **3**	The Regency **1**
The Royal Pavilion at Brighton **5**	The Restaurant at Drakes **9**
SeaLife **8**	Terre à Terre **7**

under a domed roof (painted to resemble a palm canopy) from which hangs the most amazing chandelier you'll ever see: a huge dragon breathing fire over floral lights and shards of mirror. A cafe allows you to rest amid the Regency wonders. Entry includes a free audio guide.

4–5 Pavilion Buildings. www.royalpavilion.org.uk. ✆ **01273/290900.** Admission £9.80 adults, £7.80 students and seniors, £5.60 children 5–15, £25.20 family ticket, free for children 4 and under. Apr–Sept daily 9:30am–5:45pm; Oct–Mar daily 10am–5:15pm.

SeaLife ★★ This was the world's first aquarium, opening as the Royal Aquarium in 1872. Many of the tanks are under low, vaulted ceilings, where you'll see rays, crabs, and other local sealife as well as exotic fish. You will be led into a darkened Amazonia jungle zone and eventually emerge into a glass tunnel snaking through a massive tank alive with fish, sharks, and a pair of magnificent turtles (Lulu is 70-plus years old and weighs 152kg/335lb). You can then pop upstairs to see it all from above in a glass-bottomed boat.

Marine Parade. www.visitsealife.com/brighton. ℭ **0871/423 2110.** Admission £16.20 adults, £11.40 children 3–14, £53.60 family ticket (book online for up to 25% reduction). Daily 10am–5pm.

Where to Eat

If you're going to eat in only one Brighton restaurant, it should be **The Regency ★★★**, 131 King's Rd. (www.theregencyrestaurant.co.uk; ℭ **01273/ 325014**), a fish restaurant that's been serving since the 1930s; choose cod and chips for £5.25 or have the Hot Lobster Thermidor (£20.95).

For a seafront eatery, **Due South ★★**, 139 King's Road Arches (www.due south.co.uk; ℭ **01273/821218**), boasts "organic, free-range, and biodynamic" ingredients sourced from within a 35-mile radius of Brighton beach.

For a big breakfast (plenty of bubble and squeak—mashed potato fried with cooked cabbage), with all-day snacks and lunch and dinners of Thai curry, or burgers and steaks, head to **Bill's** at The Depot, 100 North St. (www.bills-website. co.uk; ℭ **01273/692894**). **Terre à Terre ★★ 🎁**, 71 East St. (www.terreaterre. co.uk; ℭ **01273/729051**), is a place for people who like eating dishes made out of vegetables rather than wanting something coyly pretending to be meat. Closed Monday.

The smartest restaurant in Brighton is **The Restaurant at Drakes ★**, 44 Marine Parade (www.therestaurant atdrakes.co.uk; ℭ **01273/696934**), combining contemporary British style with French twists such as local scallops and black pudding purée, followed by breast of Sussex White chicken.

Shopping

It has to be the **Lanes,** a collection of alleyways and small streets behind North Street and its big-name shops. The area is full of boutiques, cafes, and arty stores of all kinds. Those in the know slide along to **North Laine**— between the Lanes and the train station—which is seen as the area for up-and-coming talent. Innumerable shops in the Lanes carry old books and jewelry, and many boutiques are found in converted backyards on Duke Lane just off Ship Street. At the heart of the Lanes is **Brighton Square,** which is ideal for relaxing or people-watching near the fountain, on one of the benches, or from a cafe-bar. Brighton

The Lanes.

Brighton's Gay Scene

Brighton has long been regarded as Britain's gay capital. It has the country's biggest gay festival (Pride, early August), and a thriving scene of bars, clubs, and hotels. Most of the action is in the Gay Quarter in **Kemp Town,** a compact strip just off the seafront. **Dr Brightons,** 16 King's Rd. (www.doctorbrightons.co.uk; ✆ **01273/208113**), opposite the pier is one of the mainstays, and has a street party during Pride. **Legends,** 31 Marine Parade (www.legendsbrighton.com; ✆ **01273/624462**), is one of the country's leading gay hotels and has two venues: **Legends** cafe-bar and **The Basement** nightclub. Of the clubs, **Revenge,** 32–34 Old Steine (www.revenge.co.uk; ✆ **01273/606064**), is the biggest, with lots of gay-friendly live acts from TV reality shows such as X Factor.

has plenty of big-name shops too. Try **Churchill Square,** which is home to major chain stores.

Regent Arcade, which is located between East Street, Bartholomew Square, and Market Street, sells artwork, jewelry, and other gift items, as well as high-fashion clothing. Bargain hunters head for the **Kemp Town Flea Market,** Upper St. James's Street, held Monday to Friday 10am to 5pm and weekends and public holidays 10:30am to 5pm. A more famous **flea market** is held in the parking lot of the train station, but only on Sunday from 6am to 2pm.

Entertainment & Nightlife

Pubs are a good place to kick off an evening, especially the **Colonnade Bar,** New Rd. (✆ **01273/328728**), serving drinks for more than 100 years. It gets a lot of theatre business because of its proximity to the Theatre Royal. **Cricketers,** Black Lion St. (www.goldenliongroup.co.uk; ✆ **01273/329472**), is worth a stop because it's Brighton's oldest pub, parts of which date from 1549.

Komedia, 44 Gardner St. (www.komedia.co.uk; ✆ **0845/293-8480**), is a venue that hosts everything from top indie bands (such as British Sea Power) to the Banff Film Festival tour, and top comedy to the Brighton Jazz Club.

The Latest Music Bar, 14 Manchester St. (www.thelatest.co.uk; ✆ **01273/687171**), combines the latest in live music with party-style club nights. **Honeyclub,** 214 King's Road Arches (www.thehoneyclub.co.uk; ✆ **01273/202807**), is a bar by day and a lively club at night with a downstairs dancefloor. **Casablanca,** 3 Middle St. (www.casablancajazzclub.com; ✆ **01273/321817**), is a club with a funk-latin-jazz feel.

OXFORD ★★★

54 miles NW of London

The city of Oxford, dominated by Britain's oldest university, is a bastion of English tradition, history, and eccentricity. Here students still get selected to join the archaic Bullingdon Club, rowing competitions attract a larger audience than soccer, and students still take exams dressed in black gowns (seriously). The creator of detective *Inspector Morse,* Colin Dexter, lives in town, and where else would you film the Harry Potter series? Oxford certainly retains a special sort of magic.

The hallowed halls and gardens of ancient colleges such as Magdalen and Christ Church are architectural gems, but not museums—students live and work here year-round. The High Street (often referred to as The High) hasn't changed much since Oscar Wilde walked along it and the water meadows and spires that inspired architect Sir Christopher Wren and writers as diverse as John Donne, C.S. Lewis, Iris Murdoch, and J.R.R. Tolkien are still here.

Essentials

GETTING THERE **Trains** from London's Paddington station reach Oxford in around 1 hour (direct trains run every 30 minutes). A cheap round-trip ticket costs £22.50 (off-peak).

If you're **driving,** take the M40 west from London and follow the signs. **Parking** is a nightmare in Oxford; however, there are five large **park-and-ride** lots (www.parkandride.net). Buses run every 8 to 10 minutes until 11:30pm Monday to Saturday and between 11am and 5pm on Sundays. Off-peak tickets cost £2.20 per adult for a round-trip ticket.

VISITOR INFORMATION The **Oxford Tourist Information Centre** is at 15–16 Broad St. (www.visitoxfordandoxfordshire.com; ✆ 01865/252200). Hours are Monday to Saturday 9:30am to 5pm, Sunday 10am to 4pm.

TOURS For an easy orientation, take a 1-hour, open top bus tour with **City Sightseeing Oxford** (www.citysightseeingoxford.com; ✆ 01865/790522). Tours start from the railway station. Buses leave daily at 9:30am and then every 10 to 15 minutes. The last bus departs at 4pm November to February, at 5pm March and October, and at 6pm April to September. The cost is £13 for adults, £11 for students, £10 for seniors, and £6 for children 5 to 14 years; a family ticket for two adults and three children is £33. Tickets can be purchased from the driver. They are valid for 24 hours and 48-hour tickets are available at a discount.

The Tourist Information Centre also offers a long list of excellent **theme tours,** everything from "Magic, Murder & Mayhem" and "Pottering in Harry's Footsteps" to 'Jewish Heritage' and 'Stained Glass': Our favorites include the 2-hour '**Inspector Morse.**'

Finally, **Oxford River Cruises** (www.oxfordrivercruises.com; ✆ 0845/2269396) runs several boat tours along the River Thames, from the tranquil 50 min River Experience (£9 adults, £6 children 15 and under) to a sunset picnic trip for £45 adults and £30 children 15 and under.

Exploring Oxford

Most first-time visitors to Oxford have trouble working out exactly where the university is. Indeed, the quickest way to sound like a dumb tourist in Oxford is to ask "Where's the university?" This is because Oxford University is in fact made up of 39 autonomous, self-governing colleges sprinkled throughout the center of town; there's no campus as such and no central university building. Touring every college would be a formidable task, so it's best to focus on just a handful of the most intriguing and famous ones (described below). Note that most of the free colleges are only open in the afternoon.

For a bird's-eye view of the city and colleges, climb the 99 steps up the 23m (74-ft.) Gothic **Carfax Tower** ★ (www.citysightseeingoxford.com; ✆ 01865/790522) in the center of town. This structure is distinguished by its clock and

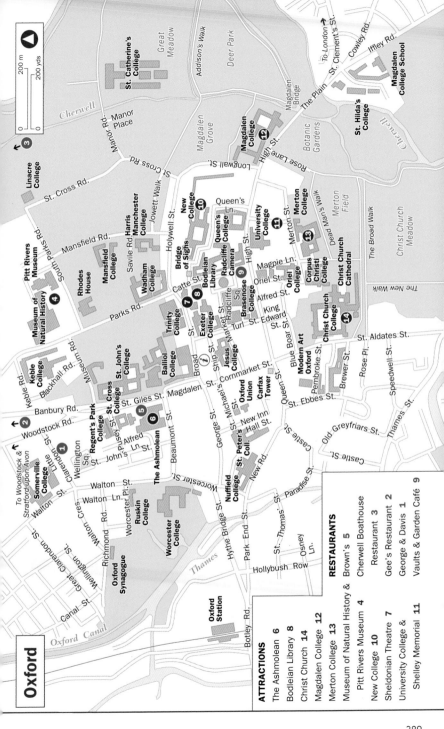

Oxford

ATTRACTIONS

The Ashmolean **6**
Bodleian Library **8**
Christ Church **14**
Magdalen College **12**
Merton College **13**
Museum of Natural History &
Pitt Rivers Museum **4**
New College **10**
Sheldonian Theatre **7**
University College &
Shelley Memorial **11**

RESTAURANTS

Brown's **5**
Cherwell Boathouse
Restaurant **3**
Gee's Restaurant **2**
George & Davis **1**
Vaults & Garden Café **9**

figures that strike on the quarter-hour. Open daily from 10am to 5:30pm (4:30pm in October), admission costs £2.20 for adults, £1.10 for children 15 and under.

The Ashmolean ★★   This oft-overlooked history museum contains some real gems, not least the Alfred Jewel, a rare Anglo-Saxon gold ornament dating from the late 9th century adorned with the words "Alfred ordered me made" (in Saxon). There are also some high-quality paintings from the Italian Renaissance (Raphael and Michelangelo among them), a large Ancient Egypt section, and some rare Asian ceramics and sculptures. The rooftop restaurant, the Ashmolean Dining Room, is a great place for a bite after a visit.

Beaumont St. at St. Giles. www.ashmolean.org. 🕾 **01865/278002.** Free admission. Tues–Sun 10am–6pm. Closed Dec 24–26.

Bodleian Library ★★   This famed library was established in 1602, initially funded by Sir Thomas Bodley, and today is a complex of several buildings in the heart of Oxford. Over the years, it has expanded from the Old Library on Catte Street and now includes the iconic **Radcliffe Camera** next door. The Bodleian is home to an astonishing 50,000 manuscripts and more than 11 million books (including a rare Gutenberg Bible).

Catte St. www.bodleian.ox.ac.uk. 🕾 **01865/277182.** Admission £1 Divinity School only; £6.50 (standard tour) or £4.50 for mini-tour (30 min); £13 (extended tour). Mon–Fri 9am–5pm; Sat 9am–4:30pm; Sun 11am–5pm. Closed Dec 24–Jan 3. Call to confirm specific tour times.

Christ Church ★★   Nothing quite matches the beauty and grandeur of Christ Church, one of the most prestigious and the largest of Oxford colleges. Christ Church has a well-deserved reputation for exclusivity, wealth, and power: It has produced 13 British prime ministers, including William Gladstone, with other alumni including John Locke, John Wesley, William Penn, W.H. Auden, and Lewis Carroll.

Radcliffe Camera.

Magdalen College.

The college chapel, which dates from the 12th century, also serves as **Oxford Cathedral;** and bowler-hatted "custodians" still patrol the pristine lawns. It boasts the most distinctive main entrance in Oxford, Sir Christopher Wren's **Tom Tower,** completed in 1682. The tower houses Great Tom, an 8,165kg (18,000lb) bell, which rings at 9:05pm nightly with 101 peals. Walk through the gate and you'll immediately face the largest quadrangle of any college in Oxford ("Tom Quad"). The two main highlights inside the college are the 16th-century Great Hall, where there are some portraits by Gainsborough and Reynolds, and the cathedral with its delicate vaulting dating from the 15th century. Many scenes from the *Harry Potter* films were shot here.

St. Aldate's. www.chch.ox.ac.uk. ℂ **01865/ 276150.** Admission £8 adults, £6.50 students, children 5–17 and seniors, free 4 and under. Mon–Sat 9am–5pm; Sun 2–5pm. Last admission 4:30pm. Closed Christmas Day.

Magdalen College ★★ Pronounced *Maud*-lin, Magdalen is the most beautiful college in Oxford, thanks to its bucolic location on the banks of the River Cherwell and some dazzling Gothic architecture, notably the elegant Magdalen Tower. There's even a deer park in the grounds and tranquil Addison's Walk, a picturesque footpath along the river. Towering over the tranquil Botanic Garden opposite (the oldest in Britain), Magdalen Tower is the tallest building in Oxford (44m/144 ft.), completed in 1509 and where the choristers sing in Latin at dawn on May Day. You can also visit the 15th-century chapel, where the same choir sings Evensong Tuesday to Sunday at 6pm.

It's another influential college whose alumni range from Thomas Wolsey to Oscar Wilde; prominent ex-students in the current Conservative Party include William Hague and George Osborne.

High St. www.magd.ox.ac.uk. ℂ **01865/276000.** Admission £4.50 adults, £3.50 seniors, students, and children. Jul–Sep daily noon–7pm; Oct–Jun daily 1–6pm or dusk (whichever is the earlier). Closed Dec 21–Dec 31.

Merton College ★ Founded in 1264, Merton College is among the three oldest colleges at the University and is the most academically successful college of the last 20 years. Merton's alumni list is eclectic and includes T.S. Eliot, J.R.R. Tolkien, unlikely Rhodes Scholar Kris Kristofferson, and even Naruhito, Crown Prince of Japan. The college is especially noted for its library, built between 1371 and 1379, and said to be the oldest college library in England. One of the library's treasures is an astrolabe (an astronomical instrument used for measuring the altitude of the sun and stars) thought to have belonged to Chaucer.

14 Merton St. www.merton.ox.ac.uk. ℂ **01865/276310.** Admission £2. Mon–Fri 2–5pm; Sat–Sun 10am–5pm. Closed for 1 week at Easter and Christmas.

Museum of Natural History & Pitt Rivers Museum ★ ☺   These two enlightening museums lie a short walk northeast of the center, well off the beaten path for most tourists but a worthwhile diversion. The Museum of Natural History houses the University's extensive collections of zoological, entomological, and geological specimens; everything from stuffed crocodiles and a giant open-jaw of a Sperm Whale, to the tsetse fly collected by the explorer David Livingstone. The Pitt Rivers Museum was founded in 1884 and displays more than half a million archeological and ethnographic objects from all over the world. Highlights include a precious Tahitian mourner's costume collected by Captain Cook in 1773–74, ghostly Japanese Noh masks, and thick Inuit fur coats.

Parks Rd. and S Parks Rd. Oxford University Museum of Natural History: www.oum.ox.ac.uk. ℂ **01865/272950.** Free admission. Daily 10am–5pm. Pitt Rivers Museum: www.prm.ox.ac.uk. ℂ **01865/270927.** Free admission. Mon noon–4:30pm; Tues–Sun 10am–4:30pm.

New College   New College is another must-see, primarily for its exceptional architecture and spacious grounds; it's also a favorite *Harry Potter* location. The college was founded in 1379 by William of Wykeham, bishop of Winchester, but the real masterpiece here is the chapel, with its handsome interior, stained glass (some designed by Joshua Reynolds), Jacob Epstein's remarkable modern sculpture of Lazarus, and a fine El Greco painting of St. James. Don't miss the beautiful garden outside the college, where you can stroll among the remains of the old city wall.

Holywell St., at New College Lane. www.new.ox.ac.uk. ℂ **01865/279500.** Admission £3 March–Oct; free during Winter.

Sheldonian Theatre   This ravishing piece of Palladian architecture stands next door to the Bodleian, completed in 1668 to a design by Sir Christopher Wren. As well as admiring the immaculate interior and ceiling frescoes, you can climb up to the cupola and enjoy fine views over Oxford.

Broad St. www.ox.ac.uk/sheldonian. ℂ **01865/277299.** Admission £2.50. Mar–Oct Mon–Sat 10am–12:30pm & 2–4:30pm; Nov–Feb Mon–Sat 10am–12:30pm & 2–3:30pm. Closed when in use.

◯ Punting the River Cherwell

Punting on the River Cherwell is an essential if slightly eccentric Oxford pastime. At the **Cherwell Boathouse,** Bardwell Rd. (www.cherwellboathouse.co.uk; ℂ **01865/515978**), you can rent a punt (a flat-bottomed boat maneuvered by a long pole and a small oar) for £14 (weekdays) to £17 (weekends) per hour, plus a £70 to £80 deposit. **Magdalen Bridge Boathouse,** the Old Horse Ford, High St. (www.oxfordpunting.co.uk; ℂ **01865/202643**), charges £16 (weekdays) to £20 (weekends) per hour. Punts are available from mid-March to mid-October, daily from 10am until dusk.

University College & Shelley Memorial ★ This modest and forward-looking college is one of the oldest in the University, founded in the 1240s by William of Durham. It's best known for the monument to Romantic poet Percy Bysshe Shelley, who came here in 1810 but was expelled the following year. The memorial is solemnly displayed in a special hall—an elegant white marble sculpture of a reclining nude and a drowned Shelley, as he washed up on the shore at Viareggio in Italy. Less romantic but equally influential alumni include Bill Clinton and Stephen Hawking.

High St. www.univ.ox.ac.uk. ☎ **01865/276602.** Free admission. Daily 9am–4pm; ask first at the porter's lodge about visiting the Shelley Memorial (small groups only).

Where to Eat

An Oxford landmark on the River Cherwell, the suitably expensive **Cherwell Boathouse Restaurant** ★, Bardwell Rd. (www.cherwellboathouse.co.uk; ☎ **01865/552746**), takes advantage of the freshest vegetables, fish, and meat. Try the pork belly with a foie gras terrine or confit of duck in a port sauce, but save room for traditional English puddings.

For more moderately priced English dining, you'll find the delightful **Gee's Restaurant** ★, 61 Banbury Rd. (www.gees-restaurant.co.uk; ☎ **01865/553540**) in a spacious Victorian glass conservatory dating from 1898 serving classic British dishes. It's worth staying for the live jazz every Sunday evening (8–9:45pm), even if you're just having drinks.

To cater to the student budget, there are plenty of inexpensive cafes in Oxford. **Brown's** ★★ at the Covered Market, Market St. (☎ **01865/243436**) is a traditional "greasy spoon" British cafe serving sausage sandwiches, fish and chips, hearty fry-ups, apple pie and custard, and mugs of tea. For dessert, **George & Davis,** 55 Little Clarendon St. (www.gdcafe.com; ☎ **01865/516652**) is Oxford's ice-cream headquarters, a brightly painted cafe serving indulgent flavors such as super chocolate, and golden secret (honeycomb and chocolate in a cream base), topped with gummy bears, nuts, or chocolate sprinkles. For something a little healthier, **Vaults & Garden Café** ★ (www.vaultsandgarden.com; ☎ **01865/279112;**) is set in the gorgeous 14th-century hall on the grounds of the University Church of St. Mary the Virgin and serves tasty soups (try the leek and potato), made with organic vegetables from nearby Worton Organic Garden, as well as salads, vegetable stir fry, and organic beef lasagna.

Shopping

Golden Cross, an arcade of first-class shops and boutiques, lies between Cornmarket Street and the Covered Market. Parts of the colorful gallery date from the 12th century; many buildings remain from the medieval era, along with some 15th- and 17th-century structures.

Alice's Shop, 83 St. Aldate's (www.aliceinwonderlandshop.co.uk; ☎ **01865/723793**) is where Alice Liddell, thought to have been the model for *Alice in Wonderland,* used to buy her barley sugar sweets when Lewis Carroll was a professor of mathematics at Christ Church. Today, you'll find commemorative pencils, chess sets, bookmarks, and, in rare cases, original editions of some of Carroll's works.

The **Bodleian Library Shop,** Old School's Quadrangle, Radcliffe Sq., Broad St. (www.shop.bodley.ox.ac.uk; ✆ **01865/277091**), specializes in Oxford souvenirs, from books and paperweights to Oxford banners and coffee mugs. **Castell & Son (The Varsity Shop),** 13 Broad St. (www.varsityshop.co.uk; ✆ **01865/244000**), is the best outlet in Oxford for clothing emblazoned with the Oxford logo or heraldic symbol.

The best bookshop in Oxford is venerable **Blackwell** at 48–51 Broad St. (bookshop.blackwell.co.uk; ✆ **01865/333536**).

Entertainment & Nightlife
THE PUB SCENE
Pubs in Oxford have a fittingly rich heritage, and you'll be drinking in the same oak-paneled rooms once frequented by Samuel Johnson, Lawrence of Arabia, Graham Greene, Bill Clinton, and Margaret Thatcher. The city does have a life beyond the University too: Radiohead played their first gig at Oxford's **Jericho Tavern** in 1986, an alternative venue that still hosts live bands.

Known as the "Bird and Baby," the **Eagle and Child,** 49 Saint Giles St. (✆ **01865/302925**), was frequented in the 1930s and '40s by the "Inklings," a writers' group that included the likes of C.S. Lewis and J.R.R. Tolkien. In fact, *The Chronicles of Narnia* and *The Hobbit* were first read aloud here. In contrast, the **Head of the River,** Abingdon Rd. at Folly Bridge, near the Westgate Centre Mall (✆ **01865/721600**), is a lively place offering traditional ales, along with good sturdy bar food. In summer, guests can sit by the river and rent a punt or a boat with an engine. The tiny **White Horse ★**, 52 Broad St. (www.whitehorse oxford.co.uk; ✆ **01865/204801**), squeezed between Blackwell's bookshops, is one of Oxford's oldest pubs, dating from the 16th century.

The Bear Inn.

The **Bear Inn** ★, 6 Alfred St. (✆ **01865/728164**), is an Oxford landmark, built in the 13th century. Around the lounge bar you'll see the remains of thousands of ties, which have been labeled with their owners' names. Even older than the Bear is the **Turf Tavern** ★★, 7 Bath Place, off Holywell St. (www.the turftavern.co.uk; ✆ **01865/243235**), on a very narrow passageway near the Bodleian Library, reached via St. Helen's Passage. Thomas Hardy used the place as the setting for *Jude the Obscure,* and it was "the local" of Bill Clinton during his student days at Oxford.

Most Oxford pubs open from around 11am to midnight.

CAMBRIDGE

55 miles N of London

The university town of Cambridge is a city of contrasts: Its historic college buildings with their magnificent chapels, turrets, and spires provide a romantic backdrop to delight even the most traveled tourist while its high-tech industries lead the way in global technology.

Visit Cambridge and it feels like a little of that fairy dust rubs off on you too, as you discover the **Bridge of Sighs** while punting on the River Cam. Walk along **The Backs** of the colleges as the spring bulbs produce a carpet of flowers and explore the narrow streets in the footsteps of Sir Isaac Newton, John Milton, Charles Darwin, Virginia Woolf, and many more. But Cambridge is not just a collection of old colleges, as inspiring as they are. It's a living, working town with many non-University residents who bring additional atmosphere to the city.

Essentials

GETTING THERE **Trains** from London's King's Cross station take 45 minutes to an hour. A return ticket costs from £22.20. Trains from London's Liverpool Street take 80 minutes and cost from £18.60 return.

If you're **driving** from London, head north on the M11. City parking is expensive so stop at a **Park-and-Ride.** Return bus tickets cost £2.40 per person from machines (£2.70 from bus drivers); children ride free. Buses leave every 10 minutes (15 minutes on Sundays and public holidays).

VISITOR INFORMATION For free information on attractions and public transport visit the **Cambridge Tourist Information Centre,** Peas Hill, CB2 3AD (www.visitcambridge.org; ✆ **0871/226-8006** or **+44/1223/464732** from overseas). Staff can also book tours and accommodation. Open year-round, Monday to Saturday 10am to 5pm, and April to October Sundays & public holidays 11am to 3pm.

GETTING AROUND Cambridge is best seen on foot, or you can join the locals and cycle everywhere. **Station Cycles** (www.stationcycles.co.uk; ✆ **01223/307125**) has bikes for rent for £7 a half-day, £10 a day, or £25 a week. There's a shop in the railway station car park and they also have left-luggage facilities. Park your bike for free at the Park Street or Grand Arcade car parks.

TOURS The **Cambridge Tourist Information Centre** (see Visitor Information) has several 2-hour walking tours of the city, from £6 to £16 for adults, and up to £7.50 for children under 12. Book tours at www.visitcambridge. org or call ✆ **01223/457574.**

City Sightseeing (www.city-sightseeing.com; ✆ **01223/423578**) uses open top, double-decker buses from outside Cambridge railway station, and has 21 hop-on, hop-off stops. Tours depart every 20 minutes from Silver Street near The Backs, between 9:30am and 4pm in summer and 10:20am to 3pm in winter. Tickets are valid for 24 hours. The fare is £13 for adults, £9 for seniors and students, £7 for children 6 to 15, and free for under-5s. A family ticket for £32 covers two adults and up to three children.

Exploring Cambridge

Scholars have been studying at Cambridge since the early 13th century, with Henry III granting the students his protection in 1231. During the late 1600s and 1700s mathematics and science began to dominate the University. This was thanks largely to Sir Isaac Newton, who formulated the principles of gravity. Cambridge University now consists of 31 colleges, all co-educational except three which remain female-only.

All the colleges are open to the public at certain times, but each has its own policies on opening times and admission prices. The colleges are almost all closed during May and June when students are taking exams. Check with the Cambridge Tourist Information Centre for opening times, or with each individual college. They are also closed during graduation ceremonies, and at Easter, bank holidays, and other times without notice.

Emmanuel College   Emmanuel, on St. Andrew's Street, was founded in 1584 by Sir Walter Mildmay, Elizabeth I's Chancellor of the Exchequer. Mildmay was a Puritan—of the 100 Cambridge graduates who emigrated to New England before 1646, 35 were from Emmanuel. The college's gardens are particularly attractive and the cloister and chapel, consecrated in 1677, were designed by Sir Christopher Wren.

Insider's tip: John Harvard, of the University that bears his name in Cambridge, U.S.A., was among the Emmanuel graduates who emigrated to New England. There's a memorial to him in the chapel.

St. Andrew's St. www.emma.cam.ac.uk. ✆ **01223/334200.** Free entry to grounds and chapel.

Fitzwilliam Museum ★★   Suits of armor, Greek and Roman pottery, Chinese jades, Japanese ceramics, and an art collection that includes Rubens, Van Dyck, Canaletto, Hogarth, Gainsborough, Constable, and the Impressionist painters; you'll find them all here in this first-class museum that's not so large that fatigue sets in. There's also a good cafe and gift shop.

Trumpington St., near Peterhouse. www.fitzmuseum.cam.ac.uk. ✆ **01223/332900.** Free admission; donations appreciated. Tues–Sat 10am–5pm; Sun noon–5pm. Closed Mondays, Good Friday, Dec 24–26 & 31 and Jan 1. Saturday guided tours at 2:30pm £5.

Kettle's Yard ★★   This oasis of calm and good taste was the home of Jim and Helen Ede from the 1950s to early 1970s. As curator of London's Tate Gallery in the 1920s and '30s, Jim built up an enviable collection of paintings and sculptures, including work by Joan Miro, Henry Moore, and Barbara Hepworth, which are still on display.

Castle St. www.kettlesyard.co.uk. ✆ **01223/748100.** Free admission; donations appreciated. Early April–late Sept Tues–Sun & Bank Holiday Mons 1:30–4:30pm (late Sept–early April 2–4pm). Closed Mondays, Good Friday, Dec 24–28 & Jan 1.

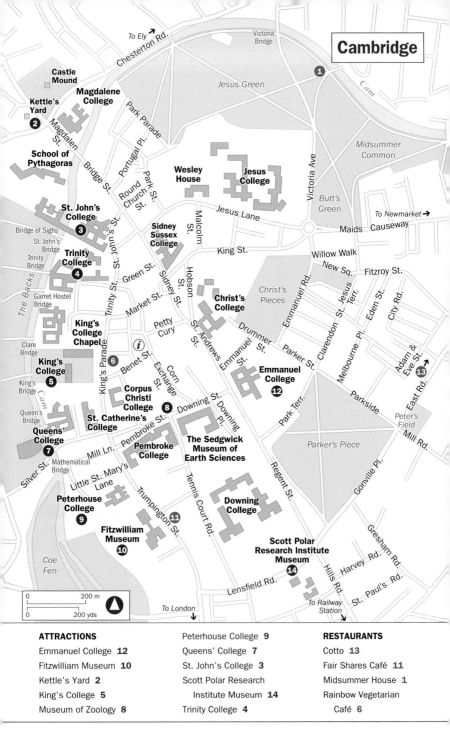

Cambridge

King's College ★★   Henry VI founded King's College in 1441 and although most of its buildings date from the 18th century and later, the world-famous **King's College Chapel** ★★★ was started in the Middle Ages and is regarded as one of Europe's finest Gothic buildings. Rubens' *Adoration of the Magi*, painted in 1634, is a highlight as are the striking stained-glass windows, most paid for by Henry VIII. Carols are broadcast world-wide from the chapel every Christmas Eve but there are concerts and organ recitals throughout the year with tickets available from the **Shop at King's,** on King's Parade.

   Insider's tip: See the chapel as it should be enjoyed by attending Evensong on an early summer's evening—one of the most uplifting experiences you'll ever have in the city. And while the chapel is beautiful inside, it is best seen from the Backs. E.M. Forster came here to contemplate scenes for his novel *Maurice*.

King's Parade. www.kings.cam.ac.uk. ⓒ **01223/331100.** Adults £7.50, students and OAPs £5, children 11 and under free.

Museum of Zoology ★★   You can see specimens collected by Cambridge graduate Charles Darwin during his voyage on the *Beagle* in the 1830s on display here, as well as rare examples of the Dodo and Great Auk.

Downing St. www.museum.zoo.cam.ac.uk. ⓒ **01223/336650.** Free admission; donations appreciated. Mon–Fri 10am–4:45pm; Sat 11am–4pm. Closed Sun.

Peterhouse College   This is the oldest Cambridge college, founded in 1284 by Bishop of Ely Hugh de Balsham. The Hall was built in 1286 but is the only part that remains of the original buildings, which were rebuilt in the 1860s in the Gothic Revival style by Sir George Gilbert Scott (also responsible for the Parliament buildings in London). The stained-glass windows were designed by British Arts and Crafts founder William Morris.

King's College.

Punting on the Cam

You haven't really experienced Cambridge if you haven't been punting on the **River Cam.** All you have to do is put the long pole, about 5m (16 ft.), straight down into the shallow water until it finds the river bed, and then gently push and retrieve the pole in one deft, simple movement. Actually, it's easy once you know how but watching inexperienced enthusiasts lose their pole or steer into the riverbed is a traditional form of entertainment in Cambridge. Rent a punt from **Scudamore's Punting Company** any time of the year to punt past The Backs from its Magdalene Bridge or Mill Lane stations, or you can punt up to Grantchester from its Mill Lane Boatyard in Granta Place, Mill Lane (www. scudamores.com; ☎ **01223/359750**). Punts cost £18 per hour (maximum of six people per punt). A credit card imprint is required as surety.

Little St. Mary's, the church next door, was the college chapel until 1632 and has a memorial to Godfrey Washington, who died in 1729. The Washington family's coat of arms contains an eagle on top of stars and stripes and is believed to be the inspiration for the U.S. flag.

Trumpington St. www.pet.cam.ac.uk. ☎ **01223/338200.** Free entry to grounds.

Queens' College ★★   Founded by English queens Margaret of Anjou, the wife of Henry VI, and Elizabeth Woodville, the wife of Edward IV, the college dates from 1448 and is regarded as the most beautiful of Cambridge's colleges. Entry and exit is by the old porter's lodge in Queens' Lane. Its second cloister is the most interesting, flanked by the 16th-century half-timbered President's Lodge.

Insider's tip: The Mathematical Bridge, an arched, wooden, self-supporting bridge, connecting the college's two parts, is best viewed from the Silver Street Bridge, dating from 1902.

Silver St. www.quns.cam.ac.uk. ☎ **01223/335511.** Daily Jun–Sep & Nov–May 10am–4:30pm; Oct Mon–Fri 2–4:30pm & 10am–4:30pm Sat–Sun. (Closed late May–late June for exams). Admission £2.50, free 11 and under, late June–early Oct 10am–4:30pm; free admission Nov–May

Scott Polar Research Institute Museum ★★   Reopened in 2010 after a £1.75 million redesign, the only word to describe this unique museum is cool, very cool. The history of polar exploration includes the last letters of Captain Scott, expedition diaries of Sir Ernest Shackleton, and artifacts from the British search for the Northwest Passage.

Lensfield Rd. www.spri.cam.ac.uk. ✆ **01223/336540.** Free admission; donations appreciated. Tues–Sat 10am–4pm. Closed Sundays, Mondays, and public holidays.

St. John's College ★★   Founded in 1511 by Lady Margaret Beaufort, mother of Henry VII who established Christ's College a few years earlier, this college's impressive gateway has the Tudor coat of arms, and the Second Court is a fine example of late Tudor brickwork. The college's best-known feature is the **Bridge of Sighs** crossing the River Cam. It was built in the 19th century, inspired by the covered bridge at the Doge's Palace in Venice. Wordsworth was an alumnus of this college.

   Insider's tip: The Bridge of Sighs is closed to visitors but can be seen from Kitchen Bridge.

St. John's St. www.joh.cam.ac.uk. ✆ **01223/338600.** Admission adults £3.20, seniors and students 12–17 £2, children 11 and under free. Daily March–Oct 10am–5:30pm; Nov–Feb Sat 10am–3:30pm.

Trinity College ★★   Not to be confused with Trinity Hall, Trinity College is the largest college and was founded in 1546 when Henry VIII consolidated a number of smaller colleges on the site. The courtyard is the most spacious in Cambridge, built when Thomas Neville was master. The Wren Library, from 1695, was designed by Sir Christopher Wren. It contains manuscripts and books that were in the college library by 1820, together with various special collections including 1,250 medieval manuscripts, early Shakespeare editions, many books from Sir Isaac Newton's own library, and A.A. Milne's Winnie-the-Pooh manuscripts.

   Sir Isaac Newton first calculated the speed of sound here, at Neville's Court, and Lord Byron used to bathe naked in the Great Court's fountain with his pet bear. The University forbade students from having dogs, but there was no rule against bears. Years later, Vladimir Nabokov walked through that same courtyard dreaming of the young lady he would later immortalize as *Lolita*.

Trinity St. www.trin.cam.ac.uk. ✆ **01223/338400.** Free admission. The Wren Library: Mon–Fri noon–2pm, Sat 10:30am–12:30pm. Various other areas are open at different times; inquire at the porter's lodge.

Where to Eat

Midsummer House ★★, Midsummer Common (www.midsummerhouse. co.uk; ✆ **01223/369299**) is the best dining in town, with a lovely riverside setting on Midsummer Common. It's the only two-star Michelin restaurant in East Anglia. For high-quality food and on the pricey side of moderate **Cotto ★,** 183 East Rd. (www.cottocambridge.co.uk; ✆ **01223/302010**), serves locally sourced ingredients.

   For less expensive offerings, **Fair Shares Café 👔**, Emmanuel United Reformed Church, Trumpington St. (✆ **01223/351174**) is highly recommended for its wholesome home-made lunches. The cafe is run in a non-profit-making partnership by the church and Cambridgeshire Mencap, ensuring a friendly community atmosphere. Some volunteers have learning disabilities.

A long-established pioneer of vegetarian eating, **Rainbow Vegetarian Café,** 9a King's Parade, across from King's College (www.rainbowcafe.co.uk; ✆ **01223/321551**), offers vegan and gluten-free food and organic wine and cider. Spinach lasagna is the Rainbow's signature dish. There is also a children's menu and free organic jars of baby food.

Shopping

Shopping opportunities start in the central Market Square. Monday to Saturday is the **General Market** with fruit and vegetables, clothes, books, and jewelry, while on Sundays there's the **Arts and Crafts and Local Produce Market** selling crafts plus home-made cakes, bread and organic food.

There's been a bookshop since 1581 on the present site of the **Cambridge University Press book shop,** 1–2 Trinity St. (www.cambridge.org; ✆ **01223/3333333**), although the bookshop **Heffers,** 20 Trinity St. (www.heffers.co.uk; ✆ **01223/463200**) is a Cambridge institution.

Rose Crescent, near the market, is pretty with clothes and cosmetics shops while the **Benet St. Area,** or Arts Quarter, off King's Parade has fashion, ceramics, and jewelry shops. The newest shopping destination is **Grand Arcade,** in St. Andrews St. (www.grandarcade.co.uk; ✆ **01223/302601**), with many high-street stores. But if you're looking for a more bohemian choice, go to **Mill Road,** off Parker's Piece, for all kinds of second-hand shops including **Cambridge Antiques Centre** at Gwydir Street off Mill Rd. (www.cambsantiques. com; ✆ **01223/356391**).

Entertainment & Nightlife

Cambridge Corn Exchange, 3 Parsons Court (www.cornex.co.uk; ✆ **01223/357851**) is your best bet for mainstream touring shows, bands, and comedians, but **Cambridge Arts Theatre,** 6 St. Edward's Passage (www.cambridgeartstheatre.com; ✆ **01223/503333**), has some wonderful stage productions. It used to be the venue for **Cambridge Footlights,** the University theatre group that produced some of Britain's best-known actors. The Footlights Spring Revue now takes place at the **Amateur Dramatic Club,** in Park Street near Jesus Lane (www.adctheatre.com; ✆ **01223/300085**), and it's the place to see other University or local drama productions.

Cambridge also has some wonderful old pubs. The oldest is **The Pickerel Inn,** Magdalene St. (✆ **01223/355068**), dating from 1432 with ceiling beams and little alcoves; and it's near the river. **The Eagle,** Benet St., off King's Parade (✆ **01223/505020**), was loved by American airmen during World War II. **The Anchor,** Silver St. (✆ **01223/353554**), and **The Mill (Tap & Spile),** 14 Mill Lane, off Silver Street Bridge (✆ **01223/357026**), are good for sitting out near the river.

SALISBURY ★★ & STONEHENGE ★★

90 miles SW of London

Long before you enter the city, the spire of Salisbury Cathedral comes into view—just as John Constable and J.M.W. Turner captured it on canvas. The 123m (404-ft.) pinnacle of the Early English Gothic cathedral is the tallest in England, but is just one among many historical points of interest in this thriving county town.

Salisbury, once known as "New Sarum," lies in the valley of South Wiltshire's River Avon. Filled with Tudor inns and tearooms, it is also an excellent base for visitors keen to explore nearby Stonehenge. The old market town also has a lively arts scene, and is an interesting destination on its own. If you choose to linger for a day or two, you find an added bonus: Salisbury's pub-to-citizen ratio is among the highest in England.

Essentials

GETTING THERE   Trains for Salisbury depart half-hourly from Waterloo Station in London; the trip takes under 1½ hours. A return ticket costs from £34.80. For more information check www.nationalrail.co.uk

If you're driving from London, head west on the M3 and then the M27 to junction 2, continuing the rest of the way on the A36.

VISITOR INFORMATION   Salisbury's friendly **Tourist Information Centre** is on Fish Row (www.visitsalisbury.com; ✆ **01722/334956**). It's open Monday to Saturday 10am to 5pm March to October (closes at 4pm Nov–Feb). For information on the wider South Wiltshire area, you should also consult **www.visitwiltshire.co.uk**.

TOURS   You can easily see Salisbury on foot, either on your own or by taking a guided daytime or evening walk run by **Salisbury City Guides** (www.salisburycityguides.co.uk; ✆ **07873/212941**). Tickets are £4 for adults and £2 for children.

The hop-on, hop-off **Stonehenge Tour** bus (www.thestonehengetour.info; ✆ **01983/827005**) picks up several times an hour (on the hour from 10am to 2pm in winter) from Salisbury railway and bus stations, passing via Salisbury Cathedral (additional cost), Old Sarum (see below) all the way to the stones, taking 35 minutes each way. A round-trip ticket costs £11 for adults, £5 for children; including entrance to Stonehenge and Old Sarum, prices are £18 adults, £15 students, and £9 children.

Exploring Salisbury

Head to the cathedral and **The Close,** some say the most beautiful of its kind, where you'll find the slightly haphazard collection at the **Salisbury & South Wiltshire Museum ★**, King's House, 65 The Close (www.salisburymuseum.org.uk; ✆ **01722/332151**). The "History of Salisbury" gallery houses a small collection of Turner's Salisbury watercolors. The museum is open Monday to Saturday 10am to 5pm, and between June and September also Sunday noon to 5pm. Admission costs £6 for adults, £2 children between 5 and 15, free for children 4 and under.

Salisbury Cathedral ★★★   You'll find no better example of the Early English Gothic architectural style than Salisbury Cathedral. Construction on this magnificent building began as early as 1220 and took only 38 years to complete. (Many of Europe's grandest cathedrals took up to 300 years to build.) As a result, Salisbury Cathedral is one of the most homogenous and harmonious of all the great cathedrals.

The cathedral's 13th-century octagonal Chapter House possesses one of the four surviving original texts of Magna Carta—one of the founding documents of democracy and justice, signed by King John in 1215.

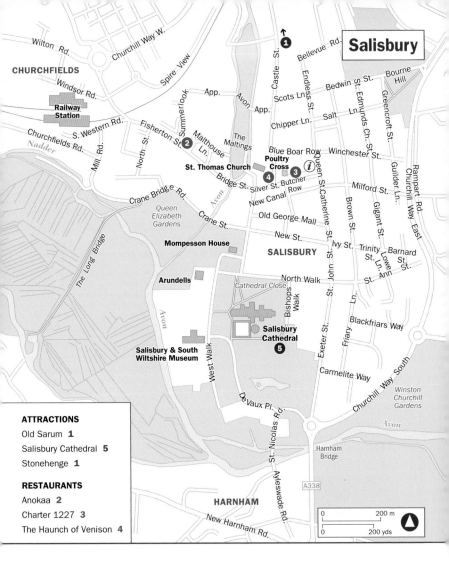

ATTRACTIONS

Old Sarum **1**

Salisbury Cathedral **5**

Stonehenge **1**

RESTAURANTS

Anokaa **2**

Charter 1227 **3**

The Haunch of Venison **4**

The 123m (404-ft.) spire is the tallest in Britain, and was one of the tallest structures in the world when completed in 1315. In its day, this was seriously advanced technology. Amazingly, the spire was not part of the original design, and the name of the master mason is lost to history. In 1668, Sir Christopher Wren expressed alarm at the tilt of the spire, but no further shift has since been measured. You can now explore the heights on a 1½-hour **Tower Tour ★★** costing £8.50 for adults, £6.50 for children and seniors, £25 for a family of five (this fee includes your cathedral donation). Between April and September, there are five tours a day Monday to Saturday (hourly from 11:15am), and two on Sunday (1 and 2:30pm). From October to March, there are usually one or two daily, depending on weather, but no tour on Sunday. Children must be aged 5 or over, and everyone will need a head for heights.

The Close. www.salisburycathedral.org.uk. ☏ **01722/555156.** Suggested donation £5.50 adults, £4.50 students and seniors, £3 children 5–17, £13 family. Daily 7:15am–6:15pm; Chapter House closes 4:30pm (5:30pm Apr–Oct) and all morning Sun.

Exploring Stonehenge & South Wiltshire

Old Sarum ★   Believed to have been an Iron Age fortification, Old Sarum was used again by the Saxons and flourished as a walled town into the Middle Ages. The Normans built a cathedral and a castle here; parts of this old cathedral were taken down to build the city of "New Sarum," later known as Salisbury, leaving behind the dramatically sited remains you see today. In the early 19th-century Old Sarum was one of the English Parliament's most notorious "Rotten Boroughs," constituencies that were allowed to send a Member of Parliament to Westminster despite having few—in Old Sarum's case, no—residents. The Rotten Boroughs were finally disbanded in 1832.

2 miles north of Salisbury off A345 Castle Rd. www.english-heritage.org.uk/oldsarum. ☏ **01722/335398.** Admission £3.70 adults, £3.30 seniors, £2.20 children 5–15. Daily Apr–June and Sept 10am–5pm; July–Aug 9am–6pm; Mar and Oct 10am–4pm; Nov–Jan 11am–3pm; Feb 11am–4pm. Bus: 5, 6, 7, 8, or 9, every 30 min. during the day, from Salisbury bus station.

Stonehenge ★★ 📷   This iconic circle of lintels and megalithic pillars is perhaps the most important prehistoric monument in Britain. The concentric rings of standing stones represent an amazing feat of late Neolithic engineering because many of the boulders were moved many miles to this site: From Pembrokeshire in southwest Wales, and the local Marlborough Downs. If you're a romantic, come see the ruins in the early glow of dawn or else when shadows fall at sunset. The light is most dramatic at these times, the shadows longer, and the effect is often far more mesmerizing than in the glaring light of midday. The mystical experience is marred only slightly by an ugly (but necessary) perimeter fence. Your admission ticket gets you inside the fence, but no longer all the way up to the stones.

Stonehenge.

The widely held view of 18th- and 19th-century Romantics, who believed Stonehenge was the work of the Druids, is without foundation. The boulders, many weighing several tonnes, are believed to have predated the arrival in Britain of the Celtic culture. Controversy surrounds the prehistoric site—in truth, its purpose remains a mystery. The first of the giant stones were erected around 2500 B.C.

Insider's tip: From the road, if you don't mind the noise from traffic, you can get a good view of Stonehenge without paying the admission charge for a close-up encounter. Alternatively, climb **Amesbury Hill,** clearly visible 1½ miles up the A303. From here, you'll get a free panoramic view.

At the junction of A303 and A344. www.english-heritage.org.uk/stonehenge. ℂ **08703/331181.** Admission £7.50 adults, £6.80 students and seniors, £4.50 children 5–15, £17.30 family ticket. Daily. June–Aug 9am–7pm; Mar 16–May and Sept–Oct 15 9:30am–6pm; Oct 16–Mar 15 9:30am–4pm. If you're driving, head north on Castle Rd. from the center of Salisbury on to the A345 to Amesbury, and then the A303 to Exeter. You'll see signs for Stonehenge, leading you up the A344 to the right. It's 2 miles west of Amesbury.

Where to Eat

Salisbury has plenty of characterful pubs, where a lunch of typical British pub grub fare awaits. **The Haunch of Venison** (see p. 406) serves up roasts and grills to hungry visitors.

For British bistro classics with some refined, French-influenced cooking in a redbrick building on Salisbury's marketplace, try **Charter 1227 ★**, 6–7 Ox Row, Market Sq. (www.charter1227.co.uk; ℂ **01722/333118**). Expect pan-roasted filet of beef with potato terrine and a horseradish velouté, or fish and double-cooked chunky chips, followed by sticky toffee "pud" with butterscotch sauce. Closed Sunday and Monday.

Or try out one of Britain's new breed of 21st-century Indian restaurants: **Anokaa ★**, 60 Fisherton St., Salisbury (www.anokaa.com; ℂ **01722/414142**). This relaxed and colorful dining room serves up contemporary cuisine from a variety of Indian regions. *Anokaa* means "different," and when you taste the chicken lababdar, flavored with coconut, ginger, and sweet chili, or the tandoori seared lamb rack, you'll understand why. At lunchtime it's a limited buffet service only, but at £8.95 it offers excellent value.

Shopping

Many shops in Salisbury are set in beautiful medieval timber-framed buildings. As you wander through the colorful **Charter market** (Tues and Sat) held in **Market Square** since 1361, or walk the ancient streets, you'll find everything from touristy gift shops to unique specialty stores.

Locals gravitate to the **Old George Mall Shopping Centre,** 23B High St. (www.oldgeorgemall.co.uk; ℂ **01722/333500**), a short walk from the cathedral and with more than 40 individual shops and high-street stores.

Another place of note, situated within a 14th-century building with hammered beams and original windows, is **Watsons,** 8–9 Queen St. (www.watsonsof salisbury.co.uk; ℂ **01722/32031**). This elegant store carries paperweights, bone china from Wedgwood, Royal Doulton, and Aynsley, and Dartington glassware.

Entertainment & Nightlife
THE PUB SCENE

Hopback is the local brewer to look out for, and the best of Salisbury's many pubs usually have at least one of their fine beers on tap. Standing just outside the center, **Deacons ★**, 118 Fisherton St. (✆ **01722/504723**), has a local reputation for keeping and serving ale the way it should be. The tiny, characterful bar is worth the short walk. Even in a city full of ancient, half-timbered inns, there's nowhere quite like the **Haunch of Venison ★**, 1 Minster St. (www.haunchofvenison.uk.com; ✆ **01722/411313**). The haphazard interior layout and wood-paneled rooms of this former chophouse ooze medieval charm—and are reputedly haunted.

BATH ★★★

115 miles W of London; 13 miles SE of Bristol

Strolling along Bath's sweeping Royal Crescent with its wide pavements and grand Georgian terraced homes, you immediately feel part of a Jane Austen novel. Tourism has been the main industry in Bath for more than 2,000 years: from Roman times to the present-day tourism, which began in the 18th century when Queen Anne came to "take the waters" in 1702. Imagine the fantastic balls and parties held in the Pump Rooms and Assembly Rooms, overseen by the dandy Richard "Beau" Nash, and then take a nose into the grand homes along the Royal Crescent, designed to fit their social status.

Essentials

GETTING THERE   Trains leave London's Paddington station bound for Bath once every half-hour during the day; the trip takes about 1½ hours: **National Rail** (www.nationalrail.co.uk; ✆ **0845/748-4950**).

National Express (www.nationalexpress.com; ✆ **0871/781-8178**) buses leave London's Victoria coach station every 90 minutes during the day. The trip takes 3½ hours.

If you're **driving,** head west on the M4 to Junction 18. Parking in Bath is expensive, and many roads are blocked off during busy times for buses, and so park at the Lansdown Park & Ride, 3 miles south of Junction 18. Open Monday to Saturday 6:15am to 8:30pm (pay on the bus).

VISITOR INFORMATION   The **Bath Tourist Information Centre** is at Abbey Chambers, Abbey Church Yard (www.visitbath.co.uk; ✆ **09067/112000** toll call, 50p per minute; from overseas call +**44/844/847525**). It's open Monday to Saturday 9:30am to 5:30pm and Sunday 10am to 4pm. Closed December 25 and January 1.

TOURS   The Mayor's office provides professionally guided free 2-hour **Walking Tours of Bath** daily (Sun–Fri 10:30am and 2pm; Sat 10:30am. May–Sept also Tues and Fri 7pm). Meet outside the Abbey Churchyard entrance to the Pump Room.

Exploring Bath

Begin your tour of Georgian Bath at **Queen Square** and discover some of the famous streets laid out by John Wood the Elder (1704–54). Walk up to the **Circus ★★★**, three Palladian crescents arranged in a circle, with 524 different

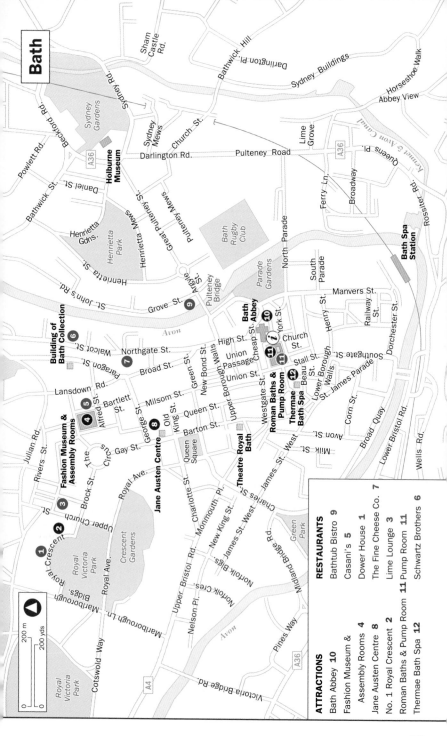

Bath

ATTRACTIONS

Bath Abbey **10**
Fashion Museum &
Assembly Rooms **4**
Jane Austen Centre **8**
No. 1 Royal Crescent **2**
Roman Baths & Pump Room **11**
Thermae Bath Spa **12**

RESTAURANTS

Bathtub Bistro **9**
Casani's **5**
Dower House **1**
The Fine Cheese Co. **7**
Lime Lounge **3**
Pump Room **11**
Schwartz Brothers **6**

carved emblems above the doors. His son, the younger John Wood designed the **Royal Crescent ★★★**, an elegant half-moon row of town houses. Also take a look at the shop-lined **Pulteney Bridge ★**, designed by Robert Adam, and often compared to the Ponte Vecchio of Florence.

Bath Abbey ★★　Completed in 1611, Bath Abbey is the last of the great medieval churches of England, and known as the "lantern of the west" for its many ornate windows. Beau Nash—honored by a simple monument totally out of keeping with his flamboyant character—is buried in the nave. For a birds-eye view of the city take the **Abbey Tower Tour** (45–50 mins), climbing 212 steps.

Orange Grove. www.bathabbey.org. ☎ **01225/422462.** Suggested donation £3 adults, free for children 15 and under. Abbey: Apr–Oct Mon–Sat 9am–6pm; Nov–Mar Mon–Sat 9am–4:30pm; year-round Sun 1–2:30pm (Apr–Oct also 4:30–5:30pm). Abbey Tower Tour: £6 adults, £3 children 5–14 (under-5s not allowed). Apr–Oct Mon–Sat 10am–4pm on the hour; Nov–Mar 11am, noon, and 2pm.

Fashion Museum & Assembly Rooms ★　The grand **Assembly Rooms,** designed by the younger John Wood and completed in 1771, once played host to dances, recitals, and tea parties. Damaged in World War II, the elegant rooms have been gloriously restored and look much as they did when Jane Austen and Thomas Gainsborough attended society events here. Housed in the same building, the **Fashion Museum** offers audiotours through the history of fashion from the 16th century to the present day. Exhibits change every 6 months. There's also a special "Corsets and Crinolines" display where enthusiastic visitors can try on reproduction period garments.

Bennett St. www.fashionmuseum.co.uk. ☎ **01225/477789.** Admission (includes audio tour) £7.50 adults, £6.75 students and seniors, £5.50 children 6–16, £21 family ticket, free for children 5 and under. Admission to Assembly Rooms only £2, children under 17 free. Nov–Feb daily 10:30am–4pm; Mar–Oct daily 10:30am–5pm. Closed Dec 25–26.

Jane Austen Centre　This small homage to Britain's favorite 19th-century writer occupies a graceful Georgian town house on the street where Miss Austen once lived (at no. 25). Exhibits and a video convey a sense of what life was like when Austen lived here between 1801 and 1806. Ladies can also learn the esoteric skill of using a fan to attract an admirer. The tearoom is worth a visit (see "Taking Tea in Bath," p. 410).

40 Gay St. www.janeausten.co.uk. ☎ **01225/443000.** Daily 9:45am–5:30pm Apr–Oct. 11am–4:30pm Nov–Mar. Allow at least 45 min. Admission £7.45 adults, £5.95 students and over-65s, £4.25 children 6 to 15, £19.50 family.

No. 1 Royal Crescent　This small but edifying museum provides a sense of life at Bath's most sought-after address. The Georgian interior has been redecorated and furnished in late 18th-century style, replete with period furniture and authentic flowery wallpaper.

1 Royal Crescent. www.bath-preservation-trust.org.uk. ☎ **01225/428126.** Admission £6.50 adults, £5 students and seniors, £2.50 children 5–16, family ticket £13. Mid-Feb–Oct Tues–Sun 10:30am–5pm, Nov–mid-Dec Tues–Sun 10:30am–4pm (last admission 30 min. before closing).

Roman Baths ★★★ & Pump Room ★　Blending Roman ingenuity and Georgian style, the best-preserved thermo-mineral Roman baths in the world have been cleaned, and the steaming (35°C/95°F hot-spring water) Great Bath now looks more like the Roman original. Audio guides, displays, and costumed actors interpret the site as you wander past the Sacred Spring, remains of a Roman

Roman Baths.

Temple, plunge pools, and the Great Bath itself. To take in everything allow at least 2 hours. After wandering the baths, visit the 18th-century **Pump Room,** overlooking the hot springs, and try a glass of the water—although be warned that it's not exactly tasty. It has been fashionable since the 18th-century to take coffee, lunch, and afternoon tea here.

Bath Abbey Church Yard, Stall St. www.roman baths.co.uk. © **01225/477785.** Admission £12.25 adults (saver ticket with Fashion Museum £15.75), £10.75 seniors, £78 children 6–16, £35 family ticket. Daily 9am–10pm Jul–Aug; 9am–5pm Sep–Oct; 9:30am–5:30pm Nov–Feb; 9am–6pm Mar–Jun. Last admission 1 hr. before closing. Closed Dec 25–26.

Thermae Bath Spa ★★ The waters at the old Roman Baths are unfit for bathing, so if you want to sample the city's celebrated hot springs make for this plush, modern spa. From the outdoor pool in the New Royal Bath complex you can watch the sun setting over Bath's rooftops while you soak.

Hot Bath St. www.thermaebathspa.com. © **0844/888-0844.** Admission New Royal Bath £26 for 2 hrs, £36 for 4 hrs. (16 and under not permitted). New Royal Bath daily 9am–10pm; Spa Visitor Centre Apr–Oct Mon–Sat 10am–5pm, Sun 10am–4pm. Closed Dec 24–25 & Dec 31–Jan 7.

Where to Eat

Dining in Bath is as fine as the architecture. If you're looking for exceptional cuisine in a wonderful setting, Bath is not short on locations, from the best of the West Country's fine dining at the **Dower House** ★★★ in the Royal Crescent Hotel, 16 Royal Crescent (www.royalcrescent.co.uk; © **01225/823333**), to the chandelier-lit **Pump Room** (see above) overlooking the Roman Baths.

For authentic French food, visit **Casani's,** 4 Saville Row (www.casanis. co.uk; © **01225/780055**; reservations required), where simple but stylish dishes are mostly inspired by Provence.

Less expensive, the fashionable **Bathtub Bistro** ★, 2 Grove St. (www.the bathtubbistro.co.uk; © **01225/460593;** closed Sun pm), features home-style British cooking with hearty plates for lunch such as ham hock, and split pea and mint stew. The day-time menu at **Lime Lounge** ★★, 11 Margarets Buildings (www.limeloungebath.co.uk; © **01225/421251**), features home-made soups and cakes, salads, burgers, and sandwiches. Hot chocolate fans are also in for a treat. In the evenings there are riffs on old Brit classics; think "posh" fish and chips, or pork with creamed apple and a cider and stilton sauce.

Made popular by the Georgians and popularized by Jane Austen, Bath is the ideal place to indulge in that quintessentially English tradition of afternoon tea, served with jam, clotted cream, and scones. Try the **Pump Room ★★** at the Roman Baths (p. 408), which serves "Bath buns" (sweet buns sprinkled with sugar), or **Sally Lunn's ★** at 4 North Parade Passage (www.sallylunns.co.uk; ✆ **01225/461634**). The latter's building itself is one of the oldest in Bath, dating from 1482, and shows little hint of any changes with its crooked, creaking floors and low ceilings. For £6.18 to £11.88,

you can sample a range of fabulous Sally Lunn cream teas, which include toasted and buttered Sally Lunn buns served with strawberry jam and clotted cream. The **Regency Tea Rooms ★** at the Jane Austen Centre (p. 408) offers "Tea with Mr Darcy" sets for £11.50 to £20.50 for two, and basic cream tea sets from £5.50. For a more luxurious afternoon tea, head to **The Royal Crescent Hotel** at 16 Royal Crescent (www.royalcrescent. co.uk; ✆ **01225/823333**) between 3 and 5pm for sandwiches, quiche, cakes, Bath buns, and champagne for £32.50 per person. Booking is essential.

For food on the go, head to **The Fine Cheese Co. ★**, 29 & 31 Walcot St. (www.finecheese.co.uk; ✆ **01225/483407**), for sandwiches made with cheese from artisan cheesemongers. If you prefer a chargrilled garlic mayoburger or an irresistible Danish blue cheeseburger, stop at gourmet burger bar **Schwartz Brothers,** 102 Walcot St. (www.schwartzbros.co.uk; ✆ **01225/463613**).

Shopping

Bath is crammed with markets, antiques centers, specialist food stores, and fashion boutiques. Prices, however, are comparable to London. Arriving by train, you'll encounter a new shopping center, **SouthGate** (www.southgatebath.com; ✆ **01225/469061**), with plenty of high-street stores.

Head to **Milsom Street** for fashion and the department store **Jolly's** (www. houseoffraser.co.uk; ✆ **0844/8003704**), or wander the boutiques along the **Corridor** and **North and South Passages,** and arty, independent stores in **Walcot Street.** Here you'll find a Saturday flea market and **The Fine Cheese Co.** (see p. 410), which sells a vast array of artisan British cheeses.

The **Bartlett Street Antiques Centre,** 5 Bartlett St. (Mon–Tues, Thurs–Sat 9:30am–5pm, Wed 8am–5pm; ✆ **01225/466689**), encompasses 60 stands displaying furniture, silver, antique jewelry, paintings, toys, and military items.

Entertainment & Nightlife

As befits one of Britain's oldest cities, there are plenty of characterful pubs in Bath and nightlife tends to revolve around them—for nightclubs, Bristol is better.

Look out for beers by **Abbey Ales,** Bath's only micro-brewery. You'll find them among nine cask ales served at the **Bell,** 103 Walcot St. (www.walcot street.com; ✆ **01225/460426**), with live music on Monday and Wednesday nights and Sunday. Vegetarians and students love the **Porter,** 15 George St. (www.theporter.co.uk; ✆ **01225/424104**), a grungier option specializing in vegetarian food, live music, open mic nights, ambient DJs, and comedy. Next door is **Moles** (www.moles.co.uk; ✆ **01225/404445**), Bath's popular dance club and live music venue.

PLANNING YOUR TRIP TO LONDON

10

GETTING THERE
By Plane

London's flagship airport for arrivals from across the globe is **London Heathrow** (LHR; www.heathrowairport.com), 17 miles west of the center and boasting five hectic, bustling terminals (numbered imaginatively, Terminals 1 to 5, although Terminal 2 is closed until 2014). This is the U.K. hub of most major airlines, including British Airways, Virgin Atlantic, and North American carriers. **London Gatwick** (LGW; www.gatwickairport.com) is the city's second major airport, with two terminals (North and South) 31 miles south of central London. As with Heathrow, you can fly to or from almost anywhere on the planet.

Increasingly, however, passengers are arriving at London's smaller airports—particularly since the proliferation of budget airlines, which now dominate many short-haul routes. **London Stansted** (STN; www.stanstedairport.com), 37 miles northeast of the center, is the gateway to a vast array of destinations in the U.K., continental Europe, and parts of the Middle East. It's also a hub for Ryanair. **London Luton** (LTN; www.london-luton.co.uk) anchors a similarly diverse short-haul network, and lies 34 miles northwest of the center: easyJet and Ryanair are regular visitors. **London City** (LCY; www.londoncityairport.com), the only passenger airport actually in London itself, is frequented mainly by business travelers, but it does have some key intercity links, including regular direct flights to New York, Paris, Edinburgh, Florence, and Amsterdam. British Airways and Cityjet are the two major airlines at London City. **London Southend** (SEN; www.southendairport.com), 40 miles east of the center, became a secondary base for easyJet short-haul services in 2012.

FROM THE AIRPORT
Heathrow Airport

Heathrow offers a range of transfer options depending on where your comfort/convenience versus value-for-money trade-off rests. A journey to the center of London via the Piccadilly Underground (Tube) Line takes 45 to 50 minutes and costs between £2.90 and £5.30—it's cheapest if you travel after 9:30am and use an Oyster Card (see "Getting Around," below). Trains leave every couple of minutes, but if you want to plan, use the online journey planner at **www.tfl.gov.uk/journeyplanner**. For Tube ticketing information, again see "Getting Around."

The **Heathrow Express** (www.heathrowexpress.com; ☎ **0845/600-1515**) train service runs every 15 minutes daily from 5:10am until 11:40pm between Heathrow and Paddington station, just west of London's West End. Tickets bought online in advance cost £16.50 each way in economy class, rising to £18 if bought from one of the ticket machines, and £23 on the train itself. First-class tickets cost £26. Children aged 5 to 15 pay £8.20 to £11.50 in economy, £13 in first class. The trip takes 15 minutes each way between Paddington and Terminals 1 and 3; 21 to 23 minutes from Terminals 4 or 5. The trains have special areas for wheelchairs. From Paddington, you can connect to the Underground ("Tube") system, or just follow signs to the taxi stand outside.

A better-value, but slower, rail option is the **Heathrow Connect** (www.heathrowconnect.com; ☎ **0845/678-6975**). A couple of trains an hour ply the route to Paddington station via Ealing from Terminals 1 and 3, where you make

a quick change for a transfer from 4 or 5. Journey time is about 25 minutes for Terminals 1 and 3, 15 minutes more for Terminals 4 or 5. A single fare from Paddington costs £8.50, with children 5 to 15 paying 50% less.

Most expensive of the lot, a **taxi** hailed at one of the airport's official ranks is likely to cost anything from £60 to £85. You can make a saving of around £10 by booking a fixed-price minicab service in advance from **Addison Lee** (www.addisonlee.com; ℂ **0844/800-6677**). Pay online or over the phone.

Gatwick Airport

The fastest way to central London is via the **Gatwick Express** (www.gatwickexpress.com), which departs every 15 minutes, daily between 4:30am and 12:50am. The round-trip fare between Gatwick and Victoria rail station is £30.80 for adults and £15.40 for children age 5 to 15. (One-way fares cost £17.90 for adults and £8.95 for children.) If you book online, you can save about 15% on ticket prices. The travel time each way is 30 minutes Monday to Saturday, and 35 minutes on Sunday. Check the website for regular pre-booking discounts, including 3-for-2 tickets.

Cheaper rail routes, operated by **Southern** (www.southernrailway.com; ℂ **0845/127-2920**) and **First Capital Connect** (www.firstcapitalconnect.co.uk; ℂ **0845/026-4700**), also operate 3 or 4 times an hour between Gatwick and Victoria, or London Bridge, City Thameslink, Blackfriars, Farringdon, and St. Pancras International. Journeys take 30 to 40 minutes. See **www.nationalrail.co.uk** for timetables and service updates.

Roughly hourly **National Express** (www.nationalexpress.com; ℂ **0871/781-8178**) coaches link Gatwick with London's Victoria coach station. The walk-up fare is £8 single, but that can fall to £4.50 if you book online. Children aged 3 to 14 pay half-price. **easyBus** (www.easybus.co.uk) connects both Gatwick terminals with West Brompton Underground station, close to Earl's Court, west of the center, at bargain rates as low as £2 if you book ahead online; the walk-up fare is £10 one way. Services depart a couple of times an hour, and there are no children's discounts. Journey time on any bus is at the mercy of London traffic, but ought to be under 1½ hours.

A **taxi** from Gatwick to central London costs over £100. Exact fares vary according to a fixed price list to various neighborhoods of London.

Stansted Airport

The quickest route to central London is via the **Stansted Express** (www.stanstedexpress.com; ℂ **08457/850-0150**) train to Liverpool Street station, which runs every 15 minutes from 6am to 11:45pm. If you book online, it costs £20 for a standard ticket and £32.50 for first class—return fares are £27.30 and £47.50 respectively. Children pay half-price. The journey takes 45 minutes. Tickets cost an extra £1 each way from a machine or teller at the station. If your final destination in London is in the West End, alight at the Express's only interim stop, Tottenham Hale, and switch to the Tube's Victoria Line. The Stansted–Tottenham Hale return fare is a couple of pounds cheaper, and the journey is 11 minutes shorter.

An alternative, slower rail route on **National Express East Anglia** (www.nationalexpresseastanglia.com; ℂ **0845/600-7245**) is no cheaper but does terminate at Stratford, ideal if you're lodging in East London. Journey time between Stansted and Stratford is 1 hour, and trains leave hourly for much of the day, Monday through Saturday.

By bus, you have several options depending on your final destination. The regular **National Express A6 Airbus** (www.nationalexpress.com; ✆ 0871/781-8178) heads for Victoria station, via the West End, 24 hours a day; tickets cost £10 one way, £5 for children aged 3 to 15. The half-hourly **National Express A9 Airbus** connects the airport with Stratford station, which lies on the Jubilee and Central Tube lines, as well as the Overground network. Tickets cost £8 for adults, £4 for children aged 3 to 15. **easyBus** (www.easybus.co.uk) connects Stansted with Baker Street, at bargain rates as low as £2 if you book online (but no child discounts). **Terravision** (www.terravision.eu; ✆ 01279/680-028) runs two generally half-hourly services, to Victoria and Liverpool Street stations respectively. One-way tickets cost £9 for adults, £4 for children aged 5 to 12. Note that because of distance and traffic conditions, any bus from Stansted to the center of London will take between 1 and 2 hours; at the lower end of that range for eastern destinations such as Stratford and Liverpool Street. If you're pressed for time, stick to the Stansted Express.

If you prefer the relative privacy of a **taxi,** you'll pay dearly for the privilege. For a ride to London's West End, a cab will charge around £100. Expect the trip to take around an hour during normal traffic conditions, but beware of Friday afternoons, when dense traffic could double the travel time.

Luton Airport

Like Stansted, Luton Airport is well served by airbuses. **Greenline** (www.greenline.co.uk; ✆ 0844/801-7261) service 757 links the airport with Victoria station via Baker Street and Marble Arch. Fares are £16 for adults, £13 for children aged 5 to 13; a return costs £23 for adults, £18 for kids. (easyJet passengers can claim a £3 discount by booking online ahead of time.) Buses leave half-hourly for most of the day. **easyBus** (www.easybus.co.uk) follows a similar route, with bargain one-way fares as low as £2 available if you book online, though you're more likely to pay around £10 (with no child reductions). Buses depart every 20 minutes or so. The **National Express** (www.nationalexpress.com; ✆ 0871/781-8178) airport bus runs a similar service, with similar frequency; tickets cost around £15 one way; children get 50% off full fare. All bus journey times are around 1½ hours, a little less if you alight at Baker Street.

It's quicker if you make for central London by train, although you first have to take the short shuttle bus to Luton Airport Parkway station (£1.50 each way, children £0.75; buses leave every 10 minutes). Both **First Capital Connect** (www.firstcapitalconnect.co.uk; ✆ 0845/026-4700) and **East Midlands Trains** (www.eastmidlandstrains.co.uk; ✆ 08457/125-678) run services to St. Pancras station. Several direct trains leave every hour, taking between 26 and 37 minutes. One-way tickets cost £12.50; children aged 5 to 15 travel half-price. See **www.nationalrail.co.uk** for timetables and service updates. Buy tickets for any of the bus or rail routes into town from the booths in the airport arrivals hall.

London City Airport

Trains on the **Docklands Light Railway,** known locally as "the DLR," make runs at 10-minute intervals from City Airport to Bank Underground station in the heart of London's financial district. From there, you can change onto the Central or Northern Line, or walk below-ground to the adjacent Monument station for the District or Circle Lines. A one-way ticket to anywhere in zone 1 costs £4.30 for adults and £2.10 for children aged 11 to 15 (substantially cheaper with an

Changing Airports

Some visitors may need to transfer from one airport to another. **National Express** (www.nationalexpress.com; *℡* **0871/ 781-8178**) buses leave from Heathrow, Gatwick, Stansted, and Luton, circum-navigating the M25 to each of the others with varying frequencies throughout the day. Gatwick to Heathrow costs £25 for adults, £12.25 for children ages 3 to 15, and takes about 1¼ hours. Check the website (click "Airports") for timetables. For transfers between Luton and Gat-wick airports, the quickest and most frequent interconnecting service is the direct train operated by **First Capital Connect** (www.firstcapitalconnect.co.uk; *℡* **0845/026-4700**). A single fare costs £24.50.

Oyster Card; see below). The journey from London City to Bank takes 22 minutes. If there are problems with the DLR, local buses 473 (alight at Plaistow station) and 474 (alight at Canning Town station) will connect you quickly with the Tube network. The cash fare is £2.30, or £1.35 with an Oyster Card (see below).

A **taxi** should cost £20 to £40, depending on how far west you're traveling.

London Southend Airport

A rail link operated by **National Express East Anglia** (www.nationalexpress eastanglia.com; *℡* **0845/600-7245**) connects the airport with London Liver-pool Street Station, via Stratford, around 3 times per hour. Journey time is 55 minutes and the fare is £15 single, £22 round-trip.

A taxi operated by **Andrews** (www.southendairporttaxis.com; *℡* **01702/ 200-000**) should cost around £100. The company uses MPVs that can accom-modate up to 7 passengers.

By Car

To anyone thinking of arriving in the capital by car, our most important piece of advice would be: "Don't." Roads in and around the city are clogged with traffic, and the M25 highway that rings the city is prone to major time-eating traffic jams at any time of day—but especially between 7:30 and 9am, or 4 and 7pm, on week-days, and on Sundays from mid-afternoon until well into the evening. And once you're in the city, just about every technology yet imagined is deployed against you (see "Getting Around" below). On top of that, and despite the complaints and grumbles of Londoners, the public transportation system is efficient.

That said, if you must drive, road maps can be deceiving. From the north, the M1 and A1 converge at London's **North Circular Road** (the A406), and then proceed in a slow, but orderly fashion into the center, with the occasional bottleneck and inevitable jam. It's horribly clogged at peak traffic hours, but oth-erwise a reasonable route into the north of the city. From the west, both the M40/ A40 and M4/A4 routes into the city are slightly more efficient. (Remember, we're talking in *relative* terms here; no one averse to sitting in stationary traffic should attempt any of these roads at peak times.) From the east and northeast, take the M11 or A12 roads into the city. Approaching the city from the south is much more problematic, however. London's supposed **South Circular Road** (the A205) is that in name only. It's little more than a collection of linked high-streets for much of its length, and very slow going. Roads from the south into the center

are similarly tortuous. From Kent and the Channel ports, such as Dover, the A2 usually clips along satisfactorily outside rush hour, although the bottleneck at the Blackwall Tunnel creates long queues every weekday. From the southwest, it's quicker to head clockwise around the M25 to enter London via the M4 or M40 (see above), unless you're heading for a southwestern suburb such as Richmond, Kew, or Twickenham. From Brighton and the south coast, the arrow-straight M23/A23 route looks inviting, but it's incredibly slow through suburbia. You're better advised to head anticlockwise around the M25 to pick up the A2 for the City and East London, or clockwise to the M4 for the West End—even though that looks insane on a roadmap.

By Train

Precisely which of London's many mainline stations you arrive at depends on where you start your journey. **Paddington station** serves Heathrow Airport, and destinations west of London—including Oxford, Reading, Bath, Bristol, and South Wales, and Cornwall. **Marylebone station** is used mostly by commuters, but also serves Warwick and Stratford-upon-Avon. **Euston station** serves North Wales and major cities in northwest England, including Liverpool and Manchester; trains also depart from here to the Lake District and Glasgow, Scotland, via the West Coast Mainline. **King's Cross station** is the endpoint of the East Coast Mainline—trains arrive here from York, Newcastle, and Edinburgh. **Liverpool Street station** is the City's main commuter hub, but also links London with Stansted Airport, Cambridge, and Norwich. The City's other mainline stations—Cannon Street, Moorgate, Blackfriars, and Fenchurch Street—are also heavily used by commuters from the neighboring counties of Hertfordshire, Essex, Kent, Surrey, and Sussex, as is **Charing Cross station,** close to Trafalgar Square. **Waterloo station** serves the southwest of England: Trains from Devon, Dorset, and Hampshire terminate here, as do Salisbury services. **Victoria station** serves Gatwick Airport, as well as cities and towns across southern England, including Brighton. South of the River Thames, **London Bridge station** is another busy commuter hub, and serves Brighton and Gatwick Airport. Each of London's mainline train stations is connected to the city's vast bus and Underground networks (see below), and each has phones, sandwich bars, fast-food joints, luggage storage areas, and transport information points.

Missing from the above list is **St. Pancras station,** the London hub for high-speed Eurostar services to Paris and Brussels, as well as some domestic services to the East Midlands and South Yorkshire. Restored and reopened in 2007, it connects England with Belgium and France through the multibillion-pound **Channel Tunnel.** Recent upgrades to the line mean you can now reach London from Brussels in 1 hour and 59 minutes, and from Paris in 2 hours and 15 minutes. It is also served by six Underground routes—the Victoria, Northern, Piccadilly, Circle, Hammersmith & City, and Metropolitan lines—as well as seven rail companies. In the U.K., you can make reservations for **Eurostar** by calling ℗ **0843/2186-186;** in North America, book online at **www.eurostar.com,** or contact **Rail Europe** (www.raileurope.com; ℗ **800/622-8600,** or 800/361-7245 in Canada). U.S. visitors arriving from Continental Europe should remember that the validity of the Eurail pass ends at the English Channel. You'll need to purchase a separate BritRail pass if you plan to tour the U.K.; see **www.britrail.com.**

The plethora of train companies running services on Britain's deregulated railways can seem very confusing to visitors—as indeed it is to locals. The best source of timetable and price information for any rail journey is **National Rail Enquiries** (www.nationalrail.co.uk; ✆ **08457/48-49-50** or 020/7278-5240). As long as you're sure of your travel dates and times, booking tickets in advance from **theTrainline.com** or **Quno.com** can bag huge savings on long-distance travel. You can collect tickets from your departure station. If you're fortunate, **MegaTrain** (www.megatrain.com) may have a seat at a deep discount.

By Bus

Long-distance buses, or "coaches," are the cheapest—but also the slowest and least comfortable—way to reach London. Just about every sizable town in the U.K. has a coach link with the capital, most run by **National Express** (www.nationalexpress.com; ✆ **0871/781-8178**). Depending on where you are starting your journey, super-budget **MegaBus** (www.megabus.com; ✆ **0900/1600-900**) may be an option, with ticket prices starting at just a couple of pounds. The **Oxford Tube** (www.oxfordtube.com; ✆ **01865/772250**) links London with Oxford 3 or 4 times an hour (a return fare costs £16, half-price for children 15 and under).

Most buses terminate at **Victoria coach station,** 164 Buckingham Palace Rd. (✆ **020/7027-2541**), although many offer intermediate stops in the capital too.

GETTING AROUND
By Public Transportation

The first London word that any visitor needs to learn is "Oyster." The **Oyster Card** is a plastic smartcard that is your gateway to pretty much every form of London public transport, from the Underground (the "Tube") and the buses to surface rail networks and even the suburban Croydon–Wimbledon Tramlink. You can still pay to use these services with cash, but an Oyster offers big savings on just about every journey. The pay-as-you-go card costs £5 for adults (see below for children's savings) from any Tube or major rail station—a charge that's refundable if you return the card after use. (In any case, you'll get almost half that investment back right away if you ride the Tube from Heathrow into the center, for example.) As well as these significant discounts, your daily bill for using an Oyster is capped at the price of an equivalent 1-Day Travelcard (see below), so there's no longer any need to calculate in advance whether to buy a discounted multi-trip travel ticket. If you're staying more than a day or so, and plan to use London's public transport network, investing in an Oyster is a no-brainer. It saves you time and money.

To use an Oyster, simply touch it against the yellow card-reader that guards the entry/exit gates at Tube and rail stations. The gates will open. On the bus you'll find the reader next to the driver. If you're caught traveling without having swiped your Oyster, you're liable for an on-the-spot fine.

You can order an Oyster in advance, preloaded with as much credit as you like, from **www.tfl.gov.uk/oyster**. Postage to the U.K. is free, but worldwide delivery costs £4.25. It's cheaper for overseas residents to purchase from the first Tube station they enter—activation is immediate. Oyster Cards are also on sale

Kids' Travel Discounts

As long as they're accompanied by an adult, children aged 10 and under travel free on just about everything public, including Tube, Overground, DLR, bus, and many local rail services. Children in this age bracket who look older than 10 should carry photo ID. Children aged 11 to 15 carrying a **11–15 Zip Oyster photocard** travel free on buses and trams, and pay child fare on Tube, Overground, DLR, and regular rail services—up to a maximum of £1.30 for unlimited off-peak journeys in one day. To obtain a Zip Oyster photocard, apply online at **www.tfl.gov.uk/zip**. There's an administration fee of £10, and you'll need to upload a photo. Postage is free to U.K. addresses, and overseas visitors can arrange to collect their card at any Travel Information Centre. It's a similar drill for anyone aged 16 to 18. The **16+ Zip Oyster photocard** gets you single tickets at half the adult price on bus, Tube, tram, and Overground services, as well as child-fare Travelcards.

at London's **Travel Information Centres,** located inside Heathrow Terminal 123 and Piccadilly Circus Underground stations, and at Liverpool Street, Euston, Victoria, and King's Cross rail stations. To top up your balance, use cash or a credit card at any Oyster machine, which you'll find inside most rail stations, at any of a network of around 4,000 newsagents citywide (see http://ticketstoplocator.tfl.gov.uk), or online if you register your card in advance.

THE UNDERGROUND AND DOCKLANDS LIGHT RAILWAY The **"Tube"** is the quickest and easiest way to move around the capital. All Tube stations are clearly marked with a red circle and blue crossbar. There are 10 extensive lines, plus the short Waterloo & City line linking Waterloo and Bank, all of which are conveniently color-coded and clearly mapped on the walls of every Tube station. The Underground generally operates Monday to Saturday 5am to 12:30am, Sunday 7:30am to 11:30pm. The above-ground extension of the Underground that links the City with points around the East End and Docklands, including London City Airport, is known as the **Docklands Light Railway,** or "DLR." This metro-rail system is essentially integrated with the Tube.

Tickets for the Underground operate on a system of nine fare zones. The fare zones radiate in concentric rings from the central zone 1, which is where most visitors spend the majority of their time. Zone 1 covers the area from Liverpool Street in the east to Notting Hill in the west, and from Waterloo in the south to Baker Street, Euston, and King's Cross in the north. Tube maps should be available at any Underground station. You can also download one before your trip from the excellent **Transport for London (TfL)** website, at **www.tfl.gov.uk/assets/downloads/standard-tube-map.pdf**. (Every smartphone platform also has a London Tube map app available in offline format—and usually free.) A 24-hour information service is also available at ℭ **0843/222-1234.** The best planning resource is the TfL Journey Planner, online at **www.tfl.gov.uk/journeyplanner**. For specific journey information on-the-move, text your start-point and end-point—as full postcodes, or station or stop names, in the format "A to B"—to ℭ **60835.** TfL will send an SMS with the quickest route and scheduled departure times.

If you don't have an Oyster Card (see above), you can buy your ticket at a vending machine or a ticket window. But note the prices: The cash fare for travel across up to three zones is £4.30, rising to £5.30 to travel across six zones. A journey from anywhere in zones 1 or 2 to anywhere else in zones 1 or 2 using Oyster pay-as-you-go costs £2 outside peak hours; £2 to £2.70 before 9:30am. Oyster will get you across all six zones for £2.90 after 9:30am. On all journeys, you can transfer as many times as you like as long as you stay on the Underground or DLR network.

THE BUS NETWORK London's buses can be a delightful way to navigate the city. Not only are they regular, efficient, and—late nights aside—comfortable, but they are also cheap compared to the Underground system. Buses also have the distinct advantage of allowing you to see where you're going—no need for an open-top bus tour when you can ride the upper-deck of an old-fashioned heritage **Routemaster** (p. 425) from Knightsbridge to Trafalgar Square on route no. 9, or past St. Paul's and the Tower of London on the no. 15. Other excellent "sightseeing" routes include the no. 8 (from Oxford Circus to the Bank of England) and the no. 11 (from Victoria Station, through Parliament Square and Trafalgar Square to Bank).

Unfortunately, the bewildering array of services and routes deters many visitors—and even some locals. There are online route maps and downloadable area maps available at **www.tfl.gov.uk/tfl/gettingaround/maps/buses**. If you have Web access, you could also try **Busmapper.co.uk**: Simply click your start and end points on an embedded Google Map and the site will suggest the best bus routes and tip you off about forthcoming departures. It's also available as an iPhone and Android app. **When's My Bus** (http://whensmybus.tumblr.com) is a handy service for Twitter users: Tweet your required bus number and location to @whensmybus and it tweets back the time of the next departure.

Annual Price Rises

January 2 is the date ticket prices for London's public transportation change, in an upward direction. Expect Oyster and cash fares, for adults and children, as well as Travelcard costs—across Tube, rail, and bus networks—to rise by around the rate of inflation, currently around 3.5%. Check out **www.tfl.gov.uk** for the latest.

Unlike the Underground, bus fares do not vary according to distance traveled—but if you transfer buses, you must pay again. A single journey from anywhere to anywhere costs £2.30 with cash, £1.35 with an Oyster Card. You can travel on buses all day with an Oyster for £4.20. To speed up bus travel, passengers in central London who aren't using an Oyster have to purchase tickets before boarding from a roadside ticket machine at most stops; you'll need the exact fare. The sign at the stop clearly marks which services halt there. Put your arm out when you see a bus approaching, just to be sure you've been seen. Once aboard, if you want your stop called out, simply ask the driver when you board—although all modern vehicles in London's fleet have automated digital information.

Buses generally run from 5am to just after midnight. Some run 24 hours, but other popular routes are served by **night buses,** running once every half-hour or so during the night, and with service numbers prefixed by an "N." Most night buses originate at or pass through Trafalgar Square.

Keep in mind that these buses are often so crowded (especially on weekends) that they're unable to pick up passengers after a few stops. You may find yourself waiting a long time. Consider taking a taxi (see below). The TfL 24-hour information service is available at ☎ **0843/222-1234.**

For **open-top bus tours** of the city, see "Tours & Special-Interest Trips," p. 424.

THE OVERGROUND AND OTHER RAIL SERVICES The remarkable improvements in London's surface rail network have been the big transport story of recent years. Especially useful for visitors to North, East, and Southeast London is the **London Overground** (marked in orange on most transport maps). The Overground connects Kew in southwest London with Highbury in North London, Stratford in East London adjacent to the 2012 Olympic Park and Westfield shopping mall (p. 278), as well as Whitechapel and Wapping in the East End, and then points south of the river as far as Croydon. The new, air-conditioned carriages and upgraded track ensure an efficient ride. Oyster Cards are valid on Overground services. See **www.tfl.gov.uk/overground** for more. Oyster Cards are also valid on the remainder of London's surface rail network, encompassing a vast web of commuter and local services. For specific journey information, contact **National Rail Enquiries** (www.nationalrail.co.uk; ☎ **08457/48-49-50** or 020/7278-5240).

TRAVELCARDS These discounted travel tickets offer unlimited use of buses, Underground, DLR, and regular rail services in Greater London for any period ranging from a day to a year. The fare cap on pay-as-you-go Oyster Cards (see above) has obviated the need to buy a short-period Travelcard, but they remain available from Underground ticket offices, Travel Information Centres, and some newsstands.

For the **1-Day Off-Peak Travelcard,** valid for travel anywhere within zones 1 and 2 after 9:30am, the cost is £7 for adults or £3.20 for children aged 5 to 15. **One-Week Travelcards** cost adults £29.20 for zones 1 and 2. For more Travelcard prices, visit **www.tfl.gov.uk/tickets**.

By Car

We suggest you confine your driving in London to the bare minimum, which means arriving (see "Getting There" above) and parking, *at the very most.* Before arrival in London, call your hotel and inquire if it has a garage (and what the charges are), or ask staff to give you the name and contact details of a secure garage nearby. Expect parking charges to be expensive, perhaps £30 for 24 hours in a West End garage. Be warned, also, that the entire city center is covered by a CCTV-monitored **Congestion Charging Zone.** All vehicles that enter this "C-Charge" zone—all of central London, in effect—between 7am and 6pm Monday to Friday must pay £10 per day (£12 if you pay after you drove into the zone). Pay online or by phone (www.tfl.gov.uk/roadusers/congestioncharging; ☎ **0845/900-1234**) up to 90 days in advance, and by midnight on the day after you entered the Zone at the latest. Failure to do so will result in an automatic fine. Disabled Blue Badge holders and drivers of electric vehicles qualify for a 100% C-Charge discount, but you need to register your vehicle in advance. There's usually a C-Charge moratorium between Christmas and New Year. There's a downloadable map at **www.tfl.gov.uk/roadusers/congestioncharging**.

London's roads are also among the most camera-dense on the planet, and you can expect to be photographed and fined if you err into a marked bus lane, park in the wrong place, park in the right place but at the wrong time, park in the right place but on a matchday at a nearby sports stadium, stop on a double-red line anytime, stop on a single red line outside designated times, turn right or left when you're not supposed to, run a red light, or come to a standstill in a marked yellow "box junction"—even if none of the above were done on purpose. And don't think you'll avoid a fine if you're driving a rental car: The rental agency will pay up and bill your credit card automatically, perhaps with an "administration fee" as well.

On top of all that, the city's roads are laid out haphazardly and plagued by road works, one-way systems are baffling and undergoing apparently constant redesign, and car-rental rates are high. Visitors from outside the E.U. might be shocked at the price of Britain's heavily-taxed **gasoline,** or "petrol." At the time of writing, it costs around £1.41 a liter (1 U.S. gallon = 3.785 liters)—and that price is on an ever upward trajectory.

CarRentals.co.uk is a handy price comparison site for London car hire, and the city has offices of all the main international competitors, including **Alamo** (www.alamo.co.uk), **Avis** (www.avis.co.uk), and **Hertz** (www.hertz.co.uk). Be sure to check whether your rental vehicle takes unleaded or diesel before refueling. Watch out for constantly changing speed limits—enforced, of course, by automatic cameras. The limit for traveling in a built-up area is 30mph (and some are marked only 20mph), but on an urban clearway that can shift up to 40 or 50mph, and then back again. So for all those reasons, we suggest you don't drive in London, unless it's totally unavoidable.

By Taxi

London black cabs are among the best designed in the world, and seat up to 5 passengers. Standard vehicles are wheelchair friendly. All drivers must pass a rigorous series of tests known as "the Knowledge," and cabbies generally know every London street within 6 miles of Charing Cross. You can pick up a taxi either by heading for a cab rank—stations, marquee West End hotels and department stores, and major attractions all have them—or by hailing one in the street. It is available if the yellow sign on its roof is lit.

Black taxi meters start at £2.20, with increments of £2 or more per mile thereafter, based on distance and elapsed time. Surcharges are imposed after 8pm and on weekends and public holidays. Expect a mile-long journey to average around £6 to £8, a 2-mile journey around £8 to £13, and so on. There's no need to tip, although you may like to round the fare upward if you receive friendly service. To book a black cab, phone **One-Number Taxi** on ✆ **0871/871-8710.** There's a £2 booking fee. Connected travelers can also summon a nearby black cab via smartphone app. Try either **Get Taxi** (www.gettaxi.co.uk; iPhone, Android, and Blackberry) or **Hailo** (www.hailocab.com; iPhone, Android).

Minicabs are also plentiful, and are useful when regular taxis are scarce, as is often the case in the suburbs or late at night. These cabs are often meterless, so do discuss the fare in advance. Unlike black cabs, minicabs are forbidden by law to cruise for business. Twitter users can employ the services of **Tweetalondoncab** (www.tweetalondoncab.co.uk). Follow @tweetalondoncab, send a Direct Message with your location, phone number, and time the taxi is required,

and they'll confirm and send a licensed taxi. Rates are competitive. If you text CAB to ☏ **60835,** TfL's Cabwise service will text you back with the telephone number of the nearest two licensed minicab offices. Premium minicab operator Addison Lee also has taxi booking apps for smartphone platforms including iPhone, Android, and Blackberry; see **www.addisonlee.com/discover/mobile.**

The Best London News & Views Websites

BBC London (www.bbc.co.uk/london)
Greenwich.co.uk (www.greenwich.co.uk)
London Evening Standard (www.thisis
london.co.uk)
London SE1 (www.london-se1.co.uk)
MayorWatch (www.mayorwatch.co.uk)
Metro (www.metro.co.uk)
Yeah Hackney (www.yeahhackney.com)

Kabbee (www.kabbee.com) is an Android and iPhone app that compares minicab prices and allows you to book from your handset.

If you have a complaint about your taxi service, contact the **TfL Taxi and Private Hire Office,** 4th Floor, Palestra, 197 Blackfriars Rd., SE1 8NJ, or call ☏ **0845/300-7000.** If it's a complaint about a black taxi, you must have the cab number, which is displayed in the passenger compartment.

By Boat

Once London's watery highway, these days the River Thames is more suited to a sightseeing trip than an A-to-B journey. However, it is used by some Docklands commuters, and that commuter service is as fun a way as any to get to the maritime sights of Greenwich (p. 170). **Thames Clippers** (www.thamesclippers. com) runs a year-round fleet of catamarans between the London Eye Pier and North Greenwich Pier, stopping at Embankment Pier, Bankside Pier, Tower Millennium Pier, Canary Wharf Pier, and Greenwich Pier, among others. Services run every 20 to 30 minutes for most of the day; journey time from Embankment to Greenwich is 35 minutes. An adult single costs £5.50, £5 with an Oyster Card, £3.70 if you hold a valid Travelcard, and £2.80 for children aged 5 to 15. A **River Roamer,** allowing unlimited travel on Thames Clippers between 9am and 9pm, costs £12.60, £8.40 for Travelcard holders, and £6.30 for children. A Family River Roamer costs £26.50. Buy online, on board, or at any of the piers. There's also a separate **Tate-to-Tate** service that connects Tate Modern, in Bankside, with Tate Britain, in Pimlico. Tickets cost £5 and boats depart each end at least hourly, all day between 10am and 5pm (p. 143). The Thames Clippers iPhone app makes comprehensive timetables available offline. Pay at the ticket office with your Oyster Card and you receive a 10% discount off all Thames Clippers fares.

For trips upriver to Hampton Court and Kew, see "River Cruises on the Thames," p. 424.

Narrowboat trips on London's **canals,** especially the Regent's Canal, are also a good way of touring less-visited corners of the city. Bus no. 6 takes you to Little Venice, where you can board several tour boats. One of the best is *Jason,* which takes you on a 90-minute round-trip ride past London Zoo to Camden Lock. The season runs April to early November, with daily trips at 10:30am, 12:30pm, and 2:30pm (also 4:30pm June through August). The round-trip fare is £9 for adults, £8 for seniors and children aged 4 to 13, free for children

3 and under. Contact **Jason's,** Jason's Wharf, Westbourne Terrace Road Bridge opposite 42 Blomfield Rd., Little Venice, W9 (www.jasons.co.uk; ✆ **020/7286-3428;** Tube: Warwick Ave.).

By Bike

The **Barclays Cycle Hire scheme** (www.tfl.gov.uk/barclayscyclehire) was launched with a fanfare in 2010. Anyone can rent a so-called "Boris Bike"—jocularly named after mayor at the time, Boris Johnson—from any of the hundreds of docking stations dotted around the center, at all points of the compass from Bow and Hackney to Olympia, and Regent's Park to the Oval. There's no need to return the bike to the docking station you collected it from, making the scheme ideal for short-range tourism. Charges are made up of a fixed access fee—£1 per day or £5 per week—and a usage fee—it's free to rent a bike for 30 minutes, £1 for an hour, £6 for 2 hours, £15 for 3 hours. Buy access with a credit or debit card at the docking station or join online. Regular visitors to the city should consider annual membership, which provides a quick-access key (£3), and allows you to run an account balance online. Bikes are suited to anyone aged 14 or over.

Follow London on Twitter

@secret_london
@glplondon
@TelegraphLondon
@ldn
@londonist
@qypedoeslondon
@visitlondonweb

For longer-term rental and better equipment, try **On Your Bike,** 52–54 Tooley St., SE1 (www.onyourbike.com; ✆ **020/7378-6669;** Tube: London Bridge), open Monday to Friday 7:30am to 7:30pm, Saturday 10am to 6pm, and Sunday 11am to 5pm. Hybrid bikes, with high seats and low-slung handlebars, cost £18 for the first day and £10 for each day thereafter, or £45 per week, and require a deposit on a credit card.

You should always ride London's roads with extreme care. Most importantly, never under-take a large vehicle close to a junction or corner. For touring London and its environs by bike, see p. 425 and **www.tfl.gov.uk/cycling**.

On Foot

London comes in two sizes: Greater London, which is huge—28 miles north to south, 35 miles east to west—and central London, which isn't big at all. Touring on foot is the best and cheapest way to get to know the smaller version. (And was the method used by quintessential Londoner Charles Dickens to get familiar with his city: He walked everywhere, even as far as Rochester, in Kent.) Do note, however, that London was created piecemeal over many centuries. The city's layout adheres to no grid or plan, and it's very easy to get lost. Arm yourself with a copy of London's iconic street atlas, the *London A–Z* (£6.95), on sale everywhere, or a smartphone with your favorite map app locked on open—though be aware that some map apps require a live web connection and are extremely data-hungry.

For organized **walking tours** of many fascinating areas, see p. 426.

TOURS & SPECIAL-INTEREST TRIPS

River Cruises on the Thames

A trip on the river gives you an entirely different view of London. You'll see how the city grew along and around the Thames, and how many of its landmarks turn toward the water. The Thames was London's first highway.

Thames River Services, Westminster Pier, Victoria Embankment, SW1 (www.westminsterpier.co.uk; ☎ 020/7930-4097; Tube: Westminster), concerns itself with downriver traffic from Westminster Pier to such destinations as Greenwich, St. Katharine's Dock, and the Thames Barrier. The most popular excursion departs for Greenwich (a 50-min. ride) at half-hour intervals between 10am and 4pm daily in April, May, September, and October, and between 10am and 5pm from June to August; from November to March, boats depart from Westminster Pier at 40-minute intervals daily from 10:20am to 3:30pm. One-way fares are £10 for adults and £5 for children 15 and under. Round-trip fares are £13 for adults, £6.50 for children. A family ticket costs £33.50 round-trip. There's no service on December 24, 25, and 26, or January 1. **City Cruises** (www.citycruises.com; ☎ 020/77-400400) operates a near-identical service at similar prices from the same pier.

A perfectly fine and cheaper, if slightly more functional, option for downriver trips from Embankment Pier to the London Eye, Bankside, the Tower of London, Canary Wharf, and/or Greenwich are the regular, fast water-borne commuter services operated by **Thames Clippers ★**. One-day, unlimited travel roamer passes are available. For details, see p. 422.

Westminster Passenger Service Association (www.wpsa.co.uk; ☎ 020/7930-2062; Tube: Westminster), which also uses Westminster Pier, offers the only riverboat service upstream to Kew, Richmond, and Hampton Court, with regular daily sailings from just before Easter until the end of October on traditional riverboats with licensed bars. Trip time, one-way, can be as little as 1½ hours to Kew and between 2½ and 4 hours to Hampton Court, depending on the tide. Round-trip tickets to Hampton Court are £22.50 for adults, £15 for seniors, £11.25 for children aged 4 to 14, and £56.25 for a family ticket; one child 3 or younger accompanied by an adult goes free. Round-trip tickets to Kew cost £18, £12, £9, and £45, respectively. Travelcard holders are entitled to a third off quoted ticket prices.

Bus Tours

For the bewildered first-timer, the quickest way to bring London into focus is probably to take a bus tour—but it isn't cheap. The **Original London Sightseeing Tour** passes by many of the major sights in a couple of hours or so, depending on traffic. The tour—that uses a traditional double-decker bus with live commentary by a guide—costs £26 for adults, £13 for children aged 5 to 15, free for those 4 and younger. A family ticket costs £91 and includes up to 3 children. The ticket, valid for 48 hours, allows you to hop on or off the bus at any point on any of three different circuits around the city. Your ticket also entitles you to a free riverboat ride with City Cruises (see above) and a choice of free 90-minute walking tours.

Tickets can be purchased on the bus or at any of the five start-points—Marble Arch, Trafalgar Square, Woburn Place, Piccadilly Circus, or Grosvenor Gardens—and from the **Original London Visitor Centre,** 17–19 Cockspur St., Trafalgar Square, SW1 (📞 **020/7389-5040;** Tube: Charing Cross). Many hotel concierges and Travel Information Centres (see "Visitor Information," p. 441) also sell tickets. For information or phone purchases, call 📞 **020/8877-1722.** It's also possible to book online at **www.theoriginaltour.com.** Do so ahead of time, especially in low season, and you may secure significant discounts on the prices quoted above.

Big Bus Tours, 48 Buckingham Palace Rd., SW1 (www.bigbustours.com; 📞 **020/7233-9533;** Tube: Victoria), operates a similar 2-hour tour, departing frequently between 8:30am and 4:30pm daily from 40 or so points around the center. The cost is £27 for adults, £12 for children aged 5 to 15; a family ticket (two adults with two children) is £66. Tickets are valid for 48 hours; you can hop on and off the bus as you wish. As with the Original London Tour, a river cruise and a choice of guided walks are included in your ticket price.

A much cheaper alternative is to seek out the two remaining London bus lines where old-fashioned **Routemaster ★** double-decker buses still operate. Only route **9**—which skirts Hyde Park and Green Park, and halts at Piccadilly Circus and Trafalgar Square—and route **15**—linking Monument and St. Paul's with Trafalgar Square and Regent Street—offer this "heritage" service. Although you can't hop on and off at will—unless you've bought a Travelcard (see "Getting Around," p. 417)—you can enjoy your own self-guided London bus tour for £1.35 per person.

For more on navigating London's bus network, see "Getting Around," p. 417.

Cycle Tours

If you prefer two wheels to four, the **London Bicycle Tour Company** (www.londonbicycle.com; 📞 **020/7928-6838**) guides groups around six separate circuits of the capital, originating from its base at Gabriel's Wharf, on the South Bank. The Central London Tour costs £16.95 and takes approximately 2½ hours, passing Buckingham Palace, Westminster Abbey, and St. Paul's Cathedral en route. It leaves daily at 10:30am; tours of the Royal West and East London run weekends only, and cost £19.95 for the longer, 3½-hour circuits. Between November and March booking ahead is essential. New tours added in 2012 include the Night Tour (Sat only; booking essential) and a 2½-hour West End tour (daily, in summer only). Hybrid bike and helmet rental is included in all tour prices.

 Save Money on Standard Tour Prices

For many of the cycle tours, bus tours, and walking tours we recommend—and a unique 1-hour tour of the city by Mini Cooper (£99 per car with up to 3 passengers) run by **Small Car Big City** (www.smallcarbigcity.com; 📞 **020/75850-399**)—it's worth checking with agent **Discount London** (www.discount-london.com; 📞 **020/8295-8383**) for savings on headline prices.

Fat Tire Bike Tours (www.fattirebiketours.com/London; ☏ **0788/2338-779**) offer a 4-hour tour of Royal London (£20, £18 students) originating from Queensway Tube station, and a 5-hour River Thames Tour (£30) starting from Waterloo Road, on the South Bank. Both offer plenty of guiding as well as cycling, and you're advised to book ahead of time; you can cancel in case of bad weather. Bike rental is included in the price—at a reduced rate for children, for whom the Royal London Tour is ideally suited.

Walking Tours

London Walks ★ (www.walks.com; ☏ **020/7624-3978**) is the oldest established walking-tour company in London—and still offers the best range of guided walks, departing every day of the week from points around town. Their hallmarks are variety, value, reasonably sized groups (generally under 30), and—above all—superb guides. The renowned crime historian Donald Rumbelow leads the daily **Jack the Ripper walk** (www.jacktheripperwalk.com) on Sundays, and occasional Mondays, Tuesdays, and Fridays; gather outside Tower Hill station before 7:30pm. Other notable themed walks include "Shakespeare's and Dickens' London," "The Beatles Magical Mystery Tour," "Hidden London" and a selection of tours covering Harry Potter movie locations. Several walks run every day, and all cost £8 for adults, £6 for students and seniors; children 14 and younger go free. Check the website for a schedule, or consult the London walks leaflet that you'll find in almost every information center and hotel in London; no reservations are needed and walks last around 2 hours.

Context ★ (www.contexttravel.com; ☏ **020/3318-5637,** or 800/691-6036 in the U.S.) takes a more didactic approach to its walking program, with smaller groups led by engaging docents who are experts and scholars in their fields. Walks such as "London: Portrait of a City" are ideal for visitors who want to dig a little deeper. Prices range from £55 to £70 per person for walks of 2½ to 4 hours' duration. Both London Walks and Context can arrange private guides for individuals or small groups.

City Guides (www.cityoflondontouristguides.com) offers a small program of high-quality walking tours based in and around the Square Mile. Themes include "London's Burning," "Highlife-Lowlife: Stories of Fleet Street," and tours of individual historic sites such as All-Hallows-by-the-Tower Church. Prices range from free to £7 per walk.

Unseen Tours ★ (www.sockmobevents.org.uk; ☏ **07514/266-774**) runs guided walks of city neighborhoods led by homeless and former homeless residents. Guides with years of local knowledge garnered on the streets specialize in giving visitors a raw look at their city from a unique angle. Tours cost £8, and are packed with alternative history, anecdotes, and peeks into corners that are too easy to miss. They last 80 to 90 minutes and run Friday through Sunday on five different routes—around Shoreditch, Covent Garden, London Bridge, Brick Lane, and Mayfair. There's no need to book ahead, unless you're in a large group—just gather at the rendezvous points at the times specified on the website. Tours are probably not suited to young children.

For in-depth or group walks, also check out **London Detours** (www.londondetours.com; ☏ **07843/498-733**). Guides specialize in leading you away from the sights into neighborhoods such as Southwark, Greenwich, or the East End. Walks last around 4½ hours and cost £25 per person. You'll need to take

Tours & Special-Interest Trips

PLANNING YOUR TRIP

along an Oyster Card or Travelcard, because they incorporate occasional hops onto public transportation.

Special-Interest Tours & Experiences

If you want to see behind the scenes of the world's most famous broadcasting organization, **BBC Tours** ★ (www.bbc.co.uk/tours; ℂ **0370/901-1227** or **01732/ 427770**) leads group visits around Television Centre in White City, and the recently renovated Art Deco Broadcasting House in the West End. The former focuses on television and includes a visit to the BBC newsroom, while the latter is all about radio and takes in the famous BBC Radio Theatre and the chance to create your own short program. The tours are restricted to visitors aged from 9 and 12 upward, respectively. There's also an interactive Children's Tour aimed at accompanied youngsters aged 6 to 11. Little ones are able to see inside a real BBC dressing room, hang out on sets of well-known programs, and even make a short TV spot of their own. All tours last between 1½ and 2 hours and cost £9.95 for adults, £9.25 seniors, and £7.75 children. Family tickets for up to four people cost £30. There's something running most days of most weeks; book online or by telephone.

Football (soccer) fans may be interested in an all-areas tour of Arsenal's **Emirates Stadium** (www.arsenal.com/stadiumtours; ℂ **020/7619-5000**). Approximately 1-hour visits around the capital's finest club ground take in the dressing rooms, players' tunnel, and directors' boxes. Tours are self-guided and available between 10:15am and 3:45pm on most non-matchdays, and cost £17.50 for adults, £9 for children aged 5 to 15, and £42 for a family of four. Dedicated Arsenal fans should consider paying extra (£35/£18) to join a tour led by a club legend such as Charlie George or Lee Dixon. These generally run once per day, twice on weekends.

There are hundreds of English cheeses, and you can discover just a few of them at themed, tutored cheese tastings at **Neal's Yard Dairy** ★ (www.neals yarddairy.co.uk; ℂ **020/7500-7575**). "Classes" are sociable affairs, a mixture of flip-chart science and informative banter, and take place above this top cheese-monger's warehouse opposite Borough Market (p. 276). There's a range of themes, ranging from "Beer and Cheese" (a favorite of ours) and "Modern Traditionals" to "Cider and Cheese" and "England vs. Spain." Booking is essential; prices are usually £50 per person for a 2-hour evening session.

In fact, whatever your niche interest, you'll probably be able to locate an expert to show you how it's done London-style. **The Intelligence Trail** (www. theintelligencetrail.co.uk) runs espionage-themed tours around the city that are ideally suited to modern history and ephemera buffs. Tours cost £20 (less if you pay ahead of time online) and are not suitable for anyone aged 17 and under. **Dragon and Flagon** (www.londonpubtours.weebly.com; ℂ **020/8554-8803**) runs walking and drinking tours of the city's historic pubs. Tours cost £10 per adult. **Walk, Eat, Talk, Eat** (www.walktalkeat.com; ℂ **020/7426-0894**) leads foodie walks, packed with insider knowledge, in the eastern part of the city that cover brunch or lunch, last 2½ hours, and cost £30 to £40 including tastings. Chocolate lovers can take a cocoa-fueled walk around the master chocolatiers of Mayfair and Chelsea with **Chocolate Ecstasy Tours** (www.chocolateecstasy tours.com; ℂ **07981/809-536**). Daytime tours usually run at weekends, costing £40 to £45 for walks of around 3 hours that include tastings and discounts at some of the world's most creative chocolate stores. **Skylon Restaurant,** inside

the Royal Festival Hall (p. 308; www.skylon-restaurant.co.uk; ☎ **020/7654-7800**), runs monthly free cocktail-making classes open to anyone.

Whatever your specialism, there will be a qualified **Blue Badge Guide** to match. It's worth searching the directory of official professional guides at **www.blue-badge-guides.com**; you can book personalized full-day, half-day, or evening tours. An equally customizable, but less formal and less expensive alternative is provided by **Tripbod** (www.tripbod.com). This web-based service allows you to connect with a trusted local for one-to-one trip-planning advice before you leave home, or to accompany them on niche experiences while you're here. Prices start from £11. The website allows you to sift London Tripbods by a wide range of special interests. Experiences might include a real ale crawl around London pubs or jogging through the Royal Parks with a local.

As well as the tours recommended above, you could also check tour and experience aggregators like **Isango!** (www.isango.com), **Viator** (www.viator.com), and **Get Your Guide** (www.getyourguide.com).

Self-Guided Walks & Trails

There are a number of options that work well, alongside this guidebook, if you prefer to lead yourself around London. **Way2Go audioguides** (www.way2goguides.com) publishes mini-guides to areas or key sights, including Maritime Greenwich, the Tower of London, and the Royal Parks. Most are priced at £3 and last around 1 hour. Buy online and download to your MP3 player or smartphone. They are also available as iPhone apps.

Part guide, part game, **Treasure Trails** (www.treasuretrails.co.uk) are a fun, interactive, and educational way to see the city if you have kids in tow. They cost £6 and are available online, via mail order or as downloadable PDFs. Each trail takes around 2 hours to complete.

For our suggested self-guided walking routes through the city, see Chapter 3.

Voluntourism & Slow Travel

If you have an interest in giving something back, try volunteering while you're in London. Conservation charity **BTCV** (www.btcv.org/london; ☏ **020/7278-4294**) runs sessions improving the city's natural spaces. Many are part of its "Green Gym" program designed to keep you fit as you work on such projects as clearing ponds and coppicing woodland. Anyone can volunteer via the website, and it's free to take part. Sessions last a few hours and run most weeks. It's also worth keeping an eye on **Timebank** (www.timebank.org.uk). This online resource helps you match your location and availability with volunteering opportunities nearby—although most are more suited to a long stay or residency.

[FastFACTS] LONDON

Area Codes The country telephone code for Great Britain is **44.** The area code for London is **020.** The full telephone number is then usually 8-digits long. As a general rule, businesses and homes in central London have numbers beginning with a **7;** those from further out begin with an **8.** For more info, see "Telephones," later in this section.

Business Hours With many exceptions, business hours are Monday to Friday 9am to 5pm. In general, retail stores are open Monday to Saturday 9am to 6pm, Sunday 11am to 5pm (sometimes noon to 6pm). Thursday is often late-night opening for central retailers; until 8pm or later isn't unusual.

Car Rental See "Getting There," earlier in this chapter.

Cellphones See "Mobile Phones," later in this section.

Crime See "Safety," later in this section.

Customs **Non-E.U. nationals aged 17 and over** can bring in, duty free, 200 cigarettes, or 100 cigarillos, or 50 cigars, or 250 grams of smoking tobacco. You can also bring in 4 liters of wine and 16 liters of beer plus either 1 liter of alcohol more than 22% ("spirits"), or 2 liters of "fortified" wine at less than 22%. Visitors may also bring in other goods, including perfume, gifts, and souvenirs, totaling £390 in value. (Customs officials tend to be lenient about these general merchandise regulations, realizing the limits are unrealistically low.) For **arrivals from within the E.U.,** there are no limits as long as goods are for your own personal use, or are gifts.

For specifics on what you can take back home and the corresponding fees, U.S. citizens should download the free pamphlet *Know Before You Go* online at **www.cbp.gov.** Alternatively contact the **U.S. Customs & Border Protection (CBP),** 1300 Pennsylvania Ave. NW, Washington, D.C. 20229 (☏ **877/CBP-5511**). For a clear summary of their own rules, Canadians should consult the booklet *I Declare,* issued by the **Canada Border Services Agency** (www.cbsa-asfc.gc.ca; ☏ **800/461-9999** in Canada, or 204/983-3500). Australians need to read *Guide for Travellers: Know Before You Go.* For more information, call the **Australian Customs Service** at ☏ **1300/363-263,** or download the leaflet from **www.customs.gov. au/webdata/resources/files/GuideForTravellers.pdf.** For New Zealanders, most questions are answered under "Coming into NZ" at **www.customs.govt.nz.** For more information, contact the **New Zealand Customs Service** (☏ **0800/428-786,** or 09/927-8036).

Disabled Travelers Your first stop should be the "Accessible London" section of the **Visit London** website: **www.visitlondon.com/access.** You'll find links to details of accessible hotels and information about which parts of the transport network are adapted to

your needs. Many London hotels, museums, restaurants, buses, Tube stations, and sight-seeing attractions have dedicated wheelchair entry, and persons with disabilities are often granted admission discounts. For £1.50, iPhone users can download the **LDN Access app** (www.myukaccess.co.uk), which reviews the accessibility of hotels, restaurants, attractions, and more across the city.

The best U.K. organization to consult for trip-planning advice is **Tourism for All UK,** Shap Road Industrial Estate, Shap Rd., Kendal, Cumbria, LA9 6NZ (www.tourismforall.org. uk; ✆ **0303/303-0146;** from overseas +44(0)1539/814-683). The website also has an invaluable list of relevant organizations to contact for advice relating to specific chronic complaints. The **Royal Association for Disability Rights (RADAR),** 12 City Forum, 250 City Rd., London EC1V 8AF (www.radar.org.uk; ✆ **020/7250-3222**), publishes a number of handy written resources and, for a small fee, sells a key that opens over 8,000 locked public disabled toilets countrywide (£4 inc. UK P&P; £6 to anywhere in the world).

Annual guide **Open London** (£10.99) is the capital's largest directory of accessible accommodation and travel services. It's widely available in city bookstores, and at the usual online booksellers worldwide. RADAR's annual **Open Britain** (£13.99) guide covers the whole of the U.K. and Ireland, and has good London coverage; buy it online from the RADAR website (see above). Companion website **OpenBritain.net,** launched in 2011, has a handy search facility for accessible accommodation countrywide. A new edition of the occasional **Access in London** guidebook (£10–£15 donation, plus $15 delivery charge to the U.S.; www.accessinlondon.org), a publication listing facilities for the disabled, was published just before the London 2012 Olympic Games and Paralympic Games.

For public transportation assistance, **Transport for London** publishes a good deal of accessibility information; visit **www.tfl.gov.uk/accessguides** for the lowdown on stair-free Underground access, large-print and audio Tube maps, a Tube toilet map, and more. There's also a 24-hour assistance telephone line: ✆ **020/7222-1234.** London's official "black cab" taxis have interiors adapted to those in wheelchairs.

London's most helpful organization for information about access to theatres, cinemas, galleries, museums, and other arts venues is **Artsline,** 21 Pine Court, Wood Lodge Gardens, Bromley BR1 2WA (www.artsline.org.uk; ✆ **020/7388-2227**). Its website and directory offers free information about wheelchair access, theatres with hearing aids, and cinemas.

Doctors If you need a non-emergency doctor, your hotel can recommend one, or you can contact your embassy or consulate. Failing that, try the G.P. (General Practitioner) finder at **www.nhsdirect.nhs.uk**. North American members of the **International Association for Medical Assistance to Travelers (IAMAT;** www.iamat.org; ✆ **716/754-4883,** or 416/652-0137 in Canada) can consult that organization for lists of local approved doctors. **Note:** U.S. and Canadian visitors who become ill while they're in London are eligible only for free *emergency* care. For other treatment, including follow-up care, you'll pay. See "Insurance," below.

In any medical emergency, call ✆ **999,** or 112 immediately.

Drinking Laws The legal age for the purchase of alcohol is 18. Over-16s may have a glass of beer, wine, or cider with a meal in a pub or restaurant, if it is bought for them by a responsible adult. Children 15 and younger are allowed in pubs only if accompanied by a parent or guardian, but may not drink alcohol. Don't drink and drive: Penalties are stiff, not to mention the danger in which you're placing yourself and other road users. Drinking of alcohol on London's **public transport network** is forbidden, and on-the-spot fines are issued to transgressors.

Driving Rules   See "Getting Around," earlier in this chapter.

Electricity   British mains electricity operates at 240 volts AC (50 cycles), and most overseas plugs don't fit Britain's unique three-pronged wall outlets. Always bring suitable transformers and/or adapters such as world multiplugs—if you plug some American appliances directly into an electrical outlet without a transformer, for example, you'll destroy your appliance and possibly start a fire. Portable electronic devices such as iPods and mobile phones, however, recharge without problems via USB or using a multiplug.

Embassies & Consulates   The **U.S. Embassy** is at 24 Grosvenor Sq., London W1A 1AE (http://london.usembassy.gov; ✆ **020/7499-9000;** Tube: Bond St.). Standard hours are Monday to Friday 8:30am to 5:30pm. However, for passport and visa services relating to U.S. citizens, contact the **Passport and Citizenship Unit,** 55–56 Upper Brook St., London W1A 2LQ (phone number as above, but the preferred method is email: londonpassports@state.gov). Most non-emergency inquiries require an appointment.

The **High Commission of Canada,** Canada House, 1 Trafalgar Sq., London SW1Y 5BJ (www.canadainternational.gc.ca/united_kingdom-royaume_uni/index.aspx; ✆ **020/7258-6600;** Tube: Charing Cross), handles passport and consular services for Canadians. Hours are Monday to Friday 9:30am to 1pm.

The **Australian High Commission** is at Australia House, Strand, London WC2B 4LA (www.uk.embassy.gov.au; ✆ **020/7887-5776;** Tube: Covent Garden or Temple). Hours are Monday to Friday 9am to 5pm.

The **New Zealand High Commission** is at New Zealand House, 80 Haymarket (at Pall Mall), London SW1Y 4TQ (www.nzembassy.com/uk; ✆ **020/7930-8422;** Tube: Charing Cross or Piccadilly Circus). Hours are Monday to Friday 9am to 5pm.

The **Irish Embassy** is at 17 Grosvenor Place, London SW1X 7HR (www.embassyofireland.co.uk; ✆ **020/7235-2171;** Tube: Hyde Park Corner). Hours are Monday to Friday 9:30am to 5pm.

Emergencies   Dial ✆ **999** for police, fire, or ambulance. Give your name and state the nature of the emergency. Dialing ✆ **112** also connects you to the local emergency services anywhere in the E.U.

Family Travel   Before you go, help your children check out the excellent **Kids Love London** directory and ideas bank, at **www.kidslovelondon.com**. It was created by the city's tourist board to give family travelers the lowdown on the city's child-friendly attractions and events. Most museums, for example, have quizzes, events, or entertaining resources for youngsters of any age, and most of the key venues are part of the Kids in Museums program (see **www.kidsinmuseums.org.uk**). We've selected London's best under "Especially for Kids" on p. 183.

Most London accommodations can provide a crib (or "cot") on request, and if you're renting a car, children under 12 and under 1.35m (4½ ft.) in height must ride in an appropriate car seat. Consult your car rental company in advance of arrival, but it's the driver's legal responsibility to ensure all child passengers comply (see **www.childcarseats.org.uk/law** for details). You'll also find babysitting available at most hotels; inquire at the concierge or reception desk. For any length of stay, you can rent baby equipment from **Chelsea Baby Hire,** 31 Osborne House, 414 Wimbledon Park Rd., SW19 6PW (www.chelseababyhire.com; ✆ **07802/846-742**).

To locate those hotels, restaurants, and attractions that are particularly child-friendly, refer to the "Kids" icon 😊 throughout this guide. Our favorite family-friendly restaurants are covered from p. 254. Hotel best bets for families are selected on p. 337. London's top

places to buy toys and games are covered on p. 297; and London's most child-friendly attractions are listed in Chapter 4. For even wider coverage, *Frommer's London with Kids* (£13.99/$17.99) is the best specialist guidebook for family travelers to the city. For a list of more family-friendly travel resources, turn to the experts at **Frommers.com**.

Gasoline/Petrol   Please see "Getting Around," earlier in this chapter.

Health   Traveling to London doesn't pose any specific health risks. Common drugs sold throughout the Western world are generally available over the pharmacy counter and in large supermarkets, although visitors from overseas should note the generic rather than brand names of any medicines they rely on. If you're flying into London, pack **prescription medications** in carry-on luggage and carry prescription medications in their original containers, with pharmacy labels—otherwise they won't make it through airport security. Also bring along copies of your prescriptions, in case you lose your pills or run out. Don't forget an extra pair of contact lenses or prescription glasses. The general purpose painkiller known in North America as acetaminophen is called **paracetamol** in the U.K.

Hospitals   There are 24-hour, walk-in Accident & Emergency departments at the following central hospitals: **University College London Hospital,** 235 Euston Rd., London NW1 2BU (www.uclh.nhs.uk; ☏ **020/3456-7890;** Tube: Warren St.); **St. Thomas' Hospital,** Westminster Bridge Rd. (entrance on Lambeth Palace Rd.), London SE1 7EH (www. guysandstthomas.nhs.uk; ☏ **020/7188-7188;** Tube: Westminster or Waterloo). The **NHS Choices** website (www.nhs.uk) has a search facility that enables you to locate your nearest Accident & Emergency department wherever you are in the U.K. In a medical emergency, you should dial ☏ **999.** Note that emergency care is free for all visitors, irrespective of country of origin.

Insurance   **U.K. nationals** receive free medical treatment countrywide, but visitors from overseas only qualify automatically for free **emergency** care. **U.S. visitors** should note that most domestic health plans (including Medicare and Medicaid) do not provide coverage, and the ones that do often require you to pay for services upfront and reimburse you only after you return home. Among many options, you could try **MEDEX** (www.medexassist. com; ☏ **410/453-6380**) or **Travel Assistance International** (www.travelassistance.com; ☏ **800/821-2828**) for overseas medical insurance cover. **Canadians** should check with their provincial health plan offices or call **Health Canada** (www.hc-sc.gc.ca; ☏ **866/225-0709**) to find out the extent of their coverage and what documentation and receipts they must take home in case they are treated overseas. **E.U. nationals** (and nationals of E.E.A. countries and Switzerland) should note that reciprocal health agreements are in place to ensure they receive free medical care while in the U.K. However, it is essential that visitors from those countries carry a valid **European Health Identity Card** (EHIC). At the time of writing, there are bilateral agreements in place offering free healthcare to nationals of **New Zealand.** However, you should always double-check the latest situation before leaving home, with domestic health authorities or online at **www.dh.gov.uk/OverseasVisitors**.

For information on general traveler's insurance, trip cancellation insurance, and medical insurance while traveling, please visit **www.frommers.com/planning**.

Internet & Wi-Fi   The availability of the Internet in London is in a constant state of development. How you access it depends on whether you've brought your own computer or smartphone, or you're relying on public terminals. Many hotels have computers for guest use, although pricing can vary from gratis to extortionate. To find a local Internet cafe, start by checking **www.cybercaptive.com**. Although such places have suffered due to the spread of smartphones and free Wi-Fi (see below), they do tend to be prevalent close to centers of cheap, backpacker-focused accommodations, such as Victoria,

Paddington, and Earl's Court. Aside from formal cybercafes, most **hostels** have Internet access, and some **public libraries** allow nonresidents to use terminals.

If you have your own computer or smartphone, **Wi-Fi** makes access much easier. Always check before using your hotel's network—many charge exorbitant rates, and free or cheap Wi-Fi isn't hard to find elsewhere. There's an erratically updated list and map of free hotspots at **http://londonist.com/2007/05/free_wifi_in_lo.php**—many are in coffee shops where you'll be expected to buy something small, but you won't raise an eyebrow if you walk into either of the city's two Apple Stores to log on (235 Regent St., near Oxford Circus; and 1–7 The Piazza, Covent Garden). That map has also morphed into the **Free Wifi London** iPhone app, available for £1.19/$1.99 from the iTunes Store. Chains like J. D. Wetherspoon (pubs), Starbucks, and McDonalds are other safe bets, as are many museum cafes. **WorkSnug** (www.worksnug.com) is another great—and free—multiplatform mobile app that helps you locate a Wi-Fi-equipped mobile workspace in the city.

In 2011, **Nokia** launched 26 free Wi-Fi hotspots around the city, most clustered close to tourist magnets like Oxford Street, busy Tube stations, and mainline rail terminals like St. Pancras and Liverpool Street. In 2012, **O2** threw its hat into the ring, with a promise to trial then roll out a massive free Wi-Fi zone across the boroughs of Westminster, and Kensington and Chelsea—an area that takes in the West End and Knightsbridge, too. **TfL** announced a 2012 rollout of below-ground Wi-Fi at between 80 and 120 Tube stations, provided by cable company Virgin Media on a pay-as-you-surf basis. Travelers on the London Overground network will be entitled to 1 hour's free internet each day at 56 rail stations via The Cloud. To locate more free Wi-Fi, it's also worth using the hotspot locator at www.jiwire.com.

Savvy smartphone users from overseas may even find it cheaper and practical to switch off 3G altogether and call using freely available Wi-Fi in combination with a **Skype** (www.skype.com) account and mobile app.

Legal Aid   If you're visiting from overseas and find yourself in legal trouble, contact your consulate or embassy (see "Embassies & Consulates," above). They can advise you of your rights and will usually provide a list of local attorneys (for which you'll have to pay if services are used), but they cannot interfere on your behalf in the English legal process. For questions about American citizens who are arrested abroad, including ways of getting money to them, telephone the **Citizens Emergency Center** of the Office of Special Consular Services in Washington, D.C. (☎ **202/647-5225**).

If you're in some sort of substance abuse emergency, call **Release** (www.release.org. uk; ☎ **0845/4500-215**); the advice line is open Monday to Friday 11am to 1pm and 2 to 4pm. The **Rape and Sexual Abuse Support Centre** (www.rapecrisis.org.uk; ☎ **0808/802-9999**) is open daily noon to 2:30pm and 7 to 9:30pm.

LGBT Travelers   London has one of the most active gay and lesbian scenes in the world. Gay bars, restaurants, and gatherings are plentiful, and a general anything-goes acceptance largely characterizes the London social scene, especially in and around Soho (Old Compton Street is considered the entertainment epicenter of gay London, although Shoreditch and Vauxhall aren't far behind; see p. 328 for the best of the gay nightlife scene). The **Lesbian and Gay Switchboard** (www.llgs.org.uk; ☎ **0300/330-0630**) is open 10am to 11pm daily, providing information about gay-related activities in London and general advice. Their searchable online database (www.turingnetwork.org.uk) lists gay bars, clubs, and other services countrywide. Homophobic crime is rare—but unfortunately not unknown—in London. You should take the usual commonsense precautions; see "Safety," below.

London's best gay-oriented bookstore is **Gay's the Word,** 66 Marchmont St. (www.
gaystheword.co.uk; ☏ **020/7278-7654;** Tube: Russell Sq.). The staff is friendly and helpful
and will offer advice about the ever-changing scene in the city. It's open Monday through
Saturday from 10am to 6:30pm and Sunday from 2 to 6pm. Local news about gay and
lesbian issues is provided by a number of reliable sources, including the **Pink Paper**
(www.pinkpaper.com) and **Pink News** (www.pinknews.co.uk). Monthly magazine *Out in
the City* (www.outmag.co.uk) bills itself as the ultimate guide to gay London, and weekly
listings magazine *Time Out* (www.timeout.com/london/gay) runs substantial LGBT events
and nightlife coverage. July's **Pride London** march and festival (www.pridelondon.org;
☏ **0844/884-2439**) is the highlight of London's LGBT calendar. Manchester-based **Gaydio**
(www.gaydio.co.uk) was the U.K.'s first dedicated radio station for lesbian, gay, bisexual,
and trans listeners.

For more gay and lesbian travel resources, visit **Frommers.com**.

Mail   An airmail letter to anywhere outside Europe costs 76p for up to 10g (⅓ oz.) and
generally takes 5 to 7 working days to arrive; postcards also require a 76p stamp. Within
the E.U., letters or postcards under 20g (⅔ oz.) cost 68p. Within the U.K., First Class mail
ought to arrive the following working day; Second Class mail takes around 3 days.

Medical Requirements   Unless you're arriving from an area known to be suffering
from an epidemic (particularly cholera or yellow fever), inoculations or vaccinations are not
required for entry into the U.K. Also see "Health," above.

Mobile Phones   The three letters that define much of the world's wireless capabilities
are **GSM** (Global System for Mobiles), a satellite network that makes for easy cross-border
mobile (cell) phone use throughout most of the planet, including the U.K. If you own an
unlocked GSM phone, pack it in your hand luggage and pick up a contract-free **SIM-only
tariff** when you arrive in the U.K. The SIM card will cost very little, but you will need to
load it up with credit to make calls. Tariffs change constantly in response to the market, but
in general expect call charges of around 20p per minute, 10p for a text message, and a
deal on data that might allow 500MB in a month for about £5. There are phone and SIM
card retailers on practically every major city street, but not everywhere will sell SIM-only
deals to nonresidents. Larger branches of supermarket Tesco sell **Tesco Mobile** (www.
tescomobile.com) SIMs for 99p that you can top-up in-store with cash or an overseas
credit card. Find a convenient branch at **www.tesco.com/storelocator**. **Three** (www.
three.co.uk) offers SIMs for £11.99, with £10 of credit preloaded, which you can top-up
further at Three stores, supermarkets, and newsagents across the city. Three SIMs work
only in 3G-compatible phones.

There are other options if you're visiting from overseas but don't own an unlocked
GSM phone. For a short visit, **renting** a phone may be a good idea, and we suggest renting the handset before you leave home. North Americans can rent from **InTouch USA**
(www.intouchusa.us; ☏ **800/872-7626** or 703/222-7161) or **BrightRoam** (www.bright
roam.com; ☏ **888/622-3393**). However, handset purchase prices have fallen to a level
where you can probably buy a basic U.K. **pay-as-you-go (PAYG) phone** for less than one
week's handset rental. Prices at the city's many cellphone retailers start from under £20 for
a cheap model, and you can find a basic Android smartphone for around £50. Expect
outgoing call charges of approximately 25p per minute to anywhere in the U.K., 10p for
text messages (SMS); receiving calls on your local number is free. **Carphone Warehouse**
(www.carphonewarehouse.com) has retail branches across the city and a reliable range of
cheap PAYG phones. Buy one, use it while you're here, and recycle it on the way home.

There are several U.K. networks offering a bewildering array of tariffs. Best for reliable
citywide voice and 3G reception are probably **O2** (www.o2.co.uk)—whose cell network is

also used by Tesco Mobile—and **Vodafone** (www.vodafone.co.uk). **Orange** (www.orange.co.uk) tends to offer slightly better-value tariffs, while **Three** (www.three.co.uk) usually has the best deals for smartphone users who want data included in their rate. Unfortunately, per-minute charges for international calls can be high whatever network you choose, so if you plan to do a lot of calling home use a VoIP service such as **Skype** (www.skype.com) in conjunction with a Web connection. See "Internet & Wi-Fi," above.

If you intend to use your mobile phone *solely* to call overseas, and it's unlocked and GSM-compatible, you may find purchasing a specialist **international SIM card** to be the most convenient option. Calls to the U.S., for example, using a SIM card from either **Lyca** (www.lycamobile.co.uk; ☎ **020/7132-0322**) or **Lebara** (www.lebara-mobile.co.uk; ☎ **0870/075-5588** or 020/7031-0791) cost 5p per minute to both landlines and cellphones. You can buy either at independent phone retailers on practically every city street, and can top-up both brands with vouchers on sale at branches of Tesco, Sainsbury's, the Post Office, and small retailers citywide.

For advice on making **international calls,** see "Telephones," later in this section.

Money & Costs

THE VALUE OF THE BRITISH POUND VS. OTHER POPULAR CURRENCIES

UK£	Aus$	Can$	Euro (€)	NZ$	US$
£1	A$1.47	C$1.57	€1.21	NZ$1.89	$1.58

Frommer's lists exact prices in the local currency. The currency conversions quoted above were correct at press time. However, rates fluctuate, so before departing consult a currency exchange website such as **www.oanda.com/currency/converter** to check up-to-the-minute rates. There's also a smartphone app available for pretty much any mobile device; see **www.oanda.com/mobile**.

London is the most expensive city in Britain, but perceptions of value for overseas visitors are at the mercy of exchange rate fluctuations. London is not as expensive as Tokyo or Oslo, that's for sure, but even an average hotel room can cost £100 a night or more—in many cases, much, much more. While certain items might seem extortionate to an experienced European traveler—such as a cup of coffee, a pizza, or a Tube fare—everyday clothes cost less than in many Continental capitals. Mobile phone charges will seem inexpensive to a visitor from North America, but the same person will shudder at the price of a pair of branded sneakers or an iPod. But with entrance to state museums costing nothing at all, London has more high culture for your buck than anywhere in the world.

ATMs are everywhere in London—at banks, some fuel stations, many supermarkets, and post offices. (Watch out for those inside small shops, however, as they charge users for withdrawing money.) These "cash machines" or "cashpoints" are the easiest way to get cash away from home. The **Cirrus** (www.mastercard.com) and **PLUS** (www.visa.com) networks span the globe; look at the back of your bank card to see which network you're on, and then check online for ATM locations at your destination if you want to be ultra-organized. Be sure you know your personal identification number (PIN) and daily withdrawal limit before you depart. Note that UK machines use **4-digit PINs,** so if your bank issues a 6-digit number, contact them before you leave home. Credit cards are accepted just about everywhere, save street markets and tiny independent retailers or street-food vendors.

	UK£
Taxi from Heathrow to central London	65.00–85.00
Underground from Heathrow to Piccadilly Circus using Oyster Card, off-peak	2.90
Double room at Claridge's (very expensive)	360.00
Double room at the Main House (moderate)	130.00
Double room at Avo (inexpensive)	90.00
Lunch for one at Petersham Nurseries Café (expensive)	25.00
Lunch for one at Ottolenghi (inexpensive)	11.00
Dinner for one, without wine, at Alain Ducasse (very expensive)	78.00
Dinner for one, without wine, at Pollen Street Social (moderate)	26.00
Dinner for one, without wine, at Mangal (inexpensive)	13.00
Pint of beer	3.00–4.00
Cup of coffee	1.80–2.50
Admission to national/state museums	Free
Movie ticket	8.00–12.00
Theatre ticket	25.00–85.00

10

However, North American visitors should note that **American Express** is accepted far less widely than at home. To be sure of your credit line, bring a Visa or MasterCard as well.

Britain has been among the world's most aggressive countries in the fight against credit card fraud. As a result, almost everywhere in London has moved from the magnetic strip credit card to the new system of **Chip and PIN** ("smartcards" with chips embedded in them). Most retailers ask for your 4-digit PIN to be entered into a keypad near the cash register. In restaurants, a waiter usually brings a hand-held device to your table to authorize payment. If you're visiting from a country where Chip and PIN is less prevalent (such as the U.S.), it's possible that some retailers will be reluctant to accept your (to Brits, old-fashioned) swipe cards. Be prepared to argue your case: Swipe cards are still legal and the same machines that read the smartcard chips can also read your magnetic strip. However, do carry some cash with you too, just in case.

For help with currency conversions, tip calculations, and more, download Frommer's convenient Travel Tools app for your mobile device. Go to **www.frommers.com/go/mobile** and click on the Travel Tools icon.

Newspapers & Magazines

Londoners love to consume news and views, and the city's "local" daily newspapers are both now free. *Metro* appears first-thing in the morning (weekdays only), and is distributed at Tube and train stations across the capital. The *Evening Standard*, long considered a quasi-national paper thanks to its berth close to the heart of government, is also now free, and appears on the streets in constantly updated editions from lunchtime onward, 5 days a week.

London is also the home of Britain's national papers (and most of their journalists), and all the quality press covers London news and events well. *The Times* and the

Daily Telegraph generally lean to the right of the political spectrum; the *Guardian* and *Independent* are to the left. All also issue Sunday editions: The *Sunday Times, Sunday Telegraph, Observer,* and *Independent on Sunday,* respectively. You'll find newspapers and magazines in newsagents, supermarkets, petrol stations, and street kiosks across the city. Most sizable central London newsagents also carry papers and publications from across the globe.

For coverage of what's on, *Time Out* is the capital's go-to weekly listings magazine. Zeitgeist-laden *Shortlist* magazine is distributed free at main transport hubs on a Wednesday. Alternatively, turn to the Web for offbeat events and news. The best of the sites is **Londonist** (www.londonist.com).

Packing   British weather is notoriously fickle, and so although it rains in London much less than in the rest of the British Isles—and nowhere close to the levels Britain's almost mythical reputation would have you believe, less than it does in Rome or Sydney in fact—only the foolhardy traveler heads to the U.K. without some rainwear, even in high summer. On the plus side, winter temperatures rarely stay below freezing for long, and summers can be intermittently muggy but nothing like as hot and humid as southern Europe or the U.S.

Whether you need to bring formal eveningwear depends on where you plan to stay and (especially) dine. Traditional, upscale West End restaurants still largely expect you to arrive in a collared shirt, non-denim trousers, and "proper" shoes—and the equivalent attire for women. Any eatery with a contemporary edge, and any eatery period in the funkier East of the city, will welcome you as you are, even if that means jeans and sneakers. For more helpful information on packing for your trip, download our convenient Travel Tools app for your mobile device. Go to **www.frommers.com/go/mobile** and click on the Travel Tools icon.

Passports   To enter the United Kingdom, all U.S. citizens, Canadians, Australians, New Zealanders, and South Africans must have a passport valid through their length of stay. No visa is required. A passport will allow you to stay in the country for up to 6 months. The immigration officer may also want to see proof of your intention to return to your point of origin (usually a round-trip ticket) and of visible means of support while you're in Britain. If you're planning to fly from the United States or Canada to the United Kingdom and then on to a country that requires a visa (India, for example), you should secure that visa before you arrive in Britain.

Passport Offices

o   **Australia   Australian Passport Information Service** (www.passports.gov.au or ℭ **131-232**).

o   **Canada   Passport Canada,** Department of Foreign Affairs and International Trade, Gatineau, QC K1A 1L2 (www.ppt.gc.ca; ℭ **800/567-6868**).

o   **New Zealand   Passport Office,** Department of Internal Affairs, P.O. Box 1658, Wellington, 6140 (www.passports.govt.nz; ℭ **0800/22-50-50** in New Zealand or 04/463-9360).

o   **United States**   To find your regional passport office, check the U.S. State Department website (travel.state.gov/passport) or call the **National Passport Information Center** (ℭ **877/487-2778**) for automated information.

Petrol   Please see "Getting Around: By Car," earlier in this chapter.

Police   London has two official police forces: The City of London police (www.cityoflondon.police.uk) whose remit covers the "Square Mile" and its 8,600 residents; and the Metropolitan Police ("the Met"), which covers the rest of the capital and is split into separate borough commands for operational purposes. Opening hours for all the Met's local

police stations are listed at **www.met.police.uk/local**. In a non-emergency, you can contact your local police station from anywhere by dialing ☎ **101.** Losses, thefts, and other criminal matters should be reported at the nearest police station immediately. You will be given a crime number, which your travel insurer will request if you make a claim against any losses. Always dial ☎ **999** or 112 if the matter is serious.

Safety   London has its share of crime, but in general it's one of the safest big cities in the world for travelers. Pickpockets are a concern, especially along busy shopping streets such as Oxford Street and on rush-hour Tube trains, although violent crime is relatively rare in the center. The east of the city has a grittier edge, especially at night; however, it's generally safe, too. If you're in any doubt, ask the bar or restaurant you're leaving to phone you a minicab—never get into an unlicensed minicab touting on the street alone, especially if you're a solo female. In addition, it is of course unwise to go walking in any empty park at night. Conceal your wallet or hold onto your purse, and don't flaunt jewelry or cash. Electronic devices including smartphones and iPods are another obvious target. In short, it's the same advice you'd follow in your hometown or native city.

Trafalgar Square and Parliament Square are usually the focal points for British political protest, and the casual visitor is advised to stay out of the Whitehall area during any demonstrations. However, only very occasionally does such protest turn violent, so if you stumble into something unexpected, there's probably no cause for alarm.

In general, the city's residents practice greater tolerance than in most parts of the world. "Live and let live" is pretty much the Londoner's maxim. As a visitor, you're very unlikely to experience overt racial, ethnic, or religious discrimination, or that based on sexual preference. However, London is by no means some cuddly, tolerant nirvana: You'll know discrimination if you experience it, so take your usual action to deal with it. It is **illegal** for any business offering goods, facilities, or services to discriminate against you because of your race, your religion, or your sexuality.

Traffic is your greatest mortal danger in the city center. Be careful crossing all roads, and be on your lookout for bikes, mopeds, delivery trucks, cars, buses, even rollerbladers when you step onto the road.

Senior Travel   London offers lots of discounts to senior visitors—those aged 60 or over. Many of the attractions recommended in this book list a separate, reduced entrance fee for seniors. However, even if discounts aren't posted, ask if they're available. Make sure you carry some kind of identification that shows your date of birth. Also, mention you're a senior when you make accommodation reservations. Some hotels offer seniors discounts—but if you do not ask, they probably won't offer.

Free journeys on the Tube are offered only to resident, over-60 Londoners armed with a Freedom Pass, but if you hold a **National Concessionary Pass** for bus travel from any local authority in England, it also entitles you to free bus travel in the capital. Show the driver when you board.

For overseas visitors, if you're continuing your journey beyond London, **BritRail** (see www.britrail.com) offers seniors discounted rates on some rail passes around Britain. If you're heading to London from the U.S., members of **AARP,** 601 E St. NW, Washington, D.C. 20049 (www.aarp.org; ☎ **888/687-2277**), can secure discounts on hotels, airfares, and car rentals. Anyone 50 or older can join.

Smoking   On July 1, 2007, smoking was banned in all indoor public places, such as pubs, restaurants, and clubs, across England and Wales. The regulations are almost universally observed and strictly enforced. If you wish to smoke, you will usually find temporary companions huddled close to the entrance door. Some pubs lay on a designated outdoor smoking area, and smoking is allowed in beer gardens and on outdoor terraces in bars.

Student Travel   Never leave home without your student I.D. card. Visitors from overseas should arm themselves with an **International Student Identity Card (ISIC),** which
offers local savings on rail passes, plane tickets, entrance fees, and more. Each country's
card offers slightly different benefits (in the U.S., for example, it provides you with basic
health and life insurance and a 24-hour helpline). Apply before departing in your country
of origin: in the U.S. or Canada, at **www.myisic.com**; in Australia, see **www.isiccard.com.
au**; in New Zealand, visit **www.isiccard.co.nz**. U.K. students should carry their NUS card. If
you're no longer a student but are still younger than 26, you can get an **International
Youth Travel Card (IYTC),** which entitles you to a more limited range of discounts, as does
the **International Teacher Identity Card,** aimed at educators.

   University of London Union, Malet St., London WC1E 7HY (www.ulu.co.uk;
✆ **020/7664-2000;** Tube: Goodge St. or Russell Sq.), is the epicenter of London's student
life. It's the place to go to learn about any student activities in the Greater London area.
The Union has a swimming pool, fitness center, general store, ticket agency, bars, inexpensive restaurants, venues for live events, and a branch of STA Travel. Bulletin boards provide
a rundown on events; you may be able to attend many, although some may be "closed
door" for London students only. You can also keep up with the latest at **www.facebook.
com/UniversityOfLondonUnion**.

   If you're studying in the city, the **International Students House,** 229 Great Portland
St., London W1W 5PN (www.ish.org.uk; ✆ **020/7631-8310**) accommodation, at the foot
of Regent's Park across from the Tube stop for Great Portland Street, is a beehive of activities, such as live music and film showings, and rents somewhat institutional rooms at fair
prices. There's also a gym. Reserve way in advance.

Taxes   All prices in the U.K. must be quoted inclusive of taxes. Since 2011 the national
value-added tax (**VAT**) has stood at 20%. This is included in all hotel and restaurant bills,
and in the price of most items you purchase.

   If you are permanently resident outside the E.U., VAT on goods can be refunded if you
shop at stores that participate in the **Retail Export Scheme**—look for the window sticker
or ask the staff. See p. 299 for details. Information about the scheme is also posted online
at **www.hmrc.gov.uk/vat/sectors/consumers/overseas-visitors.htm**.

Telephones   To make a call **within the U.K.,** the area codes found throughout this
book all begin with "0"; you drop the "0" if you're calling from outside Britain, but you
need to dial it along with the rest of the code if you're calling domestically. The area code
for London is **020.** For calls within the same city or town, the local number is all you need,
minus the area code. So, to call from one phone to another within London, dial just the
8-digit number. Calling from a mobile phone, you need to dial the full number including
area code, *no matter where you're calling from.*

   Phonecards are often the most economical method for visitors from overseas to make
both international and national calls. They are available in several values, and are reusable
until the total value has expired. Cards can be purchased from newsstands and small retailers citywide, and offer call rates of a few pence per minute to English-speaking countries
such as Australia and the United States. Follow the instructions on the card to make a call
from a public payphone. Most payphones now also take **credit cards,** but if your card
doesn't have Chip and PIN technology embedded (see "Money & Costs" above), you may
encounter problems.

   For advice on using your **cellphone** in London, see "Mobile Phones," earlier in this
section.

To make an **international call** from Britain, dial the international access code (**00**), then the
country code, then the area code, and finally the local number. Common country codes

are: U.S.A. and Canada, **1;** Australia, **61;** Ireland, **353;** New Zealand, **64;** and South Africa, **27.** For calling **collect** or if you need an international operator, dial ✆ **155.** Alternatively, call via one of the following long-distance access services: **AT&T USA Direct** (✆ **0800-89-0011** or 0500/89-0011), **Canada Direct** (✆ **0800/89-0016**), or **Australia Direct** (✆ **0800/89-0061**). For **directory assistance**, dial ✆ **118-118.**

Callers beware: Many hotels routinely add outrageous surcharges onto phone calls made from your room. Inquire before you call. It may be a lot cheaper to use your own calling-card number or to purchase a phonecard.

Time   Britain follows **Greenwich Mean Time** (GMT) between late October and late March. Daylight-saving **British Summer Time** (BST), one hour ahead of GMT, operates for the rest of the year. London is generally 5 hours ahead of U.S. Eastern Standard Time (EST), although because of different daylight saving time practices in the two nations, there may be a brief period (about a week) in spring when Britain is only 4 hours ahead of New York or Toronto, and a brief period in the fall when it's 6 hours ahead. Sydney is 10 or 11 hours ahead of UK time, Auckland 12 or 13 hours ahead.

For help with time translations, and more, download our convenient Travel Tools app for your mobile device. Go to **www.frommers.com/go/mobile** and click on the Travel Tools icon.

Tipping   Whether, and how much, to tip in London is not without controversy. Visitors from the U.S. in particular, tend to be more generous than locals—and some Londoners resent a tipping culture being "imported."

Tipping in **restaurants** is standard practice, as long as no automatic service charge is added to your bill. Leave 10% to 15% if you're happy with your server. However, be aware that a small number of places do not distribute these tips to staff as perks, but use them to pay their wages. This practice is only possible if you pay by credit or debit card, and unfortunately is perfectly legal. Ask who gets the tip, and if you're unhappy about paying the management's wage bill, have any automatic service charge removed and leave cash for your server to pick up. Earnings usually go into a communal pot to be split between everyone from the kitchen porter to the sommelier, so there is no need to leave more than one tip per meal.

There's no need to tip **black taxicab drivers.** They charge you extra for each item of luggage, and for standing in traffic—and earn more than most Londoners. However, if the driver is especially helpful, add a pound or so to say thanks. Minicab drivers, on the other hand, generally earn less, and are always grateful if you're able to top-up their rates with a couple of extra pounds, provided you're happy with the service.

Tipping in **bars** and **pubs** is practically unheard of, but if you receive table service in an upscale Mayfair nightclub or wine bar, leave a couple of pounds on the change tray.

In upscale **hotels,** porters expect around £1 per bag. Leave your maid £1 per day if you're happy with the cleaning, but only tip the concierge if they have performed something beyond the call of their regular work. Barbers and **hairdressers** will appreciate an extra pound or two for a good job, but you're not obliged. **Tour guides** may expect £2 for a job well done, although again it's not mandatory. Theatre ushers don't expect tips.

For help with tip calculations, and more, download our convenient Travel Tools app for your mobile device. Go to **www.frommers.com/go/mobile** and click on the Travel Tools icon.

Toilets   Also known as "loos" or "public conveniences," these are marked by public toilet signs in streets, parks, and Tube stations; many are automatically sterilized after each use. You can also find well-maintained lavatories in all larger public buildings, such as museums, large department stores, and railway stations. It's not always acceptable to use

the lavatories in hotels, restaurants, and pubs if you're not a customer, but we can't say that we always stick to this rule. Public lavatories are usually free, but you may need a small coin to get in or to use a proper washroom. Those at major train stations cost 30p (correct change required).

VAT   See "Taxes," above.

Visas   No E.U. nationals require a visa to visit the U.K. Visas are also not required for travelers from Australia, Canada, New Zealand, or the U.S. For nationals of, or visitors from, other countries, see **www.ukvisas.gov.uk/en/doineedvisa**.

Visitor Information   The U.K. has made huge investments in placing comprehensive, up-to-date, and inspirational visitor information online, so the Web is the place to begin your London research. The official **Visit London** online home is the excellent **www.visit london.com**. You can download PDF brochures and maps, or have them mailed to a U.K. or U.S. address, or ask any question about the city by filling out the online contact form at **www.visitlondon.com/contact_us**.

Once in the city, the **Britain and London Visitor Centre,** 1 Lower Regent St., London SW1 4XT (www.visitbritain.com; ✆ **08701/566-366;** Tube: Piccadilly Circus), can help you with almost anything, from the most superficial to the most serious queries. Located just downhill from Piccadilly Circus, it deals with procuring accommodations in all price categories through an onsite travel agency (www.lastminute.com), and you can also book bus or train tickets throughout the U.K. There's a kiosk for procuring theatre or group tour tickets, a bookshop loaded with titles dealing with travel in the city and the U.K., a souvenir shop, an Internet cafe, a foreign exchange desk, and pleasant, helpful, and friendly staff. It's open year-round Monday 9:30am to 6pm, Tuesday to Friday 9am to 6pm, and Saturday and Sunday 10am to 4pm. Between April and September, weekday closing is a half-hour later.

There are further central information points at: **King's Cross St. Pancras,** LUL Western Ticket Hall, Euston Rd., N1 (Mon–Sat 7:15am–9:15pm, Sun 8:15am–8:15pm); **Euston rail station,** opposite Platform 8, NW1 (Daily 8:15am–7:15pm, Fri 8:15am–8:15pm); **Heathrow Airport,** Terminal 1,2,3 Underground Station, TW6 (Mon–Sat 7:15am–8pm, Sun 8:15am–8pm); **Holborn,** outside Holborn station, Kingsway, WC2B (Mon–Fri 8am–6pm); **Liverpool Street underground station,** EC2M (Mon–Sat 7:15am–9:15pm, Sun 8:15am–8:15pm); **Piccadilly Circus underground station,** W1D (daily 9:15am–7pm); **Victoria rail station,** opposite Platform 8 (Mon–Sat 7:15am–9:15pm, Sun 8:15am–8:15pm); **Greenwich,** Pepys House, 2 Cutty Sark Gardens, SE1 (www.visitgreenwich.org.uk; ✆ **0870/608-2000;** daily 10am–5pm).

The Square Mile has its own visitor information center, the **City of London Information Centre,** St. Paul's Churchyard (✆ **020/7332-1456**). This striking building opposite the south side of St. Paul's has leaflets and brochures relating to sights, attractions, guided tours, self-guided walks, and the latest events. Opening hours are Monday to Saturday 9:30am to 5:30pm, Sunday 10am to 4pm.

An alternative organization to help foreign visitors with their inquiries is the **London Information Centre,** Leicester Sq., London W1 (next to tkts booth; www.londoninformation centre.com; ✆ **020/7292-2333;** Tube: Leicester Sq.). Note that it's a privately owned, commercially driven organization that may have an interest in steering you toward a particular venue. The booth is open daily 8am to midnight.

You can also call ✆ **08701/LONDON** (566366) for city information and to book London hotels. Sales staff is available daily from 8am to 11pm.

London is such a **web-savvy** city that almost as soon as we recommend an online news source or blog, it's immediately matched or superseded by another. However, there

are some phenomenally useful London resources on the Internet. You'll find the latest local news and weather at **www.bbc.co.uk/london** and **www.thisislondon.co.uk**. **LDN** (www.ldn.in) does a great job of aggregating information about all kinds of events, deals, and trivia. The **Visit London Blog** (http://blogs.visitlondon.com) manages to combine the official line with an eye for the unusual, but if you want to head off-piste and under the city's skin, bookmark blogs like the magnificent **Great Wen** (www.greatwen.com). While the remit of the **London Review of Breakfasts** (http://londonreviewofbreakfasts.blogspot.com) has expanded beyond the city, it still does what it promises. **Londonist** (http://londonist.com) remains the best source for street-level coverage of arts, events, food, drink, and London trivia, and **I Know a Great Little Place...** (www.greatlittleplace.com) is often updated with bar openings, club nights, dining ideas, and unusual tours. **Gresham College** (www.gresham.ac.uk) hosts a rolling program of free lunchtime and evening public lectures, on a vast range of topics, to which all are invited. For the latest on London's theatre scene, consult **www.officiallondontheatre.co.uk**. If you wish to attend Christian worship, **www.cityevents.org.uk** has a regularly updated calendar of services at all the City's churches. *Time Out*'s **First Thursdays** (www.firstthursdays.co.uk) see art galleries across East London open until late for cultural events and free tours on the first Thursday of the month. The Museum of London's **Streetmuseum app** (iPhone and Android) uses augmented reality and the inbuilt camera to superimpose historic images of London onto a view of the modern streets. For regular features and updates, visit **www.frommers.com/destinations/London**.

Wi-Fi   See "Internet & Wi-Fi," earlier in this section.

Women Travelers   First and foremost, lone women should never ride in **unlicensed London taxicabs,** especially at night. Recent high-profile cases have seen this method used by predatory sex attackers. However attractive the price you're quoted, flag down a black cab or call a minicab instead. **Addison Lee** (www.addisonlee.com; ☏ **0844/800-6677**) has a huge, efficient fleet, and will text you the registration plate of your cab for added security. If you're carrying an iPhone, Blackberry, or Android handset, you can book via their app. For more on staying safe, see "Safety," above.

If you want to dig a little deeper into the history of women in London, visit the **Women's Library,** London Metropolitan University, Old Castle St. (www.londonmet.ac.uk/thewomenslibrary; ☏ **020/7320-2222;** Tube: Aldgate East). Admission is free and opening hours are Tuesday to Friday 9:30am to 5pm (until 8pm Thursday).

For general travel resources for women, go to **Frommers.com**.

Index